Tales from the Embassy

Richard Arnold.
President Guild of Transcultural Studies.
1917-1922.

Tales from the Embassy

Communiqués from the
Guild of Transcultural Studies
1976 - 1991

Dave Tomlin

Tales from the Embassy by Dave Tomlin
Published by Strange Attractor Press 2017
ISBN: 9781907222566
Originally published in three volumes by Iconoclast Press, 2002, 2006, 2008
This edition edited by Paul Sieveking

Cover design by Tihana Šare & Jamie Sutcliffe
Frontispiece: Richard Arnold, Guild President (see page 81) Photo: Tim Arnett

 A CIP catalogue record for this book is available from the British Library.

Strange Attractor Press
BM SAP, London, WC1N 3XX, UK
www.strangeattractor.co.uk

Distributed by The MIT Press, Cambridge, Massachusetts.
And London, England.

Printed and bound in the UK by TJ International, Padstow.

For my son Tom who entered life through the portals of the embassy, and for his friend Poppy who followed soon thereafter.

Contents

Foreword

Barry Miles

Most people don't realise how restrictive Britain was at the start of the Sixties: this was, after all, when Mervyn Griffith-Jones asked the jury at the *Lady Chatterley's Lover* obscenity trial if it were the kind of book 'you would wish your wife or servants to read'. This is why the ideals and actions of the youth culture of the mid-Sixties were seen as such a threat to the stability of society: there was but one British way of life for the twin-set and pearls, bowler hat and furled umbrella British and that was exemplified by that of our dear Queen. This was not a multi-culture. Sixties youth culture, with its mini-skirts, mini-cars, Beatles and East End photographers could be just about tolerated; it was still about shopping and could be passed off as youthful exuberance. But the underground, with its free love, drugs, psychedelic music and anti-consumerism, directly challenged the establishment by positing an 'alternative' society. The police came down on it hard.

Dave Tomlin was a central figure in the implementation of these ideas, beginning as the in-house music teacher at the London Free School: all through the decades — as hippie merchants arose and got rich, as rock stars grew greedy and underground journalists drifted into Fleet Street — Dave kept the flame alive. Before pop became rock, a new approach to jazz was developing in the music of Cecil Taylor, Charles Mingus, John Coltrane, Albert Ayler, Pharaoh Sanders and others. This music, exemplified by *Free*

Jazz, a Collective Improvisation by the Ornette Coleman Double Quartet (1960) became known as Free Jazz. Dave Tomlin was one of its finest British players, as shown on *Pendulum*, where he plays soprano saxophone with the Mike Taylor Quartet (1965). At the UFO Club he, Glen Sweeney (hand drum) and Roger Bunn (bass) played as the Giant Sun Trolley. They were also one of the bands that played at the 14 Hour Technicolor Dream at Alexandra Palace, a benefit to support the *International Times* bust fund. He re-joined Sweeney in 1972 to play bass on the Third Ear Band's *The Magus* album.

I very much liked Dave's story about his switch from saxophone to violin. At an *International Times* 'happening' in Oxford, Dave was arrested when the police over-reacted to a bunch of hippies playing music in the streets (the hippies attempted to wrap the police up in a giant roll of Mellonex; silver foil on a plastic backing). Dave was arrested and at the station they roughly shoved him through the iron cell door, breaking the bell of his saxophone. When Hoppy (co-publisher of *IT*), arrived to bail him out he asked how the sax got damaged:

> 'They ran me into a door,' says Smith, regarding the ruined instrument. It is a bad omen. 'There's something about me the police don't like,' he thinks, and looking at his damaged horn he sees immediately what the finger of fate has so obviously pointed out: It is not *he* the police dislike. It is his *saxophone*.
>
> 'It's my saxophone!' he bursts out. 'I must be playing the wrong instrument.'[...]
>
> But Smith has plunged once more into his latest revelation. The saxophone. The most bolshie instrument on the planet. Its associations with jazz making it decidedly hip, and hipness raises the hackles amongst the Philistine. The status-quo represents the fixed; while the hip is fluid and changeable, and change is anathema to the powers-that-be.'

I would have been filled with self-righteous anger, but Dave got it right; his was a position of Zen calm. There is no point in confrontation unless it is part of a well thought-out plan of action. Reactive measures rarely work out.

Dave writes with a deceptively light touch using the present tense, and the third person — a very unusual form. He refers to himself as 'Smith', presumably a reference to George Orwell's 'Smith', the Everyman of *1984*. Dave has been a prolific contributor to the on-line edition of *International*

Times and over time regular readers have been treated to extracts from the three volumes of *The Embassy*. For 15 years, beginning in 1976, he squatted the abandoned Cambodian Embassy and ran it as the Guild of Transcultural Studies, putting on talks and concerts and offering hospitality, support and shelter to some of the most fragile members of the creative community.

Dave is a picaresque writer: this is not a straightforward autobiography. Many of those stories are richly amusing as the establishment comes face-to-face with the anti-establishment. Dave can make even a mundane court appearance over unpaid rates seem incredibly funny. He does not confine himself to the embassy days but includes stories and anecdotes about the London Free School — the best record of this idealistic 1966 project in existence — through to his reminiscences of old friends from the Sixties — many now departed: Hoppy, Harry Fainlight, John Michell. Dave is telling the Tale of the Tribe; you cannot get a more authentic voice.

Feet wandering a deserted path
While mind wonders how it got there.
The first drop of storm rain
Falls onto the centre of my brow.

Sarson 20
Harry Fainlight

I lean outward to the sky
And should tumble in it if I
Were not held here cleverly
By the threads of my identity.

Sylvia Plath

We are glad to get the good opinion of a friend,
but that may be partial;
the good word of a stranger is likely to be more sincere,
but he may be a blockhead.

William Hazlitt

O God, if somebody had to be me, why did it have to be me?

Su Rose

Part One

A Preposterous Proposition

Ready to board with a crowbar up his sleeve Jubal Smith contemplates an empty house. The basement door is nailed up fast with timber struts and he waits for a bus to pass before dealing with it, the roaring engine masking the sound of cracking boards. He opens up a gap large enough to slip through and enters. Outside, peering at a map is George O'Grass pretending to be a lost American tourist; any trouble and he will whistle.

Inside, is devastation: the house has burned and gutted from within; floorboards and ceilings fallen; the joists charred beyond redemption. They leave and walk back to their squat in Belsize Park. Ten days left before eviction they house-hunt as a team, George with his map and Smith with his crowbar.

Detouring through Regent's Park they enter an avenue of grand mansions. Foreign embassies sit in cages of decorative wrought-iron tipped with leaf of gold. They saunter along in silence until, glancing to the left Smith sees, set back from the road, a redbrick mansion. He indicates the house, pointing over his shoulder with his thumb.

'What about that then, George?'

They laugh at this most preposterous of propositions and continue walking. But something bothers Smith, and he remembers the front-door of the house. Between two stone columns and a modest portico, he recollects the small pile of yellow phone-books half covered by a drift of last year's leaves. He stops dead in his tracks.

'I'll see you later George,' he says. 'I'm going to have a closer look at that house.'

George stutters into speech. 'Oh! Oh! R-r-r right!' He nods, blinks at Smith then abruptly turns on his heel. George is a one-pointed man who strives constantly to disrupt the sedentary nature of convention, his stutter — a cosmic machine-gun mowing down the ramifications of mundane thought. However, Smith sometimes suspects him of using this device to stretch and elongate the moment in his quest for the absolute essence of now.

The front-gates of the house have been removed leaving two brick pillars through which he walks. The forecourt is circular; whilst on either side trees and bushes provide cover for the approach. To be discovered by the police in possession of a crowbar in these circumstances would not be wise, and he drops it into the long grass amongst the bushes. Trying to stay out of sight from paranoid neighbours he makes his way towards a ground floor window.

Arriving, apparently unobserved, he crouches under a bush to make sure, then examines the window for some way of entry. It is mullioned with small panes of glass held together with lead. One pane near the handle seems loose and the lead around it soft. It is enough, he retraces his steps leaving the crowbar where it lay. It will come in handy later.

Back at the squat he confers with George and a small group who will stay together when the next place is found. They do not intend to allow the new address to become known to certain undesirable characters that have over the last three years infiltrated the house, some of whom do not believe in civilisation at all. Amongst these is McCafferty, whom Smith has known since the mid-Sixties. Banging upon the front door one day he had demanded a cup of tea – and then made it last for six months. Smith has had words with him recently over his habit of milking the house lamps of paraffin for his own private use.

'Don't come knocking on the door for a cup of tea at the next place.' He had told him.

'I'll come and take one,' McCafferty had snarled in reply, as he descended to the cellar where he has taken up his abode in the room next to 'Basement Michael', an ex-circus fire-eater now gone very much to seed.

Smith had discovered Michael while first exploring the derelict house. On that occasion he had found the ground and two upper floors empty, and descended the cellar stairs by the light of a candle.

Apart from rubbish the two rooms below were empty. Going over to the coal-cupboard he had pulled open the door and peered in. There, crouching on a heap of coal and lit by the flickering candle sat a man as filthy as it is possible to imagine. Squatting amongst a collection of empty wine bottles, he was straggle-bearded and wild of eye. 'Oh,' said Smith. 'Sorry to disturb you,' and hastily backing out he had left the man to his coal and darkness.

However, once the house becomes fully occupied Michael, who hitherto had crawled through the coal-chute to gain shelter, acquires some confidence and moves into one of the basement rooms with his drinking partner Fred. Eventually he even becomes sufficiently upwardly-mobile to use the front door. His room adjoins McCafferty's, who emerges from time to time to lambast the two winos and their habit of spending their nights in a drunken stupor, with the radio continuously murmuring in the background.

'Not so much radio!' He roars fearlessly at them, which drives Michael and Fred into paroxysms of drunken rage.

'Shut your mouth you Scotch git!' and variations on this are their usual reply. Some nights their conflicts below fill the air with foul oaths and heated profanities which rise through the house above, seething like a volcano on the point of eruption.

One night such an eruption had indeed occurred. Smith, lying reading in his room on the ground floor has heard McCafferty come in and give his customary broadside. 'Not so much radio!' An utterance which he has recently began to augment by banging a house-brick against Basement Michael's door. 'Eff of you effing Scotch git!' Roars an infuriated Michael.

There come shouts and more bangs from below. 'This,' thinks Smith, 'is getting seriously serious,' and he gets up to investigate.

From outside his door the basement appears to be on fire. A bright flickering glare lights the stairs leading below in intermittent bursts, accompanied by roars of rage.

Descending a few steps he sees McCafferty backed up against a wall and wearing the countenance of a cornered wolf. Facing him stands Michael, and close behind his mate Fred. Burning in one hand Michael has a screwed-up newspaper which he swings around to keep alight, whilst simultaneously slagging off McCafferty in the vilest of terms. McCafferty weathers the verbal onslaught and bides his time, then, letting out a wild war-cry he launches himself at them. Whereupon Fred, who is holding a can of paraffin hands it to Michael, who takes a large swig and blows the contents of his mouth across the burning newspaper.

A great plume of flame shoots forth which he directs at McCafferty who is thrown back by the fierceness of the heat, his beard singed and smoking. The performance is repeated several times, during which McCafferty is never quite able to reach Michael before he has reloaded; his mate Fred is a deft hand with the paraffin can. Defeated and singed, McCafferty retreats snarling to his room and Smith returns to his book.

With the possibility of a new place in the offing there is no desire to have these unruly characters in their midst, and a small group have formed to deal with this issue. Now, gathered together, they formulate a strategy. Smith will attempt to gain entry to the new house tonight, and if he doesn't return they will arrive one by one at the side door of the house the next evening after dark.

Conception

That night, Smith loads up his pushbike with a sleeping-bag and a few possessions, included amongst which is a new Yale lock for immediate use should the mission prove successful. Arriving at the house he leaves the bike in the bushes and returns to the window reconnoitred earlier. He discovers that the loose pane will, with a little help from a screwdriver, come out. Now he can get his arm through to reach the handle, it opens easily and the window swings outward. Climbing onto the sill he drops his gear inside and quietly follows; then, pulling the window shut behind him sits on the floor to listen and wait in the darkness for a very long time.

He had made a mistake at this point a couple of years before, when, seeing a prospective squat in an obviously unoccupied house he had gained entry through a side window. Having explored a couple of disused rooms he had entered another to see, crouched over a fire, an old man and woman. They immediately began making a horrendous din; the woman screaming as if under attack, the man calling loudly for someone called Jim. Smith had left in a hurry, and as a result of this experience now exercises extreme caution.

Faintly through the window comes a distant swish of traffic, but the house itself remains utterly still as he begins feeling his way around the room. A little light is coming in from the far-off streetlamps and this reveals a large polished wooden desk and walls lined with glass-fronted bookcases filled with important looking tomes. It seems to be an office of some kind.

The door of the room opens into a front hall; a well of darkness into which he begins to grope, stumbling soon on some black bin-liners scattered around on the floor. Through the plastic he can feel what seem to be heavy metal wall-brackets of the kind used in light fittings. The panelled walls of the hall are shrouded in deep shadow, but peering into the gloom he now sees that there are large holes out of which hang bundles of electrical wiring. The thought hits him with a jolt: Burglars! And what's more they may still be in the house. 'If they catch me here,' he thinks, 'I could be in trouble. They won't be too happy with a witness to identify them, and who knows to what lengths they may go?'

Smith now has the horrors and decides that in this instance prudence is a virtue. He retires to the point of entry and unrolls his sleeping bag behind the desk. The burglars, if they are still around will surely be gone by morning, and he will then be able to investigate the house at his leisure.

The next morning he begins his exploration. Re-entering the hall he sees the bin-liners scattered around the floor, the burglars may be planning to collect them later, but for now he checks his surroundings. There is a flight of wooden stairs to the upper floors and several doors lead off the hall. He opens one at random and peers within. It is a large and splendid salon, richly furnished with huge upholstered armchairs and couches; chandeliers hang from the ceilings and large gilded mirrors adorn the walls, together with pictures of Asian dignitaries.

Two French-windows lead onto a flagstone patio and an overgrown garden, the lawn a field of hay. At the bottom of the garden is another building, its mullioned windows set in mock-Tudor brickwork. These windows overlook the garden and seeing them Smith keeps well back and out of sight. Exploring further he finds a substantial kitchen with a red tiled floor. Upstairs are two master suites and several smaller rooms, and the top floor reveals a series of attics, obviously the servants' quarters. The whole house seems abandoned, but the opulence of the furniture and fittings is impressive.

Descending by the back stairs, he begins work on the side-door. Removing the screws from the inside of the lock he pulls open the door and takes out the barrel. He cannot be seen, since there is a high brick wall outside which conceals these actions from the house next door. He replaces the lock with his own and is now by law the 'Householder.' Anyone contending this must prove in court that they have a better claim to the property.

The rest of the day is spent checking that the water and gas are on, while mulling over the chances of hanging on to this stately pile. It is obviously outrageous: squatters are confined to derelict and sub-standard buildings. You can't squat a palace.

Once it is dark he pulls the heavy red velvet drapes in the salon, and lights a few candles set into the silver candlesticks which stand on a boardroom sized table, then stands awhile outside the back door. He has not long to wait.

Looming out of the darkness comes George O'Grass, his typewriter and sleeping-bag in his arms. They mumble their way through some sort of greeting and wait until the others arrive; French Nellie, Tralee, Morgiana and Brett are soon present, and they assemble in the salon.

No one can believe this is really taking place. Their usual habitat of one lavatory plumbed with garden hose — the bowl set in concrete borrowed from a building site — is far from the tiled splendours they can see here. However, they rise to the occasion and before long someone has a kettle going in the kitchen where cupboards full of cups and plates have been found. A tea-tray is brought into the salon and everyone has tea, and then wander off upstairs to find a room for the night.

The next morning Smith descends and with his screwdriver replaces the silver-sculpted wall lights in the hall; his sense of territory already so far advanced that he feels slightly outraged by the audacity of the burglars. In the afternoon he decides to explore the conservatory, a long glassed corridor which runs from the salon down one side of the garden, and ends at a windowed door leading into the other building.

The floor is tiled and covered in a thick carpet of dried leaves, fallen from the grape-vine which grows along the rafters of the roof. He gets down on his hands and knees and begins slowly shuffling along the corridor. This takes some time, for every movement stirs the leaves and makes a loud rustling in the silence. Once embarked on this course he is vulnerable; anyone looking through from the other end cannot fail to see this intrusion and sound the alarm.

Finally, after half an hour of microscopic movements he reaches the end and all is quiet. Slowly standing up until his eyes are level with the glass of the door, he sees a large panelled hall filled with desks, on which are typewriters, telephones and a scattering of papers, but a layering of dust belies any occupancy. Quietly he tries the door; it is unlocked and opens easily.

Inside, a flight of stairs leads above where several rooms seem to be offices, but from the confusion of papers lying around, abandoned in a hurry, and from the thickly lying dust, some time ago. At this point he realises that the building is part of the property of which the main house is merely the front. Now they no longer need to pull the drapes at night; there is no one here to see them.

Plausible Logic

Into the brass scoop a stream of lentils cascade from an open sack, until, gauging the quantity by eye, Smith drops the sack to the floor and checks the balance of the scales. It seems to be correct and he empties the scoop into a plastic bag. Closing the end with a tie he writes the weight and price on the outside with a marker pen.

The shelves which line the loft are filled with rows of similar packages containing peas, beans and many hued pulses. The floor is piled with boxes of brazils, cashews and peanuts, leaving little room for the packages of dried bananas piled against the lower walls to jostle with great jars of honey, which glint a mellow amber sweetness from as far afield as Mexico and the outbacks of Australia.

He is a partner with Morgiana and their friend Mick D'Silva in a wholefood warehouse in Covent Garden which has just opened. Mick has put up the money for the operation and Morgiana is the manageress while Smith is in charge of the packing department. He has just piled the packages of lentils into a milk-crate and sent them rumbling down the chute to the shop below, when he has a visitor. Brett, who has been left to guard the house, comes in looking concerned.

'The police have just been at the house,' he says. 'They were very aggressive and said I had a choice: either leave now or they would throw me out; they meant business,' he says, 'so I left.'

This is a serious blow, but they decide to take some expert advice and make their way to Kentish Town and the Citizens Advice Bureau. A lady solicitor receives them and they tell her what has happened.

'This gentleman has just been evicted by the police without a magistrate's order from a house we are squatting,' explains Smith. 'They also threatened him with violence if he did not leave.'

The lady listens carefully and looks sympathetic, then picks up the phone. 'What is the local station?' She asks.

'St John's Wood,' says Brett, and she dials the number then... 'Hello.' She introduces herself and says: 'I have a gentleman here who claims that some of your officers have just evicted him from a house without a court order, and furthermore offered him violence if he did not leave immediately.'

There is silence as she listens to the reply then...

'Thank you very much. I'm glad to hear it. Goodbye.'

She puts down the phone her face expressing satisfaction.

'They said that they would never do that. What you do now is up to you.'

They thank her for her help and leave.

'Well that's it then,' says Smith. 'If they said they would never do it, it means that now they can't.'

The logic seems plausible if not entirely convincing, but from now on there must always be at least two people in the house until they know if there will be any more serious opposition.

Serious Opposition

Two or three days now pass in which the police seemingly having retired from the field, the new occupants breathe more easily and have begun the process of settling in; when into the forecourt sweep two large black limousines. The doors of the cars open and a tall grey-haired woman advances, followed by a posse consisting of several serious looking men in immaculate dark suits. The woman has a large bunch of keys with which she opens the front door of the house and they storm in.

'Foreign and Commonwealth Office!' The lady barks as she enters. 'This is diplomatic property and you must all leave immediately.'

Smith, who is standing in the hall, had at this point been about to join the others for afternoon tea in the salon; an aristocratic habit acquired but recently, no doubt influenced by the elegant nature of the house. Now he feels obliged to make some sort of response, having outfaced the police, this avalanche of bureaucratic righteousness will have to come up with something better than this.

'Unless you have a court order,' he says. 'We are entitled by law to remain in occupation.'

Just then Morgiana passes through the little confrontation; she is carrying a tray on which are a large tea-pot, some cups and a plate of biscuits.

'Would you like to have some tea?' She says sweetly to the woman and her entourage.

The lady is angry; she ignores the offer of tea with contempt.

'If the Ambassador or staff are not on the premises,' she snaps. 'They fall within the jurisdiction of the Foreign Office, and you must all leave at once.'

'What do you mean Ambassador?' asks Morgiana.

'This,' replies the woman. 'Is the Embassy of the Khmer Republic and as such is diplomatic property, so for the last time, are you going to leave?'

There is a short silence while this new information is considered. Then, making no sense of it, Smith speaks in what he hopes is a reasonable manner.

'I think,' he says, 'that you still need a magistrate's order, and to get that you must take us to court.'

The woman is outraged at this, she is literally vibrating in fury and is obviously used to being obeyed without question.

'Well, we'll see about that,' she splutters, and abruptly turning on her heel stalks out, her minions, who have not uttered a word, following.

At the door she whirls about and confronts them once more. Shaking her finger sternly she gives them one more blast.

'And don't think you're going to stay here!' She is almost screaming, and with a great slamming of doors they are gone.

An embassy? They look at each other in astonishment. Suddenly the whole ambience of the house falls into place; the over-opulent salon where the Ambassador had no doubt received his visitors now makes sense. A hasty search reveals that the small panelled room into which Smith had made his initial entry was indeed the Consular Office, the shelves lined with books on international law and diplomacy; the drawers full of headed notepaper. The annexe building across the garden is full of such stationary; the cupboards lined with files and great stores of international correspondence, all pertaining to this Khmer Republic. Reading deeper they discover that the Khmer Republic is in fact, the pre-communist government of Cambodia.

Having very little interest in 'world news', it takes some time to piece together the whole story. Cambodia has until recently been a monarchy ruled by a God-King. The King's son and heir, Norodom Sihanouk, had on his succession forfeited his Divine status in order to become more politically involved. Supported by the Americans against the Communists, the country had finally succumbed to the Khmer Rouge led by the Communist dictator Pol Pot, while Prince Sihanouk had accepted sanctuary in Peking.

Pol Pot: Ruthless killer of a whole class of people; the educated, the cultured and all those with dissident views, or who displayed affection for decadent Western practices; such as the wearing of spectacles. This of course included diplomats of the former administration.

No wonder the house had been abandoned in such a hurry. The Ambassador would have considered himself a marked man, vulnerable to Pol Pot's international hit men. Without the Ambassador's authority the cooks, the chauffeur, maids and secretaries would undoubtedly have panicked and made themselves scarce. The Khmer Rouge takeover had occurred in 1974; therefore the house has been empty for two years.

The new inhabitants now find themselves in an uneasy situation, founded as it were upon the suffering and bloodshed of countless people. However, there are already some signs of decay in the house: a leak on the first floor has dripped through into a corner of the salon, and the parquet flooring beneath is giving birth to some strange moulds. Left to itself the house will rot.

The Letter

It is French Nellie who comes up with the suggestion.

'Why don't we write to Prince Sihanouk to see if he will give us his approval to caretake the house?'

Nellie is a complete naïf. She stands there innocently in her flowing sky-blue chiffon robes, a disciple of Sri Muktakrishna, the 'Singing Guru'. Rarely joining in these discussions she prefers to scurry up to her attic from where her voice haunts the house as she sings the sacred songs of her calling. Now though, her suggestion is received with enthusiasm and it seems the right thing to do. These strange circumstances lead to flights of fancy which have the quality of magical acts.

Candles are lit in the salon. They reflect in the rich red wood of the polished table and cause the chandeliers to sparkle above. The residents sit formally on the elegant chairs and a sense of theatre is in the air, as around the table they fashion a letter to the Prince.

Morgiana picks up a pen and in her best managerial manner begins fielding suggestions. These fly back and forth for a while until all possible approaches have been examined. The results are then perused and from these a letter is composed.

'Dear Prince Sihanouk,

We are a group of musicians, writers and artists of various kinds who are homeless. Under English law, which in certain circumstances allow the homeless to occupy vacant or unused premises, we have taken up residence in your embassy here in London. However, we hereby give our word to vacate the premises on demand to the recognised government of Cambodia, when such an organisation is once more in place.

'Meanwhile we undertake to care for the property while in occupation, and to protect it from vandalism and the ravages of dereliction. A letter from yourself sanctioning our caretakership would give us the authority to fulfil this commitment to everyone's satisfaction, and would be most appreciated.'

George O'Grass takes it to his room for typing, after which they will all add their signatures. George types incessantly. He is close to the centre of a cosmic conspiracy which seeks to lull the population of the planet into a false sense of security, while aliens infiltrate their world. There is of course much evidence for this point of view and amongst some people it is regarded as de facto. However, George, through his world-wide network of correspondences has access to deeper levels of these cosmic machinations and is even now writing a book on the subject; an exposé of the latest developments in this field.

He types the letter on the Ambassador's notepaper and they place it in an envelope addressed to: 'His Highness Prince Norodam Sihanouk, Peking'; and by way of authenticity stamp it with the State Seal of the now defunct Khmer Republic which has been discovered in the Consul's Office.

Since it seems doubtful if the letter will reach the Prince by ordinary mail it is decided to approach the Cultural Attaché at the Chinese Legation in London, and there inquire whether they will consider carrying it in their diplomatic pouch to Peking.

Tomorrow Smith will attempt to carry out this mission.

Beyond The Crack

It will not do to turn up looking like a dirty squatter, so Smith repairs to a local charity-shop and there purchases a dark blue suit, a white shirt, and a tie. Thus apparelled he takes a tube to Oxford Circus and walks from there to Portland Place. 'The People's Republic of China', it says on a brass plate on the front of an imposing white building.

He advances a finger to the bell-push and presses. After waiting for some time with no result he is about to give them some more bell, when he is startled to notice that the door has quietly opened a little and furthermore, from beyond the crack which ensues, an eye is observing him. It is he sees, definitely a Chinese eye. Presently a voice issues forth from the crack.

'Wat you wan?' It is a voice full of Chinese inflections. Smith takes the letter from his pocket and holds it up to the eye.

'I wish to speak to your Cultural Attaché about this letter if that is permissible.'

The eye regards him for a long oriental moment, then the door swings open to reveal a large Chinese official, his face impassive above a featureless grey uniform, and with a curt nod he indicates that Smith should enter. So far so good. The Chinaman leads him through a resplendent annexe red of carpet afoot, at the far end of which is a large desk behind which waits another Chinese. The man sits bolt upright with his head held high and looks down his nose at them as they approach as if daring them to enter his awesome presence.

They halt at the desk and the two Orientals converse together. They are speaking in rapid Chinese and casting glances full of suspicion at Smith then…

'Show retter!'

The man at the desk has the voice and tone of an interrogator, as if already he has Smith's fingernails firmly gripped in his pliers. He holds out the letter and the man snatches it from him and reads aloud from the front of the envelope, while Smith attempts to explain his purpose in getting the letter to Peking. He tries to do this in an inscrutable manner, hoping in this way to inspire a more sympathetic attitude, since he knows that this quality is highly regarded amongst these people. It does not work. The man regards him icily then...

'You wait,' and standing up he disappears through an inner door.

Several minutes pass in silence then the door re-opens and two more Chinese appear, they scrutinise him from the doorway and again the door closes. More silence and Smith begins to get the horrors. This after all, is diplomatic ground, officially the territory of Communist China. If they suspect him of some kind of international plot, they have the power to detain him indefinitely should they so wish, and no one any the wiser.

He looks behind him; the way back to the street is blocked. Two large Chinese in grey uniforms stand with folded arms their backs against the front door. They look back at him without expression, and the tension goes up one or two notches. 'It is,' thinks Smith, 'like a Fu Man Chu film.'

He is trying not to succumb to his sense of danger and breathes his way carefully through several more silences, until at last the door opens and the man with his letter returns. He stands formally to attention behind the desk, his voice ceremoniously high.

'The Government of China do not wish to become involved in this matter,' he announces pompously, and hands back the letter unopened.

Smith, who is so relieved at the dissolution of his paranoia that the news does not dismay him, thanks the official, giving a slight bow as he does so, his recent association with the world of embassies making the gesture appropriate, and having escaped the clutches of Fu Man Chu a bit of James Bond suaveness seems not out of keeping.

Walking back down the long red carpet he keeps an unhurried pace, expecting any second to hear a voice from behind shout. '*Bring retter back now!*' And it is not until he is almost upon the two Chinese henchmen at the door that they move impassively aside. A moment more and he is in the street.

From Portland Place he walks through Regent's Park, and the roar of traffic fades to a distant murmur as he strikes out across the flat fields northwards to where the Church of St John rears its tower above the autumn trees of the St John's Wood skyline.

Back at the embassy he recounts the tale of his failed mission and the escape from Fu Man Chu. Now however, they must seek other means of delivering the letter. Again it is French Nellie who speaks up. She has a friend who is going to Paris, a Vietnamese girl who is a disciple of her guru. She will take the letter to her embassy there which has diplomatic relations with Red China.

It is a very long shot indeed, but their only one. The letter is handed over to Nellie who will make sure it gets to Paris. At the very least they can now claim to be in communication with Prince Sihanouk, even if it is for the moment, only one way.

Colonel D—

Colonel D— is a dapper and cheerful man dressed in the orthodox mufti of the military: Hacking jacket, check shirt, cavalry twill trousers, suede boots and a brown felt hat. He is red-faced and breezy. Smith, having spent several years in the army recognises the type immediately. He has come to inspect the troops.

The Colonel is from the protocol department of the Foreign Office, and is accompanied by the usual posse of po-faced suits and a grim-of-visage policeman from the Diplomatic Protection Branch. The policeman looks about eight feet tall, his guardsman's style peak-cap reminiscent of the Gestapo. The Colonel explains that he has a duty to inspect consular premises periodically and hopes they have no objections.

This is a surprisingly different approach, but he puts it in such a civilised manner that Smith readily complies with the request, even offering to show them around. Shortly they are proceeding from room to room, Corporal Smith in the lead, closely followed by the Colonel and his suits, whilst the policeman looms Nazi-like in the rear.

They visit Morgiana's room first, and all the niceties of polite introductions are observed, while Morgiana sits amidst a dazzling confusion of oriental carpets. She is a skilful restorer of these rugs and the room is her workshop, its walls covered with the multicoloured wools which she uses to match the complex shades of the carpets. Colonel D— is most intrigued, and asks Morgiana many questions of the kind which reveal that he too knows a bit about carpets. They are fellow connoisseurs.

Morgiana sits there prattling of Turkish knots and the subtle shades of Kelims and Bokharas, while the Colonel chortles happily away. He is much taken with her flirtatious style and is enjoying himself immensely. The suits are gathered in the doorway and take no part in the main discourse. Like minor courtiers they whisper amongst themselves and ogle the opulent fittings.

Meanwhile Morgiana and the Colonel are reaching great heights of bantering repartee, the ripples of which wash back to animate the suits and dash themselves like waves against the granite cliffs of the policeman's unmoving face.

As the Colonel takes his reluctant leave Morgiana flashes one more provocative glance at him. The look is full of meaning, as if she has arranged by some means unknown to Smith, the suits or the policeman, to meet the Colonel in a later assignation.

The Colonel is fairly beaming by now and Smith leads the way to the other master-suite where Tralee has taken up residence. Even more magnificent, it is hung with astrological charts which she peruses constantly, the room lined and piled with the enormous collection of books which she takes everywhere.

The cats, of which she has many, are perched here and there throughout the room. Some sitting basilisk-like upon the several heaps of books, while others stretch languorously along the arms of sumptuous armchairs. As Smith enters with the entourage, the cats scatter in panic and flee beneath the couches, while one, 'Whitey Moustache', even claws her way up the curtains to perch on the pelmet high above.

Whitey had acquired her name on account of her colour. 'It is,' maintains Tralee, 'exactly the shade of an old man's moustache when he smokes cigarettes down to the tip.' The smoke, rising through the white hairs to stain them a particular shade of orange, which matches exactly the shade of Whitey Moustache.

Tralee immediately asks the Colonel for his birth-date and checks the Ephemeris to verify her fix on him. He gives it to her quite meekly, and now she begins to analyse his character on the spot.

The suits are very interested in this. They crane eagerly forward so as not to miss a word, almost licking their lips at the prospect of the embarrassment and possible demolition of their boss. Tralee, aware of this, confounds them and takes great pleasure in making him out to be some kind of Sir Galahad, which flatters him no end and he blushes with pleasure.

The books now engage his interest and before very long they are delving into the esoteric world of literature, while the cats, after their initial fright at this invasion begin to approach the suits for strokes, and soon these gentlemen are bending down to finger them when they think no one is looking. All that is except the policeman, who has from the start seen this whole approach as lacking in proper discipline.

Whitey Moustache however, maintains her position on the pelmet from where she glares down at the proceedings. Smith she recognises and hates intensely, never having forgiven him for his assault upon her when as a kitten he had doused her in flea-powder. It had been a hard day; the morning milk served a little earlier than usual, and when she had returned from a prowl in the garden the other cats had drunk the lot.

'Those bastards,' she thinks. 'They drink my share of the milk and now let themselves be patronised by strangers.' She looks around and notices that the bathroom door is ajar. 'Sod this,' she thinks, and in a frantic rush is down the curtain and through the bathroom door, her dignity intact.

Meanwhile, Tralee and the Colonel are deep into the comparative merits of Thomas Mann and Proust, while the cats are fraternising with the suits, when the policeman gives a loud and obviously artificial cough. The Colonel sighs in exasperation and with undisguised regret takes his fond farewell of Tralee.

The entourage now wends its way to the top floor, and on reach the landing there comes the sound of Indian music. Someone is playing sitar. It echoes exotically down a long corridor at the far end of which Brett has his quarters. As they approach the music's source, the whispers of the suits fall quiet and all instinctively soften their footstep. All that is except the clumping boots of the policeman, who is refusing to make any concessions whatsoever. They halt and listen for a while, then Smith opens the door.

Brett sits cross-legged in the middle of the carpetless floor. His room is bare of any furnishings to enhance the acoustics, and he is playing sitar. Smith advances into the room followed by the Colonel, the suits, and the policeman. Brett takes no notice whatsoever, he is playing raga Bhairavi and is well into it, gone and somewhere else.

After a while the suits get restless; one of them says something and abruptly Brett stops playing. Carefully laying down the sitar he gazes out of the window for a while. Smith speaks.

'Brett,' he says. 'This is Colonel D— from the Foreign Office. He has come to check the house and make sure everything is all right.'

'What?' says Brett. The Colonel steps breezily forward.

'Hello,' he says. 'Is everything all right then?'

Brett cannot get his head around this either. Bhairavi is still singing in his ears and racing in his blood. These questions are faintly heard voices on the periphery of his awareness which hold little or no interest for him, and anyway, he wants to get back to the sitar.

Eventually however he must pay the price and reluctantly concedes that yes, he has spent much time in India, and the Colonel has to be satisfied with this. He can see that even as Brett delivers these few reluctant words his hand is moving to pick up the sitar. The interview is over.

As they descend the stairs, the soulful strains of Bhairavi follow them down to the front door where the Colonel seems much impressed by what he has seen, and compliments them on maintaining the house in such good order.

At the door he makes an arrangement to call in six months time. He has been a perfect gentleman and Smith shakes his hand with pleasure. He then does the same with the suits, it is all very civilised until he finds himself facing the policeman. Having shaken hands with the suits he feels obliged to offer the same courtesy to this man.

The policeman is rather put out by this, and seems to regard it as some sort of insolence. His hand comes out reluctantly. It is held stiff and flat as if about to deliver a karate blow and as Smith takes it, does not bend or return the shake. He is letting it be known that all this polite hanky-panky is not the reality to which he subscribes. They are a gang of dirty squatters who as far as he is concerned should be kicked out now!

The door closes and a minor celebration erupts; they have weathered the storm. If the Foreign Office is making six-monthly inspections, it implies that they have for some reason accepted the occupancy.

It now occurs to them what may be the reason for this change of posture. If the Foreign Office has responsibility for vacant embassies, then it follows that some sort of guard should have been made on the property, protecting it from burglars and squatters. Someone, somewhere in the hierarchy has slipped up in this, and now should they attempt to obtain a court order the incompetence will be exposed and heads will roll.

Colonel D—, with his affable approach is a damage limitation exercise.

A Sonorous Nocturne

For some time now, evenings at the embassy have been permeated by the sound of Chopin's Nocturnes emanating from the piano on the mezzanine floor. It is Phineas, a tall gangling Irishman with a small black goatee beard and round steel-rimmed glasses. He has a scholarly manner and is a congenital rebel, but the piano is his love; and particularly the music of Chopin. Visiting the house so frequently of late he now has a room on a permanent basis.

He shakes his head at the state of the piano and says it needs renovating, his rich brogue giving an ironic twist to his scholarly use of language.

'With the state that piano's in,' he says, 'A pint of porter is your best man.'

Fortunately, repairing and tuning pianos is his profession and he offers to bring it up to scratch.

'It's in the wrong place,' he says. 'It should be in a larger space.'

It is decided to put it below in the salon, and they struggle manfully downstairs with it under the direction of Phineas, who is experienced in such manoeuvres.

Once in the salon he immediately takes the instrument to pieces, the numerous parts are spread across the floor in orderly rows while he replaces worn felts and springs. Having spent two or three days with glue and pliers he begins the task of bringing the strings into tune, and by evening is satisfied with its condition.

Meanwhile, work has been going on in the garden using the implements which have been found in the garage. The lawn has been burned off, the rose-beds and shrubs trimmed, and now they gather for tea on the patio.

The french-windows are open in the salon and light spills out into the autumn evening dusk as they sip their tea, while Phineas embarks upon a limpid nocturne and the piano, after such loving treatment, rings out sonorous as a bell.

Difficulty In The Beginning

A difficult stage in the occupation has now been reached. Word has gone around that a new squat has opened up and there is a constant stream of applicants for a room. The problem is that although they do not feel justified in keeping any rooms empty, there is a desire for people of an artistic or otherwise creative nature. However, perhaps regarding these conditions as elitist, some applicants adopt a more egalitarian manner, and late one Saturday night there is a ring at the side door which is answered by Smith. Outside are three young men somewhat the worse for drink.

'We want a bed for the night,' states their spokesman bluntly.

'I'm sorry,' says Smith, 'but this isn't a hotel.'

'No,' says the man, 'it's a squat, and you can't stop us from coming in.'

His mates are rumbling aggressively and begin to push from the rear; Smith, however, has his foot against the door. What they claim is technically true, the police cannot be called upon for obvious reasons and the men know this. He attempts to explain that although the house is a squat, it has permanent residents and there is room for no more. He is attempting to be reasonable without giving cause for violence, while surreptitiously slipping a heavy chain, (which he had fitted earlier for just such an occasion as this), across the door.

'What are you then,' says their surly leader. 'Some kind of right-wing squatting landlord?'

Smith is about to reply when from behind him comes a great shriek of fury. It is Tralee: she comes flying along the corridor, her ragged gypsy skirts streaming out behind, her hair, a tangled Medusa like bush above eyes that flash with passionate outrage.

'Philistines!' She screams. 'Eff off!' And launching herself through the air she delivers a mighty kick at the door.

It slams shut with a violent bang in the faces of the men, which sends them into a fury. They begin to kick it from the outside, and then one of them draws back his fist and slams it through a glass pane.

However, he cannot reach the chain or lock and cuts himself trying. His friends gather round to commiserate before, with much dark muttering and many unimaginative curses they give up and leave, although, not before hurling a large chunk from the front rockery through the kitchen window.

Infiltration I

A beautiful young girl is at the door, she is asking for George O'Grass and says she is an old friend. Smith takes her across the garden to the annexe, where George has cleared out one of the offices upstairs and is now ensconced. She knocks and is invited in, and around an hour or so later Smith returns on some minor errand. He finds George and the lady on the friendliest of terms and they ask about the possibilities of her having the room next to his. Anyone fast enough to be a friend of George's is a friend indeed, and nobody raises any objection. The lady moves in and for a few days all is well until it is noticed that she has a boyfriend, who, by his constant presence seems to have moved in with her.

Next it appears they have a small boy called Lucifer, and furthermore many friends who come and go frequently. Now George finds his peace disturbed by the child and the endless visitors, some of whom everyone agrees, look decidedly sinister. He moves across to the main house and the couple then ask Smith for the empty room. When he refuses they become abusive, and it is at this point that George reveals that he had never met the girl before in his life. She had been recommended to him by a trusted friend who had not revealed her true motives. He has been betrayed and the residents duped.

Late night visitors now regularly call at the side-door for the couple. Taxi drivers in black leather jackets park their vehicles in the forecourt and disappear across the garden, together with a miscellany of other dodgy looking characters. They wonder what is going on and one morning Smith goes over to take a look.

He cannot believe his eyes. The hall, cleared of the desks is now filled with green baize tables in the centre of which is a roulette wheel, and from the quality of the equipment this is no amateur set-up. The place has been turned into a gambling club. Upstairs he notices that the empty room has already been taken over.

'Look,' he says to the girl and her friend, 'you've got the wrong idea about this place and it would be better for all concerned if you left.'

'You fascist!' screams the girl. 'How much of this place do you want?'

'All of it,' says Smith without hesitation.

The couple are incensed by this and appear to be on the point of committing some violence, which Smith, unwilling to engage in such futile procedures avoids by making a hasty but diplomatic withdrawal.

Returning, he is called into the kitchen by Phineas. The household are gathered there discussing the issue, it is difficult as they have no real authority. But something must be done.

'I've just been to see some friends that know of these people,' says Phineas. 'They belong to a community in Cornwall and are planning to move the whole group to London; the boy friend is the girl's husband.'

Now the future of the house is in jeopardy and there is only one way to deal with it. They must psyche the interlopers out.

Sir Andy The Valiant

Phineas has a friend by name of Andy, a poet whose writing revolves around the concept of London as a sacred city. He is steeped in Blakean imagery and centres his enthusiasm around Kings Cross, the site of one of Boadicea's last great battles, and in particular the oldest church in London, St Pancras, founded he says upon the ancient site of the pagan 'Pan Cross'.

Andy needs somewhere to live and it is suggested that he take a room in the annexe, if he can bear the close proximity of the interlopers until they leave; and thus become a major factor in the ongoing campaign to expel them.

He is doubtful of this proposition until Tralee and Morgiana begin to point out the heroic nature of this task. They cast admiring glances at him and all his poetic notions of ancient chivalry are aroused. He will be their knight in shining armour if he accepts the challenge. He cannot resist this witchery and Phineas and Smith, his two esquires, accompany him across the garden where they clear out the contents of the room and there install 'Sir Andy'.

However, an atmosphere of gloom pervades. This conflict is affecting everyone and the darkness thickens until one evening Phineas turns up with a friend from a nearby squat. He stands around six feet four and, a kindly soul, he is known amongst his friends as 'Big Eddie'.

But now, with his overcoat collar turned up and a black felt hat pulled low, he looks capable of committing a St Valentine's Day Massacre single-handed.

The men, augmented by Phineas' fearsome-looking friend assemble in the kitchen, where they wait a short while until the girl's husband comes in to put on a kettle. He is watched in a heavy silence while he fills it and seems at first inclined to wait until it boils, but the menace in the air is too much for him.

Glancing up, he meets the stony gaze of the assembled company and sees the threatening hulk of Phineas' friend. He turns hurriedly and makes for the door leaving the kettle to its fate, and eventually someone turns it off.

The next morning a van pulls up in the forecourt, the driver and his mate ring at the side door and Smith answers it.

'We've come to pick up the stuff,' they say.

'What stuff?' Smith asks.

'The card tables and the wheel,' says the driver.

'They're being repossessed. You're two weeks behind with the rentals.'

'Help yourself,' says Smith, only too pleased to smooth their way. He shows them across the garden to the hall and they begin dismantling the tables and loading them into the van. It is a noisy process, but no one comes downstairs to investigate. Smith, curious, goes up to take a look and finds the rooms all empty but for Sir Andy's.

He lies upon his bed beneath the open dormer window in the languorous pose which has become habitual to him. It is 'The Death of Chatterton'; a poet he reveres above all others whose recumbent form he now emulates, and in this position dreams of the lost spires of a mythical and mystical London.

'They've gone,' he says. 'They took off early this morning, I heard them go.'

This is glorious news, and one by one as the others come to hear of it the clouds which had hung over them lift once more. Sir Andy is feted by the ladies for his courage during the darkest days, while Phineas, in a flash of joyousness ripples through a Chopin Waltz. The house rings with the music and they toast the success of their strategy with several pots of tea.

Infiltration II

There comes a knock at the door. It is Don, who with four others of his group had lived for a while back at the Belsize Park squat. They had appeared there while Smith, (not long moved in) was still trying to put the half-ruined house into some sort of order. He is outside one afternoon clipping the hedge when the group, rounding a corner come into view, and reaching Smith stand silently watching him while looking with interest at the house. After a while Don, their spokesman, brings forth a question.

'What do you do for money?' he asks.

'Anything that doesn't get me involved,' answers Smith.

Significant looks pass amongst them, evidently they speak the same language. They are fellow combatants against the greedy maw of the so called 'world'.

The group have just been evicted from a squat just a few streets away, and being hard-line Buddhists had accepted the situation as is. Camping on the pavement outside their erstwhile dwelling and surrounded by their possessions: two armchairs, a standard lamp a table, they were only too willing to engage in discourse on the metaphysical implications of the blocked right-of-way with any curious passer-by.

Eventually the police had been called to clear the way, and as a demonstration of their non-attachment, they had walked off leaving the furniture to its fate.

The 'Psykos', as they call themselves, are now looking for somewhere to live, and Smith, impressed by their readiness to put their money where their mouth is offers them some space.

'There's two floors empty above me,' he says. 'You can help keep out the dossers and winos.'

The Psykos set to work and over the next few days there is much sweeping and banging to be heard. One afternoon when the initial phase seems over, Pike, one of the group, asks Smith up for tea, and he is heartened by the transformation. The room is freshly painted, the floorboards scoured, and the windows sparkle.

They sit round a spotless table and are served tea in immaculately clean glass cups. Everything is very orderly, and as they converse on the nature of reality Smith realises that they operate as a team, governed by their allegiance to the notion of the 'One Mind', a degree of Buddhist principles not encountered in meditation classes down at the scout-hut every Thursday evening.

However, the result of this metaphysical exactness seems rather clinical to Smith and his instinct warns him to keep his distance. They all dress the same: Dark blue raincoats, white shirts, black polished shoes, and are very precise in manner. But it is, thinks Smith, the precision of clockwork. Nevertheless he is pleased that they are there. He cannot hope to protect the house from barbarians alone, since it is very far gone and attracts such people.

One of the first things he had done on moving into the derelict house had been to give the front door a heavy coat of blue gloss paint, and every morning with a bucket and mop he washes down the tiled front steps. Inside, the banisters up the wide Edwardian staircase are gone, as are most of the windows on the ground-floor; these however, have been repaired with polythene sheeting. There is no electricity or heating, but the fireplaces work, and Smith has constructed a wheelbarrow in which to collect firewood from local skips. He has also obtained several old oil lamps, the bases of which sit on small shelves hammered into the walls of the front hall, the staircase, and the landing above.

Next to the lamps are small vases of flowers, and in the evenings at dusk it is his delight to go around lighting the lamps and placing incense among the flowers. The flames from the lamps reflect in the freshly washed black and white tiles of the hall, and the sweet-smelling smoke from the incense rises up through the still air, the Spartan simplicity invoking the serene atmosphere of a monastery.

After six months or so of polishing their room and taking turns meticulously dicing up the raw vegetables on which they live, the Psykos had decided to test their understanding of the absolute, by confronting the various gurus of whom they have read and going to India, there to challenge these gentleman face to face.

The Charlatans

Arriving in India the Psykos had visited Wey Wu Wey, a writer of Buddhist books of some renown in the West. He had greeted them kindly and given them tea. The moment of truth had come with a serious question from Don:

'And what is your understanding of enlightenment?'

'I don't believe in it,' answered Wey. Upon which the Psykos had promptly all stood up, thanked him very much for the tea and left.

'He was obviously a charlatan,' Don had said later. But Smith had thought otherwise. He was, he thinks, a wily old bird, and no doubt highly pleased to have got rid of them so easily.

Next on their hit list had been Bhagwan Sri Rajneesh, and for this operation they had taken a room in a hotel in Poona where the famous guru has his headquarters. Wishing to lure Bhagwan from his ashram which they had disdained to visit, they had issued their challenge, inviting him to have tea with them alone in their hotel room and thus be on equal terms. Rajneesh had turned them down.

'He was afraid to come,' says Don. 'Another charlatan.'

However, this had all taken place some years ago and now here is Don at the embassy door. Smith invites him in for tea.

'The thing is,' says Don. 'We've been living in the country in a large house which we have established as a monastery. But it's so far off the beaten track that no one came, except for one Tibetan monk, who had just completed a round-the-world walk with his begging bowl. However, when we invited him in and asked him to take off his boots he refused. So we had to throw him out.'

Smith cannot suppress a covert grin at this. The smile gets up Don's nose. He reddens and puffs himself up.

'But his boots were dirty,' he says indignantly.

The Psykos, continues Don, are now seeking a pied-a-terre in London, and he has come up to scout around. He asks Smith if they can put him up for the weekend, and as it happens there is a small flat above the garage, formerly the home of the embassy chauffeur. The flat is empty and Smith hands him the key.

'Let me have it back on Monday,' he says. He is not interested in having them as permanent residents as they are a tight-knit group with a different agenda, which will no doubt conflict with his own plans at some point.

The weekend passes quietly, and by Tuesday Smith is wondering about the key. Don has not put in an appearance, so he goes across the garden to check out the situation and hears the sound of sawing and hammering coming from above the garage. He leaves the house, walks around the street corner and rings the bell of the flat. Don opens the door.

'Come in and have a cup of tea with us,' he says breezily, and Smith goes in to find the whole group have moved in. They have brought their own furniture and are busily at work constructing five bunk beds in one of the rooms. Don shows off their handiwork proudly and displays no sign of guilt at his devious behaviour, and Smith hasn't the heart to pour cold water on this happy little scene by pointing out that he has broken his agreement to return the key. Although he feels indignant, he knows their argument will centre on the delusion of ownership, and having for some time himself been infiltrated by the logic of Buddhist thought, he knows that in all honesty he would be obliged to concede this point of view. He therefore says nothing, drinks the tea they offer and leaves.

He is not happy with this new arrangement, but since the flat is isolated from the main property he doesn't consider they will cause too many problems. 'At least they're clean,' he thinks.

Returning to the house he explains to the others what has occurred, and since some of them had been acquainted with the Psykos at the last place all agree to let the present situation stand.

A few weeks go by and not much is seen of the Psykos; they are keeping to themselves while fixing up the flat. One afternoon Smith meets Don in the street.

'Come up for a cup of tea,' he says. Smith complies and soon they are all sitting around a table participating in the 'English Tea Ceremony'. The Psykos sit perfectly straight and still with their hands in their laps, and a long silence ensues. 'Something is going on here', thinks Smith, and he is not wrong. Don breaks the silence.

'The fact is,' he says. 'We're fed up with you cooping us up in this small place; we propose to take over the annexe and leave you with the main house.'

Smith explodes. His principles stretched beyond their limits, he is outraged by this attempt to extend the territory which they have stolen in the first place, and he turns to Don.

'I loaned you this place for a weekend,' he says, 'and you abused the favour. As far as I am concerned this arrangement is at an end.'

Hamish stands up; he is the scapegoat of the Psykos and the butt of all their humour. Now he attempts to raise his status within the group.

'You made no arrangement with me,' he shouts, 'and what's more we're here now, and we're coming right through'.

Up to this point Smith had accredited the Psykos with some integrity, but now it seemed they have none. There is obviously no more to be said and he leaves, still sure that they can do no real harm. Some days after this fracas Morgiana decides to do a little gardening, and whilst attempting to open the garage door finds it nailed up from the inside.

'What's going on?' She asks Smith, and he goes across the garden to take a look.

It is true: the door will not budge, and he can see the ends of several six-inch nails protruding around the door frame. Peering in through the dusty window he sees a gaping hole in the ceiling, and a ladder leading down from the flat above. The Psykos are now in possession of the garage, and he sees that they also have begun tunnelling through the wall into the hall of the annexe. Hammers and chisels lie around amongst the debris. They have given up for the moment on account, it would seem, of the hardness of the wall.

Smith ventures around to the front door of the flat and rings the bell. There is no answer. 'They're out hiring a pneumatic-drill,' he thinks. Some time later he enters the salon and looks into the garden. There, striding up and down on the lawn are the Psykos. They have jumped down from the balcony of the flat and now seem bent on displaying their possession of the garden.

The five followers of the Lord Buddha are dressed in ex-army combat fatigues and boots, all brand-new and obviously bought especially for this change of strategy. Smith goes into the kitchen where Phineas is lecturing Sir Andy on the connections between the Illuminati, the Masons, and the music of Mozart.

'They're in the garden,' he says. It is unnecessary to say who, as by now they are all aware of the problem with the Psykos. This challenge must be confronted at once, and passing through the salon they enter the garden through the french-windows. Sir Andy, Phineas, and Smith stand side by side on the patio at the edge of the lawn, at which the Psykos come to a halt and both groups face each other in silence. It is 'High Noon', and no one knows what will happen next.

What happens next is a great cry of anger from Tralee, who has been watching from the salon and now comes running. She is a whirlwind of flailing arms and kicking legs as she launches herself at the nearest Psyko. He attempts to defend himself and grabs her arms, twisting them behind her back. She lets out a cry of pain which is too much for Smith, who, as it happens, is rather fond of her. He crosses the garden quickly and grabs her tormentor around the neck obliging him to release Tralee.

The two men then grapple for a while without actually coming to blows. There comes another shriek from behind Smith, and again it is Tralee. Outraged by an offensive remark from Hamish, she flies at him ferociously and again Smith feels bound to intervene. Hamish and Smith struggle crab-like around the garden for a while until another of the Psykos mounts to the balcony and shouts down into the garden.

'Well, if we can't have it then you're not having it either. I'm sending for the police,' before disappearing inside.

No one can believe their ears; the fearless slayers of Wey Wu Wey and Bhagwan are calling on the police for assistance? Sure enough, while accusations fly back and forth, two policemen come out onto the balcony and the Psyko who has made the call is speaking to them in an urgent whisper. Smith goes across the garden,

'I am the legal householder here,' he says to the policemen. 'These people are guests who have outstayed their welcome and now won't leave.'

The policemen look down into the garden while considering the situation and then announce their verdict.

'Nothing to do with us. You must sort out your problems by yourselves.'

They leave, and now it is obvious that the Psykos have shot their bolt.

'You should go back to your monastery,' says Sir Andy. 'You will never live this down.'

But it is Phineas who has the last word. His Irish lilt, a voice that still echoes its ancient poetry from the green hills and valleys of Ireland clear across the sea to the back streets of Camden Town, now comes curling pungently through the air.

'Ye've read the arse out of your Buddhist books, and to be sure, two planks still have the best of ye.'

He throws this over his shoulder as he leaves the garden, while Sir Andy and Smith follow and watch from a window as the Psykos climb one by one back onto the balcony and into the flat.

The next day they are gone, and Smith goes across to secure the doors and windows facing the street.

'Have to watch out for squatters,' he thinks, as he slides home the final bolt.

The Mission

It is decided to allow some young students to occupy the empty rooms in the house, since it is likely that they will be too busy with their work to cause trouble. Most of them are foreigners, and two girls recently arrived from Argentina are the first to arrive.

The girls have spent the last year or so in prison, having been caught in a room containing more than five people, this being strictly against the law in Argentina. While awaiting trial, they had been beaten every morning before breakfast as a matter of routine. Now they are by contrast radiantly happy, and skip about the house babbling excitedly in Spanish. They make great friends with Johnny Banana Head, another newcomer, who had lived for a while back at the Belsize Park squat and is now staying at the embassy.

Johnny had acquired his peculiar name as no doubt is obvious, on account of his strangely shaped head. He had at birth been delivered by forceps, a not uncommon procedure. But a child's skull at birth is very soft and the forceps commonly pull it askew. No matter, it is an easy task for the doctor to pat it back into the correct shape and no harm done.

However, Johnny's mother had developed complications after the birth and the baby was put aside while the doctor attended to her. Some time later, when her condition was stable, a process which had taken rather longer than usual, he had remembered Johnny, by which time it was too late to do anything about the shape of his head.

One night a few years back Johnny had taken 500mgs of LSD and gone walking in the vicinity of Primrose Hill. As the myriad tiny particles of acid infiltrated his brain and rose like a hymn to the topmost spire of his lofty head, he had suddenly realised that someone was walking alongside him.

Stopping, he had turned to confront this interloper, and had been terrified to see that it was himself. The same clothes, the identical face: Everything. Then, through his terror a voice had seemed to whisper, 'Love yourself.' As it spoke his fear gave way to a great tide of love which came sweeping over him, and before he had a chance to hesitate, he had thrown himself into the arms of his doppelgänger. There came a great crash and shards of glass fly around. He has thrown himself through the plate-glass window of an off-licence. Smith had been taken by Tralee to the hospital where surgeons had reconnected the severed tendons in Johnny's ankle, and sewn up the cuts which had criss-crossed his body. When he has recovered, Smith offers him a room at the Belsize Park squat, and a few days later he turns up with a suitcase.

Since he is still convalescing and spends most of his time lying on his bed, Smith gives him a book which he has found lying around. It is the *Tao Te Ching*, and over the next few weeks he notices Johnny sitting around, his long head bent over the book. Occasionally raising his moonlike face he stares at the wall as if beholding things of great wonder, and sighs frequently as if the sight is too much for him.

One day Smith walks past his room; the door is open and Johnny Banana Head sits on his bed staring as usual at the wall. Smith wonders if he is alright and goes in.

'How's everything?' He asks.

Johnny raises his elongated countenance, the whites of his eyes appear enormous and Smith can see that something momentous is happening to him.

'Well,' he says, 'I've done it.'

'Done what?' asks Smith.

'Got rid of everything,' answers Johnny.

Smith looks around. There are no personal possessions in the room at all. Johnny sits on the edge of his bed dressed in a scruffy blue suit and white T shirt. He stares at Smith.

'It says in this book that all personal possessions are a form of attachment. So I've got rid of everything. You see. I've done it.' He looks earnestly at Smith. 'Now what?'

'It's no use asking me,' replies Smith. 'I didn't write the book, it was written by some daft old Chinaman, and if you choose to hold those views there isn't any 'now what?''

'What do you mean, no 'now what?'' Johnny says.

'Well,' begins Smith, saying the first thing that comes into his head. 'If there was a 'now what', you ought to be able to detect it, and since you're asking me it implies that you can't. Therefore, how can you be sure that there's any such thing?'

Johnny is pleased with this and seems to be regaining his sense of humour.

'Anyway,' says Smith. 'Now what might not be the only what. For instance. What about "then what"? Once you have two "whats" you can move straight on to "Which what?"'

'And what about "What what"?' says Johnny, warming to the subject.

He begins hunting for a pen and paper to make a list of all the possible whats, but of course he has thrown everything away.

'I think there's a pen in my suitcase. I threw it in a skip but it may still be there,' he says hopefully and hurries off on his quest.

'He looks,' thinks Smith, as he watches him walk purposefully away down the street. 'Like a man with a mission.'

Looking

After this episode Johnny had disappeared for a few years, turning up at the embassy and staying for a while in one of the annexe rooms which overlook the garden. However, a few days after his arrival Morgiana accosts Smith in the kitchen, her face, usually a cornucopia of feminine intrigue now looks cross.

'Banana Head has to go,' she says. 'He's driving me mad staring out like that.'

'What do you mean?' Smith asks.

'He's staring across into my room from his window,' she complains, 'and it's freaking me out. Come up and see.'

Smith accompanies her upstairs and once inside her room she leads him over to the window.

'Look,' she moans. Smith looks out across the garden to where her finger points.

There, framed by the window of his room is the white moon-face of Johnny Banana Head. The head is motionless, and his large eyes with their enormous whites stare out with the impenetrable regard of a wax-dummy.

'I can't stand it any more,' she groans. 'He's always there staring. No one can sit in the garden because of him.' Smith looks down, it is true, the garden is empty which on reflection does seem rather unusual.

'I can't tell him not to look out of his window,' says Smith.

'But he doesn't have to do it all the time. He sits there from morning to night,' she protests.

Smith can see that Morgiana is seriously upset and decides to pay him a visit.

Johnny's kitchen-chair is pushed right up to the window, his nose almost touching the glass. He looks around as Smith comes in.

'I can see everything from here,' he says excitedly. 'It's like the bridge of a ship.'

'That's all very well,' says Smith. 'But you're freaking people out. No one likes to feel they're being watched all the time.'

Johnny looks blank. He cannot get his head around this.

'Look,' says Smith. 'Just turn your chair a little.'

Johnny stands up and Smith angles the chair to face across the next-door garden.

'Try it now.' He says.

Johnny sits down again.

'How's that?' Smith asks. Johnny tries out the new view and seems to find it satisfactory. He giggles quietly to himself at the African antics taking place in the next door garden, which is owned by Chief Mopo, the head of some small African state which he has no doubt plundered to support his opulent lifestyle.

Chief Mopo emerges from time to time to enter his stretch-limo, his gaudy robes flowing around his corpulent figure and surrounded by his acolytes, their dark glasses flashing and similarly attired. Smith hopes the Africans are not easily freaked out; he leaves Johnny to his looking and returns to the house.

Some time later Morgiana comes to Smith's room, she looks on the verge of tears. 'He's still doing it,' she complains.

Smith accompanies her upstairs to find her room now in darkness, she has drawn the curtains. He pulls them back a little and looks out. Morgiana is right. Although Johnny's body still faces across to the house next door, he has turned his head to the left and once more the ghostly visage peers forth.

'I forgot to tell him not to move his head,' says Smith.

A room is vacant in the house and Johnny is winkled out from his all-seeing eyrie and there deposited. It is at the front of the building overlooking the street, and soon his face is a familiar sight as he sits counting the traffic and observing the comings and goings of the residents.

Occasionally, when in the afternoons the local schools come out, small gangs of children congregate outside the front gate and gaze in trepidation at Johnny's head. They cannot decide if it is real or not and whisper fearfully amongst themselves.

Johnny gazes back at the children without interest. He is into looking.

Cambodian Opportunism

A trio of oriental gentleman present themselves at the front door one morning. Smith opens up and the men explain that they are from a Cambodian expatriate association in London. He invites them in immediately. John Pilger's book, *Year Zero* has been circulating through the embassy, and he is now well acquainted with the scale of Pol Pot's reign of terror. There is much sympathy in the house for Cambodians in general, and now in their presence he cannot shake off the sense of being an interloper in their embassy.

Their spokesman tells him they have heard there may be a Cambodian typewriter on the premises, something which their organisation does not have and is sorely in need of. Fortunately Smith has already noticed a machine with mysterious typeface in the former Ambassador's office. He dusts it off and brings it forth.

The Cambodians cluster excitedly around as paper is fed in, and twitter like birds as the strange characters begin to emerge. They are delighted and willingly sign a receipt for the machine, a procedure which Smith feels prudent under the circumstances.

As they are about to depart one of them lays his hand on the back of a chair which stands in the hall. It is an elegant piece, made of carved wood and upholstered in green leather, and the man asks if they may have the chair also. Smith feels he cannot refuse; after all, they are real Cambodians and for this reason have a certain moral advantage. Now they decide to leave these two items for the moment and return on the morrow with some transport.

The Cambodians arrive the next day with a van; Morgiana lets them in and then goes looking for Smith. She finds him in the kitchen.

'They're OK,' he says. 'They've just come to collect a typewriter and a chair.'

Morgiana goes back to her room and after a while Smith hears a few bumps and bangs from the hall. He leaves the kitchen to investigate and is just in time to see one of the armchairs from the salon disappearing through the front door. Following hard on the heels of the chair Smith confronts two Cambodians who are about to load it into the back of the van. Neither of the two was amongst those who had called the day before, and as he remonstrates with them is immediately aware that neither speaks English. He resorts to hand gestures and mime, indicating in a forceful way that they can definitely not have the chair and must return it to the house at once. This act, as far as he is concerned has lost them their moral advantage.

They obediently begin manoeuvring the chair back through the door and Smith precedes them into the salon where he catches two more Cambodians standing on chairs to remove a large gilded mirror from the wall, while another struggles with a small glass-fronted cabinet.

'That's enough!' shouts Smith. He can see that his open-handedness of the day before has been, to put it mildly, misunderstood, and they are exploiting the situation to the full. Nevertheless, being somewhat of an opportunist himself he rather admires the scale of their audacity. He does not however, let this approval show; one such slip now and they will be back with a furniture van to empty the house. He adopts instead the outraged manner of a violated householder.

'No more!' He says with as much authority as he can muster, striding to the door he opens it and with more gestures indicates that they must leave. They shamble out in a bunch, muttering to each other and looking slightly guilty.

Outside, the typewriter and leather chair are loaded onto the van and the Cambodians get in. Their round faces peer from the windows of the vehicle as they drive off, and Smith watches from the front-door as they depart. Bearing them no ill-will, he gives them a wave. Their oriental features stare blankly back. They do not return the wave.

Getting Away From It All

George O'Grass is on his knees in the salon. He is surrounded by maps which are spread out and taped together to represent the whole of the North American continent. He studies a list identifying the locality of every nuclear power station in the country and marks the position of each one with a coloured pin.

Having recently received an advance for the manuscript of his book, he is bent on buying a piece of land in his own country. His idea is to set up an annexe to the embassy, where a similar cast of characters can act out their dreams in an Ozark mountain setting. The problem is he has no desire to share his air with one of these monsters of pollution, and wishes to be as far away from all of them as he can get. Now, as he puts in the last pin he can see where the clusters occur, and is with the aid of compasses able to identify the space which is the greatest distance from any of these installations. He puts his finger on the spot. It is a wilderness in Missouri.

'Oh George, please don't go,' begs Tralee. There are tears in her eyes as she contemplates the hole he will make by his departure.

George shrugs and holds his arms wide as if helpless in the ruthless grip of his destiny. Tralee wails in despair and wrings her hands, but George can take it and continues with his plans. However, she does not give up so easily and is working herself up into a state; a condition she is wont to adopt by imagining how she would feel were one of her cats, Chinaman for instance, or Winkle, to die. Bursting into tears at the thought, she will rush up to her room and cuddle whichever unfortunate cat has been the deceased subject of her imagination.

But George gathers up his maps and folds them carefully with the determined air of a traveller who has but paused a moment before departing on the last leg of his journey. Tralee can't take it, her only recourse is to weep her way through the next few days until George goes, and when the sad day comes they all cluster on the front doorstep to see him off. He turns at the gate, holds up his hand in a last farewell, and is gone.

Later, letters begin to arrive bearing American stamps. George has brought himself a farm in Missouri — it is in a secluded valley far from the polluting power stations. He writes of the tin barn in which he now lives and of the hole in the roof through which rain frequently pours, forcing him to set up his typewriter on a small table as far from the leak as possible. He complains that the local rednecks have pressured him into carrying a gun. The right to carry such a weapon is jealously guarded, and non-conformists in this matter are given a hard time. However, says George, a gun without bullets is no gun at all. He has told the locals that he cannot afford the ammunition.

George has got away from it all.

Geisha

Now that the Psykos have gone the empty flat above the garage is a security risk, since it has its own front-door leading on to the street beyond and is thus vulnerable to squatters. Someone responsible must be found who can be trusted to maintain the respectable front which the residents have instinctively adopted. Hippie graffiti and rock and roll have no place in this exclusive locality, and they have engaged in a kind of establishment counter-magic by presenting a facade of extreme respectability. The front of the house is always immaculately swept, and a sand-garden near the front-gate is freshly raked each day into parallel lines around a cluster of rocks at the centre.

Tralee suggests a friend for the flat. Her name is Katarina and she has an affinity with Tralee since they are both astrologers. Smith has visited Katarina's house in Camden Town where she lives with her kleptomaniac boyfriend, and has been impressed by her sense of order, and the boyfriend's extensive collection of junk. An intensely reserved lady, Katrina is just recovering from the usual misspent youth common to her generation. She had escaped the dreary culture of the late Fifties by joining the throng of wan-faced bohemian girls who haunted the jazz clubs and coffee bars of the period.

Dressed in the obligatory flat shoes, black stockings and pencil skirts, topped with decadent eyes dripping with black mascara, she had been ready for the transition to full-blown hippie. As such she had taken off for India, Tibet, and the Far East, and has spent a large part of her subsequent life travelling in this manner. Her rooms are an Aladdin's cave of oriental mementoes picked up in her travels, and now perched precariously but carefully here and there.

Her boyfriend is also an avid collector of sorts, albeit of a somewhat different aesthetic. He has turned the cellar into a kind of indoor junkyard; it is filled from top to bottom with discarded appliances salvaged from skips and local flea-markets.

Broken washing-machines, ancient television sets and vacuum-cleaners fill every space and corner, and a great plethora of useless junk clutters the basement stairs to overflow and threaten the calm order of the house above. Katarina has decided it is time to go.

The final straw had occurred but recently when he had dragged a broken and abandoned cement-mixer into the front garden. Katarina is now seriously disturbed and may crack up unless she can find alternative accommodation quickly. Everyone agrees that she will be perfect for the flat, particularly since she is the only one amongst them who has actually been to Cambodia and made the pilgrimage to Angkor Wat.

Within a week she has abandoned her boyfriend, his junk, and the house in Camden Town, and has arranged her collection of exotic bric-a-brac around the rooms of the flat. In no time the garden balcony is lined with flower boxes and she has begun to festoon the railings with honeysuckle, amongst which, in the evenings she can be seen diligently watering her charges, her hair always elegantly coiffured, and fingernails agleam with the fresh lacquer without which, geisha-like, she will never stir beyond her door.

Garage Music

Phineas can usually be found late at night in the kitchen discoursing loud and long on the Masonic significance of Mozart's 'Magic Flute', or the hidden influences of the Illuminati on European cultural history. He has recently acquired a new obsession: mechanical pianos, and having purchased one of these relics of a bygone world has also discovered a hoard of old piano rolls, some of which had been personally cut by the great composers themselves. He spends much time at it. Pedalling away while the keys depress themselves in a ghostly manner, and the music of Liszt, Chopin, and others of their ilk pours forth from the garage where he keeps the instrument.

Recently he has obtained more of the same from junk-shops and auctions. He subjects them to his usual craftsman's skills and is now the proud possessor of eleven prime examples. Late at night, the music of a past era rings out across the secluded gardens of St John's Wood, and occasionally he will wind up several of the clockwork variety and set them all going at once.

The garage lights are on and he stands silhouetted in the doorway, grinning and rubbing his hands together in glee as the resulting cacophony thunders out around him.

The Spytower

A police inspector from the local station accompanied by a constable are at the front door asking to speak with the householder, and are shown into the salon where they stand hesitantly on the threshold, until Smith invites them to take a seat.

They perch themselves stiffly on the very edges of two armchairs and are obviously uncomfortable in this environment; the classy atmosphere has an effect on them despite having been taken over by squatters. 'They are behaving,' thinks Smith, 'like a couple of estate hands come up to the big house to complain about the smallness of the bread-ration.'

The inspector takes off his hat and opens the proceedings; he clears his throat and speaks in a broad Yorkshire dialect.

'We've coom here today because t'situation is getting out of hand.'

His accent heightens the impression that he is a farm-hand in fancy dress. He takes out a handkerchief and mops his brow, then continues.

'Usually,' he says, 'I can ignore most complaints, but when the letters reach this high,' with his hand he suggests a formidable stack about a foot tall. 'I have to do something about it.'

Smith waits in silence for what is coming next, and he wonders if Phineas has disturbed the neighbours with his massed pianolas, or perhaps Banana Head has been staring at the Africans. The inspector continues.

'The people in the house over there,' he points through the window at the house which adjoins the garage, 'have complained that someone here has thrown a car-battery up onto their roof.'

He stops speaking and looks at Smith for a response. Smith searches around inside his head for some clue as to who might have committed such a hooliganistic deed. His search is fruitless; the space behind his eyes yields nothing and seems to go on forever, while the silence in the room is becoming ominous. He imagines himself performing the act and in a flash puts his finger with Holmesian accuracy on the crux of the matter.

'Well,' he says at last. 'I can lift a car-battery all right, and using two hands could even carry it for a while. But there's no way either I or anyone else could throw it up onto a roof, even two or three people would find it impossible.'

He watches the inspector and the constable digest this, while imagining themselves trying to accomplish the feat, (something they had obviously not done before) and eventually coming to the same conclusion as

Smith. Someone is either mad or lying. The inspector scratches his head, expressing his bewilderment in this time-honoured manner and exchanges embarrassed looks with the constable.

'I see,' he says finally. 'A mistake must have been made somewhere, perhaps it is a misunderstanding.' He and the constable exchange more looks; both nod their assent and the matter is for the moment closed. The inspector addresses Smith again.

'However,' he says gravely. 'There is another more serious charge. The old lady next door,' he indicates with his thumb towards the house which stands on the opposite side from the Africans, 'has complained that you are building a spy-tower in your garden so that you can see into her upper rooms. What have you got to say about that?'

Smith has nothing to say about this, it is too insane to even contemplate and he wants to laugh, but is aware that these two men are serious professionals and perhaps not sympathetic to humour. He gets up and goes over to the French-windows.

'Look, see for yourselves,' he says, pointing into the garden. 'No spy-tower.'

It is true. The lawn stretches emptily away from the window innocent of any clandestine structure, and as they gaze forth Smith casts his eye over the brick wall separating the two gardens. There had at some time been a trellis running along the top which has long since rotted away and disappeared. However, the two heavy supporting posts bolted side by side to the brickwork still rise, green with moss three or four feet above the top of the wall.

'She must mean those posts,' says Smith. 'They've been there for at least forty years and she's only just noticed them.'

There is silence; the inspector knows for sure that he has been sent on a wild goose-chase.

'Well,' he says eventually. 'I'll just go and have a word with her.'

He sighs heavily as he turns to leave and Smith, feeling that with two strikes in his favour the ground is secure enough to hazard a touch of humour, warns the inspector.

'Be careful,' he says. 'The old lady is very paranoid, she may misinterpret something you say and cause trouble for you.'

The inspector however takes this piece of cheek seriously and nods to the constable to take note of the caution. All three exchange looks heavy with manly solidarity in the face of mad old ladies, and Smith, feeling somewhat dizzy shows them with much relief to the door.

The Alarm

Before the house next door had been purchased by Chief Mopo, the former residents had seldom been seen, and only once had there been any contact, an event which had not been exactly friendly. The circumstances having arisen late one evening when their neighbour's burglar alarm, fitted to the wall nearest the embassy, had suddenly and for no apparent reason burst into life with a loud old-fashioned clanging.

All through the subsequent night the bell had continued its clamour, making it impossible for anyone to get any sleep. The following morning Smith had gone round to complain but had been unable to get any reply. It seemed that the occupants were away.

Later, called by irate neighbours, the police had arrived. Checking the doors and windows and finding nothing amiss they had left saying that faulty burglar alarms were nothing to do with them. Evening draws on and still the bell is ringing. It can be heard from several streets away and the prospect of another night of this is intolerable. Something must be done, and Smith goes round to take a look.

The bell is high under the eaves, but there is a long ladder in the garage which should reach. He is wondering how from its top he might disable the bell, when he remembers an axe hanging on the wall next to the ladder and goes off to fetch them. When it is dark enough to make a move, he leans the ladder against the side wall of the house, and sticking the axe into his belt mounts upwards until the offending contraption is within reach.

From this close the din is deafening, but he can see no wires which might be disconnected; the clapper is designed to strike the bell from inside and thus cannot be blocked. Between the wall and the bell is gap around a quarter-inch wide, he has no alternative. Holding on to a nearby drainpipe to steady the rickety ladder he removes the axe from his belt. Raising it high he brings it down with a mighty whack at the crack. His aim is accurate, and the head of the axe almost disappears into the gap twixt the bell and the wall.

The alarm ceases its clanging immediately. A silence so profound descends that he momentarily thinks he has gone deaf, and the sense of peace this silence brings makes the preceding ordeal by bell seem almost worthwhile. From the garden of the embassy there comes a faint cheer, a small group have gathered on the lawn to witness his efforts, and he detects the morphic resonances of relief and gratitude washing over him from fellow sufferers in the nearby houses. He gives a thumbs-up and prepares to make good his retreat.

Taking a firm grip on the handle of the axe he gives a sharp pull. Nothing happens, the axe is stuck fast. He tries again, but now the drainpipe is coming loose and the ladder is wobbling so violently that he cannot get much leverage and still the axe will not budge. To all intents and purposes it is now a permanent fixture and there is no choice but to abandon it. He climbs down and returns the ladder to the garage, mission accomplished at the price of the axe.

A few days later, seeing a car in the next door driveway it is assumed that their neighbours have returned, and they prepare counter-arguments with which to refute any charges of unneighbourly behaviour in the matter of the disabled alarm. Strangely, nothing happens, and after a few days Smith looks up and notices that his axe has been removed. He thinks about this. It was a good axe, and he has other uses for it. He wants the axe back.

Walking around to the house he knocks at the front door. It is opened by a middle aged lady, her grey hair swept back into a severe bun.

'Yes?' She asks abruptly.

'This doesn't look too good,' thinks Smith and adopts his politest manner.

'I live next door,' he says, pointing to the embassy. 'And my axe got stuck in your burglar alarm.'

The lady's eyes harden from stern disdain to pure hatred as she stares in silence at him. Smith waits for a response. None is forthcoming, and feeling like a small boy asking for his ball says.

'Can I have my axe back?'

The lady's nostrils flare wildly in suppressed anger, and he has hardly got out the last word before the door is slammed violently in his face. Smith decides there and then to write off the axe and pursue the matter no further.

Temple Magic

Soon after the episode with an axe the house next door had become vacant. Smith, climbing over a wall, had been able to explore the extensive gardens and harvest the blooms from the cultivated section with which to adorn the salon of the embassy. One day, whilst thus occupied, he pushes his way through the thick undergrowth obscuring the far end of the garden and there discovers a small building, the top of which can be seen from the upper windows of the embassy. It is partly clad in ivy and has obviously not been visited for many years.

There is a small Grecian style entrance, on either side of which two sculpted female figures stand and with upraised arms support the lintel of the door. The small clearing in which it stands is uncannily quiet, even the birds seem to have fallen silent and he wonders what may be inside.

Trying the oaken door, which is sunk into a recess within the entrance, he finds that it is either locked or stuck so fast that it will not give. He goes to a small window, and clearing away the ivy and dust peers within. Inside, a small skylight sends a shaft of illumination down onto a carved stone slab which he takes from its size and general shape to be either a small tomb or an altar of some kind. In a niche in the far wall he can just make out two candlesticks, and on the floor beneath, a bunch of ancient dried flowers. There is an aura of mystery about the site, but no further clues to its purpose.

Later it is noticed that when the Chief holds his garden parties, none of his guests or staff approach anywhere near the temple-like building, but cluster in small groups near the house, as if there is some strange power surrounding that end of the garden. It is not until some months after the house had been purchased by Chief Mopo that the mystery is at least partly solved.

Tralee is sitting reading on the patio one afternoon when she gives a loud shriek and raises her eyes from the book. It is a history of the Theosophical Society, revealing the esoteric paths of the *Secret Doctrine*, and its deathless Tibetan masters.

'Madame Blavatsky!' She shouts in great excitement and jumping up begins twirling and waving the book about. 'Madame Blavatsky!' she shouts again. 'She lived next door, number nineteen. It was her house and that's where she died.'

Morgiana, Sir Andy and Smith, having witnessed Tralee's announcement gather around to see the book. It is true; there it is on the page, number nineteen A— Rd, St John's Wood.

'Then that must have been her temple,' says Sir Andy, who had been over the wall to view the building for himself.

They are delighted by this revelation. Madame Blavatsky, a founding member of Theosophy, and one of the earliest Western metaphysical synthesisers; not to mention the most outrageous and controversial woman of her time. They are all familiar with her books, and this news subtly alters their view of the whole situation.

'That's what must have drawn Smith and George to this house,' says Tralee with conviction. 'It's a power spot, and we are part of some magical plan.'

She claps her hands in delight and they have to admit that there could be something in what she says. At the very least they feel it an honour to be even geographically associated with so powerful and remarkable a lady.

Several months later, Chief Mopo, having finally settled in, begins building a high security wall around his property complete with cameras and floodlights. In the course of this work the contractors landscape his garden. To the horror of those watching from the embassy windows, they clear the bushes and undergrowth from the far end, and with the aid of a small bulldozer demolish the Temple. Within an hour it is nothing but a heap of rubble.

Madame Blavatsky's delicate temple magic is no match for Chief Mopo's bulldozer juju.

Rude Awakening

Katarina has of late become fascinated by the infinitely variable order of Islamic patterns. She had, in her former house in Camden Town, rented rooms to a lodger who was a passionate student of the subject. Wade Davenport had amassed a vast archive of these designs from which he is compiling a book, and he has recently come to roost in an attic at the embassy and there set up his drawing board.

Katarina now conceives the idea of screen-printing these patterns onto silk and making cushions of the resulting artwork. She purchases special lamps to transfer the patterns onto screens and stocks up with a collection of multi-hued inks. Wade has allowed her access to his archive from which she selects her favourite designs.

She sets to work, and having successfully surmounted the experimental stages and early failures, is now, after nearly a year's dedicated application beginning to produce work of a high order. The hard-won new skills, and her mastery of the medium is now apparent in the exquisite cushions; their lemon yellows and variegated shades of red, blue and greens contained by the pristine discipline of the patterns.

The cushions begin to pile up in her flat, and she has recently loaned much of her excess stock to the salon, where their jewel-like charms enhance the splendour of the room. Recently, a designer employed by the Sultan of Brunei had seen one of Katarina's cushions in the flat of a friend. The lady had been so struck by their quality that she had paid a visit to Katarina's workshop at the embassy and ordered a dozen or so for the saloon of the Sultan's new yacht. Having completed this assignment she is wondering what to do as an encore.

It is now late spring and Bones, a young student of microbiology who joins Smith and Katarina in their Chinese exercises every Friday evening, is leaning against the conservatory doors in the garden; he is a frequent visitor and knows the inhabitants well.

At the moment he is admiring the early roses and musing on the possibilities of isolating and extracting a particular element from the tails of certain lizards, (a substance which allows the creature to regenerate that member should it become detached). He is certain that should he succeed in understanding this mysterious process he will be able to apply the principle to the human body, stimulating a permanent regeneration of cells and thus achieving immortality for the human race. Being a modest young man, however, he usually keeps the last part of the theory to himself.

As his mind is leaping from one DNA configuration to another, he notices Johnny Banana Head emerging through the french-windows of the salon. He has picked up one of Katarina's silk cushions and saunters across, to where, overhanging the patio, is a cherry tree in blossom underneath which stands a garden bench.

Banana Head walks over to the bench and placing the cushion at one end reclines at full length, his head upon the cushion and his long greasy hair spread across the meticulously patterned silk. Pink petals from the cherry tree drift romantically down upon him as with a sigh of contentment he closes his eyes and is very soon snoring loudly. Bones shudders at Johnny's audacity. He considers him to be asking for trouble, but being somewhat cautious in his approach to life declines to meddle.

For a while nothing happens, and he has just begun to conceive of a new metabolic sequence when he hears sharp footsteps approaching. It is Katarina. She comes stalking purposefully along the patio her face set into an expression of grim determination, and Bones notices that her path will take her directly past the peacefully sleeping Banana Head. Bones senses trouble coming, and watches in fascination as Katarina reaches the bench. As she passes her hand shoots out and takes a firm grip on the cushion.

Then, without breaking her stride she gives a sharp jerk, and snatching the cushion from under Johnny's head she tucks it beneath her arm and continues on her way.

Banana Head meanwhile has had a rude awakening. The cushion, snatched so abruptly away, brings his head down onto the hard bench with a sickening thud. His eyes fly open in shock and his arms jerk around in alarm, as he sits up and stares wildly around the garden. Bones cannot aid him; he is helpless with laughter, and as he doubles over he catches a last glimpse of Katarina as she disappears up the ladder to her balcony, the cushion tucked firmly beneath her arm.

The Tao Of Pugilism

Harry Flame's poetry is sublime. His problem is that he knows he is the best; that his work stands head and shoulders above most others of his time. However, his manner betrays that he considers those others to be pygmies in relation to his own talent, an attitude which does not endear him to many, and contributes in no small way to the lack of recognition to which he feels entitled.

He stands at the mantelpiece in Smith's room some years back at the Belsize Park squat eating his lunch. He has opened a small tin of baked beans into which he crumbles a segment of Kraft processed cheese, and eats the resulting mixture from the tin with a teaspoon. With his other hand he simultaneously attempts to give himself a dry shave, his face covered with the innumerable small cuts which are the result of this habit.

'You should hate life and avoid experience.' He says to Smith, his voice dripping with disillusionment.

'Do you mean hate life itself, or the kind of world we have to live in?' Smith asks.

Harry looks at him as if he is a pygmy. There is almost pity in his eyes at Smith's inability to grasp what he is saying. He does not answer but sighs heavily as he passes his hand wearily across his noble brow. The gesture and sigh show that poor Harry, cast down and doomed to share his life with these unintelligent clods, cannot put it simpler. Smith, however, always ready to worship at the shrine of Harry's poetry, sometimes thinks what he needs is a good kick up the arse.

Unfortunately, when Harry's brilliant imagination turns negative it produces some far-fetched situations, and he had for some time suspected that the Labour Party was using his head as a kind of transmitter. But in spite of his bouts of madness he is capable of delivering the most stunning indictments.

'The politician is an amateur criminal,' he says. 'One still hampered by the bourgeois ethic.'

He goes on.

'The politician who overcomes this disadvantage is the military commander.'

Harry has a small room above the front door in the derelict house, and he later discusses the matter there with Smith.

'My mind's not my own anymore,' he says. 'You won't get any meat off me. They've eaten the flesh from my bones and now I've got the Communists to contend with. Look!'

He points excitedly over Smith's shoulder who turns and looks out of the window, and there, walking down the opposite side of the street he sees a Chinese man; a tourist perhaps in a dark blue suit.

'See what I mean?' Harry is angry. He rushes from the room and down the stairs and Smith, still watching from the window, hears the front door open and there is Harry, storming across the road towards the Chinese, whom he confronts fists up in a ridiculously stylised boxing stance.

The Chinaman is bewildered. He hasn't a clue what Harry is about and tries repeatedly to get around him. But Harry will have none of it.

'Come on,' he shouts. 'Fight me in the open!' Harry looks seriously demented. Whichever way the Chinese turns Harry blocks his path.

Eventually the man succumbs to his natural Taoist tendencies and does a runner. Harry comes scowling back in, his eyes alight with a deep and complex satisfaction. He has, as far as he is concerned proved his point. Smith is not so sure, but on account of Harry's erstwhile brilliant poetic viewpoints he gives him the benefit of the doubt.

A few weeks later he finds this tolerant attitude put severely to the test. Leaving the house one morning just as Harry is coming in he gives him a smile in passing. Harry stops dead in his tracks. He turns, and casting a malevolent look on Smith says in a voice dripping with venom: 'I'll get you for that!' Leaving Smith something to puzzle over for the rest of his life.

The Concert

It is a grey drizzling day and traffic swishes wetly around Seven Dials on the fringes of Covent Garden. The pavements are thronged with office workers homeward bound, and from their midst Smith emerges and descends the scruffy steps of a basement beneath a row of seedy shops. It is an Indian cultural centre which he has recently discovered and to which he has been drawn by his growing interest in the music of India. The centre is much frequented by Indian musicians who are passing through London and Smith, amongst other things, is looking for a teacher. He has been playing the violin for several years, dabbling with jigs and reels of the Celtic variety supplemented with a few country dances of his own devising. But he had lost heart a year or so back when certain circumstances had shattered his delusions.

While living at the Belsize Park squat he had earned his pittance busking each evening for an hour outside the local tube station, and whilst engaged in this activity had quickly realised that passers-by were not long enough within earshot to be aware of the breadth of his repertoire. He had consequently reduced the number of pieces he played to a mere two or three.

At some point, detecting an alchemical principle in this minimising process, he had further reduced this number to one; the Prima Matera. Hoping that by bringing the focus to a single point of application as the master alchemists had recommended, and repeating the process again and again, the substance itself will reach such a degree of purity that a transformation will occur and precipitate the humble student into a new and higher dimension.

To intensify the experiment further he had decided to spend a whole hour playing a single piece without stopping for rest, and for the last several evenings had been gradually building up stamina for the attempt. On the previous evening he had achieved forty-five minutes before his bow-arm, nearly dropping off had refused to function further.

Now he is making another attempt and it is but a few minutes before the hour is up. His bow-arm is in agony, when he realises that the pain comes from a subliminal layer of muscular tension in the arm. He allows this tension to drop, and is immediately rewarded with a fresh surge of energy up the arm. 'This is it', he thinks. 'This is the breakthrough'. Now he feels that he can go on forever.

Just then a couple of frail old ladies detach themselves from the passing throng. He has seen them before. They totter along clinging to each other for support, sometimes even putting a few coppers into his open violin case. Tonight they come purposefully up and stand glaring disapprovingly at him. One of them leans forward and puts her mouth close to his ear.

'Can't you play anything else?' She screeches.

Smith is shaken to his boots and stares aghast at a void, his alchemical dream in shards around him. He puts away the violin and leaves, never to return.

However, this episode is now some years behind him as he descends the shabby stairs of the cultural centre. Below, the air is thick with incense and the delicate sound of a sitar comes from an inner-room. It is Ganesh Mandra, an Indian who earns his living by day as a lawyer, and graces the drawing rooms of the underground Indian music lovers' network in the evenings.

The residents of the embassy have recently had the idea of using the premises in some creative way apart from just living in them, and have decided to turn the salon into a small concert hall. Since they find the art forms of other cultures attractive, particularly those of China and India, it has been agreed to start off with an Indian music concert, and who better to ask than Ganesh Mandra? Smith enters the room where Ganesh has just finished instructing his students and waits until he is alone, then makes his proposition.

The embassy will feature Ganesh in concert the following Saturday and charge an entrance fee of one pound. This money, less expenses for tea-breaks will all go to the musicians. Ganesh likes the idea and readily agrees, and Smith, the first part of his mission accomplished returns with the good news.

They set about designing and photocopying a small poster, and by the next day these are in the post to various friends. Next the local skips are scoured for a couple of wooden pallets with which to build a platform in the salon and this, covered with a large carpet provides a convincing stage.

The great night arrives and Tralee sits at a table near the front door to collect the money, whilst Morgiana presides over a giant tea-pot in the kitchen. Smith collects flowers from the garden and lights sticks of incense around the salon which, with a few draped saris and a scattering of Katarina's cushions now has the appearance of an exotic temple.

Ganesh arrives early with his friend Popatkar Manicrao, a tabla player in the Bombay style, and they retire above to tune their instruments. Ganesh has also brought his teenage son with him to complete the ensemble on tanpura. Soon the audience begin to arrive; there are thirty or so and when they are settled the musicians come down and the concert begins. Ganesh is the master of his instrument and plays several sublime ragas with intervals for tea. The evening is a great success and the house seems entirely suited to this type of event.

Over the next few days it is decided to form some sort of organisation with an official sounding title, which will help dispel the unfortunate image of a squat. Smith favours the word 'Study', to create an atmosphere of seriousness, while Phineas proposes that it should be a 'Guild', thus suggesting a kind of classical integrity. Since their interests include the arts of the East, the title must include a reference to intercultural activities, and the name finally emerges as *The Guild of Transcultural Studies.*

The Brass Plate

No time is now lost in establishing some credibility: headed notepaper is ordered bearing the new title in copperplate and some thought is given to a brass plate for the front door. Smith enrols the help of Sladovich, a bushy-bearded Serb with a fierce and hearty manner. Sladovich has just been dismissed from his job teaching drawing at a London art college. He had entered a competition to design a building being proposed for the South Bank complex. The plans which he had submitted to the board of governors had projected a three-hundred-foot glass sphere, in which were suspended spiral walkways meandering among waterfalls and hanging gardens; the inner side of the sphere to contain mechanisms operating a large model of the Solar System, in which the planets would pursue their orbits among the walkways and around a central sun.

The governors had chosen a simple concrete structure for the first prize, while Sladovich's effort had received nothing but sneers and derision. 'Silly'. 'Irrelevant', and even offensive to the board had been their judgement. Sladovich, with all the Balkan passion of his race was not a man to take this lying down.

During the public meeting at which these verdicts had been announced he had stormed onto the platform, seized the microphone and delivered a harangue, in which the governors were denounced as Philistines and bigots. His behaviour had caused uproar and provoked demonstrations from his students; the police had been called and Sladovich dismissed from his job and evicted from the premises. Now, out of work, he maintains himself with a few private pupils and has conceived the idea of giving a lecture on the true function of Art in society, while Smith, on the lookout for some intelligent points of view to present under the auspices of the new Guild, gives him all the encouragement he can.

Sladovich brings in a dozen or so sacks of sand which he spreads across the far end of the oak panelled hall in the annexe. When the sand, piled up against a wall is about three feet deep, he half-buries pieces of statuary so that here a Greek head emerges and there an arm or leg. White strings are attached to the window and stretched tautly in long converging lines which culminate at the protruding planes of the statues, and against the wall are placed large wooden circles and triangles. He plans to illustrate his theory that all real progress in the evolution of human intelligence has come about through the slow introduction of new ways of perceiving through Art.

'Take perspective,' he says. 'Before the discovery of geometry in perspective, people actually perceived differently in many ways, and the psychology was restricted to a plane. The view was one-dimensional, and thus it was not possible to get a rational 'perspective' on any situation. The ability to see from another's point of view is a high cultural attainment, and it can be seen from history that this faculty only emerged when artists began to use the newly discovered laws of perspective. Once these laws were expressed in art they could become part of the general awareness and internalised.'

Sladovich's conversation is full of references to vanishing points and lines of sight.

'Unfortunately,' he sighs. 'All these gains have suffered a reversal, and psychologically humans are degenerating at an alarming rate. They can no longer obtain their principles or receive inspiration from art, which has now become either a purely decorative medium, or the glorification of novelty. Draughtsmanship, quality workmanship, skill in formal composition and the significance of placement become forgotten within a few generations, and the concepts which formerly stood as ideals for living, lost to our culture.'

Smith entirely agrees with all this but doesn't give much for Sladovich's chances of influencing the present milieu.

'You're right,' he says, 'But our present social circumstances cannot justifiably be called a culture; since such a form by definition must be the embodiment of growing ideals and principles beneficial to the whole. It is more properly a compost, which is the rotting down of common sense to produce a uniform mulch, in which the PR and advertising men can make their mud pies.' Sladovich is amused by this and his great booming laugh echoes from the panelled walls and sets the strings of his display vibrating.

By now he has finished his arrangement and steps back for a final look. He has created a surreal effect, and looking at it Smith notices that the angles of the strings and the oddness of the disembodied limbs protruding from the sand have somehow altered the quality of silence in the hall. The display provokes a profound sense of enigma that is almost tangible. They walk back to the house together and Smith broaches the subject of the brass plate, a high priority and magical icon in the effort to set up a credible front.

'If we wish to operate openly," says Smith. 'We have to use the magical symbolism of the establishment, and that means a brass plate.'

Sladovich suggests setting up an engraving workshop in the basement and with the help of his friend Tiberius, a tall saturnine Swiss, they set to work. Purchasing a heavy gauge brass off-cut, and having it shaped to size at a back street metal workshop in Islington, they obtain a large enamelled tray and a flask of the appropriate acid and set up a worktable in the basement. Next, the plate is covered with a thick coat of dark shellac upon which the title of the 'Guild' is stencilled.

Some time is now spent carefully scraping off the shellac from beneath the letters with a scalpel, a task which Smith and Tiberius undertake. Tiberius takes the first shift and Smith leaves him bent over the plate beneath the cellar's single light bulb; he reckons that between them they can accomplish the task in a day or two. However, having but recently been introduced to Tiberius he has no idea with whom he is dealing. 'He is an anarchist,' Sladovich had announced with a mischievous grin when making the introductions.

Returning three or four hours later to see how the plate is progressing he goes below and opens the cellar door. Tiberius looks up from his work; he has a watchmaker's glass screwed into his right eye and now leans back to allow Smith a view of the plate. He can only just believe what he sees. The top curve of the capital 'G' of the title is all that Tiberius has achieved in almost four hours' work. But this is only part of the reason for his disbelief. For the curve of the capital is exquisite. A perfect sickle moon cut into the shellac with a degree of precision that seems not within human capabilities. The sculpted curve is cut with a knife-edged accuracy that takes Smith's breath away, and he seriously doubts his ability to follow this act.

'You can borrow my glass,' intones Tiberius, his voice solemn, a hollow gothic ring lurking in the tone.

At this point Smith wishes he had gone first to set the standard; after all, no one is going to take a magnifying glass to the plate once it is up. Nevertheless, this is a challenge, and in view of the fineness of Tiberius' work he can do no less than aim for the same standard. He takes the glass and a new scalpel and tentatively sketches in the descending curve of the 'G'. The line is very fine, a mere hairline scratch across the shiny surface of the shellac. At first the curve looks perfect, but as he focuses closer with the glass he notices a distinct waver in the line about a third of the way down, and two small blips near the bottom. Fortunately, since the initial line is so tentative as to be almost non-existent, it is easy to correct these blemishes. However, now that the lower half has such a fine look to it, by contrast the upper half is thrown into doubt. An hour or so later he reaches the point where he cannot see in what way the curving sweep of the line can be improved. Taking a deep breath and a fresh grip on the scalpel, he makes his first deep cut.

Some weeks later they reach the last letter of the title. It has been a saga in which Smith and Tiberius have lived like miners, taking long shifts at the microscopic coalface of the shellac, and now Tiberius works with profound stillness on the final full stop, while Smith wields a saw to cut a wooden backboard. When the plate is finished it is immersed in the tray of acid for around three hours or so. 'Any longer,' says Sladovich, 'and the acid will begin to undermine the edges of the shellac.'

It is then removed from the tray, washed down, and the shellac dissolved in spirit. Now the letters etched by the acid stand out boldly and when the plate, polished and mounted on its varnished wooden backboard is fixed to a pillar near the front door, it looks perfect.

New Look

On the night of Sladovich's lecture a curious audience makes its way across the garden to the annexe, where they stand around amongst his strange silences waiting for the master to demystify them. They are disappointed in this since he plunges them immediately into the unknown.

'The world you see with your eyes,' he begins. 'Is utterly silent. No sound exists out there at all. No birdsong. No soughing of the trees in the wind, or children's voices to break the profound silence of the world of sight. For eyes are not made to hear.'

'Air, however,' he goes on. 'Apart from its usefulness to gas-breathing creatures such as ourselves, is a medium of vibrations. A kinetic event sends rippling waves of disturbed air in ever-widening concentric circles of excitement around the centre of the disturbance. A phenomenon exactly represented when a pebble is dropped into a still pool of water.'

He is silent for a while, then:

'Plop!'

He lets the word hang echoing, a perfect example of what he means. He goes on... But Smith, who is standing near the door, has other things to attend to and Sladovich's masterful 'Plop' is the last thing he hears. Walking across the garden towards the kitchen he considers Sladovich's angular philosophy, which seems from its direction to lead inexorably to a universal perspective containing every possible point of view simultaneously. 'One might as well have none at all,' he thinks, and rather relishes the idea.

In the kitchen Morgiana has all the cups ready and lined in neat rows on the long table, while on the gas stove is a huge kettle. The kettle takes around forty minutes to boil, allowing her to gauge the tea-breaks in a timely manner. Smith hangs around for a bit stoking up the fire which burns on the large open hearth. Down in the cellar he breaks the legs from a collapsed chair and finds an old jig-saw puzzle of the *SS Queen Elizabeth* with three pieces missing. With these ingredients he soon has a good blaze going.

After a while he returns to see how Sladovich's strange lecture is progressing, and looking through the window sees a most curious sight. Sladovich is standing in the centre of the hall up to his ankles in sand from which various marble heads and limbs sprout. His right arm is raised and his finger points dramatically at his own eye. His voice comes clearly through the window and sets Smith's eardrums rattling.

'So you see,' he is saying. 'The answer to the question: Where is what I see? Is; On the retina of my eye... *There* ?' He jabs in a demented manner towards his own eye while his audience gape at him in silence. Then reaching out his other arm Sladovich touches a chair. 'And furthermore,' he continues, 'you may think this is a chair. But whatever I touch I feel only my own finger. Try it.'

The silence in the hall is now verging on the ominous, when from behind Smith comes the sound of footsteps approaching the annexe entrance. They come to a halt and everyone in the hall holds their breath, as squeaking eerily on its rusty hinges the door slowly opens. Morgiana stands there. She faces a sea of anxious and bewildered faces, but is quite unperturbed as she announces that tea is being served in the kitchen. This down-to-earth and prosaic statement only serves to accentuate the strange atmosphere that Sladovich's unconventional line of approach to his subject has provoked, and the audience cautiously make their way across the garden to the house.

In the kitchen the mood is subdued, with none of the excited chatter of the Indian concert, and people sit around staring into their tea or talking in hushed tones. Smith cannot decide if they are inhibited by their awe of what Sladovich has revealed to them, or shocked by the scale of his madness. He stands in a corner and overhears a conversation between Sladovich and a young man, who is attempting to prove the reality of objects through the sense of touch.

'I know this is a chair even though I cannot prove it,' the man complains as he raps his knuckles on a kitchen chair.

'Yes,' says Sladovich. 'But remember, "chair" is merely the name for something, and you cannot sit on a name, nor by giving it a name are you any closer to knowing what it is.'

The man will not accept this reasoning and sticks to his guns. 'No,' he says. 'It is definitely a chair because it is clearly nothing else.'

'That is just hearsay,' answers Sladovich. 'For instance, who told you it was a chair? You're Mother, you're Father? And did they really know what it was?'

The man seems upset by the direction this is taking, but Sladovich is bent on developing his argument.

'Take the word 'chair',' he says. 'It is an English word and therefore it follows that the inventor of the word was an Englishman. But when did he live? And what was his name? He might have lived three, four, five or possibly six hundred years ago. You know nothing; neither the who or the when, of the instigator of the chair myth, and therefore you're knowing in this matter is pure hearsay.'

The man searches around for something with which he might refute this, but the argument has moved into uncharted territory and he is out of his depth. Sladovich, however, has only just got started and plunges ruthlessly on.

'The so-called 'chair', is an interesting object,' he says seriously, 'and there seem to be two opposing theories as to its invention.'

He goes on:

'One such explanation is that there was once a wheelwright by the name of George Chair who lived in the village of Farnham. He had in an idle moment nailed together a few off-cuts of wood and found to his amusement that he could accommodate his body on a protruding portion of the construction, whilst leaning back against some vertical staves at the rear.'

The man clearly does not believe a word of this. 'And after all,' thinks Smith. 'Who would?' But he detects a subtler level beneath the surface of Sladovich's story, and wonders what he is up to. The man, too polite to show his disbelief coughs nervously and asks what the alternative theory might be. To Smith's delight Sladovich is primed to go.

'The other theory,' he begins, 'is the one I consider to be the most likely explanation, and its source is based in early Victorian times, when prevailing values made the acquiring and maintenance of dignity the greatest concern of the time. As you probably know, in the East the floor is the natural and proper place to sit, and carpets or cushions are normally supplied for this purpose. By contrast, in the West the floor, in the times of which we are speaking, would have reduced a man to the status of a beggar and robbed him of all his carefully contrived dignity.

'Therefore, dressed in their tight formal clothes and embellished with top-hats and impressive beards they were obliged to remain always standing up. This forced posture was however very inconvenient, not to say putting a terrible strain on the legs. Until some unsung genius invented a kind of prop; a small platform upon legs with a support for the back, which allowed these unfortunate creatures to take the weight off their feet without putting their precious dignity in jeopardy.'

Sladovich finishes with an enigmatic smile, and the man to whom he has been speaking stares blankly at him with a glazed expression. He is rescued at this point by a general exodus from the kitchen as it empties for the second half of the lecture, and Smith remains to help Morgiana with the washing up. By the time he makes his way across the darkened garden Sladovich is winding up, and Smith, standing beneath an opened window catches only his final words.

"What I have tried to demonstrate tonight is that at various periods in history, art has been recognised as the source of new ways of experiencing the world. The Renaissance gave birth to many of these, and further strengthened the higher ideals of the society from which it emerged.

'From the discovery of perspective to the experiments with light of the Impressionists, these new-found principles have nourished and revitalised our common human culture, and had art continued thus to reveal the true nature of existence as is its proper function, we would not be forced to live in this unholy and ungraceful mess, and the ideas introduced tonight would by now have become commonplace.'

The lecture is over and the audience prepares to leave. Smith goes up and joins Banana Head at his high front window, and they stand silently looking down as Sladovich's audience cross the forecourt and reach the front gate. There on the pavement they mill around a little; taking a few steps in one direction, then another.

'They've forgotten where they live, says Banana Head.

'And probably in some cases,' thinks Smith. 'What they think they are'.

Bid For Freedom

A female vocalist and her accompanist have been rehearsing of late in the annexe hall and subsequently invited to do a public performance for the Guild. Her name is Laura, and since she is a local is billed as, "The Nightingale of St John's Wood".

On the night of her performance she brings a far different audience to the house. Middle-class and highly respectable in appearance, they seem to be made up of doctors, solicitors, and other such worthy members of the professional establishment and their elegant wives. They have no idea, as they park their posh cars in the forecourt and enter the grand-looking house that they are in a squat. Smith has put on his suit and masquerades as the proprietor. Occasionally he shows himself in a distant sort of way; the distance being necessary; one inflexion of his working-class accent and the game would be up. Now he sits in the garden enjoying the falling dusk, as Laura's crystalline tones emerge from the redbrick Tudor facade and mullioned bay windows of the annexe.

He has long ago analysed the English class system, placing the working-class into three distinct categories:

Upper working class. That is: Where the father of the family has worked all his life (preferably at the same job until honourable retirement).

Middle working class. Where the father has worked intermittently; and:

Lower working class. Where the father has never done a day's work in his life.

During the interval Phineas introduces Smith to a young violinist. 'This is Mr Amuel,' he says. 'But his friends call him Ace, and he would like to give a violin recital here.'

This is a pleasing development; it now appears that the Guild is already building up some momentum. Smith offers Ace the same deal they had first formulated with the Indian concert, namely the artiste takes all minus expenses. Ace will give his recital on the next Saturday and the following week the bills are designed, photocopied and sent out on the steadily expanding mailing list. Ace turns up on the night to find he has an audience of around fifty people, and, accompanied on piano by a young lady he plays a selection of pieces from the classical repertoire. His playing reveals an immense love and respect for the music and his instrumental technique is formidable.

The audience love every minute of it and in the kitchen, when the concert is over, Ace becomes involved in a deep conversation with Phineas on the merits of the various composers who have influenced them. Phineas has a great fund of stories coupled with an Irish sense of humour, and Ace clearly doesn't know whether to laugh or cry when he recounts the story of Gustav Mahler's unfortunate encounter with an American newspaper reporter.

It seems that Mahler was deeply immersed in his latest great symphony, and had fixed up a large shed as a studio at the bottom of his garden into which he would disappear for days at a time. Seeking the wellspring of inspiration in the profound silence which surrounds the shed, he has given strict instructions that he is not to be disturbed for any reason.

'It is imperative,' he says sternly, 'that I suffer no distraction.' He had then disappeared into the shed and had not been seen for several days.

Around this time an American reporter arrives seeking an interview with the great composer and hoping to scoop his new symphony. At the house he is informed that the great man cannot be disturbed and he doesn't accept this lightly. He has come a long way at considerable personal expense and does not intend to be put off by this preciousness. A brash man, he inquires if Mahler is in the house.

'No,' says the lady who has answered the door. 'He is in his studio in the garden. But he really must not be disturbed.'

The American appears to accept this and takes his leave. However, he is an old hand at this sort of thing and hell-bent on getting his interview. Waiting at the side gate until he hears the door close and allowing a few minutes more to be certain, he cautiously reopens the gate. Then ducking under the trees and keeping close to the wall he creeps down the garden. Soon the shed, standing in a small clearing comes into sight. Now, hidden from the house he makes his way softly across this oasis of peace until he reaches it. Feeling a sense of triumph swelling within that nothing has succeeded in thwarting his quest, he raises his fist and gives several sharp raps upon the door, and in a loud and authoritative voice calls out: 'Mr Mahler!' There is a clatter and a heavy thud from within. Poor Gustav has fallen to the floor with a heart attack; and in the poignant silence which follows the ending of the story, the kitchen clock strikes midnight.

The clock in question is a pendulum "Westminster Chimes" and has been kept wound up since the occupation; Phineas however, had grimaced when first hearing its chimes. 'It's out of tune,' he had announced scathingly, and that night had taken down the clock and dismantled it upon the kitchen table. With a set of files he adjusts the length of the chiming-rods until they are perfectly in tune, and while at this, rearranges their striking order to produce an unusual and rather sinister sequence. He had then returned it to the wall, and now it strikes with a perfectly sonorous, yet somewhat disconcerting chime.

Ace looks at his watch and says he must be going or he will be in trouble with his landlady. They look at him blankly. It is inconceivable to these living-on-the-edge squatters that anyone could allow themselves to submit to such constraints.

'But you see,' he says. 'My mother found me the place and personally arranged with the landlady to make sure I had proper meals and clean socks. And she is very strict about what hours I keep.'

They all feel sympathy for Ace, in spite of finding his situation hilariously funny, and are now bent on rescuing him from this dismal fate.

'You don't have to go back tonight,' says Smith. 'There's an empty room you can sleep in.'

A sudden spark gleams in Ace's eye, and is as quickly extinguished.

'But my landlady will be upset,' he says anxiously.

'Well ring her up,' says Morgiana, 'Just tell her you won't be back tonight.'

Ace looks dubious at this revolutionary talk. But he is surrounded by determined faces and encouraging voices, and thus empowered, he decides to strike a blow for freedom. Taking a deep breath and clenching his fists he turns about. Then makes off to the telephone to do battle with his dragon.

The next morning they bid him farewell, while offering him the room on a permanent basis and he leaves to face the wrath of his landlady. Some days later he reappears at the front door with a bag and his violin case and confides that he has not been able to forget the feeling of freedom in the room he had slept in. The gleam is back in his eye and he looks ready to take some risks. He is given a warm welcome and shown with great ceremony to his room.

Ace will have to wash his own socks from now on.

With Love From Andromeda

Group seminars have begun to hire the salon at weekends and the Guild is now accommodating an astrological convention which has drawn several eminent figures from abroad. Prague, Berlin, and other centres of esoteric learning have sent their learned representatives to lecture on their specialities. These professors are for the most part white-haired and venerable old gentlemen, of whom the most impressive is a huge old bear of a man from Prague. He holds forth all day at a blackboard set up on the lawn, his convoluted middle European accent difficult to understand, and the students cluster around attempting to decipher his discourse for their notes. Later, during the frequent tea-breaks these gentlemen gather in the kitchen to discuss the finer points of their several theories. The old voices rise in passion, and hotly their guttural accents thicken as they dispute issues of a profound obscurity.

Meanwhile, Caspar is communing with the stars from the top of nearby Primrose Hill. He is at the moment the major moth around Morgiana's flame and thus a frequent visitor to the embassy. But his interest in stars has little to do with birth-charts or planetary influences. It is rather the poetry of magnitudes which fascinate him, the colour and proximity of globular clusters set into the awesome beauty of galactic scale. Having drunk his fill from this bottomless bowl he wanders back downhill and through the back streets towards the embassy, whilst ruminating upon the calculations in his pocket.

Marked upon a grid he has plotted the exact location of the major star systems and planets over the next twenty-four hours. The work has been produced in collaboration with the old professor from Prague, who needs these precise calculations for the lecture he will give on the morrow. In a short while Caspar reaches a zebra-crossing on the main road. It is a quiet evening with little traffic as he ventures across, deep in reverie upon the air of complacency radiating from the surrounding rich family houses, while light from the Andromeda Galaxy hurtles towards them at one hundred and eighty six thousand miles per second. He is so absorbed in this, his mind still loitering among the light years, that he does not see the car hurtling towards him at sixty miles per hour. The front of the car strikes low, scooping up and throwing him through the air across bonnet and roof, as a bull will toss an unwary matador.

Once more Caspar is communing with the stars. They turn about him in long lazy arcs as he cartwheels through the firmament. There is barely time to note the hard blue light of Altair before he sees that the constellation of

Orion is setting towards his feet at an alarming rate, and a dazzling new sun bursts into life as his head strikes the unyielding surface of the road while the rest of his body collapses around him. For the moment, Caspar is out of it.

The kitchen of the embassy is a sea of twittering astrological students, above which rises like a mountain peak the snowy-topped eminence of the old professor from Prague. He dispenses from his store of wisdom in a weary manner, as if he regards these eager young mystics as nothing more than a gang of teeny-boppers, who need sixty more years before they can even begin to understand what he is talking about. Smith is pottering around collecting cups and making himself useful, when through the mass of people he sees Morgiana waving across to him with an anxious expression on her face. 'Well, where else would it be?' he thinks, as he pushes his way through to where she stands near the door.

'It's Caspar,' she says tearfully. 'He's been knocked down by a car.'

Smith rushes out of the front door and down to the street, where, to his right he sees a group of people standing around something in the road. As he approaches he recognises Caspar, limbs asprawl on the pedestrian crossing; one of his legs sticks out sideways at an impossible angle and is obviously broken. The driver of the offending car is walking around in small circles muttering frantically to himself and anyone who will listen.

'I didn't see him, I didn't see him,' he repeats incessantly, while a bystander reports that an ambulance is on its way.

Although now conscious, Caspar lies very still, and Smith kneels down to ask him how he feels. 'I can't feel anything,' he replies weakly. Smith thinks this just as well at the moment considering the state of his leg. A wailing sound is distantly heard. It comes closer and the ambulance draws up with a great screech of brakes. Two medics and a nurse come hurrying and immediately take charge, shooing the small crowd back and giving Caspar a quick check-over. Then the medics return to their vehicle for a stretcher and the nurse remains to stand guard over her casualty.

Looking down into Caspar's pale face, lit only by the intermittent orange blink of the nearby Belisha beacons, and joined now by the less sedate blue flash from the ambulance, Smith thinks that Caspar is trying to say something. Overriding the protests of the nurse he leans down and places his ear close to Caspar's mouth. The voice comes faintly, but he has no difficulty deciphering the message.

'There's an envelope in my pocket. Can you get to it and give it to the professor?'

Smith reaches down and tries to get his hand into the jacket pocket, but although he can feel an envelope some of Caspar's weight prevents its removal. The nurse is now leaning over Caspar possessively, indicating that Smith's presence is entirely out of order. He leans down and speaks into Caspar's ear.

'You're lying on the envelope and I'm afraid of disturbing you. But maybe if I do it in small jerks it will come free, ready? I'll just give it a few sharp tugs.'

The nurse, straining to catch this exchange has misheard the last few words.

'What's this?' Her voice is sharp and accusing. 'Drugs, is he on drugs?'

Smith nips her quickly in the bud by saying the first thing that comes into his head.

'Certainly not,' he says, as if the very idea is abhorrent to him. 'My friend is a practising Christian.'

This wrong-foots the nurse a little and she says nothing more. But suspicion remains and she watches Smith like a hawk, as with a quick flip he retrieves the envelope and slips it into his pocket. The two medics return and lift Caspar onto the stretcher, his leg, still at a sideways angle of forty-five degrees being supported by the nurse, and he is carried aboard the ambulance which soon goes wailing off to the local hospital. That evening the old professor draws up a chart for the exact moment of Caspar's accident, and the next day Morgiana takes it to the hospital where Caspar lies, his leg now straight and encased in plaster. The arcane chart, criss-crossed with connecting lines showing the major and minor correspondences between the various heavenly bodies, and the particular influences of the moment of impact, point unswervingly to one simple conclusion; Caspar should have stayed home that day. However, within a week or so he is up, moving around on crutches and ready to leave the hospital.

A difficulty now arises. He has been having problems with the tenants of the house he rents from the local council. Caspar is serious about air and he likes his very fresh, the consequence of this being that he insists on having all the windows open all the time. His other tenants disagree with this policy and in the depths of winter the ladies of the household complain bitterly. Caspar is unmoved by their pleas; the survivor of an English public-school regime he will not listen to their pampered demands, going so far as to nail some of the windows open in order to thwart their efforts.

Now, however, his disability will make him easy meat for the rebels. It will take him some time to negotiate the stairs on his crutches in order to reach and open the windows on the upper floor, giving adequate time for someone below to close the lower. He lies on his bed torturing himself by imagining the noxious fug which will be building up in his absence. In his mind it takes on the presence of a stale and malignant ectoplasm, nurtured and encouraged by his triumphant tenants. It is a difficulty that at the moment he cannot face, and when Morgiana suggests he convalesce at the embassy where she can personally take care of him, he has no difficulty in accepting.

For the next several weeks he occupies a room adjacent to Morgiana's, lying in state while she flits Florence Nightingale like in and out of the room with ample trays of food and endless pots of tea. By the time he is hobbling around on a stick, he has become so much part of the house that he abandons his fug-loving tenants and accepts the room on a permanent basis.

Cabbage Pervert

Tralee has recently met an interesting painter who she thinks might be a suitable person for a room. Her name is Sukie, a French lady with decidedly bohemian leanings, who, although she has lost her youthful bloom, still exhibits the spirit of a young girl. Her eyes are darkly luminous and she flashes them mischievously at all and sundry. She works in oils and her canvases are resplendent with flowers and butterflies all painted in minute detail. The garden room on the ground floor is given over to her as a studio, since the light is good and its windows overlook the lawn. This room had probably been occupied by the embassy cook, and had been but meagrely furnished with a small iron bed and one straight-backed chair.

On first entering the room Smith had opened a large cupboard standing against one wall, to reveal thousands of empty plastic yoghurt pots. They had been washed and neatly piled in columns filling half the cupboard, the remaining half being occupied by empty matchboxes, stacked one on the other, tier upon tier to fill the space from top to bottom. To someone coming from the rural class in Cambodia, a peasant or such from which the embassy staff was no doubt drawn, these receptacles would have seemed of immense value. Sukie immediately fills the room with huge bunches of dried wildflowers, stones, leaves and branches. She sets up her easel in the window and while working plays host to a variety of birds and squirrels, which she tempts into the room with bird seed and nuts.

She has a patron, a rich American banker who pays money in advance. But Sukie's bohemian lifestyle, late nights and the ingestion of various illegal substances, means she is always behind with her commissions, and having already received and spent the money for the work in progress has no incentive to complete it. She sits in front of a half-painted still life of a cabbage and confides her tale of woe to Smith.

'I am fed up wiz cabbages,' she wails. 'Why does 'e tell me to pent cabbages? 'E is a pervert.'

Smith has quickly come to realise that Sukie regards all men as sex-maniacs or perverts of one sort or another. Some days there are other reasons why she cannot concentrate on her work.

'I need a good smok. If I do not 'ave a good smok, I lose my 'appy feeling.'

Before long Sukie has become a much valued member of the growing colony in spite of her mischievous ways, and her room soon becomes a favourite haunt. She serves hot croissants thick with black cherry jam which she dips into her coffee, while in the background her radio, which she keeps tuned to Paris, provides a muted babble of French voices and café music. One afternoon Smith calls in and finds she has a visitor.

'Zis is doctor Toledo von Ehrenhart,' says Sukie, making the introduction. ''E is a 'omeopathic doctor 'oo 'as just been deported from Chile where 'e was being persecuted as a dissident, and now 'e need somewhere to live.'

Toledo is an impressive man. He has lost his right arm and the replacement hangs limply at his side, his black hair is combed flat to his head and his equally black beard is neatly sculpted. Sukie and Smith have been conversing of late in respect of the philosophy of G. Gurdjieff, and now she announces that Toledo is a man much steeped in the subject. She has a large blackboard used to compose layouts for her paintings, and Toledo at once begins using it to list the table of elements and their associations relating to the Gurdjieffian system. He speaks in the rich deep voice of an opera singer and seems to have all the complexities at his command.

Smith is impressed and feels that such a man would be a most interesting addition to the household, and after consultation with the others offers him a room. Toledo gladly accepts, and before long he has turned the Ambassador's study into a homeopathic clinic, from where he ministers to a constant stream of patients.

Birdsong

Some time after he has settled in, Toledo confides his story. He had been employed in a Chilean Government laboratory during the regime of Colonel Pinochet. Occasionally he had noticed that a fellow scientist from the lab would be absent from work, and without explanation or warning fail to reappear. This had perplexed him a little but not given rise to concern, since he had assumed that they had been assigned to other tasks. However, one evening outside the gates of the faculty, he is approached by a woman who seems by her broken voice and tearful eyes to be in a state of deep grief. She takes him by the arm and implores him to reveal the whereabouts of her husband.

'Who is your husband?' he asks, and she mentions a name, which he recognises immediately as a fellow scientist who had until a week or so ago worked close by him in the same lab. The man had failed to appear one morning, and Toledo had assumed that as with the others he had been reassigned.

'He may have had an accident,' he says. 'Have you checked the hospitals and the police?'

'It's no good.' The woman is weeping uncontrollably. 'I am not the only one. Will you come and speak with us? My husband always spoke of you as an honourable man; will you please try to help?'

Toledo is puzzled by all this and decides to find out more. He accompanies the woman to her home where six or seven other women gather, all of whom have a similar story. Their husbands had not returned from work nor been seen again, and the police had advised them not to ask too many questions.

The story is shocking, he has known some of these men personally and decides to do what he can to help. He must however, be careful lest he share the same fate. Taking leave of the women and promising to do what he can he spends the next couple of days reviewing the options. He cannot for obvious reasons ask any direct questions, and he eventually decides to write to the International Red Cross, since they will have the authority to mount an investigation and at least demand an explanation from the Chilean Government.

The letter is written giving the names of the missing men and the circumstances of their disappearance. It ends with a plea not to reveal their sources or mention his name, for he knows enough by now to foresee that were he identified in such an act, he could expect no mercy. The letter posted he continues working as usual, until a few weeks later the police arrest him as he makes his way home from work.

At the police station he is interrogated for the rest of the night. They want to know the names of all his friends and the addresses of his correspondents abroad. To all these questions Toledo remains silent. Finally his interrogator flings a letter down in front of him. It is from the International Red Cross listing a series of accusations against the regime, and there to his dismay he sees his own name cited in evidence. They have done the very thing he had asked them not to and he is betrayed.

Fortunately, he has family connections with some clout in England, enough it seems to bring pressure to bear for his release, together with the offer of a permanent UK visa. He now has to wait a while for his deportation papers to be processed in which time the authorities are able to vent their spleen. He is led away to a prison yard in which is a barred cage around four feet high and five and a half long with a metal roof. A guard unlocks the cage and indicates that he should enter. Toledo has to go down on his knees to get through the small door, and the guard robs him of any dignity which he may have retained with a violent shove from his boot.

It is very hot, the Chilean sun beats down and the cage is an oven. Toledo is a tall man and the cage is too small to allow him to stretch his legs, but he is able to get some relief by lying at a diagonal, and of course he cannot stand up. His personal possessions have been confiscated and he has nothing but the prison mug issued soon after his arrest. After a couple of hours of this he becomes extremely thirsty and calls to the guard who lounges on a chair in the shade of a nearby building. The guard ignores him.

'I need some water,' calls Toledo. But the man does not even look up.

As the day wears on his need for water is desperate. He has never been so thirsty in his life and he wonders if they keep this up, how long he can survive. Mercifully, towards evening the sun sinks below the yard wall and the air becomes a little cooler. A new guard comes on duty and Toledo's hopes rise; perhaps this man will have a less callous nature. His voice is now a mere croak.

'Could I have some water?' he manages to call.

In answer, the guard takes up a bottle and strolls across the yard to where a tap juts out from a wall. He fills the bottle and comes over to the cage and Toledo controls his eagerness as he approaches. Stopping a foot or two away, the man lifts the bottle to his lips and slowly begins drinking. When he has consumed most of the contents he upturns the bottle, and looking with contempt straight into Toledo's eyes pours the remainder out onto the ground.

Toledo flops back to the floor of the cage. He has no doubt now about his likely fate, and he watches with feverish eyes as the guard strolls back to the tap, refills the bottle and takes another long drink. Again he lets some of the precious contents fall to the ground, and to make the torment worse he leaves the tap running a little. The gurgle and splash of falling water continues throughout the night, adding still further to his suffering.

Towards morning he falls into an exhausted sleep, but is soon awakened by the heat of the returning sun. Having been given little food since his arrest his bowels are not giving him any discomfort, but his bladder is uncomfortably full. He tries without success to attract the attention of the guard and is desperate for a toilet, he knows that if he cannot reach one soon he will be forced to foul the cage and on top of his raging thirst have to endure the resulting smell. Finally he has no option but to use his only possession, the mug, which being large enables him to relieve himself without filling it up.

He spends the rest of the day drifting in and out of consciousness, and as evening falls the resulting coolness brings a measure of alertness. His tongue has begun to swell and his throat is so dry that he cannot swallow. As he pushes himself weakly up onto one elbow his eye alights on the mug of urine.

'It looks,' he thinks. 'Like a pale China tea,' and he cannot stop himself imagining how wonderful it would be if indeed this were the case. Overcoming his revulsion he dips a finger in the mug and applies the liquid to his cracked lips. It stings so much that he involuntarily licks them with his tongue and tastes salt with a faint hint of liquorice. Without thinking he lifts the mug to his mouth and takes a sip and then swallows. But hardly any of the liquid reaches his throat, his mouth, dry and leathery has absorbed the most part. Another larger sip brings enormous relief and the taste is nowhere as bad as expected.

'It is in fact quite interesting,' he thinks. 'Rather like water in which cabbage has been boiled.'

Toledo is a doctor and knows something of the composition of urine, he is also aware that in some parts of the world this ingestion is considered to be of great benefit to health. Thus encouraged, a small mouthful at a time he slowly drinks from the mug. When only a few inches remain he puts it down.

'Better save some for later,' he thinks.

Just before dark the guard comes over and stands looking at him thoughtfully. Then, a malevolent leer spreading across his face he raises one hand. With two fingers extended he forms the shape of a pistol, and with his lips makes an explosive sound. He laughs brutally, and pointing the fingers at Toledo makes the sound again, then turning around he walks away still laughing. Toledo is disturbed by this and cannot help but take the guards action as ominous. But there is nothing he can do, so arranging his body into the most comfortable position possible he attempts to sleep, and, as a night-cap drains the contents of his mug.

'After all,' he thinks. 'I can always fill it again in the morning.'

He awakens before dawn and in the early light can just make out the grey stone walls of the compound. His limbs are stiff and aching and he has slept but fitfully. He also needs to relieve himself and does so, filling the mug almost to the top. Although once more very thirsty he restrains himself, putting it aside for a while to cool before the sun comes up. He is wondering how much longer he will be incarcerated when he hears the sound of marching feet and a squad of eight soldiers come into sight and halt with a crash of boots in front of his cage. Their officer barks an order and one of the men breaks rank and comes forward to unlock the cage. Toledo emerges, and surrounded by the soldiers is marched across the compound and through a doorway to a smaller yard. They halt at a wall pitted with innumerable small indentations which Toledo recognises at once can only be bullet holes. He remembers the guard's pantomime of the night before and knows he is doomed.

His wrists are handcuffed behind his back and he is led forward and placed with his back to the wall, where his ankles are also restrained. The squad now form a line facing him a short distance away and the officer approaches and pins a scrap of white paper over his heart.

'Do you wish to say a last prayer?' The officer asks, but Toledo, not the kind of man to ask God for anything, silently and soundly curses the lot of them. This outcome is the last thing he had expected. He had accepted his ill-treatment philosophically, but due to his connections had expected to escape with his life, and he has not even been offered a blindfold. He decides in these final moments that it is important to die with a mind as calm as possible in spite of the violent nature of his demise, and he begins ridding himself of all thought. The officer returns to his men and gives the order to load. Eight bolts rattle into place.

'Aim!' He barks. The row of rifles are raised and pointed, while Toledo, out of time, gazes into the eight black eyes of his coming death. Now he is intensely aware of the early beams of sunlight just breaking the top of the wall behind him. They illuminate the small clusters of weeds which dot the yard and brush the highly polished boots of the soldiers. As he closes his eyes he is aware that somewhere a bird is singing.

Then comes the last word he will ever hear.

'Fire!'

There follows a ragged volley from the rifles, shockingly loud in the early morning silence. He feels nothing, and a great darkness engulfs him, but he feels nothing. Opening his eyes he sees a faint cloud of smoke hovering above the line of pointing rifles; he is bewildered; from this range they cannot all have missed. Is he dead? He looks down, fully expecting to see his bullet-riddled body lying on the ground. Seeing this the line of soldiers burst into uncontrollable laughter, while slapping their legs and each other in hysterical mirth. The officer is doubled over and holding his stomach helplessly.

'Fire!' He shouts again when he can catch his breath, and once more the squad of soldiers are convulsed with laughter. It is a cruel and sadistic joke and the rifles had been loaded with nothing but blanks.

When they have recovered from their laughter, the soldiers form up and Toledo is unfettered and marched back to his cage, where amongst much hilarity they push him roughly back inside. He feels very strange. As if newly born. The whole of his previous life a superficial dream and he, nothing but a ghost. Once more his eye alights upon the mug of urine still standing where he had put it down several lifetimes ago. It is now considerably cooler, and lifting it in a toast to the rising sun he drinks deeply.

A few waterless days later he is removed from the cage and put under guard into a truck. From the open back he watches the prison buildings recede to be replaced by a long dusty road, which view remains unbroken for an hour or so until, swinging sideways the truck enters the back gates of an airport. He is taken to a small shed at a little distance from the public terminal where Customs give him a thorough search. His personal clothes, which he has not seen since his arrest are thrown to him, and he begins to put them on. As he is about to don his coat, one of the Custom men comes forward and pulls it roughly from him. It is an expensive leather jacket, finely cut and of quality workmanship. The man takes out a razor blade from his wallet and begins slashing it along the seams, then plunges in his hand and searches around in the lining. Finding nothing he flings the now tattered jacket back in Toledo's direction. They are determined that he will leave the country destitute.

Outside on the tarmac, the regular flight has been delayed for him. A guard either side, he is marched towards the plane, its door open and a stewardess in attendance. They escort him up the steps and with a final and violent shove push him into the plane. Toledo stands slightly confused by these new surroundings, the rows of seats recede down the plane, while the passengers placidly read books or newspapers and only those seated near the door have noticed this sudden and dramatic entrance. They look a little startled as he sways unsteadily after his period of near starvation, his beard and hair unkempt and the ribbons of his leather jacket festooning his gaunt frame.

'This way please sir,' says the stewardess politely, and leads him to the back of the plane where there is a small row of three empty seats. He slides in against the window and straps himself in. By now the plane's engines are running up and soon it moves out onto the main runway and takes off. Toledo is in heaven. He sinks back into the unimaginable luxury of the seat and begins once more to breathe, something he realises he has not done since the rifles of his mock-executioners had released their crashing volley a few mornings before. He notices a trolley working its way towards him bringing a smell of hot food and coffee, and revels in these exotic aromas until it reaches him, then indulges himself from the menu. A middle-aged couple are occupying the seat in front, and are complaining loudly about the quality of the food. But Toledo, sipping from a large glass of fresh orange juice can find nothing wrong with it at all.

Arriving in London he is met at the airport by a friend and taken to a flat where he can stay until he finds his feet. It takes him a few weeks to recover from his ordeal and he uses this time making connections in the medical world. Amongst his new friends is the flower-painter Sukie, and when by accident his flat is destroyed in a fire, she invites him to visit her at the embassy.

Philip, another painter, who supplements his income doing odd-job carpentry, has been constructing a new trellis around Katarina's balcony. He is afflicted with severe stomach ulcers and his face is constricted into a permanent grimace of pain. His doctor has recommended surgery as his only option, but the idea of going into a hospital and being cut open is something he cannot contemplate. Toledo engages him on the subject and listens gravely as, his face twisted in pain, Philip describes his condition.

'I can cure you without surgery,' says Toledo confidently. 'But you must follow my advice impeccably.' Philip swears to do everything he is told and begins the treatment at once. He follows a strict diet of fresh vegetable juices which he must extract himself and drink at certain times during the day and night. 'It is an alchemical cure,' says Toledo. 'And once begun the process must be a regular and continuous action.' A week goes by and Smith encounters Philip in the garden. He is smiling, his face is transformed and his eyes are twinkling happily. 'The pain's gone,' he says. 'I've not had any for the past two days.'

Toledo, it is apparent, is a man of his word. Another two weeks and Philip announces that his doctor, shaking his head in disbelief has confirmed that the ulcers have vanished. He is immeasurably grateful to Toledo, whose reputation as a doctor is now much enhanced, and looks for some means of expressing his gratitude. Having heard the story of the leather jacket he takes a needle and strong thread and begins the laborious task of restoring it to its original condition. He follows the line of the seams using tiny and meticulous stitches, and it takes him several weeks of painstaking work until it is finished.

Tralee, Sukie, and Smith, are sitting in the garden one morning when Toledo emerges from the annexe where he has his quarters. He is proudly wearing the leather jacket and cannot suppress a huge grin at his pleasure. He stands before them and puffs out his chest; the jacket looks splendid as he expresses his amazement at Philip's skill.

'This jacket is the symbol of my triumph over that regime,' he says. 'And they were not so clever after all. Look!' He reaches a hand into the jacket and undoes a strap, then removing the false arm he twists off the hand revealing that the arm is hollow. 'They did not look in here,' he says, 'or they would have found the roll of fifty dollars I had hidden inside,' He laughs heartily and a look of wistful reminiscence passes over his face.

'But you know,' he says. 'I began to quite look forward in the morning to my first cup of piss.'

Existential Viewpoints

Tiberius has now come to stay. He is a tall shambling Swiss whose face is set into a solemn mask which seldom cracks a smile. His intense introversion has driven him into a position from which his every utterance or response is so complex and obscure that no one can understand him, which makes his isolation complete. A few days after he has moved in, Morgiana comes to Smith as he sits in the garden complaining that she cannot use the kitchen while Tiberius is in there.

'Why not?' He asks.

'Because he just stands there,' she replies. 'It makes me feel uncomfortable.'

'It's the Banana Head syndrome again,' thinks Smith.

Banana Head has left a short while ago, his New Testament, the *AtoZ* in his pocket, and a strange and recently acquired obsession with street names.

'I'll check it out,' he says and goes into the house.

The kitchen is empty, apart from Tiberius who stands near the stove his back pressed close to the wall and arms hanging straight by his sides. He stares ahead and does not move as Smith enters. Tiberius is a subtle man and Smith hesitates before initiating a dialogue. He knows that whatever Tiberius is doing he will have a profound and doubtless intricate reason for doing so. Whilst pondering the correct approach, he puts a kettle on the gas and stands watching it. There is silence in the room and Tiberius remains immobile. Finally, unable to think of a suitably unique approach, Smith speaks carefully.

'Morgiana tells me that you have upset her,' he says.

Tiberius is silent for a while, then:

'She came in here.' His voice, as always, a dull monotone.

Smith considers this and is impressed. Such an existential view on the situation looks promising. He gets straight to the point.

'Why are you standing there?' he hazards.

'I am waiting,' says Tiberius.

'What for?' asks Smith.

'For a reason to move,' replies Tiberius.

Smith tries again.

'What about freaking out Morgiana. Isn't that a good enough reason?'

'No,' says Tiberius. 'That is a stimulus coming from outside and then my movements are circumstantial. I am waiting for a real impulse.'

Smith, who has struggled at various times with this conundrum himself, now knows enough of Tiberius' predicament to realise that at this point he is best left alone. Abandoning the tea he turns off the kettle and returns to Morgiana.

'He is waiting for a real impulse,' he says.

'Well, why can't he do it in his room,' she complains.

'Because you can't predict when the thought may come. Or where, and the moment it comes you are paralysed,' says Smith. 'Anyway, at some point he will need a pee, after which we will see whether he can find a reason to leave the toilet.'

Morgiana is irritated by this approach and clearly thinks Smith should put his foot down. She also suspects that he secretly admires and even encourages these existential forms of behaviour.

A few hours later he looks in the kitchen and finds the wall vacant. He visits the toilets to discover if his friend has become immobilised in a compromising position, but finds them empty, and he wonders if Tiberius has received some great revelation, which now enables him to move from one static point to another, independent of the need to consider the integrity of each impulse.

The Smile

From the sub-continent of India they come. Delhi, Madras and Bangalore. The émigrés leave the land of their gods and the ancient culture which has nurtured their ancestors through countless generations, to begin a new life in the mythical land whence had originated that rapacious race of Englishmen, who had, like Cortez in Mexico and the Pizzaro brothers in Peru, robbed them of their treasures and subjected them to centuries of apartheid. Now the visit is being repaid, and with hope in their hearts they spread themselves among the featureless suburbs of greater London. Tamils from the South settling in droves around Kingsbury and Canons Park, the Sikhs and Muslims in Southall come to seek their fortunes in the affluent West.

Amongst this throng are musicians and dancers, highly respected and even in some cases famous amongst their own people. Soon to find their gifts unwanted by a post-Victorian, quasi-American swamp of trivial pursuits, beneath which anything redolent of quality has long since sunk out of sight. And so they languish unappreciated as they scrabble for a living and do their best to keep up with the Krishnamurtis. Smith, having given up his involvement at the wholefood warehouse in order to concentrate fully on the increasing activities of the Guild, has been frequenting an Indian Cultural centre and through this association become acquainted with the plight of these immigrant artistes.

He realises that here is an untapped source of talent for their transcultural events and Ganesh Mandra informs him of one such possibility. Her name is Usha Khambhodi, a vocalist from Nagpur whose husband accompanies her on violin. 'She has a small voice,' says Ganesh. 'But in India this is not important, and she is well known for her superb musicianship. She has only been in England for a few months and as yet has little communication with anyone. You can use my name, and if she has any doubts please tell her to ring me.' Smith thanks him for his help and promptly rings the number Ganesh has given him.

On the phone he mentions the possibility of a concert while cautiously refraining from using the word 'squat'. Mrs Khambhodi agrees to see him at her home, and Smith takes a bus out Southall way where she and her husband live.

It is a late autumn evening as he enters a bleak stretch of Victorian terraced houses that stand shoulder to shoulder along the street. An elongated fortress of prison-like austerity facing onto a network of railway lines, along which trains grind and screech their way at frequent intervals and add a deafening clatter to the dismal scene. A misty rain falls softly through the dank air, wet upon the skin and seen only against a streetlamp's radius of orange light. Somewhere along this soul-shivering facade lives the lady he has come to see, and he searches among the numbers for her house.

Arriving, he rings the ground floor bell, and since he has arranged the visit by telephone need only say his name to the Indian man who opens the door.

'I am Mr Khambhodi,' says the man. 'Please to come in.'

Smith is led into the front room where the man's wife awaits him. The room is very cold and the light dim. In the fireplace is an ancient single bar electric fire, but it is not switched on and the decor has not been renewed since at least the nineteen-thirties. The lady is sitting on a shabby couch and gestures towards an armchair. Smith sits down while her husband remains standing behind her.

She is approaching middle age, wearing a dark green and gold sari, and around her shoulders is a heavy shawl to ward off the chill. Her face is stern and her eyes show no warmth as she waits silently for Smith to make his proposition.

'I have the use of a large house,' he begins, 'and have been putting on some small Indian concerts. I wondered if you would be interested in coming to sing for us there?'

A long silence follows. Then Mr Khambhodi speaks.

'How are you finding us?' he asks.

Smith mentions Ganesh, and at the sound of his name husband and wife exchange guarded looks.

'How much guarantee?' Mr Khambhodi asks.

'Well the thing is,' says Smith. 'We have little money so cannot guarantee anything. But you can have all the admission fees,' and he goes on to explain their usual arrangement. They both regard him with undisguised suspicion. Here is another unscrupulous impresario bent on using their talents for his own ends. They have no doubt experienced a lifetime of being ripped off by such characters even in their own country, and seek to discern the self-interest beneath his facade of altruism.

At this point he realises that his neat suit and tie, which he had donned to give himself a small degree of credibility, is having entirely the wrong effect, and he wishes he had not put it on. They regard him stonily. Mrs Khambhodi has not yet spoken but now she breaks her silence. Turning to her husband she speaks in rapid Hindi, a translation of which, unknown to Smith, is 'I don't trust this man. I think he is a crook,' and Mr Khambhodi leaves the room.

'My husband will speak with Mr Mandra,' she says. Her voice is low and melodious, a delight to the ear and Smith wishes she would say more, but she lapses again into silence.

Whilst waiting for the return of Mr Khambhodi Smith imagines how their new life must look. No sun, little colour, and a complete absence of the conviviality that is such a vibrant feature of their own country. Here, in these grim surroundings they are like two tropical birds trapped in a dingy iron cage; the feathers soon to lose their glossy sheen while he labours as a low-paid clerk, and she attempts to maintain her dignity at home, singing softly under her breath as she cleans their room for fear of upsetting the landlady.

Presently the door opens and Mr Khambhodi re-enters. He speaks for a while with his wife while Smith sits awaiting their verdict. By now the cold is getting to him, and he cannot repress a shiver. Seeing this Mr Khambhodi gives his wife yet another guarded look and a meaningful nod towards the fire, at which she leans forward and switches it on. The fire slowly and reluctantly comes into life with a dull red glow, but any chance of it having an effect on the icy room is minimal. Mr Khambhodi now addresses Smith.

'My wife and I will be pleased to coming and performing for you, isn't it?' he says, and a short conversation ensues regarding the timing of the concert and the location of the embassy.

Now Smith can detect the faintest hint of warmth reaching him from the fire. But no sooner has he registered this welcome but meagre boon than Mrs Khambhodi receives another meaningful look from her husband, at which she again leans forward and switches off the fire. It is evident to Smith that in this household a little has to go a very long way. Now it is time for him to leave and having settled all the details he departs once more into the night. Returning to the embassy he then begins the process of printing and sending out the bills and securing the services of Ganesh's tabla player to accompany Mrs Khambhodi and her husband.

On the night of the concert Mrs Khambhodi's voice is indeed small. But this only serves to provoke an intense silence in her audience, who strain to catch the whispering nuances which fall delicately through the hush in long loops of minutely detailed ornament. Each tone is subtly embellished in ways that send shivers of delight through her audience, and at the close of the concert she receives tumultuous applause.

Among the audience tonight are many Indians who have heard of the concert through Ganesh and the Indian grapevine of north London. They are from the more affluent class. Professional men in business suits drive expensive cars into the forecourt, and their wives, gorgeous in gold embroidered saris, emerge perfumed and bejewelled to sweep majestically through the front door and into the salon. Tralee sits behind a table in the foyer. Dressed in her finest rags and with her hair in tasteful disarray, she collects the entrance fee from the husbands. Smith has put on his suit for the occasion, and since Indians do not pick up on accents, even mingles a little. Nevertheless, he spends most of the evening dodging awkward questions.

Ownership of the house for instance, is a question which seems to dominate the minds of the Indians with whom he speaks. In this matter he strays as far as possible from the truth, imagining, not without a sense of glee that it would empty the house in a few seconds flat. From the foyer he can hear the voice of Mr Khambhodi, deep in conversation with a lady who has just regretted the smallness of Mrs Khambhodi's voice. Mr Khambhodi immediately puts the lady in her place.

'The whole world clamours for attention,' he says severely. 'A truly great singer just sings— straight into the ear of God.'

This statement confirms Smith's suspicion engendered during the concert, that Mrs Khambhodi deliberately sings quietly in order to lure the audience's attention towards her, rather than, as in the West, bellowing at them, as for example opera singers are wont to do. It is a sublime philosophy thinks Smith, for which she willingly suffers the reputation of having a 'small' voice.

Now he is cornered by Mr Lakshmimurti to whom he had been introduced at the concert given by Ganesh Mandra. Mr Laksmimurti has assumed that Smith, in spite of his denials, is the owner of the house, and pursues him around trying to sell him fire insurance. He is somewhat puzzled by Smith's inability to conceal his amusement.

'I really can't explain,' says Smith, not wishing to offend this respectable pillar of his community. 'It is too complicated.'

'Yes. Yes,' says Mr Lakshmimurti enthusiastically, and pretending to understand Smith's cagey attitude. 'I can get you werry cheap rates, isn't it?'

But Smith's attention is on the stage where the singer is surrounded by a swirl of rainbow-hued saris. They float around her like a cloud of butterflies as the ladies shower extravagant compliments on her performance. From where he stands at the back of the salon, he can see that Mrs Khambhodi is smiling.

Saving Grace

Derek and Christine have arrived. They have an old caravan parked a few streets away and the local council are harassing them. Unfortunately their car has broken down and they cannot move it. Now they are desperate for somewhere to live, and since Derek is an old friend Smith has no option but to allow them a tiny room next to the kitchen.

The room is too small for two people to live in for any length of time, but will give them shelter until they can find alternative accommodation. It is not possible to give them a permanent room since Derek's wife, Christine, is a highly strung lady and her temperament does not suit the insecure life of a squatter. Smith had first met the couple a few years back at the Belsize Park squat where one morning he hears a knock.

Opening the door he sees a middle-aged couple standing on the front steps. He, a respectably dressed but somewhat rumpled looking man who might be a provincial bank clerk, and she a bubble-haired blond with an eager-to-please smile.

'Excuse me,' says the man. 'I don't know how to put this, but we wondered if you wouldn't mind us looking inside your house for a moment. I know this might seem rude, but you see I used to live here many years ago when I first came to London as a young man.'

While he speaks his wife is listening and nodding her head in confirmation.

'Yes,' she says. 'It's always been our dream you see. Ever since we've been married Derek has been telling me about the little room he had when he was a young man, and how he used to sit looking down into the street when he felt lonely. He has always promised me that if ever we came up to London he would take me to the street and show me the house. And so after all these years our dream has finally come true.'

She has tears in her eyes and her voice is beginning to break with emotion. Derek puts a comforting arm around her.

'So you see,' he says. 'Since we were here, Christine dared me to knock at the door, and I took this liberty to ask if you would mind us having just a glimpse at my old room.'

Smith is moved by their story and with great pleasure invites them in.

'Which room was it?' he asks.

'The little one over the front door,' replies Derek.

'Right,' says Smith. 'But keep to the wall as there are no banisters,' and he leads the way up the carpetless staircase.

The stone treads have been worn hollow by the countless feet which have passed up and down since Edwardian times when the house was built, but they have been washed clean each morning and a heavy coat of white gloss is painted in a wide strip either side of the treads. On the landing he opens the door and stands back. Johnny Banana Head has just vacated the room to pursue some obscure goal, which in spite of a detailed explanation is beyond Smith's understanding.

'I'll leave you for a bit,' says Smith, gesturing for them to enter, and retires to let them relish the moment to the full.

Returning some time later he finds them standing side by side looking out of the window. Christine turns and with tears rolling down her cheeks thanks Smith.

'It has meant so much to us,' she tells him.

'No problem for me,' says Smith. 'Look, would you like a cup of tea while you're here? I can bring it up.'

'Oh no,' says Christine. 'We wouldn't want to put you to the trouble.'

'It's easy,' says Smith. 'I've got my fire on so it will only take a few minutes,' and he leaves before they can protest further. He is intrigued by their story and wants to hear more. Downstairs he breaks up some wood to replenish the fire, now a heap of dully glowing ashes upon which sits a kettle emitting a faint curl of steam from its spout. Soon the tea is ready and he ascends the stair with three cups on a tray. Derek and Christine perch themselves on the edge of the bed while Smith occupies the window sill.

'Where have you come from?' he asks.

'Reading,' says Derek. 'I had a job in a small factory and the boss allowed us to live in a caravan in the factory yard. But then I was made redundant and that meant we also lost the caravan. Unfortunately there was no other work in the area for me, so we loaded everything we could in our Robin

Reliant and drove up to London to try our luck. That's why your kindness seems like a good omen.'

'Where are you living now?' Smith enquires.

'Well,' replies Derek. 'At the moment we're sleeping in the 'Robin' up at Hampstead Heath car-park until our luck changes.'

'You can have this room if you want,' says Smith.

They stare at him uncomprehendingly; they cannot believe what they are hearing. At last Christine breaks the silence.

'But we have no money,' she says.

'That's all right,' says Smith. 'It's only twenty pence a week: ten pence for toilet paper and ten to buy paraffin for the house lights.'

'But what about rent?' Derek asks.

'No rent,' says Smith. 'This is a squat, and since I opened it up I have some say about who gets a room.'

Derek and Christine cannot believe this luck. Their dream has come true and more, they will actually be living in the very room which has for so many years occupied a special place in their imaginations. That evening Derek goes up to the Heath to collect the car before the park closes, and when he returns they carry in their meagre possessions and soon make the room their own.

'First Harry Flame,' thinks Smith. 'Then Banana Head, and now Derek and Christine'.

Over the next few days Smith discovers that philosophy interests them, which allows communication on levels other than shopping or football, and Derek turns out to be a nifty handyman. A lofty window overlooks the hall from halfway up the staircase. Unfortunately not only does it have no glass, but the wooden frame is also entirely missing, leaving a vast opening lined with rough brickwork. Smith has cut a large piece of heavy transparent plastic to the size of this space onto which he has traced and painted in colour a large-scale decorative pattern. Stretched on a wooden frame it is ready to be fitted into the window, but he cannot install it alone and asks Derek for his help.

Now it is that Derek's practical skills are revealed. He swarms up a rickety ladder perched precariously on the staircase and supported by a rope tied to a doorknob on the first floor landing. Like a spider he goes aloft and clinging to the brickwork with one arm, reaches down to take the hammer and nails which Smith hands up to him. The new window, hoisted from below by Smith and steadied from above by Derek is then nailed firmly into place. It looks magnificent. The late afternoon sun shines squarely upon the window, sending shafts of coloured light upon the stairs and across the tiled floor of the hall below. Later, when the oil lamps and incense are lit, it is sublime.

The Psykos, who inhabit two rooms on the first floor, being hard-line Buddhists have no compassion at all and treat Christine's lack of confidence with lofty scorn. Their sharp Zen wit cuts through her nervous flurries as they sharpen their swords on her compulsive desire to please, before marching off in their identical dark blue raincoats to make their daily visit to the library and there bone up on their metaphysics. Christine will not leave her room without Derek for fear of encountering them alone and thus be presented with questions which, like a few billion others, she would rather avoid.

Christine is afraid of the Psykos.

McCafferty treats Christine with a rough and theatrical gallantry. He sweeps his battered hat off to her in passing, his ragged overcoat swirling piratically around him. Grinning broken- toothed through his scraggy beard, he casts upon her a look of supercilious amusement as, fluttering madly, she presses herself against the wall to let him pass. Unlike the Psykos, he awards himself no kudos for being far above her muddled head and treats all women in the same way.

'What I like best of all,' he tells Smith with an evil leer. 'Is to get into a woman's boudoir and stretch myself out on her silk sheets with my boots on.'

Christine is afraid of McCafferty.

Christine is afraid of Basement Michael. What she doesn't realise is that with the possible exception of McCafferty, so is everybody else. Encouraged by the activity in the house above, he has had his own key cut and now uses the front door in preference to his erstwhile mode of entry via the coal-chute. Michael comes in at night much the worse for drink, and singing loudly issues violent challenges to the house at large.

'The bastards don't believe in God,' he mutters to himself as he descends the cellar stairs, and then a roar from below. 'Come out McCafferty, you Scotch git!'

But McCafferty, in spite of his legendary valour is not at times above a little discretion and keeps his head down.

Smith now finds himself continually harassed by Christine, who has an endless stream of complaints about the Psykos, McCafferty, and Basement Michael.

'Also,' she says. 'I don't like living on the first-floor. Why can't we have a room downstairs?'

She does not like having to share the one lavatory with everybody else, and complains about the lack of cooking facilities.

Smith tries to explain: 'What you don't seem to understand,' he says. 'Is that this place is pretty basic. No electricity or gas means no bills to be paid. Here, we are out of the rat-race. You must ask Derek to get you a paraffin stove if you don't want to collect firewood.'

A fastidious look comes into Christine's face and she wrinkles up her nose in disdain. 'But they're so smelly,' she says.

Soon her consensus views are in serious disarray. Daily life in the house is for her fraught with too many affronts to her sense of what is proper, and she and Derek are forced to leave before she completely loses it. Derek, however, continues to visit frequently on his own and remains a firm friend thereafter. Hence Smith's reluctance to allow Christine into the embassy, where she cannot help but create mayhem.

'We can't afford to have any internal problems now,' he tells Derek. 'It would interfere with the activities of the Guild. What I think you should do is find your own squat and let Christine choose the tenants.'

But having gained a foothold at the embassy they seem reluctant to look for a place of their own. Smith consults his *I Ching* for advice on how best to handle them. Unaware, as he finds out years later from Derek, that downstairs in their little room they have their own *I Ching*, from which they seek advice on the best way to handle Smith. Late one evening he comes upon Tiberius and Christine in the kitchen. She has obviously been working on him to gain his support for her permanent residence in the house. He knows nothing of the background to this situation, and merely sees a nice lady being treated badly by the ruthless Smith.

'She wants to put down roots,' he says, and there is a lurking tone of accusation in his otherwise monotonic delivery.

'I can understand that,' says Smith ruefully. 'But not here. The last thing a squatter can afford is roots.'

Eventually he is obliged to do something himself, and while scouting the area on his pushbike comes upon an empty row of terraced houses overlooking Regent's Park. They are boarded up but seem from the outside to be in good condition. Together Derek and Smith examine the property after dark, and with a crowbar easily gain entry. The houses are divided into flats, one of which, its windows looking across the canal they consider will please even Christine. Much to Smith's relief she becomes enthusiastic at the prospect of having her own place, and with the help of Tiberius, Ace and Smith, they fix the place up and move in.

All goes well for a couple of months and Smith even sends round some prospective tenants to help them hold the property. But Christine turns them all down. Now very possessive about the place she wants no one else there and a certain bossiness is apparent in her manner. One day Derek turns up at the embassy with bad news. The owners of their house, having spent a fortune getting rid of the former tenants are not going to allow dirty squatters to spoil their plans. They wish to keep the house empty in order to make an easier sale and a magistrate's order has been obtained. They have a week to leave.

Derek, an adventurous soul, has concocted a scheme to thwart these plans. He intends to conceal himself inside the flat so that when the workmen close up the house he will be boarded up inside, on the somewhat dubious calculation that it will be easier to break out than to break in again when the workmen are gone.

Derek is reluctant to give up the house.

Comes the day and Derek, hiding in a cupboard hears a workman arrive. The man gives the rooms only a cursory glance before beginning to nail up the front door. Derek has sternly warned Christine not to come anywhere near during this crucial phase of the operation. But Christine, overwhelmed by her indignation at thus losing her house cannot resist. She now turns up and begins to harass the workman. She wails and weeps while hanging on to his jacket and the man begins to get upset.

'I'm just doing my job,' he shouts at her. The time-honoured slogan of all who earn a living by preying upon their own kind. Parking-wardens, court bailiffs, inventors of nuclear weapons and such. Her tears and broken-hearted appeal to his conscience having had no effect on the man, Christine turns nasty.

Inside the flat Derek has come out of his cupboard, and standing on the other side of the front-door hears the ensuing dialogue.

'Where are my nails?' The workman demands angrily.

Christine has hidden the nails and he scrabbles about looking for them. Then…

'Stop wobbling the ladder.'

'Oi! Lady. LEAVE GO THE LADDER!'

Recounting this episode later, Derek cannot conceal a hint of admiration for his dotty wife, and Smith is compelled to agree that Christine has her finer points after all.

The Baleful Glance

From the Maida Vale basin the canal cuts eastward through St John's Wood. Skirting along the edge of Regent's Park towards Camden Town the towpath for much of this route is beyond the sound of traffic, and from time to time it gives the impression of deep countryside. No buildings intrude among the lofty trees either side of the still waters, while birds, relishing the pristine silence sing without interruption.

Once beyond the Zoological Gardens the canal turns sharply left and passes under a series of bridges. It is here that signs of a bygone era become apparent. As it turns beneath a bridge a curious cluster of grooves are cut into a corner of the brickwork. Deep and smoothly worn, they show where the pulling horse plodded its way around the corner, the taut rope cutting across the edge and each passing barge contributing to the wear. Further on, and just before passing beneath an iron railway bridge, a slope cuts into the side of the towpath which angles down into the murky depths. This, is the escape route used by the bargee to rescue his horse from the water when, on the sudden appearance of a roaring and hissing monster clanking fiercely across the bridge the horse, screaming in terror would fling itself panic-stricken into the water.

Now the canal enters a straight stretch. An ancient brick wall to the left, and to the right, the sloping back gardens of elegant houses dip their bottoms into the water and play host to family boats. It is at this point that on weekends the peaceful idyll is infiltrated by vibrations of a different order.

A distant as yet muffled thud intrudes upon the subtle sough of shifting leaves and soft lap in the wake of a passing pleasure barge. The thud now getting stronger as the towpath leads towards and up a cobbled slope which took the horse to a higher level of the lock. And here again the deep rope burns across the iron rail are evidence of that long-gone slow and patient work in days when job satisfaction was easy to come by.

The thud now deafening; an omnipresent beat assails the senses with an added element. Electronic wails and hoots and groans and shrieks and beeps assault the ears and curl the toes.

It's very hard rock at the Camden Lock.

The sprawling market spread across the ancient cobbled stones is a condensed mass of youthful vitality come to shop among the stalls that offer fashions from the minds of wizards tuned to the latest thing. However, a jarring note is struck amongst these festive airs; two disapproving eyes behold this ever-shifting eager throng of gaily coloured bargain-hunters. They stare unblinking at the dayglow hair of girls and silver-studded leather males who throb and jive amid a bedlam of tortured loudspeakers.

Smith is standing by a coffee stall cup in hand, when to his front the densely packed sea of shoppers parts, and for a fleeting moment a clear channel appears through the crowd which cuts straight as an arrow across the market place. At the other end of this brief parting he is startled to see the two eyes. They stare directly at him, and such is the intensity of disapproval in their look, that he feels an involuntary twinge of guilt.

Most intrigued, he begins working his way through the nose-ringed, tattooed, shaven-headed throng, to reach at last a shop contained within an arch beneath a passing railway track. The shop is full of priceless junk which spills outside and there, propped against a wall between a hat-rack and an upturned bath stands a picture framed in shabby gold.

It is a portrait done in oils. The head and shoulders of an old gentleman with an almost bald head and a short clipped white moustache. Dressed in a formal black jacket and old-fashioned stiff shirt collar he looks out from the picture in a baleful manner, and it is immediately apparent that he does not approve of anything at all.

He is just what Smith is looking for.

'How much for the picture?' he asks the shopkeeper, a green-haired fellow with a ring through his nose.

'Three quid,' the man answers, without looking up from the task he is engaged in.

He is mixing glue in an old saucer, and Smith watches silently as he smears it onto the back of a glass eye, before replacing it into the eye-socket of a stuffed bear which stands in the shop doorway.

'I'll give you two for it,' says Smith.

The man twists the eye around a few times to make sure it is well seated, then, still without looking up he holds out his hand. Smith takes two pound coins from his pocket and dropping them into the outstretched palm turns to face the contemptuous look of the old gentleman. Somehow, since he is now the owner of the picture he feels less vulnerable to the withering disdain with which the old man regards him. It is as if he is the keeper of a large and very fierce bulldog and the notion gives him an idea.

Lifting up the picture and holding it face forward in front of him he makes his way back through the throng towards the canal, his passage through the crowd made smooth by the Medusa-like stare of the old man. One look is enough and people are falling back, stumbling in their haste to avoid his malicious glance. Smith ploughs his way swiftly forward like a combine harvester through a field of wheat until he reaches the canal towpath. Here, where crowds no longer gather and the din is a fading hum he tucks the picture beneath his arm, making sure that the old man is facing the water as he walks along.

'It will do him good,' he thinks. 'And maybe cheer him up a bit.'

After a while he takes a quick look to see if the calming influence of the placid water and gentle woodlands has had any effect. He is disappointed. The old man has not budged an inch. He stares out across the canal with utter contempt, he will never, never, approve of anything. 'How dare you? How dare you?' he seems to be saying.

Back at the embassy Smith gives the picture a rub with linseed oil and patches up the gold frame. Then taking a fine haired water-colour brush and a tube of gold paint he writes in small letters at the bottom. 'Richard Arnold. President, Guild of Transcultural Studies. 1917-1922.'

The name, redolent of schoolmasters, has the right ring to it and suits the old man well. When the picture is dry he hangs it in the foyer directly facing the front door where anyone coming in will be confronted by the disapproving stare. It will stop them in their tracks and put them at a disadvantage until they reveal themselves as friend or foe.

A short while later a large framed photograph of a similarly worthy looking gentleman is discovered in the attic. An austere and self-assured military type, he is hung in the kitchen under the guise of 'George Philpot. President, Guild of Transcultural Studies. 1923-1928', and becomes another of the ghostly hierarchy which, together with the brass plate completes their cover of stuffy English respectability.

A Ghastly Shopping Bag

Smith has been accepted as a pupil by a teacher of Carnatic violin at an Indian cultural centre. He finds himself sitting down cross-legged, the violin held between breast and ankle in the Indian manner, amongst a dozen or so twelve-year-olds learning the elementary rules of the music. After some weeks he notices another late-starter amongst the pupils. He is an Indian and like Smith approaching middle age; a clipped grey beard covers his chin and he has an ambition to play the Carnatic flute.

He arrives each week with his flutes contained in a large shopping bag which carries a huge advertisement for 'Swan Vesta' matches, and is coloured a lurid red, yellow, and green. Smith hates the bag on sight, and automatically extends his revulsion for the bag onto its owner. For a brief moment their eyes meet and a vague sense of hostility hangs between them. Subsequently, Smith keeps well away from the man; he knows for sure that they won't get on.

Some time goes by and the teacher is returning to India; he assembles his pupils before him and at the end of a short farewell speech says, 'You must work together in pairs on the material I have left you,' and he begins pairing them off two-by-two. On reaching Smith he says. 'You will work with Wirril Mauratunga.'

Smith looks around. Who is Wirril Mauratunga? To his dismay he sees it is the Indian with the ghastly shopping bag, and they exchange hostile looks. 'This,' thinks Smith, 'Is going to be difficult.'

Wirril agrees to come to the embassy for their first practice session and turns up with flutes contained as usual in the dreadful bag. Smith, in order to understand the mathematical punctuation of this music has also taken some lessons on the mridungam, the double-headed drum of South India. He has been keeping time for Wirril and now they sit alone on the floor of the annexe hall. They have spoken to each other only in surly monosyllables, but have played through several exercises uneventfully and stop for a breather.

Smith feels like a smoke and decides to make himself a joint of hashish, but is aware that respectable Indians are even more affronted by this habit than the average law abiding Britisher, 'and this man,' he thinks, 'may go to the police.'

He therefore constructs the joint behind the drum which lies between them and well below Wirril's line of sight. He has just finished crumbling in the hashish when Wirril, catching Smith unawares, suddenly leans forward and looks over the top of the drum.

'Is that a joint you're making?' he asks, grinning hugely.

Instant brotherhood is established and they cement the relationship by sharing the smoke.

'I thought you were a stuck-up Englishman,' says Wirril, as they fall about laughing, while Smith reveals his distaste for the shopping bag which seems to him now, as no more than an endearing expression of his new found friend's eccentricity.

Wirril had arrived in England in the early Fifties, a youth fresh from Sri Lanka; he had obtained a place at a London college and studied there for a degree in music. However, the bright city lights had proved too tempting a lure for this innocent, and when he should have been practising his scales, was instead frequenting certain low-class dance halls. An eye or two for the ladies had completed the downfall and he had begun drifting; until the arrival of the Sixties had galvanised him along the hippie trail to Afghanistan with some friends in a Volkswagen bus.

Thereafter, an acid-fuelled caper through the subsequent years had culminated in a desire for some stability. He had attended night school to qualify as an architect and is now employed by the local council in this capacity. Wirril is no longer the naive young émigré who had first stepped onto these shores. He is a Londoner through and through, and an old hippie to boot.

'You know,' he confides to Smith, 'I used to like nothing better than dropping a tab of acid and going to my karate classes.'

At The Fulcrum Of Two Realities

A young American by the name of Bill Fortune has turned up at the embassy and stays for a few days. He is on his way to India where he hopes to get singing lessons from a teacher he is in contact with there. He attends one of the Guild's now frequent concerts and finds the setting and ambience perfect for this music.

'When I get to India,' he says, 'I will give your address to as many musicians as possible.'

A month or so after he has left, he calls the embassy from India.

'I have met the great Dagar Brothers,' he says excitedly. 'They are coming to England in a few weeks time to perform some concerts in the north, and I have told them that they can stay with you and perhaps do a London concert at the embassy.'

He requests also that they may be picked up at the airport.

The Dagar Bros? This is a stunning piece of news. They are masters of the Drupad style of singing. Developed in the 12th century at the Moghul courts and faithfully preserved thereafter by the Dagar family through many generations of singers; it is the most austerely classical amongst the many genres of North Indian vocal music. This is an undreamed of honour and much work needs to be done in order to rise to this occasion.

A room upstairs is put aside for these illustrious guests and given a thorough cleaning. Sheets for the two single beds are borrowed from friends and two armchairs carried up. The fireplace is ripped out from an alcove at the far end of the salon and the walls lined with soft insulating board. Several pallets cut to size form a low stage while Tralee contributes a half-dozen saris and a large oriental carpet from her collection of exotica. The saris are hung around the alcove and the carpet is spread over the pallets, while across the top is hung a red velvet pelmet fringed with gold, concealing a spotlight in each corner. When the lights in the salon are turned off and the stage is lit by the spotlights it seems a perfect setting for these princes of music.

The two brothers, their sister who will play tanpura, and the drummer who will accompany them, are picked up at the airport by a Rolls-Royce belonging to a lady-friend of Albert Clere, a painter of Tibetan Tanka pictures who lives locally. He has spent many years in the Himalayas learning this art, and a screen print of one of his pieces hangs in the salon. Morgiana borrows a truck from the wholefood warehouse to collect the luggage, and this entourage sweeps into the embassy forecourt in great style.

The brothers, Zahir and Fayadud, are middle-aged and dress elegantly in long Gandhi jackets with Kashmir scarves around their necks to protect their vulnerable throats from any chill. They are shown straight up to their rooms whereupon Zahir, the elder of the two immediately tests the beds. He bounces up and down a few times to try the springs then pulls back the blankets to reveal, as bad luck would have it, a tear in one of the sheets. The brothers look at each other and tut-tut disapprovingly.

'It's only a small tear,' says Smith, who is beginning to wonder if the Roller had been a mistake. 'And the sheets are clean'.

They do not answer. The Dagar Brothers are very fussy.

The next morning Smith takes them a pot of tea. They have just got up and Zahir is taking a wash in the en-suite bathroom while Fayadud sprawls in an armchair. Sounds of splashing come from the bathroom accompanied by a deep bass hum. Suddenly, the hum rises through several tones, then hovers for a moment before dropping again. A few seconds later the sequence is repeated, this time accompanied in perfect unison by Fayadud from deep within his armchair.

They continue in this way as the tea is poured, and each time the phrase is repeated it contains a new variation. The brothers do not speak; they are singing, and continue to do so for the greater part of the day. When they perform a concert, it is merely the continuation of what they have been doing for several hours anyway. There is however, one major problem. Food.

The drummer, a Hindu, is staying with an Indian family in Southall and will be fed in the appropriate manner according to his religion, while their sister will be accommodated by a family friend. But the Dagars are Muslims and are used to their own diet which it seems Indian restaurants cannot produce to their satisfaction. They turn their noses up at tandoori take-aways and are most discontented. Smith encounters them one day struggling through the front door with a large suitcase which they have just unloaded from a taxi. He offers to help as they are obviously both unused to this kind of exercise. The case is very heavy and takes some time to get up the stairs to the top floor.

'What have you got in here?' gasps Smith, as he puts down the case.

'Food,' says Zahir reverently.

A friend has taken them on a shopping trip to Southall where Indian grocery stores abound and they have managed to purchase a stock of the kind of food for which they so long. Now the early morning kitchen is heavy with transcultural cooking smells. Caspar, the quintessential Englishman, tucks in to a pair of odorous kippers followed by toast and marmalade, while Brett, a minimalist in most things boils himself a solitary carrot. Morgiana has some cabbage frying on one ring of the stove while the Dagar sister, a buxom lady who turns up to minister unto her brothers, swirls amply around in a voluminous sari juggling strange bubbling concoctions which give off the rich aroma of subtle curries. These smells when experienced separately might to most palates seem innocuous, and perhaps in some cases even attractive. Together, however, they produce a fearful stink and only the most hardy dare enter the kitchen at such times.

A few days pass and the Dagars ask if they can have a bath. A bath? This is tricky as there is no hot water. The residents, having indulged themselves during their first winter in plentiful baths and central heating, the fuel tank is now empty, and those living at the embassy take care of their personal cleanliness as best they can. However, these two artistes cannot be expected to do without these bourgeois necessities. The only source of hot water of any significant volume is a large washing machine in a passage leading out to the garden. After filling it with water and switching it on, Smith goes upstairs and risking all, knocks at the Dagars' door.

'Your bath will be ready in about half an hour,' he calls.

While the water is heating they scour the house for buckets and collect half-a-dozen or so, then form a chain between the washing machine and a bathroom further along the corridor. Soon a slowly moving series of hot water filled buckets is passing along the chain; some spillage occurs and within a short time the floor is awash. In the midst of this slapstick scenario a step is heard on the stair above. It would be disastrous were the Dagars to witness this scene, so Smith leaves his place in the chain and ascends the stairs to forestall them. As he rounds a corner in the staircase he sees Zahir just coming down.

'Is our bath ready yet?' he asks in a plaintive voice.

'Five more minutes,' says Smith who, from his vantage point at the corner of the staircase can see the long sweating and fumbling chain of sloshing buckets and above, the dignified figure of Zahir waiting with towel folded neatly over his arm. Smith is at the fulcrum of two realities.

When the bath is full and the floor mopped dry, Zahir is invited down and as soon as he has entered the bathroom the washing machine is refilled in preparation for Fayadud. The whole procedure is then re-enacted and the Dagar brothers retire clean to their room.

The evening of the concert arrives and they surpass the expectations of even the most devoted connoisseurs. From the single long, gentle and deep-throated tone with which Zahir opens, to the frenzied climax, when a raga dedicated to Shiva evolves into a crescendo of leaping firework phrases. Sitting cross-legged, their jackets unbuttoned and hair tossing wildly they call upon their Lord with passionate and masterful skill.

'It will be ten years before anyone realises what happened here tonight,' says Phineas cryptically at the close of the concert.

The brothers now become friends with an Indian devotee of their music who offers to find them alternative accommodation. They are not happy at the embassy which, although on the surface appears opulent and comfortable, lacks the basic facilities which they are used to, and is a veritable ice-box in winter. Smith accompanies them to view a room which their friend has found for them. It belongs to a concert pianist who is away touring in America. The pianist's mother shows them in and speaks reverently of the white grand piano that stands in a corner of the large room. She runs her hands lovingly over its polished surface.

'It is tuned regularly every ten days, even when my son is away,' she says smugly.

While the rent is being discussed, Smith notices Zahir wander over to the piano. He lifts the lid and plays two soft tones. It is enough, his face screwed up in disgust as if encountering a bad smell he quickly lowers the lid again. The tempered piano, in which each tone is microscopically adjusted in order to fulfil the laws of western harmonic music, is to his refined ear, badly out of tune and an affront to his musicianship.

On their last night in England the Dagars sing a farewell concert for the Guild, and are invited to partake of a dinner afterward in the annexe. Wirril

Mauratunga, as well as playing flute is also a superb cook, and he offers to prepare a selection of dishes cooked in his native Sri Lankan style. The brothers look dubious, food is an important issue with them and they are mistrustful of these misguided attempts to please them.

'Just come and have a look,' pleads Smith, when the concert is over, and they follow him reluctantly along the conservatory and into the annexe.

There, on a long low table surrounded by Katarina's cushions, is laid out a feast to tempt even the most jaded palate. The delicate aroma of rare spices in which each of the many dishes have been prepared, waft across the room and pass beneath the nostrils of the Dagars as they stand sniffing in this oriental bouquet. The look of suspicion fades from their eyes to be replaced by an eager gleam. They exchange looks and the decision is a foregone conclusion.

'We'll stay,' says Zahir firmly.

The meal is delicious and the brothers are very happy when they leave. The farewells are warm, and all memories of torn sheets and dodgy baths are forgotten in the afterglow of two exquisite concerts and the magnificent feast in which they had all partaken. As the brothers leave, the embassy residents gather in the forecourt to wave their last farewells and the taxi departs, carrying the Dagar brothers away to be swallowed up once more by the world.

The Lair Of Merlin

A letter has arrived from America. It is George O'Grass writing with an urgent appeal for action on the part of Smith. It appears that George has become deeply involved with an esoteric group known as the White Bull Lodge. They have a spirit guide known to them as 'Sitting Elk', who speaks to them through one of the inner circle. George has also obtained a book published by one of their number which speaks in some detail of the Merlin myth.

When Merlin is awakened from his enchantment, says the book, he will use his powers to restore sanity to the human race. There is however a problem, says George. Although his group have discovered the location of Merlin's tomb, there are others outside the Lodge who are also close to obtaining this knowledge. Amongst these are a group of Japanese who wish to use Merlin's power for quite other purposes.

George now instructs Smith on the whereabouts of the tomb; he speaks of a certain hill in Glastonbury and an oak tree that grows on its slopes.

Smith is instructed to insert a finger into a small hole in the tree whereupon a door in the trunk will open and give access to a lift. He is to go down in the lift and find at the bottom of the shaft a stone chamber, in the middle of which he will see the body of Merlin contained in a transparent crystal sarcophagus. On the side of the casket he will find a row of buttons each inscribed with a different rune. To awaken Merlin these runes must be pressed in the correct order.

The tomb however, is protected by a powerful booby-trap and should the runes be pressed in the wrong sequence it will initiate an explosion that will destroy Smith, the tomb, and the opportunity to awaken Merlin. The Black Elk Lodge has so far not been able to establish what the correct order for the runes is, but time is pressing and the Japanese are close to discovering the location. The correct order for the runes, writes George, is encoded in *Finnegans Wake*.

'Joyce knew exactly what he was doing,' he says. 'But before visiting the tomb, I want you to see a lady who is connected to our group. She is a witch and may provide you with a clue through her dust pictures.'

The letter concludes with a final appeal for speed and Smith sits down to try to get some perspective on all this.

George is an old friend, and in Smith's eyes a well grounded man, but the story sounds too fantastic to be true, and in truth, he doesn't believe a word of it. As for *Finnegans Wake*, he had once pursued his mesmerised way through the book and now has no intention of repeating the experience. The witch, however, seems a tangible possibility and the 'dust pictures' well worth a visit. She lives in Pinner and Smith takes the tube out to this neatly suburban enclave.

The street where the witch lives is exactly the same as all the other streets in Pinner. The front gardens are painfully manicured and the razor-edged privet hedges cut back to the quick. From behind the white lace curtains and polished letter boxes comes the fearful wailing of vacuum cleaners and Smith, entering the street, sees at the further end a hedge which seems to have entirely escaped this discipline.

To call it ragged would be a major understatement, he thinks, as he approaches. It looms menacingly over the pavement and its topmost scraggy branches reach long twiggy fingers to the sky. It crosses Smith's mind that this can be no other than the abode of the witch, but he is slightly disconcerted that the hedge makes it so obvious. Surely, a witch operating in the modern world will work under cover and seek to avoid this kind of attention. How can she get away with this blatant eccentricity amongst the uniform fascism of these suburban streets?

'She must have the whole of Pinner in her power,' he thinks, as he checks the numbers and finds his surmise to be correct. The house itself is equally derelict of care. The paint on the front door and window frames has been blistered by many a summer sun, and the windows themselves thick with grime have lost all transparency.

He knocks at the door and it is opened by what he assumes is the witch. She appears to be around forty-five years old and her shapeless form is covered by an old print dress, while on her feet she has a pair of broken down slippers. He mentions George O'Grass, and she invites him to enter in a curiously girlish voice.

The room to which she shows him is gloomy and the furniture, while depressingly ordinary is exceedingly scruffy. Smith sits down and she offers him tea. While she goes to boil a kettle he takes note of his surroundings. Next to where he is sitting is a piano, the top of which is piled high with sheet music some of which has fallen to litter the floor. He looks down and notices that it is all children's music. *A Sunny Waltz*, and *Eventide*, lay half obliterating *Fairy Polka*, and, *A Merry Ride*. The room he decides hasn't been cleaned in years. The witch returns with the tea which Smith finds passable. But the cakes which she offers him are so stale that he wonders if he is being tested.

He picks one up and gives it a bit of a squeeze between his fingers; it is as unyielding as a piece of rock. He puts it back and decides that whatever the consequences he is definitely not going to eat the cake. The witch he sees is watching him closely. She has a wide almost Caribbean mouth with large gapped square teeth and her eyes have a Voodoo strangeness. They are heavily hooded with the left eye so obscured by the dropped lid that the eye itself is barely visible. This affliction means that she is forced to throw her head back in order to bring both eyes to bear on Smith's cake behaviour. She is a strange person with the personality of a little girl and seems entirely oblivious of her sinister appearance. She talks of George and the quest for Merlin, and Smith can see that she knows all the details.

At one point during their conversation she takes him across to a small wooden bureau.

'This appeared last night,' she says.

Smith examines the top of the bureau. He has never seen household dust so thick, and there seems to be some faint marks as if made with a sprig of grass or a fine feather. A number of indistinct lines describe what seems to be a tree. Underneath the tree stands a stick man, his body and limbs are ill-proportioned and his head a mere smudge. Smith is uncertain about the picture: it could be an arrangement of abstract scuff marks so indistinct is it. But his first impression of the man and the tree lingers in his imagination. Could this be a further summons to Glastonbury, or are George and this lady setting him up? Now the witch seems to be complaining about something to do with coffee.

'It just keeps on appearing,' she says, shaking her head in wonder. Leading Smith into the kitchen she opens a large cupboard to reveal a great stock of jumbo-sized tins of instant coffee.

'Every day there are more,' she sighs, pointing to a long shelf high on the wall where dozens of the huge tins are lined up.

'I don't know what to do with it all,' she complains. 'And look at these.'

She leads Smith back to the other room and points to something he had not noticed before. There in a long row of large sweet jars full of copper coins around the walls.

'Twopenny pieces,' she says. 'Every day I have to collect them up from the floor. Like the coffee they just keep appearing.'

She seems more puzzled than anything, but is at the same time a little pleased by the results of whatever strange practices she is engaged in. Smith however is quite impressed by all this and is convinced that she has something going for her. He refrains however from suggesting that she do a deal with a local café for her coffee, since he regards meddling to be dangerous. He might for instance be struck down at a later date by a lorryload of coffee or blown up by an exploding espresso machine. But he leaves the witch with the intention of at least visiting Glastonbury to find the tomb. He will descend in the lift if he finds it but will keep strictly away from any buttons, and will certainly maintain a watch on any *Finnegans Wake*-reading Japanese. It is as far as he is prepared to go in the matter.

Arriving back at the embassy he packs a small tent and sleeping-bag for the trip; but the next morning he is forestalled by another letter from America. George is desperate; he is being castigated by the Black Elk Lodge for revealing their secrets to the world. The book, of which he had written so blithely, had been published for the eyes of the inner-circle only. George has unwittingly betrayed his oath of secrecy, and now warns Smith to stay away from the tomb and speak to no one of it.

'Don't worry about the Japanese,' he writes. 'The Lodge has already taken steps to deflect them.'

Smith feels a great relief at this and gladly unpacks his things. He has been let off the hook and the whole matter is in the safe hands of the brotherhood, who will undoubtedly deal with Merlin, the runes, and the Japanese in the proper manner. But poor George it seems is in deep trouble.

Karate Jelly

Dr Luong is an expatriate Cambodian and a successful businessman at present operating in Germany. He has knocked at the front door with a request to see the proprietor, and Smith, who usually represents the residents on such occasions invites him in. Doctor Luong is expensively dressed in a well-cut business suit with many discreet flashes of gold from rings, wristwatch and tie-pin. Since the man is Cambodian Smith feels a certain deference towards him, but this is quickly dissipated by his pompous and overbearing manner.

'This Cambodian property,' he announces the moment he is inside. 'It belong Cambodian people.' He sounds angry and Smith adopts a less forthcoming approach.

'I know,' he says, 'and they can have it back when they have a legitimate government.'

'No! Now!' shouts Dr Luong, his round Cambodian face flushing with frustration at Smith's failure to obey him immediately. 'You must all leave now.'

Smith has heard this somewhere before.

'Not unless you can produce a magistrate's order,' he replies. Dr Luong looks puzzled; he doesn't know what Smith is talking about.

'My father has share in this house,' he says. 'A consortium of Cambodian businessmen purchased it for the government for use as embassy, and now we wish to set up government in exile here.'

'Well you can't have it,' says Smith, who regards all governments as a form of social disease. 'You've been squatted.'

'What?' Dr Luong looks baffled, and has obviously never heard the word 'squat' before. His eyes narrow to slits and moving closer to Smith he hisses. 'Who is your contact at the Foreign Office?'

Now Smith has a little insight into the Doctor's understanding of the situation. He obviously thinks the tenancy is courtesy of some deal with the Foreign Office. Smith decides not to disillusion him.

'I can't tell you,' is all he says.

By now they have walked through the open doorway into the salon.

'Where has the Buddha gone?' Dr Luong points to the alcove at the far end where the stage is now a permanent feature. 'There used to be a golden Buddha standing against the wall there.'

Smith professes ignorance; he knows this to be untrue since he had taken out the fireplace which had occupied that spot himself.

'Look! Look!' Says Dr Luong excitedly, 'Cambodian sacred painting.'

He indicates Albert Clere's screen-printed Tibetan Buddhist Tanka, a work executed within ten minutes' walk of the house. Going closer he points to a prayer in Tibetan script at the bottom.

'See,' he says. 'Cambodian writing.'

Now Smith knows he is a liar and begins to manoeuvre him towards the front door. Before reluctantly leaving, the Doctor gives Smith his card and makes him a proposition.

'I will give you one thousand pounds for the name of your contact at the Foreign Office.'

Smith considers this. A thousand pounds would be useful, they could replenish the fuel-tank and he could give Doctor Luong the phone number of Colonel D—. But his instinct warns him to stay clear of murky deals of this kind and he turns the offer down. Later that evening he is called to the phone. It is Doctor Luong speaking from London airport.

'I am coming to London again soon,' he says. 'And I will want a room at the house.'

'I'm sorry,' says Smith. 'But that's not possible.'

'Why not?' asks Dr Luong.

'Because to be a resident here requires certain qualifications,' replies Smith. 'And anyway the house is full.'

Now Dr Luong's voice changes and he speaks in a weedling tone.

'If you give me the name of your contact at the Foreign Office I will give you two thousand pounds. Come to the airport now and I will give it to you in cash.' But Smith turns this down also.

Dr Luong is enraged by this and his voice splutters with anger.

'I'm going to shoot you!' He shrieks. 'I will kill you dead. I have many friends in London and I will have you karated to a jelly!'

Smith puts the phone down a little shocked by this venomous outburst, and for the next few days is very careful when coming in late at night. The front garden of the embassy is overhung with large trees and bushes. It would be easy for someone to hide in the shadows and from there leap out and 'karate him to a jelly'. Before entering therefore he stands on the other side of the road for a while, studying the undergrowth for any sign of activity before walking quickly through the centre of the gateway, ready to flee at the slightest movement.

'We should write to Colonel D—' says Morgiana, and Smith takes her advice. They compose a letter to the Colonel describing the visit of Dr Luong and of his intention to set up a Cambodian government in exile at the house, and a few days later receive a reply from the Foreign Office.

"Her Majesty's Government does not look upon the idea of a government in exile with favour," writes the Colonel's aide. He thanks Smith politely for the letter and says they have taken note of the Doctor's address and will be getting in touch with him.

Smith hopes that "getting in touch", is a euphemism for sending over a heavy from MI5 to put the frighteners on Dr Luong, who happily never shows his face again.

Desert Song

In the distance the early morning sun is just emerging from behind a far-off ridge of mountains; a low mist still lingers and for a while the air remains cool. The desert floor is broken by rocky outcroppings through which the travellers pick their way. They have been on the move since dawn and hope to reach their destination before the sun is high and this Moroccan desert becomes a furnace.

Two camels plod steadily along. The first carrying two old men swathed like their companions in the thin nomadic robes of the desert, while the second clanks along bearing cooking-pots, bedding rolls and a miscellany of musical instruments. The camels are led by two adolescent boys who frolic a little until called to order by a sharp word from one of the old men, who, from the top of the camel scans with the alertness of an eagle the way ahead. To the rear walks a middle-aged Moroccan keeping an overall watch on the whole party. They have come from the Jajouka valley, two days journey distant and have almost reached their destination, a small village where later in the afternoon a wedding is to take place, and they have been summoned to provide music for the feast which will follow.

The Jajouka take their name from the valley in which their village lies and all the men are musicians accomplished in their unique form of Arabic music. They play an assortment of drums, a wooden horn about twelve inches long with a reed mouthpiece, and a primitive oud. Traditionally they have supplied musicians to all the villages throughout the province, performing at weddings, births, and the initiation into adulthood of the village youth. Small groups are constantly forming to perform this function and leave their village to all points of the compass. Now, however, global politics have caused the government to redraw its internal boundaries and whole swaths of their former territory are now placed out of bounds to them. Visas must be obtained when answering a call to the outlying villages and these must be applied for in the city some days away. There is no post.

The visas take several weeks to be issued and are sometimes refused, since the application forms are complicated and the 'reasons for this travel' section, difficult to fill in by these illiterate people. It is hopeless. The obstacles are insurmountable and calls for their music, which for centuries has sustained their village are fast ceasing. Over the past year or two the young men have begun leaving for the city, and now the village consists mostly of the old greybeards, the women, and a few adolescents.

The travellers have now reached the outskirts of the village where they will perform. The camels are unloaded and led away to be fed and watered by eager children, while the men are warmly welcomed and led to a large stone hut which will accommodate them during their stay. Soon there come aromatic cooking smells from several large dishes which a group of women bring in and place upon the earthen floor, and the travellers sit down to eat rice, lamb, and copious mint tea, followed by chunks of halva. When they have eaten their fill they belch loudly, and the ladies beam delightedly at this satisfied sound. They quickly remove the dishes and the travellers lie down to rest a while until evening when the festivities will begin.

Dusk is falling as the last rays of sunset colour the desert sky to glow like distant fire along the horizon, and in the huts of the village oil-lanterns are being lit. In the square the central cooking fire is tended by the women who scurry back and forth carrying steaming dishes to the banqueting tent. Inside, the floor of the Bedouin-style tent is covered by a variety of colourful Moroccan carpets, and the bride and groom already occupy the dais which will be their throne for the evening. Gradually the places fill as relatives arrive for the seats of honour, while the villagers fill the remaining places. When everyone has eaten and the long speeches are done, a curtain at the far end of the tent is pulled aside, and in come the Jajouka.

The boys enter first. Dressed in their best tunics with long scarves about the waist and trailing from their shoulders, they twirl and pirouette whilst rattling their tambourines. Behind them comes the man who had travelled in their rear during their journey. He is softly beating a large drum carried on a strap about his neck. One of the old men carries an oud and the other a wooden horn. The two old men sit down and one takes up his oud and plucks an open string hard. Then, while it is still vibrating he runs an index finger up the string in a long looping motion culminating in a high tremolo on one tone, and the other old man raises his horn to his lips.

He blows, and the sound which emerges is electrifying. It is harsh, pure and uncompromising. It is also unbelievably loud. The drummer crackles into life with a flurry of beats which resolve into a steady hypnotic pattern, and the oud picks out the shape of a traditional folk-dance well-known to the assembled company. While above soars the wild voice of the horn. Piercing at times and hoarse like a monstrous crow, its wailing voice carries beyond the outskirts of the village and far out into the desert night.

The boys are performing the ritual steps of an ancient dance celebrating the union of sun and moon; intently they circle each other, whirling and jumping amidst a flurry of scarves. Clapping their hands in time the audience shout encouragement and the excitement in the tent begins to rise. It continues rising till the early hours of the morning, when it seems the tent can no longer contain the volcano of energy unleashed by the musicians. The next day when they leave, the whole village turns out to accompany them for a mile or so into the desert. This is almost their last engagement. The village they have just left is one of only three to which they now have free access, a number too small to sustain their way of life. Although the occasion has been enjoyable there is a measure of sadness in the air as they depart.

A small cloud of dust has been approaching the village from far out across the flat Jajouka Valley floor. The children have seen it first and run shouting through the village, bringing out the elders to shade their eyes with a flattened hand as they scan the horizon. The cloud of dust grows larger and begins to emit a distant hum, rapidly turning into the growling roar of a battered Land Rover, which sweeps amongst the huts sending chickens and goats fleeing in panic and comes to rest in the village square. The driver is Bill Fortune, hunter of rare musics and regenerator of dying forms. Pushing his safari hat to the back of his head he jumps from the vehicle and speaks to the small knot of villagers.

'Anyone speak English?' he asks.

The villagers look at each other and shake their heads. 'Inglese! Inglese!' They mutter to each other. Then an old woman raises her arm. 'Mustapha! Mustapha!' She shouts. With signs they bid him wait while one of the children is sent to fetch "Mustapha", and soon a figure is seen approaching across the square.

Mustapha is a middle-aged Moroccan dressed in desert garb, and since he has been guarding the small flock of goats which belong to the village commune he has an old Martini-Henri rifle slung on his back, while across his shoulder he wears a bandoleer of ammunition. He flashes his white teeth at Bill and salaams. Bill salaams in return, and is taken into the shade of an awning stretched between clusters of date palms to be refreshed with tea.

He spends the afternoon with Mustapha, explaining that he would like to set up an international tour for them beginning in London. Some weeks later Bill recounts this meeting to Smith, who imagines the conversation that may have taken place.

'London?' says Mustapha. 'What manner of thing is this London?'

'It is a place beyond the desert,' says Bill Fortune. 'And to reach it you must fly in an aeroplane.'

Mustapha looks doubtful; he has of course seen an aeroplane, indeed who has not, as it arrows across the vast blue sky of the desert leaving a long white contrail in its wake? The tiny silver dart is not a rare sight, but he cannot imagine such a thing on the ground.

'And will the aeroplane take us beyond the desert?' he asks.

'It will take you far beyond the desert and across the seas, all the way to London.' Bill Fortune replies.

Mustapha has been to a city only once, when the village was still attempting to get visas, and he had travelled there alone for this purpose. Bewildered, he had stood for an hour on the opposite side of the road to the Consulate where the application was to be lodged. The traffic had moved in a constant stream both ways in front of him and he had been unable to cross. Eventually a policeman had taken him further along and directed him to a pedestrian walkway across the road. 'Like a river,' he had mused. 'It can only be forded at certain places.'

'And is there much traffic in London?' Mustapha now asks.

'Much indeed,' replies Bill Fortune.

'Then I hope we can find many crossing places,' says Mustapha.

'Don't worry,' says Bill, 'You will travel everywhere in your own bus.'

This satisfies Mustapha and he gathers the old men together to introduce this new idea. When he finishes speaking the old men do not smile or make any other facial concessions but sit silently looking at the ground. Their small plots of arable land cannot sustain more than a dozen people and this venture promises to bring some much-needed money for the village. Only Mustapha amongst them has ever been to a city, which in their mind's eye is no more than a very large village, but a hardy life has bred in them a profound and simple philosophy untainted by greed or expectation. The eldest of the men lifts his head and looks to the others, whose eyes do not waver as his glance falls amongst them. He nods to Mustapha who returns to Bill Fortune and tells him of their decision.

'We will come,' he says, and Bill returns to the Land Rover and departs in his cloud of dust.

Smith later recounts this conversation to Wirril, who immediately advances on him, his sword of realism flashing as he cuts Smith's Arabian idyll to shreds.

'Your idea of these people is Victorian,' he says. 'In these times it would be impossible for someone as ignorant as Mustapha to exist. They probably all have transistor radios and he would have known very well what London was,' and although loath to concede this view, Smith suspects that Wirril may be right.

Bill Fortune is speaking to Smith on the phone:

'I've got some Moroccan musicians coming over and we've managed to get the Commonwealth Institute to book them. I think the Glastonbury Festival is a possibility and also a performance in Regent's Park. How about hosting a concert at the embassy?'

'No problem,' says Smith. 'When?'

'Sometime this summer,' says Bill. 'But the thing is we don't have enough money to put them into hotels, so I wondered if they can stay at the embassy while they are in London.'

'How many are there?' Smith asks, mentally counting the few empty rooms left in the house.

'About twenty,' says Bill. 'But they are used to roughing it, so your annexe hall would be perfect for them if that's all right.'

Smith can see no reason why not, and the negotiations continue until all minor details are settled.

'One more thing,' says Bill, before he rings off. 'These people have never been outside their own environment before. One day they will be in their village in the desert, and the next at the embassy, so you must be prepared for some cultural differences.'

It is late at night when the Jajouka arrive at the embassy. Their coach which has brought them from the airport unloads in the forecourt and they carry their bundles through the side door and straight across the garden to the annexe. They are tired, and unrolling their bedding on the floor, are soon asleep.

Morning comes and the Jajouka, rising early go about their business in these strange surroundings. Outside the annexe, grass, cut short to a velvet sheen by Caspar stretches before them unlike any grass they have ever seen and they venture out upon it, squatting to feel it with their hands before beginning their morning tasks. By the time Smith comes down the garden has been transformed. Long white shirts freshly washed festoon the peony bushes and hang across the garden on a rope stretched between the spy-tower and a window in the conservatory. Lengths of unwound turbans, Teureg blue or black hang from the patio vine and lie in long strips across the rosebushes.

As he emerges into the garden the Jajouka are coming to the end of a call to prayer. Kneeling on the lawn they face Mecca and the lone voice of an old man rings out across the gardens as he sings loudly in praise of Allah, and when the prayers are finished Smith is invited by common sign language to have a cup or tea with them in the annexe.

The once staid and baronial hall with its vast ornately carved fireplace is now a bandit chieftain's mountain lair. Around the walls the sleeping rolls are covered in a variety of multi-coloured drapes glittering with tiny insewn mirrors, and upon the floor sumptuous carpets glow in the light streaming through the windows. The old men lie along the walls upon the bedding-rolls. Propped upon one elbow they smoke pungent French cigarettes and drink from an endless supply of mint tea. From this position they watch the minor events of daily life unroll, occasionally making humorous comments when an occasion arises. Smith sits down with a glass of mint tea and the old men fall silent.

After a lengthy pause one of the men utters a single word in Arabic. Another long silence ensues during which the old men ruminate upon the merit of this offering. From the far end of the hall an old fellow of seventy or so takes a puff of his Gauloise and utters a precisely articulated response and the old men fall about laughing. Smith watches and listens to this sublime and unhurried game, and wonders at the civilised way in which they spend their time. Occasionally an oud will be softly played and soon the boys, who have travelled with them, are dancing to the beat of a drum. Smith stays for hours, even trying out an oud for himself.

Later, he brings across his fiddle and the Jajouka unwrap their own. They play in a cross-legged position with the violin held in the manner of a cello. Smith cannot believe the state of their instruments. They are battered and crudely repaired; the pegs lost and replaced by roughly carved twigs from which in some cases the bark has not even been removed, and he feels embarrassed by his prissy velvet-lined case. They want to try his fiddle, passing it from one to another and he can see by their faces that they do not like it at all. One of the old men has a few words of English.

'It have only one voice,' he says and picking up his own sorry looking instrument begins to play.

He pushes the bow backward and forward hard across a string in a strange broken rhythm, and the tone which emerges is not the usual clear sound of the violin. It is the cracking voice of a passionate woman, split into an infinity of tiny sounds as the hairs of the bow pass deeply pressed into the thick gut string of the violin. The sound goes through Smith's body like an unending ripple of minor shocks thrilling in its untamed fearlessness. This was a sound which did not subscribe to fashion or the polite drawing-room tone of the western violinist. It is one of the most profound lessons in music that Smith has ever had.

At one point he glances across the room and catches an old fellow looking at him intently. Smith stares nervously back for a while, until he realises that the old man is not about to start shouting: 'Who the f*** do you think you're looking at?' Suddenly the old man bursts into a long cackle of laughter. But what can he be laughing at? Smith begins to suspect that the old man finds it funny that they had not laughed before. The other old men find something amusing in this and the laughing rolls around the room. Nothing has been said. They are laughing at nothing.

'To find nothing funny is a high attainment,' thinks Smith. 'Since there is always plenty of that around.'

It is evident to him that these men are among the real elders of the human race, and he compares them to the frail and ghostly pensioners who haunt the streets and Bingo halls of London, a city that long ago left them far behind. These old men are relaxed in their bodies as they sprawl around in their robes. Lean as old panthers they are at ease, their eyes sparkling with a humour from far beyond this clamorous world, which they seem to regard with an easeful equanimity not available to the average western psychotic.

In the centre of the hall is laid a vast silver tray on which an ornate metal teapot sits upon a spirit lamp. It is surrounded by a number of small glasses, and throughout the day the two boys watch over the pot, and at frequent intervals circulate with small trays and a collection of glasses filled with sweet mint tea. The old men do not thank the boys as they reach for the tea, it is a ceremony with honour shared equally and the boys enjoy their part in it, performing the role with solemn dignity and laughing with the old men at their jokes.

The Jajouka perform their first concert at the Commonwealth Institute and Smith attends this much-anticipated event. The drummers have arranged themselves at the back of the stage and a dozen or so old men enter with wooden horns and sit in a line at the front. The drums begin to beat; the horn players raise their instruments to their lips, and a great wave of sound goes rolling across the auditorium. There is no amplification and yet Smith, sitting several rows back, can actually feel the vibrations woofing in his ears as if sitting close to a large loudspeaker. The effect is startling and the old men look very intent as they pour a searing blast of unprocessed sound into the ears of their audience. This is not entertainment, it is a call to awake! Fresh from the desert and almost reeking of camel dung it electrifies its city audience like the cry of a mad bull elephant.

Later, the two boys come out and gyrate skilfully to the plucking of several ouds. The Jajouka are magicians, they carry their charismatic desert song into the theatre without guile or deception. For a brief interlude the audience forget the grim city that lies outside, which, like a bad dream is blown away by the power of the music. At the end the audience do not clap, even they realise that this conventional form of appreciation would be pathetic in the light of what they have witnessed this evening. Some of the pure wildness of the Jajouka has passed into them, and they cheer and wave their arms aloft. The Jajouka grin and Salaam again and again.

Over the next few days they settle in at the embassy. Venturing into the house they visit everyone's room, always with their instruments and within minutes they have a party going. Sukie will not answer her door to them and keeps it locked. In a prim schoolmistress voice she orders them away and accuses them of vile practices. They understand her French very well and know what she thinks of them. At lunchtime the boys take around great door-steps of bread and chunks of meat roasted on a small fire in the garden.

Four of the old men develop a strange habit. In the front garden is a large mound of earth, the result of a pit which had been dug to bury some rubbish from the house. The mound is up against the front hedge overlooking the street, and covered now by sparse grasses and wildflowers. The four old men swathed in their desert robes, sit on the summit of the mound and watch the traffic in the road outside. They make comments to each other as the cars, lorries and coaches swish by, and seem to find it extremely entertaining. Smith notices them for the first time one morning when returning from the local shops. As he reaches the house he sees a row of four heads sticking up above the privet hedge. They are grey-bearded and gap-toothed, with turbans swathing their upper parts, and they are grinning happily, an occasional skinny brown arm raised to point out some item of particular interest. Each day they occupy the mound and the boys bring their food and keep them regularly supplied with tea.

Tiberius has a wonderful time with the Jajouka. He stands sometimes for whole days, his back pressed to a wall in the annexe his arms straight by his sides, waiting for the inspiration that will galvanise him into a new direction far removed from his habitual and obsessive responses to life. The old men treat him kindly and the boys bring him tea. In their own culture such lone warriors against the prison of human conditioning are regarded somewhat as idiot savants, and they understand full well what he is up to. Morgiana and Tralee excite much admiration from the Jajouka, who have never seen a woman's legs bared in public before, or such wanton displays of hair. The girls bask in this attention whilst lounging like film stars in deck chairs on the patio. Dressed in their glad-rags they giggle to each other but do not stray off the patio. For despite being musicians the Jajouka are hard men of the desert and there is a fire in their eyes which deter Tralee and Morgiana from entering the annexe alone.

Sukie keeps out of sight. She had taken one look into the eye of the Jajouka and scurried back to her room.

'Zey are all sex maniac!' she had complained to Smith.

Wirril Mauretunga sits amongst the Jajouka, and accompanied by an oud plays his flute, his gaudy shopping bag lost amid the riot of colour from the Moroccan drapes, while Smith wonders how the nutty old lady next door is taking all this. He imagines the police inspector at the door.

'Excuse me sir,' he says. 'We've had a complaint from the lady next door. Do you have a Mr Ali Baba and forty thieves staying here by any chance?'

Over a period of some weeks the Jajouka travel around England, performing wherever Bill Fortune has managed to secure them a booking and turning up at the embassy whenever in London. During one of their stays the Psykos arrive on a visit. They have chosen to forget their previous treachery and Smith, not to be outdone in this Buddhist approach to the past behaves as if nothing has happened, but nevertheless he keeps a watchful eye on them. The Psykos have heard of the arrival of the Jajouka and wish to test out their metaphysics. Smith lets them in and they disappear across the garden to the annexe.

Twenty minutes or so later he encounters them as, ashen faced, they depart. It seems that their uncouth delving into the doings of Allah had got up the Jajouka's noses and one of the old men had taken out a knife and threatened to spill their guts if they did not have more respect for the subject. The Psykos, leaving in a hurry had not returned for a considerable time.

The Jajouka perform a concert for the Guild and their magic transforms the salon into the court of an Arabian palace. In the tea-break the two boys take mint tea around the audience, while the old men lie around on the stage in a relaxed manner and smoke their Gauloises. Amused by this situation they punctuate the proceedings with cackles of old man's laughter as they exercise their terse Arabic wit, undaunted by the presence of an audience. In the second half, taking their cue from the old men the audience begin to sprawl and recline on Katarina's cushions, and whilst the two boys swirl around amongst them, sip their mint tea and for a moment taste the flavour of a somewhat more graceful culture.

As they had arrived, so they had left. Late one night the Jajouka bundle their luggage into the coach and climb aboard. From the windows the grey-bearded heads look forth and salaam in farewell. Their future is uncertain, but they have Bill Fortune to smooth the path to their new global village.

Pushing The Luck

Chief Mopo is dissatisfied with the high brick wall with which he has surrounded his property and he now tops it with a wrought-iron railing. When the gang of workmen who are fitting it reach the end of the wall which abuts onto the embassy, they have no choice but to secure the end of the railing into the side of the house. They set up a small step-ladder and with a hammer and chisel cut a hole five or six inches square in the brickwork, then cementing the end of the railing into the wall they go for lunch. Caspar, alerted by the banging comes out to investigate and what he sees offends his sense of propriety. Just then Smith happens by and Caspar draws his attention to the wall.

'They should have asked our permission first,' he says. Smith agrees but cannot get himself worked up about it.

'It seems such a small thing,' he replies. 'And not worth making a fuss about.'

Caspar's ire however, is well up and he will not drop it. He is an ex-public-school man with a degree in philosophy to whom ethics and form have primal importance.

'They should have asked us first,' he says again. 'It's not so much the hole in the wall, it's the principle of the thing.'

Caspar is angry, both at the wall, and Smith's apparent inability to grasp his point.

'Look,' says Smith. 'If you feel that strongly about it do whatever you think is right, but I'm staying out of this one.'

'Right,' says Caspar with a determined air and disappears into the house, while Smith hangs around, curious to know what will happen next.

Caspar is a great hand with paste-ups. He produces his own books on anything from the astronomical alignments in the megalithic monuments of obscure Greek islands, to the translation of stellar magnitudes into colour, and the workbench in his room is cluttered with pots of gum, razor blades and off-cuttings of paper. In a few minutes Caspar reappears. Under one arm he has a step-ladder and in his hand a pot of gum and a sheet of A4 paper. This looks very interesting and Smith watches the drama unfold. Will Caspar, with right on his side see the workmen off, or will he stir up a hornet's nest? Caspar opens up the ladder and ascends to where the railing enters the wall of the embassy. The cement is still wet and he wrenches the offending metalwork free, digging out the remaining cement with a piece of stick. He then plasters Cow-Gum liberally onto the brickwork and glues the sheet of A4 across the hole. Satisfied, he takes the ladder back to the house.

When the workmen return they gaze up at the wall in bewilderment until Caspar emerges to confront them. He begins a lecture on the impropriety of their actions and his middle-class accent has a disconcerting effect on them. They treat him with some deference but their eyes flicker from time to time towards the sheet of A4 glued to the wall; in their view the action of a lunatic and they don't know quite what to do. Just then Chief Mopo's Chief Wife comes out. She is a corpulent African lady dressed in an orange kaftan, and a scarf of the same colour is wound high about her head.

She listens for a while impassively as Caspar explains that permission is needed to fix the railing to the embassy wall. She cannot tell the difference between the south London accents of the workmen and Caspar's cultured tones, but she knows the embassy is a squat and in her eyes squatters have no status at all. Grasping the workmen's ladder she wobbles her way upwards, tears away the sheet of paper and sticks the end of the railing back into the wall. Standing atop the ladder with her hands on her hips she directs her rich fruity voice across the wall at Caspar.

'Don' push de luck.' she says, and Caspar, having made his point retires, honour intact.

Top Dogs

The Psykos take their metaphysics very seriously indeed and seek to identify with the void in which there are no entities.

'You might think it's me that's talking,' says Pike to Wirril one day. 'But I can assure you that there is no entity present here.'

Wirril makes no comment to this and Pike goes on.

'It's just this mouth that is talking, and I don't know what it's going to say next. It might go on and on. Or it might suddenly stop.'

He stops and bursts into laughter. Then becomes serious again.

'You might think that was me laughing,' he says. 'But I can assure you that there is no entity present here at all.'

Wirril however, uninterested in Pike's self-description lets it pass.

The position of top-dog amongst the Psykos depends on the depth of recognition and the degree of embodiment of the non-existence of the self. Their philosophy is founded upon the principle of inquiry, and the 'Top Dog' must have his wits about him. Don, the leader, although he would deny the definition, has an overall formal charm which reinforces his status, but Pike is the more brilliant. While whoever occupies the lowest position is treated like a buffoon, the butt of all their jokes and the scapegoat when things go wrong.

It is Hamish who fulfils this unfortunate role and he has not the flair to rise in the group's estimation. Frequently reminded that he enjoys the benefits of their company on sufferance, he stands in constant danger of being ejected from their midst. Don and Pike at times lock horns on the issue of entities. It may be accepted that neither of them exist as such, but the question remains: Who is more not there than the other?

'We've been here too long,' says Don, one day some years back at the Belsize Park squat. 'We need to change our surroundings for a while, and we want some real challenges.'

They are standing on a large semi-circular balcony at the back of the house. Smith is leaning against the ornate but half derelict cast-iron railings, looking out across the tanglewood back gardens.

'I have a friend in Scotland,' he says, 'who squatted some land up there in the Sixties. You could pay him a visit, I'm sure he could do with some help.' He writes down the address and gives it to Don. 'His name is Ram O'Neil,' he says.

A few days later the Psykos, having packed their few possessions, are about to embark for Scotland in a small van. Before leaving they question

Smith once more.

'What's this Ram O'Neil like?' asks Don.

'He is a cross between a mountain torrent and a babbling brook,' answers Smith, indulging on sudden impulse in a bit of flowery speech. 'But you can be assured of a warm welcome.'

The Psykos regard him sardonically. This, they think, comes dangerously close to sentiment. Pike, still striving for Top-Dog status is not for letting Smith off so lightly.

'Where's he at?' he asks.

'Well,' answers Smith, 'For the answer to that, if there is one, you must ask him yourself. But you will find him to have a sympathetic ear for any interesting ideas you may have.'

'Is there any such thing as an interesting idea?' asks Don with razor-sharp sarcasm.

'Don't worry about it.' says Smith, 'He is a kind bloke and will give you a meal anyway.'

Smith is a little sorry to see them go. They have had a stabilising effect on the other more unruly elements in the house; five people working together as a team have more clout than he alone can muster. The Psykos had for instance refused to take McCafferty seriously at all, and to his menacing attitudes they merely laugh. Smith is having tea with them one day when he comes slouching in and stands sneering at the clean glass cups and Zen-like simplicity of their room. McCafferty's definition of a bourgeois is someone who takes their overcoat off before going to bed and washes in the morning, or any other time for that matter. He slits his eyes at the Psykos. Now he is getting serious.

With his left hand he sweeps his filthy overcoat aside to reveal the handle of a large kitchen knife stuck into the back of his belt. The Psykos are, however, unfazed by this antisocial demonstration and begin making claims that they can actually see his body odour surrounding him like an aura. McCafferty, enraged, puts on some more pressure.

Striding to the mantelpiece he seizes a Japanese style vase, an elegant piece containing a solitary fresh flower. Raising it high he smashes it down onto the floor and stands amongst the shards daring the Psykos to do anything about it.

Unfortunately for McCafferty they find his action extremely funny. Linking hands around him they circle in a skipping ring-o-roses dance singing,

'McCafferty! McCafferty! La-la la-la la-laah!'

McCafferty stands in the centre, furious and baffled by their behaviour, but reduced nevertheless to the stature of a cornered playground bully.

Two days after the Psykos have left Smith catches McCafferty milking the house-lights of paraffin for his own personal use. Since he pays nothing towards their maintenance Smith feels an immediate sense of outrage. But this is tempered by the knowledge that in McCafferty's eyes he will be the respectable town-burgher bewailing the gypsies who hang around on the outskirts of town to pilfer and rob the taxpayers. Their relationship goes back a long way, to the days when McCafferty's philosophy had been in embryo and yet to reach the extremes which he now exhibits. They understand each other very well.

'Considering the circumstances,' says Smith as evenly as possible and trying not to sound like a town-burgher. 'I don't see how even you can justify what you're doing.'

But McCafferty is unmoved by this and secure in his philosophy.

'Oil is oil,' he growls as he makes his way down to the cellar, his milk-bottle of stolen paraffin clutched in his hand.

It is some time before Smith gets any news from Scotland, and he imagines Ram and the Psykos deeply engaged in complex discourses upon the nature of reality as they stroll through the pines on Ram's vast estate. He should have known better. Dialogue of this nature can only take place between equals, and the Psykos have none. Ram, quite a wordsmith himself in these matters had refuted their metaphysics, and they had decided to test his detachment. Emptying his house, they had piled all the furniture in the garden and burned it in a huge bonfire. Ram had taken this quite well, but had not been able to give it his full attention since he had been in the throes of writing a poem at the time.

'If they had wanted to test me,' he later complains. 'Why didn't they burn the house down?'

The Psykos had lingered for a while longer, doing their best to destabilise Ram and attempting to recruit some of his friends and family into their group, and failing in this had left to seek a suitable property and there establish a monastery from which they intended to propagate their own brand of reality.

Those days are now however long gone, and Pike has since then come to the conclusion that the path of a Psykos separates the acolyte from the world of ordinary people. Emphasising the void as reality it is therefore a duality and as such delusion. He has now, as a result of this enlightenment, dived head first into the 'world', and is soon up to his neck in big business.

"Missing Marble" is the name of the computer software company he has formed and his new persona as managing director sits oddly alongside his still lingering Buddhist viewpoints. Alone, he now occasionally turns up at the embassy with the tablas he is learning, and joins Wirril and Smith as they explore the ragas of Indian music. There is a break in this exotic musical quest while Smith puts aside his fiddle and stokes the fire under the kettle for tea. Pike turns his high octane attention on Wirril again. 'I seek the perfect and absolute point of view which is irrefutable and unassailable,' he says. The statement is a metaphysical gauntlet cast down at Wirril's feet.

'Listen', says Wirril. 'I'm not even interested in what I think. Never mind what deluded notions you may entertain.'

And now it is Pike's turn to say nothing.

Gymnopedies

Sukie had received piano lessons as a young girl, and although through neglect she has lost her technique, the piano in the salon has begun to attract her. For some days she speculates with odd pieces from Phineas' collection of sheet music, only to find much of it too difficult. Eventually however, she stumbles upon some music by Erik Satie, a composer whom she greatly reveres. She becomes enchanted by the spell of the Gymnopedies, one of his most famous pieces, and now plays hardly anything else. She struggles bravely with the strangely poignant music. Praying each time she begins that she can reach the end without stumbling and Smith, overhearing her efforts becomes enamoured of the piece himself and soon it begins to haunt him.

One day Sukie invites him to fetch his violin and try it out with her. He does so, and they spend hours attempting to get it right. Smith, never having had lessons on the classical western violin has trouble playing in such a formal manner, and his lack of technique is painful to hear.

'You sound like a chicken,' laughs Sukie.

They talk about Satie and she recounts many stories of his life, and Smith finds himself drawn deeper into the myth of this charismatic man.

''E earn 'is living playing in cafés.' says Sukie, 'and every night 'e walk 'ome by 'imself and nobody see inside 'is room. When 'e die all the musicians rush round to where 'e live to see inside, and what do zey find? Only a little iron bed and an old piano wiz broken and rusty strings. All around the edges of 'is room is empty bottles which 'e fill wiz 'ot water to warm 'imself.'

Smith admires such eccentricity and reading up a little on the subject discovers that this strange man with his original and highly poetic view of music had been the hidden influence behind the works of Ravel and Debussy, his young and admiring contemporaries.

Sukie and Smith now become obsessed with the *Gymnopedies* and day after day attempt to master its limpid simplicity. Since the music is French and the composer a Parisian it seems appropriate to have a bottle of Pernod present with which to refresh themselves when they play. A silver tray with water, sugar and lemon and the bottle of Pernod, soon becomes part of their ritual as they sink ever deeper into the Satie myth.

One afternoon, they are trying to recreate the delicate composition when there is a knock upon the salon door. It is Bella De Lorne, an American dancer who has performed many of her original pieces for the Guild. Sometimes she will dance to poetry, slowly weaving a graceful path amongst the words, her movements a mixture of pure inspiration and the Chinese exercises which she diligently practices.

'Hi,' she says in her slow Virginian drawl.

'Come in, come in,' says Sukie; they are a mutual admiration club and get on well. Bella recognises the awesome naiveté of Sukie's skilful oils, while Sukie considers Bella to be a true artiste and speaks of her talent with bated breath. They chat for a while and Sukie tells some more tales of the legendary Satie. When they resume playing Bella begins moving around the room, shaping her postures and steps to the fragile piece.

'I love it,' she says when they reach the end. 'Can we do it again?' The rest of the afternoon is spent in this manner and they arrange to meet again a few days later for more of the same.

Over the next few weeks they add the companion pieces to the *Gymnopedies*, the even stranger *Gnossiennes*. These new pieces are more difficult and give Smith much trouble, but with a glass or two of Pernod inside him he manages to saw his way more or less successfully through them. One day an idea arises to present Bella, accompanied by Sukie and Smith at the Guild, in an evening devoted to the music of Eric Satie. They are taking an enormous risk in this since they know that only Bella is a competent performer, but the Pernod brings out a bohemian spirit and they commit themselves to the project.

A schedule of three afternoons a week over the next month is committed to rehearsals after which will come the performance. Sukie volunteers to write a short synopsis of the composer's life for the programme, on the front of which will be Cocteau's famous drawing of the musician. Screen-printed with the help of Katarina, he is caught in the act of adjusting his pince-nez and the synopsis, which Sukie translates into her own peculiar form of English has great charm.

She speaks of Satie as an egoist and a maniac, on account of his unswerving devotion to music. According to her he wore 'binoculars and a bowl hat, and came very far by feet'. Satie walked home each night when his job as café pianist finished, and since his room was located on the outskirts of Paris he did indeed come very far by feet. ''E clean himself wiz a stone sponge', she writes, 'and 'e never use water for this. He give his music ridiculous titles to turn off immediately a crowd of mediocre spirits'. The synopsis is so pungently French that it is reproduced in her own handwriting and when photocopied is glued between the covers of the programme.

The evening of the performance arrives and although Sukie and Smith have spent many hours in rehearsal they have little confidence in their ability to do justice to the music, but fortified by quantities of Pernod they take their places in the salon. The podium has been removed and against the back wall of the alcove is hung a floor-to-ceiling drawing of Satie rendered in thick black lines on heavy white paper. The drawing is illuminated from the rear, and there is enough room behind this backdrop for Bella to conceal herself before making her entrance. Against the walls of the salon are arranged card-tables covered with red and white check tablecloths on which stand candles stuck into bottles, and when the guests have taken their seats the impression of a Parisian café will be complete.

Sukie sits at the piano with her hair piled high, dressed in a long silk gown borrowed from Tralee, while Smith sports a rumpled and collarless white shirt and a soup-stained black waistcoat. He has not shaved for a few days in order to cultivate a disreputable stubble, the better to strengthen the appearance of a scruffy waiter who doubles on fiddle for the floor-show. Sukie is very nervous and trembles uncontrollably in anticipation of the mistakes she is bound to make.

'Look,' says Smith, just before they go on. 'We're not supposed to be good; this is a back street café, unable to afford real musicians and forced to rely on the kitchen staff to provide the music.' Sukie is not much comforted by this and is sure that she will be laughed at.

'Have some more Pernod,' suggests Smith, and she pours them both a glass.

'Zis will make us feel much better,' she says as she swigs it down.

The front door is now opened for the evening and Derek and Christine are the first to arrive. Derek, dapper in a new suit and Christine, now safely housed, have blossomed and are greeted with real pleasure. They go into the salon and take a table in the corner, and soon around them the other places begin to fill. Smith, casting his eye around sees some familiar faces, and he nods across to Dylan Jones; ace barrelhouse pianist, pataphysical cyclist, and paramour of Bella de Lorne to boot. He is leaning against the wall at the back of the room whilst regarding the company with a puzzled air through a pair of antique wire-rimmed spectacles. Next to him stands Tiberius ready to dim the lights, and at a front table he notices Jay Marcel, a friend from the old days. Jay's companion tonight is Lilith, an American lady from New York who has spent many years in London producing films for the fringe theatre and now, since she lives locally is a frequent visitor and friend of the house. They chat a while with Derek and Christine until the candles are lit and Tiberius dims the main lights.

Suddenly, without anyone noticing her entrance, Bella stands silhouetted against the white backdrop. Her top hat is tilted at a rakish angle while the tails of her black evening jacket fall like elegant wings. Her shirt-front gleams white in the candlelight and she does not move. The room gradually falls silent as the audience become aware of her presence. Now Sukie judges that the time is right and begins the soft opening chords of the first *Gymnopedie*. Smith draws out the initial tones of the haunting melody and as he does so, Bella begins sinking slowly on her left leg. Then, with infinite caution she begins extending her right foot, moving forward upon it so slowly that the action is barely detectable and her silhouette seems not to have changed at all. Her head turns by small degrees to the left and again to the right, as she progresses like a disembodied shadow down the centre of the salon.

It is as if she is looking upon sights unseen to her audience. She is Erik Satie, making his way slowly homewards through the empty night streets of Paris. Her expression reflects the cafés closed now for the night; or perhaps the brief glimpse of an alley-cat as it flits across the lamplit pavement and makes its way amongst the shadowy trees of the boulevard.

This first piece is relatively easy and Smith manages to contain the neurotic chicken which threatens with every movement of his bow to come screeching from the violin, while Sukie's love of the piece steadies her nerves once she has started. Bella raises her elegant silver-knobbed walking-stick in salutation perhaps to some other late night walker as she performs the steps of her carefully composed dance. Occasionally she is inspired to introduce small variations in the choreography and her control is superb. Her audience is mesmerised as she saunters through the gaslit streets into which, with a sorceress' magic she transforms the room. Sukie stumbles once or twice during the three *Gymnopedies*, and one or two very small chickens afflict Smith's performance but nobody seems to notice. The end of the first half is reached without any damaging mistakes and Bella takes her bow to an appreciative audience.

Sukie now invites Smith to her room for some more Pernod.

'And I 'ave something else,' she says mysteriously.

She pours two large glasses and while they sip she stretches forth her hand.

'Ave one of zese,' she says, and there in her palm lie two white tablets.

'What are they?' asks Smith suspiciously.

'Zey are 'Torrinol',' she answers. 'I 'ave friends in Spain, zey send zem to me.'

'What will it do?' he asks.

'It will give you confidence' she replies. Confidence is precisely what Smith needs at the moment since the *Gnossiennes* are coming up next. He takes the pill and they wash them down with Pernod.

'We just 'ave time for a quick smok,' says Sukie, and takes a joint of grass from her pocket. She lights up and they pass the smoke one to another until it is finished.

'Now for the real test,' says Smith, as he prepares to leave. Strangely he is not at all nervous and feels he can handle anything no problem.

'Ave anozzer 'Torrinol',' says Sukie, and again she conjures up two white pills.

Smith doesn't hesitate, by now he feels quite elated. He takes the pill and washes it down with more Pernod, and leaving the room they make their wobbly way to the salon for the second half. Something strange is happening to Smith's body as they approach the salon. It feels very light as if walking on the moon, and looking down the floor seems an immense distance away. His arms are long and thin and the hands seem ridiculously small at the end of these far reaching appendages. Arriving back at the piano he picks up his violin, it seems no bigger than a matchbox and he has almost forgotten what it is for. Somehow, Sukie has managed to begin the first of the *Gnossiennes*, and Smith discovers that if he closes his eyes his minuscule violin feels almost normal.

He starts to play, and having memorised the first few bars the piece begins well, until behind him he hears a sob of despair from Sukie. She is also having problems with disarranged senses. Wrong notes begin escaping in shoals from her twenty fingers and the piece begins to disintegrate.

Smith, having come to the end of his few memorised bars is forced to open his eyes. He squints and tries to steady the dancing notes of the music which are jumping up and down from one line to another. The whole stave begins to undulate like a passing serpent and he cannot remember the tune. His bow now becomes entangled in the curtain strings behind him, and Sukie is weeping and banging the same chord over and over again. He looks out across the floor of the salon, the room is swimming and his violin is made of limp rubber.

Bella has just made her entrance and now, frozen in the midst of a delicate step she looks with horror at Sukie and Smith as they flounder around producing a dreadful parody of the music. Now Bella is angry, her dance ruined by the awful cacophony coming from her accompanists and she launches herself into a spontaneous war dance. She struts at high speed up and down the salon, her arms held stiff and swinging high in a military manner; an Amazon in evening dress. Smith decides there is nothing left but to join in this Dionysian display. 'People might think it's part of the act,' he thinks, and begins to stab with his bow, hitting the strings in staccato time to Bella's jerky movements. His left hand scuttles in random leaps up and down the fingerboard and like a demented crab wreaks an unmusical anarchy.

Bella is spinning furiously around the room, a wild choreography taking instant possession of her limbs. Smith's drug-fazed eyes are now witnessing another dimension. Sparks seem to be flying from Bella's fingertips as she gesticulates angrily; they hang in the air crackling audibly until subsiding. She is immersed in an aura of orange red light, which pulses and flames around her Shiva-like figure, and Sukie is out of it, her forehead resting on the piano fingerboard as she weeps and bangs monotonously away with one hand.

Jay Marcel jumps impulsively to his feet startled by Bella's whirling arms. His table overturns with a crash causing his friend Lilith to give a loud cry of alarm which in turn terrifies the wits out of the highly strung Christine who lets rip with a piercing scream. The room is now in chaos. People are getting fearfully to their feet and another table is overturned, while a whole flock of chickens escape squawking and screeching from Smith's violin. Sukie cannot stand it anymore, she gives a last despairing wail and flees from the room.

It is over; their weeks of careful preparation blown away by the weird effects of the 'Torrinol', and afterwards in Sukie's room where Smith, escaping from the outraged Bella and her indignance has gone to console her, Sukie is in despair.

'If only we did not take two 'Torrinol',' she cries broken voiced. 'Now Bella will never forgive us.'

Smith thinks she may be right, but stoically presents an alternative point of view.

'We could have taken three. Then you could have played the piano with your feet and I could have eaten my violin.'

But Smith has other ideas as to the probable cause of the disaster. Satie had been a mystic, and his music was often founded upon esoteric principles. He had also been an active Rosicrucian and the word *Gnossiennes*, a derivation from "Gnostique" knowledge of the mysteries. Smith suspects that the piece had been devised as a magical invocation of some kind and they had unwittingly become sorcerer's apprentices. The composer may well have intended the piece to be played softly and only late at night when the solitary pianist was quite alone. Smith and Sukie's cavalier approach to the music had unleashed a current of wilful magic and opened a portal for the Lord of Misrule to enter. Bella however is a generous spirit and once her initial outrage has subsided is able to regard the event with a somewhat wry amusement.

'In no other circumstances could I have seen you dance like that,' says Smith to her a few days later. 'Your war dance was splendid, and I wouldn't have missed it for worlds.'

Tralee

One morning Smith is returning to the embassy after a mission so excruciatingly boring that it would be of little or no interest to any other but himself, and even he is still reeling from the tedium of it. Approaching the side door he sees the postman just leaving. The man glances askew at Smith and then stops.

'I don't want to be rude,' he says. 'But are you all religious here?'

'Why do you ask?' says Smith.

'Well, the young lady who opened the door behaved very strangely.'

'What did she look like?' asks Smith.

'She had black hair all over the place and her skirt was torn at the bottom,' says the postman.

'That's Tralee for sure,' thinks Smith. 'In what way was she strange?' he asks.

'She asked me whether I was a Sagittarius,' says the postman. 'As it happens I am, but how she knew it is beyond me. Anyway, I told her I didn't believe in all that kind of nonsense and that she should get back into the real world.' He takes off his peaked-cap and scratches his head. 'I did my best with her,' he goes on. 'But do you know what? She didn't even know who the Prime Minister was!'

'Well I suppose that could well be so,' says Smith evasively — he is not too sure himself.

'I asked her whether she didn't ever read the newspapers,' says the postman. 'And she called me a Philistine and slammed the door.'

Now he seems puzzled. 'That's some sort of Bible thing isn't it — Philistine?'

'Well it is a Bible thing,' says Smith. 'But people sometimes use it in other ways.' He tries to explain. 'For instance:

'A man sits at the piano in a drawing room. The room is hushed but for the Chopin Nocturne which he is playing. French windows are open onto a garden and lacy curtains billow in a gentle breeze as the limpid tones float out across the lawn.'

The postman is now regarding him oddly. But Smith ignores this and goes on:

'A plumber has been called to the house and he is working in the kitchen. Now the drawing room door opens and the plumber comes in; he has a roll-up projecting from his mouth. Strolling over to the pianist who has just reached the most poignant part of the Nocturne he taps him sharply on the back.'

"Got a light mate," he says.'

The postman doesn't see the point.

'It's some sort of Bible thing,' says Smith. 'We're all very religious here.'

Second Coming

An American lady is running a weekend seminar in the salon and the subject of her course is the miracle in daily life. She is co-founder of a new metaphysic which views Jesus Christ as the eternal brother and therefore dispenses with a priesthood. Wirril and Smith are intrigued by this philosophy and read the book which the course has printed with interest. Three characters dominate the material: God, a concept impossibly far beyond the reach of human understanding and therefore you might as well forget it. Jesus Christ, brother of all mankind; and a benevolent will o' the wisp known as the Holy Spirit. Wirril and Smith have really taken to this third entity, and to dispel any whiff of piety have attributed to it a *nom de plume*, taking the initials of 'Holy Spirit', and retranslating them as 'Herman Schmidt', a tall hero with cropped blond hair, a heart of gold and a long duelling scar disfiguring his cheek.

They imagine him arriving on Earth with a mission to bring Love to the planet in the form of a virus carried in the blood. The planetary authorities however, recognise this threat to their earthly power and have set up surveillance systems to guard against the virus entering. Nevertheless, Herman Schmidt has distilled a serum which coats the virus in a membrane giving it the appearance of a white blood corpuscle. The effect lasts for several hours and is good enough to deceive even the most advanced bloodometer.

Bloodcheck I

SZzzztd! A laser pulse flickered briefly to his right and winked out. He checked his screen. Police or surveillance? he wondered.

SZzzzowtd! A second burst, closer this time flashed across his field of view, a stabbing beam ruby red against the night. Dipping the nose of his flitter, Herman punched for a quick landing. No use risking another shot.

The machine comes to ground on a wide floodlit boulevard that curves away in a great sweeping arc across the industrial wasteland, dwindling finally into a single chain of sparks before plunging like an arrow into the heart of the still distant city.

He lowers a window.
Outside,
Starlight glints on the black visor.
A tall dark figure.
An austere voice...

'Bloodcheck!'

The Vietnamese

Ram O'Neil has just arrived from his Scottish fastness, a long drive of around seven hundred miles. He accomplishes this in a 1937 side-valve Ford Popular, a vehicle which he can push up to a speed of almost sixty mph providing he has a following wind. He spends days rattling down the interminable motorways, chanting mantras to the tinkling of the small bells which he has strung around the inside of the car. Ram has long given up the proprietorship of 'Sam Widges' (a coffee bar in Soho where Smith had first made his acquaintance) to launch himself along the poetry highway and find in time his Shangri La in the Highlands of Scotland.

'I'm writing a play,' he announces when he arrives.

'What's it called?' asks Smith.

'*The Weft*,' says Ram. 'It's the saga of a poet's journey through the dark underworld of human deviousness to regain his eternal soul from the clutches of his negative conditioning.'

'Bloody Hell', thinks Smith, while Ram, still talking, reaches into a cardboard box which he has brought up to Smith's room from the back seat of his car. He brings forth a half loaf of bread, a lump of cheese and an onion. These items he lays on the floorboards while Smith kicks his fire into life and puts on a kettle. Ram, already chewing as he speaks is warming to his subject.

'The poet's name is Matt Phillips,' he says, 'whose character and experiences mirror my own mythical alter-ego.'

Smith reaches over and tears off a piece of bread and a lump of cheese, then with his penknife cuts a slice of onion. Compressing these three items into one lump he puts it into his mouth. Ram meanwhile is in full song, his narrative a kaleidoscopic sequence of remarkable meetings with madmen and seers. Where the hero finds himself ever domestically challenged by a succession of wilful houris and strumpets; bamboozled by new-age psychology and drawn willy-nilly into the orbit of mesmeric Indian gurus.

'Bloody Hell!' says Smith, when the synopsis comes finally to an end. It is his favourite expression at the moment and he uses it at every opportunity. Just then a knock comes at the door and Ace pokes his head in.

'There's three men at the front door,' he says. 'They say they are from the Vietnamese Embassy.' This sounds a bit odd given that it is almost midnight, but Smith makes his way downstairs to the front door. Outside it is difficult to see the callers clearly since the bulb in the lantern over the portico has blown, but he can just make out three sinister-looking Orientals wearing raincoats and trilbies and behind them a black limousine. Their spokesman is a small man, but his two companions loom hard-faced and silent behind him.

'We are from Vietnamese Embassy in Paris,' says the man. 'Now that Vietnam has annexed Cambodia, this property belong us and you must go at once.'

Smith knows the first part of this to be true, since he has been keeping an eye on the news and watching the ongoing situation. The Vietnamese are now quasi-heroes, having sent their armies across the border to liberate Cambodia from the evil Pol Pot regime, and are as a result now bathing in the warm glow of a mild international approval. None of this however has anything to do with him, not being party to any diplomatic arrangements regarding the establishment of embassies or such. As far as he is concerned he is an Englishman squatting by right of ancient law in an English house in England. He therefore resorts to his usual stance in these matters.

'Have you got a magistrate's order?' he asks. The man looks puzzled and then waves his hand in contemptuous dismissal.

'This house belong Vietnam Government,' he says, and insists that he has the authority to take over the house whenever he pleases. He is getting excited and seems to be angry at Smith's resistance to his proposition. The three now begin to press forward and look as if they intend to push past Smith into the house. To forestall this he steps quickly outside and pulls the door shut behind him, an act which infuriates the man even more. It is a dark night and only the weak light from the hall window falls upon the little group.

The three Vietnamese now crowd menacingly around him and their leader speaks again. 'You cannot resist Vietnamese Government,' he snarls. 'And I have my mechanic with me.'

He points to one of the men who regards Smith through narrowed eyes. The man's face doesn't move a muscle to Smith's polite 'Hello,' and his mouth stays grimly shut.

'You will be in big trouble if you do not obey,' says the first man, and Smith can see that his talk of magistrate's orders will not be understood by these people. He is wondering how to get rid of them, when he notices on the periphery of his vision a dark figure flitting like a shadow through the bushes at the far side of the forecourt. It slides soundlessly from tree-to-tree down to the front hedge where Ram's car is parked.

'Look, I really can't help you,' says Smith. 'The only way to gain legal possession of the house is through a magistrate's court.'

The man explodes with anger, barking out some sort of order to the other men and Smith becomes suddenly aware of his vulnerability. They could become violent and rough him up and in the darkness no one would be any the wiser.

The man introduced to him as the mechanic now steps close and is making as if to grab Smith's arm, when the whole forecourt is suddenly flooded with a brilliant white light. It transforms the scene from a sinister and ugly situation into a dramatic stage set on view to the street and the public at large. Thwarted, the Vietnamese jump away from Smith and shade their eyes from the glare, which is emanating from the far end of the forecourt where Ram O'Neil has switched on the headlamps of his Ford Popular to full beam. The men back off and retreat to their car with a final word for Smith.

'Be careful when you come in at night,' says the little Vietnamese before driving off and Ram, after switching off his headlights looms out of the darkness.

'I thought there was something suspicious about the whole thing,' he says. 'So I sneaked out the side door and it was quite obvious that they were up to no good.'

Ram deserves an accolade for this timely action. But there is one thing that puzzles Smith.

'What I don't understand,' he says, 'is why he introduced me to his mechanic.'

'That's easy,' says Ram. 'It is the jargon of the criminal underworld. The 'mechanic' is the one who carries the gun.'

'Bloody Hell!' says Smith.

No Flowers For McCafferty

A police inspector from a central London station has telephoned the embassy asking to speak with Smith.

'I understand that you are a friend of Mr Michael McCafferty,' says the inspector.

'Well I know him,' says Smith. 'But I doubt he has any friends.'

'So it seems,' replies the inspector. 'And what about relations, did he have any family?'

'I think he may have a sister somewhere,' says Smith. 'But why did you say "*did*"?'

'Because he's dead,' says the inspector. 'He was found floating in the river off Wapping Pier with a knife in his back and we're trying to trace his next of kin.'

Smith cannot help him and the inspector refuses to give any further information.

'I'm afraid the matter is still under investigation,' he says, and ends the call firmly by putting down the phone.

McCafferty dead, and in such a fitting way, thinks Smith. It seems to him almost inevitable that given his approach to life he must end this way. He imagines the shadowy hulk of Wapping Pier. A full moon hangs over the river. Street lamps on the far shore dapple the surface with dancing reflections and a black hump quietly breaks the waterline turning lazy circles in the shadows of the pier. McCafferty, face down and transfixed has gambled once too often and someone has finally called him out. Nevertheless the news appals Smith, and he sits on the stairs near the telephone casting his mind back to the time when McCafferty had first appeared on his event horizon.

It is the summer of 1966 and revolution is in the air. Something new is trying to be born and the establishment ethic is nervous, shifting uncomfortably on its ponderous foundations. McCafferty has arrived at the London Free School with a short haircut and a copy of Auden's poems in his jacket pocket from which he is fond of reading aloud. He renders the lines in a forceful manner, the words articulated precisely and delivered in a sarcastic tone, as if the poem lays bare the pathetic and sorry state of his listeners. Smith's connection with the school had begun the previous winter, when at a meeting called to found a free school in Notting Hill he had volunteered to teach a class in music composition. He had subsequently spent many chilly evenings in the dank basement in which it is housed waiting for the hoard of culture-hungry locals to come pouring through the door. His waiting had been almost entirely in vain. One or two pensioners had ventured down looking for a cup of tea, a few bolshie teenagers hang around for a while restless and looking for some action.

'I'm here to teach you how to write music,' says Smith, and they look at him as if he is mad.

'It's the Thursday night down at the scout-hall syndrome,' he thinks. 'We'd do better running a bingo club.'

Around about this time, what with the ozone in the air from the seismological shifts taking place in the culture and one thing or another, Smith embarks upon a course of madness which involves the casting away of all possessions and the abandonment of his rented room. He has decided to take to the streets with only the clothes he wears and a wooden flute. Having just finished reading Herman Hess' *Magister Ludi*, the image of its hero leaving all behind and casting himself upon the whim of circumstance has appealed mightily to his imagination. It is spring and the weather is fine; he feels confident that by nightfall of the first day providence will have provided him with some shelter.

Providence however, decrees otherwise. After spending a fruitless day wandering the streets of Notting Hill, eyes alert for the chance circumstance which will open the door into a new life, he finds himself late that night still in the same predicament. The streets are deserted and Smith is forced to conclude that nothing much is coming his way at the moment. It is getting dark and a little chilly, he thrusts his hand deep into his trouser pocket and feels a flat tapering object. It is his key to the cellar of the Free School and he cannot resist the opportunity it offers.

Letting himself quickly in he goes to the cellar below where he takes off his shoes, bundles up his jacket for a pillow and climbs upon a small billiard-table which has been donated to the school. Morning comes and he rises early and departs unseen. The next day brings nothing in the way of doors to new worlds, and since he had moved to the area barely six months before he knows no one. Night falls and he must use the key again. And again, and again, and again. But he cannot see any harm in it and no one is any the wiser. After a while he gets the old iron range working with wood taken from local skips. He finds a large can, cleans it out and cooks himself the odd stew with vegetables left by the market barrows in the Portobello Road. He is surviving in this way when he meets Bob, an old friend and trumpet player who has nowhere to stay. Smith, feeling that he has a moral obligation to help a friend invites him to shelter for the night at the school.

'But we must leave early in the morning and allow no one to see or hear us,' says Smith, and Bob accompanies him down to the cellar that night. And the next, and the next, and the next. Pretty soon a friend of Bob's turns up. He is a painter and on the street. Bob Dylan is singing, "How does it feel to be out on your own?" and Smith doesn't say no.

Things are now beginning to happen for him. He has recently collected a few interesting musicians together and formed a group called Suntrolly, and chief amongst these is Zen Glenn, a drummer who uses certain alchemical principles to reduce his technique to a minimum. He produces a simple rolling beat from which he will not deviate whatever the mode or speed of the music. The group play at various neighbourhood venues where their abstract improvisations are looked upon favourably by the freaks of the time. Zen has also picked up the sense of change which lies sparkling in the air and joins Smith one day in a spot of musical guerrilla warfare. Free concerts are the latest underground revolutionary fashion and Zen and Smith have decided to donate their talents to such a concert. They tell no one of their plans or the purity of the 'happening' would be sullied. One afternoon they descend upon Kensington Gardens where the bandstand is empty. They mount the steps to the podium.

Smith has recently borrowed an old tenor-sax from Bob's brother and now he takes it from the bag in which it had been hidden, while Zen unwraps the cloth from a flat Sufi drum. It is a sunny day and the park is tranquil, dotted only here and there by the odd dog-walker or perambulator-pushing nursemaid. 'It is a good day for a concert,' thinks Smith, and raising his horn to his mouth blows a sudden high stream of tones which whirl around each other in a tight cluster. He blows hard and long, while behind him comes a mesmerising throb as Zen applies his alchemical skills to his drum and gives support to Smith's shrieking horn. This performance is no adolescent defiance of authority. It is the creation of an event, a spontaneous happening bursting into life out of the sheer joy of living.

'Well that's the theory,' thinks Smith. 'Now let's see how many notes I can play before a park-keeper or the fuzz turn up.' He applies himself with vigour to his horn, riffling up and down on the keys his fingers striking willy-nilly where they fall, while from the horn comes a wailing stream of honks, shrieks and cacophonic bursts of iconoclastic music.

As the sound reaches them, the figures which dot the landscape turn their faces towards the bandstand and some of the dogs set to barking. But Zen and Smith play blithely on, their music permeating to the far reaches of the park where a keeper on his rounds hears the distant racket and begins his long-determined plod to put a stop to it. They see him coming long before he reaches the bandstand and continue the performance until, stern of visage he mounts the steps to the podium. Unscrewing the neck of his saxophone Smith drops the instrument back into the bag, while Zen's drum disappears with equal speed. They do not wait to hear the municipal admonitions but leave and make for the exit, the keeper's voice following them across the park.

'You can't do that,' he shouts. 'Music's not allowed in the park!'

Smith is glad to have found Zen who doesn't get nervous in these situations. He has discovered that Zen is an ex-burglar who because he is smallish in size kept watch at the bottom of the ladder while his two accomplices went inside.

'Yeah man,' says Zen, when Smith asks him about it. 'I was third man in a ladder gang.'

'Do we have to play everything at the same speed?' complains Dick, a trombonist who joins Suntrolly occasionally.

Zen's Zen emerges like the proverbial uncarved block.

'If you want to go faster, go ahead,' he snarls, and means it.

They are playing a gig at a local church hall and the audience are interested in this altercation and clearly think that the dialogue is part of some multi-media set up.

'Well sod you!' shouts Dick, who loses his temper easily and he begins speeding up, pumping the rhythm faster and faster. But he is on his own since Zen stubbornly refuses to budge. Smith, torn between the two, opts in this instance for a speed around half-way between the drum and the trombone. Now he has upset Dick for his lack of support and ditto Zen for his betrayal and they glare angrily at each other, while their audience look on with delight. The performance has real depth and the music is wonderful.

By now the Free School has become the refuge for a collection of strange misfits. They have transformed the gloomy cellar into something less forbidding and an exhibition of local artists adorns the walls. The floor now has a carpet and the bare light bulb has been festooned with coloured tissue paper. Thinking to make the place a little more attractive Smith has sawn the backs off the upright kitchen chairs to make stools around a low circular table. But the other teachers are offended and accuse him of trying to take the school over, and although the cellar is vacated for the evening classes complaints begin to circulate.

Smith however, is watching the birth of a new aspect of the school and begins to question its purpose. He can no longer close his eyes to the fact that as an evening institute distributing free education to the locals it is a failure and will never at this rate get off the ground. The concept itself is almost Victorian and nowhere matches the spirit of the time. But a " school of freedom" with a resident faculty has more of a lively ring to it, and he relishes the new idea.

The other members of the school however, do not take kindly to the concept, and one day they come storming down the cellar in a gang intent on the eviction of Smith and his friends. There is some attempt at negotiation, but, secure in their fine flats with all mod-cons they will not even consider Smith's point of view. They begin collecting the blankets and possessions which are kept stashed in a cupboard and carry them upstairs and pile them in the street. The two groups now face each other and it looks for a moment as if there will be an attempt to make the eviction physical. But, although dissenting with the school's new direction they are after all on the same side, and leave without another word. The possessions are soon carried back into the basement and now that this break with authority has occurred they feel that the Free School is well and truly launched.

Smith decides at this point to use his new musical connections to organise a children's procession down the Portobello Road each Saturday as part of the activities of the school, and they begin one Friday evening to put the plan into effect. Going out in a group they split up and call on all the houses in the surrounding streets asking for one flower from each garden for a children's procession. It works like magic and they return through the dusk laden with blossom. That night the flowers are bundled into small nosegays and put into buckets of water for the morrow, and the next day Smith goes out and purchases a dozen cheap Indian flutes and a few rolls of streamers. Walking the length of the Portobello market he distributes the streamers to the costers who line both sides of the road with their barrows.

'Throw a streamer when the procession goes past,' he asks them.

'OK, mate, throw it in there,' they say, and he tosses the tightly wound paper ribbon into the battered brass scoop of their scales.

That afternoon they venture forth, their number now swelled by a little bevy of young ladies who have attached themselves to the school. The ladies carry the boxes of nosegays and search the streets for little girls to join the procession and hand out the flowers. Smith meanwhile scours the area for small boys who he hopes to coerce into playing the flutes. It is tricky since if he gives them out too soon the boys will be sure to make off with them.

'Want to play a flute in the procession?' he asks a group of scruffy urchins who are kicking a ball around in the road. They look at him dully and are obviously not in the least interested.

'You can keep the flutes afterwards,' he says. Now he has their attention and they gather around.

'Let's see the flutes mister,' one of the boys calls out and Smith opens his bag and displays the bundle of flutes, their gaudy Indian labels flashing like a lure in the sun.

'But you can't have them till it begins.' He says, holding the flutes up beyond their reaching hands.

'When's the procession starting mister?' says another boy.

'Soon,' answers Smith. 'Come on,' and he begins walking up the road with the boys, now eager to get their hands on the flutes, following.

The plan is to meet the others at Denbigh Terrace where the tower of St Peter's rears above the quaint old facades of the Portobello Road. As the church clock strikes three they will start the procession and devil take the hindmost. Coming into Denbigh Terrace he sees a cluster of little girls distributing the posies amongst themselves, while a trumpet, a trombone, and a bass-drum are poised to go. It is a minute off three and Smith undoes the string around the flutes and waits until the opening chimes of the church clock before handing them out. Herding the boys into a loose bunch behind the musicians, he takes out his saxophone and they launch themselves down the middle of the market.

Such a din it is hard to conceive. Smith is playing his latest composition. It is called *Cacophonia*, and is an instrumental piece which has but one principle: the fingers must be moving at all times, any other consideration such as what notes are being played is irrelevant. To his front the trombone and trumpet blast away mightily and the bass-drum adds its persistent thud, while from behind comes an unearthly shrieking as the twelve flutes wail like a family of demented banshees.

The crowds that throng the market give way in surprise as the procession comes rollicking down the centre of the road, and here and there streamers arc through the air as the stallholders keep their bargain. The little girls hand out their posies to ladies in passing who smile in surprise and seem too overcome for words. It is a moment of brief sweetness, since their lively pace soon brings them to Golborne Road where the market peters out. The procession falters, stops and collapses into a melée and they call it a day.

'See you next week,' says Smith to the boys as they take off at last with their flutes. As he makes his way back to the school he can hear, floating through the alleys and back yards of the surrounding streets the shrill whistling of the flutes as the boys scatter, and still blowing make their way home.

Back in the cellar of the Free School McCafferty is holding forth. He talks only of revolution, but his purpose has nothing of the philosophy of peace and love which is stimulating the imaginations of the flower children that summer. He exhibits extreme contempt for all such ideas and wants to see blood on the streets. His appearance too has now drastically changed. Gone the short haircut and jacket, to be replaced by a ruffian-brimmed hat, a scraggly beard and a buttonless overcoat, the long skirts of which swirl around his legs like a pirate. He is now constantly harassed on the streets by the police who take exception to the dangerous looks he deliberately gives them in passing, and now McCafferty wants war.

'You and you,' he says, pointing to Nick, a young lad who frequents the school and his friend Woody. 'You are warriors, and the rest of you will be stretcher bearers and nurses.'

He gauges all other men in this way. The fighters and the wimps, and reveals an overwhelming sense of superiority in the manner in which he delivers his pronouncements. The sense of superiority coming from his own fearless contempt for the modern domesticated male, and he takes a theatrical and sarcastic piss out of the pretentious.

One of his favourite pastimes has of late been to go down to Piccadilly and stand around outside the Café Royal, or some posh hotel, annoying the chauffeurs who stand around flicking spots of dust from the bonnets of luxurious limousines with a Kleenex tissue. Walking up to a Rolls-Royce he raps sharply on the bonnet with his knuckles.

'What's this then?' he says aggressively. 'An ash-tray?'

The chauffeur is insulted and McCafferty laughs as he reads the man's eyes. 'How dare you call my Master's car an ash-tray'.

It is evening at the Free School and the cellar is a hotbed of revolutionary plots. Harry Flame has dropped in to add his cosmic convolutions to the mix.

'The pressure is building up', he says ominously, speaking as if he has inside knowledge of the cultural changes taking place.

He is fond of making these cryptic statements which few if any understand, and his social mannerisms are all designed to express despair at his lack of recognition from the fools who surround him. He throws himself down in an old armchair found abandoned in the street and gazes gloomily across the room where Nick, Woody and Smith are melting lead over a wood fire in the grate. They are pouring the molten metal into a plaster mould to produce rough facsimiles of half-crown pieces which they use to obtain sandwiches, drinks and cigarettes from the local vending machines. 'Rip off the system', has replaced 'Turn on, tune in, drop out', as the new hippie philosophy, and even McCafferty, who is usually at odds with the school's activities approves this piece of skulduggery.

He has of late been attempting to start a knife-throwing class and has hung a wooden board on the wall for this purpose, but no one else seems interested, and after a few throws under his guidance they drift away to their own projects. Having now produced enough lead discs for the moment Nick and Woody venture out to plunder, and Smith falls into conversation with Dave Arnforth, who has just turned up with some small cans of silver paint.

'They're under pressure and you can write on walls with them,' he says, and proceeds to demonstrate on the cellar wall.

Smith is not interested in this. But he tries them out on his boots and finds the effect quite pleasing.

'What I'm really looking for,' he says. 'Is a pair of bolt-cutters.'

'What do you want them for?' asks Dave.

'I'll show you,' replies Smith, and they go up into the street and walk to the end of the road.

'Look,' he says, and points to a piece of land in the middle of Colville Square. It is surrounded by a high mesh fence and contains a number of large plane trees, a scattering of saplings, and a dense undergrowth of bush and nettles.

'How about that for a children's playground?' he asks, and is pleased to see a gleam of mischief enter Dave's eye at the proposition.

'The problem is the gate,' says Smith, and they walk around to take a look.

The gate is secured with a heavy chain and padlock.

'I could get through it with a hacksaw,' says Smith. 'But it would take a long time and make too much noise.' Dave looks at the chain and agrees that bolt-cutters would be quicker.

'I think I know where to lay hands on a pair,' he says, and goes off on his errand. Dave is a reticent man who says little.

'But he doesn't hang about,' thinks Smith.

Back at the school he is greeted by a strange sight. Three youths sit on a bench facing the fire, their foppish hippie dress startling among the scruffy denizens of the cellar. They are friends of Jay Marcel who occupies a garret on the top floor of the building. Jay is a man who straddles two worlds. One foot is firmly established in the doors of stately homes where rich young hippie aristocrats gambol amidst a wealth of psychedelic goodies, the cupboards of their ancient family sideboards now host to a diverse array of expensive hashish of the finest kind.

His other foot stands in a lowlife Fagin's kitchen of dodgy vicars, scruffy mystics, and people who might or might not be working for the CIA. He is wont at times upon a whimsical impulse, to mix his two worlds and watch the resulting cocktail with a lofty and much amused smile. Now he has brought these three rich young hippies from the environs of Cheyne Walk and the Kings Road down to the Free School and introduced them to the cellar. Having performed this ritual he retires above to his garret, leaving the three young flowery boys to the tender mercies of McCafferty, who walks up and down behind them for a while in an ominous silence. The boys glance nervously at each other and Smith can see that McCafferty's smell is getting to them. He has long ago given up washing and at night, without taking off his boots or overcoat, merely lies on the floor and pulls a blanket over himself. He doesn't even take off his hat.

The youths crinkle their noses but dare say nothing. They wear silk jackets with satin lapels and their crushed velvet trousers flare widely at the bottoms to fall elegantly over their shiny patent leather boots, one pair bright leaf green, another orange, and the last, purple. Not having been introduced, Smith says nothing. This is McCafferty's show, and he goes to the fire and puts on a kettle for tea. McCafferty meanwhile comes around and stands looking contemptuously at the boys.

They won't look at him and try to talk amongst themselves as if alone. But McCafferty's menacing presence is too much for them and after floundering painfully around they soon give up. Once more falls the ominous silence with McCafferty centre stage. Smith has never until this moment heard McCafferty laugh, apart from the odd sarcastic snigger which he employs to get up people's noses. Now, like a hyena giving tongue, his ungoverned mirth makes no secret of its source. He looks pointedly at the shoes and then up into the faces of the wearers, his look of he-man derision plain to see by these deluded and pampered young rebels. He laughs at the jackets and he laughs at the trousers, while they shift uncomfortably but do not lose their poise. Their inborn sense of class superiority is impervious to even McCafferty's brutal reality.

'Did you know,' he growls to the boys, beginning to walk up and down and speaking in the precise and sarcastic voice of a pedant schoolmaster, 'that in the old days when people were Shanghaied and made to rough it for a while they grew to like it, in some cases even refusing to be ransomed?'

But the boys do not respond, and McCafferty, foiled in his attempt to engage their interest falls to giving them hard and menacing looks. He slits his eyes and bares his teeth in a fearsome snarl which sends them hurrying from the room, and McCafferty returns to his knife-throwing.

Around midnight Dave Arnforth returns with an enormous pair of bolt-cutters. They are as long as his leg and look as if they will go through anything. Wrapping the cutters in a sack they venture forth into the street and along to Colville Square. Smith is carrying some cardboard signs on which he has painted in large red letters, "Children's Playground". It is now quite dark and no one is around as they tackle the gate. The bolt-cutters go through the chain with one snip of the mighty jaws and they push the gates right back and fix the notices to the trees near the entrance.

'Now we'll see what happens tomorrow,' says Smith.

The next day Dave calls round early and they go along to the Square. Already the bushes within the new playground are alive with cops and robbers. Red Indians sneak around the undergrowth leaping out with bloodthirsty yells upon unsuspecting cowboys, and groups of little girls scold their dollies as they practise for later motherhood.

'Stop doing that,' they scream at the make-believe babies. 'If you don't sit still I'm going to give you a good smack!'

They push their toy prams about avoiding the older girls who, with one end of a rope tied to a tree skip their way through interminable sing-song rhymes. Sadly, within a few days the local Council hear of this bolshie piece of work and send a workman round to tear down the notices and relock the gates. Robbed of their playground, small groups of children gaze woefully through the mesh fence at their brief paradise so cruelly snatched away, while Dave and Smith, not about to give up yet, examine the new chain. It is a galvanised steel monstrosity, but Dave, running his hand over the massive links smiles enigmatically.

'My cutters will go through this,' he says confidently.

'Well at least we can give it a try,' says Smith.

They lay their plans and decide to cut the chain late on the next Friday night, leaving the opening of the gate until Saturday to allow the children's procession to enter and thus reopen the playground with a bang. Notices are painted, and there are many more helpers since word of the impending event soon travels round the community. In the early hours of Saturday morning Dave's bolt-cutters are again in action, and true to his word the jaws slice through the links with little effort. Smith arranges the chain so that the break is unnoticeable and leaves it for the moment at that.

Towards three o'clock the next afternoon the square begins to fill with freaks and their retinues of psychedelic goddesses. They swirl around to tambourine and flute while the local residents, drawn from their houses by this exotic collection, stand around in small groups on the pavements wondering what is happening. The tension is broken at last by the far-off bell of St Peter's clock striking three. The chimes come floating across the rooftops followed immediately by the distant, regularly repeated booming thump of a bass drum.

The boom, growing in volume is intermingled with an unearthly wailing, faint as yet, but growing momently louder. Now a tooting trumpet can be heard; a trombone too with jungle blasts joins saxophone to hoot mid the shrieking skirl of wayward Indian flutes. Louder still and louder, the metasonic wave of musical misrule approaches and the gates in the fence are opened. Willing hands nail up the signs as the procession bursts into view, turns right, and straight through the gates of the playground.

The energy is high and everyone cheers as a herd of small boys make a rush for the bushes. Soon, Mums and Dads, cautious at first, unwind and sit chatting in small groups on the grass. Guitars strum and girls dance, while a granddad or two send inside for a chair and sit in the sun with their cronies. Back onto a tree the skipping rope is tied and in goes Tracy to be girl of the moment. The little lady voices sing their way through the afternoon, while here and there a mum's admonishing command rings above the hubbub.

'Leave 'im be Kevin. I said, *Leave 'im alone!*'

'The Town Square is open for business again,' thinks Smith, who leaves at dusk and bumps into Dave at the gate.

'Not a bad pair of cutters you've got there,' he says.

'I can get them anytime,' answers Dave. 'Just let me know.'

As it happens there is no further need for them, since the Council backs down to such a strong show of community spirit and leave the gates open. Later, they send in a gang of workmen with a bulldozer who quickly clear the shrubs and wilderness. Then, like a dog marking its territory, vanquish the Red Indians forever with a thick black coat of tarmac.

Later that week Smith is walking along the Portobello Road when he passes a large building which he had not noticed before. It lies well back at the north end of the road, and large iron gates bar the entrance in a high brick wall. Looking through the bars of the gate he sees a Victorian brick structure that could be a school or institution of some kind. Suddenly he notices a pale face at one of the windows. It looks out at the world with the expression of an unwanted child, but it is old and lined, and now he sees more of these sad faces peering through the glass like lost souls.

Just inside the gate is a large black noticeboard which in gold lettering announces the function of the building. It is an old people's home directed by an order of Catholic nuns. A shiver runs through Smith as he imagines the fate of these hapless wretches whose wan faces peer so hopelessly from the windows. He wonders what can be done to inject them with a bit of life and perhaps cheer them up a little.

Outside in the Portobello Road it is 1966 and the pavements are thronged with hippies in flowered shirts. Head shops abound selling hash pipes and psychedelic posters, while incense hangs heavy in the air to complement the music of a plethora of new bands. Looking at the haunted windows of the building Smith shudders again. 'Perhaps they have no relatives or grandchildren,' he thinks, and then... 'Children, that's it. Old people love children,' and he hurries back to the Free School to clean himself up a bit.

An hour later he is back at the gate, his shaggy hair combed and tucked into his shirt-collar and wearing a borrowed pair of clean trousers. He rings the bell and brings a nun scurrying to the gate.

'What do you want?' she says, regarding him suspiciously through the bars.

'I am a teacher at a local school,' he says, sensing that a little parsimony with the truth might cast him in a somewhat better light. 'And I wondered if the old people would like to receive a visit from some young children at the week-end.'

'I will have to ask the Mother Superior,' says the nun and bustles off. Returning, she opens the gate.

'Please come in,' she says, and he follows her across a yard into the building. Everything is the grim shade of old brown paint, and the smell of pious disinfectant hangs heavy in the air. A long gloomy corridor takes them to an arched wooden door on which hangs a crucifix and a sign announcing 'Mother Superior'. He is ushered inside. Sitting at a desk is another nun; she is an elderly woman and regards him sternly through steel rimmed spectacles.

'What's this about children?' she asks, and her tight voice will admit to no excuses.

'I would like to bring some children to visit the old people,' says Smith. 'I'm sure they would consider it a treat and it would be educational for the children.'

'How many?' asks the chief nun.

'Not more than a dozen I should think,' replies Smith. 'And they're quite well-behaved.'

He describes the sunny dispositions of the children. Trying to convey an impression of prim little girls in ankle socks and satin bows, and small boys in Fauntleroy suits, without actually saying so. The Mother Superior listens to him in silence then says: 'Very well, they can come for tea in the hall. But,' and she raises a stern finger to assert her will. 'for one hour only, and then you must leave.'

'No problem,' says Smith. 'And I guarantee that we'll be gone within the hour.' The Mother Superior tells a nun to let Smith out and show him where the hall is. 'I will order the gates to be opened at three on the coming Saturday,' she says, and he takes his leave.

Again it is Saturday and almost three o'clock. Along the length of the Portobello Road the usual throng of bargain hunters and hippies looking for where it's at crowd the pavements and overflow into the road. By now, word of the weekly procession has spread, and a few more musicians have turned up to swell the ranks. The boys too seem to have doubled in number, and there are not enough flutes to go round.

'You'll have to take turns,' says Smith to two of the boys who are tussling over one of the instruments. The little girls are ready, their arms filled with nosegays, and there is just time to form up in some sort of ragged order when the clock strikes three and they are off.

Once more the crowd parts to allow the carnival of outrageous music free passage. Streamers fly and festoon the marchers and surprised ladies receive a bouquet. Down past Colville Terrace they swing and up the final stretch until Smith sees on his right the opened gates of the old people's home. At the gate stands a nun waiting to receive the visitors, but there is no time for such niceties, any hesitation at this point and the procession will lose its impetus and the children scatter. The nun shrinks back in horror as in through the gates they pour, across the yard and into the hall.

The old folk have been cleaned up for the occasion and wearing their best, but the avalanche of chaos which enters their world is not what they had expected. Ranks of nuns overseeing from the sides of the hall are sent into a frenzy of alarm as Maggie, the lady who this week is playing the bass drum, skips up and down the length of the aisle banging away for all she is worth, while the children scatter throughout the room.

The nuns have prepared tea and cakes for the children and two of them stand by with plates ready to serve, but the children are too excited for such bourgeois considerations and throw themselves onto the repast with unrestrained gusto. The boys stuff cream cakes into their mouths two at a time and the girls are giving no quarter. The old folk seem shocked by all this, their mausoleum existence shattered by this onslaught of exuberance, and the nuns are devastated. Bustling around they attempt to bring order by getting the children to sit down, but they will have none of it and flee screaming and laughing along the orderly rows of chairs upon which the old people sit.

At the far end of the hall is a small platform on which Bob now climbs trumpet in hand, and begins playing an unaccompanied ballad. It is *I can't get started.* He blows gently and with much pathos getting right through to the old folk. Tears pour down their cheeks as they remember the song which had been on everyone's lips when they were young, and here and there an old cracked voice sings the words. Smith notices the Mother Superior making her way towards him and by the expression on her face she wants them to leave at once. By now however, the old folk are loosening up, their dead eyes are beginning to sparkle and he dodges her for as long as he can. Other musicians are taking their turn on the platform, and the old people are getting to their feet and attempting to dance, despite the efforts of the nuns to restrain them.

One old fellow is even wearing his medals for the occasion. He is surrounded by a small gang of boys to whom he is recounting his wartime exploits and they ply him with gory questions, while the old ladies are being regaled with stories of street and school by the girls. The old faces are filled with such pleasure that Smith feels absolved of any guilt for his barbaric behaviour.

Now comes the sound of conflict from a corner of the room where two boys are fighting for possession of a flute. One sits atop the other attempting to wrench it away and punches are being exchanged. The Mother Superior cannot allow this and she scolds them as she attempts to pull them apart.

'Fuck off!' says the boy on top, and 'Yeah, sod off!' shouts the muffled voice of the one underneath.

The Mother Superior is aghast and retires ashen faced. It is obviously time to go, and as they leave Smith notices an ancient piano in the corner. The old folk have the lid open and one of the men is playing *The Lily of Laguna.* They cluster around him to sing while a nun desperately tries to get the lid shut. But they resist her efforts to contain them and closing ranks will not let her through. Smith is the last to leave. As he passes through the gate the Mother Superior stands ready to close it behind him. The gate shuts and her voice rings malevolently into his ear.

'And don't come back!' She hisses.

Smith is playing with Suntrolly at a venue in London's east end, and McCafferty tags along looking for trouble. After the gig he and Smith walk back through the streets surrounding the docks. McCafferty has still not attracted any acolytes to his philosophy but he has yet to give up on Smith. They are walking past a pub when McCafferty speaks roughly from the side of his mouth.

'Do what I say and I'll show you something.'

Smith, wishing to keep an open mind agrees, and McCafferty instructs him to go into the pub and watch what happens.

'Just stand against the wall and don't do or say anything,' he orders.

Smith looks at the pub. It is not the sort of place which he would happily frequent; long-haired freaks are not welcome in such places and it is asking for trouble. But he has committed himself, and swallowing his misgivings opens the swing doors and enters. The place is crowded. Full of tough-looking dockers and scarfaced villains. He stands against a wall near the door, ready to flee should his appearance upset any of these fearsome-looking characters. Presently the doors swing open with a wild-west bang and McCafferty slouches in and stands in the middle of the floor, a sneer of deliberate contempt on his face. His eyes look from face to face, a smile of derision playing about his lips as each pair of eyes meet his own and then drop. His right hand holds back his overcoat at the hip as would a gunslinger clearing the way for a quick draw, while just the tips of his fingers enter the top of his trouser pocket. Only the fastest gun in town would have the confidence to go looking for trouble in this blatant manner, and his sardonic smile says that none amongst them has the bottle to call him out.

Gradually the pub falls silent as the crowd become aware of his presence, the conversations falter and all eyes flicker in his direction. This silence attracts the attention of the bar-drinkers who sit with their backs to the room. They cease talking and turning around on their stools look to see what has caused it. McCafferty regards them one by one, throwing down his gauntlet and daring any amongst them to make something of it. It is plain that he expects there to be no takers. He is right, there aren't. Unbelievably, after a minute or so of this now dramatic silence one of the men at the bar, a crop-haired tough with arms like tattooed tree trunks, turns back to his drink and says something in a quiet voice. Following suit, the line of bar-drinkers turn back and continue talking, albeit in a somewhat subdued manner. The drinkers on the main floor, taking this as their cue, begin again the conversations which McCafferty's challenge had disturbed. He waits a while still in the provocative stance and finding no takers turns, and with a final look of dismissive scorn leaves. Smith waits a moment or two then follows him into the street, glad to be out of the place.

Outside, McCafferty swaggers along grinning. 'They won't do anything,' he says. He speaks in his schoolmaster manner and is utterly confident, as if he has discovered some hidden knowledge unavailable to the common man, and Smith cannot but admire his courage. McCafferty is not a big man, and underneath his overcoat he is as frail as a bird.

Most of each week is now spent seeking new ideas for the processions. Smith is keen on the notion of asking dog-owners to bring their pets on a lead.

'A barking section,' he says, 'between the trombones and the flutes would be unusual,' while young Nick has conceived for himself the role of totem bearer. For his totem he looks not to the traditional images of tribal magic, but rather a futuristic symbolism devoid of superstitious icons, and he seeks amongst the pure shapes of geometry which speak for themselves. Begging some off-cuts from a builder's woodyard he nails a succession of squares, triangles, and circles onto a long pole. Painting the shapes in different colours, he festoons the pole with paper ribbons and intends to exhibit it in the next procession. Beneath a large yellow disc which tops the pole, he has a blue triangle inverted, and lower still another circle and a square. The standard of a general in some geometric legion, or a sacred image revealed but rarely in a religious procession of shape-worshippers.

Come Saturday it rides high above all heads. Twisting this way and that it bestows a surreal benediction as it passes through the crowds, the high held emblem of what has by now become a serpentine throng of guitarists, drummers, whistles and flutes. Two trombones up front now vie with each other, their delicate slides probing a passage through the mass of people. On Smith's right is a guitarist who is singing a Bob Dylan song loud and clear, while on his left is an accordionist playing Irish jigs. He feels in good company and continues to blow the note 'E', in as many registers as possible. It is the only tone allowed in a new composition entitled, *One is too many*. His approach to the piece is, however, flexible to a large degree, and he had only chosen which note to play the evening before.

As ever and all too soon the procession culminates at Golborne Road, where people hang around and talk for a while until dispersing. Smith watches Nick walk off down the road until, disappearing into the throng only the high-held totem marks his course through the crowd. Later, walking back to the cellar he has a profound feeling of well-being.

'Well,' he thinks. 'It has no purpose and it's not going anywhere in particular. But it is going.'

Musing thus, he is passing a row of backstreet shops when from a deeply recessed doorway an arm reaches out and a hand grips him by the collar. The hand is encased in a black leather glove which pulls him with brutal force into the shop doorway, and he is drawn upwards onto his toes against the black overcoat of a very large man with a face to which he takes an instant dislike. His mind begins throwing up possibilities. The man is obviously a gangster and has perhaps mistaken him for a local drug runner welching on a deal. He tries to turn his head towards the street, someone may pass to whom he can call for help and there, strolling along on the other side of the street with his hands behind his back comes a policeman.

Smith tries to shout, but his voice chokes off as the hand tightens its grip, while the policeman looks sideways full into the shop doorway. Then, as if he sees nothing amiss, continues strolling on his beat. The penny drops. This is the police!

Now the man, pulling Smith higher and thrusting his face forward until they are almost nose-to-nose, speaks through gritted teeth in a voice laden with menace.

'If you do that once more,' he says. 'We're going to take you down to the station and give you a good kicking.'

Smith then finds himself hurled like a straw back onto the street and into a different world. Gone the feeling of wellbeing; the plans for future processions crushed like a handful of butterflies in the black leather glove and never now to fly. To continue in the face of such ruthless tyranny would be foolish indeed, and a kicking seems unattractive. He walks back to the Free School numbed by the experience. The streets which had been such happy hunting grounds only minutes before, now seem as grey as the Gulag and the sun has definitely gone in.

Returning to the cellar he finds Harry Flame and a young lady by name of Tralee, who had witnessed Harry's reading at the Albert Hall the year before during a festival of live poetry, and they are engaged in an intense conversation.

'But what would you have said had they allowed you to speak?' asks Tralee.

'No, no,' says Harry sighing heavily. 'It's too late anyway.'

'No it's not Harry, you mustn't give up,' says Tralee, 'I want to know what it was.'

On the evening in question, Harry had wished to place his poem in a particular context without which, he thought, it could not be fully appreciated. The other poets who wait their turn to read, regard this as too precious, they begin shouting. 'Read the poem! Just read the poem,' and Harry cannot make himself heard. But he is a Bard and will not surrender his mission to the rabble so easily. He tries again and again, but the poetry yobs at the front drown him out and he must concede defeat and release his 'fistful of feathers' without preamble. Even the guest of honour from America, the illustrious and legendary Boris Gainsborough, whose messianic presence draws all ears, pales before Harry's penetrating lyricism. His finely crafted images bring a unique and devastating insight, making most of the other contributors look like well-meaning but clumsy amateurs.

Smith hears but a snatch of this conversation before Harry's baleful glare tells him he is not wanted. Withdrawing, he mounts the stair to the garret above where Jay Marcel has his abode and can usually be found perched upon a high stool at an ornately carved sideboard. The ancient yellowed mirrors of the sideboard reflect the dusty image of a three-sconced silver candelabra, by which flickering light he works on a book he is writing on the visionary aspects of flying saucers. Smith, arriving above finds Jay already has company. McCafferty is holding forth on the function of police in society and Jay, an affable man, has turned aside from his writing to hear him out, whilst interjecting here and there a whimsical observation, the humorous tone of which does not quite accord with McCafferty's realpolitik.

In a far corner of the room is George O'Grass, he sits cross-legged in front of a large heap of marijuana laid out on a sheet of newspaper. Painstakingly separating the seed from the leaves and the leaves from the stalks he will sit thus for hours, methodically working through the heap until he has processed it into three neat piles. The leaf, the seeds and the stalks, which he further reduces to a coarse powder and boils up with sugar and flour to produce a marzipan-like sweet with a delicate euphoria. George smokes grass almost continuously and rolls matchstick-size joints which he passes around. They are fast jobs, one quick toke then pass it on, and woe betide any so foolish as to forget he has the joint. George will be onto him like a falcon to its prey. In his view the smoking of grass is an almost sacred act; not to be sullied by mawkish daydreams.

'Why do you smoke so much George?' Smith had once dared to ask him.

'I smoke to stay high,' was his unequivocal reply.

'The function of the police is to protect the property of the haves from the have-nots!'

It is McCafferty speaking in his exaggeratedly gruff voice.

'It is time for the have-nots to make a move.'

Jay disagrees with this; he is a mystic who seeks among the irrefutable laws of high geometry for his solutions. Now he launches into an alternative idea for a utoplatonic society, where lines of conflict and dispute can be channelled into circles and triangles. Smith, who has been listening, finds this idea intriguing but for one nagging doubt.

'That sounds a very subtle approach,' he says, 'and I've no doubt that it would work but for one thing. What about the yobbos?'

'No trouble,' says Jay, 'We'll form them up into squares.'

McCafferty dislikes this kind of talk and doesn't hide his sneers.

'We'll give each policeman a copy of the '*I Ching*,' continues Jay. 'And they will be able to settle all difficulties on the spot.'

McCafferty, recognising that Jay is mocking him slits his eyes menacingly, turns his head and spits contemptuously on the carpet. McCafferty is definitely not joking. He swaggers across the room to where Jay's current girlfriend is quietly reading. She is an English rose with a fair damask cheek, and her eyes when she lifts them to McCafferty's scowl are cornflower-blue and innocent. He begins strutting up and down in front of her, displaying his warrior manliness and wafting towards her in doing so a sample of his caveman odour, until Jay intervenes with a somewhat more formal introduction. The lady, a sensitive girl, blushes prettily and simpers a little. McCafferty regards her with withering scorn.

'I don't fancy you lady!' He barks, and laughs at her confusion. It is his favourite opening line with women, and he uses it ruthlessly. He has of late also devised a new torture for the bourgeois. Walking up to people in the street who have a dog on a lead, he confronts them in his usual aggressive manner.

'That dog should be put down,' he snarls. At which the owner enters into many interesting kinds of fit, which McCafferty savours with the relish of a connoisseur.

The room now begins to fill as from below come Harry Flame and Tralee. On seeing McCafferty and Smith, Harry gives a groan, as if ever finding himself plagued by this company of idiots.

'What's wrong Harry?' Jay asks.

'Oh God,' says Harry wearily. 'It's the whole thing.' He sighs heavily and then...

'You don't understand,' he moans, his voice laden with doom. 'They're all swinging their arms in the street; marching around as if they think they're on television.'

Slumping down into an armchair Harry stares gloomily at the floor. He seeks to read the archetypal symbols of the time and from this lofty perch distil a poignantly acute poetry. But his subtle antenna has been violated by the Philistine and he feels robbed of his birthright. Harry had lived for some years in America, where his unique poetic voice had brought him some fame amongst his peers as he rode high on the post-beat revolution; a promising new star in the firmament. London had not, however, granted him automatic status, and he had rapidly fallen foul of interested publishers due to his erratic behaviour and outrageous interpretations of reality. The publishers, exasperated, and in some cases offended, had given up on him, while he blames the whole thing on the Labour Party.

McCafferty, leaning now against the wall and glowering in distaste at these bourgeois deviations from his reality, makes as if to give Tralee some grief. But he hesitates and thinks better of it, having tangled with her a few days previously and found his attempts to browbeat had merely served to arouse her defiance. He contents himself therefore by giving her a blast of his piercing and threat-loaded gaze which she returns with a scornful laugh. Harry Flame is now on his feet again and competing with McCafferty to be the centre of attention. He begins pacing up and down muttering 'Oh God. Oh God.' Coming to a halt he addresses the room at large.

'Look,' he says, 'the whole thing is.' He hesitates, and in a distracted manner concentrates his brows as if gathering the primal essences of a vast and far flung cosmic vision. The room at large is hanging on his words, while with his hand to his forehead he makes several more supplications to the divinity, then:

'No, look; you see they all end up turning each other in.'

There is a long and perplexed silence at this; broken only by the faint screams of Molly, a prostitute who lives on the floor below where she is being roughed up by one of her drunken clients. Harry breaks off and stands staring at the floor while Jay, perched high upon his stool, casts a faintly amused eye over the company, as if this motley crew have been assembled here for his sole entertainment. McCafferty now clears his throat loudly and dramatically, the sound reminiscent perhaps of the way a lion or tiger might announce its presence.

'Why is it' he asks, 'that everyone says, Oh dear, it's getting a bit chilly in here? When what they really mean is, shut the fucking door! '

But Smith has had enough of this. His encounter with the police that afternoon seems to have brought him, he realises with a shudder, closer to McCafferty's world. A reduction of human nature to the rule of tooth and claw is not a path he would choose to tread and he wishes to be alone for a while. He decides to walk down to the Portobello Road to collect any vegetables which may have accumulated in the gutter after the market has closed, and perhaps garner enough for a stew. Leaving the seething cauldron of outlandish philosophies to vie for supremacy he heads for the market.

'Will it be the lines and circles?' he thinks, as he emerges onto the pavement. 'Phalanxes of street fighters led by Generalissimo McCafferty. Or Harry Flame's Ministry of Truth?'

The streets are now dark, and a fine drizzle is falling on the rubbish which after the day's trading still litters the street. Soggy cardboard boxes lie in distorted shapes along the pavements, and in the gutter spoiled fruit and spilled vegetables cluster in little sodden heaps. He has a small plastic bag which he begins to fill as he moves along the debris-strewn gutter. Squatting on his haunches and crouching low he finds first a couple of good carrots, a small turnip and a handful of sprouts. So far it is a good haul and there is a sense of satisfaction and peace in the activity.

'Rather like gardening or fishing,' he thinks, as he shuffles along the gutter, rubbing the mud from a few more carrots while musing upon the simplicity of the task, and he feels a little of his former sense of well-being returning. 'All I need now is a potato or two,' he thinks, and still squatting moves further along the gutter. Soon he spies a cabbage leaf glistening wetly in the lamplight. The leaf discloses at one corner the protruding end of something interesting, and it is therefore with a sense of pleasure that he lifts it up to expose a very fine potato indeed. Tossing the leaf aside he is about to pick the potato up, when a skeleton-like hand reaches out of the darkness and clamps itself tightly around it. The hand is covered in knotted blue veins, and the bony fingers might be the claws of a large bird. He looks up and straight into the eyes of a very old woman.

She is a pantomime witch. Dressed in an assortment of filthy woollen jumpers, her nose and chin nearly meet across a toothless mouth but her eyes are naked and fearsome. With one hand possessively clamped around the potato she glares malevolently at Smith, and is obviously prepared to go all the way over the issue. His sense of well-being rapidly withers and there falls a timeless moment. His hand still hovering over the potato he looks full into the terrible eyes, and hears in the tense silence the trickle of rain as it runs along the gutter and drops musically into a nearby drain.

Slowly he withdraws his hand and turning it over makes a courtly gesture of concession, which the old woman ignores completely. Long gone beyond such polite considerations she pulls the potato slowly towards her, still watching Smith warily as if he may at any moment change his mind and attempt to snatch it from her. One small move in this direction and he knows they will be rolling around in the filthy gutter exchanging punches and kicks. To avoid any such possibility of this he backs carefully off and leaving the dark-humped figure triumphant in the field, fades into the night.

Now the streets of Notting Hill are fading too, and the peeling facades of the once elegant neighbourhood give way to the oak-panelled front hall of the embassy. Smith is sitting on the stairs by the phone, his memories of McCafferty still fresh from reverie. Their paths had diverged with the passing of that visionary summer, and for the next ten years or so Smith had seen little or nothing of him until… answering a knock at the front door of the Belsize Park Squat, he had beheld McCafferty standing with buccaneer menace on the steps outside. Offering a cup of tea Smith had invited him in. McCafferty, once inside the house had lost no time establishing himself like a pirate in the basement, and only with their moonlight flit to the embassy had he once more been lost to sight.

'And now he's dead', thinks Smith, recalling again the dark river and McCafferty's gruesome end.

Ace, passing on the stairs, notices Smith's sombre mood and enquires.

'Is something wrong?'

Smith pulls himself together.

'It's McCafferty,' he says. 'He's dead.'

Ace looks concerned and ready to offer condolences, but first: 'Who's McCafferty?' he asks, and Smith, unable to get his head around the real answer to that makes no attempt.

'Oh,' he says. 'Just an old friend.'

Scout's Honour

Luke is a tall young man with straight black hair. His face is hawk-like and the impressive nose is sharply chiselled as any Red Indian chief's. He is about to start a lecture on the structure and dynamics of flying saucers, and the salon is filled with friends of the Guild. A peppering of newcomers have been drawn by a leaflet which Luke has been passing around, and he has hung the walls of the salon with drawings and blueprints. The predominant motif for the drawings seems to be concentric circles, containing within their sections smaller circles with lines emanating outwards from their conjunctions. Dispersed amongst these geometric figures are representations of the human body sitting cross-legged with yet more concentric circles radiating around the head. In the centre hangs a traditional Tibetan Buddha who exhibits the same effect. When all are assembled, Luke mounts the podium and takes the speaker's chair.

'I'm going to begin,' he says, 'by telling you a little of my personal history. I know this may seem a little distant from the subject on which I am to speak, but you will see that without introducing myself properly my point cannot properly be understood.'

He speaks English clearly but his accent has an odd flavour, as if unsure exactly where the inflections should lie.

'The earliest memory I have is of an enormous hall containing everything needed for life. The ceiling of the hall was a single transparent bubble through which the stars shone in the blackness of space. From the age of five when new children joined us, until the age of sixteen when we left, we were overseen by five adults who were changed each week and as far as we could tell never appeared twice. These adults taught us the mental discipline of our culture, which takes the principle of the gyroscope as the divine manifestation of perfect balance. In applying this principle to the mind they had posited that since the whole field of perception is constantly spinning, from stars and planetary systems to the electrons circling the nucleus of everything that exists, it would not be surprising to discover that the mind is, in its natural state, behaving in the same way.

'Further experiment in this field had led to the discovery that the only phenomenon which could disturb this tranquil spin was thought, and as children we were taken through many exercises for the control of this aspect of the mind's activity. By focusing on these matters we were able to understand and empathise with the peculiar qualities of the gyroscope in motion, matching resonances until the relationship became symbiotic. The last two years of our education were spent familiarising ourselves with a small disc-shaped craft and learning the intricacies of its control system. These vehicles were used for scouting far ahead of the Mother Ship (in which we were born) to detect life-bearing planetary systems and guide the ship away from such areas, else would the exhaust from the ship's plasma engines destroy all life in its wake.

'When my apprenticeship was completed I joined my fellow scouts for the first time, staying initially as befitted my junior rank, close to the Mother Ship. As I became more experienced I was allowed further afield until, through diligence, I eventually found myself among the outriders of a vast shoal of far-flung scouts. Operating alone, light-years ahead of the Mother Ship and free at last to roam where I would, I approached a planetary system for a closer look (something expressly forbidden to all scouts). I had never fallen to this temptation before, but an immense curiosity overwhelmed me and I took the craft lower. Such serene beauty lay below that not even the awesome sights of deep space, where globular clusters hang burning in the eternal darkness could match these gentle greens and blues.

'I became mesmerised by the sight, and in the midst of relishing this new environment discovered to my horror that I had never before experienced such a powerful gravity field. Aboard the Mother Ship this force is adjustable according to circumstances, but this pull I quickly saw was far beyond the recourses of my craft's capabilities. I was caught, and my only hope was to use what power I had to come down at as shallow an angle as possible. Fortunately, I touched down on water and apart from the ship bouncing across the surface several times and giving me a severe shaking I was unhurt, although rendered unconscious, and only the water pouring in through a broken door-seal brought me to my senses. I quickly checked the communications and found with relief that two scouts from my own sector were in reach. I reported my plight and asked them to relay it to the Mother ship and ask for instructions. The reply came within moments and it was anything but heartening.

"There is nothing we can do for you,' they had said, 'our mission is not equipped for rescue operations, you were given sufficient warning and must now survive as best you can.'

'My craft was now sinking very fast and I had no choice but to release the door-seals and pull myself out. The water was icy cold and I began swimming towards some land about a half mile distant across a large lake, which I found later to be in Canada. Since there was never any need for clothes aboard the scout craft I was quite naked, and thus made good time and was able to reach the shore before succumbing to the intense cold. Once there I quickly found two fishermen who spoke what seemed to be a simple variation of Anglian, (one of the commonest languages in this sector). Communication was therefore easy, and they took me to their cabin at a run and there plied me with hot drinks and food. I could not tell them the truth, since I was unsure how open to such ideas they were.

'Instead I spun a tale about attempting to cross the lake in a small boat only to have it sink beneath me, and that I had discarded my clothes in order to swim more easily. Having heard my story they shook their heads in disbelief.

"You must be mad,' they said 'to try to cross this lake in winter.' But not as mad, I thought, had I told them my true story.

'I stayed a day or two lying in a warm bunk recovering from the ordeal and orientating myself to the customs of an alien culture by listening to the radio. Leaving, I travelled south, criss-crossing the entire continent and working on construction sites while saving money for the only thing which held any interest for me. The return to my Mother Ship. I had, as an apprentice, been taught the fundamental principles of the scout ship's propulsion unit, although never involved with their construction. Nevertheless, I felt confident that with trial and error I could achieve the effect and regain my kind. Since I knew well their general course it was merely a matter of locating the Mother Ship's plasma wake, which remains almost indelibly printed across the endless depths of space. I would however, have to amplify the effect to a degree far greater than that produced by my now lost scout craft. But this was merely a matter of scale and presented no real problem.

'Finding space to begin the experiments was difficult, and for economic reasons I was forced initially to enter into the world of the miniature. I therefore invested in a small lathe and a few model maker's tools, and after a year or so familiarising myself with the medium, began to turn out the small gyroscopes which were the essence of the whole project. The scout ships or what you call 'flying saucers', are basically a circle of ten or twelve gyroscopes mounted upon a ring over which the craft is constructed. These operate in pairs, and the vehicle is steered by switching off two adjacent gyros, whereupon the craft will move in the opposite direction to the switch, while of course in space no lift is necessary.

'After much painstaking work I was eventually able to build a small working model about two feet in diameter which I assembled on a kitchen table for the first experiment. The model performed so well that I decided to gather my recourses to construct a full-scale ship. Tonight's talk is, I hope, the first of many which I am giving in the near future as a means of raising sufficient funds for the project. And now, having given a brief outline of my story perhaps you would like to ask a few questions.'

Luke is relaxed and gives no hint of awareness that his tall story might stretch anyone's credibility. He has told it in a serious manner with no lack of conviction, but there is no immediate response and the audience don't seem to know quite where to begin, until a voice from the back of the salon breaks the silence. It is a middle-aged man who seems upset by Luke's story and can contain himself no longer.

'This whole thing sounds like a fantasy.' He sounds angry and has obviously taken it personally.

'If you're really serious, you're mixing up your memory with your imagination and if you're not, then I don't think it's funny.'

'I see what you're saying,' returns Luke affably. 'But you see that was precisely my dilemma. Here I am, apparently a human amongst other humans, and yet the story I have told is the only memory I have. For some time after my arrival I had doubts about these memories and wondered if I were seriously unhinged.'

'Yes, yes,' says the man nodding his head vigorously. 'Unhinged.'

'But,' goes on Luke, ignoring him and addressing his audience. 'With the success of my working model these doubts were laid to rest.'

'What did your model do?' Another voice, a young lady this time.

'It went straight up.' answers Luke, who now moves over to the plans hanging on the wall. He begins showing how the gyroscopes are mounted and moved from the vertical to produce directional changes.

'The pilot must be mentally in resonance with the gyros to operate them with the finesse required. It all works on extremely precise measurements; one millionth of an inch out and it does not function. It is a kind of flying geometry.'

Now the questions are coming a little faster.

'Why do you have a picture of the Buddha amongst your plans?' It is Ace, who is interested in such things, and now emboldened by his sojourn amongst the squatting fraternity bravely sticks his neck out.

'Because the profound serenity of the Buddha mind works on gyroscopic principles,' answers Luke. 'It is a much atrophied faculty, but entirely similar to the methods used to propel our scout ships. All the gyros must run at exactly the same speed, a skill that takes many years to master. It is like a musical instrument and must be kept perfectly in tune.'

'Oh,' says Ace. 'But why then do some have ten gyros and others twelve?'

Luke hesitates, as if the question enters realms he would rather avoid.

'All I can say is that it is not a question of mechanics,' he says carefully. 'Amongst the races that have made their home in space there is a basic schism regarding the holy unit, which some take to be twelve and others ten. Since both systems work, the question is then one of metaphysics.'

'Oh,' says Ace again.

'Have you got the model with you?' Again it is the belligerent man, sure now that he has caught Luke out.

'No,' says Luke. 'I told you, it went straight up. Through the ceiling. Through the roof. Straight up. I never saw it again!'

This produces a long and profound silence which seems to bring the formal lecture to a close, but the enquiry goes on far into the night and many awkward questions are asked, all of which Luke fields with an innocent deftness. He has all the angles covered and leaves unrefuted.

Luke's fortunes do not take him immediately back to the stars however, and a few months later he meets a man who is interested in his machine and offers to help raise money for the project. All Luke has to do is invest a little money in a sure-fire business proposition and Luke, eager to realise his plan, invests his savings and writes the man out a cheque. It is of course a drug deal and the man is already under surveillance. When the police move in, Luke is dragged into the bust and charged with conspiracy to supply. But his plea of ignorance cuts no ice with the judge and he is given a custodial sentence. Luke does his time and keeps his head down. He finds this preferable to telling them the truth and ending up in the hands of police psychiatrists.

Manifold Secrets

The mysterious flow of circumstance bring questions to mind which seem at times imponderable to Smith. Yielding nothing by way of illumination and despite the sincerity of the seeker, they leave him no choice but to abandon the question to the unknowable. A prime example of this dilemma occurs one afternoon as he is carrying a cup of tea into the garden where he may find something interesting to watch. Just beyond the door is a trellis which boxes in and conceals the entrance. The trellis is thickly garlanded with honeysuckle, and bees diligently milk the blossom which cascades in swooping tendrils to the ground. Passing through the door, and while still within the concealment of the trellis he catches a glimpse of something which causes him to halt and peer through a gap in the foliage. He observes for a while, and then stepping quietly back into shadow stands leaning against a wall and sipping the tea, whilst maintaining a cautious watch through the leaves.

It is Tiberius who has captured his attention. He sits on the ground with his back against the outside wall of the salon staring across the garden at the facade of the annexe. His face is in profile, but even so, by the intentness of his gaze it is obvious that he is engaged in some profound inner struggle, and not wishing to complicate the already no doubt inexplicably complex nature of Tiberius' problem Smith hesitates before intruding on his awareness. The garden is quiet and nothing moves, while within the trellis Smith sips his tea and settles down for a long wait.

Several minutes pass and his tea finished he is about to re-enter the house unrewarded for his vigilance, when emerging from an open window some few feet above Tiberius' head comes a low and contented chuckle. A short silence, then another chuckle, and a swarm of giggles exit the window to float like wanton bubbles across the garden, and Smith wonders if Caspar is maybe titillating Morgiana in her room. Tiberius however remains unmoving, although Smith is sure that he has detected a minor stiffening of his posture.

Once more a silence descends, and the garden has just returned to its former tranquillity when again the air is filled with several more bursts of excited giggles which have an electrifying effect on Tiberius. As if stung by a wasp he leaps to his feet and still facing outward delivers a loud Germanic bellow. The volume is so great that Smith hears a distinct echo ringing back from the wall of the annexe. He stares through the trellis at Tiberius, dazzled and impressed by this peerless eccentricity. The words of the outburst had been incomprehensible, sounding to Smith somewhat like, "Gottsindammer Shniffellhousen!" But the delivery had been awe- inspiring.

A long moment's silence; another burst of giggles; and again Tiberius unleashes the guttural tirade, his body stiffening with the effort and his face red with apparent outrage.

'GOTTSINDAMMER SHNIFFELHOUSEN!' he roars. Then turning abruptly on his heels he heads back into the house, his brow darkened in the manner of a sent-off footballer who disagrees with the referee's decision. He strides past Smith without a look or word and disappears into the house, leaving him to ponder on the meaning of this brief and dramatic vignette.

Was it the nature of Morgiana's wanton giggles which had disturbed him? Were his parents adherents perhaps of a particularly severe form of Calvinism and had strictly reared him in their ways? And now, his puritan soul affronted by the harem tone of Morgiana's enticingly lush giggles, had a real impulse at last animated his spirit and vitalised his body? Springing to his feet he had delivered his angelic trump against the iniquities of Sodom and Gomorrah and the corrupt world at large.

'On the other hand,' thinks Smith. 'Maybe the giggles had nothing to do with it at all and he is pursued by demons which require exorcising occasionally.'

However, he refrains from asking anything directly since he knows that with Tiberius you only get one chance. Therefore it is important to get the question right, and he spends some time formulating it with care. Finally, a few days later, unable to contain his curiosity any longer and desperate to put his mind at rest he pops the question as they are passing on the stairs.

'Tiberius,' he says, slowing down to speak. 'The other day in the garden you shouted out something in German. What did it mean?'

Tiberius continues on his way down the stairs, he doesn't stop but his response is immediate and final. His solemn voice echoes back up the stairwell where Smith stands waiting for his revelation.

'It wasn't German,' says Tiberius, 'It was Swiss.'

Counting Coup

Brett, Ace and Smith are in the garden one late summer's day. The surrounding trees show a bare hint of rust, and wood pigeons compete for the red berries in a Rowan tree which shades Katarina's balcony. Ace is demonstrating his latest acquisition: a cheap factory-made Chinese violin in which he seems to have discovered a mysterious virtue. He draws a bow across the strings.

'Listen,' he says. 'The sound is more spread out and full of overtones, all of which are eliminated in a 'good' violin.'

It is true, lack of volume and brilliance seem more than compensated by a tone resonant of the mournful cry of a distant goose far out on a twilit marsh. Ace is getting excited.

'I'm going to form a string quartet using only cheap Chinese factory-fiddles.' It sounds like a great idea and Smith is enthusiastic.

'But what will you call it?' he asks and Ace sobers for a moment, then…

"The Cheapo Chinese Factory-Fiddle String Quartet',' he says. 'But if the musicians are good, and we play the music perfectly we can introduce audiences to a completely different sound.'

He is seriously enamoured of the idea and is thoughtfully putting away the violin when there is a ring at the side door and he goes to answer it. Outside, a man and a lady are asking to speak with someone in relation to a project which they have in mind, and he invites them into the garden.

'You see,' says the man, a middle-aged, scholarly-looking sort, 'this lady has come from America on a mission which her people have entrusted her with.'

Smith glances at the lady and encounters a look of unusual intensity. Her skin is copper-coloured and her hair, a glossy black, is woven into two braids which frame her lean face, while her eyes are dark and piercing.

'She is from Dakota,' explains the man, 'Her family are Shamans of the Oglala Sioux, but she speaks in the name of all the tribes. Her mission is to redress a great wrong done to her people by the English. She intends to count coup and claim these islands for the tribes.'

'Bloody hell,' thinks Smith and addresses himself to the lady.

'Why do you want to do that?' he asks.

The lady's face does not move a muscle as she gazes at him steadily, and he wonders if she has understood.

'She will not speak until her mission is completed,' says the man. 'She is not here to negotiate, but to perform a magical act to wipe out forever the insult to her peoples committed when the emissaries of Elizabeth the First dared claim the tribal lands for their Queen.

'The planting of that Royal Tudor flag upon the soil of their homelands was, in the eyes of the people, equivalent to a warrior from an enemy tribe planting his coup stick in the centre of the home village. It was an insult which could not be countered at the time since the homelands of their enemy were far beyond reach. But now, with the return of their national and ethnic consciousness, they aim through this lady to redress these matters with a symbolic magical act. The counterpart to Elizabeth's shaman Raleigh and his like stands before you, and her name is Lo Wahn Sah, which means 'Singer'.'

Smith looks at the lady again. She is just standing there, and the distant look on her face says that she couldn't care less and is asking for nothing. She appears to be in her mid-thirties and wears a simple black skirt and T-shirt of the same colour. Shod in simple plastic sandals there is nothing ethnic about her dress and not a bead in sight. Her face however, says it all. A sense of deep sobriety and the penetrating glance give an unmistakable warning: this lady is not interested in small talk. He notices for the first time that she is carrying something long and slim wrapped in a piece of embroidered cloth, together with a small bag decorated with strange geometric patterns.

'Before you say any more,' says Smith, turning to the man. 'Let me say now, I like the sound of the whole thing. But what exactly is it she wants to do?'

'She wants to plant her coup-stick somewhere there,' replies the man pointing at the lawn.

'Is that all?' asks Ace.

'It is no small matter,' says the man. 'I am a director of the Institute of Ethnic Studies, but our offices have no land attached, otherwise they would have been made available to her. Somebody told me of this place and suggested that since you run a cultural organisation yourselves your attitude might be sympathetic, and the fact that this is quasi-diplomatic ground and also British soil, it would seem a most appropriate spot for the act.'

Beginning to see the scale of this thing, Smith attempts to express himself with the formality he feels the situation deserves.

'We would be honoured to be host to such a ceremony,' he says. 'Please feel free, and if there is anything you need you have only to ask.'

A tiny smile flickers briefly about the lady's lips and she lets out a slow breath.

'Perhaps we can have some tea first,' says Ace making for the kitchen, and the man speaks again.

'It would be helpful if we could have something in which to burn some herbs,' he says, and Smith fetches a silver tray from the house. 'For an occasion like this', he thinks. 'Only the best is good enough'.

The lady solemnly takes the tray and lays it on the flagstones of the patio, then, undoing the drawstring of her bag, she takes out a bundle of dried leaves and crumbles them into a small heap on the tray. Now Ace arrives with the tea and they sit in a circle to drink. The lady's bag now lies in full view and the patterns woven into it shimmer with a strange gloss. Seeing that it has caught their attention the man speaks.

'It is quillwork, an almost forgotten art. Although the American Indian is now almost always associated with beadwork decoration, those beads were obtained in the first place from Europe through the settlers and frontiersmen. Prior to this they worked with dyed quill, which as you can see produces a subtler effect.' Indeed it is true, the quills are translucent in the sun and the bag glows with a sombre richness far from the gaudy primary colours of the manufactured beads.

'This bag and these herbs have been in her family for many generations, and the herbs were picked from her tribal lands long before the roads and railways came.'

There is very little talk after this, and when the tea is finished the lady rises gracefully to her feet and walks out onto the lawn. She stands at the centre for a while her face turned up to the sky, then returns to the tray and taking out matches applies a flame to the heap of crushed leaves. The herb flares up briefly and subsides into a smouldering glow; blowing upon it she sends up pungent clouds of thick white smoke into the still afternoon air. Into this smoke she thrusts the cloth-wound object and begins to unwrap it, emitting as she does so a low hum. It is not a musical sound but comes like a growl from deep within her body, and as the last of the cloth falls away the hum rises in pitch and volume until it is a full-throated howl which rings like a savage aria across the sedate back gardens.

She rises to her feet holding high in her left hand the piece of cloth and in her right a stick of some sort. It is about two feet long, pointed at one end and decorated down its length with bundles of feathers which hang like tassels from the shaft. Her mouth is wide open as with head flung back and voice pitched to the sky she stalks slowly to the middle of the lawn. Her companion leans forward and speaks in a quiet voice.

'She is calling upon all the ancestors who lost face when those regal standards were planted, and she will ask them to bear witness to the act which will grant them peace.'

Standing in the middle of the lawn Lo Wahn Sah now breaks into a torrent of strange words.

'She is speaking Lakota,' says the man, 'and has begun to make her claim.' He continues to translate. 'She is naming all the chiefs of the tribes who have succeeded each other back to the time of the first European contact, and in calling their names aloud she claims the right to represent them.'

Now she begins stamping her feet, whilst intoning a single stream of broken syllables repeated endlessly in a wild mantra.

'This is her dedication,' says the man. 'She is promising to make the act with full intent and a pure heart.'

The lady has stopped moving and is now silent. Still with both arms in the air she stands and seems to be waiting for something. Brett, Ace and Smith hold their breath and the silence in the garden is profound, even the pigeons in the Rowan have stopped squabbling to cast a sharp eye on the proceedings below. Suddenly, Lo Wahn Sah gives forth with a loud and piercing shriek, whilst simultaneously plunging the coup-stick downward with all the strength of her lithe body, sending the pointed shaft deep into the embassy lawn.

'It is done,' says the man, smiling in quiet satisfaction. 'She has declared the sovereignty of her tribe over all the territories of these British Isles in perpetuity, and her people have regained their honour.' Lo Whan Sah comes towards them; she is smiling and rewrapping the coup-stick speaks for the first time.

'Now,' she says, 'I can die satisfied.'

Her voice still contains something of the howl, although now with softer resonances. The accent is American, but she speaks as if the language is foreign to her and seems to be choosing her words with great care.

'I am not going to thank you for this opportunity,' she says gravely. 'Neither did Raleigh thank my ancestors, but I appreciate the respect which you gave the occasion. I could have performed the ritual in a park, but this might have attracted the wrong kind of attention, and it was necessary to enact it in a place shielded from the gaze of the everyday world.'

The haughty disdain has gone from her eyes and her voice is almost friendly as she continues.

'I have been trained since childhood in the old tradition to perform the task enacted today, and that is why it has given much joy. When I return that joy will pass to many.'

She falls silent, and soon the man gets to his feet and they begin to take their leave. Lo Whan Sah opens her bag and removes another bundle of herbs which she leaves on the tray.

'Burn it only amongst good company,' she says in parting, and they are gone.

It has been an honour to witness such a historical event and everyone is pleased to have been associated. All that is except Caspar, who, not being present at the time hears the story from Ace, and the next day he tackles Smith in the kitchen. Caspar, in spite of his impeccable manners is not one to beat about the bush. He comes straight to the point.

'I hear you gave England away yesterday.'

He sounds cross, and Smith can see that the notion has really got up his nose.

'It wasn't England,' he says. 'It was the British Isles, and anyway, I didn't give it away. She came and took it!'

Principles

The floorboards outside the toilet on the ground floor have become afflicted with wet rot, and fearful that some visitor may go through Smith is considering how to replace them. Finding an old door in the garage, he discovers that it is exactly the right size to fill the space from wall to wall and begins tearing up the boards. They come away easily being for the most part soft and rotten, while releasing as they are removed a damp miasma of secret fungoidal aromas. When the joists beneath are exposed he examines them for any signs of decay and finds that fortunately they have not been affected. However, the nails which had secured the boards remain protruding upwards from the joists in long rows, and he begins hammering them in, preparatory to laying down the door. Just then Tiberius happens by and asks if he may help.

'You can bang down these nails if you like,' says Smith. 'It should only take fifteen minutes or so, then we can lay down this door and replace the carpet on top.' He hands Tiberius the hammer and goes off for a cup of tea. Returning around twenty minutes later he finds Tiberius struggling with a pair of pliers to pull each nail from the joists.

'What are you doing?' asks Smith. 'It will take all day to do it like that. Just hammer them in.'

'I am doing it properly,' says Tiberius solemnly.

'But it won't make any difference when the door is laid on top,' says Smith. 'No one will ever see it.'

'That isn't the point,' says Tiberius. 'It should be done properly; it is a matter of principle.'

'But I want to get the job done quickly,' says Smith, 'I've got better things to do.

Tiberius, however, will not budge; he continues the laborious task of removing each nail and Smith can see that nothing will deter him from his course. He makes a final attempt.

'Look,' he says. 'Principle is all very well, but there are times when it doesn't apply.'

'Principle always applies,' replies Tiberius doggedly. 'It is the most important thing.'

'But you can get bogged down with it and lose your flexibility,' says Smith. 'For example, imagine a man of principle who organises his life according to certain habits. In order that he always has clean clothes he may do his laundry every Wednesday as a matter of principle. One day a friend rings him up and says that he has booked a villa by the sea in the South of France with two gorgeous young ladies as company, and the whole thing has been paid for. Unfortunately, some unexpected business has turned up which makes it impossible for his friend to go. He is offering the ticket free of charge and the plane leaves on Wednesday.'

'I'm sorry,' says the man of principle. 'But I can't go. I always do my laundry on Wednesdays.'

Tiberius is unmoved by this and not even looking up he continues stubbornly with the pliers. Smith knows he won't get through to him in a million years, and it is not until the next day that he can drop the door in place and bang in a few nails to hold it down. He has just put back the carpet, and is stamping up and down to test the repair when he looks up and sees Tiberius watching him. He stands with his arms hanging straight by his sides and a grave expression on his face. There is a long moment of silence before he speaks, then...

'He could have taken his laundry with him.' He says.

The Magic Drum

A master drummer from India is visiting London and his friends arrange with him to perform a solo concert for the Guild. It will be part lecture and part demonstration of the double-headed drum as used in the ancient Carnatic music of South India. Alone he sits upon the podium, displaying the consummate skill required to master the mathematical techniques of the instrument. He is an austere-looking man, who gazes fiercely out at tonight's audience, his concentration so intense that it seems he might explode or burst into flames at any moment.

Watching his performance, Smith is reminded of a time many years before in the early Sixties, when as a young jazz musician he had haunted the late night jazz clubs in London's West End. Dressed in the obligatory sharp two-piece suit, slim Jim tie and dark glasses he had, in company with Chris, a young trumpet player, tramped the night streets of Soho looking for a 'blow'. From club to club they wander, checking in each to see who is playing and looking for an opportunity to get up on the stand when an interval arises.

One night in particular they are drinking coffee in 'Sam Widges', a café in Berwick Street with a basement below which plays host to any jazz musicians who care to drop in. They are leaning against the juke-box, and Chris has just inserted a coin and pressed the button for a 'Jazz Messengers' track. They are ardent aficionados of this music and seek to emulate the same saxophone-trumpet partnership in their playing. The clientele of the café look up approvingly; the disc has been playing almost non-stop for the last several days and is the latest thing. Chris gives a nod to Jimmy Fochs who comes over carrying his trumpet case.

'Want some grass?' he asks from the side of his mouth, but they are both broke and after a few words he wanders away looking for customers. Jimmy has a false bottom in his trumpet case in which he stashes his ten shilling deals. The trumpet works, but he has never been seen to play it.

The café is full of the usual nighthawks. Painters and poets, musicians and mystics, scarfaced villains and painted ladies of the night. From behind the counter Ram O'Neil the proprietor is lambasting his assistant Reg, a short and rotund fellow.

'You piece of unmitigated shit!' roars Ram, a man who takes his poetry seriously. Reg, having fallen foul of some local gangsters has been obliged to supply them with free meals when Ram is absent, and now there is no bolognaise left for the customers.

'But they'll kill me,' whines Reg, and indeed Smith, tuning in to their conversation knows this to be quite likely, since he had witnessed only a few evenings before the dramatic entrance of Reg into the 'Nucleus', a jazz cellar in Monmouth Street. White as a sheet and shaking in terror he had begged for somewhere to hide. There being no place but the kitchen he had quickly scuttled out of sight. No sooner has he disappeared than a voice shouts violently down the cellar entrance. 'REG!' It bellows, followed by heavy steps down the stairs.

Sitting near the piano is Dave Grey; guitarist's guitarist and king of the folk and blues clubs. He is weaving his way sinuously through the chords of *Funny Valentine*, while, adding his ultra-modern flurries on muted trumpet is Chuck. He is a friend of Reg and has a tough hawk-like face topped with a bristly crew cut. Up jumps Chuck and trumpet in hand goes to see who is threatening his friend. He reaches the bottom of the stairs just in time to thwart the entrance of a hard-looking character with a sawn-off shotgun in his hands and the obvious intention of using it on the fugitive.

'Where's Reg?' The man demands, menacing Chuck with the gun. Chuck doesn't even glance at it.

'He's not here,' he says calmly, looking the man in the eye.

The villain hesitates and glancing down sees the trumpet, which, although no match for the shotgun if it comes to battle, nevertheless gives Chuck a certain credibility in the eyes of the gunman. Musicians have a kind of immunity and can usually pass unharmed, and in some cases are even respected amongst the local gangsters of the time.

'He's not been here all evening,' says Chuck without moving.

'I'll just come in and have a look round then,' says the man trying to push past him. But Chuck will have none of it.

'You can't come in here with that,' he says, acknowledging the gun for the first time and standing his ground.

This is the moment of truth and Chuck is fearless. The man respects this and backs down, lowering the gun and retreating a step or two.

'Tell Reg he'd better keep running,' he growls, before turning back up the stairs. Chuck walks back to his chair by the band which is still playing the same piece and calmly resumes his playing, while the grateful Reg keeps his head down for the next few days. Now, however, he is in trouble with Ram O'Neil. 'You appalling parody of an ape!' Ram's voice comes echoing from the kitchen in the back and Reg hasn't a leg to stand on. This is clearly but the beginning of a long tirade and Ram is choosing his words carefully.

'You're a fucking liability, do you know that?' he roars. But Smith is getting restless and decides to go down to the cellar below to see if there is any chance of a blow, and Chris, being of the same mind leads the way.

'You scraping from the inside of a wino's toilet!' Ram's voice, full of passion follows them below.

'You fat bloated piss-pot!'

'Who does he think he is?' thinks Smith, as he descends the cellar stairs, 'Baudelaire?'

The cellar is but dimly lit by shaded lamps above the tables which line two sides of the room. A scattering of musicians sit among the shadows hunched over the tables their instruments in cases below. Light glints in their dark glasses as they rabbit endlessly over their Nasetone-laced coffee, cracking the plastic inhalers in their teeth like walnuts and dropping the Benzedrine wad into the brew. Against one wall a small platform hosts a piano and a drum kit. A double bass is being plucked to accompany the sparse extended chords of Mike Butcher at the piano, who seems free for the moment from the demons which frequently plague him.

He is a strange genius of a man, a superb pianist and much admired by the young musicians who hang around listening to his sophisticated approach. Mike, however, is afflicted with a constant inner dialogue which oftimes bursts into the open, his ghostly antagonist an unseen presence goading him into a stream of obscene expletives. Smith and Chris have on occasion played with Mike who at times is released from his devils to reveal a quiet man, kindly and always willing to impart his musical knowledge to younger musicians. However, it frequently befalls that halfway through a piece there will begin an ominous muttering from the vicinity of the piano. The musicians glance at each other: they know what is coming.

'Fuck Off!' says Mike, his voice rising above the music. He begins to shout.

'I told you before, leave me alone. Just get out of it! Jesus! Fuck off!' Chris and Smith attempt to drown him out by increasing their volume, hoping that Mike's fit might subside before the music completely disintigrates.

Their efforts are in vain. Now standing up and still playing, Mike directs his demented stare at the bare wall above the piano.

'I've had enough!' he bellows at the wall, '*Fuck Off!*'

He has become so involved with the dialogue that he stops playing altogether, and with hands thrust deep into his jacket pockets gets off the stand and walks out of the club, trailing behind him to the astonishment of the club's clientele, a stream of pungent oaths and vile expletives, leaving the musicians to finish the piece as best they can. Playing with Mike is always a risk since it is never certain whether once started, the piece will be completed.

In one corner of the cellar sits Dickie De Vere, a junkie so far gone that he is barely surviving between one fix and the next. He has the reputation of having once been a drummer of some note, but now, slumped in his tatty raincoat over a cup of coffee he is a pathetic object of derision to all. During one of his more lucid moments, Mike Butcher had spoken of Dickie and the man he used to be.

'He was the governor,' says Mike. 'I'm telling you. He was the greatest.'

But Chris and Smith, acolytes of the avant-garde in their own music have heard this sort of thing before from the old timers, and although Mike was playing round the clubs while they were still at school they doubt his judgement. Dickie de Vere is a hopeless wreck, who in their opinion could never have amounted to much.

Chris now moves across and steps up onto the stand. He takes out his trumpet and begins to infiltrate the piano's meandering while Mike, as if divulging the secrets of some esoteric rite whispers the progression of chords into his ear. Drawn by this rare opportunity to acquire some of Mike's vast fund of knowledge Smith takes out his tenor-sax and joins them.

'Can't we play something up-tempo?' says the bassist, who has become bored with these mystic proceedings. 'I'm going to fall asleep in a minute,' he adds sarcastically. But Mike isn't interested. 'Not without a drummer,' he says. 'It's too much like hard work.'

'Well I'm fucking off then.' The bassist lays his instrument down and begins to get out the case.

'Can't we just try?' asks Chris. But Mike doesn't want to know.

Suddenly they are aware of a figure standing in front of the podium. It is Dickie de Vere, and he is asking if he may join them on drums. There is some consternation at this. It is embarrassing for them both since Dickie is an elder in spite of his deteriorated condition and is also something of a legend among the older musicians. But the last thing either of these two cool young blades wants is to be associated with an old-fashioned clapped-out pro like Dickie. Nor do they want to be laughed at by any of their peers who may be present. However, neither have sufficient bottle to say no, so onto the stand shambles Dickie and arranges himself behind the drums, while the bassist with a patronising sneer rejoins the group.

Smith has never really looked at Dickie, finding the usual bombed-out nature of junkies to be unrewarding to any interest. But Dickie's eyes, he is startled to see, are clear as a schoolboy's, with a strange puckish glint that entirely belies his ravaged face.

'We'll play something simple,' says Mike. 'What about Lester Leaps In?' It is an up-tempo number conventionally played at a furious pace. Chris begins the fast count in, but before they can start Dickie calls across. 'I'll count it in,' and he begins at once to bring his sticks into action.

There seems to be nothing regular about the collection of loose raps which he delivers on his snare drum, and his sticks fall as if without intent. Yet from this apparently uncoordinated and aimless clatter, there miraculously appears a loose pulsing rhythm which seems now to have been there all the time. But the tempo is far too slow for this upbeat piece. They will have trouble holding it together without the momentum which only speed can supply, and they will have to work hard to carry their obviously disoriented drummer.

Smith begins to play in a staccato manner, attempting to pump some life into the dirge-like tempo, when he suddenly feels a peculiar sensation moving through his body. It is as if he is standing up to his waist in the sea, while the swell of each wave moving shoreward is physically lifting him and giving a gentle push in passing. These rolling breakers of invisible pulses are emanating from behind him where Dickie, a puckish grin on his face is invoking a sorcerer's brew. Smith has never before experienced such an invisible force.

'So this is what it means to swing,' he thinks.

After years of playing with the young whiz-kid drummers of his generation, their avant-garde techniques delivered amidst great flurries of virtuoso display, the sheer simplicity of a beat that swings is a revelation to him. They ride now effortlessly on this magical pulse, the long lazy troughs, peaks and crests need just a few notes here and there to adorn their undulations. Dickie is barely giving each beat a passing caress; it is as if he is tuned to a universal standing wave which only he has the power to detect.

When the piece is finished, Dickie stands up and with a casual wave leaves the stand and takes off into the night. Smith and Chris watch him go, shaken, and not a little awed by the experience.

'See what I mean?' is all Mike will say, and a month or so later Dickie is found dead in a phone box, a needle still hanging from his arm.

Smith's ruminations return him to the embassy. The lesson learned on that momentous occasion remains a vivid memory and here in the salon, he listens to a drum speaking the language of a culture far removed from the hip city beat of jazz. The drummer is dealing in Yogic principles. Juggling with number and dividing his drum patterns into fractions and multiples which must resolve themselves to coincide with the completion of each time cycle, and his mind must not deviate for an instant from the calculations. This is more than just rhythm. It is the ancient music of a system devised to enhance the human intelligence by engaging the whole consciousness into a single focus. The drummer speaks at times; explaining some of the techniques he is demonstrating to an increasingly interested audience. He pulls them beneath the surface of drum beats to a substratum of numerical reasoning, which, without this kind of instruction would be inconceivable.

Autumn

Looking into a mirror one day Smith notices that his hair is thinning. 'Autumn whispers at my heels,' he thinks, and likes the phrase so much that he decides to write a poem on the subject.

Autumn whispers at my heels
Whene'r, whilst mounting
High upon a stair
The leg doth falter in its stride,
Slows the eager upward bound
To more sedateful pace...

'I don't think I'll bother with the rest,' he thinks.
And indeed one can well see why.

The Tempest

White froth tips the waves of a tempestuous sea in which the small yawl-rigged barque is tossed. The mast tilts far over as the boat yields to the tumultuous rollers, and from its stern there ripples a large red banner emblazoned with a white cross. Further out, a large three-decker, its sails billowing wildly in the blustering wind yet sits more sedately upon the violent waters, its huge size dwarfing the waves and reducing them to mere ripples against its lofty timbered sides, while seagulls swoop along the troughs of heaving water and rise to skim the spume-raddled crests.

Were this troubled scene real, then surely would the seagull's piercing cry come skirling through the boisterous air to join the groan of straining timbers as the barque labours amongst these elemental forces. Happily, these dark and threatening waves are motionless, and the barque, leaning heavily to the wind maintains eternally its perilous angle, and the seagull's fly forever still, trapped by a white-tipped brush against the raging oil-painted waves of a picture that stands leaning against a wall in Smith's room. It is a reproduction Dutch seascape by B. Peeters (1614-1652) and is glued to a piece of stiff card.

Down at the far end of the room Smith is operating his broom. The bare wooden handle leads down into an equally unadorned and fibrous head. It had been chosen with care and although the plastic varieties are abundant in local skips, he had resolutely turned down all these offerings. Until one day, whilst passing a house in the throes of renovation, he had seen, emerging from a heap of stony rubble in a builders skip, the head of a broom to delight the eye.

No pastel shaded monstrosity of extruded plastic, which under the least stress is liable to lose its head completely, without —glue how you may— hope of redemption. No, this broom was of another order entirely. Its honest yeoman wood bereft of any deceit, and proudly displaying like a medal of honour a half-inch of rusty nail protruding from the head at its intersection with the pole. Smith had found his ideal broom, and stepping forward to grasp the head had withdrawn the shaft from amongst the stone and carried it triumphantly off.

Now the broom is being wielded in a masterful manner and a long swathe of dust retreats before his advance. He aims for a maintenance-free environment, and sweeps the broom in long arcs to drive the line of dust before him. As he approaches the picture, he gradually brings the two flanks of the line inwards towards the centre, and when this is accomplished stands for a while as if contemplating those raging seas. But it is not the picture itself as such that has engaged his attention, rather a spillage of dust which is leaking from either side, and he wonders if he can get away with one more day before a major collection.

Leaning down he lifts the picture aside to reveal a considerable pile of dust, the accumulated sweepings of several weeks. He gauges possibilities. 'Perhaps if I pile the heap just a little higher I can get away with one more day,' he thinks, and taking up the broom once more he sweeps the morning's collection onto the main pile, then carefully shapes the sides into a steep incline before replacing the picture. Unfortunately, the base of the pile now juts so far forward at the inclusion of this latest addition, that the bottom of the picture is forced forwards and is within a hairsbreadth of falling flat to expose this talent for procrastination. 'Tomorrow for sure,' he thinks.

He has from time to time considered the appropriateness of using the picture for this purpose, imagining the artist painting his perhaps solitary way through the seasons with infinite care, to produce in time such an impeccable and fine seascape. 'Could he have imagined,' he thinks. 'That in some far distant future, an alienesque technology would reproduce facsimiles of his precious work and deliver them like potato crisps into the hands of riffraff?'

Concealment is however, only one of two aspects of the picture's function. For, when the heap of dust attains a bulk which it can no longer contain, the picture is reversed and serves thus as an excellent dustpan. Smith, a reductionist where maintenance is concerned derives much satisfaction from this duel function. Once a major collection has been accomplished and the dust disposed of, the picture returns to its former position against the wall, albeit at a somewhat more austere angle, and the whole process begins again.

He relishes this economy of function, although he knows for sure the artist could never have approved. He has recently been considering ways to extend the periods between major collections, and has soon realised that a larger picture might double or even treble this interval. He has almost as quickly seen where such an extension might lead. 'If I go that way,' he thinks. 'I could end up with a picture as big as the room,' and he decides that the opposite direction better suits his nature.

'I'll look out for an even smaller picture,' he thinks. He enjoys imposing such yogic axioms upon himself, and is pleased with the sense of self discipline with which they endow him.

Katarina

Streams of light from a bank of mullioned windows fall across a rich brown floor in an oak-panelled hall to illuminate the central figure. Kneeling in the foreground, she is bent as if in silent supplication or prayer, while the light leaches without depleting the deep blue from her smock, sending a cobalt shimmer across the glossy floor until it disappears into the black maw of the carved wooden fireplace beside her. A Dutch interior perhaps. The painter's brush a magic wand which cobalt loaded touches here the smock, and there the floor. A hint of yellow through the leaded panes to spark a highlight in the figure's hair, intensifying the shadows. But painters, whether Hollander or no, can work but a single plane, and movement does not fall within this limitation. The smell of varnish too is in the air, and sound: a soft, barely perceptible brushing whisper in the hall's hanging silence as the figure's arm sweeps to and fro. The wide brush replenished from time to time from a tin of varnish at her side.

Katarina: overall-clad, hair carefully coiffured and fingernails adding only a brief flash of scarlet, has spent two days on her knees at this. Slowly working her way backwards down the floor of the annexe, leaving before her an impeccable glossy surface, in preparation for a forthcoming concert to be given by a famous *bharat natyam* dancer from India. The annexe has a well-laid hardwood floor which will gleam under coloured spotlights when the performance takes place.

A Light Step

The varnishing, when finished, is soon hard enough to take some polish. Smith rubs in a whole tin, and then spends the afternoon before the performance skating around with cloths tied to his feet giving the floor lustre fit for a queen. When the dancer and her musicians arrive, he proudly shows her into the annex where the beautifully polished floor awaits her. The musicians arrange themselves in one corner, but the dancer gives no sign of pleasure at the floor. She stands looking at it thoughtfully and frowning a little, then, removing her shoes she brings forth from her bag a large bottle of Coca-Cola. Walking to the centre of the floor she shakes the bottle vigorously and begins squirting the cola all around her.

'What are you doing?' shouts Smith, leaping forward to save the precious floor. But it is too late; the sticky liquid bubbling and seething has already destroyed the sheen. Now she is stamping up and down working it in with her feet and spreading the cola to every part.

'I cannot get grip with my feet on polished floor,' she explains as she stamps around. 'And so I always take Coca-Cola with me isn't it.'

Smith steps hurriedly back and hastily re-arranges his value system. He gives a lame smile but she does not notice, busily continuing to spread the cola into every nook and cranny. He leaves her to it, and occupies himself in putting the finishing touches to the throne, which stands in a prominent position against the great carved oak fireplace.

The throne is a large wooden chair with ornately carved legs and arms. Thinking to provide a seat fit for The Indian High Commissioner, who will be present for the performance, it has been painted gold. The red velvet seat and padded high back is given a regal air by the nailing on behind of a large scarlet and gold Indian umbrella. Resplendent with tassel and fringe it will, it is thought, be appropriate to the status of their illustrious guest. Somehow, word of the embassy's hospitality towards eastern artists has reached the ears of India House and finding the venue of sufficient grandeur the administration has arranged the evening in honour of this visiting star.

As late afternoon wanes the first guests begin to arrive and flit sari-clad around the twighlit garden, while across in the annexe the windows light up and musicians can be heard tuning their instruments. The guests are all here by invitation and the High Commission is footing the modest bill without any idea that the place is a squat. As the hour for the performance approaches the guests filter across to the annexe, and by the time the dancer is ready the hall is almost full.

No one, of course, dare sit on the throne since it occupies such an exalted position. Thus empty, it awaits the man himself. A few anxious moments later the door opens to reveal the High Commissioner and his small retinue. He is white-bearded and wears a simple long Indian shirt. At the door he removes his sandals and advances into the hall. His eyes flicker across the throne and dismiss it with a single glance. There are no flies on this man. He can see that it is some sort of set-up, and ignoring it completely he walks across the hall to a gap amongst the cushions and sits on the floor, while his retinue ensconce themselves around him. The throne, erected with such thoughtful care, has now become a faux-pas of mind-boggling proportions and nothing can be done to resolve it.

However, as sometimes happens when all seems lost the house doorbell rings, and Morgiana slips across the garden to see who it is. She is confronted at the door by Johnny Banana Head. He is still wearing his St John's Ambulance overcoat, now strung like a silver buttoned cloak around his shoulders, and his searchlight eyes seek Morgiana out and bathe her in their manic glow. Morgiana, however, knows exactly how to handle Banana Head, and focusing all her matriarchal authority into one intense beam she delivers a stern ultimatum.

'You can come in,' she says. 'But we are having a concert tonight and the Indian High Commissioner is here, so don't get up to any of your usual antics.'

Banana Head buckles under her formidable clout and humbly promises to behave himself, then follows her across the garden to the annexe. Entering the hall he looks around for a seat, and without a moment's hesitation heads straight across the room and lowers himself into the throne. The audience of Indians look puzzled. They had initially assumed it to be for the High Commissioner, but since he had ignored the honour it must therefore be for some higher personage, and lo! This must be. Banana Head lounges back in the throne completely at ease, his silver buttoned "cloak" glinting in the coloured spotlights. He is entirely unaware of the circumstances, and undiscomfited by all the interest he is attracting nods his head around in a benevolent manner, as if quite used to such attention. Smith begins to uncross his fingers. It looks as if Banana Head has saved the day and might just pull it off.

The High Commissioner however, upstaged, is frowning across at Johnny, while his aids whisper amongst themselves to discover who he might be.

'Now nobody knows what's happening,' thinks Smith.

Suddenly, a crackling flourish from the drummer electrifies the room and all heads swivel to catch the entrance of the dancer, whose footwork matches perfectly the complicated patterns of the drum. 'kita taka ta,' beats the mridungham. 'kita taka ta,' stamps her feet. And then in unison, 'kita taka Thom!' She uses the same language for her feet that the drummer employs for his hands, a not uncommon custom in the south of India, where even the sacred statues are carved in exact proportion to their musical scales. Wide leather bands are strapped around her ankles upon which rows of tiny bells are sewn. These add to each percussive step and now her singer, who has been quietly venturing out along the lines of a raga, raises her voice and begins her song.

It tells of a beautiful girl, who, whilst wandering alone in the forest catches a brief glimpse of Krishna and falls desperately in love with him. The dancer holds her arms before her beseeching him to return, imploring him once more to show himself. But though she weaves into her dance the most alluring of her wiles he does not come and she is inconsolable.

Sinking low, her face cast down and listless, she seems about to abandon her efforts when the flute, silent till now, rises bird-like through the song, and in her eye comes a sudden spark of hope. It must be, her Lord. She turns towards the sound and radiance brightens her features as she catches sight of something denied her audience, who can only gaze spellbound at her joy.

After the performance, Banana Head corners Smith and wants to know which of the Indians is the High Commissioner. He begins expounding his new theory on street names, in which he thinks the Commissioner might, for some obscure reason, be interested.

'Look at this,' he says, pulling out his *AtoZ* by way of demonstration. 'I've marked all the streets called "Willington" and look what you get when they're joined up.'

He opens the book to show a network of fine lines drawn across the map. But Smith can make neither head nor tail of Johnny's spiel and has long given up trying. 'A sub-borderline Asperger,' he estimates. 'With perhaps just a dash of bipolar disorder.' He excuses himself, and in the kitchen where tea is being served he has a word with Caspar.

'Johnny Banana Head is asking who the Commissioner is. Whatever you do don't let him anywhere near him,' he says. 'He might let the cat out of the bag and blow our front.' Years ago, back at the Belsize Park squat, Smith had helped set Johnny upon his lotus-eating, pinko-nihilistic path and now feels a mild responsibility for him.

'The Commissioner has already left,' says Caspar. 'He went out the side door the moment the concert was over.'

Smith is relieved by this, but he notes a mischievous gleam entering Caspar's eye.

'I'll just go and have a word with him,' says Caspar, and leaving Smith to help Morgiana pour the tea makes for the open garden door. He waits for a while, leaning against the door-jamb until Banana Head looms out of the darkness. The black-cloaked figure slowly takes shape as Johnny transverses the lawn. First a glint of silver buttons on the shouldered overcoat. Then two white eyes to dominate the emerging moon-like countenance.

Banana Head comes to a halt, one hand moving swiftly to his pocketed *AtoZ*, as if he is a gunslinger ready for a quick draw. Caspar, however, a mite faster, forestalls him.

'There's tea and biscuits in the kitchen,' he says, by way of a diversion. He had once tried to understand Banana Head's obsession with street names, and tried vainly to grasp the theory. But after an hour or so on the subject he had admitted failure. Caspar has a degree in philosophy, but Johnny is beyond even his well-governed intellect.

Banana Head looks past Caspar into the crowded kitchen.

'Which one is the High Commissioner?' he asks.

'He's in the salon,' says Caspar. 'I'll point him out to you.' Leading the way he takes Johnny past the kitchen and opens the door of the salon. The room is full of expensive saris and well-cut business suits abound, as Caspar stops, and... 'There he is,' he says, pointing across the salon to Mr Laksmimurthi, an insurance salesman who attends all these occasions hoping to do a little business on the side. He has yet to give up on selling some insurance for the house, and cannot understand Smith's reluctance to talk about it.

Mr Laksmimurthi: sober-suited, grey-winged horn-rimmed glasses has sufficient gravitas to qualify for this exalted role. He stands in a little circle of prosperous Indian businessmen, their elegant wives in discreet but gorgeous attendance.

Johnny doesn't hesitate. He strides across the room and as he reaches Mr Laksmimurthi joins his palms together before him in reverent *namaste*. Halting, he bows low. Mr Laksmimurthi looks startled, and his friends gaze on with astonishment as Johnny pulls his *AtoZ* from his pocket.

'Your Excellency,' Johnny says pompously, and bows deeply again. But Mr Laksmimurthi is embarrassed by this over-the-top respect and sycophantic body-language. He is not sure if he is being made fun of, and refuses to consider Johnny's book. Now his wife is pulling him away, one look at Johnny had been enough. In the softly lit annex, certain blemishes in his appearance had not been apparent among the shadows. But here in the salon, the bright chandeliers above cast a merciless light on the stained overcoat, shaggy hair and whiskery jowl. Mr Laksmimurthi allows his wife to take him off, leaving Johnny standing alone in the middle of the salon. Book in hand, he now surveys the room, until, noticing Caspar watching him, he lurches towards him, and holding out the *AtoZ* he points at a page.

'Look, I've joined up all the Willingtons, and see what I get.' Caspar, feeling a little guilty, allows Johnny one more chance, and peers at the tangled lines overdrawing the map. He tries to see some sort of picture or design but can make no sense of it at all. Finally, 'I still don't understand,' he says.

'Understand?' says Johnny, puzzled. But that isn't the point; you're not supposed to *understand* it.'

Caspar, clean bowled, is out, and Johnny walks off shaking his head in despair.

Bones

A conservatory runs along one side of the embassy garden. A long glassed-in cloister with red tiled floor and an old grape-vine swathed about the timber rafters above. Against the outside wall are a few garden benches, and upon one of these sit Caspar and Bones. Bones seems immensely pleased about something which to Smith, as he enters the garden, is a welcome sign. Bones has been somewhat morose of late, going through the motions but dully with the Friday evening's Chinese exercise group. He has lost confidence in his profession as a microbiologist, and is beginning to wonder if he has chosen the wrong path.

His peers, with whom he had gained his Ph.D., are turning out wonderful papers at the teaching hospital where he is employed. The place is buzzing with excitement over the brilliance of these newcomers and their papers are hotly discussed in the staff canteen. Bones, however, hasn't done so well. He works in a mysterious microscopic world, where jellyfish-shaped creatures float down to rest upon great smooth plains of white bone. There they settle and begin to consume the bone beneath, until a sizeable crater has been eaten away, whereupon the bone-devourer lifts off for fresh pastures. The moment it has gone, however, another "jelly-fish" lands athwart the crater, and begins diligently to fill it in with fresh bone matter, a process by which the skeleton is constantly renewed.

Bones watches all this carefully to discover how certain imbalances occur, whereby the devourers gain dominance and begin to outnumber the builders. For here lie the problems associated with age in the female skeleton. The work is slow and painstaking and as a result his papers are few and not easily understood. He becomes despondent, and feels miscast amongst this band of young geniuses whose papers, unlike his own, sparkle amongst much acclaim.

'I don't think I'm really up to it,' he had confided to Smith. 'They're all turning in such brilliant papers it makes my efforts seem amateurish'. Smith has been watching him sink lower and lower over the past six months, until he must concede that for Bones, this does look like the end of the road.

But now, venturing into the garden, he sees that Bones is smiling; Bones is grinning; Bones is laughing!

Caspar waves him over. 'Come and listen to this,' he says, moving along the bench to make room, and Smith sits down to hear the news.

Over the past year the new papers have been circulating around the scientific community at large, and during this time, and one by one, they had been returned with negative results. Suspicion had been gradually aroused that all was not well, and all papers of Bones' class had been called in for the most severe scrutiny.

'They all failed,' says Bones. 'In their eagerness to prove their theories, they had brushed aside and fudged their way through anything which tended to disprove them.'

He is quiet for a moment, and Smith waits for the punchline.

'The only papers that fulfilled all the tests,' he says, with a modest but irrepressible grin. 'Were mine.'

An Interesting Morsel

It is some years since Colonel D— had made his first visit, and true to his word has arrived at six-monthly intervals for his "Inspection of the premises". He has by now become familiar with all the residents, asking by name after those not present or who have left. This fraternisation with the representative of a potential contender for the house has the appearance of playing into the enemy's hands. But they trust him, and giving him credit for the sense of fair play which he displays towards them they take him at his word and treat him as a friend.

His final visit occurs one afternoon when Smith is sitting in the garden drinking a pot of tea. He has a packet of digestive biscuits opened before him and is dunking them into his cup. This process is engaging his instinct to the full, since he scorns to use the counting method when gauging how long to leave the biscuit submerged in the tea; a period subject to minor variations depending on the type of biscuit, different brands of the same type, and the heat of the tea. He prefers to play a dangerous game, risking the loss of an over-saturated biscuit which, sinking to the bottom of the cup will form a disgusting sludge and make the tea undrinkable. He takes a biscuit and immerses it half-way into the cup then, a timeless moment later and daring to hesitate no longer he withdraws it dripping from the tea.

The biscuit holds together, well soaked but still firm enough to survive the passage to his mouth, where the finely ground mix of flour cementing the whole dissolves into a thick sweet paste, leaving the larger granules of unmilled grain to be ground in a ruminating manner between the front teeth. He is isolating these particles on his tongue and passing them forward one by one to be dealt with in this manner, when one of the granules proves more resistant than its fellows and he bites down harder. The particle is brittle, and at this sudden pressure cracks asunder with a minor shock, which evokes the memory of a past occasion when he had been engaged in the identical act.

A festive gathering has occurred in the salon and many friends of the Guild are present. Prominent by way of his exuberant nature is Paul Bloomfeld, a rotund supercharged fellow with a card up every sleeve and a tendency to go over the top at a breakneck speed in everything he does. He has recently spent some time committed to an asylum for persistently writing alarming letters to the Queen. Feeling somewhat low in spirits he had embarked on a course of Bach homeopathic flower remedies, and is soon clinking around with his pockets full of small bottles from which he continuously doses himself. His faith in the remedies however, had faltered when he found himself feeling really ill and confined to his bed with scarcely the energy to get up.

Discarding the flower remedies he had taken a couple of aspirins and is on his feet hale and hearty in no time, and had thus come to suspect that the remedies are part of a nefarious plot to incapacitate those who, scorning the consensus reality, seek outside the accepted forms and thus create a threat to the social order.

'We're being slowly poisoned,' he had said earnestly. 'This thing must be exposed.'

He begins by writing to the manufacturers, accusing them of conspiring to lay waste to the brightest and best and receives bland letters in reply suggesting politely that he might try their Rescue Remedy. Bloomfeld goes over the top at this and fires off a series of vitriolic letters to his M.P. who, suffering these in silence for a while recommends that he see his doctor. Infuriated by the extent of the conspiracy which he now realises even the government is party to, he has but one recourse: he will write to the Queen. Letters begin arriving at Buckingham Palace describing the sinister machinations of the plot and entreating Her Majesty's co-operation in defeating this subtle threat to her realm. The letters apparently cause some concern, since poor Bloomfeld had been investigated and in short time finds himself sectioned by the health authorities.

In the asylum he had quickly realised that the doctors were also part of the plot and that his only way out was to convince them that he has been mistaken about the whole thing. He may be mad, but he is no fool. This takes a considerable time since the doctors are well aware of this ploy, but he diligently pursues this course until somewhat doubtfully they allow him out to live in a halfway house until he has satisfied the authorities that he is fully recovered. He has arrived at the embassy tonight wearing a black flat-brimmed Spanish hat. His latest love is Flamenco music and the poetry of Lorca and these suit well his excitable nature.

'My name,' he declares as he comes swanning into the salon, 'is El Bongo,' and he pulls out a pack of cards and begins to demonstrate his latest illusion.

On some occasions he can be coerced into playing fragments of jazz improvisations on the piano, his grasshopper mind jumping from piece to piece, but he will not be tied down to anything for long. The sole exception to this is the *Asturias* by Albeniz; a piece full of electrifying effects and on the piano producing great storming waves of passionate sound. Like a team of nervous horses it can, at the least slackening of control, break into a wild and frenzied gallop. Bloomfeld plays it like everything else at a furious speed, and his flamboyant style as he attacks the piano is a spectacle not to be missed. Ace now enters the salon carrying a cup of tea.

'I've just made a fresh pot,' he says, as he passes Smith who is watching Bloomfeld's antics.

Smith acknowledges this important piece of information with a nod and wanders into the kitchen, where, in the centre of the long table stands Ace's teapot. It is an antique, girded round with gold lines and garlanded with leaf-wreathed roses; it is obviously a prized possession. Ace has an eye for fine objects, and only a day or so ago had returned from Camden Market with an old piano stool of magnificent workmanship. The four delicate legs are turned in graceful spirals with rounded knobs along the way. They are spindly, and support the velvet-covered seat which is scalloped around the edges by the chisel of some long dead master cabinet maker.

'Look,' he says excitedly when he shows off his new acquisition. He lifts the seat to reveal a hollow box-like interior.

'Its for keeping music in.' He caresses the velvet top and beams with pleasure. 'It was only fifteen pounds,' he says, and proudly carries the stool into the salon and places it at the piano.

In the kitchen, Smith pours himself a cup of tea from the magnificent pot and noticing a plate of digestive biscuits helps himself to a couple. Returning to the salon with the tea and biscuits he is just in time to see Bloomfeld being dragged towards the piano by some of his admirers intent on hearing him perform the fearful *Asturias*. He is remonstrating loudly as they pull on his jacket and push from behind.

'No, no,' he protests. 'I can't do that one. The last time I played it all the fillings in my teeth jumped out.' He struggles for a while until, still protesting he allows himself to be seated at the piano. Pulling up his sleeves he takes a deep breath while casting an anxious look around the expectant faces, as if seeking courage before embarking alone on a dangerous undertaking.

Smith sits down on a couch near the piano and takes a sip of his tea as Bloomfeld, his rattlesnake fingers striking the keys with dazzling speed begins the piece. Smith takes another sip of tea as the music rapidly gains its own momentum in great swirls of rippling tones. He then takes one of the biscuits and immerses it in the cup as Bloomfeld, already in trouble, is desperately trying to rein in the *Asturias* which is going rapidly out of control. He sways around on the stool and his fingers strafe the keyboard with stabbing chords, while Smith, removing the biscuit from the tea conveys it successfully to his mouth and begins isolating the particles of grain from the dissolving flour.

Finding a large and interesting lump amongst them, he takes it between his front teeth and bites down. The particle of grain is hard and cracks apart with a grating sensation, but he is startled by a simultaneous cracking from without. A loud snapping sound emerges from beneath Bloomfeld as, his eyes wild with excitement he rides the *Asturias*, his heavy body bouncing around on Ace's stool which was never built for such treatment.

Elegant young ladies by the score had no doubt sat with straight backs to play Mozart upon its equally elegant legs. But Bloomfeld, his jaws tightly clenched to hold his fillings in place whilst rampaging around upon those frail and spindly legs is insupportable. With sharp pistol-shot snaps the legs give way and the *Asturias* comes to an abrupt and spectacular end as Bloomfeld, a look of terror on his face crashes to the floor amidst the dismembered and broken pieces of the stool.

There is a moment of shocked silence as prostrate upon his back amongst the shards of the stool, 'El Bongo' waves his arms feebly and looks with bewilderment around him. Then, apparently unhurt, he struggles to his feet and Smith, frozen in the act of grinding the particle of grain swallows it down and joins in the general laughter. It is pure slapstick, and carried out in such a dramatic way that the humour is irresistible. To all present that is except one. For simultaneous with the laughter comes a piercing cry of anguish which cuts through the humour like a knife and brings it to a speedy end.

It is Ace. Standing in the middle of the floor with cup still in hand; his voice breaks on a tragic note in the silence.

'But it was my stool!' he wails.

Ace is not laughing. He finds nothing amusing about Bloomfeld's antics and it is not until a few days later, when Caspar and Tiberius get together with a tube of strong glue and carefully fix the stool back together that he is mollified.

This event, rekindled in Smith's mind by the brittle particle of biscuit which his teeth encounter as he sits in the garden comes complete. As if the memory of the incident had been stored embryo-like within the particle and waiting only for his teeth to release it. The concept is intriguing, and he is about to pursue it further with the second half of the biscuit from which he might release further forgotten episodes, when he hears from within the house a knock at the front door.

Faux Pas

Friends know by now to come to the side door, where a bell-pull sends a loud clang ringing through the house which can be heard from even the furthest attic. The front door however, is another matter entirely and a cautious decorum is essential when opening it to unknown knockers.

It is Colonel D—, his ruddy face beaming with affability and his hand held forth ready for shaking. He has four youngish minions with him, but no Gestapo. This Neolithic appendage has been long dispensed with, but the minions change with each visitation. Smith, having over the years observed their eager-eyed manner as they gawk like tourists through the house, has come to the conclusion that this little bi-annual tour of the squatted Cambodian embassy has become a much valued perk amongst the Colonel's younger staff, and he suspects there may be some competition amongst them for the assignment. The Colonel, having shaken Smith's hand enters the front hall, and his dark-suited staff follow close behind as Corporal Smith leads off.

'I'm afraid there's hardly anyone at home at the moment,' he says over his shoulder as he mounts the stairs.

'That's all right,' says the Colonel. 'I don't have much time today anyway. It was something else I came about, but maybe I'll just look in and say hello while I'm here.'

They stop outside Ace's door, through which they can hear two violins working their way through a duet, stopping starting and repeating as they master each section.

'Ace is giving a lesson,' says Smith. 'But I'm sure he won't mind if we look in for a moment.' He waits for a while until a pause occurs in the music then knocks and enters.

Ace is sitting on his refurbished piano stool which he now keeps in his room for safety. Lying across his lap is his violin and bow, while opposite him sits a young man with his violin still held beneath his chin. Ace looks up and smiles a greeting at the Colonel who he has met many times before.

'Hello! Hello!' booms the Colonel as he follows Smith into the room, and his minions spread out and form an observant circle around the Colonel and the two violinists. He greets Ace and they exchange pleasantries. Then, turning to the young man he says: 'So. Learning violin are you?'

The young man seems a little confused at this. He hasn't a clue who the Colonel or any of these people are, and it is doubtful if Ace has even told him it is a squat.

'Well yes, I suppose so,' he replies politely. 'There's always more to learn.'

The Colonel beams happily at this, and confident of the rightness of his view blunders on.

'I suppose you want to get into a band one day?' he asks, his manner kindly but now a little patronising.

The young man looks at him blankly for a moment then...

'Well actually I am in a band.'

'Oh yes,' says the Colonel, looking mildly surprised. 'And what band is that then?'

'The BBC Philharmonic Orchestra,' replies the young man, and there follows a long silence while the Colonel tries to rearrange the furniture in his head. He is struggling manfully with this when Ace comes to his rescue and explains that he employs yogic principles in his teaching which allow greater depths of subtlety to be coerced from the instrument, and not a few professionals come for his help in this refinement. The Colonel, now much subdued is profuse in his apologies for the disturbance and makes a somewhat less breezy departure.

At the top of the house they discover Brett in his room. He is sitting in the middle of the floor surrounded by the pieces of his now completely dismantled sitar. He has been engaged for the last few weeks in stripping the varnish from the body and replacing it with a hand-finished french polish. His first attempts to do this had been a failure, since it is a process requiring much skill and takes some time to master. After many days trial and error, rubbing in the polish with small circular movements of cotton pads he had laid down a rich glossy surface but...

'It's the wrong shade.' he mourns. 'I will have to do it again and mix my own polish.'

Further days had been spent gathering the pure ingredients before, surrounded by bottles and mixing bowls he had begun once more to lay on the polish. At one point Tiberius had come upon him sitting in the upper corridor polishing his sitar with the required minuscule circles, whilst taking advantage of the sunlight streaming through a nearby window. Tiberius comes to a halt and stands silently watching for a while, but Brett does not look up. Deep in his dream of an ideal rich dark colour, he dips his pad into the polish and rubs around in silence. Standing, his arms straight by his sides Tiberius speaks in his hollow monotone.

'Why don't you buy a chair?' he intones. Brett looks up startled, so deeply absorbed with his task that he hasn't heard.

'What?' he says, reluctant to stop his polishing.

'Why don't you buy a chair?' repeats Tiberius. 'Then you can polish the chair and play the sitar.'

But Brett's quest for perfection is impervious to this kind of absolutism and he doesn't suspect sarcasm. The two stare incomprehensibly at each other for a long moment but neither says anything more.

The Colonel is wary of Brett and aware of his monosyllabism. He hesitates awhile before speaking and then goes for the obvious.

'What are you doing?' He asks in a cheerful manner, having by now recovered a little of his aplomb. Brett stops rubbing, he knows he cannot avoid this and holds out his polishing pad for the Colonel's inspection.

'It's french-polish,' he says. 'I'm trying to polish the sitar to a particular shade of brown. But it must have just the right degree of red in the lustre and I keep getting the ingredients wrong.'

He begins explaining in great detail the contents of the bottles and the little heaps of reddish-brown powders amongst which he sits, but the Colonel has had enough. He has blundered once more into a quagmire of obscure viewpoints and quirky values and he doesn't want to know. Backing hurriedly from the room the entourage descend the stairs and gather in the front hall where the real reason for the visit is revealed.

'Would you sign a statement,' asks the Colonel. 'Guaranteeing to vacate the house when the Cambodians return?'

'Of course,' replies Smith. It is a subject he and the Colonel have discussed many times before, and he had already confided to him what personal pleasure it would give to hand over the keys in such circumstances. The Foreign Office have obviously become aware that the house has been occupied for almost twelve years and are concerned that a claim for adversarial possession could then be lodged by Smith. The signed statement which the Colonel has suggested will of course waive this right and prove he has no such motive. But he has no intention of making any such claim and indeed, with the other residents has fantasised often upon the small ceremony which they hope may one day take place.

A small band in the forecourt consisting of Jake Naylor on trombone, (an instrument which he had mastered for a joke and later abandoned, since few had found it funny) Ace and Smith on violins, Brett on sitar, and Wirril Mauretunga soaring above all on his flute. Standing in the portico Tralee and Morgiana carry trailing bouquets of jasmine and wild roses, while the other residents stand formally dressed in their best. Facing the house are a small group of smiling Cambodians. They are diplomats and their wives, and foremost amongst them is the new Ambassador and his lady. Jake Naylor loosens a brazen fanfare from his trombone and Katarina emerges from the house leading little Moss who bears a small velvet cushion on which lies the key to the house. The Ambassador steps forward and accepts the key from Moss, while the band strikes up and everybody claps, etc., etc.

In the light of this whimsical but feasible ending to the affair, it is not surprising that Smith willingly concurs in this matter, and the Colonel leaves promising to post the document to him for his signature.

The Diva

No sooner has Moss attained his first steps than Morgiana, encouraged by Katarina's delight in her son, allows one of her amorously circling moths close enough to initiate her into a similar state of motherhood. The lucky man is Jack Rawlings, a swashbuckling Buddhist who runs an office for the "Free Tibet" organisation and is an active supporter of the Dalai Lama's efforts in this cause. He transfers his office to a spare room in the house and moves in with Morgiana to help bring up their daughter Penny. The two children become inseparable and Moss is soon spending much of his time in Morgiana's room where, leaping monkey-like along the backs of chairs and couches he entertains a delighted Penny with his little boy circuses. One afternoon around this time Smith is clipping the hedge in the front garden when a neatly dressed old lady approaches him.

'Excuse me,' she says. 'But would you mind if I took some of that grass?' She points to some clumps of grass which sprout along the edge of the entrance to the forecourt.

'You see it's for my cats. They have to eat it to cleanse their stomachs. None grows where I live and it's too far for me to go to the park.'

She carries a brown paper bag and a pair of scissors, and Smith tells her she is welcome to help herself. She thanks him, then stooping down begins cutting the grass with her scissors and putting the harvest into the paper bag. Smith continues cutting the hedge until the old lady, clasping the bag of grass to her chest calls goodbye.

'Help yourself anytime,' he says, and the old lady smiles.

'I used to work there you know,' she says, nodding towards the house. Smith's shears freeze in mid-clip; she has his immediate attention.

'When was that?' he asks.

'Oh, years ago when Maria Callas lived here,' she replies. 'I was her cook.'

Smith thinks the old lady is maybe a little mad. The great Callas, Queen of the Opera, one time resident of their house? It sounds too far-fetched to be true.

'This must have been a long time ago,' says Smith cautiously. 'The house was an embassy for some time.'

'Oh yes,' replies the old lady. 'This was before the Cambodians came; Callas had just broken up with Aristotle Onassis, and this is where she came to live while she tried to get her voice back. But Onassis had stopped her singing for too long and she was never able to recover it fully. It was so sad.' The old lady's eyes are filling with tears.

'I used to listen to her struggling to reach the high notes in the annexe hall where she would go each day to practise, but it was no good, she was never able to get it back.'

'Why did she stop singing in the first place?' asks Smith. This new dimension to the story of the house is overcoming his doubts about the reliability of the old woman's mind.

'When Maria and Onassis had been together for a while,' she answers, 'she had begun to miss singing and wanted to do a few recitals, but Onassis forbade her. He said, "you don't need to sing no more baby, I got plenty money.' The old lady grimaces at the story she has told and shrugs her shoulders.

'But I know,' she sighs. 'I was here and used to hear her crying when she realised that she could sing no more.'

The Exorcism

Passing this dubious piece of information on to the other Guild members Smith is accused of making it up, and his story of the old lady, since nobody else had seen her, is viewed with great suspicion. The myth of Callas at the house however, spreads, and before long is confirmed and becomes an accepted fact. This has the effect of shifting the very foundations of supposition upon which their tenancy has, since the beginning, been founded. The dreadful legacy of Pol Pot, by which the house had become vacant in the first place has not been easy to dispel, and his shadow has never been completely banished. But now, like a sudden illumination, the light of the great Diva falls like a healing mantle over the embassy. This was the house, long before Pol Pot had begun his genocide, where the voice of Callas, out of practice and faded with misuse had echoed around the very walls.

'She must have lived in my room,' says Tralee, and is undoubtedly right since she occupies the master suite. Now a tide of Callasmania hits the house and they collect and listen to recordings of her performances. Gradually the historical orientation shifts back to an earlier and less gruesome period in the story of the house. This new perspective, however, needs formalising in some way, and an exorcism is proposed by Toledo and Rawlings who have been seriously discussing the matter. Rawlings' tendencies favour a Buddhistic approach, while Toledo regards a Christian style as more appropriate.

Neither however, are fundamentalists, and soon agree on a minimal form which will at the least include candles and incense. Smith likes the sound of this and offers to bring his small tape-recorder with a compilation of Maria's greatest arias. They will take her voice right through the house and drive out the Cambodian ghosts once and for all. Ace now arrives to join the cabal and they retire to the kitchen to finalise the details.

'We must harness all the power we can,' says Rawlings, who is knowledgeable in such matters and has his finger in many a Buddhist pie.

'I'll bring some Tibetan incense,' he continues. 'It is made by monks who have devoted their whole existence to the path and imbue everything they touch with power.' Toledo regards Rawlings quizzically.

'What do you mean path?' he asks, and Smith, not to be outdone in these metaphysical gymnastics says. 'What do you mean, "what"?'

Rawlings looks confused. 'And after all who wouldn't?' thinks Smith, who had often wondered himself what "what" actually was. However, he puts the thought aside for the moment determined to pursue it later, and returns to the main issue.

A simple ceremony soon emerges in the form of a procession visiting every room in the premises with the voice of the Diva in the lead. Smith ties a long red dressing-gown cord, resplendent with tassels to either end of the machine on which he fixes several sticks of incense. This will allow him to swing the recorder around trailing the fragrant smoke and the voice of Callas in the manner of a censor. Behind him, Rawlings will carry the sacred flame in the form of a three-stick candelabrum in which burns the candles which Toledo has acquired on a visit to a Castilian monastery. Ace wants to bring a bell which he will ring as they process and this is recognised as adding just the right touch, while Toledo will tackle any bolshie demons from the rear.

It is dark when they set off from the kitchen, and Rawlings' candles flicker and throw grotesque shadows along the corridors as they move from room to room. Ace rings his bell continuously, its fragile tinkling adding to the sense of solemn ceremony which the thick clouds of incense invoke. While overall the majestic voice of Callas comes soaring at full volume from the swinging and smoke-plumed censor, echoing around the walls and rafters from the darkest basement in the annexe where the great boiler rusts in the dank air, to the attics at the top of the house.

Only the passage to Katarina's flat had presented any difficulty in their tour. Not being able to reach her front door from the street in their present mode, they are forced to enter from the garage below via a rickety ladder, and up through a hole in the ceiling cut by the Psykos so long ago.

They mount the ladder one by one, a perilous operation encumbered as they are with censor, candles and bell. The ladder is unstable and sways and shakes about as each climbs carefully to the top. There are some doubts that Toledo can make it and it is suggested that he give it a miss, but he isn't listening. His one hand grasping the wobbling ladder like a steel clamp he slowly and invincibly mounts towards the hole, and when his head comes up out of the darkness they reach down and help him to his feet. Toledo has never given anything a miss.

Katarina's flat is their last port of call and the mission has been accomplished. The little group, giving the ladder a miss, blow out the candles, switch off the tape-recorder and exit through the front door. Rawlings and Toledo walk ahead as the exorcists stroll through the night streets and around to the embassy. They are discussing an earlier point.

'You still haven't answered my question,' says Toledo. 'What do you mean by path?'

Rawlings blinks owl-like through his horn-rimmed spectacles and wonders how he can convey such subtleties to the uninitiated, unaware that Toledo had been travelling in Tibet trawling for "Secret Masters" while he, Rawlings, was still a schoolboy.

'Well,' he says at last, deciding to play for time. 'It depends on which way you're facing.'

Ace walks slightly behind and following this dialogue closely but, with his fingers around the clapper of his bell remains silent. Snatches of this conversation float back along the quiet lamplit street and Smith, loitering in the rear catches only a fragment or two, but he can make neither head nor tail of it. Such lofty considerations are far above his muddled head and he returns to his ruminations upon the origins of "What?"

Entering the house they sense a difference in the atmosphere. The voice of Callas, ringing like the clarion call of a Goddess has permeated the embassy from top to bottom and still hangs tingling like ozone in the air. It is purged of ghosts and free now forever of those once murky connections.

Morning

Morning comes to the Free School, but precisely what morning is a consideration long abandoned by the faculty and whatever guests they are entertaining, who themselves have been drawn here by their desire to attain the same exalted state. At the Free School, or 'School of Freedom', as Smith prefers to think of it, the ruthless eye of this collective regard had quickly identified the first major obstacle to that freedom, and time, together with day of week, has been entirely excluded from their discourse and eradicated entirely from any serious consideration.

Serious because the occasional visitor, wandering into the cellar on some local errand might innocently enquire: 'What time is it?' To be met with much mirth from the faculty. However, this nameless morning infiltrates the blanket of sleep which enshrouds the recumbent forms and first one, and then another yawn their way up into a sitting position and begin warily watching each other to see which will succumb first to the desire for tea.

P. B. Rivers sits up and runs his hands through his hair.

'Why have we woken up?' he asks the room at large.

P. B. Rivers teaches 24hr existentialism at the school and frequently starts the day with difficult questions of this kind. Smith, always ready to stick his neck out says the first thing that comes into his head.

'Well why not?' he asks. 'You've got to start the day somehow.'

P. B. Rivers fixes him with a long, cold look.

'Have you ever considered,' he says. 'That there may be other ways to start it?'

Smith hasn't considered this and it is way too early to do so. What he wants is a cup of tea and he leaves this challenge to the others. 'As Jane Austin might have said,' he thinks, 'P. B. Rivers has no small talk.' Finally, conceding defeat, young Nick gets up and puts on the kettle and before long is handing round the cups.

Nothing is now heard for a while but the grateful slurping of tea until a bell rings out twice. Everyone looks at P. B. Rivers, for had the bell rung once it would have been Smith who received this attention. As a small notice on the doorbell indicates: One ring for a music lesson. Two rings for a dose of 24hr existentialism from P. B. Rivers. Should Smith be called upon he will begin at once explaining the fundamental laws of music to the visitor. 'Music,' he begins on such occasions, 'can only do either one of two things. It can go up. Or it can go down, no other direction is possible.' So far he has not been refuted, although sometimes among the contentious he encounters a suggestion of volume or speed as alternatives, but these he easily dismisses as secondary considerations.

However, this morning the bell has rung twice and P. B. Rivers goes to open the door. It is Scipio Hawkins, one of the prime-movers in setting up the School, and he seems to be the bearer of some exciting news. But P. B. Rivers forestalls him, he has a duty to perform and he takes the role seriously.

'Why did you wake up this morning?' he asks. But Scipio nimbly fields the question.

'To come and tell you something, I only rang the bell twice because I didn't want a music lesson,' he says.

'Then speak on,' says P. B. Rivers magnanimously.

'There's an event coming up next week in Oxford,' says Scipio. '*International Times* is supporting a movement for spontaneous street theatre which a group of undergraduates are fomenting. A few of us are going up to give our support and some music would be really cool.'

P. B. Rivers is interested in none of this, his mind focused entirely on the present he has no room for such poncey notions as some "other" place called "Oxford".

'If that's all you got up for then you should have stayed asleep,' he says dismissively. 'But now you're here you can have a cup of tea, which is the real reason that you and everybody else wakes up.'

Smith's ears have pricked up on hearing of this opportunity to take his guerrilla music to the streets, for now that the Portobello is closed to him he is at a loose end.

'I'll see if I can get a couple of Suntrolly men' he says, and later, when the London contingent arrives at Oxford, Dick and Zen have come to stand shoulder-to-shoulder.

Through the warren of narrow streets the revellers march, their banners waving amongst a sea of hippy flowers and a whiff of incense is in the air. Scipio, his silver lamé jacket discarded and dressed now in an outrageous suit of psychedelic camouflage moves here and there, flickering through the crowd like a crackerjack with camera at the ready. And Zen, somewhere behind Smith is punctuating the whole thing with his alchemical beat.

Booma, booma, dinga, booma
Booma, booma, dinga, booma

Dick is prancing well ahead, his trombone swinging from side to side as he bellows out a military march, which, conceding a little to Smith's musical approach, he is making up as he goes along. Smith is playing in precise five second bursts, a sudden swirling cluster of random tones, followed by five seconds of silence; he finds these kinds of yogic disciplines a satisfying contrast to the exuberant circumstances.

The grey stone walls of church and college echo back the trombone's roar and the piercing squawk of saxophone. Back and forth from steeple to tower the echoes ring and Dick is in his element. Forgetting all his good intentions and carried away in his excitement he now begins putting in a bit of elephant.

'Oh, no,' thinks Smith. He had warned him about this. 'Whatever you do, don't put in any elephant,' he had told him. 'Oxford is a quiet city and if you start rampaging it could lead to serious trouble.' In his next five seconds of silence Smith moves forward to restrain him.

Dick however, is far beyond any constraint; he is unleashing the raucous trumpeting of a mad bull-elephant as it lays waste to all around. Smith gives up, resigned to the disaster that must surely follow. Then, the wild bellows suddenly cease, and Dick stops dead in his tracks. He shuts his slide with a snap, turns, and runs off down a side street as fast as he can. Smith stares after him wondering what has got into him.

'Maybe he left the gas on,' he thinks, and is about to formulate more theories of this kind... but he is only allowed the one shot, for the next moment he feels a firm grip on either arm and he is in the hands of the police.

They bundle him roughly into the back of a van and through the back window he watches as a line of policeman link arms and attempt to funnel the crowds into a side street. Suddenly from amongst the students a huge roll of 'Mellomex' silver plastic film appears and begins to unroll. The students take it at either end and hold it up like a long mirror stretching from one side of the street to the other. The police cannot get past this barrier, for as they attempt to push through in one place it only tightens it in another, and now the two ends begin an outflanking movement. Getting behind the police they start to roll up their line and try to wrap them up like a gigantic parcel, but just in time to avoid this they withdraw to mount an offensive elsewhere. Smith sees no more for the van starts up and he is on his way to the police station. Sitting in the back he is puzzled by only one thing. How did Dick get warning in time to do a runner?

At the station they push him towards a heavy iron-sheeted door and his saxophone, still slung around his neck, tilts forward and a bunch of daffodils, slipped into the bell by a young hippy girl during the march, slides out and falls to the ground. Smith stops abruptly, and the policemen who surround him come to a halt and watch, as slowly and deliberately he bends down, and collecting up the daffodils places them carefully back into the bell of his saxophone. He is just about to put the final touches to the arrangement, wondering how long he can spin it out, when he receives a violent push from behind. He is launched forward straight at the iron door and only just manages to get his hands up to save his face, but his saxophone, hanging loosely before him smacks into the unyielding door with a nasty crunching sound.

The delicate shell-like bell crumples on impact. 'Well, I suppose I asked for that,' he thinks, and having conceded this, wonders if the gesture had been worth it, and then... 'Probably not,' he thinks.

The police station is small and ill-lit and the desk-sergeant looks up as they enter. His nameplate, gold lettering against the varnished wood says: Sergeant Hillter.

'Name?' he barks and then... 'Address?' Smith gives him both and the Sergeant looks at him with narrowed eyes. 'London,' he says. 'Come down here to stir up some trouble have you?'

Smith doesn't answer; he no longer feels so bolshie. 'Have you got any identification?' asks the Sergeant next, but Smith has nothing of the kind about him, he knows no one in Oxford and cannot even provide a phone number to check on.

'Then we shall just have to keep you till we find out who you are.' says the Sergeant, handing a bunch of keys to one of the constables, and Smith is taken along a short corridor to a cell and locked up.

The cell has a small barred aperture through which he can watch the reception area; he doesn't even want to think about his saxophone. A long boring hour has gone by when a sudden flurry of activity seems to electrify the dark-uniformed denizens in the reception and a swirl of bright colour lights up the gloom. Smith catches a flash of something at the front-desk and the Sergeant stiffens in his chair. It is Scipio Hawkins, his psychedelic camouflage amplifying the low-wattage bulbs of the room to mesmerise the Sergeant with its dazzle.

'I think you're holding a friend of mine here,' he says. 'A certain Mr Smith.' His manner is confident and there is the suggestion of an edge to his voice.

'We do have such a person here,' says the Sergeant stiffly. 'But he has no identification.'

'I can vouch for him,' says Scipio.

'Oh, yes,' says the Sergeant. 'And who might you be Sir?'

Scipio takes out his wallet and hands over his card. The Sergeant takes it and reads:

Mr Scipio Hawkins.
Editor, International Times.
London.

The Sergeant frowns, he has never heard of the paper, but these are London people and the International sounds impressive.

'There will be a report in tomorrow's paper about today's event,' says Scipio, 'I shall write it myself and it can come out one of two ways. We can thank the Oxfordshire Constabulary for their wise forbearance etc., since I don't suppose anybody wants to be accused of Gestapo tactics. And,' he goes on, placing a significant finger on the Sergeant's nameplate. 'Names might well be mentioned, and typographical errors are endemic in the newspaper world.'

The Sergeant makes no answer to this, Scipio's psychedelics seems to have completely thrown him. After all, anyone with enough bottle to wear such a garment might well have a lot of clout and he wants no trouble. Getting to his feet he retires to an inner-office from where, after a brief conference with its occupant he returns with a bunch of keys. 'We're letting him go,' he says, and his tone gives nothing away. Smith watches as the Sergeant comes to his cell and he hears the welcome sound of a key turning in the lock.

Outside, evening is falling and the setting sun paints the old stones of the ancient city in a ruddy glow as Scipio and Smith walk back to a flat where their friends are gathered.

'What happened to your saxophone?' asks Scipio, noticing the smashed bell of the horn.

'They ran me into a door,' says Smith, regarding the ruined instrument. It is a bad omen. It looks as if, like it or not, he is being drawn in McCafferty's direction and the thought is depressing. 'There's something about me the police don't like,' he thinks, and looking at his damaged horn he sees immediately what the finger of fate has so obviously pointed out: It is not he the police dislike. It is his saxophone.

'It's my saxophone!' he bursts out. 'I must be playing the wrong instrument.'

Not being party to Smith's inner thought processes, Scipio has to take this at face value.

'Yeah. Wow man,' he says.

But Smith has plunged once more into his latest revelation. The saxophone. The most bolshie instrument on the planet. Its associations with jazz making it decidedly hip, and hipness raises the hackles amongst the Philistine. The status-quo represents the fixed; while the hip is fluid and changeable, and change is anathema to the powers-that-be. Now Smith can almost hear the voice of the establishment raised to admonish.

'If there's any changes to be made around here, we'll make them. All right? Then we'll tell you about it.'

Smith is now at the edge of a major shift; his saxophonic days are over for sure. But what next? 'Something you don't have to put in your mouth,' he thinks 'The Banjo? No. Something more respectable like the violin. Then... That's it; the violin of course.' Having made this decision, the mere intention has given him an inner gravitas. As a violinist his credentials will be assured, already he feels the sense of dignity appropriate to such a respectable member of the musical community.

'I'm going to take up the violin,' he announces, and Scipio, a man who has rung many changes himself, takes it in his stride.

'Wow man, yeah,' he says.

Back at the flat Smith catches sight of Dick and Zen.

'How did you know they were coming?' he asks when he gets Dick alone.

'I saw them reflected in my trombone,' he says. 'The bell is like a rear-view mirror and I saw them coming up from behind.'

'Why didn't you warn me?' asks Smith.

'There wasn't time,' answers Dick. 'You had just started a burst and I wasn't going to hang about counting up to five till you'd finished.'

But Smith is not mollified. 'Well if you hadn't put in so much elephant we might have got away with it.' he says.

Flamenco Highway

Late one night as Smith is diligently sawing away on his violin, Wirril comes knocking at his door. The pair have been studying Indian music for some years, and Smith has not long returned from Madras where he had gone to get some lessons. But now he sees with some astonishment that Wirril is brandishing a guitar.

'I've been having a couple of Flamenco guitar lessons,' he says, sitting down and demonstrating a few moves.

Smith's ears prick up. He had himself attempted to play this music some years ago, and had given up after struggling for three days to make sense of a page or two of sheet music. The staves had been so thickly clustered with black notes that barely any white paper had shown through, and he had given up in the face of this impossible barrier. Now, here is Wirril making sounds that restimulate his interest in the music, and his blood is stirred as once before. But how has Wirril done it?

'The class is in a local evening school, and the teacher is from D'Alba in the south of Spain,' says Wirril. 'He's only here for a few months, but he shows you how to do it without reading music.'

Smith puts down his violin and wonders if he will ever pick it up again.

Within a few days he has acquired a boot-sale guitar, and one evening accompanies Wirril for his first lesson. The teacher, going right to the roots, begins with a few simple techniques, and it is not long before the pair are tackling their first full composition: Soleares, and Smith knows at once that this is going to take him some years to master. The music itself is not difficult to learn, but for a beginner it is impossible to play correctly and he settles down to the long haul. He must play the piece impeccably before having the credentials to move on to another. He visualises these new circumstances as a vast dusty plain, simmering under a broiling Andalusian sun. Before him, a great timbered door shod with iron bolts is set into the looming battlements of a mighty fortress. It is the fabled city of Soleares, and this the gate through which all aspiring flamencos must pass; with perfection as the only key. Broken guitars are strewn around in front of the gate, while the white bones of failed aspirants lie bleaching in the merciless sun, and his too, no doubt, will one day lie here. His chances of ever playing the piece authentically are minimal, and he is therefore a little disturbed, when a few days later Wirril turns up and begins playing the opening bars of Segeureas. This, the most solemn form in the whole genre; the Canté Jondo or deep song, where the Canté sings: 'I go out into the fields at night, and I sing until the stones cry.' However, Smith thinks Wirril is jumping the gun a bit.

'The chronologically advantaged haven't got time for all that,' says Wirril, when he expresses his doubts. 'If we hang around trying to get it right first we'll never get any further.'

This reminds Smith that they are both getting on a bit, and the proposition alters his dusty plain considerably. The impregnable gate of Soleares still stands before him, and the white bones slowly crumble beneath the sun. But now he sees a great cleft in the masonry, and many fallen blocks of stone litter the plain around, as if some passing army has breached the wall with siege-guns and taken the city. 'Bloody Hell' he thinks, as he walks along to take a closer look. However, wishing to imbibe an Andalusian flavour more fully, he has recently translated the expression into Spanish, and now uses it at every opportunity.

From his new position he can see into the gap, and there is El Wirril, scrambling his way amongst the fallen stone, as he makes his way through the breach and onwards to Segeureas, whose lofty towers and formidable walls show like a distant mirage across the vast dusty plain. Smith, unwilling now to clank his way alone and forever at his impossible task, doesn't hesitate long in following his friend along this dissolute path, and with a muttered 'Sangriento Infierno', he too takes up the new piece.

Meanwhile other pressing concerns now assail him, for he has discovered that his fingernails are nowhere strong enough for this style of playing, and the nails must be long in order to attain the edgy sound required. Smith's nails are weak and keep breaking, and it is not until he reads a guitar magazine devoted to Flamenco that he discovers that most players apply glue to their nails to get the right effect.

Here the problem bifurcates among the many types of glues available. He tries them all with minimal success. Some dry too rubbery to produce a hard sound, while others crystallise into an inflexible sheath that flakes off under pressure. He consults Brett on the matter. Brett knows all about glue, and when repairing his sitar will only use bone-glue in which he mixes iron-dust, lime, and various other esoteric substances. 'There's a ship's chandler down at Seven Dials,' he says. They have every kind of glue in the world.'

The chandler has indeed a comprehensive stock of glue, and when Smith arrives to make his purchase he has some difficulty making the correct choice. Noticing his hesitation the chandler takes up a small cardboard carton and holds it out to him.

'This glue,' he says. 'Will stick anything to anything indefinitely.'

Smith takes the box from him and opens one end. There is a tube inside and a folded leaflet of instructions.

'It dries as hard as glass yet still retains its flexibility,' says the man, and Smith, convinced by his expert testimony makes the purchase.

Later that evening he gets out the tube of glue. He unfolds the leaflet and there, as if in confirmation of the chandler's endorsement, is the acclamation: 'As tested out on Elephants!' He wonders a little about this as he applies a thick coat to his nails. 'Do they stick the elephant's feet to the ground? Or perhaps glue two elephants together?' But these theories soon fall apart when he discovers that the glue, although strong and flexible takes three days or more before completely drying, and is therefore, for his purposes, useless. Then a breakthrough. An article in a guitar magazine in which the nail problem is discussed in detail, extols the virtues of *Pegamento Imedio*. Which Toledo translates from the Spanish into: *Superglue*.

No problem now. The superglue dries quickly to a hard and flexible finish, but being a little thin needs several coatings. He is in his room strumming the guitar one evening when Kissinger, his peg-leg pigeon who spends most of his time perched on the chandelier, stretches his wings and detaches a feather. It floats to the floor at Smith's feet and he leans forward and picks it up. It is still warm, and as he bends it between his fingers he notices that the quill end is composed of a very similar substance to fingernails. He splits the quill and cuts off a thin strip which he glues to a fingernail. When it is dry, he rubs it down with fine sandpaper until it merges in with the nail. It has just the right feel on the guitar strings, and soon all four fingers and thumb of his right hand are tipped with Kissinger's quill. However, this discovery is not quite the end of the road. A day or so later he had, whilst walking in the park noticed a crow-feather lying in his path. Picking it up he had seen at once that the quill was of superior quality to pigeon, and hunting round had found a few more.

That night he slices the crow-quills into thin strips and glues them along the tips of his right-hand nails. The glue dries quickly, and he files them down to a smooth and almost unnoticeable finish. Retiring, he switches off his light and lies thinking with relish of the morrow and his first day of "Crow Flamenco". Now he remembers the moment of finding the crow-feather down at the back of the zoo. And then... the *Zoo*? —Elephants, zebras, lions and — Birds! A new idea is taking shape at the back of his mind and he explores it with growing excitement. Somewhere in the aviary section will be the king of all birds. The thought bursts into life and sends a ripple of exultation through him — 'Eagle Flamenco!'

For the moment however, crow must do and he calms down a little. He lies looking through the window across the garden and sees Toledo in his room above the annexe, where he pores until the early hours over his alchemical texts. From somewhere below comes the wistful sound of Ace's Chinese factory-fiddle, to mingle with the distant thunder of Phineas' wind-up pianola in the garage.

'How did I ever get mixed up with this gang of weirdos?' he thinks.

The Feast

Food has run low and it is late. The local shops are all shut and Smith, ravenously hungry, goes looking for a bite to eat. Brett never has any food and so calling upon him is useless. He knocks on Ace's door, but he only has a few slices of bread for his breakfast and none to spare. The house is quiet and everybody else seems to be out. Smith stands in the kitchen listening to his stomach rumbling like a far-off thunderstorm, punctuated now by the odd crack of lightning. *Lightning*? No, this cannot be. He attunes his ears and becomes aware of a distant snap and crackle which sounds not unlike wood burning. He leaves the kitchen and follows the sound. At the end of a short corridor is the small garden room now occupied by Jason, an old India-hand, who is resting between his far-flung journeys. Jason has spent many years in India, meeting all the famous and infamous gurus and sampling all manner of exotic substances. Smith notices a light beneath the door. He knocks. 'Yeah,' says a gruff voice, and he goes in.

The room is filled with leaping shadows which vie with each other from their separate sources: a guttering candle set directly on the hearth, and a fire of broken chair-legs in the grate. Upon the fire sits a small bubbling pot, watched over by the Lear-like figure of Jason.

'I thought you might have a spare bite of something,' says Smith.

'I've got a couple of potatoes and a carrot,' answers Jason. 'Have you got any tobacco?'

Smith has been saving enough tobacco for one last roll-up, but he brings it forth and unwrapping the packet on the floor exposes his small hoard. Jason leans forward to examine it.

'I'll give you one potato and half a carrot for a bit of that,' he says.

Smith looks in the pot. Two potatoes jump around, each no larger than a billiard ball, but the carrot is considerably larger. Too heavy to dance with the potatoes it lies sluggishly rolling from side-to-side at the bottom of the pot.

'Done,' says Smith, and sinking to the floor joins Jason at the fireplace.

Jason's early days at Oxford had promised a brilliant future, but at his finals, although achieving high marks in other subjects, he had failed his logic paper and had left without a degree. He had merely seen this as a sign from the gods that his path lay otherwise than logic, and therefore perchance to its opposite. The way of irrationality and mysticism had thus beckoned him, its siren voice singing him along the yogic trail to India, and straight into the arms of a succession of charismatic gurus, each of whom welcome him into their inner circle of disciples.

But footloose, he dips here and dabbles there, absorbing the teaching of each before moving on. Spending half his life in this manner he has returned to Oxford where he now has a room. The room also has another occupant: a mouse, which Jason feeds and pampers. He has grown much attached to the mouse and worries about it when, as now, he spends a few days in London.

'Can't stay long man,' he says, 'I left the mouse some food. But if it runs out what will it do?'

Jason, who has returned after so long in India with the mindset of a *naga baba*, should on this account have been far above such things as attachment to mice. 'Or anything else for that matter,' thinks Smith. Jason's aura of a master yogi is somehow at odds with his attachment to the mouse, until Smith realises that a simple saintliness lies at its heart.

Now by the candle's flicker Jason looks the part indeed. His beard and shaggy hair frame a large aristocratic nose, and his two searching eyes reflect the dancing flames of the fire. He reaches among the shadows for the fire-irons which lie like the implements of Shiva on the hearth, and holds up a poker with which he prods the fire until the potatoes begin to knock loudly in the pot. 'I think they're done,' he says. Pulling the pot from the fire he takes a fork and hooks the potatoes onto two saucers. With a knife he then carefully bisects the carrot into two equal halves.

Having received his portion, Smith breaks a small piece from his potato and applying a pinch of salt conveys it to his mouth. It is delicious, the meat white and floury, the skin no more than a fine earthy membrane. Jason is staring into the fire as he chews. Presently he swallows and announces: 'The greatest pleasure lies at the equidistant point between nothing and something.'

He looks at Smith, as if gauging whether he has understood this offering. But Smith's attention, fixed until this moment on his potato, is beginning to waver in the direction of his half-carrot. He is well aware that Jason was up at Oxford, and is not fazed by these lofty intellectual statements which are anyway far above his head. Jason tries again.

'True pleasure,' he goes on. 'Is found in fulfilling a need; not in attaining a want.'

Smith, still concentrating on the food, now tackles the carrot. He breaks off a piece with his fork and finds it less malleable than the potato. Hard and woody, its fibres are tough and he has difficulty swallowing it. Jason, however, has no trouble with his, his great lantern jaws munching effortlessly on the carrot, whilst continuing his discourse between mouthfuls.

'Think of a man,' he goes on, 'who is driving his second-best Rolls-Royce. Do you think he is enjoying himself more than we are enjoying this simple meal?'

Now he has asked a question and Smith feels obliged to answer.

'Well,' he says. 'I wouldn't enjoy driving a Rolls if I were starving hungry.'

Jason looks disappointed. Smith hasn't quite got it.

'It's a simple equation,' says Jason, giving Smith a hard stare. 'The greater the indulgence, the less the pleasure.' He makes these pronouncements with a great deal of authority, and Smith, having with great effort disposed of his carrot, is now contemplating the small morsel of potato which he has left to last. He holds back a moment in order to relish this final pleasure the more. Taking advantage of his hesitation Jason begins to reminisce.

'When I was up at Oxford,' he says. 'My professors gave me a programme to fulfil. I understood immediately that to attain a degree in logic would be the most illogical thing I could do.'

'So what *did* you do?' asks Smith, really interested now.

'I crashed out sideways,' laughs Jason. 'Left them to sort out their little boxes of therefores and took off for India.'

His plate is empty and he gazes into the fire, while Smith rediscovers to his great delight the remaining morsel of potato. He forks it in and begins chewing. A small mouthful, it doesn't take long. But he savours each tiny fragment and follows its flavour, until, he thinks, like the declining echoes of a sonorous bell, it fades and is gone.

'India,' goes on Jason, is the place where I learned to drop my wants and find satisfaction in my needs.' He grins at Smith. 'And what I need now is tobacco.'

Smith brings himself back from India with a start, and unwrapping his small hoard divides it with great care down the middle. When the two tiny heaps are as equal as he can make them he gestures to his host to take his pick. Jason, like a true Master takes the nearest, and rolling it up sets a piece of glowing chair-leg to the end. Then, blowing out a great cloud of smoke he closes his eyes and begins chanting a Hindu mantra, whilst gently beating time with his poker against the fire-irons. Now the candle is guttering and the fire is low. Jason's shadow flickers on the wall and his voice, deep and unapologetic, intones its litany like a priest of Shiva at his fiery altar. Smith lights up himself and looks around for tea. On the mantelpiece he finds one tea-bag, and boiling up some fresh water he dips it alternately into two cups. No milk, no sugar, but it is hot and goes down well. Jason's chant, meanwhile, is gaining impetus. Swaying backwards and forwards he begins shaking his head from side to side. He is in for the long haul and Smith, leaving him to it, retires to his room upstairs and consigns himself to sleep.

Priestly Rites

The high street is lined on both sides with angry Christian priests who are demonstrating their disgust at affluence wherever it displays itself.

'Walk, walk, walk,' they chant, as the congested traffic files slowly past. The drivers have their windows tightly shut and stare stonily ahead. Further down the road a Rolls-Royce is coming under heavier flak. For now the priests, revolted by this indulgence, have began spitting, and the driver, an expensively dressed and portly man with a cigar clamped between his podgy fingers is visibly seething, as his highly polished Roller is rapidly covered in dribbling saliva.

'Walk fat pig,' shout the priests as they advance, hawking throatily to deposit the results on the windscreen of the Rolls.

'Let his tyres down!' shrieks a woman from the rear, and as if released from restraint a small shoal of little girls push themselves between the priests and surround the Rolls. Within moments a loud hissing is heard as the girls apply their hair-pins to the valves of the tyres. The Rolls begins to visibly sink and the driver blows his top. Outraged, he flings open the door and emerges shaking with anger.

'Off! Off! Off!' shout the priests and surrounding the man begin to pull off his expensive silk-lined jacket. Next he is pushed to the ground and debagged. Without his trousers he has lost his gravitas. He tries to climb back into his car, but it has been pushed to the side of the road and he is held back by the crowd that now surround him.

A woman comes forward. She shoves into his hand a saucepan in which is one potato and a carrot. He stares at it in bewilderment, and then into his other hand in which has been placed a tea-bag. Now a blanket is thrust under his arm and with a shove from behind from the priests he stumbles away to begin a new and somewhat more austere life.

Somehow, Smith finds himself standing next to the Rolls. Its door still stands invitingly open, and seizing the opportunity he slips into the front seat and pulls the door shut with a satisfying clunk. Now the sounds of the street are but a distant memory hardly noticeable in the expensive hush which surrounds him. The pigskin seat moulds itself to his every movement and he relaxes into its exclusive embrace. He is beginning to enjoy himself; already regarding the crowded pavements with disdain, as if, from his newly elevated status these low-lifers are far beneath his consideration.

He idly wonders what it would be like to drive such a dream machine, and imagines himself swooping majestically around the outer circle of Regents Park. Casting his eye along the elegant brushed-rosewood fascia, he notices that a key still occupies the ignition. He considers it for a moment, and then... 'Well, why not?' he thinks, and leaning forward turns the key.

A tiny shudder ripples briefly through the great car, a faint mechanical whisper emanates from the far-reaching bonnet and he is ready to go. Pushing in the clutch he is startled to hear a violent banging on the side window. Turning, he sees the angry red face of a priest, and behind him there are more.

'Out, out,' they chant and begin rocking the car. Smith searches around desperately for the lock but cannot find it. He tries to put the car into gear but it is too late - the priests have managed to get the door open.

'Out fat pig,' they shout, and begin pulling him from the car.

'No, wait,' begs Smith. 'You've got it wrong, I'm not...' But the priests aren't listening.

'Off, off,' they chant, and soon he is jacketless.

Now his trousers are under threat, but he swings around and for a moment evades their clutching hands.

'No,' he tries to explain. 'I was just...' But they are, he sees, in for the kill and he hesitates no longer. Leaping between their over-eager grasp he makes off down the road as fast as he can. A howl of rage goes up, and soon the pavement behind him rings with the pounding feet of angry priests. Closer and closer they come and Smith is in real trouble. For some strange reason his legs are getting shorter, and he must run ever faster to escape. Now his feet seem to have fallen off and he staggers along like a truncated clothes-peg until, his legs twitching in nervous spasms he wakes up drenched in a cold sweat and gasping with horror.

Recovering slowly from the ordeal, he lies recapitulating the dream and castigating himself for his failure to resist the temptation of the Rolls. Remembering the moment intensely, he realises that in the dream he had had no choice whatever over his actions. The insight brings a degree of self-exoneration, and he sighs with relief.

'It must have been the carrot,' he thinks.

Lacuna

The embassy has now become host to a constant stream of visitors. Members of yoga groups who use the salon in the week-day evenings, patients calling to see Toledo, or violinists coming for a lesson with Ace. This public aspect of their daily lives has an effect on the dress of the residents, their outer charade of establishment values and the fact that few of the visitors have any idea that the house is a squat, causes them to dress as well as their poverty-stricken circumstances will allow.

However, this front is a double-edged sword, as they discover one day when there is a knock at the front door. Smith answers it to a grey-suited man who introduces himself as Mr Tinsdale from Westminster Council, and asks if he may come in for a moment. Smith obliges and beckons him to enter, leading him into the kitchen where a few of the residents are just finishing breakfast.

'I really want to speak to Mr Smith,' he begins.

'That's me,' says Smith, ever gullible. The man accepts a cup of tea from Caspar and sits at the long refectory table.

'I am Chief Accountant at Westminster Council's rating department, and it has been noticed that this house has been occupied for a considerable time without the payment of rates. The rateable value of the house is three thousand, three hundred pounds per year, and I'm here to find out if you are willing to pay.'

This is, to the residents, a ridiculous sum and there is no way of raising it.

'But it's useless asking us for money,' says Smith. 'We're minimalist squatters, and only have enough money for our simplest needs.'

The degree of disbelief written on Mr Tinsdale's face is plain for all to see. They do not fit into his image of how squatters live. He can see no graffiti, lurid posters or accumulated rubbish, and the people in the kitchen look like respectable occupants of a carefully maintained property; he clearly has the impression that they are maybe rich eccentrics or the like.

'Well,' he says finally. 'As long as the house was empty a reduced rate was being billed to the Foreign Office, but since the house is now occupied, the burden of payment shifts to the occupants.' He takes a form from his briefcase and writes something at the top.

'If you will just give me your names I'll finish my report, and I'm sure we can sort the whole thing out.' His manner is pleasant but they are not fooled.

Morgiana, frying some cabbage at the stove speaks in a hollow ghostly voice.

'I am the nameless one,' she intones, and giggles at her own precociousness.

There is much laughter at this, and even Mr Tinsdale manages a smile. But in the silence which follows no names are forthcoming and he adopts a firmer manner.

'As it happens,' he says. 'I really only need one, and I already have that.' He looks at Smith.

'If the Council prosecute we can claim two years retrospectively, and therefore your arrears are six thousand, six hundred pounds and payment is due immediately.' He takes out a sheaf of papers containing the relevant accounts and lays them on the table.

'I must get back now,' he says standing up. 'If we receive a cheque over the next few days no more will be said, otherwise you will be hearing from me again.'

He leaves, and sure enough a week later comes a bill with notice that Westminster Council intends to prosecute Smith for the unpaid rates. It now seems appropriate to get some advice on their legal position and Tralee speaks to a solicitor with whom she has family connections. When she has given him the gist of the situation he agrees to look into it as a personal favour. This involves an interview for Smith at the lawyer's office where he explains the situation in detail.

Mr Priest is a solicitor who specialises in land and property and the story intrigues him. 'And what we're looking for is someone who might find the case interesting,' finishes Smith.

Mr Priest stands up and holds out his hand.

'Well,' he says, jovially. 'You've found him.'

Smith rises to take the man's hand and the lawyer goes on.

'I've never heard of squatters being liable for rates; this situation being without precedent I will need to seek Counsel's Advice, and meanwhile we will apply for legal aid.'

A week or so later Smith arrives at the Inns of Court in Holborn for an interview with a barrister. He is an elderly man who seems not at all sympathetic and obviously takes a dim view of squatters; each time he mentions the word he makes no attempt to hide the sneer which curls his lip. He has already written his report and reads it out with obvious relish. In his view, he can see no legal reason why squatters should not pay rates.

'And it is my opinion,' he concludes, 'that since the wilful non-payment of rates is a civil offence which can receive a custodial sentence, Mr Smith is liable to go to prison.' And what's more, his tone seems to suggest, quite right too.

'How long might I get?' asks Smith, somewhat taken aback by this.

'For the first offence, six months,' says the barrister with obvious relish, 'And you would still owe the money.'

Smith leaves, considerably downcast by this pessimistic view. He returns to the solicitor's office where Mr Priest has already received the barrister's advice.

'I think we should seek an alternative opinion,' he says. 'I'll see what I can do,' and Smith returns to the embassy to reconsider his position.

He could just disappear and they would never find him. But he is reluctant to abandon all they have worked for, and he therefore decides to stay put for a while longer and see what transpires with the second opinion. Westminster Council, however, moves too fast for them and a few days later a summons drops through the letter-box. It is addressed to "J. Smith. Guild of Transcultural Studies" and orders him to appear at Westminster Magistrate's Court the following week on a charge of wilful non-payment of rates. Smith phones Mr Priest who seems not at all flustered.

'Don't worry,' he says calmly. 'I have engaged another Counsel and arranged an interview on the day before the hearing.'

'The day before,' thinks Smith. 'This doesn't sound too hopeful.' He is torn between the instinct to flee, and an underlining stubbornness in the face of these Philistines. On the appointed day he returns to the Inns of Court to be received by Mr R. Barnfield the new barrister. Mr Barnfield is a much younger man than the first; he is tall, slim and elegant.

'Now remember,' he says. 'I cannot coach you as to how you answer the questions which I will put when you are on the stand, but what I can do is subject you to a dummy run.' He stands and begins pacing up and down his office.

'Now imagine you are in the box,' he says. 'Here comes the first question: How did you get into the house to establish occupancy?'

'I broke in through a window on the ground floor,' answers Smith.

Mr Barnfield looks aghast. 'Oh no!' he says, clapping a hand to his forehead in dismay.

'But that's how it happened. What else can I say?' Smith asks, uncertain what line he should take.

'I can't tell you what to say, but I can see that you will prejudice yourself the moment you open your mouth,' says Mr Barnfield. He thinks for a while then... 'I'm not letting you on to the stand,' he says grimly, 'which means I will have to go straight onto the attack.'

These words sound heartening to Smith; it looks as if they have found a champion for their cause.

'What happens if I lose?' He asks, trying to grasp the odds.

'Technically,' says Mr Barnfield, a foxy gleam coming to his eye. 'A custodial sentence is possible, but as the case is without precedent there are many loopholes to exploit.'

This sounds much better and Smith cheers up a little. Returning to the embassy, however, he takes precautions and in spite of Mr Barnfield's encouraging manner, packs his possessions into bags and arranges for them to be looked after should the worst happen and he does not return on the morrow. That night they order two taxis to convey them, since they do not trust public transport to get them to the court on time.

The following morning they rise early and meet for coffee in the kitchen. Smith must present himself at nine o'clock in the court and around eight-fifteen he begins to worry. The two taxis ordered the night before have not appeared, and when Morgiana telephones the company she is told that it is a busy morning and their cars might be late.

'But it is essential that we have them on time,' she says. 'They are wanted for a court appearance,'

'I'm sorry,' the girl replies. 'But all our cars are out at the moment.' It is now getting late and Morgiana puts on her no-nonsense managerial manner.

'This is the Guild of Transcultural Studies' she says sternly. 'We ordered those cars last night and if they're not here within five minutes I shall recommend all our associates in the area to boycott your company.' There is silence for a while, then a man's voice.

'I'm sorry for the inconvenience,' he says politely, his voice oozing with social grease. 'But as it happens we do have a large limousine on call which we can let you have for the same price as the two taxis.' Morgiana accepts the offer and tells the man to get it to the embassy as fast as possible.

They wait in the forecourt for the transport to arrive and have not been standing long before the front of an enormous car comes nosing cautiously in. It is so long that when the bonnet comes to a halt at the door, its rear is only just through the front gate. Feeling a little bemused they pile in and spread themselves around its spacious interior.

It is morning in Regent's Park. The copper dome of the mosque is bright in the early sun as around a curve in the road sweeps a white Mercedes stretch-limo. It purrs majestically along; the kind of car used by celebrities and film stars when arriving at premiers and grand openings. But the dark-tinted windows give no hint as to the identity of its passengers. Inside, the car is upholstered and lined with thick white fur, and reclining across the vast back seat are Tralee, Katarina, and Morgiana.

They are enjoying the ride immensely, putting on queenly airs, and waving in a regal manner to the imaginary crowds which line their route. They giggle together amongst much banter from the others, but Smith sits staring gloomily from a window and wishes he had gone on his pushbike. He doesn't like this turn of events and feels as if he is being set up. A sacrifice, garlanded with flowers and drawn in a splendid chariot to the altar and place of execution. It is the pride of hubris before the fall, and he finds it difficult to join in with the festive air that has pervaded the interior of the car.

'The gods are with us,' booms Toledo. 'The signs are all around.' But Smith is not convinced, still feeling that he should have done a runner when he had the chance. As he gazes morosely through the window a red light brings their stately progress to a halt. 'I could jump out of the car now,' he thinks. 'This is my last chance.' But his body doesn't respond to this dictum, no minor tremor occurs to be seized upon and rapidly mobilised into a full-blown go-for-it. The fingers of fate hold Smith firmly in their grasp and he knows it.

Outside the court, a group of grey-suited legal representatives of Westminster Council huddle at the top of the court steps waiting for the great wooden doors to open. In their forefront stands Mr Tinsdale, looking very important and carrying a large and bulging briefcase. They stare disapprovingly down as the great white whale of a car draws with silent majesty to a halt, and watch stonily as a door opens and Katarina, Tralee, and Morgiana emerge, looking ready to face the cameras and still hamming it up a little. Toledo, Caspar and Ace then step out, and Smith, wishing more than ever that he had come on his pushbike is last. He can see that turning up in this ridiculous car has created the worst impression possible and done little good for his image as a poor squatter.

Inside, he must report to the Sheriff's Office, where, after registration he is led below to a small cell to await his appearance. The door shuts with a thud. 'They've got me again,' he thinks. Now the smell of damp stonework, and the far-off sound of freedom percolating faintly down through a grating from the street outside, amplify the horrors which had descended upon him since waking this morning.

Fortunately he has not long to wait before the cell door opens and a policeman tells him to follow a long narrow corridor at the end of which is a flight of wooden stairs.

'Go up!' shouts the policeman, and Smith, wondering what will happen next climbs the stairs.

What happens next is that he is in the dock. The stairs were a trap and he is high up somewhat to the centre of a large courtroom. It is panelled in light oak, carved with scrolls and curlicues around the swords, axes, and occasional portcullis which are the emblems of these powers that be. Apart from the odd policeman, the courtroom is as yet almost empty, but across the far side of the room Mr Tinsdale and his minions are gathered at a table and laying out their papers, whilst chatting with them in an affable manner is his champion, Mr Barnfield.

Dressed in a long black gown and wig and looking very impressive he seems to be sharing some sort of joke with them. Smith is a little let down by this. Why is he fraternising with the enemy? Just then he catches sight of Smith and strolls over to have a word.

'So,' he says, looking up at him with a grim smile. 'What does it feel like up there?'

Smith doesn't answer. The barrister is obviously taking the piss.

'I've often wondered,' muses Mr Barnfield. 'What it felt like to be in there,' then turning away he sits down at a table and, his long legs stretched beneath it contemplates his steepled fingers. He doesn't seem to have any papers at all and Smith is very worried indeed. The court now begins to fill with clerks and officials of various kinds, and he watches as the embassy contingent take their seats in the public gallery, the women giving him a wave which he doesn't dare return. When the magistrate enters, the court rises until he is seated and a clerk comes forward to formally announce the case. In a loud and theatrical voice he proclaims:

'The Lord Mayor and Citizens of the City of Westminster, versus Mr J. Smith, and "The Guild of Transcultural Studies".'

Hearing the full title of the Guild read out in this way seems to confer immense credibility upon it, and he is glad they did not indulge in anything more fanciful. When the clerk has finished the magistrate calls upon the Council to present their case, whereupon Mr Tinsdale rises to his feet and in a pompous manner explains that Westminster Council have a duty to collect rates from all occupied properties within its domain, and that this requirement does not exclude squatters. Therefore, he reasons, since Smith is an occupant together with others, of a large house in St John's Wood with a high rateable value, he now owes the Council exactly six thousand, six hundred pounds in unpaid rates. Mr Fawkes, the magistrate, seems to be in full agreement with him, punctuating his indictment with the occasional, 'Yes. Yes. I see,' whilst taking copious notes, and Mr Barnfield appears to be fast asleep. Smith feels doomed and is sure he won't be going home tonight.

Now Mr Tinsdale's exposition reaches a climax in which irresponsible squatters are shown to be parasites on decent society, and ends by calling upon the magistrate to deal with Smith in a properly severe manner. 'Yes! Yes!' The magistrate says enthusiastically; as Mr Tinsdale sits down to receive the congratulations of his colleagues. He smirks a little and flashes a look of vindictive satisfaction across the room, where Smith knows now for sure he is done for.

'Mr Barnfield,' says the magistrate. 'Might we now hear from you?'

Mr Barnfield slowly retrieves his long legs from beneath the table, and rising elegantly to his feet formally thanks the magistrate.

'The Court will notice,' he begins. 'That the Respondent is in this action titled, "Mr Smith, Guild of Transcultural Studies", and I should like to point to a fact that Westminster Council have singularly overlooked. The aforementioned "Guild", is an unincorporated body and if, Sir, you will look in the relevant authorities you will find that in the case of Verral v Hackney, 1983, the magistrate found that an unincorporated association may not be proceeded against for rates.'

The magistrate now receives a weighty tome from a clerk and after reading for a while looks up and says. 'Yes, yes, absolutely right Mr Barnfield. The authorities seem to be very clear on this point.'

Again Mr Barnfield thanks the magistrate.

'And now to deal with the remaining point,' he says. 'The question of Mr Smith himself, and again the law is very clear on this point. In order for an occupancy to give rise to a liability for rates it must be both exclusive and permanent. However, the Council have by their own admission shown that Mr Smith shares the property with others, and therefore I would suggest that the action fails on both these points. But,' he says, raising a finger aloft. 'There is a far more fundamental issue at stake here, and to bring it to light I would like to put a question to Westminster Council if I may?'

The magistrate gives his consent to this and once more Mr Tinsdale rises to his feet, looking now decidedly unsure of himself.

'Mr Tinsdale,' says Mr Barnfield. 'It is odd that the only name you have from amongst the considerable number who inhabit the house is Mr

Smith's.' He begins pacing the well of the court looking at his feet as if deep in thought, then coming to an abrupt halt posits his question.

'Exactly how did you acquire that name?'

Mr Tinsdale looks flustered. 'By the usual channels,' he answers evasively.

'I see,' says Mr Barnfield. 'And will you please tell the Court what those usual channels were?'

Mr Tinsdale is red-faced; now it seems as if the whole thing has turned around and it is he who is defending himself. He makes several false starts before announcing in a much chastened voice.

'We asked the lady who lives next door.'

'I see,' says Mr Barnfield again, then dismissing Mr Tinsdale in an offhand manner he turns again to the magistrate. 'We have here, Sir, an action where the only evidence that Mr Smith is an occupant at all is based upon mere hearsay, which in this circumstance matters not a jot or tittle. Were the Council to have kept watch and observed him perhaps taking in the milk over several days, or collecting letters from the postman, there might then have been sufficient evidence for at least a prima facie case.

'As we have seen there is no such evidence; neither is there any proof that Mr Smith's occupation is permanent or exclusive, and the testimony of Mr Tinsdale has I would suggest, no relevance whatsoever in law. I therefore call upon this Court to dismiss the case against my client.'

Mr Barnfield sits down and the magistrate, after consulting his notes, declares a short recess while he considers the matter, and Smith, feeling a nudge in his back turns to find the policeman standing behind him. Taking him by the arm the policeman escorts him back to the cell where he is brought some tea, and while sipping from the enamelled mug he stares at the whitewashed wall. He is aware that in some far-off room and sipping tea from a probably more elegant cup, sits a man who is even now contemplating his fate, but of his chances he has no idea. His deliberations come to an end as a key turns in the door and again he walks the corridor and mounts the stair to the dock. The magistrate enters and once more the standing up sitting down ritual is enacted.

The magistrate first reiterates the accusations of Mr Tinsdale, and then the refutation of Mr Barnfield. 'And I find,' he concludes, 'that Westminster Council have failed in their application. The case is dismissed,' and he brings his gavel down with an irrevocable thud. Mr Tinsdale is crestfallen and Smith can't believe his ears.

'Mr Tinsdale,' says the magistrate, leaning over and fixing him with a stern eye. 'If you ever bring such an ill-conceived and badly prepared case before me again, I shall come down very hard on you. Is that understood?' Mr Tinsdale hangs his head. 'Yes Sir.' He mutters then, followed by his colleagues he hurriedly leaves the Court.

Outside in the foyer they all shake hands with Mr Barnfield. The ladies cluster admiringly round the elegant barrister, who seems a little bemused by their attentions, modestly declining the accolades which they shower upon him. 'It is a Lacuna.' He says mysteriously.

Morgiana flashes her most wicked look, but to no avail. It is Katarina who has caught his eye, and she, seeking to lure him deeper, pretends she has not noticed. The ploy works, and Mr Barnfield succeeds in extracting an invitation to visit her for afternoon tea in her flat at the embassy. Smith feels born again, and as he descends the front steps of the Court and stands free upon the pavement a great weight lifts from him.

'There you are,' says Toledo, beaming heartily. 'I told you the gods were with us.' And Smith, considering the day's events, cannot disagree.

This, however, is by no means the last they hear from Westminster Council, since a few months later warning is given that they are appealing to a higher court and soon notice of the appeal arrives in the post. This time Smith must appear at the Divisional High Court in the Strand. Mr Barnfield is too busy at the moment and puts them in touch with a colleague, a Mr Brace. He is a young and energetic barrister who in court proves himself the equal, if not more, of the formidable collection of barristers and legal advisors that the Council have arrayed for the second round, but to no avail. Mr Brace sees them all off and once more the Council's case collapses.

'It is a Lacuna,' says Mr Brace. 'A case without precedent, and therefore a choice morsel for learned magistrates to haggle over and perhaps even make their name in the statute books. So they won't want to end it too quickly.'

The issue drags on over the years, finally being brought to judicial review. The sum owed rises in time to a peak of twenty eight thousand pounds and once a year or so the Court appearances are re-enacted, becoming in time a ritual, in which they ceremoniously foregather to watch their new champion pit himself alone against the massed ranks of the Philistine.

First Love

A pigeon limps around pecking amongst the table legs of an outdoor café. It seems to be alone, unable by reason of a crippled claw to keep up with its fellows. At times it attempts to preen its feathers, but, supported by only one leg cannot maintain a balance and its plumage lacking this attention is seriously bedraggled. The pigeon's eye now alights upon a few crumbs of toast fallen from a nearby table, and it begins a clumsy one-legged hop to reap this small harvest. However, as it nears the feast it notices that there is a pair of shoes within a few feet of the crumbs and it hesitates, cocking an eye at the shoes and up the trouser legs of the occupant of the table. Inside the shoes and trousers is Smith, who has been watching the pigeon for some time.

He has noticed the lameness and solitary existence forced upon the bird and feels a growing empathy for it. The pigeon dithers around but cannot quite summon the courage to approach within pecking distance of the crumbs. Smith keeps absolutely still while attempting to exude an aura of benevolence and good will. The pigeon watches him closely, and finally convinced for one brief moment that he represents no threat darts recklessly forward, snatches up a crumb and hops clumsily away.

With this success comes growing confidence and again the sudden rush and quick retreat, while Smith continues with his immobility. He notices that the retreat is becoming less anxious; perhaps even desultory, and soon the pigeon is pecking around between his feet. He admires the courage of the bird, handicapped in this way and deprived thus of the association of its fellows. Ragged of plumage yet undaunted of spirit the pigeon takes on the challenge of life without self-pity or despair. He feels a growing warmth for the bird; it swells up from within and permeates his whole body. He looks at the pigeon and allows the feeling to radiate outwards towards it. He has never felt the like of this before.

'This must be love' he thinks. 'The first time in my life I feel love, and it's for a bloody pigeon!'

Matador's Dilemma

The embassy now plays host to a succession of Gurus and Yoga masters from India; Lamas and venerable Rinpoches from Tibet; and various New-Age philosophers who find the salon provides a sympathetic ambience for their discourses. Amongst these is Rinpoche Ubron, a Tibetan Master who has founded a monastic community in Italy. He teaches Dzogchen, a form of Buddhism which has the reputation of being direct in approach and devoid of any hanky-panky. The Rinpoche has many disciples in England who have arranged to bring him over for a ten-day teaching, and they turn up on the day before his arrival to festoon the salon with maroon drapes and large Tibetan Tanka paintings.

Late afternoon of the following day there is a knock at the front door and Smith opens it to see a man wearing a tan windcheater, light khaki trousers and a red shirt. The man is eating an ice-cream lolly on a stick. He pulls the lolly from his mouth and licks his lips.

'You're a bit early,' says Smith. 'But come in and have a cup of tea while you wait.'

He guesses from the man's high cheek-bones and general oriental features that he is one of the illustrious Rinpoche's disciples.

'You can sit in the kitchen if you like,' he offers, and looking at his watch says: 'You probably have an hour or so to wait.'

The man seems amused by this, but says nothing as Smith leads him into the kitchen, where he shows him the tea-making equipment and leaves him tending to the kettle.

Later, curious about the teacher who is gracing the house that evening he enters the rear of the salon and finds a hushed room in which a single voice is speaking. Sitting cross-legged on the podium is the oriental man with the now long-consumed ice-cream lolly. Speaking quietly and keeping completely still he radiates an unpretentious dignity; whilst his disciples, eager to catch his every word silently listen. He speaks in fluant Italian and an interpreter is translating. Still wearing the windcheater and red shirt; Rinpoche Ubron is speaking his mind.

'A master who passes himself off as a punter is well worth watching,' thinks Smith. But, since he doesn't understand Italian and mistrusts the translation he withdraws and confines himself to the kitchen, where, during breaks he can watch the Rinpoche relaxing with a mug of tea amongst his disciples; fielding their questions and playing a straight bat to even the subtlest hint of sycophancy.

'Here is a man,' thinks Smith, 'who will never fall into the trap his disciples will weave around him.'

The Rinpoche sits casually relaxed, and seems not to follow the general conversation at all, speaking only when spoken to, as if words were the playthings of children which he had long outgrown. But his English is better than he claims.

One of the disciples questions him on the fundamental difference between the “Absolute” and the “Relative”. A look of amusement passes across Ubron’s face and he gives forth to a burst of hearty Tibetan laughter, as if someone has told a particularly good joke. When his laughter subsides he begins to speak of the inseparability of anything from everything else.

‘Only with language,’ he says, pointing to his mouth. ‘Can such impossible concepts arise.’

Now he has their full attention. He is taking them to the edge of an abyss. Standing up and placing his mug in a tray he begins walking back towards the salon. As he passes through the kitchen door he turns his head and speaks over his shoulder.

‘Without, or beyond language we have only what is. And within that, there are no distinctions at all.’ Having delivered this bombshell he exits for the salon, where he remounts the podium and awaits the return of his disciples.

Over the next ten days the Rinpoche, Master of the highest of the “Nine Vehicles of Dharma”, discourses at length upon the nature of absolute reality, which viewpoint he holds as impervious to the superficial changes occurring in modern culture. He speaks from an ancient tradition, but makes it plain that he is not bound by it and seems well at ease in the modern world.

Smith enters the salon one afternoon and spies Ubron sitting on a couch. He is surrounded as usual by an avid flock of seekers who are engaging him in metaphysical banter, when, putting his hand into his pocket he brings forth a bar of chocolate. Unwrapping it he takes a bite, and one of his followers jumps excitedly to his feet and takes out a camera. He will get a scoop! A picture of the Master eating a chocolate-bar. But when he raises the camera to his eye Ubron stretches out a hand to stay him, then, unfolding the wrapper so that the brand name can be clearly seen he poses, mouth open for another bite. Foiled by this master-stroke and deprived of his scoop the man takes his picture, but cannot disguise his chagrin.

The Rinpoche smiles serenely on, his matador mind equal to the horns of any dilemma.

A powerful shamanistic mantra is emanating from the salon, where Ubron is conducting a ceremonial invocation of the Great Wrathful Deity Dorje Legpa. He is one of the guardians of the gates to paradise, and Ubron is engaged in an ancient ritual which will set this fearsome entity to watch over and protect the embassy from any harm. Ubron sits on the podium and behind him hangs a large Tanka painting of the deity. The mouth of Dorje

Legpa is open in a fearsome grimace which displays pitiless fangs wreathed in smoke and flames, while his many arms bear the mighty weapons which threaten the evildoer.

The ceremony is a long and serious matter, and Ubron conducts the proceedings with a small drum mounted on a handle which he twirls rapidly in one hand. The drum has two thongs fixed to the sides, at the ends of which are threaded a pair of large beads. As the drum is twirled the beads swing rapidly around beating the drum with a sharp rattle. Thick incense rises in clouds through which the strange Tibetan chant floats to the accompaniment of the drum, while the terrible visage of Dorje Legpa looks on.

Smith, impressed by all this cannot refrain from imagining what might happen should Mr Tinsdale from the Council be foolish enough to come knocking at the door again. He won't stand a chance. Confronted in a cloud of smoke and flames by Dorje Legpa he will have no choice but to leg it back through the front gate and up the road towards Regent's Park with the monster close on his heels.

Towards the end of Ubron's stay Johnny Banana Head re-appears. He says he has been tramping around "Up North", and now wears a long St. John's Ambulance Brigade overcoat. Silver buttons resplendent he struts around in it like a commissionaire, his well-worn copy of the *AtoZ* projecting from a side pocket. A room is found for him, and since he now spends most of his time with nose buried in the book of street maps, has no time for looking.

'I've done that,' he says to Smith. 'But the *AtoZ* is much more interesting. Look at this.'

He pulls out the book, and after a brief and expert search places his finger on a maze of streets and holds it out for inspection. Smith takes a look at the page but cannot see what Johnny means.

'Look. Can't you see it? Acacia Avenue.' he shouts, and bursts into hysterical laughter. Smith is trying to understand what is so funny and struggles to get the joke, but to no avail.

Acacia Avenue! says Johnny again, articulating the name slowly and clearly as if relishing a fine fruit of a word, and then again convulses with laughter. Smith hasn't a clue and still doesn't get it, while Johnny, enjoying the joke all the more for Smith's bewilderment refuses to explain. Johnny seems now to have granted himself the status of a higher being, too lofty of intellect to be bothered with an explanation to simpletons such as Smith, and he, having better things to laugh at leaves him to it.

Later that evening Ubron's disciples give him a last supper before he returns to Italy where his order is settled, and the embassy's residents have been invited to partake of the feast. The kitchen table is heaped high with food and illuminated by several branch candlesticks and a great fire blazing in the spacious hearth. Ubron sits at the head of the table, his wise Tibetan eyes regarding this motley collection of trivial pursuits with the infinite patience of a kindergarten supervisor. Occasionally he will speak in answer to a question, and one such has just been posed relating to boredom.

'A moment comes,' says the Lama. 'Where there is nothing to do; and there arises a restlessness which is called 'boredom'. These occasions are the most valuable moments of your life, and offer the opportunity to go deeper into the reality of existence. These moments are also when you are most likely to seek some form of entertainment and thus throw away that opportunity,' and, as if proving a point he stabs downward with his fork and conveys a carrot to his mouth.

Johnny Banana Head sits half way down the table amongst the disciples; but like Ubron, takes no notice of the conversation around him. He has his *AtoZ* open by his plate and peruses it intently while he eats. During a lull in the general conversation he suddenly gives vent to a maniacal burst of laughter and all eyes turn his way. The disciples stare in bewilderment. Banana Head is cracking up. Tears stream down his cheeks as he laughs helplessly. Occasionally, when he can catch his breath he shouts:

'*Willington Road!*'

Tête-À-Tête

Sometimes of late in the afternoons, Mr Barnfield can be seen taking tea with Katarina on her balcony overlooking the garden. Coming from an orthodox middle class background he is fascinated by the bohemian atmosphere within the embassy, (although he has admitted to Katarina that he writes the occasional English sonnet) and he watches through her leaf-shrouded trellis as if from the observation box of a wildlife preserve. Caspar and Smith are about to fence on the lawn below, and swish their foils in a salute before crossing blades and taking each other's measure. Caspar is dressed immaculately in snow-white fencing jacket and trousers, while Smith wears a rather frayed and worn jacket which he had obtained second-hand and thus has not the visual panache of Caspar. They have fenced many times before and Smith knows that Caspar has innumerable tricks up his sleeve. He is therefore somewhat wary of committing himself to an overt attack.

Caspar begins to probe Smith's defence, feinting in carte a few times and watching Smith's response and Smith, well aware of what he is up to responds with the same parry each time. Caspar is trying to lure Smith into a trap. Tempting him into a repetitious movement and thus a false sense of security. Whereupon he will make a sudden change in the line of attack and catch Smith off guard. But Smith knows this, and pretending that he has not noticed the strategy continues with the same parry. He is hoping to lure Caspar into a trap, and watches for the moment when he makes his move. What the movement will be he has no idea. But he knows it will be lightning fast and lo! Here it comes.

Caspar's blade swings up again to threaten Smith and seeks to draw another parry carte, to which Smith, who guesses what is coming, does not respond. Sure enough the blade swings down again as Caspar, leaning forward until he is almost falling over bursts into the fast short run of a flèche, his point coming straight for the middle of Smith's jacket. Waiting until Caspar has reached the point of no return, Smith sinks to his haunches and catches Caspar's blade high in prime, cuts under, presents his point, and Caspar runs right on to it.

Bones, who is sitting on the patio, himself in fencing whites and waiting to challenge the winner, claps in appreciation at this piece of deviousness, and the two combatants square up again. They are playing best out of three hits, and now Smith is one up. He threatens Caspar in sixte, evades the parry and lunges in carte. But the lunge is merely an extension of the feint, for, allowing Caspar to parry him he reprises, disengages, and lunges in septième. Caspar dances lightly back, beats Smith's blade aside and scores a direct hit. One each.

Smith now attacks with a long sequence of complicated feints, seeking to fluster his opponent with the speed and precision of his onslaught. His blade flicks rapidly into a threat to carte, then downwards in a semi-circle to octave, followed by a dazzling display of rapidly changing alternatives, but all to no avail. Unfazed and barely moving, Caspar lazily reaches forth his arm and with a nonchalant air flicks the point of his blade to another direct hit and Caspar has the best of it. They remove their helmets, salute and shake hands, and Bones, eager now to try his hand with Caspar steps forth for the engagement.

Back on the patio Smith cools off on a bench. Putting his hand into his trouser pocket he brings forth a collection of curious objects which he sits idly running through his fingers. They are a gift from Bones who has just returned from an assignment in America. Taking advantage of the high-tech laboratory equipment available there, he had acquired a lump of granite from the Manhattan bedrock upon which the city is built, and with the aid of a diamond saw sliced out eight small cubes of the hard black stone. Four of which he has covered in a few nanoseconds of 24-carat gold. Smith is fascinated by their uniqueness and doubts that their like exists anywhere else on the planet.

There is, however, a subtle poignancy in this, since, unlike the rich banker who takes his after-supper guests down to the vaults to view his Renoirs and Monets, no one else on the planet, apart from Bones and himself, knows that the small dense black and gold cubes exist at all, far less that he, Smith, is the proud owner. Therefore the pleasure is a secret one and it would seem poignant to boot, an exclusive glow which endows the cubes with added charisma. Until he imagines proudly showing them to "Mr Richard Arnold, President, Guild of Transcultural Studies (1917-22)".

'So what?' he would shout angrily. '*SO WHAT!*'

The door of the annexe now swings open and Toledo emerges. Pointed black Cortez beard held at a jaunty angle, he looks as if he might be Ambassador at the Court of the Archduke himself. He evades the lawn where the two white-clad figures dart in and out of each other's range, and coming to the patio sits on the bench next to Smith, where he watches with interest the dialogue of blades. He also has been a recent recipient of Bones' skill with the diamond saw; a minor accident had robbed him of a front tooth which his dentist had replaced with a plastic facsimile. Toledo had been unhappy with the replacement, but cannot afford better work.

Around this time Brett had been cutting a new sitar bridge from a short animal tusk of some kind which he had found in a junk shop, and Bones, catching sight of it had expressed curiosity as to its origin. At his request Brett had allowed him to take it for analysis to the teaching hospital in which he does his research.

'It's a hippopotamus tooth,' he reports a week later, and offers to cut some bridge-pieces for Brett if he can have the remainder for the hospital museum. It is a good deal and Brett agrees, while Toledo, who has been listening, picks up the tusk and weighs it in his hand.

'It's very heavy,' he says, and Bones, entering into his field with enthusiasm leaps into a detailed description of its qualities.

'The teeth of the hippopotamus,' he says, 'are the hardest form of ivory in the animal kingdom, and that is why we want it for the museum.'

'Could a human tooth be made from it?' asks Toledo, an odd gleam coming into his eye.

'Of course,' says Bones. 'And it would outlast every other tooth in your head.'

Toledo reaches inside his mouth and removes his plastic replacement.

'Could you make a replica of this from it?' he asks, holding forth the tooth. Bones takes a look.

'No problem,' he says, 'I'll let you have a copy tomorrow evening if I can take this now.'

Toledo takes the plunge and hands over the piece of plastic, which Bones, true to his word returns the following evening together with the hippopotamus facsimile, and Toledo takes the tooth to his dentist who completes the process. It is at the moment his party piece, and he challenges all comers to guess from what substance it is made.

Now, in the garden the sun is sinking below the rooftops and shadows are lengthening. The discreet chink of teacups emanate from Katarina's balcony where Mr Barnfield enjoys his well earned tête-à-tête with her, and the foils of Caspar and Bones click lightly together, to mingle with the sound of Smith's granite cubes as he rattles them around in his hand. Beside him, Toledo grins with pleasure at the scene, his hippo-tooth gleaming whitely in the last moments of the sun.

The Garden

Over the years the embassy garden has become resplendent in summer. Toledo, enamoured now of roses, orders special cuttings of rare varieties by post. He tends them lovingly, treating the blooms as if they are a bevy of young girls.

'Come and see this,' he will say, pointing to a newly flowering bush. Then, with a bow and sweep of his arm invite his guest to have a sniff, as if, his manner seems to suggest, he is introducing a young lady whom he finds particularly delightful. His herbs, which he cultivates for his homeopathic remedies line a path down one side of the garden, and he keeps the plants in line with secateurs, trimming them with long neat edges straight as a Prussian guard of honour.

Caspar on the other hand, has an approach to gardening of quite a different order, and adheres faithfully to the mystical laws of Feng Shui. His Japanese lily is strategically placed to deflect the lines emanating from an angle in a nearby wall of the house. A crystalline rock is placed close by to absorb the psychokinetic charge, while a thin line of small pebbles meander among the foliage of sundry clumps of bamboo placed, it would seem, purely at random, but in reality occupying minor nodal points in a network of invisible energy lines. On the periphery of his corner of the garden, where the laws become so subtle as to be beyond representation, loom the massed ranks of Toledo's Prussian herbs. Their menacing razor-edged presence seeming to mock and even threaten Caspar's subtle arrangement, obscure as it is to the point of inscrutability.

At some point Caspar has come to suspect that Toledo's immaculate ranks are doing more than just loom. For over the last few days he has noticed that his garden seems to have shrunk a little at the edges. He begins to spend more time tinkering in the soil with a trowel whilst keeping a watch on Toledo, who, kneeling down at the other end of the path is running his eye along his ranks of herbs, checking to see that no leaves are out of place. Still convinced that somehow he is mysteriously losing territory Caspar gives vent to his suspicions.

'He must be doing it at night,' he tells Smith, who is interested in this conflict of horticultural philosophies. 'He must be mad!'

Caspar seems to have really taken the issue to heart, but Smith, sympathetic to his point of view, whilst simultaneously admiring Toledo's Napoleonic will, takes no sides and watches with interest the strategies of the combatants. Strangely, nothing of all this passes between the two. They behave affably when in conversation, wishing each other a good morning without rancour, and no hint of any subterranean angst is evident upon the surface. A few days after Caspar's remarks Smith is sitting in the garden watching an ant, when Toledo approaches him in an agitated manner.

'What's wrong with him?' he says angrily.

'Who's that?' Smith asks.

'It's Caspar,' says Toledo. 'Each day he is taking small pieces from the edge of my herbs, and I have to keep replacing them.' His voice deepens and his black eyes flash with anger. 'He must be mad!'

They walk over to the corner where the battle is taking place, and indeed, it is immediately apparent that much skirmishing has recently occurred. The earth is freshly turned where the two ideologies meet, and a thin line of pebbles accompanied by a single stalk of bamboo have infiltrated into the outer ranks of Toledo's army. Toledo's nostrils quiver and he adopts a somewhat militant stance, his black pointed beard and moustache giving him the look of a conquistador. 'He means business,' thinks Smith, and imagines Toledo's armies marching forthwith straight over Caspar's Lotus-eating Japanese Lily, and giving no quarter in the process.

Before Toledo can make a move however, Caspar inexplicably retreats. Even taking a few of his bamboo clumps from the edge of his garden and moving them to the rear. Toledo, suspecting a trap, holds his hand, and the situation remains tense for a few days. But since nothing further occurs Smith surmises that either the two have reached an unspoken armistice, or, they have taken the conflict to a higher level of subtlety which, without a thorough and lengthy briefing lies beyond his comprehension.

Of the two theories he considers the latter more likely, and suspects Caspar of arranging his bamboo clumps into an alignment which will send a shaft of invisible negative energy in the direction of Toledo's marshalled ranks, thus thwarting his attempt to acquire lebensraum in the north.

Smith however, is only an observer in this battle. A non-combatant whose gardening inclinations are limited to a few orphan plants arranged in pots on the patio, he therefore does not feel threatened by either of his fascist neighbours.

Love's Ordeal

It is a Saturday evening and from the salon comes the sound of a harpsichord as it traces a delicate filigree path through a Scarlatti sonata. A concert is in progress and the performer has the audience in his thrall. He sits on a stool in an unconventional cross-legged position, and peers at the music through the thick lenses of a rather strange-looking pair of spectacles. He is Jake Naylor, an instrument-maker who lives in a nearby squat, and the spectacles are a pair which he has hand-carved from boxwood. They are a light honey in colour and of a smooth satin finish, an effect only achievable through the use of a razor-sharp knife and much rubbing with the fingers. Jake is a craftsman in the old manner; a style that leads to many difficulties in the modern off-the-peg world in which he finds himself and the spectacles are a case in point.

Having obtained a NHS prescription for the lenses he had noticed a clause permitting the customer to supply his own frames should he so wish, and finding a log of seasoned boxwood on Hampstead Heath had carefully whittled himself a magnificent pair of frames. Taking them along to an optician he had asked for them to be fitted with the prescribed lenses. The optician is dubious. Picking them up he casts upon them a cynical eye and asks Jake where he had got them.

'I made them myself,' says Jake.

The answer is enough to turn the optician right off; Jake is obviously a nutter and he wants nothing to do with him. Jake however, persists. He produces the prescription and points out the relative clause and the man is forced to concede the point. A week later he returns to collect his glasses and finds the optician in an irritable mood.

'I've broken one of the lenses on the grinding wheel,' he states. 'It's an awkward shape to work with so you will have to pay for a new blank lens.' Jake considers this for a moment then again brings out his prescription.

'It says here,' he begins. 'That the optician must supply the lenses for the customer's frames. If you break one it is your responsibility to replace it.'

The man does not answer. He is incapable of such rational behaviour. Red-faced and spluttering he erupts with an angry bellow.

'Out! Out! Get out of my shop!' Throwing Jake's frames onto the counter he shrieks. 'And take your bloody silly wooden glasses with you!'

Jake had eventually found a more sympathetic optician and now the spectacles adorn his face above a scraggy white beard as he brings the sonata to its close. It is time for an interval and the audience make their way to the kitchen to refresh themselves with tea. Jake stays where he is, uninterested in such conventional forms as intervals. He remains upon his stool sipping from a cup which Morgiana has brought him, whilst running his fingers along the keyboard and watching the action of the mechanism to check for minor malfunctions.

A keen observer might have noticed a distinct similarity between the colour of the harpsichord keys and Jake's spectacles, and indeed this similarity goes deeper then mere colour, since he had carved the keys from the same log of boxwood from which he had whittled the spectacle frames. It should not be assumed here that this curious matching had anything to do with style in the way for instance in which a man might choose a handkerchief to compliment his tie, or a lady her handbag to match her shoes. Jake's sense of style belongs to a different order altogether, as is evident by the army-surplus khaki shirt which he is wearing, and the woollen hat sitting atop his head which he has knitted himself.

Over the past year or so when Smith has visited Jake, he has invariably found him sitting in front of his fire, where, atop a huge heap of ashes a couple of logs are smouldering beneath a large black and steaming kettle. Jake will make tea from coarse dark Chinese leaf which he obtains from a warehouse in Bermondsey, a journey which takes him several hours on his pushbike. He scorns sugar or milk, and Smith, sipping the powerful brew knows better than to even mention such decadent substances.

The floor at these times is covered in long lines of the small parts which will, when assembled, form the mechanism of the emerging harpsichord. Each piece has been subjected to the immense patience and skill which he applies to his work. All accomplished with nothing but a very sharp knife, since he refuses to use any power tools, and even sandpaper he regards as beyond the pale.

Now, however, the harpsichord is working perfectly, and the pure iron strings with which the instrument is fitted respond with an authentic ring. Jake had taken an obsessive care over the final sound, produced not as in the piano with a hammering mechanism, but rather a plucking action accomplished with a strip of goose quill. However, the quill of an ordinary domestic goose does not have the required flexibility for this purpose, and it is necessary to look as far afield as a marshy area in a remote part of Turkey, where a rare species of goose provide quills of the required mixture of firmness and flexibility. Jake's problem therefore had been almost insurmountable; but not quite. For Jake is a man who will go to extremes in the quest for perfection and if a perfect ingredient is available only in Turkey, then to Turkey he will go. And does. Packing a small tent and sleeping bag he had boarded a coach overland to Istanbul, and from there by local buses made his way to the region in question. From a small village he had then set off on foot for the marshy area where the geese have their habitat.

Dawn is but an hour away and first light is illuminating a low sandstone cliff which stretches along the rocky foreshore of a marsh-edged lake. Dense bushes cluster at the foot of the cliff, almost obscuring a small tent which has been pitched amongst them. There is movement from within. A flap opens and the head of Jake Naylor emerges. He looks around and finding the coast clear pulls himself out and begins putting on his boots, whilst simultaneously munching upon a cold chapatti which he had cooked over a small fire the evening before.

These tasks accomplished he collapses the tent and folds it into a small bag concealed amongst the bushes, then makes his way down to the edge of the marsh. It is still quite dark and the ground is strewn with rocks and stones as he cautiously makes his way towards the reed beds. It is essential at this point to make no sound which may too soon disturb the geese.

Moving slowly forward until the firm ground gives way beneath his feet, and lifting one leg at a time he removes boots and socks, then, leaving them on a flat rock rolls his trousers to the knee. The soft mud squelches between his naked toes as he moves deeper into shallow water amongst the thickening rushes.

Still in total silence he squats on his haunches and begins his long wait. Around him there is an occasional muffled honk and squawk as the coming dawn begins to awaken the sleeping geese. After some twenty minutes or so he perceives a rosy glow beginning to flush the horizon and redden the surface of the lake. It is almost time, and he gathers his energy for the release that will come when the moment is ripe. This is the third morning in which he has performed this ritual, and since it will be the last he is determined to conduct it with all the power he can muster.

Now a bright spear of light is just breaking the skyline and the hour is come. Gathering all his strength Jake suddenly rises to his feet. Waving his arms wildly, his wooden glasses flashing in the sun he gives a great bellowing shout.

'*Haroooh!... Haraaagh!*'.

Long and loud his voice rolls out across the surface of the lake and echoes again and again from the cliffs behind him.

Amongst the reeds is desperate panic as the geese, rudely awakened, flounder madly around in terror. A great cackling and honking fills the air from all sides as in their haste to get airborne the birds crash and blunder into each other. And a great cascade of white feathers drift and swirl thick as a snowstorm around Jake and fall like manna to float upon the surface of the water.

Within ten seconds the geese are gone and, honking their outrage and indignation are a rapidly diminishing flock far out across the marsh. Jake spends some time picking and choosing amongst the plethora of feathers which float around him until he has collected a large bundle. Then tying them with string he returns to his bag amongst the bushes and packs them in with those previously obtained by the same method. He has sufficient for his purpose, and slinging the bag over his shoulder begins the long trek to the village where he can board a bus on the first leg of his journey home.

Now the audience in the salon take their places as Jake begins the second half of his recital. However, he has chosen a rather ambitious piece, of which the middle section is tricky with much complicated fingering, and Jake, having plunged heroically into a quagmire of notes begins to stumble, and is brought eventually to a halt.

The audience show signs of embarrassment, but Jake appears totally unconcerned. He peers closely at the page in silence while analysing the fingering and arrangement of tones. When he is satisfied, he tentatively begins first with one hand then with both to pick his way slowly and carefully through it. Again and again he works at the section until he is satisfied, upon which, returning to the beginning he plays the piece faultlessly through. Later, during the next piece, an even more complex composition, the same situation occurs, and once more the audience exhibit signs of acute embarrassment. This kind of thing is not done. A performer is expected to play without these fumblings and they are bewildered by his manner. He is behaving as if he is in his own room at home and seems entirely oblivious of their presence. Nonchalantly he works at the difficult sections until they are perfect and then continues.

What they don't realise is that Jake couldn't care less what they think, and were he to be tackled on the subject would no doubt tell them that if they don't like it they should go home. Smith, standing at the back of the room knows this well, and relishes this assault upon conventional thought with pleasure. Jake has now reached an easier section of the sonata and is swaying around on his stool, the white braces which hold up his trousers gleaming in the candlelight against his khaki shirt. He has cut the broad strips of the braces from coarse white canvas, to the end of which flat leather loops have been sewn in an inverted V shape, the ends slit to accommodate the buttons sewn onto the outside of his trousers.

The harpsichord sounds superb. Its iron strings sending their pure vibrations around the room, sped on their way by the finely cut quills so generously donated by the Turkish geese. But of these levels of rich circumstance which surround the instrument the audience is for the most part oblivious. Smith feels a movement beside him. It is Sukie. She has come timidly into the room and now stands close by as if seeking his protection. She gazes at Jake with a mixture of awe and trepidation. The awe on account of her admiration for his faultless eccentricity, which, somewhat of a bohemian herself she appreciates to the full. The trepidation resulting from the recent ordeal which she had experienced in his company.

Jake has been visiting the embassy for some while now, and since he has spent time in India studying the flute has been joining Wirril and Smith in their attempts to master this music. Coming in through the side door and thus passing Sukie's room, his frequent presence had begun to attract her attention. One day she grabs Smith's arm and pulls him into her room.

''Oo is ze little man?' she asks in an urgent whisper.

'Jake Naylor,'says Smith.

Now Sukie attempts to be casual in her manner.

'And what do 'e do?' she asks.

'He is an instrument maker and musician,' replies Smith.

She absorbs this in silence as she makes some coffee and Smith knows she is preparing her next words carefully.

''E seem wery nice,' she says in an offhand manner, 'I would like to meet wiz 'im.'

Smith can see that she is concocting some sort of romantic fantasy in her head and decides to be her accomplice in the affair.

'I'll bring him to your room next time he comes and you can talk with him.' he says.

Sukie is excited by this and cannot conceal her pleasure at the idea, and a few days later Smith suggests to Jake that he might like to meet a lady painter who lives on the ground floor. Jake is non-committal about this, his interest in women is negligible, being far too busy for such fripperies, and Smith knows that Sukie will have her work cut out trying to lure Jake into her amorous plans. He takes him to her room a few days later and performs the introduction. Sukie is fluttering nervously around as she makes them coffee, but Jake is unmoved and doesn't suspect that her nervousness has anything to do with him. After a while Smith makes some excuse and leaves, wondering if she will succeed in making an impression on Jake. Later she confides her hopes to him.

''E is wery nice,' she says. 'And 'e might take me wiz 'im on one of 'is journeys.'

Smith doubts this. Jake is a hard man who takes off alone into the countryside every few weeks, equipped only with a small tent and a bag of maize which he hand-grinds in a stone mortar, plus a frying pan in which to cook the chapattis which is the only food he takes. Somehow he cannot visualise comfort-loving Sukie surviving such an ascetic regime, but she has stars in her eyes and is determined to get her own way in the matter. When she proposes the idea to Jake he gives her a firm no.

'You will never keep up,' he says. 'And you will create problems for me.'

'Oh please,' begs Sukie. 'I will keep up and I promise to make no problem for you.' But Jake is adamant; he knows she is not up to it. However, Sukie perseveres and over the next couple of weeks she uses all her feminine charms — which are as it happens quite formidable — and eventually succeeds in wearing down Jake's resolve.

'But,' he warns her sternly, 'I will not wait for you, and you must bring nothing but a sleeping bag.'

Sukie is delighted.

'I am going wiz 'im,' she says, clapping her hands with pleasure, her eyes dancing with the dream of being alone with Jake and already wondering what dress to wear; she is convinced that in these circumstances romance is sure to blossom. Smith, however, knowing Jake's principles has certain reservations in the matter. But not wishing to spoil her dream says nothing more.

At middle distance a large hump-backed field has been freshly ploughed, and although it is late summer the sky is overcast with a fine drizzle which falls in sweeping veils turning the long furrows of rich loam into the consistency of chocolate mousse.

Along the skyline trudges a figure carrying upon its back a bag containing a tent, a sleeping-bag and a bottle of water. At its belt hangs a bag of maize and a small frying pan. It is Jake Naylor, his wooden glasses thrust aggressively forward as he maintains the steady pace which will carry him for many miles each day. Not stopping to eat or drink, and looking neither right nor left he plunges purposefully on. Some few hundred yards to his rear another traveller dogs his footsteps in a somewhat different manner. It slips and staggers in his wake and from time to time a thin wail emerges from its mouth.

'Jake. Jake.'

The voice is faint and does not carry far.

'I cannot go any furzer.'

It is Sukie, struggling to lift her sodden semi-high-heeled shoes across the furrows, each foot encased in a great wad of heavy clay which her slim stocking-clad legs can hardly move. She is soaked to the skin and in utter despair; a night spent shivering in a damp sleeping-bag had devastated her. One cold chapatti and a swig of water is all she has eaten and it is now late afternoon. She is possessed by a fierce hunger the like of which she has never before experienced, and the desolate landscape stretches endlessly before her holding out no hope of any comfort.

Jake is now almost out of sight and she is feeling utterly abandoned, when she notices a small country road running parallel with the edge of the field and begins to slither and squelch her way towards it. After an immense struggle she staggers from the edge of the morass onto the verge of the road, and whilst standing there whimpering quietly to herself and wondering what to do next she hears in the distance a faint humming.

The sound grows louder and she sees, bumbling around a bend in the road a little Morris Minor. The driver, a well-dressed matron, seeing this distraught lady standing by the road stops her car and winding down the window addresses her.

'Are you alright dear?' she says kindly. 'Do you need any help?'

'Oh,' wails Sukie. 'I am so 'ungry.'

She clasps her hands together as she says this and her voice is so piteous that the lady's heart is touched.

'Would some sandwiches help?' she asks. 'I'm just going to a church fair and am in charge of the tea-stall so I can easily spare some.'

'Oh yes please,' moans Sukie, her pleading eyes over-brimming with gratitude.

The lady reaches into the back of the car which is crammed with food and brings forth a large package of sandwiches wrapped in greaseproof paper. She offers them through the window and Sukie takes them her hands trembling in anticipation. However, the woman now seems a little distracted, her eyes flicker over Sukie's shoulder where she can see a wild-looking figure approaching across the field. It is Jake, angry at what he considers Sukie's betrayal of the principles to which she has agreed. Noticing that she is no longer following, he had retraced his steps and finding her in this compromising position is furious and stalks fiercely up to the road.

The lady is alarmed by the apparition and her eyes widen in growing apprehension but Sukie is unaware of any of this. With shaking hands she unwraps the package and takes out the topmost sandwich. Raising it to her mouth she is just about to sink her teeth into the fluffy white "Mother's Pride" slices filled with succulent sardine and tomato, when Jake's hand reaches over her shoulder and snatches it from her grasp. She makes an attempt to hang on to the package, but the angry Jake wrenches it from her hands and hurls the whole lot to the ground and with his heavy boots stomps them methodically into a brown mush.

The lady is terrified. Slamming the car into gear she puts her foot down and the little Morris lurches away up the road as fast as it is able, soon to disappear in a cloud of smoke. Jake furiously admonishes Sukie who stands there sobbing helplessly. He now gives her a long and stern lecture on the evils of white bread.

'You can have a chapatti this evening!' he shouts, then turns abruptly and stomps back off across the field with Sukie, having no alternative, following meekly behind.

A few days later Smith witnesses Sukie's return to the embassy. Her shoes are shapeless clods of mud, the stockings, torn by brambles hang in shreds around her scratched legs. Her hair, in which twigs and leaves are tangled falls in rat-tails about her face, and from her eyes long black streaks of mascara trace their tearful course down to her chin.

'How was it?' asks Smith.

'Oh, 'e is a monsteir,' she groans, ''E is a terrible monsteir.'

She staggers to her room and it is a few days before she recovers enough to show her face again. Now, standing beside Smith in the salon her feelings are mixed.

''E play wery nice,' she whispers. 'But, 'e is a monsteir.'

Jake is now reaching the end of his last sonata and with a final flourish of fragile tones brings it to a close. There is warm applause and a small group of enthusiastic music-lovers cluster around him as he sits on his stool enjoying the compliments with which they shower him. Suddenly on the edges of this crowd occurs a minor disturbance as a large-bosomed woman pushes her way imperiously and rudely to the front. Her cultured voice booms out silencing all others.

'Wonderful, wonderful,' she gushes. 'Thank you so much for a wonderful performance.' Jake is amused by this and a wicked gleam comes into his eye as she touches the unpolished case of the harpsichord. 'But,' she continues. 'It's rather an unorthodox looking instrument wouldn't you say? Where did you acquire it?'

'I made it myself,' replies Jake.

'What?' her eyes bulge. 'You made it yourself?'

She is at a loss for words. Jake leans back on his stool and hooking his thumbs into his canvas braces pulls them proudly outward as if demonstrating their flexibility.

'Yes,' he says. 'And I made my own braces too!'

The lady backs off spluttering. She has blundered unknowingly into a value system around which she cannot even begin to get her head.

Gloria. Oh! Gloria

Someone is ringing at the backdoor, and Brett—, who has seen a willowy form flit past the kitchen window goes with more than a passing interest to open it. A young and delectably attractive lady stands there. She looks at Brett across the top of a large cardboard box that she carries in front of her, and her blue eyes are the most startling he has ever seen. She smiles sunnily, and the gorgeous eyes blink in demure flashes beneath long lashes. Brett cannot say a word. He is captivated by this vision and it is not until she speaks that the silence is broken.

'I just want to leave this here for a couple of weeks while I go away,' she says.

'What is it?' asks Brett, finding his tongue at last.

'It's just a television set,' she says brightly. 'I've arranged with Smith to leave some stuff in the cellar. She begins to step over the threshold but is obstructed by Brett who holds his ground. In normal circumstances he would be only too pleased to spread his cloak before her dainty step, but the burden which she carries has set alarm bells ringing.

'You can't bring that in here,' he says, reluctant to thwart such a vision. But she gives him a dazzling smile. 'Oh that's alright,' she answers. 'It can stay in the box.'

Brett is not so sure. There are very few rules in the house, but there is one which has followed them from the Belsize Park squat and still draws a strict cultural line in the sand: No television.

'I'll be back in a moment,' says Brett, and ignoring her rising protests closes the door.

In the garden Smith is watching Caspar mow the lawn. Caspar reserves this function strictly for himself and no one would dare to even touch the mower, which he diligently oils and sharpens regularly. The result of his zealous attention is a velvet lawn bisected into immaculate stripes that run from edge to edge until reaching the razor-sharp boundaries of Toledo's fascist herbs.

'There's a girl at the door who says she has arranged to leave some stuff here.' Brett announces to the garden at large. Caspar is half-way along a swathe and dare not stop lest he leave a mark and destroy his elegant sheen.

'Oh, that's Gloria,' says Smith. 'Let her put it in the cellar.'

'But it's a television set,' says Brett.

'What?' Smith is on his feet at once.

'It's OK,' says Brett, 'I didn't let her in.'

Smith makes straight for the backdoor a "stand by to repel boarders" look on his face. Brett accompanies him, partly to provide back-up should it be necessary, and partly for another glimpse at the delectable Gloria. Caspar, halfway along one of his careful lines had given a start at the mention of Gloria's name. He has only seen her once or twice from a distance but has yet to speak with her. Now the allure of her maidenly charms breaks his concentration, and a distinct and wayward blip occurs in his impeccable line. He gives up, and abandoning the mower follows hard on the heels of Brett and Smith.

By the time they get to the door Gloria is showing signs of impatience. She taps her foot and a fleeting shadow of annoyance passes across her face.

'You said I could leave some stuff here,' she says, 'and he won't let me in.' Still holding the box before her she nods her head towards Brett. Caspar, meanwhile, is craning his head over Brett's shoulder, trying to catch Gloria's eye with his most chivalrous look.

'What's in the box?' asks Smith, thinking that Brett has maybe misheard her.

'It's my television set,' she replies. 'I just want to put it in your cellar for a couple of weeks.'

'Well I'm sorry but you can't,' says Smith, shrugging an apology for this unpalatable fact. 'Television isn't allowed in the house.'

'But it can stay in the box,' says Gloria indignantly, she cannot quite grasp what Smith is saying.

'It makes no difference,' says Smith. 'We have a rule: No television. So you can't even bring it through the door.'

Gloria stares at him in outraged disbelief, and Smith knows this will not end well. 'Look,' he says, 'it's a long story, and I'll explain it to you some time, but right now there's no way you can bring that in here.'

Gloria explodes, 'You bastard!' she screams. 'What kind of friend are you?' She cannot believe Smith's attitude and is now seething with fury.

Smith has helped Gloria many times in the past; for instance, by looking after her enormous bolt-cutters when she goes away. She suspects other tenants in the building of entering her flat when she is not there, and fits her door with a heavy hasp secured with a large case-hardened padlock. Into this lock she squeezes an entire tube of epoxy resin, and when this dries it is impregnable to anything but her enormous bolt-cutters which she collects from Smith on her return.

Such resourcefulness however, is seldom unaccompanied by other extremist qualities: and in Gloria's case, the ability to fight her corner without quarter is a talent not unknown to him. Her eyes flash and dance like a warrior-princess and her voice crackles with fury as she shrieks another war cry at him.

'You mean, rotten bastard!'

Smith accepts this philosophically. He had known almost word-for-word what would follow the rejection, but he has no choice. To allow the tv into the house may turn out to be the end of a very thin wedge. For instance, she might return later saying there is a programme that she simply cannot miss and wants to watch it in the cellar. Under such circumstances, would he have enough bottle to tell her she cannot switch it on? No. This is the time to confront the issue and Gloria is raging.

'You're a lot of filthy pigs!' she screams, and Brett looks a little upset at being included. He has fallen for Gloria's many charms and now sees he stands no chance with her. While Caspar, maligned before he has opened his mouth and cast in the role of a filthy pig is more than a little upset. Smith however, is merely grateful that owing to the large box which she carries Gloria cannot get within striking distance of him. Having delivered her verdict on the swinish trio she turns and flounces off, hurling pungent insults over her shoulder as she goes.

The issue of television had first arisen years before at the London Free School, which, back in 1966 had occupied a dank basement in the crumbling backstreets of Notting Hill. Here, a tv donated by a local shopkeeper sat on a high shelf displaying an unusual and even existential programme, for the screen has been removed and replaced with a cardboard sign.

P. B. Rivers and Smith are in the basement one evening when they hear footsteps coming heavily down the stairs. Presently the door opens and a man comes puffing in carrying a tv.

''Ere you are,' he says, lowering it with relief to the floor. 'Somebody told me you 'adn't got one and this is going spare.'

He stands up and waits for some sort of response. But none is immediately forthcoming and the two faculty members regard him in silence. Smith is attempting to formulate a polite response: 'Thank you very much, it's very kind of you,' seems appropriate. But the silence and lack of enthusiasm puts the man onto the defensive.

'It works,' he says indignantly. 'It's not rubbish.'

'Thank you very much,' says Smith at last. 'After all,' he thinks, 'we can always throw it out later.' But the man is not so easily mollified.

'I put myself to all this trouble because I thought you needed a tv,' he complains. 'And you don't seem very grateful.'

'Oh, we're grateful for the gesture,' say Smith carefully. 'But you see we don't actually need one.'

The man looks around him, puzzled.

'But you 'avn't got one,' he says.

'No,' says Smith, 'and although it's very kind of you to bring it. We'd rather do without.'

The man is baffled. 'But you've got to have a bit of entertainment,' he says, his voice rising in exasperation. He looks to P. B. Rivers for support, but P. B. Rivers has had enough. He runs a course in "twenty-four-hour existentialism" at the school and does not hold diplomatic views.

'Entertainment?' he says scathingly. 'Entertainment! You stand there, a gas-breathing creature on a planet in space, while out there infinite numbers of giant stars spin in a void of nothingness, any one of which were it as close as the sun would fry our arses right off, and you talk of entertainment.'

But the magnificent perspectives that P. B. Rivers has opened up are reduced in an instance by the man's implacable complacency.

'Well,' he growls. 'That's all very well, but if you think I'm going to carry that bloody thing back up those stairs you've got another think coming,' and he stomps back up the stairs leaving the tv where it lay. Smith waits a while before carrying it up to the street to look for a skip. But P. B. Rivers has a better idea.

'There's enough wallpaper in the world to blot out all the stars in the Universe,' he says, as he prises open the back of the tv with a large screwdriver. Then ripping out the tube he replaces the screen with a cardboard placard reading:

WE DON'T WATCH TELEVISION,
WE WATCH EACH OTHER!

Standing on a high shelf it dominates the room and has, since its installation, given rise to many sociologically weird spaces and much consternation to first-time visitors. They wilt a little under such an intense regard until, noticing the tv and its message, shed their paranoia and do a bit of watching themselves.

McCafferty doesn't approve of the sign at all. 'Is that the best you can do?' he sneers. P. B. Rivers draws himself up and mounts his high-horse. 'Well, what would you have it read,' he asks. 'Turn off the tv and have a punch-up?'

McCafferty scowls and slits his eyes menacingly. He doesn't like being found out.

It is Saturday evening a few days later when into the basement come Smith and Dick. Dick is an ex-military trombonist who had introduced himself earlier in the day up at Denbeigh Terrace, from where the school begins its processions.

'What are we playing?' he had asked.

'Don't worry about that,' says Smith. 'It's dead simple. All we're doing is playing with each other. But that doesn't mean we play together.'

'Well then, what are you playing?' asks Dick.

'I'm playing three notes,' answers Smith, 'E, F and B'.

Dick is puzzled, 'Why only three?' he asks.

'Because I've already done one. I did it last week,' says Smith. 'I've missed out two since it only gives one alternative, and one, under any conditions, is still one. But three gives access to three pairs of two and thus three alternatives.'

This approach to music seems entirely alien to Dick, who looks about to question further but is forestalled by Smith:

'What are you going to play?'

Dick looks belligerent. 'Well, I'm going to play a Sousa march.' He says this in an aggressive manner, as if challenging Smith's airy-fairy abstractions.

'Great,' says Smith, 'In that case you should lead from the front.'

And so the procession had begun. In the vanguard three young girls, garlands in their hair and coloured ribbons fluttering from their dresses, skip with naive and sylvan grace. They carry baskets of flowers, which they scatter before them amongst the crowds that throng both pavement and road. Behind them, and treading a now flower-strewn path comes Dick. Prancing along in an odd quasi-military jive, his trombone slide probes the sky above and dips to reach the ground below, as he blares out *The Thunderer*. Watching his performance Smith begins to see that there is more to Dick than meets the eye. For now he takes the leading role, as the usual avalanche of banjos, bongos, guitars and trumpets go swarming raucously along, hotly pursued by a rabble of small boys tootling enthusiastically on Indian flutes.

When the procession is over Smith invites Dick back to the school. He is promising material, and Smith intends to recruit him for his regular Saturday night gig at UFO, the psychedelic venue run by Skipio Hawkins in the Tottenham Court Road. Each week his group Suntrolly is composed of different members, accumulated at the whim of circumstance during the preceding week. But the gig is tonight and so far Dick is his only likely accomplice.

The Magus

Entering the cellar Dick and Smith walk into a seminar on twenty-four-hour existentialism being conducted by P. B. Rivers with whom this is a continuous process. Smith, taking no notice of the lecturer puts on the existential kettle for tea.

'And so you see,' P. B. Rivers is saying. 'Thinking is rather like knitting. The intellectual designs his woolly hat with complex patterns, whereas the common man knits his with mundane squares and stripes. Eventually, in either case, the hat gets too large and falls over the eyes to obscure the wearer's view entirely.'

His audience of one however, stands in a corner tapping his fingers rhythmically on a small table and taking no notice whatever. The man's eyes have a mesmeric cast, which now fixes upon Smith. He has obviously taken the tv's message to heart and is watching with hawk-like intensity. Smith, however, who had quickly learned that to watch someone watching oneself, is a dead-end, watches Dick. Dick has not seen the tv yet and begins to get hot under the collar when he comes under this sustained regard. Now P. B. Rivers breaks off his monologue and joins Smith in keeping an eye on Dick. Dick is getting very uncomfortable, his face goes red and his anger is beginning to show. He looks to be on the point of walking out, when P. B. Rivers lifts an arm and indicates the tv. Dick looks to where he points and his face changes visibly as he absorbs the message. He grins, and taking this new freedom with both hands turns and begins to watch the man in the corner, who still taps out his *booma-booma dinga-booma* upon the table top. Taking their cue from Dick they now all watch the man, who speaks for the first time.

'This is where it's at,' he says, his fingers continuing to send out their pulsing rhythm.

'This looks like promising material for Suntrolly tonight,' thinks Smith. But now P. B. Rivers attempts to swing the attention back to where *he* thinks it's at.

'What did you play in the procession?' he asks. He has serious misgivings about Smith's musical theories and usually manages to refute all his concoctions. Smith begins to explain his latest three-note theory, but P. B. River pours instant scorn on the idea.

'You can't even play one, let alone three,' he says. 'There's no such number, and you cannot define a thing by itself.'

Now he is getting into his stride and begins to gesticulate like some old-time ham actor as his poetry runs away with him.

'I can *say* one,' he begins. 'But that doesn't define what "one" is. You might agree that I can define it mathematically by: one times one is one, but that's like saying red is red *because* it's red. If you agree with this you are mistaken, since you would not have taken into account the fact that there are three "ones" in the proposition. And since "one" itself is not defined until the conclusion of the equation, where did the first, not to speak of the second, come from?'

'Well, I just put the horn in my mouth and blow,' says Smith, who cannot get his head around all this and couldn't care less whether "one" exists or not.

'Look,' goes on P. B. Rivers. 'The whole of mathematics is founded upon a profound existential misconception. Without "one", which as we have seen has no real existence, all the other numbers, two, three, four, five and six etc., are nothing but foibles of the human imagination and as theories go are seriously flawed.'

Noticing Smith's lack of interest he falls silent and directs his gaze upon the man in the corner, who, without a pause in his *booma-booma dinga-booma*, repeats in the tone of a Magus:

'This is where it's at,' and then, a considered afterthought: 'All the rest is funny hats and hoo-ha.'

Smith later recruits the man, whose name is Zen Glenn, to accompany Dick and himself that night at UFO.

'What will we play?' asks Dick. Again Smith can only speak for himself. 'Well I'm going to be a bird,' he says, 'probably a seagull.' The idea of rending that desolate squawk intrigues him no end and his saxophone will lend itself well to the task. Dick is beginning to relish this new approach to music and his naturally zany nature leaps at possibilities.

'I'll be an ostrich then,' he announces. 'It has to be a big bird because of the size of my trombone.'

'But ostriches don't sing,' says Smith. 'And anyway we don't both have to be birds.'

Dick thinks for a bit, and then... 'A lion,' he shouts with glee. The idea excites him, 'I'll be a lion roaring in the jungle,' he says. Now Smith knows he has struck gold and found two worthy companions for Suntrolly's Saturday night sojourn into the ridiculous, the outrageous, and the incomprehensible.

Putting their heads together they work out the finer details of the coming performance. 'Dick will go roaring through the jungle,' says Smith. 'Zen will let them know where it's at, and I'll soar around screeching and squawking. It will be a riot,' he says. Zen now leaves to pick up his drums while Dick goes off for something to eat, and they arrange to meet later in the Tottenham Court Road.

UFO

From the left a large magenta blob comes wobbling across the field of view. The upper part is swollen and barely able to contain its fullness, while below it trails nebulously away into a long trail of misty red particles. Soon, however, two bright orange discs, close together and following parallel trajectories speed into view and head directly across the path of the blob. A collision is unavoidable, and when the impact occurs the orange discs sink deeply into the blob and seem about to pass right through to continue their course beyond. But the greater mass of the blob slows their progress, bringing them to a halt barely half-way across. Captive to its greater momentum, they now yield all independent movement and join the blob in its stately progress to the right.

This however, is a minor incident in comparison to the larger threat that now challenges the blob. For behind it there appears a fast-moving wave of emerald green, the trailing wake of an even larger blob which, unable any longer to contain its huge mass spills over from above and engulfs the magenta blob in a great wave. For a few moments the entire field is green, and then: Blip! From deep within its emerald centre the magenta blob re-emerges, and: Blip! Blip! Its two orange eyes appear.

Light shows of this kind are the latest thing, and in every available corner enthusiasts set up their screens and drip their coloured blobs onto slides held in the beam of a projector. The medium is evolving fast as they vie with each other to produce different effects and like alchemists guard their techniques closely. The venue is dimly lit but for the splurging colours from the light shows; and the air is perfumed by clusters of incense sticks which project smouldering from every cranny, sending their smoke to drift in languorous clouds across the flashing projector beams.

The concourse is crowded with a carnival of revellers dressed in a motley of freaky costume. They come to trip, to dance and chew the psychedelic fat. It's Friday night at UFO! This is where it's *really* at.

Upon the podium a black-clad figure leaps, its bowler hat aflame with candles perched around the rim. An amplified voice thunders out across the concourse, and a demon drummer wildly flails his sticks. The figure whirls around and round the candles spinning a wheel of fire as if, shape-shifting, it has stepped from another and crazier world.

A silk top hat projects like a chimneypot above the sea of mop-headed hippies, bobbing around on the head of a lone dancer in full evening dress. Complete with silver-topped cane he dances a solitary jig, as if unaware of the rebel costumes of his compatriots. Foxy girls with heavy mascara slink in the candlelit shadows, where sugar cubes receive their globule of nectar from the tip of a glass dropper, to be sucked like lemon-drops by hopeful trippers intent on adding spice to the night.

Tralee, her usually wild hair combed and piled high for the event, has dressed in black and stands regal as a duchess talking with Harry Flame. Harry has made no concessions to the carnival air, but wears his usual tatty raincoat and grubby collarless shirt. He is above and beyond such irrelevancies and is here merely to sniff the psychic atmosphere, and perhaps distil a potent line of poetry from some small but significant incident.

Skipio Hawkins, impresario and host of these weekly revels flits here and there, his silver-lamé flowered jacket flashing as he goes about his thousand-and-one Saturday night scams.

The podium is hosting a succession of flamboyant groups, who each take the stage with their retinue of devout followers. For this is the breeding ground of future superstars, and from here they launch themselves like rockets high into the new musical firmament.

'What time are we on?' asks Dick.

'Around four o'clock,' says Smith. 'Only when the dancers are completely exhausted will they be in a fit state to hear what we have for them.'

'Right,' says Dick. 'And then we blast them with the jungle stuff.'

'Don't be too sure,' says Smith. 'That's only plan "B". Plan "A" is whatever happens when we get up there.'

Suntrolly waits and bides its time. The energy is still too high and the atmosphere taut with an expectation which they will not even attempt to fulfil. Suntrolly is something else altogether.

Much later, Smith goes looking for Zen and Dick. Their moment is fast approaching and the dancers are working themselves up into a final frenzy. The podium is now bathed in a ruddy glow from a bank of rosy-hued spotlights, while the latest avant-garde of psychedelic rock-groups reflect this colour and cavort, strutting like pink flamingos amidst a maelstrom of electronic guitars.

'Get ready,' says Smith, having found Dick and Zen. 'This is their last number and we're on next.'

The dancers, now utterly exhausted, are dropping like flies to the floor and seem, to Smith's eye, to be about ready for an earful of Suntrolly.

Suntrolly

Zen sets up a simple mid-tempo beat:

Booma-booma, dinga-booma
Booma-booma, dinga-booma

He closes his eyes and is off, drifting away into his own rhythmic self-hypnosis until oblivious to anything else at all.

Dick raises his trombone and lets forth a terrible roar; then, as if not satisfied with this he unleashes a torrent of roars and fearsome growls.

Smith is already squawking away in his highest register. Up here above the clouds he dips and soars, sending his harsh call out over the recumbent figures that litter the floor before them. Ten minutes of this and Dick, not one to hide his feelings looks fed up. He walks across the podium and speaks into Smith's ear.

'I'm going to put a bit of elephant in,' he says truculently, as if daring Smith to object.

'Brilliant,' says Smith, much heartened by his new friend's genius. Dick starts screeching in his upper harmonics before descending into a trumpeting bellow, which, were the space not confined, could have been heard as far afield as Farringdon or Charing Cross. Smith however, sticks to his seagull and flies now above a bleak foreshore where craggy rocks sit in white necklaces of broken sea, as his forlorn avian song comes echoing from the bell of his tenor-saxophone.

Eschaton

When Suntrolly has blown itself out Dick puts away his trombone and makes off. Smith is about to leave the podium himself, when he notices that Zen, eyes still shut, continues to beat out his...

Booma-booma, dinga-booma
Booma-booma, dinga-booma

Smith taps him on his shoulder and Zen, from deep within his bongo nirvana opens startled eyes.

'What's happening?' he asks.

'We've finished,' says Smith.

Moment Of Truth

Back at the Free School the faculty and those who have tagged along from UFO sit in a circle, while George O'Grass rolls an endless succession of thin ones. At gatherings such as this he is the master of ceremonies and newcomers are faced with an acute learning curve. 'Take one pull and pass it straight on,' is George's dictum, and he watches, ready to fall upon any unfortunate who lingers overly long in the process. When he passes the joint it must be taken immediately, a moment's hesitation and it goes to someone else.

Zen has brought a small drum with him and sits quietly tapping away, while Dick is getting more stoned by the second. He is also looking distinctly paranoid, casting suspicious looks about him from red-rimmed eyes and obviously the victim of some weird "stoned-out-of-his-skull" interpretation of the situation. His earlier "king-of-the-jungle" stance seems to have deserted him and he looks shrunken and withdrawn.

Suddenly, he sits up straight as if struck by some new insight, and then leaps to his feet and clenching his fists like a little boy he stamps his foot. 'I don't care what you think!' he shouts to the ring of faces. Now he cackles with laughter and begins jigging around the circle, flinging his arms around and shouting: 'I don't care what any of you think,' at the top of his voice, until brought to a sudden stop by George O'Grass.

'So what?' George's voice cuts through Dick's euphoria like a razor, bringing him to an abrupt halt and silence while he considers this new point of view. George rarely allows his clout to show but when he does it is devastating. However, before Dick can consolidate George gives him the other barrel.

'Now sit down and behave yourself,' he says, and Dick, chastened by such good sense sits down.

'Join the club,' says Smith.

Gloria Again

Gloria's attempt to breach these time-honoured tv canons although summarily rebuffed had not, it seemed, been as traumatic for her as might have been thought. For a few months later she rings the embassy asking for Smith. She seems to have forgotten her erstwhile low opinion of him and her voice is honey sweet.

'Will you help me with something?' she asks, putting Smith straight on his guard.

'What is it?' he asks suspiciously.

'Well you see my boyfriend got into a fight the other night in a pub over in Brixton,' she says, 'and I want you to come and swear in court that it was the other man who started it.'

Smith can't believe what he is hearing.

'What?' he says. 'But I wasn't there.'

'That doesn't matter,' she says. 'You can just swear that you were.'

'Sorry,' says Smith. 'You'd better ask someone else.'

'But I'll pay you sixty pounds,' says Gloria.

'Look, the answer's no,' says Smith firmly. 'Definitely, no way.'

'You bastard,' screams Gloria. 'You filthy rotten pig, what kind of a friend are you?'

Cut Off

The Westminster Magistrate's Court is an imposing building and the courtroom itself, oak-panelled and hung about with the impressive regalia of law and the judiciary has the kind of atmosphere to strike terror into the heart of any miscreant unfortunate enough to find themself at its mercy. The magistrate enters, and when all are seated the court usher announces the first of the day's culprits.

'Mr Richard Arnold, Guild of Transcultural Studies.' He announces in a solemn and stentorian voice.

There is a long silence, and Mr Arnold, in spite of the authoritarian tone of the usher, remains, of course, absent.

There is however, a perfectly good reason (apart from the fact that he does not exist) for this. Finding himself burdened with the responsibility of having the gas and electricity bills in his name, Smith had attempted to spread this burden a little by writing to the Electricity Board informing them that he was going abroad, and that the account should be transferred henceforth into the name of 'Mr Richard Arnold.' As long as the bills get paid no one should be any the wiser.

The letter had worked, and soon the bills had begun to arrive in the name of their illustrious, but entirely fictitious past president. Mr Arnold of course had not twitched a muscle of his stern face at these devious strategies compounded in his name, but had continued to glare out of his portrait in the front hall of the embassy with utter contempt for everything within his disapproving sight. All had proceeded smoothly until a quarterly meter reading had fallen due, and on the day in question Smith lets the meter reader in.

He shows the man down to the cellar where the meters occupy the wall at the end of a short passage. The only light at the foot of the stair is weak and cannot dispel the shadows at the far end. The man gets out his torch and passes it to Smith to direct while he copies down the numbers. When he has finished he reclaims the torch and shines it around.

'You should sweep away some of this,' he says, flashing the beam around the walls where ancient cobwebs hang thick as stranded seaweed. 'And look at this.' The light has settled beneath the two meters where the Company seals are threaded.

'They're rusted right through,' he says, pulling at the wires upon which the lead seals are clamped. Smith leans forward to look, and sees that rust has eaten right through the wire.

'That needs sorting,' says the man. 'I'll have to report this back at the office.'

'OK,' says Smith, 'and then I suppose they'll send someone to fix it?'

'I dunno,' says the man. 'I just read the bloody things.'

A few days later two men from the Board turn up with a large tool bag.

'Come to check your meters,' says the first of them, and Smith shows them below. He is not interested in this phase of the operation and retires above to the kitchen where he brews a cup of tea. Just about to take the first sip he hears from below a heavy banging and ripping sound. A moment later and the men's heavy boots are coming up the cellar stairs. Leaving his tea he goes to investigate and is just in time to see them leaving, each carrying a meter beneath his arm.

'When are you going to replace them?' he calls out.

'We won't be replacing them,' shouts the last man over his shoulder. 'You've been cut off!'

Telephone calls to the Board had been frustrating and answered by a girl who would give them no more information than that the Company regarded all broken seals with great suspicion and treated such cases as 'deliberate tampering.'

'But the meter reader saw that they were rusted through,' complains Smith. The girl knows nothing of this however and he makes a final appeal. 'But there are children in the house and winter is just starting.' The girl denies all responsibility. 'Well that's nothing to do with me,' she says. 'You must write to Head Office.'

Smith takes this advice and writes a letter in which he puts the whole case carefully, but when the answer comes the Board is ruthless: '... and further to this matter,' they write. 'You will be receiving a summons in due course for illegal tampering with our meters.'

The Lamplighters

The first week of the cut-off brings dark, cold evenings. The fireplaces and chimneys in the house all work but any loose wood around the place quickly disappears and the residents resort to smelly old paraffin fires for heating. Candles provide some light, but it is weak, and only Caspar with his solar panel is unaffected. By the second week, oil-lamps make an appearance, scavenged from junk-shops and markets, but the art of tending to wicks and glass chimneys has been long forgotten, and it is some time before they reacquire this basic skill. Eventually even the most inept among them learn to trim their wicks just so until the lamp produces the optimum brightness, without however, blackening the glass chimney. It is a very subtle balance and the lamps become the focus of intense interest, while they adjust them with all the finesse of a master violinist fine-tuning his instrument. Smith's flea-market lamp is old and battered, the teeth on the ratchet wheel that raises and lowers the wick are worn and do not engage properly, resulting in the wick being always just a little too low and thus giving insufficient light, or just a fraction too high and blackening the chimney. 'Jake Naylor is the man to see,' he thinks, for Jake has never been known to use electricity which he considers an abomination, and always lights his room with oil-lamps. His opinion on this aspect of modern society is scathing: 'They all go into their houses,' he says. 'They flick on a switch and... Lo! There is light. — Huh!' He sneers. 'They think they're Masters of the Universe.'

Smith packs his dodgy lamp into a bag and walks around to pay Jake a visit.

Cutting Edge

Jake takes one look at the lamp and hands it back. 'It's clapped out,' he says. 'There's only one optimum point on the wick and you'll never find it with this piece of junk. Chuck it out,' he advises, while handing Smith a cup of tea.

Jake's room is in a north London house, built in Edwardian times and originally designed to accommodate a standard family of that time and of a certain class: The Master, no doubt impressively bewhiskered, and his moll, the Mistress; always dressed to perfection and shrouded below in many layers of petticoats, while above, her bosom tightly corseted, and her chin constrained by the pretty ribbons which secured the demurely flowered bonnet.

The upper floors would have contained the main bedrooms, the nursery and the children, with perhaps a spare or two for guests. House and parlour maids occupying the higher reaches where narrow and meagrely carpeted stairs led up to their quarters in the attics above. But here below, the cook was sole mistress of her inviolate domain.

Those days of elegant propriety have, however, now long passed and 'Cook' would have thrown a fit and given her immediate notice could she have but seen the state of her kitchen now. For in the centre of the room is a great pile of woodchips, growing momently as Jake Naylor chisels curly strips of wood from a *saraswathi veena* which he is making. He sits cross-legged on the floor, his home-made canvas braces stretched across the army surplus shirt. His chisel bites firmly into the wood, and slowly but surely the instrument emerges from a log of cedar which he had discovered on Hampstead Heath after the great storm of 1987, when black thunderheads had gathered darkly as if for some fearsome black mass to hurl their windy temper across the heights and cut the ancient trees to the ground in swathes.

Smith sits on the floor near the fire, which Jake encourages occasionally with a handful of shavings, and the flames flicker upwards around a blackened kettle which hangs above. This is the kettle from which Jake had poured boiling water onto coarse Chinese leaf to make tea for his visitor. Smith tastes the tea and suppresses the shudder of revulsion which arises at the first sip of the malodorous brew, for the flavour is rank and the pungency too strong for his sensitive nature. This brings a predicament, for the tea is well nigh undrinkable, and he can see no way to get it down him. He could of course ask for milk or sugar to temper the sourness of the tea; but knowing Jake of old he is not tempted for a moment to even mention such foolish things. Jake would raise his head to deliver a look of such utter contempt for these twee considerations, that Smith would have had to leave at once and never darken the door again; a fate which Brett had once endured after questioning the musical status of Jake's home-made ocarinas. Therefore he takes minuscule sips from the tea whilst holding his breath to avoid the awful taste. It is a sacrifice he is willing to make since his visit is not without an ulterior motive.

Being near to the fire he now conceives of a plan to bring his ordeal to a close, or at least shorten it considerably, for close by him a pile of ashes is heaped in a neat cone. Jake keeps his fireplace meticulously tidy and although the fuel crackling in the hearth is of rough logs and twigs, he rakes the ashes diligently away from the flames into the pile which is now just a few inches from Smith's left knee, and he wonders if he can, without being seen by Jake, pour some, if not all of the tea onto the heap. He moves his cup surreptitiously into his left hand, keeping a close eye on Jake the while. Now, if he moves the cup so that it overhangs this heap, he may be able to pour it onto the ashes where it will be absorbed to leave very little trace.

However, Jake, although seemingly intent on his task has very sharp senses, and were he to look up and catch Smith pouring away the tea might be incensed beyond reason, *and he is sitting between Smith and the door!* He decides, all in all, not to attempt this highly risky act and shudders in horror at the mere thought that he might, in a foolhardy moment, have tried it. He turns his attention instead to the chisels which lay in a row by Jake's side.

'Can I have a look?' he asks, stretching his hand towards one of the tools.

Jake nods his assent and Smith picks up a chisel and looks closely at the working end. It is a mirror-like angle of brightness leading down to the finest of edges. He slits his eyes to bring the thin silver line into sharper focus. But the edge itself eludes him, as if it is so sharp that it extends into a further dimension far beyond the puny reach of his eyes. He imagines the invisible edge of Jake's chisel reaching down into a sub-molecular world to slip smoothly between the atoms of the wood, an action not dissimilar to a shark nosing its way through a shoal of jellyfish. Jakes chisel is cutting effortlessly through the hard cedar wood as if it were cheese, and Smith casts aside all these irrelevances; the tea and the chisels are but side-issues while he bides his time for the right moment to ask Jake if he has a spare lamp which he might borrow.

The moment comes closer as dusk falls, and soon it is too dark for Jake to continue with his work. He looks up. 'Do you want another cup of tea?' he asks, and Smith declines the offer politely. 'I've still got some left.' hc says, pretending to take a mouthful, and Jake gets up and takes the shade off his lamp. Smith, seizing the opportunity shows much interest in this, as Jake pours a little oil into a thin metal channel that runs in a ring just beneath an element of some sort.

'This is a wickless lamp,' says Jake, noticing Smith's interest. 'It emerged with the discovery of 'incandescence' and made lamps with wicks obsolete.'

He points to the element, a white dome-like object.

'That is the mantle,' hc says. 'It is made from woven silk saturated in a solution of lime. When it is fired the silk burns quickly away leaving a fragile net of calcified lime which becomes incandescent when a flame is applied.' He puts a match to the channel which ignites, and the flames reach upwards in a smoky trail.

'We have to wait until the metal parts heat up enough to vaporise the oil,' he says, and they watch in silence until a faint hissing becomes audible. 'The oil is heating up,' says Jake, as the ring of fire begins to leap up in regular puffs.

'Soon it will reach the element,' whispers Jake, pointing at the flame as it licks the lower edge of the mantle, which is now turning black with the sooty smoke. As they watch, the soot catches with a swarm of red sparks which eat their way speedily through the soot, leaving the whitened mantle to burn with a dazzling radiance too bright for the naked eye. The ring of oil, its task now accomplished, flickers out, but the mantle, fired now directly from the lamp's reservoir shines gloriously on, filling the room with hard-edged shadows, until Jake replaces the glass chimney and shade and returns with a satisfied air to his work. This looks like an opportune moment, and Smith is about to pose his question when he is foiled by a timid knock on the door.

'Hallo!' shouts Jake, and the door slowly opens to reveal Sukie who comes shyly into the room holding a plate.

The Third Croissant

Sukie: flower painter, and long-time resident at the embassy has fallen deeply in love with Jake. Hearing of a room going vacant in his squat, she had coerced Smith into smoothing her path with Jake to acquire the room, which is directly below Jake's. Packing her paints and easel she has taken up residence and now listens for his every move, dreaming of the time when he will recognise her devotion. She notes his departure each day and desperate to make contact, watches anxiously from her window, to catch him perhaps on the stairs as he comes back. Some days she weeps sadly and cannot paint.

'If 'e love me just a little,' she moans to herself, 'I will be so 'appy.'

Sometimes of an afternoon she will spend long hours at her window, watching the street for his return; lingering there until light fades and the street lamps go on and flicker among the restless leaves of the London plane trees. Here and there a passer-by might feel her ardent and steadfast glance, and looking up see her wan face, pale against the window pane and wonder at the air of melancholy in which the lonely woman seems enshrouded. But her eyes are empty of all but her desire for Jake, who she imagines might, as he returns, look up, and seeing her sad figure, ghost-like against the shadows of the room behind, smile, his face lighting up and his arm raised to give her a friendly wave. Oh! How she would fly down the stairs, heedless of all but the heartfelt need to be at last held close in her lover's arms.

But Jake is entirely oblivious of all this; he isn't the least bit interested and wonders why she pesters him so. Now the knock on the door and Sukie's entrance with a plate.

'I sink you will liking some of zis,' she whispers meekly, and kneeling down in front of Jake, lays the plate at his feet.

On the plate are some toasted croissants; they are dripping with butter and spread thickly with black cherry jam. The croissants are her speciality, and at the embassy she has long entertained her friends with this French delight. Now she assumes her gift will be received with pleasure. But Smith sees at once that Jake is mightily displeased. He bakes his own bread with wholemeal grains which he grinds in a primitive stone mortar, and this foreign muck gets right up his nose. To make matters worse, there are *three* croissants on the plate!

Sukie has obviously heard Smith arrive, and by providing a croissant for herself, has revealed her intentions to be included in a little threesome, with possibly a cosy chat thrown in, and perhaps a smile and the kind touch of Jake's hand upon her knee. But she has miscalculated badly, and the error is compounded by the third croissant. She may have got away with it had she brought only two, and then made a discreet exit... But *three*?

'She is really pushing it a bit there,' thinks Smith, and has a premonition that this will not end well.

He is right, for Jake's anger is coming to the boil as the implications of this unwanted intrusion sinks in. Rising to his feet he gives the plate a kick sending the croissants flying.

'Get them out of my room' he shouts. 'They're made with white flour!'

Sukie, terrified, now begins fielding the croissants and returning them to the plate, she cannot understand why her love is treating her so ruthlessly. When she has recovered them all and they lie in a jammy mess on the plate Jake pushes her roughly from the room. He slams the door behind her, but still her piteous voice can be heard outside.

'But 'zey 'ave good jam,' she wails.

Jake strides to the door and opens it.

'It's got sugar in,' he roars, and slams the door again.

Smith waits in silence until Jake's breathing has calmed down before posing his question. Finally: 'I wonder if you have a spare oil-lamp to loan me for a while?' he asks.

'Well I have two of those,' says Jake, pointing to his lamp, which is now giving off as much light as an electric bulb. 'I can't use more than one so you can borrow the other, but you must replace the chimney or shade if they get broken.'

Smith accepts this condition and leaving with the lamp, returns to the embassy, discarding the old one in a skip along the way.

Flag Of Convenience

The summons from the Electricity Board had taken several months to arrive and when it comes it is addressed to Mr Arnold himself. Smith shows it to Mr Priest, the local solicitor who has many times overseen their conflicts with the powers that be.

'There is nothing we can do at the moment,' he says. 'Meanwhile I will show this to Mr Brace and get some advice, but we cannot get legal aid so you will have to come up with some money this time.'

Fortunately there is a full-sized billiard table lying dismantled in the garage and this raises a few hundred pounds from a local dealer, enough to fund a day in court for Mr Brace and a consultation with the barrister in his chambers behind the ancient facades of High Holborn. Smith lays out the whole story and holds back nothing of his ploy with Mr Arnold. Mr Brace frowns.

'This complicates things,' he says. 'False signatures will arouse suspicions before the case even starts.'

'I considered it to be a kind of signature of convenience,' says Smith. Mr Brace gives a legal snort.

'Signature of convenience? There's no such thing.'

'But what about flags of convenience?' asks Smith. 'If a ship wants to get around regulations it can register in Panama. It then sails under the Panamanian flag known as a "flag of convenience", and as far as the law goes it is entirely legal. It's the same thing with Mr Arnold, a signature of convenience.'

Mr Brace shakes his head and looks dubious. 'It's a nice story,' he says. 'But it won't wash with the magistrate. Let me just see who we've got.' He takes down his court roster and runs a finger down the cases.

'Ah! Mr Ponting,' he says. 'Well he's a hard man but I suppose he does have a little humour.' He looks out of his window stroking his chin for a while, then... 'Mmm, well I suppose I could try it on as a last resort.'

Smith, encouraged by this now overplays his hand.

'We could bring the portrait of Mr Arnold to Court and you could show it to him to prove our sincerity,' he suggests.

'What?' Mr Brasce's face breaks into shards, and then, after many failed re-arrangements settles finally into an expression of shock overlaid with a look of deep suspicion. He thinks Smith is making fun of him.

'No, look,' says Smith hastily. 'I could bring it along so that when his name is called he would at least have some substance.' But he can see that although the suspicion has left the barrister's face the shock remains, and the suspicion has been replaced with a look which cannot be misinterpreted. He thinks Smith is a complete lunatic.

'Forget the picture,' he snaps. 'We shall just have to play it by ear. All I can really do is attempt to mitigate the outcome.'

Chinese Whispers

The courtroom is filled with a low level murmur of voices. The solicitors' clerks huddle to one side, sniggering together over something, while one or two barristers enjoy a somewhat more lofty and dignified form of chaff. The 'Guild' is out in force, occupying the front bench in the public gallery, high up and overlooking the central well of the Court. A young policeman stands close to Morgiana, sent no doubt to keep an eye on this raffish-looking group. Morgiana turns her head and flashes him a deliberately long and seductive look, and the young man blanches and turns bright red; she gives one or two languid flutters of her long eyelashes and a visible tremor shakes him; he can't take it and walks off a little.

'What was all that about?' asks Katarina, who sits beside her.

'He was breathing down my neck,' says Morgiana dismissively.

'What was that?' It is Tralee, who has seen this surreptitious interchange and Katarina turns to her and passes it on.

Noticing this minor ripple Ace, who sits next to Tralee wants to know what's happening.

'What's going on?' he asks, and Tralee fills him in.

No one wants to be left out of the circuit and so Morgiana's quip travels down the line until reaching Caspar, last but one at the other end of the bench. Smith, the last, hasn't noticed any of this, too worried at the moment to consider anything other than the fact that he may this time have stuck his neck out just a little too far. Caspar nudges him with his elbow and whispers into his ear:

'In this breeze there'll be a wreck.'

'Bloody Hell,' thinks Smith, then with heavy sarcasm: 'Well thank you very much,' he says, glaring angrily at Caspar. 'That's just what I needed.' He feels betrayed; the remark has increased his paranoia considerably and not for the first time in his life a sense of foreboding doom overcomes him; innocent or no, the whole thing could be easily misunderstood.

The Elusive Mr A

The court now rises as the magistrate enters and when all are seated an expectant silence falls, broken at last by the usher, who in solemn and ringing tones announces: 'Mr Richard Arnold, Guild of Transcultural Studies.'

Nothing happens and the silence is pregnant. The magistrate waits, he is the only person in the Court who is unaware that Mr Arnold is never going to grace him with his presence, for of course Mr Brace has spoken with his counterpart and told him of the circumstances, and they have agreed upon the best way to present it to the magistrate. However, this information had quickly filtered down to the other minor officers of the court, and hence the sniggering of the clerks. Even the usher is in on it and is aware that his announcement is purely rhetorical. He had thus delivered it with rather more gusto than usual, while thoroughly relishing every word.

Counsel for the prosecution has agreed to speak with the magistrate, but waits until the last moment, drawing this unusual drama out as long as he can until the magistrate begins to show the first signs of irritation. Then... 'Might we have a word, Sir?'

The magistrate looks up, nods and calls the two barristers over. The three heads draw close together and an unintelligible murmur rises from the conjunction. Presently they step back.

'Very well,' says the magistrate, 'I will hear the plaintiff's case, and we can deal with the other matter later.' But he looks up into the public gallery where the embassy contingent is putting on their most innocent expressions. Caspar and Ace are the most convincing, while the rest are rather overdoing it, and the magistrate slits his eyes and his look is venomous. He is going to throw the book at them, and it will probably hit Smith the hardest. The 'Guild' shrivels under his scathing glance and even Morgiana looks subdued.

Morgiana

Morgiana: Specialist repairer of exotic oriental carpets, whose room at the embassy displays small piles of exquisite hand-woven rugs and carpets from the arid lands of Afghanistan to the depths of the Mesopotamian deserts. Her walls are hung with the multi-coloured skeins of wool from which to choose the exact hue for each replacement knot to match the skill of the original weavers. Worn patches are replaced with new wool and when finished cannot be detected by the untrained eye. The repaired carpet then leaves her hand in the same pristine condition that it had left the loom.

Baluchies from the Turkoman tribes of Afghanistan and silk *kilims* from Arabia, their complex designs directed by the master-weavers from their book of carpet poems; each knot and its colour codified within the stanzas of a poem and chanted aloud by a grey-bearded elder; while the row of weavers listen diligently to the lines and wait for their cue for the colour and timing of the next knot. At the end of the verse when the row has been completed, the weft thread goes across, the heddle comes down to lock it in place, and the Master begins another stanza of the poem for the next row. The old man sings out the traditional designs from his book which has been handed down through many generations, while the desert winds billow out the walls of the nomadic tent, or scour the narrow streets of mountain villages as the work goes on.

While Morgiana learned her craft, her teacher had pointed out the necessity of imbibing this knowledge in order to have the degree of respect for the ancient art; she had spent much time practising her knots on inferior materials, and can now assess the quality and provenance of her customers' carpets at a glance.

Evidence for this had been given to Smith one afternoon when he had been returning to the embassy from the local shops. As he comes through the gate the front door opens and a man comes hastily out. Before the door slams shut behind him, he hears Morgiana's voice hurling some choice abuse after him. He cannot distinguish the words but the tone gives him the gist at once: the man is definitely not welcome. As Smith approaches the man is red-faced and angry.

'What's wrong with her?' he shouts.

'Why, what's up?' asks Smith.

'She must be bloody mad,' says the man. He is outraged and cannot contain himself: 'I telephoned and told her I was bringing a carpet for repair, and when I bring it round she tells me to fuck off!'

'Show me the carpet,' says Smith, already suspicious. The man holds out the carpet. 'It's just a small worn piece here,' he complains, pointing to the place. Smith takes a look and his suspicions are confirmed when he sees the gaudy pattern. He turns the carpet over and examines the back where the tight and regular knots give the game away immediately: It is machine woven. 'Probably made in Manchester or Birmingham,' he thinks.

He is about to give the man a lecture on the difference between this modern rubbish and the poetic source of the genuine article, when he notices that the man is dressed like a used-car salesman, and such efforts therefore are liable to be a waste of time.

He resorts instead to a subtler approach.

'You're lucky she didn't give you a good clump on the ear,' he says.

Meanwhile Back In Court

Now counsel for the prosecution calls his witness: a man from the Electricity Board who identifies himself as a servant of the company's legal department. The barrister asks him to lay his complaint, which he does, although not without including a description of the trouble the company has with recalcitrant squatters. At the mention of the word his lip curls disdainfully as if there is something dirty about it, which only present circumstances force him to utter. He looks at the magistrate as if seeking verification for this attitude, but the magistrate merely nods impartially.

'Tampering with our meters is common amongst such people,' the man says, 'and the company are bound to prosecute wherever it occurs.'

Mr Brace now takes over:

'My clients claim,' he begins. 'That the wires holding the seals were rusted through, and that your meter reader noticed this and reported their condition at your depot.'

The man knows nothing of this and draws himself up importantly. 'As far as the company is concerned the wires were broken.' he says. 'Our meter men visit anything up to fifteen or twenty addresses a day, and the last reading occurred several months ago.' He turns to his clerk who hands him a thick file which he then consults and is able to give the precise date.

Something in his manner interests the magistrate; he wants to see the file himself, and the man reluctantly hands it over. Pushing his glasses high on his nose the magistrate begins perusing the file while the court looks silently on. After a while he breaks the silence:

'Well as far as I can see the bills seem to have been paid regularly.' He continues to riffle through the file and stops suddenly with a frown on his face.

'This is most interesting,' he says. 'Here is a letter which I would like the court to hear,' and he begins reading aloud.

"Dear Sir," he begins. "I am afraid I have mislaid my last receipt from you, and am wondering if we have perhaps not yet paid the current bill. Please oblige and let me know how our account now stands." And the letter is signed J. Smith.'

He looks sharply up at the man from the Board. 'This hardly sounds like people who are stealing electricity,' he says.

Smith feels his heart leap at this unexpected twist. He had completely forgotten the letter, which had been written in his zealousness not to fall foul of the company, and now he sees that the magistrate is beginning to smell a rat. The magistrate looks down at the file in silence for a while, then comes to a decision. 'I want to see the evidence,' he says.

The man from the board is taken aback. 'But everything is in the file which you have,' he blusters. But the magistrate is after bigger game than this.

'This is just paperwork,' he says. 'I want to see the evidence — I want to see the meters!'

Now the man from the board is really floundering. 'But I don't have them,' he splutters.

'Well how long will it take to get them?' snaps the magistrate, and now the tide seems to have turned, since there is a certain aggressiveness in his tone. The man splutters some more: 'It means going back to the depot,' he says.

'Yes, yes,' says the magistrate irritably, 'But how long will it take? Better still can you get back here in an hour and a half?'

The man agrees to do his best. 'Very well,' says the magistrate. 'The court will now recess. Be back here by two-thirty.' He gets to his feet and the court rises.

Outside in the foyer Mr Brace gathers the 'Guild' together. 'I was afraid of this,' he says. 'Have you noticed who's sitting behind you? Look over there.' He points to a cluster of clerks who are now emerging from the courtroom, and there, a smug look on his face is Mr Tinsdale from Westminster Rating Department. 'They're bringing all their guns to bear,' he says, 'and it explains why the summons took so long. If Westminster Council is putting pressure on the Board to keep you cut off, they may, since you have children in the house, be able to close you down on health and safety grounds. Why else is Mr Tinsdale here?'

There is more here than meets the eye, but Mr Brace is highly pleased with Smith's letter. 'That letter was the best thing you ever did,' he says. 'It's aroused the magistrate's suspicions and I know him of old, he is like a terrier dog and won't let it go now.'

When the court reconvenes the magistrate fixes the man from the board with a stern eye. 'Well,' he demands. 'Have you brought the meters?'

'No, Sir.' The man is now drained of his former superciliousness and his manner is chastened.

'Why not?' the magistrate's voice is sharp.

'Because we don't keep old meters,' admits the man. 'They are sent back to the manufacturers for refurbishment and then re-used.'

There is a long pause as the ramifications of this sink in.

'I see,' says the magistrate grimly. 'And you have brought these people before my court accused of tampering with your meters and by implication stealing electricity, with absolutely no evidence whatsoever.'

The man from the board looks demolished.

'I am going to throw this case out now,' says the magistrate. 'And further, you will restore their electricity supply *at once!*'

'And Mr Brace,' he says turning to the barrister. 'You will tell Mr Smith that I want no more of this Richard Arnold nonsense.' Then... 'Case dismissed!'

The Fugitives

It is late spring and the flowers in the embassy garden are coming into bloom. Standing near the house, and growing through the flagstones of the patio is a cherry tree laden with blossom. In a perambulator beneath, a baby gurgles and swats at the petals which fall like pink snow from the branches above. Smith, seated on a bench nearby is drinking his first cup of tea of the day whilst reading a newspaper. The headlines from China are dramatic: Tiananmen Square is still on the front page, and tales of the ruthless treatment of dissidents dominate the news. From time to time he raises his head from the paper to cast a wondering eye at the pram where the baby, a boy called Moss, is enjoying the first part of his long introduction to life and the world.

Moss is the firstborn of Katarina and Smith is the boy's father. He had been a little nervous when she had first announced her condition, his idea of fatherhood fraught with images of domesticity: frilly pinafores, vacuum-cleaners, and meditation bedsocks. But Katarina has made few demands, and now, relaxing, he is beginning to quite enjoy the role.

Brett now emerges through the French-windows of the salon carrying his sitar, throws down a cushion and sitting cross-legged prepares to play. The garden is a cloistered sanctuary and the early sun is strong as he pulls his sitar close, straightens his back, and taking a deep breath begins his morning raga. As the first tones of the sitar waken the silence Smith catches from the corner of his eye a sudden movement behind him where the window of the garden-room overlooks the patio. The room, vacated recently by Sukie who has retired to a cottage in France, now has two fugitive tenants which accounts for Smith's sudden interest in the newspaper, and the recent events at Tiananmen Square.

He had received a telephone call from a member of the Chinese London Students' Association. The man had visited the embassy some time before during a performance of Chinese dancing and was familiar with the situation there. He explains that four activist Chinese students implicated in the Tiananmen affair, whilst being hunted by the police had avoided arrest by smuggling themselves aboard a plane to London. Discovered at Heathrow and speaking only Chinese, they had been detained by the police in a holding room to await deportation back to China on the next flight out. The room however, is only being used temporarily for this purpose and is no prison. They quickly discover that the toilet window gives onto a vast and poorly-lit field, which extends into the darkness to a distant perimeter fence and the lights of a highway beyond.

The four young Chinese, seizing once more their opportunity had slipped through the window and keeping to the shadows crossed the field without being seen. The perimeter fence had caused them no problems, and soon they are standing in the grass verges of a busy road and there, less than a hundred yards away stands a telephone box. They have but a single contact; the number of the Chinese Students' Association and one call had brought a car to pick them up and deliver them into the arms of friends.

The man now explains his problem. They can put two of the fugitives up amongst their members, but the other two need somewhere to hide for a few days until safe places can be found for them. Smith doesn't even think about it. 'Of course,' he says. 'Bring them round. We'd be honoured.'

'We will bring their food each day,' says the man. 'But they must not go out. If they are caught they will be deported straight back to China and then...' he leaves the unspeakable unsaid.

'Don't worry,' says Smith. 'We'll keep an eye out for them.'

The next evening after nightfall two shrouded figures had appeared at the side door. Accompanied by a couple of Chinese from the Students' Association they had flitted like shadows into the room prepared for their stay, and for the last two or three days nothing more had been seen of them. Dutifully, each evening a couple of young Chinese turn up at the side-door with steaming bamboo baskets of rice, sundry wooden pots, and bowls of oriental-smelling good home cooking. They say little, but bowing themselves in with conspiratorial smiles carry the food into the room and close the door behind them, and for the next half-hour or so the Chinese voices, rising and falling like exotic songbirds come muffled from within. When their friends leave, the room reverts once more to a tense and brooding silence, and neither hide nor hair is seen of the two young Chinese inside, who, fearful of their fate should they be discovered are keeping their heads well down.

Now however, Smith has a sudden glimpse from the corner of his eye of a Chinese face hastily withdrawn from the window. He turns fully around to take a better look, and again an anxious oriental face emerges from the shadows of the room and peers with fugitive eyes into the tranquillity of the garden. Smith ventures a smile but it is not returned. 'Well,' he thinks. 'They're on the run and the penalties are grim, they won't feel much like smiling.' Then, 'Sod this! I'm going to break protocol. They'll be safe if they keep to the patio.' He rises and entering the house knocks upon their door.

From within, he hears a sudden conspiracy of urgent Chinese whispers before the door carefully opens and the face from the window looks out. Smith begins to mime, pointing first to the man, then beckoning with both arms for him to leave the room, but the Chinaman is fearful and hesitates. 'Come, Come,' says Smith, his gestures becoming more eloquent as, walking backwards he invites them to follow. Now the second youth appears and there is a tense sing-song exchange before they both step timidly out. Keeping closely together they begin to follow the still-gesturing Smith into the garden, where they stand blinking in the sun and gazing cautiously around them.

They look at Moss, gurgling as he battles with the falling cherry-blossom, and at the figure of Brett, now deep into his raga, and some of the tension drains from their faces. Smith points to them again and making sweeping arm movements indicates that they should feel free to use the patio, and their faces break into pleased smiles as the meaning of this escapade becomes clear. He returns to his tea, and the two Chinese take a garden bench behind Brett and sit for a while looking happily around them.

Presently one of them gets up and goes back to the room to return a moment or two later with a long bamboo flute. He sits cross-legged a foot or so from Brett and waits quietly for a while head bent while he listens, then, raising the flute to his lips he begins with soft owl-like tones to infiltrate the brocaded inflections of the sitar. The flute, full of emptiness, floats through the spaces of the Indian raga at the whim of a Chinese muse and the music is rare.

Knick-Knackary

Italy has proved to be an Eldorado of the imagination for Leon Boch. He has for the past few years been running summer courses at a coastal resort for affluent acolytes of poetic mysticism who can afford the airfares and pricey registration fees. There is however, a nasty fly in this luxurious and creamy ointment. Leon has a well-appointed flat halfway up the hill to Hampstead; it is full of expensive knick-knacks and he is afraid of burglars.

Smith has occasionally visited Leon in his twee little den; it is an experience which he has not enjoyed, since the whole flat is strewn with what he regards as useless clutter. He has been invited on these occasions to sit on a silk chintz-covered sofa strewn with little cushions. But to reach this indulgently appointed item he must negotiate a delicate path between spindly-legged little tables — each graced with a real lace doily and crowned with a cut-glass bowl; or perhaps a small table lamp — its pretty shade edged with brocade and strung around with delicate silken bobbles. Leon serves fine vintage wines in fluted Venetian glasses, and he plays muted Mozart upon his state-of-the-art hi-fi, while his lady hovers butterfly like in the background. Smith loathes the whole set-up and usually avoids such visits, but had on one occasion spent a week alone in the flat.

Leon had prevailed upon him to caretake the flat and garden while he was enjoying his Italian seminar among his well-heeled poetry punters. The idea had appalled Smith, but the notion of a friend in difficulties had overcome his reservations.

'You can help yourself to anything from the fridge.' Leon had offered, and Smith had felt unable to refuse. But he had not enjoyed the experience and spent most of the time in the garden reading, avoiding entering the flat until dusk.

On the first evening, having watered the garden — a chore which went with his caretaking role — he enters the kitchen to check out the fridge. It is a large appliance standing on the floor with the capacity of a small wardrobe. He pulls open the door; the light goes on and he is presented with an Aladdin's cave of tv dinners. Shelf-after-shelf of chicken roasts; wild salmon steaks; oyster flan and baked saddle-of-lamb fill the space above, while frozen cheesecakes jostle with black forest gateaux and strawberry tarts to crowd the shelves below.

Smith is staggered by the opulent display, but bravely overcoming this trauma chooses for his first course a chicken roast with potatoes and green beans and for desert, a peach tart with brandy sauce. The oven soon renders these piping hot and he retires to the parlour where he speedily despatches the lot. The next day he tries the salmon with strawberry cake and sherry cream and so on. Nevertheless he is relieved when Leon returns and he can shake the stuffy atmosphere from his heels once and for all.

'Never again,' he thinks as he descends the hill to the embassy.

A year passes and once again Leon has organised a collection of well-heeled mystics for a seminar on the art of imagination, to be held in a romantic Italian villa which he has hired for the occasion. When Smith receives an invitation to call on him at his flat, it is only with the greatest reluctance that he agrees to come.

'I've got a great new Flamenco tape to play you.' says Leon. And Smith, allowing this tempting offer to lure him, ascends the hill one evening and rings Leon's doorbell.

'Come in, come in,' gushes Leon, beaming in such a benevolent manner that Smith is put on his guard at once. He is shown into the living-room, and there threads his way precariously around the indulgent obstacles that block his path, trying not to knock over any of the occasional tables with which the room is booby-trapped.

'To call them "occasional" is a major underestimation,' he thinks, as he sits and regards the spindly forest of twee monstrosities which surround him. Leon puts the tape into his hi-fi. The Flamenco is good and Smith is glad he has overcome his reservations. 'Maybe I'm just a bigot,' he thinks, as he sips the wine and sinks back among the cushions. 'This is not so bad. But still, I'll go as soon as the tape is finished.'

Leon however, has other plans, and leaning forward to replenish Smith's glass he says. 'You know, I'm going to Italy in a few days, and I wondered if you would stay here again while I'm away?'

'Sorry,' says Smith at once, clutching at straws. 'But I'm a bit busy at the moment with my pigeon.'

The pigeon in question is called Kissinger, he has lost most of the claws on one foot and Smith has glued a little plywood sole onto the stump. It works well, and the bird is beginning to walk around with barely a limp. The new foot serves Kissinger well, but at night proves to be a minor irritant for Smith, who, lying in the darkness cannot sleep if the bird is restless. Clop-clop-clop goes Kissinger's wooden foot against the floorboards as he meanders up and down the room.

He explains all this to Leon who frowns at the mention of the bird. Kissinger has the habit of flying up onto a chandelier in Smith's room from where, perched among the light bulbs he carpet-bombs unwary visitors who unwittingly stand directly beneath. Leon had been the victim of such an attack while visiting Smith, and no doubt remembers the expensive sweater that Kissinger had christened in this way. He thinks for a moment and then...

'He can stay in the garden shed,' he says. 'And it will only be for one week.'

Smith searches around for another excuse but Leon piles on the pathos. 'I don't dare leave the place empty,' he complains. 'I might come back and find the place stripped.'

'And a bloody good thing too,' thinks Smith, but Leon looks so stricken by the possibility that he begins to warm to him and eventually caves in. 'Okay,' he says, 'But only for one week.'

Leon beams with pleasure and again applies the bottle to Smith's glass in generous measure.

'Can you come at midday on Wednesday?' he asks: 'And please don't be late as I'll have my plane to catch.'

Smith nods, resigned now to this duty to a friend. 'I'll be here with Kissinger,' he says, and stands up to leave.

'I've made a little list of important items,' says Leon, passing Smith two sheets of paper neatly clipped together.

Smith sits down again while he peruses the list. The first page deals mostly with the garden. It seems that his casual hosing of the year before had not been up to Leon's standards. The roses, for instance, "must be done every two days in the late evening, except for the ramblers — every three days with a little plant food in the *CAN — Use the hose only on the lawn*", it admonishes, while the flower borders and pot plants each have their separate instructions. Smith is feeling the first pangs of regret for his capitulation. 'He'll have me mucking out the stables next,' he thinks.

The list of does and don'ts now moves into the flat.

"*Open the windows for one hour every day and make sure the alarm is on if you go out.*

Don't put your feet up on the couch (you made a hole in the coverlet last year)."

The list goes through several more of these petit-bourgeois strictures and Smith is feeling a rising tide of resentment gathering within, but he manages to keep the lid tightly on until reaching the final clause on the list.

"*Replace anything you take from the fridge.*"

Smith's lid flies off. Like a spark in a barrel of gunpowder this final insult transforms the resentment into full-blown anger. Full of furious indignation he rises to his feet and begins tearing the list into small pieces.

'You can get someone else to guard your bloody knick-knacks,' he splutters. Scattering the pieces in the air he makes for the door and Leon is aghast.

'It's too late to get anyone else,' he moans But Smith has the bit between his teeth; his considerate tip-toeing now flung to the winds his inconsiderate foot brushes against a dainty little table as he passes. The table, although prettily set upon slim legs by a craftsman is also somewhat knock-kneed, which adds a certain fragility to its equilibrium. It teeters for a moment on one foot and then topples sideways. A glass flower-bowl crashes to the floor and a lace doily goes sailing. Leon jumps up as if to protect his clutter from this barbarism but Smith is already out of the door.

'That's it,' he mutters, as he storms down the hill to the embassy.

'That's definitely it!'

This experience gives rise to many thoughts on this episode, which emerge a little later as a sonnet.

Ballad Of The Bourgeois

Don't blow your nose on the curtains
No spitting on the stair
Stop fiddling with the doilies
And feet down off that chair
Make sure you put the seat up
Do not forget the chain
Then get a proper haircut
And come straight home again.
Keep an eye on what you say
No 'Bloody Hell' or such
And take your shoes off at the door
My floors they must not touch.
Look down now! Check that all is well
If they're undone you'll hear me yell...(repeat)

Symposium

'Moon,' says Smith, pointing through a window into the night sky.

'Min,' says Moss. It is his first word.

Excited by this notable event Smith immediately begins to exploit the newly born talent.

'Wimbledon,' he says and, 'Wim-be-din,' answers Moss.

A seed has been planted and the next day, supplied with cream buns and a flask of tea they board a tube for Wimbledon. Smith usually avoids this rushing, clanking, claustrophobic wormhole-world whenever possible, but in the cause of higher education he willingly makes this minor concession. The train emerges from tunnels to desolate industrial wastelands and passionless suburbs, where the rows of terraced houses stratify the landscape in waves of sediment like a pink coral girdle around the outskirts of the city.

Wimbledon is the end of the line and they detrain and wander along the platform to a vacant bench. They have no intention of leaving the station, but once the cream buns have disappeared and the flask is empty, Smith reopens the dialogue of the evening before and there perchance to align the abstract with the real.

'W-I-M-B-L-E-D-O-N,' says Smith, indicating with a finger the sign above the back of the seat, whilst enunciating each letter in turn. Then, standing up, he stamps his foot on the platform and pointing dramatically to the ground.

'This Wimbledon!' he says.

Moss gazes around him in delight.

'Wim-be-din.' he says happily.

Nuts In May 1

There are many avid theorists of one sort or another amongst the Guild's expanding circle of friends, and the idea for a series of lectures has been born and taken root. A forum for far-flung ideas presented in a credible manner and given serious consideration by an invited audience. The series is presented under the title of *Nuts in May*, and each year between April and June, those who have something to say are given the floor. Subjects as diverse as the significance and effect of the barber's shop on Western culture by a visiting French schoolmaster; to a description of his experiences as the disciple of a Tibetan master in the high Himalayas by Leon Boch, a local therapist. The lectures take place each year, and gathering momentum becomes in time a minor festival unto itself.

Leon Boch, as a disciple, had worked hard to convince his master that he was serious, and humbly carried out the chores which he was given to do, but the old man rarely spoke and taught him nothing. Becoming restless after a year or so of cleaning the toilets and peeling potatoes he had voiced his complaints and was told that he must now perform the 'Ten Thousand Prostrations', a ritual undertaken lying face downwards upon the ground, whilst pulling the body forwards for ten full paces using only the forearms. Rising, the acolyte walks backward ten steps and repeats the process ten thousand times.

'It took me weeks,' says Leon. 'And by the time I had finished my sleeves were in tatters and my arms were bleeding from wrist to elbow.'

Leon had not, it seemed, profited from the ordeal, for when he had drawn the Master's attention to the state of his arms the old man had roared. 'What, you're still complaining? You didn't do it properly, go and do them again!'

Now safely home he lives in Hampstead, giving therapeutic advice to the troubled in mind, and believing that imagination is the only escape from madness writes poetry to prove this so. His forays into sanity express themselves at times in unusual ways. He had been heard for instance barking like a dog whilst in the toilet. Wirril and Smith, noticing this behaviour with admiration, even try it themselves with most satisfactory results. The lectures follow one after another as each year when May comes around, a harvest of "nuts" are gathered.

Two Men And A Boat

Jay Marcel has volunteered to open this year's series with an investigation into the true authorship of Shakespeare. This is a subject which has long interested him, and he conjures forth the various contenders for the roll of wielder of that masterful pen, while a whiff of Elizabethan intrigue and the suspicion of courtly plots bring an atmosphere of mystery to the salon. He dreams of opening an "Alternative Shakespeare" bookshop in the heart of enemy territory at Stratford-upon-Avon, a town which jealously guards its myth of the "glovemaker", and will not take kindly to his shopful of heresy. Having presented his case he now turns to another matter entirely.

'The crop circles for instance are another mystery worth looking at and the geometry is fascinating.' He goes on for another hour or so with the help of a blackboard to delve into the arcane mysteries of sacred geometry; the inexplicability of crop circles, and the marriage of pentagons. Jay's ideas on mundane marriage had long ago distilled into a somewhat pithy view.

'They're all living with their mothers,' he had remarked to Smith some years before, whilst they are rowing a boat from the island of Lusty Beg in Lough Erne to the distant shore where they have arranged to pick up a couple of passengers. Smith says nothing to this, somewhat preoccupied with the foot-rest which, being a good deal shorter than Jay he cannot quite reach for purchase. The rest of Jay's words are lost to him, torn by a stiff breeze from his mouth and whisked in an instant far out across the choppy surface of the lough.

They are in Ireland at the time to attend a flying saucer conference which is being held on the island, and many old friends have been drawn to the event and camp in the woods on the shore of the lough. Ram O'Neil, released for some time from his sojourn amongst the low life of Soho is now bent on trekking north to Scotland, where he hopes to find an abandoned croft on which to settle with his wife and daughter. He imagines a community of truth-seekers living far from the sound of traffic and the polluting philosophy of the cities.

'We're going to pack our essentials into haversacks,' he had said, whilst unfolding his plan around a camp-fire the evening before. 'Then we'll take a train to the Highlands and start walking.'

His wife Melissa is earnest in her support for the pioneering quest and speaks of her hopes for the new life. 'We can change the whole world,' she says, 'and create a new society in which lies and greed have no place.' It is the mid-Sixties and such ideas have yet to be laced with the cynicism of later generations. But it is a young hippie girl of no more than sixteen who has the last word. Gazing into the fire, her eyes dreamy with possible futures.

'Wow!' she breathes. 'Just imagine, if truth became fashionable, and honesty the latest thing.'

Wade Davenport and his lady, the passengers waiting for the boat, stand on a small jetty and are soon aboard for the return journey. With an oar each and sitting side by side, Jay and Smith pull hard for night is falling fast and ominous storm clouds are massing in towering formations across the lough, bringing a menacing darkness and almost obliterating the distant island for which they head. Halfway across and subject to the volatile nature of the open water, the darkening sky is rent by a sudden lightning flash which zigzags downwards in a brilliant fractal of elemental power, and the now threatening waves rise more steeply as the offshore wind blusters with quickening strength.

Jay pulls strongly; his tall body leaning into his oar with ease, but Smith, shorter by a foot or more is sweating like a one-legged man in an arse-kicking contest.

Fearful Symmetry

The next lecture in this year's series is a comparison of the structures within the sub-molecular configurations of DNA and the cell-like arrangements in the geometric patterns of Islam. The lecture is entitled "Fearful Symmetry", and is given by Bones in league with Wade Davenport, and "Nuts in May", once begun, evolves into a cavalcade of propositions outrageous to the world at large. But amongst the aficionados of the Guild they are considered high art, and those who stick their necks out in the cause receive the accolades of champions. Derek and Christine have bravely contributed to the series by seating themselves in two armchairs on the podium and from there reminisce aloud about their life together.

The evening's event has been entitled, "Fields of Association," and sitting side by side they recount the ups and downs of their long married life. Christine is too naive to recognise the surreal nature of the situation, but Derek knows it well and plays his part with much humour, until Christine is overcome with emotion and breaks down whilst recounting her memories of the death of their dog, a pet for many years.

'He understood every word I said to him,' she says, with a sob in her voice, and bursts suddenly into tears. Derek extends a consoling arm around his wife and gives her a pat; but she rallies bravely, dabbing at her eyes with a small handkerchief.

'I don't know what came over me,' she says.

The Celestial Couch

Caspar and his colleague Nostro combine their talents in a talk, "Summer Brings Changes," an evening's exploration of the use of computing in the construction of star maps, and by way of contrast, the *I Ching* seen as a novel.

'It is all according to a cylindrical sequence of the hexagrams devised in the Han dynasty,' says Caspar, as he holds forth in front of a large Chinese star map, the constellations strangely grouped by an alien mythology.

'From the "Celestial Couch", down here, to the pole.'

His hand sweeps upwards across the map as he explains his point, and like a university don goes on to speak of the oriental myths which formed the constellations of the ancient Chinese astronomers, their ceilings painted to represent the night sky. Each star placed with unerring precision and painted with infinite care, so that the occupants may lay abed, and gazing above imagine themselves alone amongst the unimaginable reaches of deep space.

Swansong

The last lecture in the series has been given by Seamus McFinn who feels the pull of the ancient stones in his bones. He has been living at the embassy for some time, and ensconced in the room from which Banana Head had been wont to stare he writes poetry and ponders upon the mysteries of the megalithic landscape. He has but recently returned from an expedition among the islands in the far north of Scotland where the remains of long-forgotten civilisations can still be seen, and following the trail of an old legend has discovered the magic spot whence, owing to a devastatingly precise freak of nature, the moon can be seen to rise twice. Having witnessed the phenomenon for himself he is elated by the experience, and his poetic descriptions of that mystic and twice-moon-visited landscape have entranced his audience.

Bella De Lorn brings a graceful end to the evening with a succession of wind-blown postures linked by the merest gossamer thread of interwoven steps. She dances to a poem which is read aloud and translates each word into sculptured adrenaline.

The audience are breaking up and tea is being served in the kitchen where in a corner sits Strimmer, actor and star of Ram O'Neil's play. Now turned gardener, he has overseen the transformation of a large piece of wasteland behind the half-life housing where he lives into a magnificent garden, where fairy-like grottoes hide amongst exotic plants and bushes and paths meander beneath trees and ponds to create a leafy world which has become famous for miles around. Now, his rake and secateurs put aside, he sits in a corner and plays a Bach Sonata on his concertina, and its piping voice rises like a lark above the clatter of tea cups.

In the salon, people stand around talking in small groups or lounge on the couches waiting for some transcultural action. But Bloomfeld, who has followed the lectures with great enthusiasm cannot be tempted to go anywhere near the piano, and his place is taken there by Dylan Jones who sits Strauss-like in his antique spectacles, while rendering some fine barrelhouse piano; the music sets the tone and a party is in the air.

Near the door stands Nostro, friend and colleague of Caspar and a man with a natural affinity for electronics. Together they map the heavens and classify the stars by magnitude. Feeding this data into computers they devise programmes to correlate colour with scale of magnitudes and have produced many star maps of fine quality. Tonight however, Nostro has brought along his latest toy. It is a machine which registers proximity, and emits a spectrum of musical tones dependant upon the density and closeness of an approaching object. He stands near the machine watching pensively as the interacting movements of the people in the room are translated into a cacophony of weird hoots, whistles and groans, which mingle strangely with the barrelhouse piano.

Dylan launches now into a piece made famous by the old Mississippi Delta blues singer, Deaf Willy Wilkinson, and his croaking voice adds a subtle pungency to the words

'Woke up dis mornin
gotta start the day somehow.

Woke up dis mornin
Thinking' bout who, how, what, when and why?

Don't know if I'm comin or goin
got dem Ludwig Wittgenstein Blues.'

And little Moss, taking advantage of a brief lull in these proceedings shows his musical talent by mounting the podium with his recorder and delivering a verse or two of *Pop goes the Weasel.*

However, this festive air has a slight overcast and a sense that the powers of officialdom are gathering their strength for an all-out assault cannot be banished. Westminster Council have given notice of a watertight case, and intend to prosecute once more for the unpaid rates, which have over the years accumulated alarmingly. While their solicitor has received intelligence that the Foreign Office legal department have been in conference with the Council's lawyers.

Further portents of disaster emerge when a girl from one of the yoga groups which use the salon most evenings of the week had drawn Smith aside during a tea break in the kitchen.

'Do you see those two men?' She asks, pointing covertly across the room. He looks and sees two ordinary looking and casually dressed men.

'They work for Westminster rating department,' says the girl. 'I work in the typing-pool and recognised them immediately.'

The embassy has been infiltrated; and even though they take money only for services, and proceeds generated from the concerts go directly into the pockets of the performers, they cannot prove any of this and evidence of money changing hands could, in the possession of the Council's lawyers, be transformed into proof of commercial use and deployed as a legal clincher. A damage limitation exercise is in order and the groups are told that the salon is no longer available, while the concerts, for so long now a much enjoyed part of their routine are terminated. Tonight's finale to this year's "Nuts in May", in view of these gathering clouds, may prove to be their swansong.

The Blitheness Of Ants

It is a mellow autumn evening and the rays of the setting sun stream across the mock-Tudor facade of the annexe, flooding the lawn with golden light and favouring with a light-fingered touch the patio, where Smith sits watching an ant. He is fascinated by the degree of ingenuity displayed by the insect as it negotiates the various (to Smith) minuscule obstacles which strew its path and its ability to do this at high speed. The ant now holds his full attention and he is leaning slightly forward the better to see, when from an opened window in Chief Mopo's house comes a soul-searing wail. It fills the tranquil air around with loud and terrible moans, and rising and falling like the groan of a wounded Kraken rends in an instant the serene atmosphere of the garden and turns his blood to ice.

It is a vacuum-cleaner: scourge of Adam and triumphant song of Eve, as she daily scours her fitted carpets in homage to 'Domestos' — god of hearth and bane of domestically challenged man. Smith, dismayed by this assault is torn between a desire to retreat from the din and his curiosity in the progress of the ant, which in spite of the fearful noise blithely continues upon its way. He has noticed that a leaf, fallen from the vine above, will be a major impediment if its present course is continued. The ant however, rapidly increasing the distance between itself and Smith's eye, soon becomes nothing but a tiny speck which he has great trouble following.

Meanwhile, the vacuum cleaner has now come closer to a window and its wretched voice, bellowing in lusty disregard for all, emerges as would a wild beast's from a cave. For Smith, who is wondering if the ant will attempt to scale the steep sides of the leaf and traverse the wide expanse of the interior, or skirt the outer edges and give it a miss, the choice is obvious. He goes for the ant and does his best to ignore the nauseous interruption. But now it is too late. The ant has shrunk to an invisible mite, and having nothing else with which to combat the awful noise he is about to flee, when the Frankenstein voice is cut off. Strangled in mid-scream, the dragon is vanquished by finger's touch of a simple 'on-off' switch, and he sinks back onto the garden bench with relief.

'The lot of common man,' he thinks. 'A sound from which few escape,' and he wonders if even Prime Ministers must face this torture and concocts a scenario.

'The Prime Minister lolls in the back seat of his Bentley and allows his body to relax into the sumptuous leather. He slips a hand into the front of his silk-lined suit and then, changing his mind withdraws it, deciding not to have a cigar just yet while his stomach was so full of caviar. He sighs with pleasure, everything is going his way and now he can really play. Glancing from the window as the chauffeur tools the mighty Bentley through rolling countryside, he notes with satisfaction the neatly rowed houses which cluster the outskirts of small country towns. Here and there a glitter where industry strives, aluminium and glass in a light factory frame.

'And where are all the little men who live in the houses?' he muses to himself. The question is rhetorical.

'They're all in the factories,' he thinks. 'And where are the wives? They're all in the little houses busily at work with their vacuum-cleaners.' And he wonders at the din that must ensue, those fearful wails echoing like a chorus of lost and hungry souls down the quiet suburban streets. A further sigh of pleasure escapes him; he likes the image and decides to write a poem on the subject later in the evening...

By now the ant is quite out of sight and the garden is once more silent. Smith is on the point of leaving when he notices the delicately balanced leaf give a small flutter, then another, yet the air in the garden is still. Again the leaf moves, its farther edge rising high as if some small weight disturbs its equilibrium.

'It's the ant,' he thinks. 'It went straight over.'

Now the leaf slowly sinks back to its former position, while after an interval the nearside begins to rise. Higher and higher it ascends until in an instant the weight is removed, the leaf falls back, and Smith knows now for sure that it *was* the ant.

Symbiosis

The park bench is constructed of thick wooden slats supported by wrought-iron legs fashioned into curlicues, which sweep up from the ground and form armrests at either end. It had no doubt long ago provided a resting place for elegant gentlemen with top hats and side whiskers, accompanied by prim ladies in bonnets and silk gowns, who sat upon it on summer Sunday afternoons taking a genteel piss out of other promenaders. The bench stands by the side of a narrow asphalt path which wanders between shaved lawns and manicured flower beds on the north side of Regent's Park.

Two figures approach from the interior and seem to find the bench of more than passing interest. It is a man and a small boy, who slow their steps as they draw near, while the boy points to the bench and laughs. To a casual observer it is unremarkable and looks like all the other benches in the park, but the man, coming to a halt also seems to find it particularly amusing. A middle-aged couple give the bench a quick glance as they pass, then look at the man and boy as if they are mad. But Moss and Smith, impervious to these forms of stuffiness continue to regard the bench with amusement.

'Joe Storyteller must be gone home,' says Moss, having by now mastered a little more of the lingo. 'We just missed him.'

Smith looks towards the park gates.

'Perhaps if we hurry we can catch him up,' he says. But Moss will have none of it.

'No,' he says firmly. 'He was walking too fast.'

Smith accepts this fact with equanimity and they continue strolling at a leisurely pace. Joe Storyteller is a fictitious character whose daily life is controlled by the two, and the bench is his favourite spot.

The story so far...

Every afternoon Joe Storyteller goes for a walk in the park. He has a dog called Alice. She is a scruffy middle-sized mongrel with a shaggy coat. Alice has a friend called George. He is a beetle and spends most of his time hidden in the fur upon her back. George is good company for Alice, since she doesn't get on too well with Joe who thinks she is retarded.

Joe doesn't know about George, who loves Alice and doesn't know what he would do without her. He always goes with Alice to the park, hidden deep in her fur with just his head poking out to see what's going on.

Alice can pee when and where she likes. In the gutter, on the pavement, or, (while in the park), on the grass or in the bare patches around the bases of large trees. Alice has no problems peeing.

George on the other hand is not so fortunate and when taken short needs Alice's help. On such occasions she will run under the nearest bush where George climbs down to relieve himself, while Alice returns to Joe Storyteller's side and waits a little until she is sure that George is finished (George likes his privacy).

One day Joe is sitting on his favourite bench and Alice is dozing on the ground before him, when George creeps up the fur of Alice's neck and whispers into her ear.

'I need a pee.' he says, and Alice quickly jumps up and runs for the bushes behind the bench. Once there George climbs carefully down and stands in the middle of a leaf.

'I won't be long,' he calls, as Alice returns to the bench.

Joe looks down at her in puzzlement. He has been watching her more closely of late and noting her increasingly weird behaviour. Only a minute ago she had been snoozing at his feet when, for no apparent reason, up go her ears and she scrambles to her feet and makes off into the bushes, only to return with a purposeful air a moment or two later. He doesn't know what has got into her lately but has given up trying to understand.

'It must be some form of dog psychosis,' he thinks, as he watches her return from the bushes.

Joe now looks up and notices a bank of dark rain clouds filling the sky from the east, and having no umbrella decides he will just have time to get home before it reaches him. Standing abruptly to his feet and giving Alice a whistle, he makes off for the park gates as quickly as he can. Alice trots after him trying to keep up and wondering what has got into him all of a sudden. She begins to think of her blanket which waits at home and Joe is anticipating a pot of tea and some toast. When they arrive Alice makes straight for her corner where lies the cosy blanket, and circling her spot a few times is about to drop with a final sigh when she remembers George.

George?...

GEORGE!

She starts up with a feeling of anguish. She had forgotten him; left him under a bush in the park and now he will be alone. She rushes to the window. Outside it is already getting dark and a fine drizzle is falling. She begins to whine and fret at the door.

Joe Storyteller watches her in a bemused fashion and tries to calm her down.

'We've already been out today,' he says. 'If you want a pee go into the back garden.' But Alice is freaking out, she barks and pulls frantically at Joe's trouser legs beside herself with grief and remorse. She has betrayed her dearest friend, and now...?

It is a sad story, and Moss and Smith leaving the bench turn their steps in the direction of the embassy. They walk along in silence, somewhat downcast by this minor tragedy in the ongoing myth of Joe Storyteller, whilst wringing it of as much melodrama as possible. After a while Moss, introducing a note of optimism, speaks.

'Maybe George will meet some friendly beetles under the bush and perhaps even find a girlfriend.'

Smith doubts this, and suspects that poor George will have a hard time of it. Living with Joe and Alice will have accustomed him to comfort and the warmth of central heating. The night for George will be dark and cold.

'The other beetles might think he is a foreigner and give him a hard time,' he says. 'His accent will sound strange to the park beetles.' Moss considers this in silence and they continue walking sadly along. Then, thinking to lift the mood a little Smith proposes a positive outcome.

'Never mind,' he says brightly. 'Alice will remember the bush where she left George, and when they go to the park tomorrow she can go and rescue him.'

He smiles happily and opening his arms wide says. 'Think how pleased they will be when she finds him. George can climb up onto Alice's back once more and they will all live happily ever after.'

Moss ponders this for some time in a sober manner, then:

'But maybe Joe Storyteller fall down and break his leg and can't go to the park. Or Alice will forget which bush George is under and they never ever see each other again.'

Smith views this grim outcome gloomily, but is finally forced to concede that this may well be so.

A Strip Of Light

At the end of a long and dark corridor which transverses the high attic floor at the embassy, a strip of light shows beneath a closed door. As Smith's head, rising slowly as he climbs the stairs from below reaches the uppermost step, his eyes are brought level with the top floor, and there at the far end of the corridor is the strip of light.

'Caspar is working late tonight,' he thinks, and knows that behind that door Caspar will be bent diligently over his charts, the points on his dividers reaching across from star to star and gauging in micro-measurements the macro-dimensions of deep stellar space.

'I am a star clerk,' he had once been heard to say, and Smith had at once imagined him dressed in his official fur-trimmed Star Clerk's gown, whilst attending the Astronomer Royal at some great court. Caspar has been drawn into the mystic contemplation of deep space and the mighty suns which ply its furthermost reaches. His only escape from the powerful gravity of these studies is his sideways explorations and analysis of ancient stone formations on obscure Greek islands.

Caspar is an erudite man and can, at the drop of a hat, produce an edifying lecture on his subject, and given the opportunity practises this art on Smith whenever he visits his room. An evening or two before Smith had called upon him and had received a most interesting discourse.

'Interstellar space,' Caspar had begun, 'is an awesome subject for the human mind to even begin to contemplate. For instance: due to the inconceivably vast distances between stars the familiar constellations as seen from the Earth look very little different from anywhere else within our own Solar System, and therefore the conventional star maps now available would do the job when travelling between the planets.'

Caspar's words had cracked open Smith's vague and limited sense of stellar scale. He had not realised that he had so much space inside his head. Caspar, encouraged by the look of incomprehension on Smith's face had launched further into the significance of his project.

'The solar system is a nursery,' he had said with an air of dismissal. 'A playpen in which we will be able to move safely around without getting lost.

Orion will always be Orion, standing like a sentinel and forever pointing the way home, with the Sun a beacon at the centre of all. However, when ships attain the necessary propulsion devices to move between the stars themselves all such geocentric maps will become useless.

'My charts are projected for a distant future when the Solar System has been surmounted and star ships venture out into the limitlessness of deep space.'

The subject had intrigued Smith and now, viewing Caspar's strip of light from the top of the attic stairs he decides to pay him a visit, and perhaps glean a little more information on the topic.

Caspar, perched high on a stool, is poring over his star maps which litter the top of his work table. He has only one light, a low-wattage car bulb wired to a battery which is charged up daily by a solar panel fixed to the outside sill of his window. Caspar, in spite of his philosophising at Cambridge is an out-and-out maverick.

The chart over which he is bent, a dark blue ground upon which the stars are arranged and colour-coded, can by means of this code be read at a glance. Smith, however, in spite of this scientific front suspects deeper levels to the maps, as if Caspar is studying for his Master's certificate aboard some future star ship. Looking over his shoulder; he knows the general theory of Caspar's colour code, but now by way of small talk homes in on some detail.

'What colour represents the brightest magnitude?' he asks.

'My charts are not like that,' replies Caspar. 'Unlike geocentric star maps that use magnitude or brightness as a distinguishing feature, which after all is only a relative value that changes according to viewpoint, these charts are concerned with the spectral type which is a constant value and not subject to distance or apparent magnitude.'

Smith is getting out of his depth but blunders on regardless, since he senses that he is getting closer to the esoteric centre of Caspar's stellar secrets.

'Then what is your colour system based on?' he asks.

Caspar begins walking up and down, hands behind back and pontificating like a university don as he goes.

'Violet,' he says, drawing the word out with relish. 'Blue, green, white, yellow, orange, and red,' he intones. 'These colours are not arbitrary, but correlate to the actual subtle colour of the spectral type.'

As Caspar is speaking, Smith is perusing the map while attempting to make some sense of it, and he is reminded of a similar state of mental affliction encountered when attempting to understand the network of lines drawn in Johnny Banana Head's *AtoZ.*

Caspar goes on: 'The small reddish symbols are red and orange dwarfs, not visible to the naked eye. But colour only defines the spectro-type. The next important value is distance. Again, a natural scale is appropriate and size becomes the distinguishing factor, the greater the object, the larger the symbol and vice-versa.'

'But I still don't know what you mean by 'actual subtle colour,' says Smith.

Caspar walks over to his side door which opens onto a balcony outside.

'Come out here,' he says, 'and I'll show you what I mean.'

Outside the night is dark and the nearby street lighting is discreet. Above, the gulf of space hangs its yawning abyss over their heads, while beneath their feet the planet rolls through its long orbit about a central sun.

'Do you see there?' asks Caspar, pointing out among the myriad specks of light, and Smith sights along his finger in what he hopes is the right direction.

'That group of bright stars is Orion,' says Caspar. 'Now look at his right shoulder. Can you see the reddish one?'

Smith cannot see any red stars, and even with the best of intentions they all look the same to him.

'Keep looking,' says Caspar. 'After a while, as the eyes adjust you will see the colours.'

Smith stares until his eyes begin to water and is on the point of giving up when he sees it. Among the twinkling white sparks, one has a distinctly pinkish tinge, and as he continues to look its ruddiness increases.

'I see it,' he says. 'It's definitely red.'

'That's the red supergiant *Alpha Orinors*, spectral class M21A, otherwise known as Betelgeuse, says Caspar. 'Your eyesight can't be that bad since it's 490 light-years away. 'And over there,' he continues, sweeping his arm across the sky, 'is a green.'

Smith follows his finger and within moments is able to distinguish a bright star with a pronounced greenish hue.

'That's Vega,' says Caspar, 'a spectral 'A' type. The eyes have to be trained to see the colours.' He goes on: 'Fortunately it's easy; all you have to do is keep looking.'

'But why isn't this commonly known?' asks Smith, who feels that for him the night sky will never be the same again.

A look of irritation passes across Caspar's face. 'Most people hardly ever look,' he says dismissively. 'They seem to regard the night sky as if it is some kind of dotty wallpaper.'

Back in the room they stand looking down at the charts.

'These are the first genuine space-travel maps,' says Caspar, and taking up his dividers he places one point on a star. 'Light,' he says, 'travels at over 186,000 miles per *second*. He looks quizzically at Smith as he says this, and struggling to get his head around this unthinkable speed Smith nods his head and tries to look intelligent.

'And yet,' Caspar goes on. 'Even at that incomprehensible speed, light from this star takes four years to reach us. 'Its name is *Proxima Centuri*, and it might further surprise you to hear that it is the *nearest* of all the stars.'

Caspar looks satisfied, he has blown Smith's mind with his spectro-colours and knows it, but now he turns to his window and gazes up into the far-flung starfields; he looks wistful and seems now to have all but forgotten his visitor. His lips begin to move and coming closer Smith catches only the faintest of whispers.

'One day,' murmurs Caspar.

'Maybe one day...'

It has been supposed that electricity might be the means of conveying intelligence, but, ingenious as the experiments are, they are not likely ever to become practically useful.

Encyclopaedia Britannica (1824)

My lord, I have too much love for my poor people who obtain their bread by the employment of knitting to give my money to forward an invention that will tend to their ruin by depriving them of employment and thus make them beggars.

Queen Elizabeth I

Toleration is not the opposite of intoleration, but the counterfeit of it. Both are despotisms. The one assumes the right of withholding liberty of conscience, and the other of granting it.

Tom Paine

A hermit called Hsu Yu was invited by the Emperor Yao to take over the government. The suggestion was so distasteful that Hsu went down to the river and washed out his ears.

Old Chinese tale

Ghosts are the discarnate parts of those who die inebriated.
Finding themselves able to pass through walls and shut doors, they fail to realise that they are dead; they just think they're pissed.

John Dyas

Part Two

Lone Ranger

A deep gravelly hum is coming from the salon of the embassy, where three teachers from an order of Tibetan monks are dispensing their ancient wisdom to groups of Western devotees. It is a controlled growl, rising and falling like the grumbling of dissatisfied granite boulders. The chief monk, who speaks excellent English, is staying in the house during the period of this seminar, together with a young Tibetan acolyte who waits upon him. Brett has disappeared off to India again in quest of the perfect sitar. 'The one I've got is OK,' he says, 'but the tone's not quite right.' He has been searching for years to find the perfect instrument and takes off for India whenever he becomes dissatisfied with his own. The two monks are occupying his old room at the top of the house in close proximity to Smith, who often passes them on the stairs.

One day he is making his way along the corridor to his room when he sees the chief monk sitting on a bench in an alcove. As he passes he briefly meets the old man's eye. Patting the seat the monk invites him to sit beside him. Smith sits down wondering what the old man wants with him but says nothing, sensing he will not be interested in the usual chit-chat. They sit for a while in silence, until the monk leans forward and places his ear close to Smith's chest. He remains for some time in this position as if listening to something. Smith imagines that on some enigmatic psychic level the old man is giving him the once over. After a while the monk sits up and speaks:

'Are you alone?' he asks.

The question goes off like a fire-cracker in Smith's head, giving birth to a succession of secondary queries.

'Does he mean: do I have a girlfriend?' he wonders. He dismisses this immediately, the old man's gravitas points to more profound considerations than this. He imagines a world in which there are no lovers in particular, no blood relatives or familiars known as 'friends', and realises that only under these circumstances could anyone claim to be 'alone'.

He stares into the abyss, assailed by metaphysical vertigo, until a chuckle from the old man breaks his fall.

'Your answers are useless,' says the Tibetan. 'It is the question that is important.'

Smith absorbs this and likes the sound of it. But the old man hasn't finished.

'Here in the West you lost all your real questions long ago, as we Tibetans lost our function when the monks became lazy.'

Now a bell rings in Smith's head, and he remembers Toledo's account of his journeys in Tibet before the coming of the Chinese.

'It was disgusting,' he had told Smith. 'The monasteries were living off the fat of the land, while the peasantry were barely surviving in abject poverty. The monks creamed off the best of everything and exacted a punishing tithe on the rest of the population.' Toledo had narrowed his eyes at the recollection before repeating: 'It was disgusting.'

Now Smith catches a glimpse of a larger picture. It swims in and out of focus until the old man speaks again.

'We have the Chinese to thank for ending our procrastination and scattering us to the winds,' he says, and Smith's mindset is suffering a major reorganisation.

'Now,' continues the old man, 'we have established monasteries throughout the West and have resumed our work in the world, which means we have to ask many awkward questions,' and Smith, having been the recipient of one such, still has nothing to say. The old man stands up to leave and feeling something still unresolved Smith takes a chance.

'Are *you* alone?' he asks.

The old man bursts into laughter. 'Thank you, thank you,' he says, beaming with pleasure, and placing his palms together he gives a little bow and departs grinning to his room.

Later, Smith comes upon Sukie in the kitchen, where she stands by the stove waiting for a kettle to boil. He is still mulling over his recent encounter with the monk, and decides to give her a taste of the old man's technique. Taking no notice of her attempt to greet him, he bends forward to place his ear against her chest. She jumps back nervously. 'What are you doing?' she demands, looking at him suspiciously, and he realises that she has misinterpreted his motive. He must act fast or be forever dishonoured in her eyes.

'No, no,' he says, 'look, are you alone?'

Sukie looks around the empty kitchen and then back to Smith. Now she seems a little frightened, and gives a quick glance at the door as if thinking of escape.

'No,' says Smith again. 'What I mean is, are you, Sukie, alone?'

Now she looks at him seriously and he waits for her response. When it comes he is thrown into confusion for her eyes are filling with tears; they overflow and roll down her cheeks, then...

'Oh yes,' she wails, 'I am alone, I 'ave nobody.' She begins wringing her hands together, 'I am alone and it is 'orrible.'

Now she is really sobbing and Smith knows he can never explain. 'Never mind,' he says, patting her on the shoulder by way of comfort. 'You've got lots of good friends.'

Sukie has her hands over her face and her voice is muffled.

'It's not the same,' she weeps.

Sweet Dreams

From an upstairs garret window high among the eves and chimneypots on the embassy roof, Smith is looking out across the neighbouring gardens. A dash of bright red meets his eye from an overgrown yard several houses down. The garden is extremely unkempt, but a thick flourish of poppies sway in the wind and wave in rippling folds above a wasteland of rank weeds. The house itself is a small consulate representing some far-off state somewhere on the borders of Afghanistan and its occupants are rarely seen. Smith wonders if the Afghans are up to something with the poppies and is well aware that it is their favourite flower. He thinks perhaps he might go along and warn them that they should be a little more discreet, but on reflection decides not to meddle. These reflections however, once begun, continue, biting deeper as they go until the scarlet poppies fade as he recollects his own long-ago encounter with the intoxicating flower...

Lamplight spills through the branches of leafy plane trees which line an avenue on the outer rim of Kew Gardens. The night is warm and three figures which flit amongst the shadows are but lightly clad. Two men wear psychedelic shirts and their hair hangs to the shoulder, whilst the third, a foxy girl in a silk caftan, walks slightly ahead counting her steps as she goes. It is the late summer of 1966 and these adventurers are on a mission of liberation. Earlier in the day they had visited the gardens to trip amongst the flora, discovering a small museum of vegetable substances in the process. And there, housed within a glass case, a large block of the finest opium sat within its own pungent aura of unrequited potency.

They gaze at it in awe, aware of the mystical dreams which lay locked within its sticky mass.

'What's the point in letting us look at it?' says one of the three young hippies who crowd around the case, their noses pressed to the glass like children at the window of a cake shop.

'They've no right,' he continues, 'to tease people in this way.'

'They're just showing off how much they've got,' says the foxy girl, 'it's a form of hoarding and they deserve to lose it.'

They are past-masters of this language game and regard logic as an art form, to be elegantly arranged in graceful folds around the object of their whim.

'We could get the case open easily enough,' says the third of the trio, as he peers closely at the light wooden frame. There is a simple lock on the lid and not an alarm wire in sight.

'Watch it,' says the foxy girl. 'The attendant has his eye on us.'

The attendant, noticing their unusual degree of interest in the opium, and having a personal dislike of men with woman's hair and poncey shirts, has heaved himself up from his chair near the door and began to pace slowly towards them. They see him coming a mile off, and filter away between the cases to disappear amongst the other visitors.

At the rear of the room there is a window which overlooks a dense shrubbery. It is an ordinary old-fashioned sash window with a simple catch as they find out when one of them runs his hand along the middle of the frame. He gives the catch a pull, and offering no resistance it slides easily to the "off" position. Providing there are no evening security checks, the road to Xanadu now lies open. From the wall outside the museum the foxy girl paces to the exit, counting her steps as she does so, and once outside they lay their plans for a little nocturnal raiding.

That night, and well past the witching hour, they recount the steps from the entrance, until they reach a section of the wall directly opposite the museum. Overhead, great oaks and beeches reach low, and it is simple work to swing up from a branch to the top of the wall and drop quietly into the gardens below. The museum lies in dense shadow amongst thick shrubbery and the sash window at the rear slides noiselessly open. One or two blinks of a pencil torch bring them to their objective and a screwdriver is brought to bear upon the lock. With a sharp snap it gives and the lid swings open. They listen in the darkness for signs of alarm but all is still, and lifting the opium from its plinth they slip it into the foxy girl's bag.

'Next time they get some opium they won't be so ostentatious about it,' she says.

Close friends are soon aware of this good fortune and visitors begin arriving at their flat in Holland Park to view the precious substance and perhaps receive a small piece for themselves. Amongst these visitors is Miriam, an art student who has been staying at the Free School and now passes this juicy bit of gossip on to Smith.

'They're sharing it among their friends,' she says, she has been a close friend of the foxy girl for some time.

'Well I don't know them,' says Smith, 'so that counts me out.'

'Would you like some?' asks Miriam, 'I'm sure I can get you a piece.

Smith has never tried opium, but tales of the Orient had fascinated him as a schoolboy and given the Shanghai Poppy a good press.

'I wouldn't mind trying a bit,' he says, but I had better come with you in case you get stopped with it.'

Miriam agrees to this and Smith is soon joining the stream of surreptitious visitors who each receive a morsel of the precious lump. Then like ants from a honey-pot they scurry back to their nest at the Free School where Smith regards with relish his latest acquisition.

The opium is a dark brown lump of what looks like hard toffee, he bangs it on the stone hearth and a few fragments break off. These he crumbles into a cigarette paper and adds a little tobacco for tinder. Rolled up with a cardboard tip it looks quite innocent, but when he lights up the dense white smoke and exotic aroma tell another story. He draws in a rich mouthful and inhales; the smoke has a sweet and pungent fragrance; an elusive flavour which haunts his palette with a ghostly and unnameable presence.

Intrigued by this experience he takes another long pull and then attempts another; but it is too late, Miriam, not about to let him smoke the lot reaches out and takes it from his nerveless fingers. He watches her as, taking deep drags, she applies herself diligently to the joint. He considers retrieving it for another pull but cannot be bothered to move, having become intensely interested in the stunning view now that one wall of the room seems to have dissolved. Miriam has begun humming to herself. 'Mmmmm, Mmmmm,' she goes, her voice rising and falling as she dips lower and lower down the wall against which she sits.

The door now opens and McCafferty comes in. To Smith's dislocated eyes, his dreadful overcoat with its patina of stains and impacted filth has now a sheen upon it like flowing velvet, and his battered headpiece resembles a three-cornered hat. He is a dead ringer for Long John Silver; all he lacks is a parrot. His eye alights upon the lump of opium which lies among a paraphernalia of papers and tobacco.

'What's that?' he demands, pointing at the lump. Smith pulls the remnants of his faculties together. 'Opium,' he says, 'help yourself.'

McCafferty is good at helping himself and loses no time putting this talent to work. Soon his head is enveloped in the swirling white smoke that now hangs in the room like a thick fog.

As far as Smith can see, Miriam is now right out of it. Lying back, a smile of unmitigated satisfaction upon her face she emits little 'Oohs', and 'Aahs', as she contemplates her own private pleasure dome. Smith meanwhile, is observing an escarpment of low hills which occupy the far horizon, when an ear-splitting crack of thunder shatters the peaceful landscape and rumbles across the plain towards him. No sooner has its echoes faded than it is followed by another — and then a third.

McCafferty gets to his feet, he is swaying a little and his hat has fallen off. He opens the door to Julian, whose knocking had discharged itself amongst Smith's distant hills. He is a poet, a frequent visitor at the school and the most sober man Smith has ever met. He enters and stands looking curiously at the three incumbents who have now reached a degree of relaxation unknown to even the most diligent couch-potato.

'What's going on?' he asks, and Smith, having by now almost completely transcended his speech centre attempts some repartee.

'*It's* going on,' says Smith, 'On, on, and on.' He waves his hands around generously as if introducing Julian to the world for the first time.

'Yes but it must be something, otherwise it couldn't go on,' says Julian, standing over Smith and looking disapprovingly down at him, 'and anyway, what are you on?'

'Have some opium,' growls McCafferty, pushing the brown lump and a packet of cigarette papers towards him. Julian sits down on the floor, his knees and feet properly arranged before him; he is not a hippie and maintains a conservative suit-clad exterior amongst the riot of forms which flourish around his freaky friends.

'Oh no, I couldn't,' he says primly, holding up his hands as if to ward off even the suggestion of such a thing.

'Smoke some opium,' says McCafferty. This time it is an order and McCafferty is not a man for negotiation. He sticks two or three papers together, puts in some tobacco, and slowly rolls an opium joint which in size and streamlined perfection would not have disgraced the workshops of Count Zeppelin himself. He lights it up and passes it to Smith who looks at in wonder, he has forgotten what it is for.

'Smoke,' says McCafferty, and Smith raises the joint to his lips and once more draws within a long fragrant toke and offers it to Julian, who refuses to take it. 'No really,' he protests. McCafferty reaches forward and taking the joint holds it out to Julian. 'Smoke,' he growls.

'No thank you,' says Julian, still maintaining a polite distance.

'Smoke,' says McCafferty again.

'No, I er, it's just that, er you see...'

'SMOKE,' roars McCafferty, and Julian shrinks back as the joint is thrust upon him. Too polite to refuse such a direct command he takes the joint and sits looking at it as if it is a poisonous snake, then, his innate bohemian spirit asserts itself and he gives a faint grin. 'Oh well,' he says, and taking a good pull or two at the joint hands it back to McCafferty. He expels the smoke in a great cloud and gazes around him with interest.

'Hah!' he says presently, he looks pleased with himself. 'You see, it doesn't work on me.'

Now, as if to prove his point, he retrieves the joint from McCafferty and draws deeply upon it again. There is a slight bravado in his manner and he grins as if at some secret insight.

'You see, nothing,' he says, and standing up begins raising and lowering his arms and then rotating them in contrary directions.

'These are the two arms of poetry,' he says dreamily. 'With the right arm I sift the winds of the south-east; from the bleak foreshores of Canvey Island out across the deep to the kiss-me-quick promenades of Southend-on-Sea.'

Smith hears his voice as if it is coming from the depths of a deep pond, bursting like verbal bubbles upon the surface and releasing their cargo of encapsulated words one by one.

'My right arm,' continues Julian, his voice slipping into a sing-song chant, 'is the poetic wind spirit of the north-west which climbs like a lark into the air above Newcastle, then, in one vast parabola swoops southwards and down to the gull-swept skies and balmy shores of Cornwall.'

He begins to decrease the arm movements until they are barely moving.

'The poetry is slowing down,' he says, 'and I'm getting off.'

He sits down, his knees and feet no longer primly side by side but sprawled in an abandoned manner amongst the wayward limbs of the room's other occupants. McCafferty now lies flat on his back, his eyes gazing towards the ceiling. Occasionally he gives abrupt bursts of private laughter, as if the ceilings blank surface plays host to some cinematic epic which here and there tickles his fancy.

McCafferty is out of it.

Miriam, also supine, has been out of it for some time.

Julian, lying face downwards his head cradled in his arm lets forth an occasional musical groan, but is otherwise out of it, and Smith, reclining back in his leafy bower views the golden minarets and domes of a far-off mystical city — and now he too is out of it.

A Fair Cop

Morning is a very grey affair. A low key and brooding dawn filters through the grimy windows of the small room and throws the four heavily sleeping figures into an as yet uncoloured relief. Above, the weathered and long suffering front door now receives a major assault upon its faded dignity, for there comes a great hammering upon it. A further series of crashes bow the door inwards upon its only lock, which, unable to maintain a grip upon the ancient wooden frame, scatters its rusty screws like rotten teeth and the door swings back with a bang.

Smith sits bolt upright. His head is swimming and he doesn't want to even think about opening his eyes. But the crash from above is ominous and particularly so since it is closely followed by a loud stamping of boots upon the cellar stairs. A university rugby team looking for its ball. Or—? Smith tries to gather his scattered wits but is given no time. There now comes some heavy knocking on the door of the room and a hard and authoritative voice announces: 'POLICE! Open the door now!'

Smith panics. He remembers the opium. Where is it? He cannot remember who had it last, it could be anywhere and it is too late to look. McCafferty sits up, and slitting his eyes menacingly at the door says in a grating roar several degrees harder than the policeman: '*WHAT'S THAT MISTER?*'

That's it. Softly softly is over, and the door crashes inwards under the beefy shoulder of a bull-like copper, whose body language indicates that there's nothing he'd like better than a bit of a rumble right now. Moving slowly and deliberately McCafferty stands up as if performing before an audience. He draws back the flaps of his overcoat to insert just the tips of his fingers into the tops of his trouser pockets, and looks the policeman up and down in a studied and contemptuous manner. But the focus has already shifted to an immaculately turned-out Inspector, who leads a posse of several more constables. Miriam is led off into the back room by two grim-faced policewoman, while Julian, Smith and McCafferty are given a cursory search. Suddenly there comes a shriek of feminine laughter from the other room. Smith recognises the laugh; it is Miriam for sure, but what in a situation like this can she find so funny. This sudden outburst of hilarity freezes the police and their victims into a tableau. For a long moment, their roles forgotten at this demonstration of female inexplicability, they stare uncomprehendingly into each other eyes. Until, remembering himself with a start, a constable continues his rummaging through Smith's pockets — nothing — then it is McCafferty's turn. He holds his arms high as if he has done this many times before, while the policeman checking his pockets does so at arm's length. McCafferty's aggressive manner might not frighten him, but his aroma is formidable.

Julian is next, but apart from his *Manual of Pataphysics* his pockets are empty. The constable is about to report back to the Inspector when he suddenly notices Smith's shirt pocket. His fingers dip within and emerge a moment later holding a dark brown lump between finger and thumb. It is, sees Smith with dismay, the opium, and the policeman holds it out for the Inspector's attention. The Inspector comes over to take it from him, and holding it up to the light twists it around a little in a speculative manner and then asks: 'Anyone know what this is?'

No one has anything to say, the question is obviously rhetorical. He calls Miriam back into the room and addresses the four. 'You are under arrest,' he says, 'on suspicion of being in the possession of an illegal substance.' They are read their formal rights and led up the stairs to the street, where a Black Maria stands at the curb. Further along Miriam is being pushed into a car, and the two policewomen who restrain her are not being gentle. She has obviously got up their noses.

At the local station the Inspector lines them up. Once more he brings out the lump of opium and holds it up. 'Well,' he says. 'Anyone going to tell me what it is?'

'*What's that mister?*' says McCafferty, in his best Dangerous Dan McGrew voice. But the Sheriff ignores him and continues to toy with the opium. He gives it a sniff and addresses himself to Smith.

'This was found in your pocket.' he says. 'Is it yours?'

Giving him no time to answer McCafferty steps forward and swings around to face Smith. His stiff-fingered hand chops downward like a sword as he speaks.

'You don't do deals with these people,' he grates. 'You tell them nothing!'

The policemen seem hypnotised by this internecine drama and stand around viewing the scene with great interest, even the Inspector is waiting for McCafferty's next move. But Smith has had enough. He knows he is at the fulcrum of several possibilities, some of which he will prevent at all costs. 'The opium is mine and it's a fair cop,' he thinks. 'McCafferty can grind his own axe, and anyway, who does he think he is, Humphrey Bogart?' If he doesn't make a move now McCafferty's little gang are going down the tubes big time. Disregarding McCafferty's tough line he says the first thing that comes into his head. 'It's mine,' he says. Now the die is cast he feels relieved, the admission has cleared the air like a dash of cold water.

'In that case,' says the Inspector turning to Julian, 'you can go.'

A policeman steps forward and leads him from the room. 'You should choose your friends more carefully,' the Inspector shouts after him. McCafferty is, however, not pleased with this turn of events. He seems disappointed by the release of Julian, as if a member of his mob has betrayed him and reduced his status as gang-leader in the eyes of the police. Miriam is led away to another room and the Inspector turns to the desk-sergeant.

'Book them,' he says. He doesn't even look at McCafferty, who, as far as Smith can see should have been released with Julian. Now the desk-sergeant takes over whilst the remaining constables look on in a studied silence. An unspoken conspiracy is afoot. McCafferty's wild-west approach to authority has really upset them and innocent or not, no way are they letting him go just yet.

McCafferty is led away to a cell and after a while Smith is taken to another. They cannot see each other but it is not long before McCafferty's voice, now polite and supercilious to an exaggerated degree, comes echoing along the brickwork of the corridor outside the cells.

'Could I have a cup of tea please?'

In spite of the sarcasm there is a hint of pathos in the tone, gauged to a nicety to touch even the most hard-hearted jailer. And lo! Smith's cell-door opens and a policeman enters with two mugs. He hands one to Smith and leaves closing the door behind him. In the next cell he hears the door open.

'Most kind of you old chap,' says McCafferty. His voice, a caricature of twee sensibility seems to be mocking not the policeman, but rather the profound and utter stupidity of the whole situation.

Later in the day they are told that they will be taken before a magistrate in the morning. McCafferty, who is experienced in this field sends a harsh whisper of sound advice along the corridor.

'Prison?' he says. 'Nothing to it! You just eat your way through it.'

Morning comes and Smith awakens upon a hard mattress with a prickly blanket for company. Already a policeman is unlocking the cell doors and awakening the other occupants, a raucous prostitute and a couple of surly alcoholics.

'Come on then,' he shouts into each cell, and the occupants emerge to queue for the toilets and a spartan morning ablution.

Breakfast comes soon after. A sausage sandwich and a mug of tea go down passably well, before they are led out to a back yard where a prison van stands waiting. The van is divided within into tiny metal compartments into which the prisoners are locked one by one. There is just room to sit and a window high up in the side of each cell admits a little light. Smith stands on his seat but cannot see more than a few roof-tops, so he sits down to await his fate.

The journey is not long, and the van's doors open for the occupants to be led into the back of a courthouse. Here they are shown into several rows of benches at the back of the court. Miriam is already there and she comes and sits next to Smith.

'Why have they still got you?' he whispers.

Miriam rolls her eyes. 'It's something to do with my attitude,' she grimaces. 'They're really giving me a hard time.'

Gradually the benches fill as more miscreants are decanted from local police stations in the district, until the trio is compressed within a tight bunch of woeful human wreckage. Bloody noses, black eyes and grazed cheekbones abound among these unfortunates, who slump in hopeless contemplation of their miserable lives.

The entrance of the magistrate brings a little life into the courtroom which dutifully shuffles into attention. One by one the captives are brought before him, and he treats them with the bored air of a ticket-collector. Prostitutes predominate and outnumber the drunks considerably. They mount the dock nonchalantly. 'Guilty,' they say, without missing a single chew of their gum, as if asking for a ticket to Camden Town or Tooting Beck. 'Ten Pounds,' says the magistrate. The prostitutes really have their act together; they and the magistrate are "just doing their job", and they prance off afterward like ponies in a dressage competition. The drunks however, seem barely aware of their surroundings and whine their abject excuses without success.

'Ten pounds,' says the Magistrate monotonously, dismissing each one as they shuffle off.

Now the three miscreants face him and the charge is read out to the court. 'Possession of an illegal substance Sir, namely four grams of resin.' says a policeman handing the magistrate the charge sheet. The magistrate mumbles to himself as he peruses the sheet until he comes to an abrupt halt. He looks up and views the occupants of the dock with a stern and disapproving eye.

'Opium,' he says, rolling the word around on his tongue as if he is getting high on the mere mention of this taboo subject. He looks around the court and exchanges meaningful looks with the policeman and sundry other minor officials present.

'Opium,' he says again, and then: 'What are the facts?'

'We're still looking into the background of this case Sir,' says the policeman. 'Perhaps an order of remand might be suitable.'

'I agree,' says the Magistrate. 'You will be remanded in custody while further enquiries are made.'

The Walnut

Again Smith finds himself aboard the judicial charabanc. His seat not quite as comfortable as might be and for sure, not on his way to the seaside. Brixton Prison is in fact his destination, and soon the van rumbles through an archway at the main entrance. He gets out of the van and finds himself being herded with a group of other captives into a cavernous hall divided into sections. The guards who ride this herd wear black uniforms with stiff-peaked caps and flaunt a heavy key chain at their waist as if it were a badge of office.

'These must be the screws,' thinks Smith, feeling that as a genuine incarcerate he now has the right to use this familiar term. At the door civilian skins are shed and their clothes bundled up and taken away. A shower comes next to be followed by an issue of prison clothing. Smith puts on the trousers and finds them far too long. He rolls the bottoms and pulls up the waist which reaches to his armpits, whilst the ballooning crutch still hangs to his knees.

'I could get right inside them,' he thinks, sorely tempted to try. But the grim atmosphere in here seems not conducive to humour; and besides, the trousers as a means of escape does not convince even someone as gullible as himself. He looks for some buttons or other means of fastening but there are none. Bunching the trousers in one hand and holding them as high as he can he joins the queue for footwear. Everyone else, he sees, is holding their trousers in exactly the same way, and he begins to feel a sense of kinship with his fellow detainees. The screws, however, are an alien species in comparison; they give their orders like schoolmasters and watch over the inmates with a petty eye.

"No talking," seems to be at the top of their hit-parade. They bark like dogs as they issue curt commands, waving their silver chains as they walk up and down and casting a merciless eye at their prey.

'Take yer boots,' shouts a screw, as Smith comes up to a large wicker basket full of footwear. He looks within and begins searching for something in his size, which irritates the screw no end.

'Take yer boots,' he shouts angrily. 'They're all the same.'

It is true. Smith now realises that the boots are all the same size — extra large, and he takes one and inserts his right foot. It has no laces and is so large that he cannot lift his foot without the boot falling off. He looks around for the left-foot basket, but now the screw has had enough of his philandering.

'Take yer boots,' he roars. 'THEY'RE ALL THE SAME!'

Now the penny drops and Smith is stunned; the man actually means what he says. Big, small, left and right: the boots, like shapeless leather boxes, are indeed all the same. He joins a queue for the mess hall and now he hears it. A low monotonous scuffling sound as the prisoners shuffle by, their trousers gathered in one hand at the neck as they slide the boots along the ground. Smith quickly gets the hang of it and is soon shuffling along with the best of them.

The food is disgusting. Cardboard trays of dried salted fish; boxes of bread cut into doorstep-size slices; a mug of tea to wash it down and eat as much as you like. No one seems to be taking advantage of this largesse and Smith finds out why when he tackles the fish. It is tough as old leather and the bread is only just edible. Several cubicles line the room in which favourite lags can sit and eat. They are also allowed to talk, whilst the remainder must sit chewing in silence at the long table in the centre. The old screw presiding over all this has let his institutional authority go to his head. He is severe with the newcomers but relaxes the rules for his favourites who make sycophantic remarks and he smiles tolerantly. Later,

Smith is marched to a cell and behind him hears the key turn in the massive door. 'Now they've really got me,' he thinks.

The cell has one other occupant who lies on his bunk humped beneath a blanket. Smith tip-toes to the other bed where he sits for a while allowing himself to catch up with the speed of recent events. The situation is ominous, his charmed life has come to an end and he will be lucky to emerge from this predicament unscathed.

Presently, the blanket on the other bed heaves upwards to reveal the scowling face of a heavily built middle-aged man. He is a cartoon criminal with the broken-nosed countenance of a villain. The man glares at him with bloodshot eyes.

'What're you in for?' The Irish brogue is heavy and his voice so aggressive that it is almost demanding to be offended.

'Drugs,' says Smith, hoping that directness will end the interrogation sooner. The man gives him a hard look, and it is easy to see that he is unimpressed by what he sees.

'You, drugs?' he sneers. 'You're in the wrong business fella.' He obviously thinks that Smith is some kind of drug baron and doesn't give much for his chances as such.

Smith, encouraged by the success of this exchange and his newly conferred status as drug baron, attempts to venture a little small-talk himself. 'What are you in for?' he asks.

The man glares suspiciously at him, and his brow darkens as he spits out his reply.

'You mind your own soddin' business,' he says deliberately. 'Just you mind yer own soddin' business.'

'Now he thinks I'm a police informer,' thinks Smith, and disliking the direction the conversation is going he takes the man's advice.

Having dealt with Smith the man gives him another threatening look and turning his face to the wall pulls his blanket about him. Smith, now that this confrontation is over feels free to do the same. Reclining back on his bed with hands clasped behind his head he studies without much enthusiasm the ceiling of the cell; there doesn't seem much else to do.

The next day the heavens open and Brixton is treated to a long grey and dreary day of relentless drizzle. Smith's cell-mate has not uttered a word since the day before, and he diligently avoids all eye contact with the man. In the early afternoon there is an exercise period which today, on account of the rain, will take place inside. There come the sounds of rattling locks and a jangle of keys, while the curt commands of the screws echo along the row of cells.

'Out! Out!' they bark. Soon Smith's cell-door opens and he is herded out onto the metal landing. The prisoners huddle in groups until arranged into a long line, then, turning to the right they are set in motion. The walkway outside the cells is a heavy iron grid which runs around the four walls of a cavernous interior. There are four floors of this and the walkways overlook a vast central well, spanned at each floor with wire netting to catch any would be self-terminators. The line begins to move, and Smith, his trousers clasped to his neck and his feet lost in the huge boots scuffles along behind the man in front. Round and round they go under the eyes of the screws, who stand at each corner of the landings. Hundreds of semi-vacant boots scrape around the iron walkways making a continuous background rumble, while the screws keep their zombie-like charges moving with many encouraging remarks.

'Keep moving,' they shout, and on a more personal level, 'YOU! SHITHEAD! I said, NO TALKING!'

Smith looks up. High above, the wired-glass panels of the lofty roof run with streams of rain and a ghastly grey light illuminates the scene. He looks sideways across the central well where the line scuffles along in the opposite direction and there catches a glinting eye. It is McCafferty, whom he has not seen since leaving the magistrate's court. McCafferty returns the look with a knowing grin, his shoulders are hunched and in spite of the boots he manages to swagger a little. Smith realises that at last he is in his own element; now the cards are on the table and the chips down, McCafferty is *really* enjoying himself.

A few miserable days later Smith is led from his cell and taken to the main entrance hall where his clothes are handed back to him.

'You've got bail,' says the screw. 'Get changed and go through there.' He points to an office door, and Smith loses no time in walking out of the boots and trousers. He puts on his own clothes and follows the screw's pointing finger into a glass-boxed office at the main gate, where Jay Marcel and a few friends have brought the documents for his release. Skipio Hawkins, the editor of *International Times* has organised a collection at UFO, his enterprise in the Tottenham Court Road, and with a few other donations sufficient funds have been accumulated to grant Smith bail.

'Miriam got out yesterday,' says Jay. 'Some friends bailed her and she's staying over in Fulham'.

Smith wastes no time in hunting her down. There is something he wants to ask her; it is a question that has been plaguing his mind since their arrest. She is however, not in a good mood when he sees her. With her legs up on a couch she launches immediately into a long tirade against the police and her time in Holloway prison where she had been remanded.

'They hated me,' she complains. 'Just because I thought their hats were funny, and look at this.'

She lifts her dress to expose her upper-legs.

Smith gives the legs an appreciative glance and notices some red chafe marks around the thighs.

'How did you get those?' He asks.

She grimaces with distaste.

'Prison knickers,' she says. 'They were so stiff they may as well have been made of cardboard.'

Smith suppresses a grin, 'cardboard knickers,' he thinks, and then aloud: 'Cardboard knickers.' He laughs at this amusing thought. But in her present mood Miriam doesn't find the image funny and she glares angrily at him.

'There's something I wanted to ask you,' says Smith, when she signals the end of his examination by pulling down her dress. 'When they arrested us and you were taken into the other room. What where you laughing at?'

She looks at him, puzzled for a moment, and then, sore legs forgotten bursts into peals of laughter.

'They asked me...' she can hardly speak for laughing.

'They asked me...' she splutters. 'Which of you three was my husband.'

Again she roars with laughter. But Smith, being one of the three doesn't think this particularly funny, and he glares angrily at her.

The episode however, is not over yet, since all now hinges on their appearance at Marylebone Court. Jay worries about McCafferty. He attempts to drum up support to get him bail, but McCafferty is not a favoured son and no one seems very interested. Smith however, knows better. 'He won't be well pleased to have his holiday cut short,' he thinks. Bail, as far as McCafferty is concerned, is for the wimps.

The day of the hearing arrives and Smith stands in the dock. McCafferty and Miriam have been released and the charges of accessory dropped. The magistrate reads the charge-sheet, and fortunately it seems that no connection has been made with Kew Gardens.

'Hmm,' he says, you have been found in possession of four grams of opium, have you anything to say?'

Smith decides not to wriggle and says nothing. The magistrate looks serious. 'Four grams,' he says gravely, and then again. 'Four grams.' He is searching for an image of what this might be, and Smith realises the magistrate has no idea what quantity one gram represents, let alone four. As far as he is concerned Smith may have needed a wheelbarrow to transport it and nobody present seems able or willing to enlighten him. There is a moment's silence and Smith knows he must speak.

'It was about the size of a walnut,' he says, as clearly and distinctly as he can.

The magistrate bangs down his gavel. 'SILENCE!' he orders, angry that anyone thinks he has the right to tell him anything and Smith closes his mouth. But the bird has flown. The image of the walnut has winged its way around the Court and cannot now be recaptured. The walnut, a homely item, with its common associations of Christmas and Santa Claus leaches away the aura of criminality which the "four grams" had woven around Smith — reducing him to the status of an amateur, a mere dabbler in the game. The walnut appears to have done its work, for after a little silent consideration the magistrate barks: 'Twenty-five pounds.'

Smith, hiding his elation beneath a suitably chastened exterior asks for, and is granted time to pay, and leaves the Courthouse to rejoin his friends outside. That evening McCafferty comes crashing down the cellar stairs at the Free School. He swaggers in grinning. 'Got any opium?' he growls with a leer, before retiring to the back room, from where soon comes the thud of his throwing knives as they bury themselves deeply into the target which he has hung on the wall.

The Grove

The environs of the London Free School are a maze of narrow streets, stretching to the north in a fine network and lined with the humble dwellings of Irish canal-diggers and railway navvies of a long-gone era. The houses, dark and cramped, now house the riffraff of the area; a shifting population of Irish voices tempered by the quasi-criminal jargon of the streets, and overlaid with the lilting patois of the West Indies.

A crow flying northwards from the School across the maze of streets, might take at most a minute or two before alighting on the roof of Lettie Ronson's house, which stands in a seedy street close by the railway line. It is the summer of 1966, and the small gang of scruffy hippies who emerge from the school to head in this direction take, however, some time longer. They are conferring urgently together over an unforeseen crisis which has arisen in their midst.

An idea for a local hippie newspaper had emerged, and soon bursts into print. It is called *The Grove*, and bears articles on the latest "happenings" and verse from a plethora of local poets. Significantly in this case, many of these poets — perhaps carried away by the spirit of the times — have made oblique references to certain illegal substances in their poems which in the current milieu seem not out of context.

Lettie Ronson is a local community worker with a great deal of clout in the area. She also runs a boarding-house for Irish labourers over whom she wields a formidable discipline. She has however, a heart of gold and many times — when the lead has run out or busking fails — she has provided the denizens of the school with thick sandwiches of the heavy-duty spam which she feeds to her lodgers. The lodgers are a surly lot who regard hippies as scum and cannot understand why Lettie lets them into the house.

Now however, Lettie has displayed a hitherto unsuspected facet. *The Grove* has been printed up and is ready to go onto the street, carrying the hopes and aspirations of the community at large. Lettie being a respectable house-holder with a proper address, it had been arranged for the entire first issue to be delivered at her house. But then, travelling like a flash along the grape-vine came the outrageous news that Lettie had decided to ban and confiscate the whole issue, on account of its references to these "certain substances". It is a situation which demands instant action. Negotiation favours the status-quo, and by now the School faculty are well aware of this.

'We should just go and take them,' says P. B. Rivers, who runs a course on twenty-four hour existentialism at the school. 'She's assumed a right,' he says, 'and by doing so confers the same right upon us.'

It is a brilliant argument and Smith is easily won over, but Nick has his doubts. He has carried his totem fearlessly through the crowded streets of Notting Hill, when the Saturday processions erupt on the stroke of three and parade downhill to the kind of music that you can't quite put your finger on. But now Nick has some reservations.

'We can't just take them,' he says. 'Her lodgers are just waiting for us to put a foot wrong. They'll tear us apart and Lettie would show us no sympathy.'

It is a sobering thought and each contemplates this outcome without relish, until P.B. Rivers snaps his fingers. 'Given the circumstances,' he announces with existential finality. 'We have no choice but to try'.

This kamikaze strategy galvanises the trio into action, and before Nick can voice further doubts they set out to raid the enemy camp.

Smith had first heard of Lettie's *fait accompli* from Ram O'Neil, whom he had encountered earlier in the day while watching a march as it passed Notting Hill Gate Station. He had no idea what the purpose of the march had been, but when he spied Ram amongst the marchers discovered that he had no idea either. Ram is draped in a white toga and has a wreath of leaves about his head. He is playing an Indian flute and pauses for a moment to exchange a few words with Smith.

'The march passed my window,' he says. 'I was in bed but the energy got to me and I took my flute, wrapped myself in this sheet and grabbed a bit of privet-hedge on the way.'

'Where's the march going?' asks Smith.

'Don't know that either,' says Ram. 'But I feel committed to see it through.'

Smith wonders if he too should join but decides, what with one thing or another, to give it a miss.

'Don't forget *The Grove* comes out today,' he says. Ram has contributed a poem for the paper which burns with the naive fervour of the time, whilst perhaps hinting here and there at a knowledge of altered states of consciousness and thus in the eyes of any respectable person, to the issue of illegal substances.

'It's not coming out,' says Ram. 'Lettie Ronson says she wants nothing to do with drugs and she won't release it.'

'But the paper isn't about drugs,' says Smith. 'It's about art and creativity. Anyway, it doesn't actually mention drugs directly, just the odd obscure reference to Congo bush or the delights of tripping, which could mean anything.'

'She was probably tipped off,' says Ram. 'Otherwise she would never have noticed.'

Ram has begun to move off, swirled along by the impetus of the march and piping for all he is worth. His leaf-swathed head disappears into the throng and Smith, unwilling to follow lest he too become swept along with the momentum returns to the School with the bad news.

Now the rescue expedition nears Lettie's house, and P. B. Rivers adds a Machiavellian flavour to his usual existential approach.

'We could send in a couple of decoys,' he suggests. 'All we have to do is keep Lettie occupied in the kitchen while someone else looks around for the papers. She has probably dumped the lot in her hallway.'

This sounds reasonable, and soon a strategy is outlined. Nick will ask Lettie for a sandwich and with P. B. Rivers' help try to keep her in the kitchen as long as possible, leaving Smith free to search for the confiscated paper. Conspiring thus, the small but determined band makes their way towards the dragon's lair, whilst finalising the details of this plan.

'Let Nick do the talking,' says P. B. Rivers. 'She has a soft spot for him.

Nick is a fresh-faced young lad and Lettie clucks over him like a mother hen. P. B. Rivers maintains a convincing facade of politeness over his existential nature and Lettie thinks he is a gentleman. Smith she regards with suspicion, there is something about his looks she does not like.

Arriving at her house they ring the bell and Lettie opens the door. She steps back when she sees who it is. P. B. Rivers stands close behind Nick, while Smith, trying to keep out of sight stays to the rear.

'We thought you might give us a sandwich,' says Nick. Without hesitation Lettie leads the way along her narrow hall to the kitchen, while Smith enters and closes the front door quietly behind him. From the kitchen comes the sound of cupboards opening and knives rattling as Lettie brings forth her great block of industrial-strength spam and P. B. Rivers is in full song.

'How fortunate,' he gushes, 'that such unlucky persons as ourselves can still find kindness amongst our fellows.' He is fond of making these elaborate and stentorian remarks. But Lettie loves it, and she watches indulgently as Nick, making the most of the situation, gets as much spam and bread down him as he can.

Smith, lurking in the hall, listens for a while to see if there is any movement from upstairs where the Irish workmen have their abode. One or two floorboards creak, and only a single rough voice comes from above.

'Jesus and Mary,' it complains. 'Will ye get off me foot now?' But there seems to be no immediate threat.

He quickly scans the hall. The papers are not in sight but a wooden chest stands beneath the coat-rack. He checks it out and finds it contains only shoes. There is nowhere else they could be hidden and he glances up the stair; no way is he venturing up there. To his right is the door to the front room, and he quietly turns the knob. It is unlocked and the door swings open to reveal the parlour, a sacrosanct place from which even Lettie's lodgers are barred. He dare not enter. The old polished furniture menaces him with its unquestionable respectability, while photographs of Lettie's obscure relatives gaze down in stony silence from the discreetly papered walls.

He stands in the doorway gazing with sickened fascination into the awful room, and is about to close the door when something beneath a plushy chair catches his eye. It gleams whitely from the shadows beneath and looks to be a large bundle of newspapers. In a moment he overcomes his reluctance and valiantly faces down the disapproving furniture. Darting beneath the cannon of hostile family faces he reaches quickly under the chair and pulls the bundle out.

It is tightly bound in string, but the topmost paper proclaims all he need to know. The Grove, it announces. He picks the bundle up and tests the weight. It is quite heavy, but he will manage as long as he doesn't have to run. Emerging clumsily from the parlour the front door seems far away. He can hear P. B. Rivers and Nick, like courtiers skilled in the fine art of flattery, buttering Lettie up for all they're worth, and from above the lilting voice again comes wafting.

'I said: *WILL YE GET OFF ME FECKIN FOOT NOW!*'

Smith staggers along the hallway as quietly as he can. This is the most dangerous part. To have been caught in the parlour would have been difficult, but his ever useful ploy of saying the first thing that comes into his head might have stood him in good stead; but here... He won't stand a chance. Bereft of any excuse, with Lettie's screams raging in the background he will hear the dread clump of Irish boots on the stair. He is half way down the hall before he is able to devise a strategy to deal with this misfortune should it occur.

'I'll do a runner,' he thinks. 'I'll just drop the papers and run.'

Now he feels marginally better, and soon his ponderous steps bring him to the front door. With great difficulty he gets it open and emerges into relative safety, then closing the door behind him with his foot he makes off down the street.

The paper retrieved, retribution may follow fast and they dare not take the time to sell it. But by that evening it has been distributed free along the Portobello Road, where for a few days it causes a stir amongst the local hippies. However, this single issue is also the paper's swan-song, and the impulse for such an organ, passing into more capable hands, finally brings forth another radical publication with the title of *International Times*. With a firm foundation and wide support this paper is a great success; flourishing its psychedelic values not just under the very nose of the establishment, but even venturing at times to go a considerable way up it.

However, these bolshie expeditions generate a growing reservoir of affront and irritation from the powers that be, until, unable to contain itself any longer, it overspills and sends the police in to turn over and close the paper's office, while fitting up the editor, Scipio Hawkins, with a large spoonful of porridge for his trouble. This show of municipal righteousness however, is far too late. The paper had done its work and the baby has flown, while the establishment is left with nothing but the bathwater. The Free School, however, had thereafter given Lettie Ronson's spam sandwiches a miss.

The Outlaws

Thick box-trimmed hedges surround a stand of tall trees at the junction of several paths. It is a quiet summer day and pigeons koo among the high branches. Then, from within the thicket a woman's sudden scream. High and piercing it splits the air and carries far across the well-groomed lawns without. A man's voice, rich and deep now follows fast upon the scream and in passionate tones exclaims:

'Madam, hast thou no regard but to send these mewling shrieks to bring thy father's servants hastening to thy aid? And yet, did I not but lightly touch thy knee?'

Now a woman's voice, haughty and disdainful.

'Fie Sir, an if that wert my knee, then surely should'st thou study better thy anatomies. Or doe'st thou confuse the very names of these maidenly parts?'

Man: 'Tis but an unrequited love that blind the eye.

And see... I kneel, and take thy hands to kiss thy...'

Another and louder scream.

It is a matinee performance of *Omphalia*, a tragedy from the pen of an obscure Elizabethan poet, and the passionate voices cause much consternation among a group of Japanese tourists who, having sampled the rose-garden are now passing the open-air theatre in Regent's Park.

As the first scream rents the air they freeze, and huddling closely together stand looking fearfully around them. The man's voice, loud and full of passion, does nothing to reassure them, and at the second scream they turn and with one accord make hurriedly off towards the park exit.

Some little way off, but still within earshot of the theatre, an ornate fountain plays at the end of an avenue of lawns, flower-beds and tall hedges. It sends a jet of water high to break at the tip into a spray of myriad drops which fall into the deep stone bowl of the pool which surrounds it.

This too, attracts its quota of tourists, who snap their cameras, and lingering beside the pool enact the international ritual of throwing in a coin and making a wish. The bottom of the pool is lined with pebbles, amongst which now lie an appreciable sprinkling of one-pound coins. These, accumulated through the summer season, now lie like shellfish at the bottom and barely visible through the murky depths. At the rear of the fountain a dense hedge provides a backdrop behind which lurk a man and a small boy. They are engaged in some furtive activity and seem nervous of being overlooked, giving them the air of definitely being up to something. Moss and Smith are in "hunter-gatherer" mode.

From a nearby waste-bin Smith has retrieved two throw-away plastic cups, and these he is binding onto the ends of long sticks with some rusty wire, while Moss keeps an eye open for park-keepers or tourists. When finished, they intend to apply these instruments in a worthy cause which will furnish them with the wherewithal to buy a coffee for Smith and an ice-cream or two for Moss.

'Go and see if the tourists have gone,' says Smith, and Moss goes sloping off along the hedge, hamming up his role for all he is worth. Reaching the end of the hedge he peers carefully around the corner for a while and then comes sneaking back.

'They're still there' he hisses. 'Come and see.'

Smith crawls along with Moss and sticks his head around the corner. It is true. A large group of Japanese schoolgirls crowd the edges of the fountain, and their excited twittering is punctuated by the plip-plop of pound coins as they hit the surface of the pool.

Moss and Smith continue to watch from the thicket, waiting for a natural lull to occur in the tourist traffic. Moss is tense with suppressed excitement; this is better than football and the possibility of an ice-cream has given a high degree of reality to the action.

'They've gone,' whispers Moss at last, and Smith takes another look. The area around the fountain is now clear and the long avenue in which it stands, deserted. There is not a moment to lose. Rising stealthily to their feet, the two hunters leave the shelter of the hedge and emerge into the open to cross a lawn and wide gravel path. Carrying their cup-on-sticks like spears and crouching low they reach their objective unseen, and perching on the stone surround thrust their sticks deep into the pool.

Moss has immediate success. His cup, dredging the bottom of the pool, has disturbed in passing a large pebble upon which three pound coins are precariously balanced. The pebble loses its equilibrium and falls on its side depositing the three coins neatly into his cup. Smith however, has no such luck. But after much scrabbling about manages to bring one, then another coin to the surface. It is enough, and not a moment too soon. For along the avenue a hoard of wish-hungry tourists are fast approaching who may, should they catch sight of the cup-on-sticks, put two and two together and send for the park-keepers. Leaving the fountain Moss and Smith dodge once more behind the concealing hedge where the cups are removed and deposited back in the bin. While the sticks are pushed deep into the hedge for use should a financial emergency of this sort occur again.

Cutting through the park a wide boulevard is lined at frequent intervals with benches. Half-way along and surrounded by tables and chairs a café stands a little back from the path. At one of the tables sit a man and a small boy. The boy is on his second ice-cream and the man sips his coffee with relish. Moss and Smith are in their "dad-and-his-boy" bourgeois mode, and are enacting the roles so well that none of the other patrons suspect their recent outlawry. Now, well satisfied, they feel grateful to the Japanese tourists and hope all their wishes come true.

Later, walking across the open parklands that lie between the café and the embassy the two hunters are still in bourgeois mode, that is: walking straight and swinging their arms in the appropriate manner. They are making for the banks of the canal, which on the park side is heavily wooded with trees and dense undergrowth. Here and there and well hidden amongst the bushes are the dwellings of winos and derelicts. Constructed from sticks and ragged sheets of polythene the flimsy shelters are abandoned during the day, and only the odd filthy blanket or sodden sleeping bag give evidence of occupation. Moss and Smith now plunge into this unfrequented wilderness and down a steep wooded slope to the edge of the canal. From here, peering through the bushes they can see the towpath on the further side. Abandoning their bourgeois fronts, and now in full hunter-gatherer mode they crouch, moving from bush to bush and taking care not to be seen from the tow-path. Soon Moss dives beneath a bramble bush and emerges a moment later pulling a small two-wheeled hand-barrow, upon which is tied a rip-saw which they had stashed here earlier in the day. All along these banks trees have fallen to lie neglected in the undergrowth, and Smith has for some time been putting them to good use. Now he gets to work on the remains of a large tree blown down in some long past and forgotten storm. The sound of the saw cannot be heard from the park since the canal lies in a deep rift. But, just as a precaution, Moss keeps watch from the bushes at the edge of the canal to give early warning of strollers along the towpath from where the sound of the saw might be heard.

Smith is sawing vigorously away when Moss comes scrambling up the slope with an urgent message.

'People coming,' he whispers, and Smith stays his hand until a small familial group of innocents pass. Chatting idly amongst themselves, their voices come floating across the water and up the slope to where Smith crouches behind a tree. A woman's voice full of resentment is complaining:

'I only had it three weeks and the thin bit on the end for getting into corners broke right off.'

A man's voice answers her:

'I'm not surprised the way you bang around with it, it's a wonder the whole thing doesn't fall apart.'

This response annoys the woman and her voice becomes shrill:

'Why do you always have to argue with me?'

Man: 'I don't always argue with you.'

Woman: 'Yes you do, you argue with whatever I say.'

Man: 'No I don't.'

Their two children lingering far behind have no interest in this grown-up dialogue. The little girl is floating leaves on the canal, and she has a small flotilla of such craft making their way serenely towards Camden Town when there is a horrendous splash amongst the frail vessels, while the surface of the water heaves as if struck by some mighty comet. The leaves violently disperse or sink and the girl is in tears. The boy, a year or so younger, laughs and throws another stone which upsets her even more.

'Well I'm telling mum,' she screams, running to catch up with the parents, while the boy, unwilling to let her malign him out of hand follows hard behind.

This little group are entirely unaware of the intense scrutiny focused upon them as Moss, observing their every move from behind his leafy screen keeps a careful watch. Close on the heels of this contentious little group a young well-dressed couple follow while conversing loudly upon this and that. The man is pontificating in lofty tones.

'No darling,' he is saying. 'You've quite got the wrong end of the stick there. It wasn't Marcel Proust who initiated the Post-Modernist movement. It was Marcel Duchamp.'

The woman is having none of this. 'What's the difference?' she snaps, 'you always quibble over unessential details and refute everything I propose.'

Man: 'Oh darling, *of course* I don't.'

Woman: 'Yes you do.'

Man: 'No I don't.'

Their voices fade and Moss, slithering up from his observation post returns to Smith.

'They've gone,' he says.

When the barrow is loaded with logs they haul it up the slope and wait, still in the shelter of low-hanging trees. This is the most dangerous part of the expedition. A park-keeper might catch sight of their illicit cargo and be the cause of unhelpful complications. Keeping well hidden beneath the concealing branches they exit the park unchallenged, and with enough wood for two or three days return to their secret lair at the embassy.

Heavy Weather

Somewhere a few miles off the Netherlands coast a storm is brewing. No minor squall this but an elemental disturbance of serious proportions which gathers in towering black clouds above, and into a dark lightning-shod presence beneath. Moving south-eastwards it broils the face of the sea and lashes across the Friesian Islands, twisting the sandbanks into ever changing forms and riddling the dunes with treacherous tides.

Heading over the Dutch lowlands and sweeping southwards across the German boarder, the flashing thunderheads trail their heavy drenched skirts across Düsseldorf, Cologne, and further south to Frankfurt and Mannheim. An autobahn stretches its pale ribbon of concrete directly in the path of the storm, and is now receiving the full blast of its powerful winds and torrential rains.

Along the autobahn speed two small saloon cars, which rock on their springs as they are buffeted in the fierce crosswinds. The lead car is being driven by Smith, who has much difficulty keeping it in a straight line. By his side sits Wirril Mauretunga, who has borrowed the car from his girlfriend Aurora; but his glasses are lost and he cannot drive without them. The car which follows close behind is a rust-bucket old Fiat driven by Ram O'Neil. Beside him sits Strimmer, who is a little worried concerning the car's roadworthiness. Ahead the air is darkening and flashes of lightning are crackling around them, while the rain is lashing down so furiously that Smith's windscreen wipers cannot deal with the sheer volume and he sees only momentary glimpses of the road ahead.

'It's like driving through a waterfall,' he remarks to Wirril, who is never short of some good advice.

'Well slow down then,' he says.

Smith eases his foot off the accelerator and immediately the conditions become less fraught.

'That's better,' says Wirril. 'Only a maniac would drive fast through a storm like this.'

As he speaks a sudden flash of headlights in the rear-view mirror catches Smith's attention and he feels the car rock as he is overtaken by the Fiat. It passes so closely that the door handles lightly click together as the Fiat, doing well over 100mph flashes past. Having a friend at his local garage who turns a blind eye when issuing his M.O.T. Ram had carefully hidden the car's innumerable rusty perforations with plasticine covered with a thick coat of paint, and his friend had not pried too deeply. But now the force of this downpour is rapidly returning the car to its true condition. Shedding blobs of plasticine along the way, and spraying water through the many rusted holes in its bodywork it sashays wildly on its bald tyres across the road ahead. Smith catches but a brief glimpse of Ram bent over his shuddering steering wheel as he hurtles past, and beside him Strimmer, who, with white-knuckled hands gripping the edge of his seat stares with horror-stricken eyes at the road ahead. The Fiat disappears in a great cloud of spray and is soon lost to sight.

'See what I mean?' says Wirril.

They are heading for a village just outside of Mannheim where an avatar has taken up residence. She is from southern India, and was born into that exalted mental state which some spend a lifetime trying to achieve. She is in her early thirties and ravishingly beautiful as only Tamil girls can be. But she lives quietly, receiving devotees from all over the world in her home. She dispenses no teaching beyond recommending a simple life, and the individual interviews with her devotees are conducted with a silent eye-contact. Wirril, Strimmer, Ram and Smith have all seen her photograph, of which there are many versions and they each have their favourite. By the time Wirril and Smith arrive at the Gasthaus into which they are booked, the ramshackle Fiat, sagging on its clapped-out springs, already stands dripping in the forecourt.

Heavier Weather

'Ach so,' says the hausefrau as they enter the foyer, 'Herr Shmidt, und Herr Wire Tongue.'

She is a formidable woman with a severe manner, but Wirril is not happy with this "Wire Tongue" business and is foolish enough to try to put her right.

'No,' he says. 'My name is Wirril Mauretunga.'

The housefrau's mouth shuts like a steel-trap and her eyes narrow to a flinty hardness.

'Ach Ja!' she grits scathingly. 'Herr Wire Tongue.'

Turning on her heel and rattling her keys like a wardress she stomps off.

'Kommen sie,' she commands, and they follow her apprehensively along a corridor, until she flings open a door and points an imperious finger into the room where Ram and Strimmer have already set themselves up.

'Herr Shmidt,' she snaps, and Smith meekly enters and flings his bag into a corner.

'Kommen sie,' the hausefrau orders, and leads Wirril off to another smaller room further along. They watch as she marches him off, 'Schnell! Schnell!' she barks.

'She's putting him into an isolation cell,' says Strimmer.

Outer Sight

That evening they drive to the small village where the avatar has her abode. They have been instructed to gather in a car park on the outskirts, and warned that on no account must they enter the village without a guide. Ma Neera lives quietly, and although thousands of devotees make this journey each year she is careful not to upset the Germans.

In the car park small groups of people are already huddled together in the darkness and it is bitterly cold. There are around a hundred people present: Danes and Swedes, Americans and French, and the odd sannyasin from everywhere. But the chatter of excited tongues is halted mid-babble as the official guide turns up, and they gather around to hear his instructions.

'From here to the house,' he says, 'there must be absolutely no talking, and you must walk very quietly as we pass through the village.'

He arranges them into a long line of pairs before taking his place at the head and leading off. But the devotees, talking forbidden, resort to an animated whispering which hovers around them in an audible hiss. The village, as they enter, is deathly quiet. Street lamps cast a mellow light through ornamental trees standing in small plots of well-trimmed grass, and only here and there does a curtained window show a discreet light. Hissing like a snake, the long dark line of devotees weaves a serpent path as it threads its tiptoe way to the house.

Arriving, they enter a wide front door which leads into a long and spacious room. There are rows of seats at either end, and against a far wall is a large chair standing on a low platform. The devotees arrange themselves on the seats and await the appearance of Ma Neera. A hush falls as a door opens, and she comes in.

She wears a sari, and is barefoot with her hands clasped loosely before her. As she walks demurely towards her chair she holds her head so low that it is impossible to see her face. When she is seated a helper comes forward with a small cushion and places it on the floor in front of her, then kneels and briefly places her hands on Ma Neera's feet. She waits patiently as slowly, slowly, the avatar raises her head until they are eye to eye. They hold this pose for perhaps a minute before Ma Neera's head begins to dip. Lower and lower it falls until once more her face is hidden. This demonstration over, the devotees form a short queue, and one at a time are permitted to gaze for a few fleeting moments into the eyes of a living avatar.

Smith hangs back. Now that his own interview is imminent he is assailed by doubts. How will he be able to hide his appreciation of her voluptuous femininity. For she is desirable beyond words, and he is not sure of his ability to suppress lascivious thoughts. From the lofty heights of her serene mind she will read him like a book, and he fears this exposure. 'After all,' he thinks, 'It's not done to fancy God.'

Already, Ram, Wirril and Strimmer have gone forward to take their medicine, and Smith knows he might wait here for years before his moment comes. He decides willy-nilly, to go for it now. With wildly beating heart he rises from his seat and takes his place behind two devotees who await their turn. Each go forward and Smith's moment, right or wrong, has arrived.

He steps up, kneels on the cushion, and reaching forward touches the avatar's feet then waits, ready to stamp on any inappropriate thoughts which are sure to arise. He can see only the top of her head, her glossy black hair swept back and held behind in a small garland of Jasmine. He has barely a moment to gather himself before her head begins slowly to rise. Higher and higher it lifts until her forehead comes into view, a little more and he can see her brows, and then... her eyes!

He had expected destruction from a Medusa-like stare, or feel his bones crushed to powder beneath the terrible gaze of Kali. Anything but this, for he can read no intent whatsoever in her face. Her voluptuous lips are relaxed in the faintest of smiles, and her eyes seem fixed on a vanishing point lying somewhere a few million miles behind him; Ma Neera hasn't just gone beyond. She has never been anywhere else.

Smith on the other hand, his mental processes sucked into the vortex of her vast spaces experiences a profound relief. For he sees in an instant that his thoughts are to her, inconsequential. She is not looking at him; she is allowing him to see her. Of course, he realises, she is an avatar, one born into that unfallen and exalted state which does not recognise the duality of "this" or "that". Or "one thing and another". From where she views the "world" she does not distinguish between Smith and the pattern on the wallpaper behind him. No sooner has the monkey in his mind fled — gibbering at this revelation, than her head begins to drop. Lower and lower it descends, her eyes as it does so lifting upwards to meet his, so that never for a moment does she withdraw them from him. Only, when like twin moons they have sunk beneath her brows, is the interview over.

Smith, cast back into the world of this, that, and sometimes even the other, is left with an impression of impeccable grace; and the question of her divinity he leaves for the monkey to sort out.

The Whim

The next day Smith gets up early to accomplish a personal whim before heading back to London. He has become enamoured of late with the life and poetry of Wilfred Owen, and has a copy of the poems in his pocket. Poor Wilfred, cut down by a machine-gun to fall dying in the mud of the Sambre Canal one week before the Armistice of the 1914/18 war. Having found at last his poetic wings he might have risen to the status of a giant among the English poets, had not his death become the saddest story of all. Now Smith brings some small retribution, for he intends to read one of Owen's poems aloud in a German field.

Crows

A country lane passes the isolated Gasthaus and Smith follows it until out of sight. Beside him, an enormous ploughed field rolls into the distance. Climbing a gate he begins the long plod to the centre, where foraging crows are gathered in large numbers. As he approaches they hop away, maintaining a precise distance and calculating to a nicety the time they need to take off against his assumed ability to reach them. However, the issue does not interest him, and he leaves these calculations entirely to the crows.

From the centre of the field the hedges which surround it are but a thin dark line on the curving horizon. Apart from the crows he is alone in the landscape. Taking the book from his pocket he opens it to the poem which he has decided to read. Then taking a deep breath, and reciting as loudly as he can, he fires off the first salvo:

Red roses are not so red
As the stained stones kissed by the English dead.

As the lines leave his lips the crows are startled into sudden flight. They rise cawing furiously into the air to circle in a ragged black orchestra above him.

Brett

The small bamboo and rattan house stands almost invisible amongst a grove of palms, and although mosquitoes swarm in clouds its shady interior remains insect-free. Sitting inside on a rush mat is Brett, and facing him an elderly man is playing sitar. He is Aktar Ali Kahn, master of the *Ranpur Garana*. This style of sitar playing has passed through Aktar's family since the time of the Mogul emperors, and Brett has the recent good fortune to have been accepted as a pupil by this illustrious musician. The ceremony had been simple. Brett had merely to bring an offering of flowers and fruit to lay before his new Maestro, and receive in return the sacred red chord of the *Garana*, which the old man had formally tied around his wrist.

'Now you are serious musician,' he had said sternly. 'Don't going to chase after moonbeams.'

Noticing Brett's puzzlement over this enigmatic statement the old man elucidates.

'The best sitar players are not always the most famous,' he says. 'To achieve the best one cannot allow the distraction of fame, or you will ending up just being clever. Then you will be very entertaining, but your music will have no depth.' He nods his head to Brett. 'Now you play.'

Brett has his sitar beside him, and he picks it up and slowly begins to enter the raga Aktar had been playing. But questions are rising in his head which will not allow him to concentrate. He stops. 'Then who is the best,' he asks.

Aktar smiles tolerantly as if he had been expecting the question. 'He is a musician,' he says, 'who lives away on the far side of the city.' He waves his arm towards Calcutta, which can be seen through the window distantly shimmering beneath a broiling sun.

'If you are near his house you will know he is playing even if you cannot hear him.'

Brett looks a little doubtful at this, but Aktar fixes him with a stern eye. 'I can tell when he is playing from here,' he says. Brett, catching a glimpse of the red chord about his wrist is reminded of his commitment to this man, and decides to give him the benefit of the doubt. But he cannot refrain from one more bolshie question.

'Is he playing right now?' he asks.

Aktar is silent for a moment then... 'No, at the moment he is not playing,' and as if to forestall the next question... 'He is probably having his supper,' he grins. 'Or maybe he is making the toilet.'

Brett, however, is still confused. 'But if he's the best, what about Shavi Rankha?'

Aktar shakes his head sadly. 'Shavi Rankha? he says. 'Werry nice man but... rubbish sitar player.'

At the end of the lesson Brett gets to his feet and puts on his sandals. Looking outside he sees the mosquito swarms waiting to ambush his meat and remarks on their absence inside.

'They do not like the wibrations of my sitar,' says Aktar, 'and so they will staying outside.'

Returning to London Brett had recounted the whole episode to Smith, who had been a little shocked by Aktar's dismissal of such a revered figure as Shavi Rankha. 'It's rather like saying: Albert Einstein? Very clever man with numbers, but thick as two planks,' he thinks. 'Nevertheless,' the thought continues. 'His contribution to Nagasaki and Hiroshima could scarcely be considered intelligent.'

Power-Freak

Indian music has for several years been the major preoccupation of both Wirril Mauretunga and Smith, who have been taking lessons with Indian teachers in London. However, they are both somewhat wayward of mind and having begun this quest with the high diligence of purists, have now sunk — albeit with even more diligence — to the low pleasures of deviants.

They have discovered in their studies that the raga formations are based upon simple scales, camouflaged beneath a bewildering arsenal of ornament and subtle inflections and had, on account of this revelation, devised for themselves a mathematical system to calculate every possible combination of tones. The lure of striking out into this unknown territory had proven too much for the wilful pair and they had become, in the eyes of their eastern mentors, deviant.

The scales that emerge from their system are of many kinds. Ranging from the serenely beautiful to the blandly boring; and from the brightly enervating to the distinctly sinister. There is, however, one category which has been attracting them of late, and it is here that they have reached the very dregs of deviancy. They have stumbled upon a family of scales so preposterously ugly and unmusically weird as to be almost unplayable. But, seasoned travellers amongst the highways and byways of the myriad combinations they are rapidly developing a taste for these abominations.

An acquired taste implies an initial repugnance. For instance, that which may be encountered at the first taste of Gorgonzola cheese; or the semi-rotten flavour of jugged hare and a preference for birds hung until distinctly "off". Wirril and Smith now disport themselves amongst these perverse sounds, vying with each other to devise ever more bizarre atonalities, and often falling to the floor in helpless laughter in the process. There is however, a further element involved in all this: they are also seeking amongst these tonal relationships for the universal principles which govern the nature of existence itself.

Axioms such as balance, expediency and timing— three principles which influence the circumstances of their everyday lives — are observed amongst the tones as their values change and shift in a moving relationship. Having classified the most fundamental of these qualities, they have entered the field of more obscure and subtle distinctions, and are now engaged in pursuing the dynamics of:

1. That which on the surface appears perfectly sensible and proper, but is actually quite silly. For example: Top hats or economic growth.

2. That which on the surface looks silly, but in fact makes very good sense. For instance: the first man to construct and use an umbrella was laughed off the streets.

3. That which looks sensible and indeed is so. (This boring category is immediately discarded.)

But it is the depths of their degeneracy and the scale of this deviance which reveals itself when they pounce with delight on the fourth dynamic:

4. That which on the surface appears quite silly and indeed is in fact, *Bloody Silly*.

It is commonly held that certain principles can be seen and even proposed intellectually, but which in the "real world" are considered ridiculous, and which only a fanatic would attempt to put into practice (love, peace etc.). However, fanaticism of this order is the cherry on the cake for Wirril and Smith. Hence, emerging now through the door of the salon there come rambling improvisations upon scary scales, each tone of which is antipathetic to every other, with not a jot or tittle of affinity between them.

A flute leaps an interval of outrageous proportions then drops a half-tone and repeats the figure over and over again, slowly descending through every possibility: while a violin does the same in reverse order; gradually ascending until the two instruments meet at the middle and come to an abrupt stop. A round of hearty applause follows, intermingled with enthusiastic shouts and whistles. But their audience appear strangely unmoved.

Upon the podium sit Wirril, Smith, and Wirril's lady-friend Aurora. She is strumming the tanpura, its deep and stable drone providing the only lifeline in their jaunts into the unknown, and many times has saved them from becoming lost forever in the unknowable.

A large placard is centrally placed on the podium which reads: *Analytical Cubist Palm Court Orchestra*. Beside Smith is a small tape-player with a loop of pre-recorded applause, which he activates at the conclusion of each piece. The audience however, in spite of all the orchestra's efforts remain entirely unmoved, and the finely drawn features of an elderly lady betrays no emotion at all on her austere and haughty face. She is Wirril's protégé, existing from the waist up only, and she sits propped up from behind by a hinged wooden strut. Wirril has cut her out from heavy white card and drawn her features with a marker-pen. Behind, and a little to the left of the lady is Aurora's contribution — a life-size sheep which stands complacently cropping its cardboard grass. And Smith, wishing to introduce an extra-terrestrial aspect to the proceedings has fashioned a cut-out of a bright red Martian, its single eye glaring from the centre of its forehead.

The orchestra now embarks upon a piece so excruciatingly unbearable to the ears that Wirril and Smith, hardened as they have become in their explorations, bring it speedily to an end. Smith leans forward and presses the play button on the recorder and the room resounds with a storm of applause. Claps, whistles and shouts of encouragement echo round the salon, which gratify the musicians no end and they wave their arms dismissively as if too humble to receive such an accolade. Their audience however, make no response and sit staring stonily back at them. Aurora too sits rigidly; she stews with inner fury and cannot keep it from her face. She is giving Smith hostile looks and he wonders what is getting up her nose. Wirril, also aware of her anger makes a hesitant enquiry.

'What's up Aurora?' he asks, but she will not answer. Her face is set as she bottles up her fury.

Exasperated, Wirril tries again. 'Come on, what is it?' he demands, and the floodgates open.

'It's him,' grits Aurora through clenched teeth and nodding her head fiercely at Smith. 'He's a power-freak!'

Smith is startled by this, what can she be talking about? And his face registers the innocence of the falsely maligned.

'In what way am I a power-freak?' he asks. This infuriates Aurora even more and she jumps to her feet. Pointing an outraged and quivering finger at Smith she screams her answer:

'If you're not a power-freak. THEN WHY IS IT ALWAYS YOU WHO PRESSES THE CLAP BUTTON?'

Smith is dumbfounded. He cannot even begin to muster the defence which her unexpected attack has called for, and in the sudden shock had even considered for a moment that she might be right. However, such notions as defence and explanation he has long given up, complex arguments of this sort usually result in the issue becoming ever more complex. He now recognises this situation as a familiar syndrome which he knows perfectly well how to handle. Saying nothing more he stands up, and taking the recorder over to Aurora hands it to her with a small bow. He does not overdo the bow lest he provoke her to further umbrage.

This little difficulty overcome the orchestra take up a new scale. It contains an interesting dichotomy: its lower section is as solemn and funereal as a church crypt, while above, it narrows as a steeple to a cluster of three harmonious tones which ring like bells at the top. Up and down they go from crypt to the belfry and back again until, having exhausted all possibilities the piece comes to an end.

There is a moment's silence. Then, with a look of righteous satisfaction on her face and a new-born lust for power gleaming in her eyes, *Aurora presses the clap button*!

Poseidon's People

Two pasty-faced young men descend from their lofty sit-up-and-beg bicycles and stoop low to remove the clips from their trouser bottoms. They wear black raincoats and white shirts, while upon their heads are stiff-peaked Water Board caps. Leaning their machines against the front gate of the embassy they approach the house

A large and heavy iron knocker adorns the oak-timbered door, which one of them lifts and lets fall a few times. A short pause, and the door swings ponderously open to reveal Morgiana, who at the sight of the peak-caps adopts a severe manner which has immediate affect — for one of the men touches his forelock in a servile manner and takes a sheet of paper from his pocket.

'What do you want?' barks Morgiana; she seems about to send them around to the tradesmen's entrance, but the man forestalls her by holding up the paper.

'You have a major leak,' he says, 'and this is an order from the Board. You must get it fixed immediately.'

Morgiana has managerial talents and in no time her synapses are firing away at super-speed.

'How do you know we have a leak?' she asks. She regards all officials as troublemakers who devote their lives to irritating everyone else.

'We've checked,' replies the man. 'Our meters show there is a major loss of pressure at this point, and the piping is sound until it reaches your property. The leak is somewhere between your inlet and our junction in the pavement outside, so it's your responsibility.'

Morgiana listens to this puerile excuse with little sympathy and doesn't give an inch. 'How do you know that your meters aren't at fault? She asks sternly. 'Have you had them checked recently?'

'That's not our job,' replies one of the men, absorbing her clout as would a pond deal with a tossed pebble. His manner seems to yield on the surface, rolling back and gathering strength before returning to crash like a wave on Morgiana's beach.

'We're from flow regulation.'

By now Morgiana has been joined by Caspar and Smith who watch her handling of the issue with admiration: but Caspar, having by now got the gist of it puts his finger unerringly on the crux of the matter.

'Why don't you just send in some men to repair it then?' he asks.

'Because you are responsible for all piping under your property,' replies the man. 'You must get it fixed yourself.'

'But where exactly is the leak? Asks Caspar. The forecourt is large; they can't dig the whole thing up.

'It'll be over there,' says the man, his hand drifting slowly upward to wave vaguely over to the side-hedge. 'And you'd better get a plumber to fix it quick or you'll be cut off.'

This is an ominous threat. To be without running water will bring the public-health authorities down upon them, and eviction could follow on sanitation grounds alone. Is this some new ploy by the Council to get them out?

Smith has said nothing so far, relying on Morgiana's formidable clout and Caspar's English common-sense to get them out of this predicament. But the two men have their orders and this conversation is getting them nowhere. As he listens to the exchange he becomes aware of something deep beneath the surface of these men. He detects a quality in their response which moves like the current in a stream. Their allegiance to a watery god guiding them through mental sluices and over mossy weirs to a world of water-levels, variable pressures, and even possibly through tidal forces to the Moon itself.

'They will have water-diviners and psychics on the pay-roll,' he thinks. Mystics from a world of pressure and flow. An accumulated knowledge of ancient courses and water-tables, united into an alchemical wisdom under the unassuming title of "The Water Board." Blithely categorising them amongst the usual dry and logical servants of the state they have badly misjudged the situation. Now Smith casts his mind upon the deep and attempts a more fluid approach, sprinkling his words with all manner of watery terms the better to strike up some sort of affinity with these men.

'Look,' he says, stepping forward and saying the first thing that comes into his head. 'We don't want to jump in at the deep-end over this. We might start digging in the wrong place and end up the creek without a paddle, so at least show us where to start.'

The two men walk to the corner of the house and begin scuffling their heels into the ground around the side path. Soon one of them uncovers a small metal plate upon which is embossed a large "W".

'This is your inlet-cock,' he tells Smith, 'and our junction is there,' he points along the side of the garden to where it joins the pavement. 'So your leak is somewhere along that line.'

Smith looks to where he points and the sight is daunting, a good thirty yards at least. 'How deep?' he asks.

'Four feet standard,' replies the man.

'Does that mean we have to dig down here to four feet and carry a trench all the way to the street until we find the leak?'

'That's right,' says the man.

'But isn't there any way to find where it is before digging?' asks Smith.

The two men exchange glances and reach an unspoken agreement.

'We'll see what we can do sir,' says the spokesman. Returning to their bicycles they begin undoing some straps, and Smith notices for the first time the long slim bags affixed to the bicycle cross-bars. They look like cased fishing-rods, and walking back they loosen the bags and withdraw long pieces of pipe not unlike lengths of curtain rod. Into one end of the pipes they thrust what appear to be trumpet mouth-pieces. He has no idea what to expect next: will they raise these strange instruments high and sound a fanfare to invoke Poseidon to their aid? Or are they about to perform some mysterious rite from the Water Board's book of magic spells?

With the solemnity of high priests they step forward and place the ends of the rods upon the ground like walking sticks. Then, removing their caps they place their ears upon the mouthpieces, and Smith sees his mistake. A far away dreamy look comes into the men's eyes as, with heads held awkwardly sideways they gaze blankly off into some mysterious inner- world. Up and down the line they go, occasionally conferring and shaking their heads.

It seems however, that these strange operations are unsuccessful. For one of the men returns to where Smith stands watching while slowly returning his rod to the bag.

'We can't get a direction,' he says.

'Why not?' asks Smith, his mind awash with questions. But the man puts him off. He looks away shiftily. 'It's very difficult,' he says.

'Can't you try one more time,' begs Smith, immersed in the magnitude of this leviathan task and desperate to avoid digging the trench.

'Have you got a phone?' asks the man. 'I'll see if the Governor will come out.'

Smith shows him to the telephone, and when the call is made they return to the forecourt and await the arrival of the "Governor".

Ten minutes pass. Then in through the gate appears a third bicycle upon which sits a middle-aged man dressed exactly as the first two, except that his clothes appear somewhat more formal and his hat sits square and firm upon a short regulation haircut. His bicycle is a formidable machine: old-fashioned and high, with lever-operated brakes. Its sober black frame a splendid foil for this dignified-looking man.

The two young men approach the Governor respectfully and a few remarks are exchanged as they point along the course of the water pipe. The Governor looks and sagely nods his head. Then, with a great sense of ceremony, and as if disrobing for the priestly functions of a hallowed ritual he stoops and removes his bicycle-clips, giving each leg a practised flick to loosen his trouser bottoms. The tension in the forecourt is rising, and Smith senses at once that a Magus has entered the scene. This man has depths of such a profound nature, that his mere presence is enough to strike awe into them all.

From his bicycle the Governor now unstraps his own instrument, removing its bag to reveal a highly polished black rod. It gleams like old ebony and he holds it reverently under his arm. From his pocket he removes a small chamois-leather pouch and takes out his ear-piece. Unlike the common brass of his apprentices, the Governor's appears to be carved from solid ivory with a tiny wreath of leaves inscribed about the edge. He twists it into the end of his gleaming rod and steps forward to the line. An apprentice is on hand to take his hat, and with immense dignity he puts the rod to the ground and applies his ear.

Unlike the other two men he does not enter into a trance-like state, but slits his eyes, darting them from side to side while he tests each spot up and down the line. When he has finished his survey he shakes his head, and after a few words with the men returns to his bicycle, cases his rod, replaces his trouser clips and departs.

Smith, comes forward for the verdict.

'It's no good,' says the man. 'The Governor says that your tarmac forecourt is like a giant pie-crust; it's distorting the surface and absorbing the vibrations. I'm afraid sir, that this makes it impossible to get a directional reading.'

The Master has spoken and Smith, his imagination flooded in the undertow of the great man's departure, can find no further arguments. The two men return to their bicycles, strap up, and with a final admonishment that the leak must be stopped soon they mount up and depart.

Fortunately there are some tools in the garage, amongst which are a couple of spades and a pickaxe. Smith and Brett begin probing the ground around the inlet plate. It is stony and the clay concrete hard. But with the help of a hammer and chisel they manage to sink a hole a foot or two deep.

'That's enough for today,' thinks Smith, 'but at least it's a start.'

The next day Brett joins Smith in the trench again, and later Caspar and Tiberius take a turn. For a few days they work like navvies, until they have exposed the pipe and covered a third of the way to the street. From time to time an official from the Water Board comes to inspect the progress; he stands on the edge of the trench looking down where they labour, running his eye over the exposed water pipe.

Two days later it is noticed that the hard packed clay and stone has less resistance; the ground is becoming damper and soon gives way to a slushy mud. Trickles of water runnel their way in tributaries through the stone until finally, when the next few shovelfulls have been lifted, a thin but powerful jet of water shoots upward, reaching high into the branches of a nearby tree and dripping like rain from the leaves. The leak has been found, but now comes the hard part. How to repair it? A professional plumber is out of the question; there is nothing at all in the kitty, and Smith sits on the side of the trench looking down at the exposed pipe as it gushes forcefully skywards. The leak itself must be very small, 'probably no bigger than a pin-hole,' he thinks. Without further thought and purely on a whimsical impulse, he leans forward and gives the soft lead pipe a sharp tap with the hammer.

The leak stops at once.

He avoids giving it another "just to make sure" tap, and backs carefully away. Then stands listening to the drops still falling from the foliage above, until they too cease.

Throughout the rest of the day they make frequent visits to the site, but the pipe remains dry and no leak is apparent. The next morning they support it from beneath with a house-brick, lest it sag and the leak re-open. Finally, to protect this sensitive spot, an old cupboard door is sunk above the pipe and the trench filled in and tamped down.

When the Water Board men return with their listening tubes the sunken pipe gives no sign of a leak. They seem a little suspicious. 'You shouldn't have filled it in,' they admonish, before ticking their clipboard and mounting their bicycles.

'We like to see the work is done properly.'

'Sorry about that,' says Smith. 'You should have said so. But you were right about one thing. It definitely needed a plumber.'

The Hydronium

Jake Naylor is bringing over a newly constructed instrument that he has spent the last few weeks inventing. Wirril and Smith sit in Smith's room at the top of the house and await his arrival. They are slightly apprehensive, since Jake has the reputation for possessing a fearsome temper and he is very serious about his instruments. Brett had recently visited Jake, who had at the time been working on his ocarinas which he makes from the best clay and fires in an electric kiln. Jake is very proud of his work in this craft, and takes immense care to produce ocarinas capable of sounding all the overtones. Brett, a serious musician himself with a life-long relationship with the sitar, had suggested to Jake that the ocarina is not commonly regarded as a proper musical instrument. He had expected, at the best, an interesting argument. But what he got was the worst.

'He began throwing stuff around and roaring,' says Brett. 'I got out as quickly as I could.' He admires Jake's musicianship, but since this experience has been a little wary of him.

Wirril and Smith are also on their guard when Jake's step is heard outside the door. When he enters he is carrying a collection of glass tubes and some sort of frame to which is attached a small one-octave keyboard. 'I'll just go down and get the water tank,' he says, and leaving the equipment on the floor stomps back along the corridor, his home-made boots making a strange rattling sound on the floorboards. The boots are made of some heavy sailcloth, nailed around the welts with broad-headed tacks.

'They have articulated soles,' Jake had said when demonstrating them to Smith, and lifting a foot had shown a series of heavy wooden slats running across the bottom of the boots. 'They're made of beechwood.' he had explained, 'and bend on hinges.'

'Don't the hinges hurt the bottom of your foot?' asked Smith doubtfully.

'No,' Jake had said, regarding him scathingly through his hand-carved wooden spectacles. 'The hinges are countersunk on the underside'.

Now Wirril and Smith stare at the jumbled heap of glass pipes and the spindly frame of what looks like a modified clothes-horse. Wirril looks at Smith. 'Water tank?' he says. But the only thing that comes to Smith's mind what with the clothes-horse and all, is some kind of musical washing-machine. However, he is saved from further speculations of this sort by Jake, who comes clacking into the room carrying a small metal drum of water and various other wooden parts. He sets the drum up on three long legs and pulls the clothes-horse arrangement to stand beneath it. Then he begins fixing the glass tubes to rubber sockets racked beneath a row of tiny spigots, which operate on spring levers attached by long thin dowels to the keyboard below. Underneath, he places a long ceramic trough into which he pours an inch or two of water. When he has made a few minor adjustments to the springs and spigots he reaches up, turns the water on, winds a handle to get the pressure up, and announces solemnly: 'I call this the 'Hydronium''.

He kneels at the keyboard while Wirril and Smith seat themselves on the floor in front of the instrument. They can see Jake watching them closely through the intersections of the tubes and rods and wait with bated breath for him to begin.

'I'll just show you what it can do first,' he says, and presses a key high up the board. A rod ascends to activate a lever and turn one of the miniature spigots, which releases one tiny drop of water to roll down a glass tube and fall into the trough beneath.

'Plip,' it goes.

'That's the high register, but if I put in some bass.' He presses down a key at the lower end of the keyboard. Again a rod ascends; a lever is pushed; a spigot turns and another single drop of water is released. This second drop is, however, of considerably larger proportions, and rolling down its tube falls with a deep 'PLOP!' into the trough below.

'I can play Scarlatti on it too,' says Jake. 'Although it's difficult with only one octave.'

Now he concentrates on the music and soon his fingers are tripping up and down the keyboard as he attempts one of the great man's sonatas.

'Plip, plip, PLOP! Plip, plip, 'PLOP!'

'Plinka, plinka, plip plip PLOP!' plays Jake.

Smith has a pain in his stomach where the laughter is building up and threatens any second to come bursting out. His lips are buttoned up tight, but he is terrified that his stomach muscles may give out at any moment. Wirril is silently shaking as he too is forced to apply the strictest discipline. For should either fail, Jake's wrath might fall upon their innocent heads and Smith doesn't want his room smashed up. However, Jake finishes the piece without incident and leaving the contraption where it stands joins the two for a cup of tea. They sit sipping the tea and contemplating the instrument, while Jake explains the mechanism and tells of the difficulty he had carving the spigots.

'I used a tiny piece of broken razor-blade bound onto half a matchstick to carve them,' he says proudly. 'They work OK, providing I don't overfill the tank and send the pressure up too high.' Now he is getting serious again. 'If the pressure gets too high the spigots can't take it and the tubes burst from their grommets.'

Wirril looks uncomfortable. He is sitting very near the instrument, which is giving the occasional ominous gurgle, and he is not sure how safe it is.

'What's the pressure like now?' he asks nervously.

'Oh, it's very low at the moment,' says Jake. 'I couldn't carry much water upstairs. But if I fill it right up I can show you how much the volume increases.'

'No that's alright. I believe you,' says Wirril, getting hastily to his feet and helping himself to more tea, while Smith, now that the demonstration is over feels it safe to venture a harmless comment.

'Well I suppose it would be alright for giving concerts to tadpoles,' he says, hoping to get a laugh from Jake. But Jake is not amused.

'What would be alright?' he asks suspiciously, and Smith, hoping to extract himself from this tight corner blunders on.

'Your —er, Dripaphone.' he says.

Jake steels his eyes. 'It is a H-Y-D-R-O-N-I-U-M! He says through gritted teeth, and Smith thinks his room lucky to have got off so lightly.

Unrequited Love

The Hydronium makes a great clatter going back down the stairs and Sukie, still hopelessly in love with Jake, comes out of her room near the backdoor and hangs around hoping to get a smile from him. Jake, however, is entirely uninterested in her and doesn't want to know. She had once accompanied him on one of his country hikes, but she had been unable to bear the primitive conditions of the trip and had arrived back at the embassy wet, dishevelled, and totally demoralised. Nevertheless, she still cannot get Jake out of her head and yearns hopelessly for a more intimate relationship. Smith had recently asked Jake how he feels about Sukie.

'She can't keep up,' he had said dismissively.

Jake does not cast the usual male eye upon women, and a well-developed bosom cuts little ice with him no matter how enticing the proportions. Jake has other criteria, and his eye will sometimes be caught by a couple of sturdy legs with good thick ankles. Or a pair of brawny arms capable of carrying the frying-pan and a sack of coarse flour for the chappatis in one hand, and in the other, a sleeping bag and *her own* tent.

Sukie fulfils none of these conditions, and huddling in a wet sleeping bag while the wind outside flings torrential rain against the side of her tent, plus cold shoes thick with yesterday's sludgy clay to put on in the morning, is not her understanding of the ideal honeymoon. But Sukie is not for giving up, and won't believe Smith when he tells her of the hopelessness of her dreams.

''E is shy,' she says firmly. 'And 'e do not like to show 'is feeling.'

Smith leaves her to dream on, until one day she pulls him excitedly into her room.

''Zere is a room going free in ze 'ouse of Jake Naylor,' she says. 'And I want to 'ave it.

'Okay,' says Smith, 'I'll have a word with him and see what he says'.

The next time he visits Jake he waits for a break in their conversation and casually puts the question. Jake hardly gives it a thought. He couldn't care less who lives in the house, which is a squat. As long as the new tenant doesn't make a nuisance of themselves the question of who it may be is irrelevant. Smith returns to Sukie with the news, and he has never seen her look so happy. 'Oh, it is wonderful,' she says, clapping her hands together with delight. 'Now I can be near 'im'.

Smith watches her drive off in her battered old Citroen her bags and easel crammed hurriedly into the back. Now that she has gone her room looks abandoned. He will miss her coffee and croissants, the black cherry jam which she spreads thickly on top, while her radio, always tuned to Paris, plays café music quietly in the background. Nevertheless, he crosses his fingers for her and hopes that her dreams come true. But somehow, knowing Jake, he doubts this new arrangement will last, and suspects that it won't be long before she is back.

Meanwhile, round at Jake's squat Sukie moves into the new room and sets up her easel in the window. The room, which is directly beneath Jake's, is spacious, and as she sits painting she can often hear his articulated boots as he rattles around on the creaking floorboards above. She is in heaven: so close to her love that she hears every movement he makes. Outside in the street all is quiet as her fine camelhair brush moves stealthily along the outer edges of a morning-glory blossom which adorns the centre of her new painting. 'I am so 'appy,' she whispers to herself as she works. Soon Jake will be back from the Heath, where he goes most afternoons looking for pieces of seasoned wood for his instruments, and she listens intently for his step. When she hears him put his kettle on in the room above she too does the same, and drinking her tea feels at one with her lover. She looks at her clock, Jake is later than usual and she becomes a little worried. The morning-glory loses its charm and cannot compete with her rising anxiety. She sighs and lays aside the brush, then walks restlessly over to the window. Pulling aside the curtain she looks down into the street where the late autumn trees hold their few remaining leaves against the setting sun. She sighs and imagines herself and Jake walking arm-in-arm beneath them, perhaps on their way to the cinema or the park, where they will visit the café and drink tea together while gazing happily into each other's eyes.

She steps back from the window; her task now is to overcome Jake's shyness. She will catch him on the stairs as if by accident, and casually invite him into her room for coffee. He will not be able to resist such an invitation.

'I,— I,— well, I don't know,' he will splutter shyly. But she will be kind and firm until he capitulates, acknowledging that at last he has found his true soulmate. However, she doesn't often catch him on the stairs, and during this first week at the house she has only passed him twice. She had given him her most alluring smile each time, but he had not seemed to notice and had gone by with hardly a look in her direction, thus proving to her the depth of his shyness.

Jake makes a bit of money on the side giving lessons on the bamboo flute, a skill he had learned in India. One of his pupils is a young girl, who, having purchased such a flute arrives one day for her first lesson. Jake is very stern with her and won't countenance any sloppiness. When she makes mistakes he doesn't pull his punches.

'Keep your little finger down whatever the other fingers are doing,' he orders. But she keeps forgetting, and the little finger waves around each time she plays the exercise he has given her.

'Keep it on!' He says angrily, and the girl, nervous at his irritation gives a giggle. Jake steps behind her and holds down her little finger with his thumb and she giggles again with embarrassment. Now Jake is impatient with this silliness, and he squeezes harder to produce an even more hysterical giggle.

In the room below Sukie is listening intently. She had heard the front-doorbell ring, and peeping through the crack of her door watched Jake lead the girl up to his room. She is thrown into a terrible turmoil, and her heart pounds as she waits, listening with anguish to the sound of voices from above.

How can he do this to her? What has she done to deserve this kind of treatment from her lover? Through the ceiling she now hears a distinct giggle and a floorboard creaks suggestively. She throws down her paintbrush and stares at her work in despair. Another giggle from above, and then, with a bit more body to it, another. Her imagination begins to construct lurid pictures of what is obviously taking place in the room above. In her mind's eye she can see it all and the sight is insupportable…

Jake has the girl bent backwards over the bed, and his horny craftsman's hands have already torn through the fragility of her lacy bra as if it were tissue paper, thus releasing her ample pink breasts to his lustful gaze. Now, one hand fumbling with the buttons of his home-made canvas braces, while the other, with ruthless force pulls her knickers elastic to breaking point, he presses home his suit upon the girl.

A fury of volcanic proportions erupts within Sukie such as only a scorned woman can know. Tormented by jealous demons and wearing the ravaged mask of anguish she mounts the stair and crashes open the door to her betrayer's room. The girl sits upon a kitchen-chair, and behind her stands Jake with his hand upon the flute which she holds to her lips. But Sukie is blind to this innocent tableau. Everything for her is in shades of red, and her pent up fury explodes.

'Get out! Get out!' she yells at the girl, and then strides across the room towards Jake.

'Tell her to go,' she screams at him and points imperiously towards the open door.

'Tell her to get out!'

It takes a few seconds for Jake to register what this outburst means, but when the penny drops his outrage is awesome. A fury so terrible that Suki's flaky effort pales and shrivels before it.

'*ARRRRGGGHHHH!!!*' he roars, baring his teeth and looking around for something to break. His eye alights upon a wooden stool, and picking it up he raises it high and smashes it down with all his strength upon a table. The stool shatters into pieces while shards and splinters fly. The girl is terrified and runs into a corner where she crouches huddled against the wall. Suckie knows now for sure that Jake doesn't love her; has never loved her; and what's more, never will. Sobbing she flees the room; sobbing she packs her things into her old Citroen, and sobbing she returns to the embassy. It has been a very hard lesson for Sukie. But she manages to survive and comes in time to develop her own unique philosophy on the incident.

''E is maniac', she says bitterly. 'An' I 'ave finish wiz 'im.'

However, after a suitable interval in which she seems to have pondered deeply upon the end of the affair, she comes to some private conclusions. Undaunted, she now sets out once more and begins to probe Smith on the suitability of another prospect.

''Zis man Ace,' she says softly, plying Smith with coffee and croissants. ''E seem a werry nice man?' She glances slyly at Smith as she speaks, and he knows at once that she is concocting some new amorous design.

'Ace?' says Smith, 'Yeah, Ace is OK, why?'

'I sink 'e is werry nice too,' says Sukie.

Smith waits for more but none is forthcoming, and he wonders what she has in mind. Has she fallen in love again? Ace is a safer proposition by far, since he is unlikely to rage around smashing up stools whatever the circumstances. But she will face stiff opposition from his Chinese factory-fiddle. Nevertheless, over the next few weeks Smith notices that Ace is spending more and more of his time in Sukie's room and has become increasingly silent in company. Something is going on between the two, and this is revealed one day when Smith is sitting idly in the kitchen. Ace bursts in looking distraught, he peers anxiously up at the clock and then at Smith.

'Has Sukie been in?' he asks, his face expressing acute anxiety.

'I haven't seen her,' answers Smith. 'She might be in her room but she hasn't been in here.'

Ace looks at the clock, which is just striking five, and there is something akin to fear in his manner. 'She told me to meet her in the kitchen at ten-to-five.' he says, 'and I'm late.'

'Well so what?' says Smith. But Ace is too distressed to even consider the question.

'But she told me to be here,' he says bleakly.

Smith can see that Sukie has profited from her encounter with Jake Naylor. She is testing a newly found power, and Chinese factory-fiddle or no, is already twisting Ace around her little finger. 'You're in for a terrible telling off now,' says Smith with a grin. But Ace is too agitated for levity. He frowns and looks even more upset.

'I know, he says hollowly. 'She's going to be so angry with me.'

Inhibitions

Smith is returning from the local high street where each morning he visits a café for a cup of tea and to keep in touch with the "world" by perusing a newspaper. Some item amongst the usual stupidities has engaged his ire and he is talking to himself aloud as he walks along. He has only recently fallen into this habit, a process which had begun with the odd blurt when arriving at a particularly engaging item. Now however, he cannot be bothered to remove his finger from the trigger and delivers his opinions loudly in a continuous stream somewhere just below the top of his voice. This new habit had worried him at first and thrown a little doubt upon his sanity. But rather than curtail what he is beginning to find rather enjoyable, he has devised a rationalisation for the indulgence.

On the grounds that silent and thus private thoughts could be construed as a little sneaky, and further, cannot really be considered to exist at all unless grounded in some form of physical manifestation, he had finally concluded that thoughts themselves are incomplete unless spoken aloud. This analysis therefore, has absolved him from madness (at least in his own eyes) and freed him to engage wholeheartedly in the practice.

In the privacy of his own room there is nothing to inhibit him, although visitors will sometimes look around on entering and seem a little surprised to find him alone. On the street however, it is another matter entirely, and in spite of his convincing logic he does not push it too far. Seeing someone approaching he lacks the courage to persist, and gradually tones down the volume as they draw near. Once they have passed him by, little by little he turns it up until he is once more going at full spate.

He has by now become something of an expert at this, although on occasion, while engaged upon some especially interesting thought he has been reluctant to use this technique and had cut it rather fine, the result being that the other pedestrian may have caught a few words and regards him somewhat askance as they pass. They suspect that he *had* been talking to himself. However, as far as Smith is concerned *had* is not *is*, and he has enough innate bravado to bear these consequences. On one occasion he had nevertheless, and in spite of all precautions, received a threat from a new and totally unexpected quarter; for, walking along the street one day and loudly engaged upon a particularly juicy thought he had suddenly become aware that someone was passing him, *from behind*!

The man had been wearing trainers and therefore Smith had received no warning of his approach. He had been suffused with embarrassment and his voice had faltered and died. Rationalisation or no, there was no escape; the man obviously *knew* that Smith was talking to himself. Put on his guard, he now casts an occasional glance over his shoulder lest some other sneaky bastard creeps up and catches him out. These early exercises in his apprenticeship now culminate in an event which transforms his whole approach in one fell swoop, and without a shadow of doubt he meets his master.

On the day in question, whilst pursuing his thoughts at probably a higher amplification than usual, he notices a man approaching along the pavement towards him. Gauging the distance expertly, he is just about to lower his volume when he hears, whilst still at some distance, that the man's voice is raised somewhat above his own. The man is talking to himself very loudly indeed and seems not as yet to have noticed Smith. He coughs loudly to give the man time to forestall any embarrassment. The man takes no notice whatsoever and Smith makes a momentous, and for him, daring decision.

'Well if he doesn't stop,' he thinks. 'Then neither will I.'

The man doesn't stop. And though it takes all his nerve neither does Smith. He cannot hear what the man is saying since his own voice, raised now in competition drowns out the other's; but they pass each other still talking to themselves at the top of their voices. Smith walks on, exonerated; vindicated, and suffused now with a perverse and exultant joy.

Nevertheless, he examines this new confirmation with a critical eye. 'Maybe I've started a new social trend,' he thinks, 'and everyone will soon be doing it.' He imagines where this might lead and the prospect is appalling. No one would be able to hear anybody else and the resulting din would be unbearable. 'Perhaps things are better as they are,' the thought continues.

'At least it is still possible to think of something else entirely when being addressed, although in many cases this means that one has no idea what the other person is talking about at all.' This however, he considers a small price to pay and decides, in spite of the sneakiness of the practice, that he will keep his thoughts to himself in public from now on.

Nuts in May II

Here we go gathering nuts in May
On a cold and frosty morning.

A strange little ditty and nonsense to boot, since cold and frosty mornings are rare in May and of nuts there will be as yet none. The residents at the embassy however have pounced with delight on the whimsical rhyme, and when May comes around invite interesting speakers to mount the podium and deliver one of the "Nuts in May" lectures which take place each year.

The subjects of the talks are preferably of the more bizarre kind, whilst nevertheless retaining a modicum of credibility; for instance one of last year's speakers, a French professor of linguistics had entitled his exposition "Hair". He had begun his talk by making a simple observation, 'Have you noticed?' he had asked, 'that the barber's shop is the only place where you pay money and come out with less than when you entered.'

This year alas, April is already upon them and so far only two "nuts" have been gathered. The first, a talk by Dr O'Reilly from the Irish Institute of History entitled, "The Real Gunpowder Plot", an exposé of the true nature of the Guy Fawkes conspiracy. The second, given by a certain Professor Van Horne, who has in his studies of Elizabethan culture stumbled upon some heretofore unnoticed facts about Shakespeare. His lecture, "The Real Shakespeare Mystery," will take place on the second weekend of May, and now, with only one week to go they are looking to snatch a final nut out of the air.

One afternoon a small gathering occurs in the kitchen where they sit around the long refectory table wondering where their third lecturer might come from. Ace has been giving a violin lesson and now he brings his student down to the kitchen for a cup of tea. The young man sits at the end of the table and listens in on the discussion. After a while he breaks in with a question.

'What are the lectures supposed to be about?' he asks.

'Well it's Pataphysics really,' says Caspar. 'The application of impeccable logic to support outrageous and hopefully even unacceptable points of view or fact.'

The young man looks thoughtful, gazing at the wall in front of him with his chin in his hands. 'Mmm,' he says, 'I see.'

'Why?' asks Smith. 'Do you have any ideas you'd like to air?'

'Well, as a matter of fact,' says the man, still looking intently at the wall, 'I think I see what you're after and I might be able to come up with something interesting.'

'What subject?' asks Caspar.

'Mmm,' says the man again, a gleam of mischief coming into his eye. 'I would entitle it: "The Tomb of the Real Unknown Warrior".' This sounds intriguing and without more ado he agrees to give the last lecture in this year's series and thus the programmes can now be designed, copied and sent out from the mailing list.

The Real Gunpowder Plot

Doctor O'Reilly is the director of a Dublin historical society, a tall man with the detached and lofty manner of a headmaster, which oddly conflicts with the rebel gleam in his eye. He steps onto the podium and without more ado launches straight into his lecture: 'I shan't talk for long,' he opens. 'I only intend to speedily run through a series of historical events without going into too much detail, after which we might discuss the ramifications of what I am going to tell you.

'In present times,' he begins, 'the general public has become aware of the machinations of power. Through the media and press, the deviousness which power demands from those who hold and wish to keep it, has become glaringly obvious even to the common man. I am, however, going to speak of a time when politics was a matter for Court and Parliament alone, when the common man lived his life without this knowledge and received at face value whatever he was told by his betters, believing without question the word of the King: God bless him.

'Tonight I will attempt to show how the natural arising of folk-myth in a culture can, and has, been manipulated by government propaganda into producing figures of national derision which then, having served their purpose, go on to become entrenched in the hierarchy of folk-heroes and villains. I am going to leave Father Christmas out of this, since he seems to be a figure upon whom no suspicion is likely to fall, and I mention his name merely in order to indicate the direction of this enquiry. One such folk-myth might serve as an example of the syndrome, although not having made a wholly indelible mark and long since faded from sight, it illustrates how this sleight of hand is done.

'I am speaking now of Tom Paine, a man who, having been a prime mover in the French Revolution, then went on to perform the same service in America's War of Independence. An irritating thorn in the side of the British government of the time, he was given the full treatment of dirty politics and demonised to such an extent that Tom Paine, the champion of good sense and the rights of the common man, was through political propaganda, transformed into public enemy number one and burned in effigy throughout the land; he then entered folk-law as the new bogeyman. "Behave yourself or Tom Paine will get you," was a common threat wielded over their recalcitrant children by mothers in that time. However, he only held this satanic position for a short period before being driven from centre stage by a new contender: Napoleon Bonaparte — "Watch out or Boney will come for you."

'The most interesting example of this syndrome and the focus of tonight's talk is a gentleman from an even earlier time whose myth nevertheless has survived even to the present day, and, through political propaganda is seen as the villain who tried to blow up Parliament, although actually it was the House of Lords. Like Father Christmas and the Easter Bunny he appears every year, and unlike them is burned in effigy amidst much pyrotechnics. Guy Fawkes, the dupe and scapegoat for a conspiracy of far-reaching proportions in international politics.

'In order to examine this figure more closely we must look back to a time before investigative journalism, before in fact any journalism at all, when only one story, and one story alone, was disseminated to engage the simple minds of the population at large. Most of what is now known about this sequence of events has come about lately from the scholarly collating and piecing together of family letters written at the time, some stored unseen through many generations in attic trunks and storerooms. Letter writing was then the only medium of communication between the far flung families and much correspondence concerning the issue has recently come to light to expose at last the machinations of the government of the day.

'It is 1605 and King James I is on the throne, having just succeeded Elizabeth I and inherited her anti-Catholic policies. With the monasteries sacked and their lands seized for the state, the Monarchy and Parliament now greedily eye the vast estates of the Catholic gentry. Moves towards their sequestration must nevertheless be made with extreme caution, since any further suppression if made overtly, might call forth an Armada and thus lead to war with Spain, who, through her spies keeps a close watch on the plight of English Catholics. Forbidden already to stand for Parliament, and represented only in the House of Lords where they might speak but not vote, any further disenfranchisement might lead to serious consequences and England, depleted by its conflicts in support of the Protestant Dutch in the low countries has not at the moment the wherewithal to fight another war.

'Enter Guido Fawkes, a military gentleman with many years service in the armies of Spain. He is a lapsed Catholic who still retains many contacts among the leading Catholic families of the time. Through these connections he meets Robert Catesby, Gentleman, of Ashby St Ledgers and the mastermind of a plot to blow up the House of Lords when it reconvenes on the fifth of November 1605. The King and Queen will die in the explosion and a simultaneous uprising be fomented in the Midlands, together with the abduction of the King's young daughter Elizabeth, who will replace the King as a puppet Queen under a Catholic Regent. Fawkes however, is in the pay of the government and reports all his findings to Sir Robert Cecil, Earl of Salisbury and Secretary of State, who sets his attorney general Sir Edward Coke to investigate the further reaches of the plot. Now Cecil lays his careful trap. Guido Fawkes, using his family connections and taking advantage of the many invitations which he receives from the Catholic aristocracy will reveal the plot to his hosts and seek their help in the matter.

'In return for this service Fawkes will receive certain monies and extensive estates in the new colonies of Virginia. It will of course be necessary for him to be arrested, tried and condemned with the other plotters to safeguard the integrity of the conspiracy and hide the government's hand in the affair. Then, at the last moment, a Herald will appear, as was not uncommon in those days, to grant him the King's pardon and he will be transported to America, never to return. Guido Fawkes accepted these terms and began to go about his devious work. Naturally the Catholic gentry whom he approached with the plot had shied away in horror at such a dangerous undertaking but, a fatal error, had refrained from betraying a fellow Catholic.

'On the fifth of November 1605 the plot was sprung, and Guy Fawkes was arrested as planned in the vaults beneath the Lords, and since the plotters had already been infiltrated at a lower level by government agents, the "barrels of gunpowder" had contained nothing but earth. A cover story was then fabricated telling of Fawkes' betrayal of his accomplices and those in the know under torture, and their arrests followed immediately. According to the law of the land, knowledge of a plot against the King without informing his Majesty was considered High Treason, and falling straight into Cecil's trap they were forced to confess this knowledge.

'After a show trial in which all eight of the major figures had been condemned, the first four had been hanged in the churchyard of St Paul's, and the second four, with Fawkes as agreed, to go last, were to be hanged in Old Palace Yard at Westminster, since it was thought that otherwise Catholics might justifiably accuse the government of desecrating the holy places.

'Imagine the scene then: The first three condemned men have already mounted the ladder and hang jerking and gasping at the end of ropes, and now it is Guido's turn. He waits confidently for the King's Herald to step forth with his proclamation of a pardon and casts his eye expectantly over the crowds that swarm around the scaffold.

"Traitor!" they shout, and... "Dirty Papist dog!" And the cry is taken up among a sea of bloodthirsty faces.

"Any minute now," he thinks, as the hangman's firm grip closes around his arm.

"Come now Sir," says the man in his ear. But Guido hangs back, surely now the Herald will appear. The grip on his arm tightens and..."Come Sir if thou wilst," comes the hangman's voice again. "The sooner ye mount the sooner 'twill be over."

'Guido is desperate as, unable further to resist he mounts the ladder, and now a terrible truth dawns upon him. As he feels the rough rope slip about his neck he knows that there will be no Herald to bring him succour. He is betrayed. For knowing what he does how can the government let him loose? Virginia too will be infiltrated by spies from Spain's possessions in the South, and one slip of the tongue, should it reach the Spanish Court, may plunge England into war. Poor Guido's enlightenment is soon however mercifully cut short, and then he too jerks and twists at the end of a rope.

'His fate we now all know, but the reason for it has been carefully hidden and Guy Fawkes seems as firmly ensconced in the national consciousness as Father Christmas, a man who only realised at the last moment the dreadful fact that power has *no* scruples. However, in spite of the facts that support this historical revision, it is doubtful if the truth will have any effect on the myth, which will continue to let off its fireworks each year and burn what is certainly the right man, albeit for entirely the wrong reason.'

The Real Shakespeare Mystery

Professor Van Horne is quite obviously unhinged. From the moment he steps onto the podium it can be seen that he contains an almost messianic intensity. He glares at his audience from beneath shaggy brows; his white hair has an electrical wildness, and his large ears stick out like open window shutters. He stands silently for a while as if choosing with care his opening words.

'The title of my lecture,' he begins, 'is "The Real Shakespeare Mystery", which itself may lead you off on the wrong track. Let me explain. I am not speaking of the authorship controversy, for whoever wrote Shakespeare will of course always be "Shakespeare". The name is so deeply embedded, and the literary correlations now so finely woven, that whether it be Edward de Vere, Kit Marlowe or Norman Jenkins of Dagenham, the work will be forever known by that name.

'I am putting that whole question aside tonight since as far as I am concerned it is of no interest *WHATSOEVER*!' There is a small table on the podium and he brings his fist down upon it with a crash at the last word.

'The mystery I am going to speak of has similar echoes, but the subject matter is of far greater import and I will introduce it now by making a statement. To those who find the statement of little or no interest I would say: Then leave now and don't waste my time!' He is almost shouting now and brings his fist down hard upon the table again.

There is a silence in which many delighted looks are surreptitiously exchanged among the members of the audience. They have collected a most interesting nut and the evening looks to be very entertaining. The professor draws himself up, takes a deep breath and announces:

'Shakespeare never wrote a sonnet in his life!'

A subdued muttering arises from those present, for his statement has sent a small shock amongst them and Tralee is on her feet at once. She is a Shakespearian *aficionado* and will leap passionately to his defence should some small slur be occasioned upon the Bard.

'You may be a professor,' she heckles, 'but to make such a philistine statement about the poet who enlightened our culture with such a shower of heavenly insights doesn't say much for your taste.'

The professor smiles, 'I admire your loyalty,' he says. 'But you see I am not speaking of the poetic content, or the shower of heavenly insights of which you have so eloquently, and might I add, so poetically reminded us; I too consider the contents of the "sonnets" sublime. I am speaking however, of the form in which the poems are cast, which is a quite different argument.'

Tralee subsides, she is unwilling to accept the separation of content from form, but not wanting to make trouble at the moment gives him the benefit of the doubt, while the professor, having fielded her heckle successfully has now been put on his guard, and keeps a wary eye upon Tralee as he continues.

'Before I clarify my statement it is first desirable to know something of the sonnet form, and how the English version came about. If you pay attention and listen to what I have to say, you will at the end of the evening be able to identify a sonnet from more common-or-garden poems, and what's more, even tell what kind of sonnet it is. As we know, rhyme is the most fundamental device upon which poetry can be constructed, the last word in each line providing the key. And I paraphrase for example:

Mary had a little tent a
Its colour white as snow b
Everywhere that Mary went a
The tent was sure to go b

'A simple, even childish arrangement which nevertheless as a rhyme is difficult to avoid. Then — bursting into the poetic firmament came the Italian sonnet, unleashed by Petrarch, and gaining rapid success on the continent during the sixteenth and seventeenth centuries it brought a new rhyming scheme. Instead of the pedestrian a-b-a-b, it twisted the order and became a-b-b-a. And thus:

Mary had a little tent a
Its colour white as snow b
The tent was sure to go b
Everywhere that Mary went a

The Italians then doubled this quatrain of four lines to:
a-b-b-a-a-b-b-a
to produce the Octave, or first eight lines of the sonnet.
Next comes the six lines of the Sestet.
c-d-c-d-c-d
Or: a Quatrain c-d-d-c and a Couplet e-e.

'So we have an eight, a four and a two, a reducing figure rather like a downward-spointing triangle, which is the very reason why a sonnet has fourteen lines. A fourteen-line poem however, is not necessarily a sonnet, since such poems already fell into a well established genre of their own: namely the Quatorzain.

'The Italian or Petrarchan sonnet form was introduced to the English court by Thomas Wyatt, and it was then transformed by the Earl of Surrey into what we now know as the English Sonnet. This transformation was unavoidable, for while in the Italian language there are a plethora of rhyming words: Spaghetti, Macaroni, Bughatti, Maseratti, Baloney, Vermicelli etc; English has a dearth of such correspondences. Moon, spoon, June, and that's about it. The difficulty of finding four As and four Bs for the first octave speedily used up the available rhymes, and thus Surrey broke the octave into two quatrains, and the English sonnet form emerged as three quatrains and a couplet:

a-b-b-a c-d-d-c e-f-f-e g-g

'This process was of course a major issue at the time, and later courtiers like Raleigh vied with each other to produce the finest and impress the Queen with their brilliance. Playwrights and poets too joined the fray and competition was fierce. Surrey's earlier innovation was, under the circumstances, entirely justified, since without it the form might have quickly been strangled by the demands of the Italian octave. The next change however, had no such justification; the reduction of a-b-b-a back to a-b-a-b and our old nursery friend "Mary".

'Of course such further simplification was bound to occur as poets struggled with the form whilst still trying to remain within the parameters of the sonnet; but it cannot be seen as anything more than a dumbing-down of the rules. The writing of a classical Petrarchan sonnet taxes the ingenuity of the greatest of poets, and even up to the present day it is still attempted.

'One can see then, that in the midst of this highly visible controversy poets might pen perhaps one, or even two, of the dumbed-down and childishly simple version as a kind of poetic statement, or protest at the strictures of the form, and indeed Wyatt himself used it. But to deny the challenge of the Petrarchan form altogether would be something no poet worth his salt would have possibly contemplated, since he would certainly lose credibility amongst his peers for such simplistic efforts. And yet, one amongst the masterful poets of the time did exactly that; not once, but one hundred and fifty-four times. Every single one of Shakespeare's "sonnets" is written in that dumbed-down form:

a-b-a-b c-d-c-d e-f-e-f g-g.

'How could this be so? How could that genius playwright have been satisfied with such a simple format without once trying his hand at the more taxing Petrarchan sonnet? How could a man of his vast talents not have taken up the challenge? But no, he wrote one hundred and fifty-four "sonnets", reduced in form to the commonest of denominators, until nothing remained of the original, and that which is left no sonnet at all. This then brings us to the question to which my lecture is addressed: Why?'

The professor's audience have been impressed by this avalanche of information and his question hangs in a thick silence.

'All right,' he says. 'Let us look at a few of the reasons that might explain his tardiness: One: Ignorance,' he glares at the audience as if daring any to dispute him.

'Is this possible?' he asks. 'Could he perhaps have been so besotted with writing his plays that the controversy around the emerging sonnet form completely passed him by, to such an extent that he was unaware of the technicalities of the issue? Had he lived an isolated life such ignorance might be acceptable. But he did not. London in those times was a hotbed of poets and playwrights all vying for attention and struggling to conquer the difficulties of the Petrarchan form, while giving birth at the same time to the new and more poet-friendly English version. One need look no further than some of his closest friends. Ben Jonson for instance, who himself took up the challenge with his sonnets to Lady Margaret Wroth, which are cast in the pure Petrarchan mode. Or Richard Barnfield, another close friend, who did the same with his "Cynthia" sonnets. Then there was Sir Philip Sidney and later John Donne, both writing Italian sonnets. In the midst of this poetic upheaval, how could Shakespeare have remained ignorant for one moment? Therefore we have no choice but to discard the notion.

'Let us look then for another possible reason: that of "Cocking a Snook". Perhaps he was giving the finger to all this prissy Italian stuff, reducing the form to its lowest common denominator as a gesture of his contempt for such strictures. But surely such a gesture need be stated only once or twice to make the point, a common syndrome in every art form.

'Take Marcel Duchamp's famous urinal for instance, an artistic statement of great validity, and one necessary in a world where pretentiousness is a common fault. However, he needed to make the statement only once to illustrate his point, for to exhibit a hundred and fifty-four urinals might have been considered overkill, although this view has been largely ignored in our own time by those that followed after, giving birth to the present glorification of rubbish which now exists in Duchamp's shadow. No, this excuse won't wash. But there is another interesting possibility.

'Perhaps he considered the Italian sonnet a dying form and no longer important. But we have only to look at the long list of poets who in subsequent generations have pitted their skill and produced fine Petrarchan sonnets to see the fallacy of that. From Byron to Keats, who wrote seventeen of them; to Wordsworth, Coleridge and Christina Rossetti, whose "Sonnet of Sonnets" contains twenty-eight pure Petrarchan poems, and so on up to modern times with Auden and Ezra Pound. For four hundred and fifty years the Petrarchan form has been a constant challenge, never losing its allure, and therefore hardly a dying form.

The professor's eyebrows are working overtime and his eyes glitter manically.

'Well,' he asks. 'Any ideas?'

There is silence for a while until Morgiana puts up her hand. 'Maybe he couldn't be bothered,' she suggests. She laces this proposition with a few choice giggles as if in compensation for her cheek. But the professor is impervious to the giggles and her offering gets right up his nose.

'Couldn't be bothered?' he snaps. 'A man who couldn't be bothered would hardly have written a hundred and fifty-four quatorzains in the first place, even though he did call them sonnets.'

There falls another silence in which Smith decides to give a little support to Morgiana's bolshie attitude.

'Maybe he was an Asperger,' he suggests. But there are no flies on the professor; he has been there before him.

'No Asperger could have written the "Dream",' he says dismissively. Again he sternly surveys his audience. 'Any other brilliant suggestions?' he enquires.

'Maybe he didn't write them at all.'

The dolorous voice belongs to Tiberius; he sits at the back well hidden with his head sunk between his knees and staring steadily downwards. His words excite the professor. 'What, what?' he shouts striding up and down while glancing keenly around. 'Who said that?'

'What does it matter?' answers Tiberius, still not looking up.

The professor likes this. 'Just so, just so,' he says, looking pleased. 'We have come at last to the real question: If Shakespeare didn't write them, then, who did? And more importantly: Why?'

'Let us first address ourselves to the why, since if we can discover that then the answer itself may reveal the who. Consider for a moment the human frailties that afflict the world of art and letters, even to the present day. Amid the struggle for recognition and fame, jealousy and envy undoubtedly haunt the path of those who, rising above this clamour succeed in making their unique mark upon a wayward and fickle public. This natural dissidence among others in the same field who, although perhaps possessing a similar or even greater talent, fail to reach an equal eminence; and might well remain a minor background annoyance, providing no catalyst emerges to galvanise this general angst into action. In Shakespeare's time he was the man. The anointed one, whose name was synonymous with the world of theatre and poetry. Famous in his own time at Court and on stages throughout the land. Consumed perhaps by the fire of his creativity, and sitting very pretty with the world without, he became a little careless, for at the age of thirty-four in 1599, he published a folio of twenty poems entitled "The Passionate Pilgrim" under the name of William Shakespeare. There was an immediate uproar led by his friend Richard Barnfield, then aged thirty-six, who claimed that two of the poems were his. — And here, I suggest, we have our catalyst!

'Modern scholarship now recognises only five of these poems as authentically from Shakespeare's pen, while two and possibly three are indeed Richard Barnfield's. The remaining twelve are anybody's guess. One can only speculate on the strength of Barnfield's feelings at this outrageous and blatant plagiarism. He might also have had no difficulty finding like-minded accomplices to evolve a scheme and redress the balance; bring William to heel and take him down a peg or two in the process. Certainly Ben Jonson would have joined the plot; his views on Shakespeare were well known, for when told that the Bard never scratched out a line he was heard to remark: "Would that he had scratched a thousand." And further that: "He flowed with that facility that sometimes it was necessary he should be stopped."

'Well he would say that wouldn't he?' It is Katarina, who although maintaining her usual impeccable facade is not above a little heckling herself.

'Oh yes,' says the professor, a little taken aback. 'And why is that?'

Katarina had read some Jonson in her student days and is primed to go. 'Because his plays, unlike Shakespeare's, were written to be readily understood. They are as clear and relevant now as they were in his own time, and for that reason were deliberately lacking in Shakespeare's flamboyance. That's why.'

The professor claps his hands together boyishly, delighted with Katarina's observation and sensing an ally for his view he continues.

'Exactly, exactly,' he says, rubbing his hands together in satisfaction. 'Ben Jonson was also known to be of the opinion that Shakespeare's plays marked the beginning of a decline in English theatre. Such views might well have brought him out in support of Barnfield, and there would likely to have been others of similar ilk. Take Christopher Marlowe, then aged thirty-four, whose lines from *Hero and Leander* were plagiarised by Shakespeare to appear in *As You Like It.* He can certainly be considered a likely contender, and being the adventurous soul he was would hardly have turned down such an opportunity to turn the tables.

'It is my contention that a plot was hatched among several disgruntled men of letters to write between them, and then to publish, a collection of "sonnets" in the simple dumbed-down version under the name of William Shakespeare. None amongst them of course would publish such simplistic concoctions under their own names, lest they become objects of ridicule amongst their peers. Naming Shakespeare as the author however, should have made him the laughing-stock of London.

'Unfortunately they were too late, for the great name was already branded deeply upon the national consciousness and was therefore impervious to such attacks. Like Picasso, anything which flowed from his hand was already seized upon ecstatically and revered beyond any criticism. And so the plot backfired, with Shakespeare, far from being taken down a peg, exalted to even greater heights, and such is the irony that in our time should anyone speak of "The Sonnets", they can surely be referring to no other than William Shakespeare.

'This brings me back to the statement with which I opened this lecture and with which I intend to close it. The statement is justified as we have seen by two allegations: First, "The Sonnets" are not sonnets at all, but more properly "quatorzains", and secondly, no poetic genius of Shakespeare's calibre could have undertaken such an undemanding and overstated exercise. Therefore I say again: Shakespeare never wrote a sonnet in his life. He may have written many fourteen line poems, but that is as if I owe somebody five pounds and repay them with five potatoes, claiming that since there are five, our debt is settled.'

In the face of such erudition no further quibbles arise from the audience, and the professor slowly nods his head in satisfaction. 'One more thing,' he says. 'Having delved so deeply into the technicalities of the sonnet form, it would be remiss of me to leave tonight without offering one of my own. It is cast in the original Petrarchan mode and illustrates the argument with which we have been engaged in.'

The professor takes a piece of paper from his pocket, clears his throat and begins to read:

Sonnet to W S

Fourteen lines doth not a sonnet make
Much more required to shape that mode
And form the old Italian ode
Preserve the rules for Petrarch's sake.
So if we would tradition break
Upon the path Lord Surrey rode
It should remain within that code
While following his Lordship's wake.
But yet, an English sonnet must
Contain one octave, one quatrain
Seek twice four rhymes and seek in vain
Has no resource but break that trust
Thus split the octave in two parts
And free the poet to his arts.

Sonnet To A Hat

When the lecture is over and the professor has departed Smith goes up to his room. Much inspired by the evening's revelations he decides to try his hand at this intriguing exercise and write a sonnet himself. Putting pen to paper and after much head-scratching he writes:

In which a gentleman of humble birth
Takes umbrage at his wife's new hat.

'Ere, watcha fink yer doin' wearin' that?
It looks just like a saucepan on yer 'ed
The colour too, a mucky shade of red
It's 'orrible, I really hate that hat.
So take it off, I'd rather I was dead
My mates will laugh if we go walkin' out
You pair of silly buggers,' they will shout
That hat will lose me all of my street cred.'
'Don't talk to me like that you bloody lout
This hat's the only one I've got to wear
While you go out and spend your dosh on beer

I do with less and not much left to flout.'
'Blimey, love, just pop down to the deli
We'll stay at home tonight and watch the telly.'

The Tomb Of The Real Unknown Soldier

Tonight is the last in this year's series, and it is the turn of Ace's violin student Allen to hold forth. He asks for a small armchair to be placed on the podium from which, dressed in a simple dark suit he tells his story.

He begins by explaining that a few months before he had received a letter from an old university friend who had found something of interest while sorting through his deceased parents' belongings. His friend had been very mysterious about the discovery but implied that, knowing his interest in such things, a visit might prove well worth his while. He had been intrigued by the offer and set a day or so aside to pay his friend a visit, and on his arrival his friend had wasted no time in bringing out his find.

It is a tattered old notebook written in indelible pencil on the now yellowing pages. His friend had explained that the notebook was an account of his last days on the battlefields of Flanders, written by his great-grandfather, Lance Corporal Arthur Howers of the Rifle Brigade, at the conclusion of the First World War. While waiting for demobilisation his battalion had been set the task of guarding the many ammunition dumps around the Arras area. With the war now over and restrictions on keeping a diary lifted, he had decided to write down his impressions of France before going home. However, amongst his various observations amongst the shattered trees and rusty barbed wire of a shell-scarred plain of treacherous mud, one episode contains an event with truly explosive connotations.

His friend had allowed him to read the diary and even copy the most interesting parts, but wisely, as will be revealed, he would not let the original out of his hand, and so inflammable are the contents that he is even considering the possibility of destroying it altogether.

The speaker leans forward in his armchair and takes from his pocket a small notebook. He holds it up. 'This,' he says, 'is a word-for-word transcript of my friend's great grandfather's notebook.' He settles back and opening the notebook begins to read:

'*Wednesday. Lucheux. St Pol. Arras.*

Same old thing. Up and down up and down all day keeping me eye on the sentries. What they want guards on this lot for I don't know, there's nobody here to nick anything anyway, just mud for miles around.

Thursday. Same place.

Got clobbered for special guard-duty tomorrow, Sergeant Rowley told me to smarten meself up and get a polish on me boots. 'There's some big brass coming down from H.Q. so I want you well turned out.' he says. So tonight I'll have me work cut out getting some of this mud off meself.

Friday. Same place.

The Sergeant came and got me early this morning. 'Not bad,' he says when he's finished giving me the once over and he leads off right away, threading his way between the shell-holes two or three miles it must have been till we gets to a wood. Not much left of the trees but on the other side is the Chapel of Pol. It's not knocked about too much, except of course the windows is all blown in and some of the roof has gone. The Sergeant pushes the door open and we goes in. A section of stretcher-bearers are bringing in some bodies, lying them down on two trestle tables and covering them with Union Jack flags. Four of them there were side by side on the tables.

'Come on then,' says the Sergeant to me. 'We have to make sure there are no bits missing, everything must be right when the officers get here and I can't trust these dozy bastards.'

He begins lifting the flags off one by one, and when he gets to the third body he gives an angry shout and calls in some stretcher bearers.

'What's this then?' he roars. 'This one's got two left arms. He picks up an arm and throws it on their stretcher. 'Go and find a right arm.' he says. The bearers go off grumbling that they can't see what difference it makes anyway. But the Sergeant won't have any of it. 'Get on with it!' he shouts and then continues checking the bodies. When he gets to the last one I couldn't believe me eyes. It was Private George Philpots, who I hadn't seen since the Vimy Ridge days. I knowed him anyway on account of his ginger hair. His face was a bit messed up but I recognised him straight away and the Sergeant saw me gaping.

'What you looking at then?' he says. 'Haven't you seen enough dead 'uns to last you a lifetime?' So I tells him it's George on the end there, who was in my platoon at Neuve Chapelle and Vimy Ridge.

'Oh is that so?' says the Sergeant. 'Then you'd better just forget all about it see. The officers are coming up here to choose an unidentified body from this lot and you'd better not upset the apple-cart.'

One of the stretcher bearers come in then with a right arm and the sergeant takes it over to the table and fixes it more or less in place. Then he steps back and takes a look. 'That looks all right,' he says. 'As long as they don't muck about with it.' He straightens all the flags up so they looks neat and we goes outside and he locks the door.

'Right me lad,' he says. 'You wait here until you see the staff-cars coming and mind you give a good snappy salute, these are bigwigs from the Army Council and we don't want to upset them.' Then off he goes along the duckboards leading up to the road.

Once he was gone I took it easy, I could see the road from where I was so would get plenty of warning. I pulled an empty ammo-box against the wall and sat down to have a fag while I thought about poor old George. I'd known him as a kid, he only lived a few streets away and we both went to the same school. When we left he got a job at the local milk-depot and I'd often seen him leading his nag around the streets on me way to work of a morning. Anyways, he started dipping into the till and fiddling his books. But he got rumbled right quick, not being very bright he hadn't covered himself. So he got given the choice of two years' hard or take the King's shilling. So that's how George joined up, and now he's lying under that flag and won't be delivering any more milk.

I sat watching the road and the long line of ambulances from the War Graves Commission which blocked it all along one side. They were loading up with bodies brought in by the stretcher parties who were crossing backwards and forwards like ants across the mud as far as the eye could see. I thanked God to be on such a cushy number and not out there digging those poor buggers out of that muck. After a while I see two staff-cars and a special ambulance stop on the road, so I put out me fag and got meself into position beside the door.

Two Staff Officers and the Sergeant got out of the cars and walked along the duckboards with two bearers with a stretcher between them following. The officers looked like poncey peacocks strutting along with boots as polished as new conkers and red hatbands and tabs the only bit of colour for miles around. I comes to attention when they gets close, then shouldered arms and slapped me butt so hard I hurt me hand. The Sergeant comes forward and unlocks the door and in goes the officers. They're not in there for two minutes before one of them comes to the door. He has a silk handkerchief up to his nose and doesn't seem too happy. He beckons to the two bearers and they trots forward and goes in. Two or three minutes more and out they come again. I gives another smart salute but I needn't have bothered, the officers looked as if they were about to throw up and left in quite a hurry with the stretcher-bearers following with a body. Back into the cars they get still waving their silk handkerchiefs around while the bearers put the body in a coffin, threw the flag over it, puts it in the ambulance and they was gone.

The Sergeant comes back to me. 'Come on,' he says, 'Let's get rid of the ones they left,' and we goes inside.

I only needed one look to see they'd taken George, and so I mentions it to the Sergeant. 'They've taken George Philpots,' I says. 'What are they going to do with him?'

'Oh, that's right,' he says. 'You knowed that one didn't you.' He goes over to the door and shouts over a stretcher detail. 'Get rid of these,' he orders, pointing at the three bodies left on the tables and they go to work. Then he turns back to me. 'They're going to take that body back to Blighty tonight, there's a French destroyer waiting at Boulogne to take it over, and then they're going to bury it in Westminster Abbey,' he says. 'It's going to be the tomb of the Unknown Soldier. If you've got any different ideas about that you'd be sensible to keep them to yourself. So keep your bloody trap shut tight about it. All right?'

I saw what he meant. If one word of what I know gets out my life won't be worth living. I felt sorry for George's mum though, such a nice old lady and she would be so proud to know her son George, the ex-milkman, was going to be buried in Westminster Abbey. I'll be going home soon, but even if I see her in the street I won't say a word. She would be bound to go around boasting about her son George, and then the cat will be out of the bag. The Sergeant knows but he'll soon forget it, and me, I'm not saying nothing. I'll probably burn this diary when I get back, just in case.

'The interesting part of the diary ends here,' says the speaker. 'And fortunately or not as the case may be, he seems to have forgotten all about it in the aftermath. The diary ended up in a drawer in my friend's parent's house, and there it lay for years until he found it.' Alan lays the notebook down on the table.

'And that's the whole story as far as I know it,' he says. 'I hope you found these revelations as interesting as I did, but as to what, if anything to do about it, my guess is as good as yours.' He finishes and stands up. There come a storm of questions from the audience but he brushes them all aside. 'I'll leave the transcription with you,' he says. 'I have already made a copy for myself, but I must go straight away because I'm playing a concert in Manchester tomorrow and have to get up early in the morning.'

He gets down from the podium, puts on his overcoat and with a hurried farewell takes his leave.

Denouément

Later, the embassy faculty drink tea in the kitchen and discuss the evening's lecture.

'There's going to be such an uproar when this gets out.' says Morgiana, and all agree that it will cause a seismic earthquake amongst the Great and the Good.'

'The Queen will be terribly upset,' says Tralee. 'All those years paying her respects at the tomb of a dodgy ex-milkman.'

'The first thing they'll do,' says Smith. 'Is march up to Westminster Abbey, dig up the tomb and throw poor George Philpots out on his ear.'

'Well the only way it can get out is if the newspapers get wind of it, and we have no evidence apart from a copy of the diary, which anybody could have written,' says Caspar.

Ace is saying nothing, deep in thought he is staring intently at the wall in front of him. Suddenly he knits his brows into a frown as if at some inner puzzle, then cautiously he frames a tentative question. 'Alan was sitting right here wasn't he,' he says. 'On the evening when he first suggested doing his lecture. He was sitting right where I am now.'

'So what?' says Tiberius.

'Well look,' says Ace.

All eyes in the kitchen follow his finger and Smith gets up to take a look. There hanging on the wall is a large framed photograph of a stern military-looking gentleman which had been found some time ago in a cupboard in one of the upper rooms. At the bottom of the picture and written in gold with a careful hand is the legend: *George Philpots, President Guild of Transcultural Studies. (1923—1928)*

Smith had written it there himself some years before when they had first moved in, and were in the process of creating a phantom lineage of past presidents. 'Bloody Hell,' he mutters. No wonder the name had sounded familiar.

'He must have made the whole thing up,' he says.

Shibboleth

The last lecture in the *Nuts in May* series has given Smith much food for thought. The sheer audacity of the straight-faced presentation has inspired him to look in this direction himself, and he casts around for a similar outrageous subject on which he may, next year, give a lecture himself. He hunts among the firmly ensconced shibboleths which stand like immovable rocks in the ever-changing stream of cultural forms, and homes immediately in on one such example which seems tailor-made for his purpose:

Supposing there were to emerge a previously undiscovered and delectable body of work from an unknown German poet. Scholars from Heidelberg to Frankfurt might be thrown into ecstasies of excitement by the magnificent verses, and European critics declare from on high that not since Goethe has such purity of line and impeccable form been expressed. Supposing further that at the height of its fame the poetry was discovered to be from the hand of Adolf Hitler. How the critics would frantically back-pedal: 'No, no' they would loudly clamour. 'I didn't think they were *that* good.'

The idea amuses Smith, and after all, he had once seen some reproductions of Adolf's watercolours and had considered them not without insight, and certainly marginally better than those of Prince Charles. He begins working on the idea and wonders what Hitler's poetry might have been like had he written any. With all the sensitivity of youth the poems could well have been of a pastoral nature and full of innocent romance. But then, even at this early stage in his life, the dark angel that was later to possess him could well have been already lurking beneath the surface to show its hand in subtle ways not apparent at first glance, but easily detectable by the discerning eye.

Smith tries his hand at a Hitler poem:

Dark Angel

The Little Cloud *(by Adolf Hitler)*

Hurry, hurry little cloud
Across the deep blue sky
In which, at night, the stars are hung
Pig-Dog Englanders
Achtung!

Ace

'Listen to this,' says Ace, and raising his violin to his chin he draws the bow across the strings and Smith hears an entirely new sound. At its core is a pure and delicate tone which fades towards its edges into a whisper so faint that Smith can barely detect it. Ace lowers the violin.

'I've fitted it with gut strings,' he says. 'They have a softer effect than the edginess of metallic strings and release a whole new spectrum of resonances.'

'It sounds fantastic,' says Smith, and indeed it does, but he is on a mission and presses Ace a little.

'You don't have to do very much,' he says hopefully, but Ace is no longer listening.

'*And* I can still get my wolf-tone,' and raising the violin he applies the bow to a string and presses down hard. The sound is so painful that Smith is forced to put his hands over his ears.

'Not only that,' says Ace. 'But I've discovered that the gut strings are very good for backing poetry, since the softer vibrations blend well with the human voice.'

He picks up a tattered and coverless book of poetry. 'I've been experimenting with some of these. See what you think.'

He begins to play, and the violin lays down a poignant setting for the poem which he reads as he plays.

Whatever they said,
Whatever they did,
Everyone just laughed.
So, to have the last laugh,
The clowns turned nasty.*

As he reaches the last line his bow bears heavily down and the ghastly wolf-tone screeches forth.

'See what I mean?' says Ace. 'I can punctuate the punch lines.'

'Yes I see what you mean,' says Smith. 'But would the poet approve?'

'I don't know who the poet is,' says Ace. But it doesn't really matter; he must be a nutter anyway to write stuff like that. The point is that the violin makes anything sound good. Listen to this one.'

But Smith is already half-way out of the door, Ace's way of punctuating the poems with his wolf-tone may well be the very height of surrealism, but the experience is not necessarily a pleasant one.

* From *Night of the Child*, By Allan Samuel

The Golden Road

Poetry frequently brings subversity to the salon of the embassy, where readings often take place. One such, to celebrate a summer solstice, has attracted a good bunch of songsters to the podium, and now Ram O'Neil occupies that spot.

'Gree - ee - ow.' He is reciting a shaman's chant, and his voice grows louder as he warms to his task.

'GREE - EE - OW!' He bellows again, and then.

'*Mmumm* -EE - Ow!'

'What about some real poetry then?' Some of the other poets present are annoyed with Ram's choice of material and impatient to mount the podium themselves they try to shout him down. But Ram is in full song and ignores these barbaric interjections, until, depleted of his fiery inspiration, he ends with a long low '*Hiiissssss*.'

Now, seizing the opportunity, a poet who accompanies himself on swanee-whistle jumps to his feet and eager to perform makes for the podium. But he is outwitted by P. B. Rivers who gets there first and begins reciting Flecker's *Golden Road to Samarkand*.

The poem's splendid cadences ring around the salon and Smith, listening from the garden through an open window, is drawn along the neurone paths of memory to recollect his own long-ago travels on the road to that fabled city.

Romany Rai

Dartmoor is very much larger on the ground than can be seen on any map. The distant hilly horizon fades into a low mist from which an occasional craggy tor breaks through. A path winds its way across this bleak landscape, cutting between the hills and tracing a snaky path through the wiry heather.

Along this path a distant figure trudges leading a small pony and cart. It is accompanied by a girl dressed in a psychedelic patchwork of grubby silks and satins, while some distance behind comes a young fellow riding a chestnut gelding. The man who leads the cart is Harry Flame, the girl is Miriam, and Smith rides the gelding whose name is Babylon.

The little band have travelled up from St Germans on the Cornish coast and are making for the vicinity of Chagford, where they hope to meet up with more of their kind who are camped there. It is the summer of 1967, and travelling in this way has captured the imagination of a sizeable group of hippies. Drawn mostly from the environs of the Kings Road and Chelsea, they have the wherewithal to be the owners of such expensive things as horses. Although Smith is penniless he had attached himself earlier in the year to one such motley gang, borrowing the pony and cart from Count Marco de la Paloma, who leads the group they are now seeking. Babylon has been obtained with a loan from Miriam, from a gypsy at the Exeter horse-fair, and Smith spends as much time as possible on his back. Since saddles are regarded as decadent and bareback riding puts much strain on the coccyx, it is necessary to accustom said bone to this painful new relationship as frequently as possible.

Harry Flame had turned up at St Germans expressing a desire to travel along with the cart, and for the past few days has kept his gaze gloomily fixed on the ground in front of him, and rarely speaking a word in the process. He had however, briefly dropped this pessimistic view when passing through Princetown, with its great grim prison standing like a fortress upon the high ground. Their path had led them under the very walls and front gates of the prison where the guards could be seen strutting around, an occasional white face peering from the small grated windows that dot the steep granite walls. Miriam has a portable recorder and a tape of Donovan on the cart which she insists on playing at full blast as they pass the prison. The strains of *Mellow Yellow* echo across the heather and bounce back from the prison walls. Dismounting from Babylon and tying him to the back of the cart, Smith had began dancing a jig to the music, while Miriam, her crazy chiffon fluttering had lost no time joining him. On the hill above the forces of oppression had observed these capers with disdain, and a few more white faces had appeared to join their fellows at the windows.

Even Harry was inspired by this joyful expression of freedom. A smile, the first one in days had lit up his face, and unbelievably he had broken into a weird disjointed shuffle, his torn raincoat fluttering around him like the garment of some god-possessed dervish and even the horses had become friskier. This event, having energised the usually morose Harry, he is dissatisfied with merely following the cart and now has ambitions to lead the horse. But Smith has his doubts, Harry may be the poet's poet, but he doubts his experience of the wilful nature of horses having only recently become familiar with them himself.

As a boy Smith had, of course, been acquainted with the local milkman's horse — a docile creature that spent most of its time staring dejectedly at the ground. Recently, however, among a certain band of scruffy aristocrats led by Count Marco de la Paloma, he had endured a crash course in horsy-politics. As a new member of the band he had been required to lead Rizla, one of the enormous workhorses that pulled the Count's cart. Rizla's feet are great soup-plates of hair and bone shod in crescent bars of heavy steel. Leading the cart whilst avoiding these mighty hooves is a feat which had taken him some days to master. But eventually he had developed enough confidence to forget them altogether; until one day the cavalcade had entered a sunken lane which as it descended a steep incline began to narrow at an alarming rate.

Smith had noticed that his walking space was being rapidly reduced as the sides of the lane became steeper and higher, pushing him inwards towards the crashing hooves of Rizla. Now he had very little space left to walk in, causing him to fall back and allow the halter to slacken. The horse, sensing this lack of control, while similarly encouraged by the weight of the cart behind and the steepness of the incline ahead, began to increase speed and Smith was soon out of it. With the rear hooves of the monster almost upon him, and behind them, the heavy steel-rimmed cartwheels waiting to grind his bones, he had let go of the bridle and leaped for an overhanging bush, from where he was able to raise his legs high until the cart went hurtling by.

'Don't let go,' shouted the Count, who was riding just behind. But it was too late, and shedding pots, pans, sleeping bags and kettles, the cart had rumbled and bumped its juggernaut path to the bottom of the hill and out of sight. The Count came riding up, his white Arab stallion, Sagittarius, is highly strung and danced nervously, a little freaked by the runaway cart. The Count was irritated; horses had been a familiar adjunct to his noble family for generations and he handles them with panache, as if indeed they were nothing more threatening than a bicycle. But it is doubtful if he has ever even seen a suburban milk-cart.

'The horse won't hurt you!' he had shouted as, putting his heels to the stallion, he galloped off after the cart.

'Well, you know that better than I do!' Smith had retorted. It was the first thing that came into his head, a statement that for once seemed surprisingly true. He began descending the lane on foot, collecting a miscellany of items that had been lucky enough to escape the hoofs of Rizla and the heavy wheels of the cart. A few bent forks and spoons emerged from the earth, which he picked up and attempted to straighten; whilst here and there a dented pewter plate — the Count will eat from nothing else — lay like leaden leaves down the muddy track. Engaged thus he was overtaken by the other carts, their halters held in the firm grip of more seasoned travellers.

'Throw them in the back of my cart,' shouted the Count's *aide-de-camp*, a shaggy-haired Welshman named Muldoon, as he rumbled past. And Smith, tottering beneath his load of kitchen hardware had pulled the tarpaulin up at the rear and dumped the lot onto the floor of Muldoon's cart.

Over the next few weeks he had become more intimate with the horses, watering them in the evening and staking them out for the night. These chores which, as the newest member of the band he was expected to perform had quickly acclimatised him to their nature. But Harry Flame?

And Rommel? — Forget it.

Rommel is a small pony that for the last couple of years has done nothing but pull a tiny trap on Sundays. Doubtless he had rightly considered his hard working days were over and that he might continue this pleasant idyll indefinitely. The Count however, had other ideas. Smith has been travelling now for some time with his band and the Count had decided that he should be responsible for a rig of his own. He had offered Rommel and a light cart, providing that Smith collect and drive it up from Cornwall to rejoin the group somewhere northeast of Dartmoor.

Smith had jumped at the chance, and together with Miriam and Harry had manoeuvred through the spaghetti- junctioned highways of Portsmouth, until reaching the green fields and shadowy lanes leading inland to the great grey sweep of Dartmoor beyond. Smith had been forced to give his whole attention to Rommel every inch of the way. He does not like pulling the cart. He does not like waiting when he is hungry; and he does not like cars. Standing stiffly his legs spread wide, Rommel had come to a halt halfway across the Tamar Bridge and refused to take another step. With an increasing din from a jam of frustrated long-distance lorry drivers, who, with their horns blaring aggressively had offered Smith a variety of solutions, the little cart had brought the entire lane to a stop.

'Give the bloody thing a kick!' They had shouted, and from down the long line of halted lorries came other similar advice.

Smith is against cruelty to animals. But in this instance — his experience of horses being limited — he wonders if maybe the lorry drivers know best, and taking a piece of stick from the cart had reluctantly given Rommel a hefty whack.

It worked a treat, and Rommel, snorting his indignation and to the heartfelt cheers of the drivers had broken into a brisk trot, which Smith and Co had difficulty keeping up with. The drivers each sounded their horn and waved as they had passed which had upset Rommel even more, and he swerved erratically from side to side in a zigzag course until they were over the bridge.

But this wilful behaviour is merely the first introduction to his truculent nature and once into the countryside Rommel will, at the slightest inattention, fling himself violently sideways and begin wrenching great mouthfuls of leaves and grass from the roadside. Each time he does this, Babylon, when tied on behind pulls over to do the same. The effect on many occasions has almost had the cart over and it is some time before they are able to move again.

'It's not as easy as it looks,' says Smith to Harry. 'And Rommel is quite a handful.'

But Harry is not to be dissuaded. He has felt his spirit rising and now wants to demonstrate that he is no mere camp-follower but a card-carrying Crusader. Reluctantly, Smith hands over the halter. 'Keep him on a short rope, otherwise he will jerk it out of your hand and be off,' he advises.

Harry takes the rope and leads off, while Smith takes the opportunity to mount Babylon and test the calluses on his coccyx, while keeping an eye on Harry's progress with Rommel at the same time. They pass through a small Legoland estate, the rows of council houses each with its highly polished little car parked outside; and it is while negotiating this ghastly terrain that the disaster occurs. Harry has fallen once more into his morbid entrancement. The halter rope hangs slackly in his hand and with eyes cast down he seems to have entirely forgotten Rommel, who, fancying a bit of privet hedge on the side is angling nearer and nearer to the pavement. There is a horrendous metallic screech, and, snapping out of his trance, Harry brings Rommel to a halt.

Smith trots up to take a look and to his horror sees a long gash in one of the cars. The steel hub of the nearside wheel of the cart has torn open the whole side of the car like a can-opener. They hold their breath, but no one comes to investigate, and it seems on reflection that the best course of action is to disappear as fast as possible. Smith ties his horse behind the cart and learning fast about these things gives Rommel another whack with the stick. Again Rommel responds satisfactorily and they are soon gone.

Once onto the moor proper Harry takes the halter again, there seems nothing here that he can damage. But he soon falls prey to some inner conundrum, or perhaps he is composing a poem: for he stares dreamily around him and seems once more to have forgotten Rommel, who, slowly and subtly has been pulling at his halter to gain more slack for a quick snatch. Smith is about to call attention to this, when, looking for a moment behind he sees something coming towards them.

Still far-off, and looking like a pale blue ladybird against the distant heather it slowly bumps along in their track. It is a police car, a little Morris Minor beloved of Noddy which makes its way towards them up the narrow path, a strange little machine and so oddly out of place. The driver and a police sergeant look gravely through the windscreen as they make their final approach and come to a stop. The doors open and the sergeant gets out, followed by a man and a woman from the back. The woman is crying and the sergeant looks serious.

'Excuse me sir,' he says to Harry. 'This lady says you have damaged her car with your cart.'

Harry pulls himself together. Gathering his faculties into one intense focus and looking at the policeman as if he is some sort of alien. 'Er car?' he says vaguely.

The sergeant turns to Smith for help. But he is tying Babylon to the cart and looking as innocent as he can, while definitely not saying the first thing that comes into his head. He shrugs his shoulders as if he doesn't even understand English, while the woman wails the louder and her presumed husband tries to comfort her.

'I'll have to take your names and addresses if you don't mind,' says the sergeant, and turning back to Harry says, 'Your name please sir.'

Harry concedes this and the policeman writes it in his notebook.

'And your address please.'

This is getting too much for Harry. A navigator on the outermost edges of the poetic psyche, he must now subject himself to this clod. He claps his hand to his forehead. 'Oh God, oh God,' he moans.

'You can use mine,' says Miriam stepping into the breach, and giving the address of a friend in London who has anyway long since moved. The policeman notes it down and after taking her name turns to Smith.

'Name please,' he says, and Smith complies.

'Occupation?'

This is a tricky one. He has been occupied now for some time keeping Rommel on a straight path, but he doubts if the policeman will find this acceptable.

'Well,' says Smith, 'I am between occupations at the moment.'

'On holiday then sir?' says the sergeant, giving Smith a perfect off-the-shelf answer.

'Yes, that's right,' he answers. The sergeant looks relieved at this. Out here in the middle of the moors, Rommel and the cart with its ragged crew seem to be more real than the little Noddy car and its uniformed attendants, while the man and woman, he in a suit and she still wearing her apron seem to be the oddities, and he is grateful to bring this charade to a satisfactory conclusion.

'There will be an insurance claim for this,' he says sternly. And turning to the couple he says, 'I'm afraid I can't do any more for you at the moment, you must get in touch with your insurance company and explain the circumstances to them when making your claim.'

The woman bursts into renewed weeping as they return to the car. And soon it is bumping its way slowly back whence it came, shrinking once more into a tiny blue dot and gone.

Smith stands looking after it, then giving Rommel's halter a tug looks around for Harry. But he has wandered off while the police and their guests were making their exit. Evening is drawing in and the bleak moor is threatened by a heavy overcast — except towards the west, where the setting sun streaks the horizon with a foreboding red. This is the territory of strange legend, for the moor is host to many fearful myths. Trolls and troglodytes in league with all manner of ghostly phantoms have for centuries kept local villagers off the moor at night. But Harry, secure in his own unique universe is, it seems, impervious to such things.

Casting his eyes further afield, Smith catches one fleeting glimpse of his distant figure. He stands atop a small hillock silhouetted like a lone sentinel against the lurid horizon while he gazes off across the moor, his tatty raincoat swirling wildly around him in the rising wind. Then, without a backward glance he strikes off towards the northwest.

Smith wonders where he is going. 'Probably heading for Wales,' he thinks. When things get too hot for him in town, or his estimation of his fellows drops to a new low, Harry retires to a derelict cottage in a remote area of Wales, there to replenish his vision, until, with renewed optimism he can descend once more upon the city and re-enter the arena of human affairs.

Unfortunately, these sojourns amongst his fellows quickly drain his precious store of optimism, and a certain sourness enters his view. He has but recently fallen out with a local Notting Hill poet who had been overheard referring to him as "The Goul". Learning of this, Harry's sourness had developed a bitter edge, and thus, stewing over this latest insult as he walks the night streets of Notting Hill he had chanced to pass his tormentor's flat. The curtains are not drawn, and he sees within a softly lit room exuding an aura of comfort and security. Standing in the dark street with only a small and squalid room to call home, Harry is infuriated by this show of smug conformity and looks around for something to throw.

Outside the front door two milk-bottles catch his eye. He lifts one in each hand, and retiring a step or two takes aim. Bringing back his right arm like a javelin thrower and casting a calculating look at the lighted window, he lets fly. His aim is accurate, and the milk-bottle — sailing in a high arc through the darkness — crashes in a most satisfactory manner through the glass. Harry is delighted with this, and like a cowboy he lets off another shot which shatters a further pane. From inside the flat comes a bellow of outrage, and feeling vilified Harry gallops off towards the sodium-lit streets around Ladbroke Grove, while behind him the poet, like a "blear-eyed burgher brought bellowing to his door"* hurls his futile curses into the night.

This episode had brought Harry once more into the field, and thence to Dartmoor. No doubt this latest encounter with the police has been the last straw, and striking off to the northwest he now seeks the peace of his Welsh sanctuary.

*'*Culture Hero*' Harry Fainlight

Rommel's Offensive

The battle which takes place next evening between Babylon and Rommel is fearsome to behold. Unaware of any angst between the two horses, Smith had tethered them rather too closely together half-way along the lay-by where they are camped for the night. No sooner has he begun hunting for wood in a nearby copse, than there comes a fearful racket from the animals. Babylon, a young and inexperienced gelding had allowed his rear quarters to project into Rommel's available circle of grass; and Rommel, squealing with anger had immediately gone onto the attack. Turning around he had unleashed a series of sharp and vicious kicks on the unsuspecting Babylon, and it is his screaming protests which bring Smith running.

By the time he arrives on the scene Babylon is in full retaliation. But being somewhat taller than Rommel his kicks are pitched much too high and Rommel, looking over his shoulder comes in underneath his guard and puts in a couple more hard ones. Babylon screams again, Rommel's little hooves are sharp and although not always accurate are painful when they land. The reason for the general inaccuracy which inflicts both horses is that to deliver a kick at full power they must face away from each other. They therefore strain to look over their shoulders for accuracy, and the more they stretch their necks in this way the more misaligned become their attacks. Rommel is kicking vigorously away while Babylon, terrified out of his wits, responds accordingly. Their hooves lash high as they flail the air, whilst the occasional thud followed by a scream of rage and pain tell of another one getting home.

Dodging the rain of muddy clods which fly from their hooves, Smith runs forward and grabs Rommel's chain close to the iron stake to which it is tethered. He pulls hard, taking advantage of each minor lull in the battle. Eventually he has enough slack to wind around the stake and bring him out of range. He now unstakes Babylon and taking him further along hammers it back in. As he leaves the battlefield he notices Babylon gazing up the lay-by to where Rommel has returned to his grass. There is a puzzled look in his eye.

The next morning they set off again, intending to meet up with the Count who is camped in a drove northeast of Chagford and close upon Castle Drogo. Smith's coccyx has by now found a comfortable home somewhere between the knuckles along Babylons's spine, and he is riding behind the cart when a shout from Miriam brings him trotting up. She points ahead, and Smith sees winding upward through still distant trees a long wayward plume of smoke. As they draw closer they see the mouth of a drove which exits into the lane far ahead. It is the Count and his motley crew of turncoat aristocrats who, drawn toward the peaceful egalitarianism of the "New Age" in which they find themselves, have rejected their gracious backgrounds and riding on the prevailing high tide of hippy optimism launched themselves with cart and horse along the winding lanes and secret droves of the southwest.

These ancient pathways, once the province of the drover and his string of pack-horses, still criss-cross the surrounding countryside. Some, grown almost to invisibility through disuse, whilst others, closer to the main arteries are still usable. Rommel has now got wind of the Count's horses. He trots eagerly forward looking no doubt for an opportunity to get the first kick in and Miriam struggles to hold him back, while Babylon too pricks up his ears and snorts with excitement.

They find the Count sitting on a log beside the communal fire. Behind him stands his caravan and guarding the entrance lies an enormous hound, a giant Lurcher called Alph, who raises his great muzzle high to taste the air as Miriam, Rommel, Babylon and Smith come clattering in. The Count is pleased to see them, now the whole entourage can get back on the road again. Muldoon leads them further up the drove where Smith tethers the two horses far apart. Rommel must be kept well away from the Count's two great Shires , Rizla and Molly. For should he tangle with either he won't stand a chance. One kick from either colossus will blow him entirely away.

Later, rice and veg are served on the Count's battered pewter plates, and afterwards a coffeepot goes round. The coffee is made from the ground and roasted roots of dandelion, and although Smith, brought up on a diet of sausage, egg and chips finds the rice and veg to be definitely food, he is less convinced by the "coffee", and it is some days before his tastebuds adjust sufficiently to concede the point.

Hospitality At Bickleigh Castle

It takes a few days to get moving; harnesses have to be checked and made ready, and the horses' shoes examined for wear or looseness. Smith spends this time seeing to the wheels of Rommel's trap. Some of the spokes are loose and he has only been able to keep the metal rims on by binding them with wire, which on the move must be replaced every few days. These chores accomplished they harness up the horses, back them into the shafts and hook up. The Count, his four-wheeler nearest to the mouth of the drove leads off. He rides in the vanguard upon Sagittarius while Smith leads Rizla pulling the Count's cart. They seldom ride in the carts out of consideration for the horses which are led from the head. Ten miles per day is usual, but now, having been at rest for a while the horses have to get back into their stride and this takes a few more days.

The lanes which wander between Castle Drogo and Bickleigh Castle seem wilfully devised to make the journey from A to B as long as possible. This seeming irritation, which on a map may look like an idiot's scrawl, produces quite a contrary spirit in the traveller on the ground. For these meanderings offer a delightful succession of minor revelations as each bend in the road displays, as it is rounded, a new and unique vista, lending a subliminal excitement to each journey.

The Count rides out ahead towards each evening, scouting for a pond or stream with plentiful grass for the horses. Sometimes an unfenced wood comes down to the road, with a broad strip of grass running alongside. Here the carts are run up under the trees and the horses tethered to cool off before being watered. In no time a fire is crackling and a large black kettle is showing steam. Then, harnesses hung and horses watered they settle down to their rice and veg.

The village of Shobrooke lies in the early morning spring sunshine, nestling sleepily in a fold of the land some few miles from Castle Drogo. It witnesses little of the traffic which plies the higher ways. The odd doctor's car, an infrequent country bus or a more familiar tractor are all that disturb its centuries-long sleep. But now a new sound permeates the morning air and the village stirs uncomfortably. For it is a sound which awakens old memories in the ancient stones — the heavy measured tread of draught horses, and the gritty rumble of iron-shod wheels. Dogs bark and run towards the source of the sound as the Count, leading the way on Sagittarius, trails his rumbling carts through the village.

A small gang of village dogs come snarling to bark at the horses. But seem a little put off when, from beneath the Count's wagon a great tawny beast lurches to display its huge fanged mouth. It is Alph, whose menacing presence is enough to scatter them with puppy yelps like straw. He doesn't put himself out much over this, but treats these tin-fed pets as if they are but small-town hicks. Here and there a cottage door opens and an enquiring face appears, some occupants even coming to their garden gate to witness this strange cavalcade. One look however, at the bearded and ragged young men and dangerously wild looking women is enough, and they quickly retire to safety. Some, the more elderly amongst them, hurriedly crossing themselves and averting their eyes as the carts rumble past.

Once through Shobrooke they pursue a serpentine course through Cadbury and on to Bickleigh Castle, little more than fifteen miles in a straight line from their starting point. But following the winding convolutions of these minor by-ways more than doubles this distance, and it is three days before they arrive late one evening on the outskirts of Bickleigh.

It now appears that the village gentry wish to play host to the Count and offers him the use of a meadow for the horses and hot baths into the bargain. The Count accepts this hospitality and opening a gate leads the travellers into a large paddock. The proprietor, ruddy of face, fat of hacking jacket and ex-of-military is a jovial type. Puffing and blowing happily he is obviously pleased as punch to have the Count on his land, and no doubt his local standing will undergo a degree of inflation as a result.

They water the horses and get the rice on but nobody goes up to the house for a bath. After dark when the campfire lights up a circle of faces, the "Colonel" brings a few of his guests down to the paddock to view the "Hippies". They stand just beyond the firelight and refuse to come nearer. But the Colonel, waffling away, comes and sits on a log next to the Count and basks for a while in the admiring gaze of his guests, but refuses the offer of "coffee".

Nomad's Law

The next morning they are off early.

'The longer you stop, the harder it is to get going again,' says the Count. 'It is the first law of the nomad.'

They snap into action at these words, and within twenty minutes the paddock is empty and the fire turfed over. All that remains, dotted here and there across the meadow, are the generous donations left by the horses as payment for the grass. Now they strike out for the slopes of the Blackdown Hills some fifteen miles distant to the northeast. As he trudges at the head of Rizla, Smith mulls over the Count's words and sees the truth in them whatever the circumstances. 'So we are re-discovering the laws of the nomad,' he thinks, 'learning to travel quickly and with skilful efficiency.'

He tries to imagine where such accomplishments might lead and the answer strikes him at once. Of course! When they have perfected their techniques with the carts they will take them aboard a ferry and thus to France. Then a southwards trek to Spain and on through to Morocco. Now he sees it all: the horses, useless in the desert will be exchanged for camels, and from there all roads lead to Samarkand. Meanwhile back at camp, he knows that these are yet very early days, but his trudging step has been lightened by this visionary glimpse, and he wonders what the second nomadic law might be.

The Count Jumps To It

Towards evening and several days later, they reach the early slopes of the Blackdown Hills and camp for the night in a wood just before Cullmstock. They stay out of sight of the village in order to pass through on the morrow at dawn, when all will be asleep and the horses fresh for the hills. Next morning the ruse works and they exit the village without the usual fuss. The horses tackle the hills with no trouble, although many rests are called, when a large rock is placed behind the rear-wheels to hold the carts and give the horses a breather. By late evening the crest of the last ridge is topped and they gaze down the transverse slopes into Somerset. Here, camped along a convenient drove they spend the night, and in the morning, after conferring with Muldoon the Count announces that they will stay here for the day and give the horses a rest.

The Count is at one with his horses and rides them in a fearless manner, thinking nothing of putting Sagittarius to gate or hedge and soaring smoothly above all such obstacles while secure as a limpet on his back. Smith has never tried jumping and doesn't intend to. Riding bareback, it is as much as he can manage to stay on at a trot, which mode gives his coccyx no end of a bruising. However, he has recently discovered another gear. Babylon had for some reason misunderstood the rein, and instead of slowing from his present bone-jarring trot into a more sedate walk, had increased his speed and broken into a canter. Suddenly Smith's whole perspective on the riding of horses, with its constant discomforting jog and unpredictable jerks, was transported in an instant into a long, slow rippling movement, rolling beneath him so smoothly that it is easy to fall in with and his coccyx is rejoicing. Now he canters whenever he gets the chance, but, being a newcomer to this game he draws the line at fences.

Alph Takes It On The Chin

Their journey continued - the carts roll smoothly down long gentle slopes towards Avelon, passing through Staple Fitzpaine and beyond to set up camp halfway across West Sedgemoor. Here, far from any road they spend a few more idle days, repairing broken harness and riding out across the moor with the dogs. Alph has a consort called Phly. She is barely half Alph's size but she keeps him well in hand. When she is in an irritated mood and snarls at him as if he means nothing to her he stiffens and stands looking around him in a long-suffering manner. But he has never been known to retaliate, and obviously considers such a response beneath him.

Blacksmith

Once more on the move the offers of hospitality become more frequent. The Count's family name is well known in these parts and the gentry hereabout fall over themselves to provide sanctuary. At Stoke St Gregory, having spent the previous night on the moor, they are offered a large old tithe barn with adjoining fields and water-troughs. Here Rommel has a small field of his own with en-suite trough, while Babylon mucks in with Rizla and Molly, with whom he gets on well, since they seem to have adopted him as a surrogate son. Here a halt is declared while the Count finds a blacksmith to attend a loose shoe on Molly, Rizla's equally gigantic consort. The village smithy is now a thing of the past, and rarely in the numerous villages through which they have passed has one been seen. But within a few days a blacksmith arrives in the small flatbed truck from which he plies his trade. His ready-made shoes hang in rows by size, and his bellows is a large cylinder of propane gas. He deals with Molly and then checks the other horses.

'This will have to come off,' he says, digging with a spike at one of Rommel's rear hooves.

'Watch him!' Smith had warned, when the man had turned his attention to Rommel. 'If you get behind him he'll kick.'

The man, letting him know with one scathing look that he is sucking his granny's eggs, darts suddenly in upon the wary and suspicious Rommel; and before he can lift a hoof he grabs the lower part of a rear-leg and hauls it into the air. Now he twists himself around and brings the hoof up, to be held firmly between his burly knees.

Rommel is helpless; there is nothing he can even try. He is standing on his only other kicking leg. Smith admires the man's fearless Kung-Fu, but the smith is all nonchalance and holds the hoof in the matter-of-fact manner one might give to a faulty washing-up brush or something similar. While behind him Rommel, seething in fury will erupt into a dangerously violent fit the moment he is released. The man takes pincers from his belt and wrenches off the faulty shoe. Two or three of the nail-heads have worn away and remain standing proud of the hoof. He removes these, and exchanging the pincers for a large coarse file, he scrapes away a good part of the dead surface leaving a smooth face for the new shoe.

'Hold him tight,' says the blacksmith, and throwing over his leg had dropped the hoof and in one swift movement is at Rommel's head. Smith is holding on tight as Rommel, now free, bucks and kicks. But the blacksmith will have none of it. 'Shuddup,' he growls, giving Rommel a sharp slap on the nose. Backing up his truck he takes a new shoe and shuts it in his little furnace. Within minutes it is a bright orange crescent, and bringing Rommel up to his truck the smith again performs his black-belt manoeuvre. Rommel is ready this time: he has been watching him closely, clearly ready to kick out if the man gets anywhere near his back legs. The smith, however, stands pulling Rommel's ear and patting the side of his neck until, with no warning he walks briskly back down the flank of the horse, and in one swift and complicated movement secures the hoof once more between his knees. Rommel gives up. He stands head hanging low, looking dejectedly downwards as if he no longer cares what happens to him. While the smith, grabbing his pincers, seizes the shoe from the furnace, and while still a sparkling cherry-red places it with precision onto the horny rim of Rommel's hoof.

A dense cloud of white smoke arises, obscuring Smith's view as he stands holding tightly to the halter and waiting for Rommel to start screaming. But the smith knows what he is doing, and the hoof is nothing more than an overgrown slab of toenail. There is a heavy smell of burning in the air as the red-hot metal meets the horn and the shoe sizzles itself into a perfect fit. The smith now drops it into a bucket of water and when it has cooled slips it onto the hoof and bangs in the nails, whose ends then emerge higher up on the side of the hoof, and these he turns over to provide extra holding power.

Blacksmiths can charge what they like. And this man, a highly skilled specialist who looks after the local children's ponies and services the riding-schools in the area isn't cheap. But Smith notes that the Count's eyes register no flicker of shock when the bill arrives. Neither does his hand shake as he writes out the cheque.

Now You See It, Now You Don't

Bright young things from London begin to come down to stay for a few days, and Belgravian debutantes flaunt their haughty limbs around the camp. Merchant princes, who ply their trade from hippy shops along the Kings Road, take the weekend off and come to let it all hang out with the Count. For word of the carts and the happy-go-lucky travellers has spread afar, and the hippy grapevine keeps those in town aware of his whereabouts. The Count views all this with wry amusement. Few of these visitors last more than a few days on the road, where the everyday tasks of caring for the horses whilst trudging a daily ten miles soon dampens their party spirit and they take themselves off, "Granny takes a trip" dresses fluttering and crushed velvet bottomed trousers flapping, as they head for the nearest railway station or accept a lift from their peers. It is seldom that the small band is without these visitors and only on the long treks are they shed.

The core group have recently acquired another permanent member. He had arrived driving a 1934 MG which he had lavished much expense on, and the engine is tuned like a violin. But three days later, lying lazily propped against a tree, he had viewed his MG with a new and pensive eye. He has lost one of his two-tone shoes in the slime of a pond while learning to water the horses; and Muldoon has given him an old pair of rubber boots which have done little to keep the mud from his satin flares. His camel hair overcoat is now much the worse for wear, and he hasn't shaved since he left London.

'Look at it,' he says, languidly pointing at the MG where it is parked amongst some dense bushes, the great chrome headlamps gleaming amongst the leaves and the pristine bodywork reflecting the forest floor.

'Look at it,' he says again. 'There it is. But what is it for?'

The Count leans forward and offers his hash-pipe, and Pete, the owner of the MG, takes it and has a long toke before handing it on to Smith.

'It's for gullible people like you to buy?' suggests the Count.

Pete blows out a long plume of smoke and holds up his finger. 'No,' he says. 'That's all very well for the manufacturers. But what's in it for me?' Nobody answers and he goes on.

'I'll tell you what's in it for me. It's to get me from here to there very fast. Wherever I am is here, and wherever I'm going is there. And that is a machine devised to make the journey between as short, in time, as possible.'

But in spite of this brilliant analysis Smith is considering an alternative view. 'Maybe it's an umbrella,' he says. He enjoys philosophical discussions and is always ready to make helpful contributions of this sort.

'What?' says Pete, slightly irritated that his theory is being questioned.

'Maybe it's an umbrella,' Smith repeats. 'For instance, the car also protects you from the rain, which is exactly what an umbrella does.

Therefore, it might be some kind of brolly.'

Pete can't quite get the gist of this. He is taking this thing very seriously indeed and cannot get his head around Smith's umbrella theory.

Now Miriam places her stake in this field of speculation. 'Maybe it's not there at all,' she offers: 'Maybe we only think it's there.'

Pete stands up. 'I know it's there because I've spent a whole lot of money on it, and now I'm beginning to wonder why.' He is getting very excited and seems to be close to some powerful interior revelation.

'If you don't know why you spent the money on it,' intercedes the Count. Then you shouldn't be asking what it's for, but why it's there at all. If, that is, it is.' The Count speaks slowly between puffs of his pipe as he lounges back on his pile of sheepskins like some New Age Celtic prince, but Pete is a practical man, and this kind of mysticism is not, as yet, in his repertoire.

'Well, I'll soon settle whether it's there or not,' he says, and striding over to the car bangs his hand down hard on the bonnet. 'So much for that,' he says firmly.

'So much for what?' says Smith. 'That doesn't prove anything.'

'THE CAR IS THERE I CAN FEEL IT!' shouts the red-faced Pete, banging the bonnet with each word.

'Maybe you only think you feel it,' says Miriam, and Pete, unhinged a little by the argument and stoned out of his head on the Count's hashish loses it.

'That's it,' he shouts. 'I don't want to talk about it any more.' He jumps into the car which starts with a muffled roar and pulling out of the bushes he stops for a moment. He seems to have calmed down a little, but there is a determined look in his eye.

'I really don't know anymore what the car's for, and I'm beginning to doubt I really want it.'

He gives a parting wave and zooms off without a backward glance, the roaring exhaust fading rapidly into the returning forest silence. A log collapses in the fire with an ashy puff, and Muldoon throws on a couple more pieces of wood and readjusts the kettle.

'Well it's not there now.' says the Count, refilling his pipe and passing it round.

'So what?' says Miriam. 'There are many other things that are not there either.'

'Are you saying there's no difference between what was there, and what wasn't?' asks Muldoon, a no-good Welsh boyo and the Count's right-hand man. 'You couldn't make your minds up about that when it was *really* there.'

'What do you mean *really*,' asks Smith, ready once more to enter the fray, 'It's either there or it's not.'

'Well it's not there now.' says the Count again.

The pipe has done its work well. Unlike the Mafia cheese that Smith is accustomed to, the Count's hashish is of the best quality and he never runs out. Thus speculating they while away the rest of the afternoon, giving little more thought to Pete, who by now must be well on his way to "there".

'They all get caught when they go back,' says the Count from time to time, and by now Smith knows this to be true. "The City"; the greedy maw that has swallowed up many a would-be traveller. Turning up at the camp with sleeping bags they profess radical life changes and total committal. Then, after a week or two, they have "just one last thing to do in the city" and are never seen again.

'They all get caught,' says the Count. 'You should never go in there alone.'

By now the city, which had once represented daily life to Smith, has faded into a distant memory. The woodlands and fields; the hedgerows strung in a pale graffiti of convolvulus, with only an occasional church to spike the soft line of distant trees, have so long been his familiars that he cannot recall it to mind. In his imagination it has become a place of gilded spires and fretted marble domes. A palace of obscure temptations and sophisticated pleasures, where wicked-eyed houris lean simpering lasciviously from the windows of sumptuous boudoirs.

When in a more sober state however, he knows precisely why he had made this move. For the streets of Notting Hill no longer bubble with spontaneity, and the Portobello Road now swarms with weekend hippies. Young suburban clerks, their hair fashionably long, throw off their weekday grey and don psychedelic shirts. They grow moustaches and sport the latest in granny glasses, whilst Carnaby Street, the Height Ashbury of Barking, is doing a roaring trade.

A day or two later they are about to embark across Kings Sedgemoor, when a man comes walking along the lane towards them. It is Pete, now wearing jeans and carrying a bag he gives a casual wave of his arm when they greet him.

'I only got as far as Warminster,' he says. 'The carburettor was playing up so I took it into a garage and a chap there made me an offer.' He holds up his arms in a slow and elaborate shrug, but his eyes are dancing excitedly.

'I saw immediately what the car was for. Don't you see, the Count was right. The car was for selling to someone as gullible as me.'

'And,' says Muldoon sardonically.

'So I sold it' says Pete. 'And now I'm here.'

'Yes, but are you *really* here?' asks Muldoon.

'What do you mean *really*?' says Smith.

The Count steps forward and holds out his hand. 'Well,' he says. 'Whether you're really here or really not, you're welcome to stay as long as you like.'

They shake hands all round, and later Pete takes Smith's place at Rizla's head leaving him free to walk or ride as he chooses. This is a minor elevation of unspoken status within the group. He is no longer the beginner, but can, when the Count and Muldoon are away, harness up and get the whole cavalcade on the move, meeting up later at some pre-arranged spot and supervising inexperienced visitors whilst on the road.

Chop

The gypsies, who inhabit a twilight world between regulated farmlands and the extended suburbs of local market towns, have become aware of the Count's band of travellers as they move on the *drom* through the Romany territories. They turn up in pick-up trucks looking for things to "chop"; rural barrow-boys who follow lorries around on the chance that something may fall off the back, and they do not agree with society's philosophy of private ownership at all.

A young fellow drives up one evening as they are pitching camp in a grassy lay-by. They are a few miles beyond Godney and are heading acutely north to Priddy, where in a few weeks' time there is to be a country fair and the Count is looking to pick up a few spare wheels.

The gypsy pulls a large bundle from the back of his truck and dumps it onto the grass. They all gather round as he unties the packing ropes then stands back and silently waits for offers. Like his fellows he wears a mismatched lounge suit, the trousers held by a wide leather belt with a large brass buckle. Around his neck is a red handkerchief and to complete the ensemble, a flat workman's cap. They all dress in a vaguely similar manner, with its own interior code of sartorial values which does not exclude a plentiful spattering of mud. But they carry their wealth around with them and their fingers are ringed with heavy gold.

Muldoon comes over and gives the bundle a kick.

'What is it?' He asks. The kick conveying in an instant that whatever it is, as far as he's concerned it's not worth a penny of his money. It is a superb display of perfect communication. But the gypsy is entirely unmoved and shows not the slightest sign of having seen the gesture, for he unrolls the bundle and pulling it flat, displaying a large ridge-tent complete with lofty poles and a bundle of pegs. No one but Miriam seems interested and she stands looking down on it thoughtfully. Sleeping in Rommell's trap with a piece of canvas laid across the top is taking its toll of her feminine sensibilities and the tent has taken her fancy. She goes over to the trap and soon, as the gypsy exchanges local chat and boasts of the horse he is taking for sale to the coming fair at Priddy, there comes like a singing ghost of the city left behind, the banana-coloured strains of "Mellow Yellow". The gypsy stops in mid-boast and cocks his head towards the music. In these days the domestic tape-recorder, appearing but recently on the London scene has yet to reach this winding country lane somewhere between Godney and Wookey Hole. He walks over to the trap and stands looking down at the primitive reel-to-reeler. He has never seen one before. He tries the fast forwards and reverse, while she shows him her collection of Dylan tapes: then, standing back in silence, he gives her a long and steady look. The rules of "chop" are simple and unambiguous —— she has the next move.

'Chop?' she says, turning up the volume to display the power of her machine.

The man's expression does not change. His poker face as still as any redskin Chief's as he signs away the odd cheating treaty. He lifts his right hand to shoulder height and waits. It is a ritual as old as any Masonic Order's, and he enacts it with panache. But by now Miriam has been around the horse-fairs a little herself and has picked up the jargon. Grinning, she holds out her hand palm upwards and the gypsy gives it a smack.

'Chop,' he says.

When the truck pulls away, *Mr Tambourine Man* bellowing from the passenger seat, the tent, under Miriam's watchful eye, is brought to its feet. She wants to be able to erect it herself and carefully takes note of how it is done. Now at long at last she can unpack her bag of delights, with which she could transform a garden shed into a courtesan's parlour within minutes. Saris of many colours and Moroccan drapes with twinkling mirrors soon line the austere inner canvas walls. Bags are covered in cloth-of-silver to cushion the striped Navajo rug which covers the floor. And best of all, she can stand up.

Smith looks in and she invites him to have coffee. Significantly, she has her own fire going at the tent's mouth thus indicating, in the unstated language of that nomadic rule which still haunts the genes of even the most sophisticated city dweller: she is leaving the boy's gang and setting up on her own.

Muldoon now enters and she serves him coffee and bustles about her fire. They are sipping this and admiring the tent when the Count comes in. He has remained outside, watching the road lest the gypsy come back and make off with one of the horses. Should this happen the whole countryside would close ranks and the horse never be seen again.

Now the tent seems to expand around them, for they are all standing up and can even walk around a little. It is getting dark and Miriam lights a couple of oil-lanterns and hangs them from the ridge-pole, and Smith gets out his fiddle. He is only playing one tune at the moment and is still at work on the composition. The second part is open to further speculation but he begins playing *Priddy Fair*, a piece he is concocting to use while busking at the coming fair. It is, at the moment, his only way of earning any money, and although he eats courtesy of the Count's largesse, he can rarely buy himself the odd packet of tobacco or illicit jar of Nescafé.

He tunes his fiddle and begins the piece, a circular dance with a second part, which, since still incomplete, varies with each repeat. Round and round he goes shutting out all else and seeking a sympathetic rhythm. He hits on a pulsing jig-beat and is off. The music is lifting from his hands and the tent becomes alive with dancing people. The Count offers his hand to Miriam who queens it amongst her cushions. This is her place and things are changing around here. They dance apart, gyrating and swaying: with here a country bob of the knee, and there a sophisticated shimmy from the night spots of London. Muldoon stomps away in the corner doing some kind of Welsh clog-dance while Smith plays on, his battered fiddle wailing through the walls of the tent and out across the darkened fields beyond.

When his bow arm hurts beyond endurance he is forced to stop, and the dancers fling themselves down while Miriam refills the kettle. The Count stretches himself out and gives a whistle, the tent flaps part and Alph's great head appears. He does not want to come in, but Phly, recognising the female ambience within enters and sprawls at the Count's feet. Smith watches Miriam closely. This is a telling moment. Will she allow the Count's dogs into her "house", or will his august presence deter her from making such a ridiculous suggestion? She has a tray of coffee ready at the fire and turns with it to push past Alph who still stands in the mouth of the tent, reluctant to go back alone to his den beneath the Count's wagon. He humbly moves aside as she enters and then returns to his former position. He has drawn his line and now stands with just his head through the flap, occasionally withdrawing it to cast an eye about the camp while his ears are turned to catch the slightest rustle. Miriam passes around the tray and then reclines once more. The tent has given her no end of clout and she lolls like Cleopatra amongst her silver cushions. She looks across; sees Phly; and Smith holds his breath. Then, stretching out a nonchalant arm towards the dog, she clicks her fingers. Phly comes running and drapes herself across her lap and Smith lets out his breath. Miriam has trumped the Count this time. She has played her hand so well that he wonders if, now that she has her own place, she will take over the whole camp.

Leaf

Smith lies back on a grassy bank his head inclined against the trunk of a tall elm. Babylon is tethered to a nearby branch and the wild thyme blows around him in the summer breeze. The limbs of the elm reach outward above him, its branches slimmer as they rise, and only about their bifurcating tips does a skirt of flouncing leaves occur.

'It's like looking up a woman's dress,' he thinks, and registers a twinge of guilt. He has taken advantage of this stately presence and now lies looking unabashedly up between her naked limbs. There is but one escape from ignominy: He plays the gentleman and pretends he hasn't noticed.

As he lies staunchly ignoring the tree's embarrassing position a leaf detaches from high above and begins a gyrating flutter to the ground. He watches idly as it twists from side to side then turns and lifts in the breeze. For a moment it hangs suspended, as if undecided whether to rise or fall, then drops and spins, flashing tiny points of light as its shiny upper surface catches the sun. Now it glides in a zigzag path pulled here and there by the vagaries of the wind, until, the high-class performance over, it swoops in at an oblique angle and lands at Smith's feet.

His imagination is working overtime. The tree is aware of his impeccable discretion and has in the subtlest way shown her appreciation. Like a lady dropping her handkerchief the tree has shed for him a piece of her skirt. It is obviously a come-on. But, no nodding violet in matters of the heart, he feels that in this instant he doesn't want to take the relationship any further.

Untying Babylon he jumps astride, his thighs now grown strong to grip the horse's belly. Trousers wear out fast in these conditions, and the travellers sew pieces of raw cowhide up the inner-leg that soon become stiff with horse-sweat, an aroma which surrounds them at all times, and mingles well with the pungent reek of wood-smoke which permeates everything else. They smell of the woods with a sharp tang of mud, and their skin wears a protective patina of dirt with natural dignity. For when living on the road these matters of personal hygiene become much simplified, and city values falling away are soon forgotten in the realpolitik of the countryside.

But a smell which goes down well at the local horse-fair, where such a thing is not unusual among the gypsies and gamey old farmers, has not always, in Smith's experience been met with this comradely attitude. During his early days with the Count they had passed near the castle of a local noble Lord, who, an old friend of the Count, had offered them Christmas dinner. The Count had accepted the offer on their behalf, and securing the horses in the castle-yard and leaving Alph and Phly to guard the camp, they had turned up at the castle ready to start eating.

An Inappropriate Question

Approaching the castle Smith had fallen into his latest preoccupation; he is obsessed with the desire to obtain some boot-polish for Babylon's harness. The straps are old and much the worse for wear, but he knows that with a tin of black boot-polish he could bring a shine back to the leather and give Babylon, not the prettiest of horses anyway, a much needed bit of class. Now as they pass through the ancient stone gates into his Lordship's domain and the iron rims of the carts bite deeply into the well-tended gravel of the great tree lined avenue, all Smith can think about is boot-polish.

A butler opens the massive door to the Count's knock, and the noble Lord stands waiting to greet his guests. He is of the Count's circle and they know each other well. He shakes hands all round, but a curious expression is beginning to overshadow his welcoming smile. He gives a cautious sniff or two, wrinkling up his nose and trying to maintain the smile at the same time, a most peculiar effect, and his eyes go blank as he steps back to introduce her Ladyship, who has just reached the bottom of the grand staircase. An elegant creature she moves with languid dignity, and the long satin tea-dress gathers in controlled ripples at her feet as she holds out a lily-white hand to the Count and his friends.

The noble Lord can't take any more. Handing them over to the butler he retires to his study while her Ladyship gracefully turns to remount the stairs. This is Smith's chance. He has waited long for an opportunity such as this and now is the only one on offer. Stepping forward he halts her stately step upon the stair and says the first thing that comes into his head.

'Have you got any boot-polish?' he asks.

She stares at him blankly for several moments as if he has spoken in Chinese. Then, her thin nose held at a scornful angle, she looks down the long length of it at Smith and answers with massive disdain.

'Ask the butler,' she says frostily, waving a careless hand at the impassive man who stands silently beside them, and turning, she once more mounts the stair.

Smith follows the butler to the kitchen where to his delight he is handed a large tin of polish. Within five minutes he is in the stable with Babylon's harness around him, engaged in a lustful orgy of boot-polish. Soon the straps begin to glow; with the buckles polished it will look quite smart next time he rides out.

Now he is very hungry and wonders about the Christmas dinner. Returning to the castle he is met in the hall by the Count, who wears a bath-robe and his long wet hair is held in a pony-tail. He shows Smith up to a room on the first floor.

'We've been asked to have baths before sitting down at the table, and you must put these clothes on,' says the Count, pointing towards a chair.

Smith looks at the chair, over which are hung a well-laundered pair of smart pressed jeans and a high-neck powder-blue sweater. He pulls up short; his hands are covered in boot-polish and he had even for the occasion, considered washing them. But this...

He stares with some misgiving at the clothes, while the Count tells him that he can't eat unless he puts them on. 'His Lordship insists on it,' he says. Smith capitulates, his rumbling stomach up for any compromise. He takes his bath and dons the nice clothes, leaving his own dirt and sweat-stiffened garments leaning against the chair. Socks too have been provided, their inner-labels advertising some Jermyn Street gentleman's outfitter. This is just as well, since there is nothing much left of his own below the ankle.

Thus attired he joins the others similarly clad in the great baronial hall below. He feels an idiot, padding around in poncey expensive socks and wearing this bloody silly jumper. He doesn't really enjoy the meal, which seems to him like some strange eating exhibition put on for the amusement of the servants, who stand along the walls watching their every move, while waiting like vultures for the inevitable embarrassing *faux-pas*.

When dinner is over they retire to the games-room, where mince pies and real coffee are served. Then, the bourgeois disguises shed, they return to camp and prepare for an early morning start. Smith is glad of the early start, since he is still wearing his Lordship's poncey socks and would be reluctant now to give them up.

The Count

The Count, although of noble blood and certainly not a leveller, has an egalitarian spirit. He is "Marco" to his fellow travellers and never pulls rank; although he puts the local gentry through the social hoop of addressing him as "Sir". He is wise in this matter, for familiarity would destroy the very framework by which these gentry attain esteem amongst their fellows.

Priddy

The Count has many connections in the country around Priddy, and he and Muldoon ride now a day or so ahead, leaving markers at the mouths of usable droves and looking for a site to camp for a few weeks. He hires a field for the horses and a triangular piece of land for the carts, at a site which lay out near Wookey Hole and not a mile from Priddy. On arrival the carts and caravans are set into a semicircle, a central fire is lit, and they're free to lounge around, explore Wookey Hole or mend a bit of harness on the side. The London crowd have heard of the fair and they turn up in force, bringing the latest records for the Count's portable player.

They like T. Rex, and late at night Marc Bolan's considerate voice leaves the open door of the Count's caravan; while inside, a ring of candlelit faces are pale amongst the ruddy travellers as they roll big joints and take another puff at the Count's formidable pipe. The camp soon generates the air of a small village, with Miriam's tent like a mini town hall standing beneath an overhanging tree. At night, when logs blaze at the central fire and vegetables sizzle in the wok, her glim can be seen, and behind it, with flaps tied back the tent's lamp-lit interior is exotic as any bower bird's.

On the day of the fair the big village green is swarming with gaitered farmers, while gypsy lads with horses show them off. They ride bareback and control the beasts with a rope noose about the muzzle, and pulling on this single rein put their mounts through their paces. The horses are rough looking and half-wild, but the gypsies flaunt them with the panache of circus riders. The Count is not interested in any of this. He knows the best horses are held far out beyond the village where private deals are done, and only word-of-mouth reveals the location of the real stuff.

Dry-Stone Wall

Miriam is looking for a horse. She now wants a proper caravan but prices are high for a good puller. Though she too still eats at the Count's "table", she has a little cash in hand, but hardly enough to buy what she needs. The fair, however, is quite small and there is little for sale anyway. A couple of children's ponies are sold and the gypsies, having no luck, soon ride off. A few stalls and rides collect the country girls. They giggle around the coconut shy, and eye the local lads in their Sunday best as they compete with each other to much raucous laughter.

A low dry-stone wall, its grey surface lichen-patched in mottled orange-yellow, surrounds the hostelry that stands on the edge of the green. Inside, hoary old farmers push their grunting way to the crowded bar. Elderly scions of family gypsies flash their gold teeth and beringed fingers as they down the pint mugs of local scrumpy cider. It is fierce stuff and many a drunken voice bursts into song.

Outside, sitting on the wall is Smith. He has his fiddle with him and is waiting for the right moment to do a bit of busking. He wants to maintain the spirit of his spontaneous performances of the summer before, when the Portobello Road had rung with mad and unscheduled music. But at the moment the pub and the sideshows hold the crowd and timing is important.

Miriam is trying out the scrumpy. She has brought herself a small glass and is pulling a face at its sourness when the Count comes by. He has heard of some horses held out on the edge of the Mendip Forest and been given a name for reference. Now he is on his way to take a look and has secured a lift on a gypsy's truck.

'Do you want to come?' he asks.

Smith is set on his busking, but Miriam, eager for any opportunity to acquire a horse, jumps at the chance. The gypsy's truck is waiting and she and the Count get aboard.

The Surreptitious Chequebook

A mile or so from the village they enter the mouth of a concealed drove: its entrance is overgrown but the gypsy jumps out, pulls aside the ragged foliage and noses in his truck leaving little disturbance to be seen. He drives in a bit deeper and then parks.

'We'll walk from here,' he says.

Soon the winding lane is left behind as the drove bends and twists among the fields. Sometimes they reach a junction, but the gypsy knows his way, turning to plunge right or left among the long-forgotten ways until smoke is seen rising above the high hedges, and the dull thudding stamp of bored horses can be heard. A heavy rope fences off the drove, and behind it a small camp is set up. Several gypsies squat around a fire, and further up the drove their animals are corralled.

The driver introduces the Count, but the gypsies nod knowingly. They already know who he is. Tea is offered and local gossip aired before the conversation gets serious. They know where he is camped and whom he travels with. Their network is as fine as MI5.

'Oo arr,' they say. 'That were when you were camped over near Burrow Bridge.' But they give nothing of themselves away.

Preliminaries over the Count goes with Miriam to check out the horses, but sees nothing that he wants. He has enough pullers himself but helps Miriam assess what is on offer. There is one beast which really takes her fancy, a fine big old chestnut that seems oddly out of place amongst this shaggy herd.

''E be old carriage-'orse,' says the owner. He gives this information reluctantly, trying to look as if he doesn't want to sell, while the Count on his part exudes an aura of total disinterest. Miriam, however, loves the horse on sight, and ducking beneath the rope corral puts her arms around its neck.

''E's very well trained,' says the gypsy, now a little more enthusiastic. He can see that Miriam is smitten and senses a sale. ''E'll pull anything you put 'im to.'

The horse stands still and does not fidget under her hands. He is a gentleman and yet to pick up the coarser habits of his less well-bred kind. The Count whispers into the gypsy's ear and the man nods his head in agreement. The Count is offering to top him up should Miriam's funds prove insufficient. She, however, knows nothing of this, and would not accept if she did. They confer in further whispers and haggle over price, but there are no flies on the gypsy and he picks up the Count's tactics straight away.

'How much for the big chestnut?' asks Miriam, as, reluctant to leave the horse she comes back to where they stand. The gypsy names the price agreed with the Count and Miriam is delighted. She can manage the sum with a little to spare. Enough if she's lucky to buy an old four-wheeled farm-cart, and perhaps with a little help build a caravan of her own. She gets out the small purse which she wears round her neck and gives the gypsy a bundle of notes. He counts them slowly and carefully, then, fetching a rope halter he throws it about the horses head.

''E used to pull a smart carriage over in Wells,' he says. 'A big house it were with coachman and all.' He hands her the rope and the horse is hers.

Now she leads it back along the drove and it follows her without fuss. 'I'm going to walk him back on my own,' she says, as the Count hangs behind to write out his surreptitious cheque. Then, with the truck-driver in the lead, they retrace the droves which lie like a hidden maze between them and the nearest road. When they reach the truck the Count climbs in for the ride back, and Miriam takes off along the verge of the lane for her long walk back to Priddy. She and the horse do not hurry; she wants to spend some time with him alone.

A Question Of Logic

Miriam calls the new horse "Danny" and Muldoon asks her why.

'Because he's so sweet,' she says. Smith can't see the connection, but Muldoon seems to have swallowed it without effort.

'Where's the logic in that?' asks Smith, not wanting to start an argument but unable to put such an intriguing mystery down.

'What do you mean logic?' she snaps. 'I'll call him what I like.'

Smith allows himself one more try.

'No, what I mean is. What is the connection between the name "Danny", and sweetness?'

Now she knows that he is trying to undermine her, and her feminine intuition sees through his sly tricks.

'Danny, Danny, DANNY! ' she shouts. 'There, is that sweet enough for you?'

Smith gives up. What little understanding of women he thought he had is now unravelling at an alarming rate, and he backs off, while

Muldoon grins in a knowing way, but refrains from any further question on the matter.

Priddy Fair

Towards evening, when the cider-house begins to disgorge its rowdy contents, and red-faced farmers with half-cut wives tumble their way out into the sunset, Smith feels his moment approaching. Twilight is deepening and lights are coming on over the coconut shy and twinkle around the awnings of the tombola stall and lucky dip. Two or three revellers exit the gate in the wall and Smith opens his violin case and lays it open at his feet. Then, a quick tune-up and he is off. *Priddy Fair*, now finalised, leaps into life and his bow-arm is fresh and feels strong. He will play till his arm drops off, thus ensuring that the music will be curtailed in a natural and unpredictable manner.

Tipsy farm lads surround him and mock-dance to the tune, but some of the gypsy wives are moved to lift their skirts saucily as they kick their legs high, while their husbands dance catchy little jigs and stamp their hob-nailed boots. Smith is going like the clappers but knows he cannot stand this pace for long. The dancers spin ever faster, driving up the tempo with claps and stamps and copious juice is spilt from sloshing cider-mugs. Now the Count and a few London girls turn up to further animate the dance, and Muldoon clomps away on the edge of the crowd.

But Smith is already beginning to tire, the effort to maintain this speed soon depletes his energy and his arm is in agony. 'One more time,' he thinks, gritting his teeth and plunging once more around the circular piece, and he is only just able to reach the end before his arm drops, squeaking like a rusty hinge to hang throbbing and useless at his side. The dancers want more but he cannot oblige, and unable to persuade him they drift away across the green, still jigging and hopping to try out their luck on the coconut shy. Back at camp Smith counts the takings, almost seven shillings. Not bad, he will live like a lord for some days.

The Wake Of The Phoenix

That night, as crackling sparks rise swirling upwards to twist and fade above the camp-fire, a festive air falls upon the camp. Tralee has driven down from

London bringing Hannah, a skilled masseur, and an old friend of Miriam's, who offers her tent as a massage parlour. Word of the fair has spread and several other visitors turn up, and Hannah soon has them queuing up for treatment. Tralee is Tralee; her dark gypsy eyes flashing she strides about the camp, hair wild to the sky, skirt ragged to the ground, she is in her element and looks ready for anything.

A group of young geomancers turn up and sit around the fire animatedly discussing their latest theories. There is much talk of ley-lines and the mysterious connections linking steeple-to-hill-to-spire in a web of subtle earth currents which once, they say, governed the paths of those who in ancient times were without the "benefits" of technology. Maps are produced overdrawn with straight lines which these geomancers nod wisely over, until Tralee takes the floor. She is renowned for asking New Age lecturers difficult questions, and some have even banned her from their discourses on this account.

'You say that the ley-lines are natural formations of energy,' she says: 'And if so, how do you relate them to the astrological landscape around Glastonbury?'

Nobody seems to have thought about a connection between the two, and an argument develops which rolls fiercely around the circle, until, arriving at a consensus view a young hippy stands up and denies any such relationship.

'It's got nothing to do with it,' he says. 'What we're into are the ley-lines, and the Glastonbury Zodiac has no connection with us at all.

'*No connection?*' Tralee sounds exasperated. 'Draw a line from Butleigh at the centre of the zodiac, northwards past Wookey Hole to the camp here at Priddy, and it will pass directly through the Phoenix on the cusp between Pisces and Aquarius.' Drawing upon her fine insight into the astrological mysteries she delivers her clincher.

'The Phoenix flies barely four and a half miles south of where we stand, and were it to rise from the earth and flap its wings right now you would feel the heat alright.'

But the notion of the great firebird rising from the landscape, and scorching a path above their heads through the soft Somerset night, cuts no ice with the geomancers. They are obsessed with straight lines, which, according to Smith's small knowledge of the subject is all very well as an abstract concept, but its application as a fact yields only a circle. All lines when extended must perforce follow the curvature of the planet, which only serves to confirm his suspicion that they are a lot of closet flat-earthers.

Proof Of The Pudding

Now out of the darkness stumble two figures. It is Dick, trombonist with Smith's old band Suntrolly, and his new girlfriend Joy. They have hitched down from London to visit the carts and see what travelling is like.

'We want to find some way of making a living in the country,' says Dick. 'Maybe get an old bus or some kind of motor-van.' He lowers his voice to a whisper and looks guiltily around. '*Joy doesn't like horses very much*,' and Smith only just hears the whisper. Dick is no fool, and senses already that such provocative talk among the Count's ménage will swiftly throw them out of favour.

'We'll just stay for a few days and then move on down to Glastonbury,' he says.

Glastonbury is a quiet market town. Yet long before the coming of the festivals an infiltration has occurred and hippies, escaping the city, have set up communes and rent cottages in and around the town. There is even a café decked out in New Age themes where the newcomers gather to swop the latest UFO stories.

And people of the crystal came and those who favour trees. Ogham alphabets they skryed and with the *I Ching* sought for subtler resolutions than the lawyers could devise. Their minds now free of city lore dipped deeper into ancient things and dreamed of long-gone days when Arthur's court and Merlin's spell held all the land in harmony.

Dick hears of Smith's fiddle work earlier that evening and asks if he intends to busk again on the morrow; for if not, he would like to try this disreputable gig himself.

'I know quite a few marches on the trombone,' he says, 'And it will be a novelty for the gypsies.'

Smith doesn't think the gypsies will be interested in marching, but he encourages Dick all he can and gives him some sound advice.

'Keep your back to a wall when you play.' he warns.

'You're sure you don't want to do it?' Dick asks again.

'One-offs is what it's all about,' says Smith. 'Do it too much and you're on the slippery slope to habit and dependency.'

A sudden thought scurries across his mind. 'It is the second nomadic law,' he adds solemnly, as he delivers this bit of arcane fiction.

Joy has been listening to this and doesn't agree at all.

'You can't go through life without routines.'

Her tone is a little hostile, as if she senses a threat in his attitude. Smith doesn't answer. His recent clash with Miriam has made him wary of arguing with women, and he keeps his opinions to himself. 'Well,' he thinks, 'the proof of the pudding is in the eating.' But he dare not offer his pudding theory to Joy. He knows she will not understand.

Once more on the move the travellers head down below Shepton Mallet, then up in an arc to the Roman Road at Wanstrow and on to the castle village of Nunney, where the Count has arranged a short stay to get Miriam's caravan together. She has found a four-wheel flat at a local farm and snaps it up cheap. The wheels are sound but the flat-bed needs some rotten planks replacing before the top can be built. She now drives Danny with her baggage on the flat, and once the wheels are greased he has no trouble pulling it.

Bruton Beast

Smith has acquired two chickens, purchased from a gypsy for a few shillings each. They are Bantams and she, white with speckles becomes "Mrs Speckly," and he, glossy black shot with iridescent green is "Paganini." They both now live and travel in a cage slung beneath his cart and come out each evening to scavenge around the camp.

''Im come from fighting stock,' says the gypsy. ''Im's dad were the "Bruton Beast", and there weren't a bird for miles around that could last a minute with '*im*.'

Smith looks at the little black cockerel as he struts proudly around, and agrees that he looks ready to take on all comers.

''E'll guard yer camp well. With 'im around you don't need no dog.'

Rallying Points

Looking over the Count's shoulder one evening as he peruses his map Smith notices that they are passing over a Civil War battlefield, and realises that the little band of travellers, with their scruffy carts and ragged clothes, would pass unnoticed were they to turn a corner at just the right angle and precipitate themselves back to 1642.

In the very earliest stages of the war Cromwell had sent Alexander Popham to recruit an army at Shepton Mallet, while the King had despatched the Marquis of Hertford to Wells to rally the royalists. A bare six miles between these polarities and an unhappy encounter between representatives of the two sides had quickly led to action. But Smith, knowing little about English history is unaware of these details, and sees the whole thing as an expression of the conflict between the toffs and the yobs, brought to a head by a haughty King who regarded Cromwell and his Roundheads as nothing more than trailer-trash. However, calling in at a local library in one of the villages they had passed through, Smith had discovered that in this instance, having been sorely provoked by Cromwell's representative, the Marquis had sallied forth from Wells and descended in force upon Shepton Mallet, driving out the Parliamentarians and disarming the town. Satisfied with his plunder he had then withdrawn to Wells.

Smith, regarding all this, cannot help but imagine that unhappy initial encounter between two powerful men which had set the Marquis upon this action.

A Touch Of Class

The cobbled town-square is full of bustling commerce. Stalls ply their trade around the edges, and the great iron-shod wheels of heavy farm-carts grumble as they pass. In front of the hostelry at the sign of the "Stag", is placed a large plain wooden table, and behind it sits a severe-looking man with cropped hair. He looks as if he might be a clergyman, but he exhibits an air of great authority.

He is William Strode MP who represents Cromwell's trusted minister, the great Alexander Popham, here to recruit in Shepton Mallet for the Parliamentary Army. He deals quickly with the farm lads and village yokels, swearing them in and despatching them out to the surrounding fields, to receive elementary training from the Sergeants-at-Arms and their troops. As he is dealing with the last of the day's influx of recruits, there is a clatter of hooves as a body of richly dressed cavaliers ride into town. Behind them a company of heavy dragoons keep tight formation, and the townsfolk fall back before them as they approach the table and halt.

It is Sir Ralph Hopten, representing the Marquis of Hertford, now recruiting for the King barely six miles away in Wells. Sitting on his horse haughtily, frilled with much fine lace and hung about with silken sashes, he disdains to even look at Strode, but speaks an aside with his *aide de camp*. The man, dressed in no less finery than his master and wearing a wide-brimmed feathered hat, dismounts and approaches the MP.

'Sir Ralph wishes to use the hostelry and you will remove this table at once.' He speaks in the arrogant manner reserved by aristocrats for servants and other underlings.

Strode doesn't move a muscle. But his voice, long familiar with public speaking rings out hard so that all present may hear.

'This table,' he says. 'Is the Parliament of England, and no other power in the land may move it!'

Sir Ralph snaps an order to his Captain of dragoons, and trotting his horse forward a little speaks in a contemptuous manner to Strode.

'If you will not remove this table at once, I shall order it cut to pieces. Together with you and the rabble that support you.'

A half-dozen troopers trot forward, their horses dipping and plunging, as with drawn sabres they form into a threatening line. Behind Strode, a crowd of townsfolk have gathered in his support, and many pitchforks wave above their heads. But Sir Ralph knows that his troops can handle any number of these, and he awaits the inevitable outcome with confidence.

Strode rises slowly to his feet, and as if he is addressing the full House speaks:

'If I die at your hand this day,' he says. 'Neither you nor your men will leave this place alive.'

Sir Ralph stiffens in his saddle at this and wonders at the fellow's insolence. But looking more closely at the MP's supporters, he notices for the first time that here and there a military pike rears its fearsome head. Dotted through the crowd a glint of armoured breastplate and flash of polished helmet draw together, and as he watches, form an unbroken line behind Strode. He looks again. These men are no ill-trained yokels. For Sir Ralph, a man skilled in arms recognises the grim battle-hardened look of men who have faced cavalry before. A small forest of pikes now support strode, and in the trained hands of a skilled fighter one of these weapons, with its butt firmly grounded, can lift a man from his saddle and send him in a high arc to struggle like an insect impaled on the point of a pin. Sir Ralph turns around and sees many more armour-clad men forming into companies behind him. This is a small army, and looking once more at the pikes behind Strode Sir Ralph makes his decision.

He orders a retreat, but gives stern warning of another day.

'You will hang from yonder tree,' he says, pointing to an old oak which grows nearby, but Strode, returning to his seat is unimpressed.

'We will see who shall hang,' he says dryly.

This was the insulting episode that had stung the Marquis into a fury and led to one of the earliest actions of the Civil War. Gathering a large Royalist army about him the Marquis had driven out the Shepton Mallet Roundheads and disarmed the town. Then, laden with plunder, he had retreated again to Wells, while the unhanged Mr Strode MP made good a tactical retreat with his troops, to join with the main Parliamentary armies to the north.

And now the travellers cut across the very tracks which the Marquis' plunder-laden carts had taken on their retreat to Wells. Between Dalcote and Dinder they pass, two villages through which his troops must have ridden in triumph, closely followed by their heaped wagons of booty. Smith scans the ground closely, hoping to spy the odd jewel-encrusted goblet fallen peradventure from the back of a cart, to lie hidden perhaps for centuries in the undergrowth. But he is out of luck, and soon gives up the search to cast his eye ahead where the Count rides point on his white stallion as haughtily as any Marquis. And indeed, there is little doubt that his ancestors had all been of the King's Party. His wide-brim feathered hat and sheepskin jerkin, his long locks and pointed beard, all conspire to endow him with the cavalier looks of any of the King's men. But, luckily for him, there are no gangs of armed yobbos marching around the countryside to challenge his stance.

Contrary Oscillations

At Nunney a local bigwig has offered a yard and a couple of fields for a few days, and they go to work for Miriam. The two ends for her caravan are built with overlapping planks in the manner of a gardenshed, with a door in one section and a window in the other. When finished and erected, stabilisers are fixed across the top, a canvas is stretched over the whole thing, and Miriam goes inside and shuts her door. The caravan rocks a little on its springs as she bustles around inside arranging the decor of her new travelling boudoir.

East now through Fisherton-de-la-Mere, where beds of watercress line the road. Here, a new tune springs to Smith's mind and he names it after the village. Then north across Salisbury Plain to Horton and all along down the beautiful Vale of Pewsey. The valley is wide and steep-sided as the carts wind their way along the narrow lanes which skirt its edges. And here another catchy tune comes floating through Smith's head. They are now travelling astride a major ley-line, to the left of which streams an oscillation contrary to that of the right. He builds this contra-flow into the music, changing from 3/4 to 4/4 throughout the piece to represent this anomaly. But he keeps this esoteric aspect to himself, feeling somehow that the world is not yet ready for such notions. They are moving now much slower as the summer wears on, and the Count says he will spend the winter near Newbury, where a rock-star friend of his has a large house and grounds.

'We can take our time on the next bit,' he says. 'We've got till autumn to get there.'

Medieval Showdown

Autumn, and the Hampshire trees are going for gold. The house of the Count's friend is a noble pile with extensive grounds. The owner spends little time there himself, but a live-in gardener keeps his eye on things. Here, Smith intends to build himself a little cart of his own and manages, with the help of the Count, to get himself the chassis and wheels of an old milk-float. He builds a small flat-bed on the float's chassis and cuts two saplings for the shafts. When these are bolted to the bed of the cart and some hooks fixed beneath he has a nifty little rig. Babylon, after a bit of practice hauling logs around a field to accustom him to pulling, handles it easily. With a couple of movable hoops and some canvas on top, he has room to stretch out and a place for a candle. Now he can feel at home anywhere.

Come spring and the talk is of leaving. But over the winter the Count's visitors have been many, and some, much taken with the idea of travelling, have sworn to acquire carts in the spring to join up with him when he moves, and this may make getting started a little difficult. Even some of Smith's old friends arrive. A battered coach with Dick and Joy drives up, and young Nick of Portobello totem fame hitches down from London.

'This is our Medieval Fair,' announces Joy, standing proudly in the doorway of the coach. 'We're travelling from village to village putting on shows.'

'What kind of shows?' asks Smith.

'Oh, all kinds of things,' she says airily. 'You can join us if you like, but you must get a girlfriend first.'

'Why?' asks Smith.

'Because we're only going to have couples,' she replies firmly.

A chill runs up Smith's spine at this blatant and sinister bid for matriarchal power. But he doesn't show his hand.

'I'll think about it,' is all he says.

Joy has a strange tendency to muddle her words, and as Smith is talking later with Dick, she sticks her head out of the bus window and orders him off to get something for her at the nearby village.

'Go and get me a "cartoon" of milk,' she shouts, and Dick shrugs and rolls his eyes.

Smith accompanies him to the shop and asks him about their performances along the way.

'Well,' says Dick, 'it's not too good yet, and the last two places we got nothing. They didn't like Joy dancing to my trombone very much, and in the last place somebody shouted out that we were bloody mad. Joy got angry and called them "ignorant bumpkins" and the police turned up.' He shakes his head sadly. 'What we need are a few more people.' He looks hopefully at Smith, who knows now for sure that he is giving the "Medieval Fair" a miss.

However, young Nick is more than ready to join the Count, and within a few days he goes off to a local sale and blows his savings on a horse. With a float and harness thrown in he gets a little mare and prepares himself for the road, harnessing up each day and leading his cart around the estate until he has the best of it.

Miriam, restless after an idle winter yearns for a bit more sun. Anyway, the wheels on her cart are more rotten than she had thought. So she goes off to Morocco, leaving Danny in the secure hands of the Count. Meanwhile, the travellers begin checking over their carts for the road. The Count has arranged to meet the new influx on Hungerford Common, which is large enough to take the ten or so carts which he expects to arrive. But he doesn't look too happy about it. 'Most of them haven't a clue,' he grumbles.

A day or so later, and with spring in the air they make an early start, and taking it easy on the way arrive to pitch camp on the common. It is a sizeable piece of grassland with plenty of grazing, and staking out the horses they wait for the new members to arrive.

A road borders one side of the common. Built on a raised embankment, its entire length can be seen from the camp, and the next day three lorries arrive to disgorge a couple of carts and a pair of horses. The Count helps his friends see to the horses, and after examining the carts and harnesses he shakes his head in disbelief. 'They're not ready for the road at all,' he says. 'The wheels on that one are very dodgy and one of the horses has a loose shoe. 'They haven't got a clue,' he says.

Two more vans arrive the next morning, and in the afternoon, another three. The horses that emerge are a mixed bunch, and the carts, dilapidated and unused for years, look as if they will fall apart. The Count is in despair, but he calls the townies together and gives them a few rules of the road.

'Rule one,' he says. 'Don't let you horses eat from the hedgerows or go into any wood. Otherwise they will get stoned out of their heads and you won't be able to control them.' Smith has already had some experience of this back along their previous summer's route. Rommel had suddenly gone berserk. He had refused to back into the cart, and had kicked and bucked for no apparent reason. 'He's been into the woods,' said the Count, and Smith had admitted this to be so. He had staked his two horses in a shady little dell for an hour or so a few miles back. 'There's all kinds of stuff that they like in the woods,' says the Count, 'and they know exactly how to find it.' Babylon too was inflicted this way. For when Smith rode him later, he jumped at a fly passing too closely; then danced and reared at a twig in the road. 'He's hallucinating,' he had thought. But he intends to follow him next time to see what he eats, and maybe try a little himself.

Difficulty In The Beginning, The Middle, And The End

Everyone has an early night in expectation of a dawn start, and when morning comes the task of getting this whole entourage on the road begins. Smith and Nick watch from their carts, they can be ready to go in five minutes flat and they wait for the others to get up onto the road. But there are problems with harnesses which do not fit properly, and the horses are jumpy in these new surroundings. Two of the carts get up onto the road and the drivers try to keep their horses still while they wait for the others. Another cart attempts the embankment. But half way up the horse freaks and gallops off shedding blankets and pots which then have to be gathered up. Two more make the attempt, and one, its harness too loose, overturns the cart and makes off trailing its harness behind it.

Now the carts on the road are in trouble. A tractor passes closely and the horses jump; the two carts collide and frighten them even more, and they take off in different directions. The field is soon littered with overturned carts and freaking horses, while ladies dressed for the Kings Road run around screaming. It is total chaos, and come tea-time they're still trying. But it will get dark soon and thus too late anyway to get away today.

'The best thing is for you two to get started tomorrow on your own,' says the Count to Nick and Smith. 'This lot will never make it, so I'm going to send them off in small groups to get some practice in.'

Smith acknowledges the sense in this, and they agree to meet later when the townies have dispersed. 'This'll keep you going for a bit,' says the Count as, generous to the last, he hands Smith a ten-pound note.

The next morning Nick and Smith are off at dawn before the inevitable chaos can begin again, and since they are travelling light reach the appointed spot as dusk is falling. Here they leave their markers and set up camp in a dingle hidden from any road to await the Count.

For Smith, a problem has arisen which looms larger every day. He has overheard odd references to the Count's future intentions whilst listening to his friends talking amongst themselves. They seem to think that he is "looking for a place of his own," there to "settle down," and, piecing these fragments of conversation together, he is beginning to suspect that the place which they assert the Count is looking for is far from Samarkand.

"Settling down," is the last thing on Smith's mind. The notion has in fact given him the horrors, and he looks to see what may lie in store if his suspicions are correct. Nick and he will probably end up as the Count's stable boys with daily chores to do about the place, and the prospect of this is giving him serious doubts about the whole thing.

Two days pass and the Count rides in with Muldoon. They stay for coffee and discuss the recent events.

'It was hopeless,' says the Count. 'Most of them have sold up and gone back to town, and the others won't last very long.' He stands up. 'We're camped by the Queen's Oak in the Savernake Forest for the next few days; we'll wait for you there.'

When they have ridden off Smith contemplates his dilemma. He has reached, he knows, a crucial crossroads in his life and must make his choice quickly. Back with the Count and the security of his benevolent chequebook. Or forward to Samarkand without a pot to piss in. He had never felt entirely comfortable living under the Count's friendly largesse, and had sensed something unreal about the arrangement. He confers with Nick and proposes that they go it alone.

'We can work along the way,' he says. 'Mending chicken-runs or fences. We can clip hedges, cut grass, weed and sweep, maybe even save enough to get the horses shod.'

Nick is game. He doesn't know the Count well enough to turn up by himself, so throws in his lot with Smith, whose golden road is opening up once more. Turning their backs on the Queen's Oak they head southwest, and the Count's tenner lasts them to Warminster, but there is not a little difficulty along the way. Now, no longer beneath the umbrella of the Count's illustrious name, the country folk are hostile and treat them like vagabonds. Camping has become a problem. No jovial "colonels" open wide their gates; word goes round quickly if they set up on a the verge of a lane and the police are called to move them on. With their money gone they will begin work on the morrow, heading for Glastonbury where the droves are more welcoming, while offering their services in villages on the way.

Bob-a-Job

The next morning they hit Upton Nobel, eager and willing to do a day's work. Smith confidently knocks on the door of a cottage on the outskirts of the village, and a woman opens up. She is not the usual country type; her hair is set in a tall beehive and her pinafore is neat and frilled.

'What do you want?' she glares suspiciously at Smith as she speaks and narrows her door to a crack.

'Do you have any odd-jobs you need doing?' he asks, as politely as he can. She opens the door a little wider at this and looks past him to where stand Nick with the carts, and makes up her mind at once.

'No,' she says firmly, 'and if you don't get out of my garden right now I'll send for the police.'

Smith backs hastily off. The police are always difficult to handle on the road, since their basic assumption is that travellers should not really exist. He tries a few more cottages as they pass through the village, but is met with more hostility. One woman had immediately called her husband to the door. He is a large surly-looking man with his braces still dangling. Taking one look he had rudely and fiercely ordered them to "Eff off". And Nick too fares no better.

They get the same cold shoulder at Boscombe, and Smith begins to suspect that telephones are giving warning of their coming. For in Evercreech, a police car had been waiting on the outskirts of the village, following them slowly until they had passed through, and now worse befalls them. Babylon has cast a shoe and another is giving the ominous "clink" of coming loss. Smith ties some rags around the unshod hoof and hopes the other will last. Nick too has a few loose ones, and Rommel is "clinking" like mad. By the next day they are both stopping every mile or so to re-tie the rags, which wear through quickly on the hard road. Now the police are popping up everywhere. "Names and addresses," and "Where are you going, and why?"

In Which Paganini Shows His Mettle

Just below Glastonbury they evade the law, and go to ground along Cinnamon Lane to camp by the side of the River Brue. Here, out of sight, the police will not find them while they decide what to do next. Travelling without shoes for the horses is out of the question, they will quickly go lame and the supply of rags won't last forever. Glastonbury however, is quite nearby, and soon word of the camp beside the Brue spreads. Who should now turn up but Harry Flame, his moroseness seems to have passed and his sojourn in Wales done him good. He has news of Joy, who now leads a small convoy of buses and vans, and she rules her subjects, it is rumoured, with a rod of iron.

While they are talking around the fire, Mrs Speckly comes close and begins acting most strangely. She bobs and ducks and seems to be straining at something.

'She's laying an egg,' shouts Harry. But Smith cannot believe this. In all the time he's had her she had never done any such thing, and now he doesn't think her capable. Harry grabs a frying pan to hold beneath the bird, and sure enough a moment later an egg drops to break neatly open into the pan. Harry picks out the shell and puts the pan on the fire, and when it is cooked he divides it into three equal parts and serves.

A day or two later a fox takes a fancy to Mrs Speckly as she pecks around beneath a hedge. She cackles in alarm but the fox moves in for the kill. Smith, too far away to help, shouts at the fox and looks for something to throw. But intent on its supper it ignores him and prepares to seize the bird. Suddenly, there comes another screech, but this of banshee proportions and filled with the lust for battle. It is Paganini. Straight at the fox he flies, a glossy black whirlwind of flashing feathers, stabbing beak and striking talons. He is a fighting bantam cock and battle is in his blood. Up in the air above the fox's head he goes, then downwards with stabbing beak and talons for the eyes.

The fox won't take on the furious bird and turns tail to run. Mrs Speckly however, now that the danger is passed, returns to her complacent foraging as if nothing has happened. Paganini struts closely around her in small circles, his crowing beak held skywards and his proudly strutting feet lifted high. Mrs Speckly however, unimpressed by her husband's valour ignores his noble courage, and even chases him angrily away if he encroaches too closely on her pickings.

The Charioteers

The horses are now in a sorry state with hardly a shoe between them. Smith, realising that the end is nigh takes Rommel, now entirely shoeless, up to a farm close to Glastonbury where old Charlie, a friend of the Count's, has extensive fields. Smith opens a gate into an orchard where the little horse can do no harm, and Rommel, sensing freedom ahead darts through the gate and soon disappears amongst the trees where the Count can pick him up at his leisure. Back at camp Nick's new girlfriend, a recent acquisition has turned up with some disquieting news. The police have been asking questions around the town about the carts and their location.

'They're looking for you,' she says. 'You should move from here quickly.'

This is now a serious issue, since they had been threatened recently with a charge of vagrancy.

'Stay out of our patch,' a policeman had warned them. 'Or you'll be in trouble.'

Here, camped in a bend of Cinnamon Lane they can be seen by anything passing, and it is only the remoteness of the spot that has protected them so far.

'We must go into the droves,' says Nick. 'They'll never catch us there.'

The nearest entrance to these long-forgotten byways is no more than a mile away, but to reach it they must get up onto the lane where they are vulnerable. Little time however is given to decide, for in the distance a police siren can be heard and it is fast heading their way.

On go the collars faster now than ever before. Belly-bands are tightened, bits quickly inserted into reluctant mouths and horses backed into shafts and hooked up. There is no time for walking, so they climb aboard and swing across the wide grassy verge and up onto the road. Nick gives his horse a smack and she's off, clattering shoeless up the lane at a fast trot. Smith gets Babylon going, but before he can hold him in he breaks into a gallop. The siren is now very close and freaking him out. Smith stands up in the cart the better to see across the tops of the hedges, and there, some way behind but gaining rapidly, the pale blue top of a police car skims.

'Come on!' he shouts, now at a full-blown gallop and fast catching up with Nick, who glances over his shoulder to see Smith almost upon him. Rising to his feet Nick begins spurring his horse with the slack of his rein, and now both are standing up as they race for the mouth of the drove, galloping their two-wheeled carts like chariots, while the hedges fly past in a blur. One more corner to round and the police will see them. But now the drove is in sight and Nick slows for a moment, turns abruptly to the right, and promptly disappears. Smith, only a few yards behind pulls Babylon in, gives a tug on the right rein, heads straight into a clump of bushes and on into the drove beyond. Within seconds they are hidden from sight, and within seconds more the police car flashes past.

Heading deeper into the droves, casting left and right until secure from any pursuit, they stake out the horses and set up camp. They are safe here, but too far from a road with easy access for visitors on whom they have become dependant for food, and the next few days bring the lowest point of the whole saga.

Nightingale

Smith sits alone in the drove and evening is falling fast. Nick has found a girlfriend in Glastonbury and spends much time of late canoodling in her flat, where no doubt he is making fast and loose among the sandwiches. Smith envies him his good fortune and is gazing morosely into a small fire, equating his lot with the long-gone drover, who, each evening unpacked and staked out his horses and sat before his solitary fire watching night fall, and so far from any road that not even a cheery cottage window shows its beacon of fellowship. He is considering his own position in this light, when out of the gathering dusk looms a shadowy figure. Once into the firelight Smith recognises the man, a gypsy who plies the surrounding countryside in his pick-up truck looking for deals and anything that isn't nailed down. The gypsy squats and Smith offers him tea.

'Nice spot,' the man says. 'No one can reach you 'ere. I saw the glim of yer fire across the fields. But I know these droves well and they're no mystery to me. I could travel from 'ere clear across to Wanstrow without a soul being any the wiser.' He taps his head. 'Oo arr,' he says. 'I've got it all in 'ere, but none o' they house-buggers will go into the droves at night, even if they do catch sight of yer glim.'

They sit gazing across an adjacent field and dusk is deepening fast, when from the far side, where a hedge draws a ragged black line of real darkness comes a long, low and liquid burbling. It rises and falls through delicate intervals to end in a sustained and melodious whistle. Smith doubts his own ears; no bird can sing music like that. But again comes the call. First the burbling, and now rising higher, until at its peak it trails away on a single plaintive tone. Silence falls again and the gypsy leans forward. 'That be nightingale,' he says quietly. His voice is rough and not given to sentiment, but Smith is surprised to hear a hushed note of respect in his tone. 'Just about now 'im likes to sing.'

Smith has heard stories of the legendary bird and is aware of its lofty reputation. But he had imagined something prettier than this, the sweet prattle of a talented young songstress perhaps, and as the bird begins its unearthly song again he realises he has nothing of the same order to compare it with. No other bird he has ever heard is in its class, for the song has all the pathos of a torch-singer, tempered by the fluting purity of a renaissance angel.

He looks sideways at the dark figure which sits beside him. The gypsy is roughly dressed, his hands gnarled around the handle of the mug and his feet encased in great hobnailed boots. Smith is aware of having received a priceless gift, for the man has given him his first nightingale and he is still reeling from the magic of it. Wishing to express his appreciation, there is sincerity in his voice when he speaks.

'Thanks for telling me,' he says. 'I'll never forget it.'

The gypsy shifts uncomfortably at this borderline sentiment.

'Oo arr,' he growls.

No Direction At All

Smith has made himself a Bedouin style tent. It has a flat top supported by a central pole, with a strip of canvas sewn around the edges for walls. He wakes early one morning to the sound of heavy rain. It has been coming down for days without break and all the wood is wet, so he is without even a morning cup of tea.

He lifts himself onto one elbow and pulls aside a flap. There before him stretches the drove edged each side by ragged hedges. The rain has made the long rank grass sodden and the clouds are low and of a cheerless grey. Some way further up the drove Babylon stands dejectedly in his circle of trodden grass, water dripping from his mane and tail. He looks forlorn, and in spite of Rommel's cantankerousness Smith suspects Babylon misses him greatly.

Smith misses everything. 'Bacon and eggs would go down well now,' he thinks. 'And mushrooms, tomatoes, bake-beans and toast, and butter and *real* coffee.' He is very hungry and tortures himself in this way, but he stays where he lies. There is nothing to get up for. A few melancholy hours later he sits up and notices that his sleeping bag is wet at the bottom. A soaking patch is fast spreading up the bag and there is no way he can dry it. It is the very last straw. He gets up and puts on his boots, then sets out for the long walk to Glastonbury.

Nick comes to his girlfriend's door and Smith tells him that he is finished with travelling. His road to Samarkand has ended; bogged down amongst the sodden grassy marshlands of the Glastonbury plain.

'I'm selling Babylon,' he says. There is a gypsy lady who runs a local children's riding school who has made him an offer. 'And I'm taking it,' he says.

'What about the carts?' asks Nick.

'Well, if you've had enough too we can run them up into old Charlie's cowshed, he doesn't have any cows anyway and he can use them as he likes.'

Nick, who also has had local offers for his horse has no problem with this. His girlfriend is looking after him nicely and he looks as if he is feeding well.

'We'll do it tomorrow,' says Smith. 'And now, what are the chances of a bacon sandwich?'

The next day the deed is done, and Smith leaves Nick to travel the domestic path while he hitches eastwards to London. That fabled city of gilded spires and fretted marble domes, where houris hang lasciviously simpering from the windows of their sumptuous boudoirs.

However, dropped off at the Cromwell Road, in a city where poets languish in a Philistine landscape and troubadours go mad in their rooms, the stink and roar of traffic and the constant neurotic wailings of the police quickly bring him to his senses and leave him with no direction at all.

Double Entendre

Sukie has a large black tomcat she calls Black Jacques, who under pain of being literally thrown out must vacate her room each morning and not return till after dark. Sukie sits painting in her garden room with the windows, shrouded at one corner with overhanging bushes, wide open. Before the window she has a large table at which she works and it is strewn with nuts, fruit and pieces of bread, a daily banquet for local squirrels when, losing their fear of her they enter to partake of this convenient buffet. Robins too hop in and peck amongst her brushes, while the odd blackbird, its watchful eye missing nothing makes darting forays amongst this abundance.

Visitors to her room must knock and wait until the crazy fluttering of wings and mad scramble of tiny claw has abated before entering. The room is decorated with bundles of dried flowers which she uses as the models for her flower paintings. Cut flowers she will not tolerate for fear of upsetting her nature Goddess.

'She will be angry wiz me if I cutting flowers alive,' she says.

The only fly in this idyllic ointment is Black Jacques, who will kill every bird and squirrel in sight if he gets half the chance and is therefore banished during daylight hours. Each evening at dusk she goes into the garden and calls for him. 'Black Jacques. Coming 'ere,' she calls banging upon a plate with a spoon, until out of the shadows he bounds.

'The cat, she love me,' says Sukie, whose English doesn't run to correct gender. 'She is werry friendly wiz me.'

At some point Black Jacques, chafing perhaps under the restrictions at home, had began to spend the odd night away, and Sukie's plaintive evening call had remained unanswered.

'She 'ave find some ozzer place, but what can I do?' she complains.

This errant behaviour now becomes serious, for Black Jacques hasn't been seen for three days and Sukie is distraught.

'Black Jacques, she 'ave gone,' she moans. 'I know she 'ave gone.'

It is during this mini-drama that Ace is passing the telephone in the hall when it rings and he picks it up.

'Hallo,' he says.

The voice which answers is male and obviously of middle-eastern origin.

'I want to coming for black pussy,' says the man.

Ace thinks he has misheard. 'Black what?' he says.

'Pussy,' says the man. 'I wanting black pussy.'

'You must have the wrong number,' says Ace, he is innocent of any double entendre in the man's request.

'No, I 'ave dis number,' says the man reading it out. Not a wrong number then.

'Well I'm sorry but I don't know what you're talking about,' says Ace.

The man becomes abusive:

'You no telling people things and then telling don't know,' shouts the man angrily.

Puzzled, Ace puts down the phone. 'Perhaps it's a nutter,' he thinks, but before he can leave the phone rings again. Rather tentatively he pick it up again. This time the accent is London English, a young man who seems a little nervous.

'Er, um,' he says. 'I... er... I'd like to visit the black... er...pussy.'

He almost whispers the last and Ace is now very confused.

'Look,' he says. 'I don't know what this is all about but please don't ring here any more.' He hears a click as the caller puts down the phone and leaves the hall as fast as he can before it rings again.

In the garden he comes upon Smith.

'We're getting some very weird phone calls,' he says.

'What kind of weird?' asks Smith.

'Well it's men,' says Ace.

'What do they want?' asks Smith.

But by now Ace, for all his naiveté is beginning to have his suspicions and putting his hand to his mouth as if making an aside he whispers: 'Black pussy.' He looks very embarrassed.

'Probably just nutters,' says Smith.

'No,' says Ace. 'They had the right number.'

Smith is just about to tell him not to worry about it when from inside the house comes the ring of the telephone.

'I'll get it,' he says.

Inside he picks up the receiver.

'Hallo,' he says.

The man who answers is a Scotsman.

'Jist gie me yer address,' he says. 'I want to come for nice black pussy, and I'd like to come the noo.'

He stresses the 'noo', and the accent is so thick that Smith can barely understand him.

'What makes you think we have black pussy?' he asks.

'Ye should no put up the cairds if ye canna come up with the goods,' says the man aggressively.

'What cards?' asks Smith.

'The cairds ye put up in the bliddy street ye ken weel.' The man is very angry; he thinks he is being made a fool of.

'I'm sorry,' says Smith. 'There must be some mistake. I'll check it out.'

'Aye, you check it oot the noo, and dinna make a fool o' me agin.' The line goes dead and Smith heads for the street to 'check it oot.'

As he leaves he sees Tralee on her way out and gives her the gist of this latest mystery.

'Maybe it's someone playing a joke on us,' she says, but when they reach the pavement they see white postcards pinned to the roadside trees in both directions. Turning to the nearest they read:

NICE BLACK PUSSY
I like for you to see her
Please ring...

There follows the embassy telephone number.

'It's Sukie,' says Tralee. 'Black Jacques is missing and she must have put these up this morning.'

The cards are a disaster and Tralee and Smith go from tree to tree taking them down. 'Your English is difficult for people to understand,' Tralee tells Sukie and she helps her to write a new card with a somewhat less suggestive message.

All this however, to no avail, since Black Jacques never comes home and not hide nor hair is seen of him again. 'Probably blackmailing some old lady,' thinks Smith, but Sukie is disconsolate and it is this sad event which drives her to make a momentous decision. A wealthy businessman commissions a large painting from her, and since she gets paid up front she decides to buy the lease on a small cottage in the Massif Central area of France.

'I am going 'ome,' she says happily. ''Ere is too difficult to speaking.' And away she goes.

A year or so later Smith is invited to rehearse with a group who have a farmhouse in France and while there he calls in on her.

She lives in a wood on the outskirts of a rural village, and as Smith approaches he sees that the firs surrounding the cottage are hung with a variety of coloured bags filled with nuts. Apples swing like Christmas tree baubles from every branch and a minor forest of bird-tables mushroom upwards from the forest floor. It is an avian paradise and the surrounding trees are full of birds which are feeding from the bags and hopping down to the ground to forage amongst the squirrels for pieces of fruit. The cottage itself, however, is so densely covered in foliage that he has difficulty finding the door. He had telephoned from the village and so Sukie is expecting him when he knocks.

'Wait, wait, don't come in yet.' Sukie's voice comes from within. then... 'Get away, get away,' she shouts and there comes a series of bangs as if she is wielding a stick around. The door opens about a foot and Sukie's face appears at the opening. She is kicking backwards vigorously with both legs as she speaks.

'Come in wiz your side forward,' she says. 'I cannot open ze door any furzer.'

Smith edges his way through the crack avoiding her kicking feet and sees a circle of restless and malevolent cats pacing backwards and forwards and only held at bay by Sukie's kicking feet. Once he is inside she picks up a broom and begins laying about her with it as she drives them back. Occasionally, one cat will notice a gap in her defences and streak for the still open door, but she is too fast with the broom and using it like a hockey-stick she swoops it up and sends it tumbling back amongst its fellows.

'Get back! Get back!' she shouts as she slams the door and the cats retire to various parts of the room growling and flicking their tails angrily.

'I cannot let zem out in ze day,' she says. 'Ozzerwise zey will killing ze birds.'

Inside the cottage it is dark and lit only by a single bare bulb, but her radio, still tuned to Paris renders a low murmur of French café music. Although it is daylight outside, the windows are so shrouded with creepers that no light can penetrate.

'Why don't you cut the creepers from around your windows?' asks Smith.

Sukie looks shocked. 'The goddess will be angry wiz me if I cutting them,' she says.

Smith stays for coffee but after a while he needs to relieve himself.

'I'm just going for a pee,' he says, making for the door.

He has not moved more than a step or two in this direction before the cats are upon him, and they crowd around the door waiting for it to be opened.

'Don't open ze door!' shouts Suckie, grabbing up her broom and coming to his rescue. She sweeps the broom around in wide arcs, keeping the cats away as Smith squeezes through the smallest possible gap. Outside he breathes in a great lungful of fresh air, for inside the cottage there is a terrible stink. The cats, of which he had counted at least seven, do not seem to keep to any definite toilet arrangement and relieve themselves anywhere that pleases them, and the result is the aforementioned stink. There are, however, kinds and degrees of stink, from the mildly offensive, to the downright unbearable, but this stink goes beyond either of these to a region where words such as appalling or even ghastly would be more appropriate, and now, having tasted fresh air Smith is reluctant to go back inside.

He knocks on the door and when Sukie opens it a crack he tells her that he must be on his way. She comes outside laying around behind her with the broom.

Before he leaves she gives him a sly look and makes a request: 'I wanting you to find me some acid and sending it to me, zen I shall be werry 'appy,' she says.

Smith promises to do his best, but back in London he has no luck. Writing to tell her the bad news he erases a few errors with correction fluid leaving some white marks upon the paper. A week goes by and he gets a phone call from France. It is Sukie and she seems very upset.

'I cannot reading your letter,' she complains. 'I sink you hide ze acid under ze white stuff and so I eat one of zem and nossing 'appen. So zen I eat anozzer and nossing 'appen. Zen I eat zem all and still nossing 'appen. So zen I sink you 'ave put it on ze paper. So I eat ze whole letter. 'AND STILL NOSSING 'APPEN!' She sounds very indignant, as if Smith has deliberately deceived her.

'I am werry disappointing,' she wails. 'Now I 'ave lose my 'appy feeling and I am trap.'

'What do you mean?' asks Smith.

'I cannot leave or ze cats will immediately kill ze birds.'

'Why not get rid of the cats,' Smith suggests, realising that she has painted herself into a tight corner.

But this solution is out of her reach. 'I cannot.' Now she is in tears. 'I 'ave too much love for zem, and so now I am trap.'

She sobs for a while into the phone then... 'Oh, I am trap. I am trap,' she weeps.

Anterior Viewpoint

The embassy garden is patio'd at one end with a wide swathe of worn and weathered old paving stones. Lichen and moss clad those parts which lie outside the most frequented routes, and in the deep cracks between, tiny creeping plants surreptitiously extend themselves. One such crack, somewhat wider than its fellows, has at one end a small heap of finely worked soil hardly noticeable to a passer-by, but a closer focus reveals a dark hole at the summit of the heap. From time to time an ant comes scurrying from the hole and down the side of the heap, to hurry off along the crack about some minuscule task.

One however, takes a different route. Up the side of the stone it goes until emerging from the crack it reaches the flat surface at the top, and there halts, sentry-like, to survey the world above. Apart from the delicately waving antennae it does not move again, its head held fixed at an oblique angle it remains still for many moments. The ant is watching Smith, who sits on a garden bench close by. He has just made himself a large pot of tea and carried it into the garden where he intends to sit — and no matter what — remain until the pot is finished.

He leans back and pours himself the first cup while waiting for circumstance to challenge his resolve, and if daunting enough, perhaps even break his vow. Above his head Ace's windows are open and some musicians can be heard tuning up. An oboe is joined by a violin, and a guitar riffles through a few slow chords. Ace has just joined a new group and offered his room for rehearsals. The group are leaving for a tour of Italy soon and Ace has been asked to accompany them. Now, delighted with the idea, he is looking forward with pleasure to the trip.

'They're a funny lot,' he had told Smith. 'And I don't think they really like me very much.'

'Don't worry,' says Smith. 'Just keep your head down and enjoy the tour.'

Smith's teapot holds five cups and he has already disposed of one. Deeply ensconced in his pose of immovability he leans forward to pour a second, when a new sound issues forth from Ace's window and causes the teapot to freeze mid-pour.

Booma booma Dinga booma
Booma booma Dinga booma

Smith puts down the teapot and stares sightlessly before him. Where has he heard this before? It has the familiarity of a well known voice from long ago. He searches back through his memory and there! He has it. This precise and hypnotic rhythm can issue from the drum of only one man: Zen Glenn, his old percussionist from Suntrolly whom he has not seen in many years.

This challenge is more than his resolve can meet, and abandoning teapot and yogic ideals he leaps to his feet and makes his way into the house and up to Ace's room, while the ant, now that the coast is clear, turns and descends once more into the crack.

Smith stands outside Ace's door listening. The band has now began an ensemble piece and Ace can be heard softly filling the spaces with his Chinese-made violin, of which he is intensely proud. The violin is a cheap plywood factory job and has little carrying power, but the voice, though weak, has certain tonal qualities which a properly built instrument lacks. There is hollowness in the timbre which lends itself sweetly to the gentle tone, and Ace, much taken with this quality has resolved to form a string quartet of similar instruments.

'I'm going to call it the Chinese Cheapo Factory-Fiddle String Quartet,' he says. But Ace has now embarked on something a little tougher, and knowing Zen of old Smith wonders if he has bitten off more than he can chew.

Smith pushes open the door and looks in. The oboist stands with his back to the other musicians and seems to be playing to himself. In fact he now sees that they all have their backs turned against each other, as if they find each other's company unbearable. Only Ace stands innocently in the centre, playing steadily but with a frown of uncertainty on his face. The musicians, half-crazed to a man, are however, superb virtuosos. Their improvisations swirl around the room filling spaces others leave, and creating a collective song as fine as any dawn chorus. But it is Zen's magnetic aura and "*Booma booma Dinga booma*", that provides the glue which holds these wayward geniuses together.

Smith is pleased to see Zen again, but senses that the feeling is not entirely reciprocal. After a bit of affable chat Zen comes out with it.

'You went off and left us,' he accuses. 'You left me to keep the whole thing together.'

This is true. For Smith had indeed abandoned Suntrolly and embarked upon a motor-cycle journey for Peru. However, owing to certain unforeseen and diverting circumstances, he had ended up marooned on the Island of Fernando Poò, some way off the African coast at the mouth of the Niger River. He had then been forced to take a job as deck-hand on a rig-supply boat to earn his fare home. Of this he has no regrets. Looking at this collection of highly competent misfits he doesn't envy Zen, and is glad he didn't "Keep the whole thing together".

Antithesis

Arriving in Rome, Ace and the band retire to rest at their hotel. They will not give their first performance until the following evening, but already the fans are at their door. Zen's group, Third Ear Band, have made several CDs which sell well in Italy and gained for them a considerable following. Polanski's film *Macbeth* had featured Third Ear Band on the sound track, which gives the band a certain celebrity, and now the musicians are looking forward to a rapturous welcome. 'Be at the theatre at six-o'clock.' Zen had instructed before disappearing off to visit a friend, leaving them to amuse themselves as best they may.

The next evening Ace gets to the theatre early; he wants to experiment with something that he has only just discovered. Whilst practising in his hotel room he had stumbled upon the precise spot where his violin's "wolf-tone" occurs, and intrigued, now seeks a way to exploit it. The wolf-tone is the one point on a violin's spectrum of tones which brings the vibrations from the string into direct conflict with the geometric structure of the instrument. The result is a dreadful howl which strikes terror into the heart of every violinist. Usually this effect can be avoided by the judicious adjustment of the bridge or sound-post; often a combination of the two. But Ace's fiddle, cheaply made with scant regard for inner geometry cannot be doctored in this way, and the wolf-tone emerges ungoverned when he directs his bow a little above the G sharp.

By the time the rest of the band arrives, Ace has mastered the wolf-tone. He can descend onto it from above, or slowly climb until he can detect the beginnings of the howl. From there, plunging deeper, he can push on until his violin is on the point of shaking itself apart, and his teeth are vibrating in his jaw. When the entire band is present, they tune their instruments and play a little to warm up until the audience begin to arrive. Then, off to the coffee-shop for a last cup before the concert starts.

The auditorium is vast and the audience large, brought here by the extensive advertising invested in by the management. Tonight is important, first impressions count for much in this business and word spreads fast. As the curtain rises there is much clapping and whistling from the fans, and when Zen opens up with:

Booma booma Dinga booma
Booma booma Dinga booma

They go wild.

The first piece features the oboe. He twitters a little on two or three high notes and the guitar strikes a chord. Now the keyboard holds down two deep bass tones and Ace softly strokes his Chinese strings. It is as if a forest is awakening as more voices seek attention until, again they swirl around each other in a dawn chorus which at its epiphany sends their audience into raptures. Much applause comes from the excitable Italians, and a row of young girls in the front are trying to see up Ace's trouser legs. But, embarrassed, he steps back out of range.

The second piece begins well enough. It is almost entirely experimental and relies on the guitarist's stabbing chords which he holds one after another until a new tonality is established. Ace, not having played this piece before, looks for suitable openings in which to insert his contribution, but he feels no affinity with any of it. Then he remembers his wolf-tone. Of course, the piece is experimental, what better opportunity to put it to use? His finger slides up a string until it reaches G sharp, and then a nanatone higher, until the most dreadful sound imaginable begins to emerge from the fiddle. Ace is delighted, the tone is powerful and he is sure that it can be stronger yet. As he pushes on inwards towards the centre of this monstrous sound a demonic howl fills the air around him. It is picked up by his microphone which immediately feedbacks and amplifies the howl many times. Now at an unbearable level, the powerful speakers send the wolf-tone directly at the audience and they can't take it.

Ace, eyes fast shut, is now totally absorbed in his experiments. Reaching the centre where the tone is at its most awful, he has discovered that with a little more pressure from the bow it will leap up through the harmonics, and what is more, take the wolf-tone with it! Harder he presses and up and up he goes, until the violin is shaking in his hands. It is a banshee scream as if echoing from the mouth of hell itself. The roadies at the control desk are going frantic, and wildly fiddle with their knobs and levers to identify the source of the racket. But they have no success and the outraged members of the audience are getting up to leave in droves.

On the podium the musicians are giving each other paranoid looks, and Zen is scowling at them all with equal suspicion his drum getting louder under his furious hands.

Booma booma Dinga booma
BOOMA BOOMA DINGA BOOMA!

Behind the band long red and gold curtains are a splendid backdrop, but their serene folds are now violently displaced to make way for the manager, his face apoplectic above an immaculate dinner suit. He has invited the Mayor and City Aldermen for the performance, and he is being humiliated in front of his guests. He begins shouting at Zen, who shakes his head and shouts angrily back but does not stop playing. Now, almost beside himself, the manager stands listening behind each musician in turn in a furious attempt to find the culprit. Until, reaching Ace, he comes to a halt and stabs repeatedly an accusing finger at him. Ace, his eyes shut and unaware of the accusation, screeches higher and higher as he bears down harder on the bow. The other band members have had enough and stop playing. They begin shouting at Ace and several of the few remaining audience join in.

'*Fuori Via!' 'Fuori Via!* Come musicista sei un bravo idraulico!' and similar Italian obscenities they shout. But it is not until Zen, bringing his *Booma booma DINGA..!* to an abrupt end, and standing up roars: "SHUT UP!" That Ace senses something amiss and his composure disturbed, lowers his bow and turns to face a circle of angry faces. He has no idea why.

'You've spoilt our fucking gig! They shout vehemently and... 'Traitor!' This from the guitarist, who has suspected all along that Ace is the agent of dark forces sent to disrupt their tour. Lastly a snarl from Zen: 'It's down the tubes for you mate.'

By now most of the audience have left, and there is some talk with the manager of refunds and a free concert by way of compensation. That night back at their hotel a kangaroo court makes short-shrift of Ace. Zen as leader, attempts to give the proceedings a touch of democracy and even justice, by asking each band member in turn what should be done with Ace.

'Shall we give him one more chance?' he asks. 'Or kick him out?' He makes no attempt to disguise his preferred option in the matter.

'Kick him out,' had been the unanimous response, and Zen as leader, and nothing loath, gives Ace his plane ticket home and "Kicks him out."

Anti-Hero

Arriving back at the embassy in late afternoon, Ace had dumped his bags in his room and ventured into the garden. Brett and Caspar are examining a solar panel which Caspar intends fixing above his window, thus taking one more step in his quest for total independence. Caspar straightens up as Ace approaches.

'Why back so soon?' he asks. 'We thought you'd be gone for weeks.'

Ace decides to take it on the chin.

'I got kicked out on the first night,' he says, slightly shamefaced at the admission. He hangs his head a little but Caspar looks delighted.

'You got kicked out?' he says, grinning, and there is a hint of admiration in his tone. Brett too looks suitably impressed, and Ace is somewhat confused by their response. His confusion grows as Morgiana and Smith, brought on to the scene by Brett come and congratulate him.

'Got kicked out eh!' says Smith. 'Fantastic. How did it happen?'

Ace begins his tale and speaks with awe of the power of his violin's "wolf tone", and the subsequent hairy ride upon its vibrating back. At the end of the story he receives several pats on the shoulder, and even gets a kiss from Morgiana. He grins; suddenly he sees it all in a different light. Now he has a little genuine charisma, hard-won though it had been, and thenceforth is sometimes heard to say:

'Third Ear Band? Yes, I used to play with them.'

A pause... and then with just a touch of pride:

'But I got kicked out.'

The Tarts

Smith moodily sits on a bench in the garden one evening. He stares morosely at his feet idly looking for an ant to watch, but for some strange reason, possibly a late afternoon siesta, their presence is unusually scarce. He decides to sit, staring at this same piece of ground until an ant chooses to cross it, while knowing that such a vigil may well turn out to be a lengthy one. But his yogic instincts are now fully aroused and he commits himself totally to this austere discipline, intending with all his will to let nothing distract him. However, a moment later he drops the whole thing, since by his side the overhanging honeysuckle which shrouds the garden door parts, and accompanied by a small swarm of wanton giggles, Morgiana appears with a plate in her hands. She holds it out to Smith.

'Would you like a tart?' she says. There is an element of provocation in her voice and she flashes him a wicked look. But already the ants are out of it; for on looking up he sees that arranged tastefully on the plate are several luscious jam tarts. The jam looks like raspberry, but it is the shape that gives him a start, for they are moulded and cooked in the form of five pointed stars.

'Startarts,' says Smith, snapping out of his gloom at once.

'Caspar has eaten most of them,' says Morgiana, she tosses her head wilfully. 'But he's not having them all.' and she giggles again.

Smith considers the relationship between Caspar and Morgiana as if it is some kind of dance. He, like a moth to her candle is tempted ever closer. But her stellar gravity, although powerful, cannot overcome his centrifugal force, and just in time, he lightly skips with wings unsinged to a distant orbit from where once more, however far removed, he turns his face towards her flame. Morgiana is of course well aware of his manoeuvres and knows exactly what he is up to.

'Hence the startarts,' thinks Smith. 'It is obviously some capricious ploy she is playing in the steps of their ongoing dance. She will get Caspar hopelessly addicted to jam tarts and then sneak up on him from behind.' He takes a tart and conveys it to his mouth, while Morgiana carries the plate off in search of Ace whose tooth she knows is sweet and will be unable to resist the offering.

Smith finds the tasty morsel very good; the pastry is rich and short while the jam, with just the right consistency is set into a disc on the star-shaped tart. As he chews he raises his eyes skywards and notices that while he has been conversing with Morgiana the shades of evening have fallen and above, the real stars are coming to light.

The constellations are strung in twinkling skeins across the vaulted evening sky like sequins on a torch singer's gown; caught in their nebulous spotlight she reveals her spacious limbs, and Smith, his mind swirling with Morgiana's starry tarts and Caspar's stellar deeps is moved to write a tart poem.

Startart

Startart.
Fully fashioned moonbeam.
Plump white arm of a truly galactic collection;
Standing in her red shift
Wantonly beckons,
The Pleiades, a pool of lamplight at her feet.

Long-limbed coercer of naked stars.
One cheek's glimpsed highlight

Radiance from a Nova's heart.
White hands lingering
Among the dusty remnants of ancient systems
Trailing through languid fingers
Their tenuous veil
Rearranging life essences
Into unimaginable combinations.

Love Bug

Many outrageous and bizarre theories receive an airing from the podium in the salon, and one such had been the visit of an American psychologist. In her lecture she had proposed a world in which, with the right attitude, miracles were a natural phenomenon of daily life. The details of this re-alignment are contained in a course of daily lessons which Ace, Wirril and Smith peruse with much interest. One of the entities in the book is known as "The Holy Spirit", and in order to exorcise the pious cultural charge on this concept, they have taken the initials of "Holy Spirit", and renamed their new hero "Herman Schmidt", a tall crop-haired champion, his face disfigured down one side by an old duelling scar. Smith had wanted to add a monocle, but Wirril's disapproval had vetoed this idea, and Ace is reluctant to adopt this flippant attitude at all. Most of his bourgeois corners have by now rubbed off, and a new growth of suitable eccentricity is already flourishing, but for him, Herman Schmidt, let alone the monocle, is a step too far.

Wirril and Smith, however, long-time reprobates with nothing to lose, imagine their scarfaced hero combating the Earthly powers with Scarlet Pimpernel nonchalance. Herman has brought a love-virus to the planet Earth, disguised by a serum as a common corpuscle in his own blood, and evading the authorities he is now going about his work. He has already spread the virus far and wide, contaminating a considerable number of people in the process. But the authorities have now detected the effects of his presence. The all-pervading atmosphere of foreboding which they seek to maintain has, here and there, mysteriously lifted. The gloomy trudge replaced by a lighter and springier step. From many sub-stations there have been similar reports, and several instances of people actually *whistling in the street!*

The system goes on red alert and the iron fist closes. Now *everyone* is the prime suspect.

Bloodcheck II

Herman has no time to lose, the protective serum which disguises the love virus has worn off and the next bloodcheck will reveal his identity. He has hidden his flitter in the shrubbery of a small park while he stretches his legs for the last time before leaving.

It is dark as he steps from the park onto a lamplit pavement and sees, too late, the sleek black vehicle parked in shadow across the road. Before he has time to retreat a beam of intense light bathes him in its glare, and he freezes.

'*Bloodcheck!*'

The voice, hard and cold galvanises him into action. Taking two swift steps and grasping the top rail of the park fence he springs high, his long-legged duelling muscles hardened on the piste of many a fencing salle, carry him clear across the fence and streaking through the darkness towards his flitter.

Herman Schmidt doesn't do crucifixion.

A Scrambling Of Image

Herman jumped into his battered flitter and leaped vertically through several traffic levels at full power.

Beneath him a cluster of sparks climb like fireflies in his wake and spiral upwards towards him.

Police, or surveillance? he wonders, and leaning forward switches on the image scrambler.

Now they'll have trouble finding him.

Pursuit

Behind him, through the dissolving cloud of image particles, Herman saw five dim glows brighten into radiance once more. He was surprised; they must have the latest reassemblers and were still in pursuit. He plays his last card and switches context.

The coffee is finished and he feels like another, a waitress comes at his signal and pours a fresh cup. The night is clear, and through a vast circular window set into the wall of the restaurant the lights of the city glitter from far below.

He takes a sip of coffee and something catches his eye. It is a large crystal chandelier hanging just a few feet above him sending random flashes of brilliance from its multi-faceted drops. But in the centre of the cluster there occurs a consistent set.

Five bright and incandescent jewels far outshine the rest!

He rises hastily to his feet and makes for the door. This is no mere surveillance. They must be jumpmasters at the very least.

Camouflage

Outside the restaurant throngs jostle on the crowded pavements. He'd not realised there were so many humans. To his left a dingy tea shop, and on a torn piece of paper glued roughly to the window a mis-spelt message: "Wosherup Wantid." He takes a chance, there is little choice at the moment, and enters the steamy interior. The atmosphere reeks of grommet and rotting vegetables. The clientele, mostly down-and-outs guard their teacups with clawed fingers, and a bunch of grommet-poopers, their inhalation tubes hung with beads and dyed feathers shudder in a corner.

He approaches the counter, slouching a little, and speaks roughly from the side of his mouth.

'Stiw needa wosherup?' The grotesque human behind the counter gives him a quick glance.

'Yerfood antennerday.' He jerks his thumb. 'See Joe.'

Inside the back room, a pale-skinned figure looms among piles of filthy plates. The place stank.

'You Joe?'

The other points silently to the sink.

He removes his jump-jacket and gets to work.

Now they'll *really* have trouble finding him.

A Question Of Gravity

On the floor of his room at the top of the house Smith is lying flat on his back. In order to improve the acoustics and to facilitate his Chinese exercises he has removed the carpets and thrown out all the furniture. In the mornings he merely has to sweep with a soft broom, an activity which he enjoys, since he equates it with other elemental actions such as rowing or reaping with a scythe, a graceful and wholesome movement entirely different to the jerky and mechanical motions forced upon the operator of a vacuum cleaner, a device which he heartily loathes.

Somewhere below him Morgiana is giggling in her room. The giggles come curling up in short spirals, a silence, then another outburst and a small shoal of tiny giggles emerge, wriggling like bedsprings up through the floorboards. But the giggles, although intriguing, and emerging so wantonly from below as if from the boudoir of a rich and pampered courtesan do not distract him from the issue which has caused him to adopt this supine posture.

He has recently deduced a startling fact. In this position he can feel no strain whatsoever and the muscles, which in any other stance are required to manipulate and propel his meat-clad skeleton, are entirely at rest. Gravity, that fearsome foe of all creatures that go on legs has, in this pose been defeated, and the lifelong struggle which is the lot from birth to death of the human species is resolved. 'Seen from here,' he thinks. 'Standing up is just silly. A subconscious balancing act maintained by a combination of muscular tension and a scaffolding of articulated bones'. He stares for a while at the ceiling then...

'Well, I suppose you need something to hold the meat up.'

Looking down the length of his body he sinks deeper into the speculation. Lying down, he is convinced, is surely the most profound and primal position which the human body may adopt, since there is no element of effort involved. 'One might,' he considers, 'even fall unconscious in this position without coming to any harm.'

He turns now to the matter of other postures which may reveal some justification for their adoption. Standing up he regards as too weighty an issue to inquire into without first tackling something a little less radical, as for instance "sitting". It becomes immediately apparent that there are two variations of this posture. Sitting up, and sitting down, but it is obvious upon further examination that this halfway position is merely a covert version of lying down and therefore does not qualify as a primal posture. Thus he concludes: 'Sitting is merely the desire to retain the benefits of lying down, whilst simultaneously enjoying the advantages (if any) of standing up'. Feeling now sufficiently grounded in the fundamental dynamics of the issue he is ready to inquire into the complex nature of "Standing up".

Seeking first to discover what advantages this upright stance may offer, he soon perceives that considering the expense of muscular effort involved in moving the body into an erect posture, and the subsequent balancing act required to maintain that position, there seem to be no advantages at all. 'One might as well be lying down,' he thinks. 'But hang on a bit,' the thought continues to evolve. 'There is a missing link in the equation,' and after some further pondering he realises what it is.

'It's the legs,' he mutters.

Now he has his finger upon the crux of the matter, and the first fact to hit him as he considers these appendages is that they are two in number, implying the possibility of locomotion; for, were standing up meant by nature to be a static arrangement, one leg would have been sufficient for the purpose. 'Therefore,' the thought concludes: 'Walking is the only justification for standing up.' The logic is inescapable. 'Standing up,' he thinks, 'is merely a kind of motionless walking.'

Feeling that he has stretched his brains enough for one day he relinquishes any further purely mental perusal of the subject and rising on a sudden impulse puts the theory into practice. 'At least,' he concludes. 'I know now for sure that if I'm not walking I may as well be lying down.'

Putting his legs now to their proper use he exits the room, and leaving Morgiana's giggles to fade away behind him, turns his attention fully onto the act of walking.

'It's easy,' he thinks. 'Merely a matter of displacing one of the two legs at a time and providing they are alternated, walking takes place. He is pleased with this discovery and, speculating further realises that he doesn't even have to think about it; in fact he can think about something entirely different and still his legs continue to operate in a smooth and reliable manner.

'Whatever next?' He thinks, raising a hand to scratch his puzzled head and in so doing inadvertently brushing an ear.

Smith looks as if he cannot take any more.

'What are these weird trumpet things fixed to the side of my head?' he thinks.

The Case Of The Plundered Slipper

November sweeps a gloomy pall across the narrow London streets north of the Euston Road, bringing an early darkness to mingle with a thick fog rolling in from the river. Streetlamps penetrate this gloom but weakly, and outside the door of a certain address in Baker Street, muffled figures pass, wrapped against the cold to appear and disappear like phantoms into the fog. Above, a first floor window shows some light through a drawn curtain, and against this curtain two figures cast their shadow. One bends, and straightening, holds a violin in a dark hand, and in the other a bow. Putting violin to chin the figure begins to shadow play.

Inside the room and close against the curtain stand Moss and Smith, who are visiting the Sherlock Holmes museum at number 221b Baker Street, the home of the great investigator. Smith has been reading the collected stories to Moss each night, and by now they are familiar with the genre. Holmes' violin however is a mess, and Smith is disgusted that better care is not taken of the instrument. After all, the man who, surviving his tumble over the Reichenbach Falls at the hand of Dr. Moriarty, then went on to earn a living incognito as a concert violinist can have been no less than a master musician, and his instrument should be accorded more respect. But here, lying beside the great man's armchair, the violin has been allowed to fall into an appalling state. The strings are loose and rusty, and when Smith picks it up he can hear the sound-post rolling around inside. Moss is looking worried, he thinks an attendant may spot Smith with the violin and get them into trouble.

Smith, however, has seen enough. The thing won't play and he makes a mental note to speak to the management on the way out. Moss, meanwhile, is almost overcome by his surroundings. The room, "Just as the great man left it", is for him very real, and he tugs at Smith's sleeve and excitedly points into the fireplace. There, nestling at one side is a red leather slipper. They both know to what use it is put and Smith, taking a quick look around, stoops and thrusts his fingers into the slipper. Yes, down in the toe his fingers encounter Holmes' stash of tobacco. Taking a small pinch he brings it forth to show Moss who, still nervous that Smith may get caught, nevertheless gazes with wonder at "The real thing".

'Don't worry,' says Smith. 'Everyone nicks some; Mrs Hudson probably fills it up every night.'

Moss is unconvinced by this until, standing concealed between two glass cases, one containing Holmes' swordstick and Watson's service revolver, the other, Moriarty's death-ray fountain-pen and exploding toothbrush, they watch an elderly couple approach the fireplace. The two old people halt and exchange urgent whispers, then, while the woman darts anxious looks around the room, the man painfully crouches and thrusts his hand deep into the slipper. A moment later he withdraws it, and before he can convey it to his pocket they see, held between the shaky old fingers, a few shreds of Holmes' tobacco. Moss cheers up at this, but now he doesn't want to go. This is living theatre and he wants some more.

Smith, too, is enjoying the show, and they linger awhile until a young Japanese couple enter to wander around, pointing enthusiastically here and there as they recognise the exhibits. When they reach the fireplace however, a hush falls upon them, and while she darts her oriental eyes this way and that he, swift as a ninja, swoops downwards and in one lightning strike further depletes Holmes' stash.

Smith is holding back Moss, whose excitement threatens to expose their concealed position at any moment. His left ear is no more than a few inches from Dr. Moriarty's exploding tooth-brush and he has had enough. 'Come on,' he says. 'Let's go and get a coffee somewhere.' Moss knows that for him "coffee" means "cream-bun", and having witnessed to his satisfaction the plunder of Holmes' slipper, seems not unwilling to go.

As they are leaving the room Moss suddenly stops and stiffens. Smith glances down to see a look of childish reverence on his face. Moss' trembling finger points upwards and Smith turns to see, hanging from a nail driven into the wall, a long shrivelled and mottled snake-skin. As he stares at the skin Moss' voice comes from below:

'The Speckled Band', he whispers in awe.

Management had not been sympathetic to Smith's recommendations concerning the violin.

'It should be restrung and kept properly in tune' he had advised, even offering to come in and do the job himself. Management had regarded him with the stony eye of the Philistine.

'Mind your own business,' it had told him.

Night Of The Vernal Equinox

The eighth King Henry, standing atop the battlements of his Tower beside the Thames and looking northwards to the heights of what is now Hampstead, would have noticed rising like a green nipple from the flat farmlands about, the rounded cone of Primrose Hill. Great oaks clad the gentle flanks and flourished densely in a small forest at the crown. Impenetrable bushes further added to this wild and unfrequented place, with only an occasional footpath to meander across its lower reaches.

Here, among the many smaller woodland creatures resides the fearsome wild boar; bristle-haired, sharply tusked, and always ready in an instant to charge fearlessly upon anything that crosses its path. No man may venture near its lair without a fleet horse to bear him swiftly away should perchance he encounter the ferocious beast, and a gentleman afoot for an evening stroll does well to take his wolfhounds for company.

But with Henry dead and the passing of much time, the hill has lost its verdant woods and now, denuded of those dark thickets raises its almost bald summit above the Regent's well-regulated parklands. In this new setting a gentleman may stroll without fear, and even ladies come to exercise their canine friends. A woman trips along hauling behind her a little toy dog that with such tiny legs cannot, no matter how it tries, keep up. 'Come on Fifi,' she orders crossly, each time she turns to give another pull on the lead. Further across the park a blue-brindled lurcher has caught wind of Fifi and comes loping across the grass towards her. He approaches cautiously from behind until his nose is but an inch from her tail. Fifi is nervous of this rough-looking creature and begins walking sideways to keep an eye on him. But his skilful nose darts in and before she can stop it the lurcher takes a long ruminating sniff.

'Yip, yip,' goes Fifi, terrified by this close and very personal liberty. The woman looks round and begins screaming at the lurcher:

'Get away you filthy beast,' she squeals, swinging her handbag at the interloper. But the lurcher, wise to the ways of "owners", and full of the sharpness of a coursing hound, gauges expertly the length of the strap on which her bag is suspended and stays well out of range.

From far across the park a man begins waving his hands and calling the lurcher.

'Genaro!' He shouts. 'Come here.'

But Genaro hasn't seen such a tasty little piece in a long time, and ignoring the man continues to follow Fifi, albeit keeping a safe distance between himself and the swinging handbag. The woman has had enough. 'Get away you dirty dog,' she screeches, and picking Fifi up carries her towards the park gates with Genaro, still enamoured, following closely behind.

In this bourgeois environment however, such microscopic events are a common occurrence and attract little attention, although in the time of that eighth Henry such plump morsels as Fifi would no doubt have brought the boar from his lair, and sent him charging red-eyed and lusting for battle down the slopes of Primrose Hill. One dreadful crunch of those fearsome jaws and Fifi would have been no more.

Towards evening the park begins to empty, and as darkness falls a group of figures gather on the hilltop. They are masked, and some carry flaming torches which light up the summit and reveal the ordered motions of a ritualised dance. An evening wind carries the sound of a violin and the rattle of tambourine, while the dancers solemnly circle about, as if enacting the movements of some ancient pagan ceremony. It is a planet dance, with each participant representing one of the bodies of the Solar System, whose movements and steps have been carefully worked out and co-ordinated.

Smith had stumbled upon a conveniently empty house, when his failed attempt to reach Samarkand had left him directionless in the Cromwell Road. It had seemed a good omen when, after walking a bare three hundred yards, an overgrown hedge had attracted his attention. Behind the hedge a large house lay abandoned and the cellar door had given to his push. Inside, a long lofty room had met his gaze. At one end an iron stove stood rusting, and down some steps a great pile of coke. The house is close to Earls Court station, where each evening he now takes his violin to do a little busking. Catching the commuters as they head for home he can generally make enough to buy tea, sugar and milk, a loaf of bread, cheese, and maybe even an onion, and once he has fired up the stove he can boil water and keep himself warm. Later he meets up with some old London friends, and an idea arises to dance, on the night of the Vernal Equinox, the movements of the planets through one solar year. Smith's basement is an ideal place to rehearse, and here masks are made and painted under the direction of Tralee, who knows the correct colour symbolism. Here too, the steps are carefully worked out, so that each dancer moves precisely at the correct speed relative to the others, and Smith's violin provides the music.

Drawn in chalk upon the cellar floor are the elliptical orbits upon which the dancers will launch themselves spinning, while governing their speed by taking precisely measured steps. Mick Da Silva in his role as Mercury must make four circuits around the Sun, whilst the Gazelle-like Jenny, paramour of Wade Davenport, makes one circuit representing the Earthly year. Tralee dances Venus, and her length of step is calculated to accomplish one and a half orbits to Jenny's one. George O'Grass is Jupiter, and takes only the smallest of steps, since in one year he will complete barely a twelfth of the circuit. Each of the more distant planets takes progressively tinier steps until reaching the outermost. There, the dancer will spin, but barely move from the spot to dance Pluto, following a lonely path along its two hundred and forty-seven year orbit. A ring of candles flicker on the outer circle as Mick, a silver-masked Mercury spinning closely round the Sun turns his flashing face to the light. Tralee as Venus, her mask painted in bands of delicate colour soon loses ground to his quicksilver movements, but gains on Earth, the long-legged Jenny, who sets the benchmark by which the other dancers maintain their positions.

Night after night they practise the steps in their attempts to precisely mirror the movements of the solar planets. Sometimes, when all goes well, and just for a few moments, the dancers manage to hold their relative speeds and the whole thing comes perfectly together. Like figures on a clockwork music-box they whirl accurately and gracefully along their prescribed orbits, until one small error here or there provokes a flurry of uncoordinated re-adjustments, which, like a demonic Mexican wave, swiftly sends their well-laid plans awry. However, it is considered that if they can accomplish perfection for but a second or two, it will serve as a psychic beacon and perhaps trigger who knows what magical effects.

Darkness falls on the night of the Vernal Equinox, and the great stars hang over Primrose Hill where the dancers gather to fulfil their primary purpose: to reflect with their carefully co-ordinated steps, the movements and exact positions of the planets above. The chalk lines are measured and torches lit in the hands of friends who are not participating. The dance begins, and Smith, fiddle to chin, begins playing Vernal Equinox, a piece he has devised for the occasion, and by his side someone wields the tambourine.

The dance starts well, and for a minute or two the stately masked figures proceed along their well-ordered courses to spin as serenely as their counterparts above. Until George O'Grass, who cannot see his chalk-marks clearly, takes Jupiter blundering across the path of Mars who speeds up to elude him, only to overtake Earth, who, feeling she is losing too much ground accelerates past Venus. This disturbs Tralee, who also has trouble seeing her chalk-line, and she wobbles across the orbit of Mercury, who in order to avoid her promptly jumps into the Sun. Their well-ordered universe, in which each body moves along its preordained path, is reduced in seconds to a disorderly chaos of colliding planets and stellar disasters of appalling proportions. Smith plays on. The dance is turning into a free-for-all, as the heavenly bodies throw reason to the winds and prance, wildly spinning around their new and eccentric orbits.

More torches arrive and once lit add their illumination to the outlandish scene, and now the Lord of Misrule enters, as is his wont wherever the best-laid plans of men are cast. The spectators, content until now to watch the astrochoriography, notice the quickening tempo and begin to infiltrate the summit to join in the celebration. Jigging away for all their worth, the last vestige of Apollonian order is cast to the winds and a Dionysian wildness enters the dance. At the height of this frenzied offering to the vernal night a dark-cloaked figure stands revealed before a cluster of flaming torches. Long white beard hanging almost to its waist it flings back the wings of the cloak to stand with arms widely upraised. It is the Chief Druid, the charismatic Dr Maugham, who has come to lend his support and give his venerable benediction. Now his voice, strong against the skirling fiddle, but carried quickly away in the rising wind, is heard calling upon the elements in an ancient pagan invocation.

But Smith's bow-arm is reaching its limit and soon he can play no more, which under the circumstances is just as well. Down at the main park gates a couple of flashing blue lights indicate that they have aroused the attention of local authorities, who will no doubt take badly to this unauthorised event. Smith puts away his fiddle and makes off, while the dancers and their supporters filter quietly away along the shadow-meshed paths towards the rear exit.

Policeman's Ball

Once more onto the street, the masked figures seem under the lamplight to resemble Venetian revellers out upon a night of Carnival, and from the park gates a small group gather to watch the police gather on the summit of the hill. They are making a great din up there, shouting down their radios, and torches flash as the dark-uniformed constables examine the site. Investigating the chalk circles suspiciously they mill about, and without reference to those splendours which hang above them, seem to be dancing their own strange and perverse ritual.

Wisteria

An early morning breeze sweeps across the west face of the embassy and sets something tapping against the window of Smith's room. He lies, still abed, wondering what the tiny sound might be. His curiosity aroused he rises and takes a look. The panes of the window are set in small squares one of which is cracked. A fragment of glass has fallen out and beyond, tapping around this hole, is a slender tendril of the wisteria which clads the wall outside from its roots two floors below. The tendril is of the palest green. Young and tender its touch is light, but to Smith it seems to be seeking entrance via the broken pane. He extends a finger through the hole and hooks the would-be intruder through and into the room.

For the next few days it just hangs there as if resting after the long climb, but then he notices a few leaves which it appears to be trying to pull through the hole. He admires such persistence, not to say insolence, and taking off his shoe knocks out the rest of the pane. The leaves, pushing tightly against the glass now spring into the room with a green flourish and stretch themselves out into the newly acquired space.

A week goes by and he notices a distinct purpose in the leading tip of the tendril. It is stretching out towards another window which leads onto the balcony outside and lies at right-angles to its entry point. Having diligently and successfully gained an entrance, it now wants to get out again. He sees at once that it will never make it, for the further it reaches into the room the heavier it becomes and the lower its increased weight causes it to sink. It needs some assistance. Banging in two nails he stretches a length of string between them and loops the tendril around it.

Now the questing interloper has something to wind itself around it begins to inch its way along the string, and each morning Smith measures its progress and notes the ever thickening leaves which accompany it. Soon a dense rope of foliage extends a garland half-way across his room, sprouting pale violet blossom here and there to hang like Chinese lanterns along the way.

But summer is fast moving and autumn brings a halt to this progress. The blossoms wither and the leaves drop to the floor, while the questing tendril shrivels at its tip, still only three-quarters of the way to its goal. At the point of entry, however, it has consolidated itself into a thick woody stem and Smith begins to worry about the coming winter. The broken pane will let all his hard-won heat escape and he wonders if he should cut the tendril and replace the glass. He is dubious about the ethics of this. It is rather like inviting a guest to enter, giving them bacon egg and chips and a cup of tea, and then chopping their head off. He balks at this and attempts to push the stem back through the hole. But further growth across the window outside bars this solution.

He makes a decision. He will adapt to the conditions imposed by the tendril, and when winter is at its height and the house is blanketed in thick snow, he hammers a few six-inch nails into the floorboards for pegs and pitches a tent. The mouth of the tent is a mere foot or two from the fireplace, and from there he manages to put a kettle or stew pot on the wood fire without emerging into the room. The winter is exceedingly cold, but inside the tent with the flap closed he is quite comfortable. A 100watt light bulb suspended inside a cardboard box provides ample heat, while outside the wind whistles through the window bringing flurries of snow which settle across the tent and surrounding floor. In the morning he takes a broom and sweeps the snow into the fireplace where it will melt and dry, and by the time he is drinking his first cup of tea the night's fall has gone.

With the passing of winter the temperature loses its edge and he collapses his tent and waits, carefully watching for signs of a renewed effort on the part of the tendril which, so close to its goal must succeed as spring unfolds. But, though outside the trees and even the main body of the wisteria are putting forth new leaves, the tendril remains inert and shows no signs of life. Examining it more closely he suspects it may be dead.

He applies a little pressure and it breaks with a dry snap. Somewhere, two floors down and deep within the hoary old roots a decision has been taken to withdraw support for the errant explorer. No doubt this kind of speculation is frowned upon below and the noble attempt at fraternisation has been discontinued.

Trouble And Strife

Chief Mopo, who occupies the house adjoining the embassy is holding a garden party, and from a long patio veranda which runs along outside the attic floor the whole colourful spectacle can be surveyed. The unabashed reds and fiery orange yellows, the deep greens and rich browns mingle in a mixture of tribal robes and business suits. Swathed about the head with matching cloth the robed figures flash their dark glasses and dazzling displays of white teeth at each other, and their voices float full-throated across the neighbouring gardens.

Smith is watching the event from the balcony, and is screened from below by a thin veil of wisteria which has climbed up the side of the house and now sends its questing tendrils high into the air above the chimneys. Here, finding no further grip they turn gracefully over and descend to cover the roof in dense foliage.

Stretch limos pass through the Chief's electronic gates and the doors open to reveal more gorgeously attired African dignitaries, who sweep into the house and out at the back to join the other guests in the garden. Smith has been standing on the balcony alone for some time when he senses movement nearby. There comes a rustling among the leaves and he looks around.

There with one hand resting on the parapet, pushing aside the fronds with the other he stood: Smith's old friend P. B. Rivers; an existentialist. He now owns a junk shop in St Leonards-on-Sea and turns up to stay at the embassy occasionally when hunting for bric-a-brac. 'I have not given up my lectures,' he explains. 'Whether they are buying a chipped teapot or a cracked mirror, I still do my best to disturb the complacency around me.

'And now look at that lot,' he points downwards to the dark gathering in the Chief's garden. 'They're all the same, whatever the colour of their skin or the shape of their hats; they all suffer similar breakdowns in dynamics.'

'Dynamics?' says Smith.

'Relationships,' says P. B. Rivers. 'The dynamics of relationship can become so complex that they drive most people mad, be they English, Africans, or Chinese for that matter. They're all the same.'

Smith doesn't follow. 'Give me an example,' he says.

'It's simple,' says P. B. Rivers. 'He falls in love with Her and she with him. They marry. Love until death us do part etc. The subtext to that is of course: "I promise to love no other," and thus to the error that love can be controlled. But love is like a sneeze, an involuntary sensation arising spontaneously from the co-ordinates of divine circumstance. A natural phenomenon which can only be matched by total honesty.' He is beginning to wave his arms about and his voice gets stronger as he warms to his discourse.

'And what is the result?' he says, looking expectantly at Smith who shrugs his shoulders indifferently. He still can't see the point.

'The result is,' continues P. B. Rivers, 'after a year or two the relationship loses its charisma; complacency rules and it gets to be Tuesday or Friday or something. He meets an attractive girl at the office, falls in love, and they have a steamy affair. Then one day he discovers that his girlfriend is also having an affair with someone else; he goes into paroxysms of jealousy and that night when his wife says: "Have you had a nice day, dear?" he finds it difficult to answer.

P. B. Rivers holds up his finger to summon all Smith's attention. 'Question:' he says, 'Does the husband in all honesty attempt to explain why he is in such a foul mood? Question: Will his wife be understanding?'

He waits for a while in silence while Smith thinks about this, and he, having pondered upon the proposition gives his considered response.

'First,' he says. 'I really don't think the wife will be very understanding, and therefore he had better keep his mouth shut and pretend a headache or something.'

P. B. Rivers is taken aback by this finely worked analysis. 'Oh well,' he says. 'That was an easy one. Now here's another example: In an entirely different situation, and remember we are speaking of total honesty here. Does He tell Her that he is having a sexual relationship with her mother? And secondly,' he ticks the possibilities off on his fingers. 'Does he tell her father?'

Smith is getting confused. 'Do you mean that it is his wife's father who is having a relationship with his girlfriend?' he asks. 'Because if so he should tell the father first about his relationship with his wife's mother, man to man etc. The father could then persuade his wife to confess to her daughter.'

'No, no,' says P. B. Rivers, shaking his head in despair. 'You're mixing up the two examples.'

Smith could think of many more examples but refrains from mentioning any, since he knows that it will only encourage P. B. Rivers to get deeper into this futile argument, and anyway, for some strange reason the excited chatter from the Chief's garden is having an odd *déjà vu* effect on him, for he has heard these kind of voices before, from somewhere long ago, and then he remembers.

The memories come in disjointed fragments, each piece separate and whirling in a kaleidoscope of disconnected images; only slowly do they begin to form into coherence. He closes his eyes and the voices from below, and the wisteria above take him back in time and space — to Africa...

Journey To Fernando Poo

Just one day out from Douala where the Niger meets the sea is an African wave-washed island long possessed of Spain. Dreaming colonial town and barely legible remnant of days when Spain had majesty, gone now to seed. One indolently fat policeman; one gloriously Catholic cathedral; a plethora along waterfront bars of archetypal Texan oilmen come to plunder the sea-oil fields two days further out with expertise and rigs.

Galleons laden with goodies once careened their hulls, replenished biscuit and water here, not to mention the odd bit of treasure buried no doubt on the side. Now, several rig supply boats bob, squat, grey and powerful; crated victuals piled on high, big men with spanners at sea get hungry. Spanish deck hands, Spanish cooks, American captains, American cooks. Swedish captains and Mexican mates. These etceteras throng the bars in the native shanty town which slowly creeping through the outer suburbs relentlessly overcomes ancient Castilian dignities in the main town of Santa Isabel.

Black Africa, long-suffering and patient, bears secret assegais waiting to plunge with the spirit of Chaka into the heart of the Cathedral; transforming it perchance into the most glorious bazaar on the island. Fortunately for fun the island's blue meanie only comes when called, six-guns are not apparent, knives seem obligatory and the whiskey flows.

Santa Isabel: African sunsets embarrassingly magnificent. Evening lamplight among blossoming mimosa. Seedy Spanish villas line quiet streets; trailing wisteria tresses through balconies of iron filigree once black and proud against the white, now neglected facades drip rich red rust to mingle with the African dust.

Exchanging now this fertile dust for the grime which settles thick and black some way round the planet on London Town, late summer 1966 and flowers rule OK. Bead-bedecked and belled, youth and young of heart usurp the open spaces and secret interiors with joy. An exotic quest at once emerges, two tip-toe tripping minds devise a quest to venture far and seek the ancient cities of an older world. South through the tragic kingdom of Montezuma and on down to Peru. The hippy grapevine carries tales of a cargo boat from Barcelona outward bound which slowly wends its way, faithfully emulating the ancient route of stately Spanish galleons which plied their trade to the coast of the new Promised Land, where gold, jewels and spices abounded in days of yore for the taking with cannon, musket and sword.

Steams itself surely to a South American shore, an old cargo tramp with room for passengers providing they're not adverse to peeling a potato or two, plus ten pounds in cash to pay their way. On such small snippets of fantasy whole lives re-arranged. Overland by motorbike through France and into Spain to their seaport, Eldorado.

Next: Bombing down the Dover road, long black tarmac ribbon slipping smoothly by, between the legs a powerful purr from an old 500cc BSA. Smith, hair uncoiffured and wild to the shoulders, frayed denim jacket and jeans, silk fringed Indian shirt. Miriam, crazy fluttering patchwork, diaphanous chiffon caught like a cloud of butterflies in the bike's slipstream.

Dover harbour and the evening lights at sea, wind tasting of oysters and tar. A ferry lies waiting, they're questioned suspiciously by customs clean and uptight, but are allowed aboard with tickets to their name. Dover Castle slips astern and thus to France with nothing to declare and on their charmed life's way. This is the dream until...

Two stern Gendarmes single out their machine from mums and dads, and kids excitedly contained within Morris Ten and Austin of England. Fix Miriam and Smith with French and merciless eyes,

'Zis way plis'.

Long empty hangar of a shed, small glass cubicle and office paperwork. Harsh glare from arc-lights in the roof, they want to look at the bike. Within minutes tent, toiletry, food and books lie exposed on the concrete floor, already as ants minutely searching to squeeze each toothpaste drop and smell each roll of bread. Standing desolate as spanners appear. Off comes the seat, plumbed in the tank, oil dipped to its core. Her voice comes sibilant in his ear where they stand, watched by the demons of Liberty, Equality and Fraternity, the bleak eyes waiting for the least hint that their nonchalance is feigned. It is! And it is then Smith hears Miriam's voice, quiet as a moth through unmoving lips yet sharp and clear.

'*Get rid of it!*'

Before the seasons of acid rain the world was nearly Eden, a covenant with the gods emblazoned in the sky, a great and healing rainbow, bright with acid's burning colours, therefore, it isn't much amiss that in Smith's mouth eleven trips silver-foil enwrapped, plus half an ounce of good black Pakistani hash. Get rid of it, but how? Beneath their snake regard the merest flicker of muscled jaw in this arc-light dazzle, and he knows for sure he'll be on his back, teeth snugly fitted with tyre-lever, cruelly wrenching into sight his mouthful of poetry. And now the anger ripples through these puzzled men. They are convinced that what they seek is here. They're right. It is. With innocent eyes Miriam and Smith clock their logic.

'Zese people are 'ippies, no? Zey 'ave ze long 'air wiz jeans and Indian shirts. Ze woman she is also a 'ippie. A terrible trollop; an outrageous strumpet. Zey are 'ippies, Zerefore, zey must 'ave ze drugs, no?'

Their eyes fasten on the last sanctuary for interesting substances. Curt French commands, Gendarme either side Smith is marched to where a final corridor, death or something very like upon his shoulder perches, hippie dreams annihilated. Measured footsteps echoing, grim floor of tiles, barred cells lie either side his hour is nearly come when...

Sudden thrill of new awareness, his intrinsic hunter takes command, shapes what's next, for subtly without losing rhyme shortens by fractions his pace, unnoticed loses some ground. Their hardly concealed eagerness and his hard-won regression combine outside their peripheral vision. Opens this tiny respite, at last his jaws can shift and move and chew. Hurriedly crunched eleven silvered keys to heaven, down hard to the stomach. Quickly, oh quickly black gums of Pakistan gag his throat as years-old treacle would, nausea lurks, yet icy and serene no spasm rises to give the game away.

Down down into the guts rode the black and silver, frantic toothsuck moments, stopped at sunken door with bars, the rack? An iron maiden? A bare cell, one light bulb and a chair. His jacket off and trousers too they search each tiny seam. Feel his body over but surprisingly refrain from becoming too intimate. Now his teeth are clear he can open his mouth to the world. The world comes in, torches and teeth tapping probes. Nothing. His ears examined unkind and rough. Nothing. His hair? Nothing. His... His what? There's nothing left and their anger comes moaning, grinding its fury incarnate. Head down he stands, the least bolshie look he knows in this grim little cell and a good French kicking comes his way.

Back to the shed he's once more marched to stand in their hateful regard. This is France, no flighty flipping tripping hips, their youth we'll not corrupt, and so at last the passports reappear. But now it seems they cannot pass, their filthy English decadence returned without a by-your-leave —without a by-your-leave. And then the final act, his passport opened to the entry stamp, this bitter convoluted man takes strong red pencil in hairy primate hand. Draws huge red cross across the almost virgin page. Not draws, too delicate a word for such a violent act. No. Rips with venom, torn remnant to a shredded red and back into Smith's hand.

The BSA restored is packed again, the ruined toothpaste cast aside; escorted back to ferry; did they think they would try to escape? By this time a wet paper bag could have contained Smith easily. Large quantities of good black Pakistani hash let loose amongst his veins turn limbs to honeyed magma, and as if this were not enough the rainbow keys begin their song, kicking in with a glorious sound and firing on all eleven cylinders. Her guiding hand, a secluded corner in the deserted night saloon. He will live or die here but manages to stay in his tree. Till through shimmering eyes a pale hint of dawn, a long grey-green hump's far-off shore, and she leads his colour-blinded step to mount their steed once more.

Smith's body knows each function of the friendly BSA one kick and she roars into life. Slowly through early morn Dover it chugs, the occasional juggernaut a bellowing dragon, finds it too insignificant to swallow. Traffic lights a puzzling extraterrestrial logic. 'Green for danger,' thinks Smith, and accelerates slightly to pass before losing the red. Then her voice in his ear reverses the logic, how wrong can he be? He watching the road. He watching himself watching the road. Signalling to a passing lorry Smith cannot tell which of his multiple arms to move, but learning fast moves all those on his right side simultaneously, co-ordinating kaleidoscope eyes get through the next second safely.

Dover petering out to a country town, then townless. Welcoming green of England, soothing summer air of Kent and a wood. The bike skirting bushes, headlight flickering 'gainst trunks of shadowy trees, brambles and thistles, to a quiet space, a dingle, nook or dell. The switched-off bike gives a few coughs, stops, and the silence comes.

As The Romans Do

This trouble with the border-guards and Smith's narrow escape from the custodians of Liberty in no way diminishes the lure of Peru. Back in London it is not long before its siren song is heard again and now, he grey-suited and white collar tied; she sensible in frumpware; both look square and straight as a die. Dressed as Romans they board a plane Barcelona bound.

Barcelona: juggernaut cranes stretch dinosaur necks across cobbled waterfront streets as they hunt these jostling ways for the shipping agent who handles the boat to Peru. When discovered in a narrow side street, the seedy office is found to contain just one man, a desk, and a chair. He speaks no English, but between them he and Miriam have enough French to make sense. Smith doesn't understand a word of what is said, but he can read the man's face like a book. He is shaking his head in a puzzled way and frowns as if being asked directions to the Moon.

'What's he saying?' asks Smith.

'He says he's never even heard of it,' says Miriam, the Inca-light fading from her eye. They have been duped by a goose-chasing myth; and now this moment of truth.

'Led up the garden path by airheads again,' thinks Smith. 'When will I ever learn? Well, that's it then,' and he turns abruptly about and sees, stretched upon the wall behind him a large coloured map. Straw huts and fishing canoes, palm trees and spears, monkeys and coconuts, these images crowd the jungle-clad island which dominates the map. It lies not many miles off the West African coast where the Niger comes down to the sea. And there beneath the map a name...

The Island of Fernando Poo.

Smith peruses the map with growing excitement, while Miriam is pushing the man a little harder, her eyes moistly pleading, as putting on the pressure she calls upon his chivalry to rescue this beautiful damsel in distress. But this wilful strategy, although brought to bear successfully on numerous prior occasions, has no affect at all on the man.

He continues to shake his head firmly. 'Non!' No matter how hard he may try he cannot, even for her, concoct a boat bound for Peru out of thin air.

'Come and look at this,' says Smith over his shoulder, and Miriam, turning around sees the map.

The exotic colours, the parrots and the palms; the very name itself casts its spell and a new spark arises in her eye from the ashes of a lost Peru. It is a pivotal moment and Smith knows that even to look at her now would be seen as a challenge. Nevertheless, fate turns his head and he looks. He sees at once that she is daring him to make the obvious suggestion, but he is saved from this fatal responsibility by the agent who comes around from behind his desk and begins explaining the provenance of the island. Smith doesn't understand any of this either, but watches the man's finger as it follows the coastline to a bay between headlands where lies a small town. The moving finger stops and... 'Santa Isabel,' he says.

'Santa Isabel,' thinks Smith and... 'Isabella of Spain,' he whispers, his souped-up synapses crackling from one misbegotten association to another.

'Drake,' he thinks, 'and Hawkins the scourge of the seas.' Long John's silver pirates are yo-ho-ing in his ear as the man continues. From time to time as she listens Miriam turns to Smith and gives him the gist.

'He says it is an island colony; a Spanish possession.'

'He says there is a boat which calls in there every two months.'

'He says that it leaves from here in the port of Barcelona.'

And then the clincher:

'He says the next boat sails tonight with the evening tide.'

And now, folly upon folly, Smith glances at Miriam again. Catching his eye she rises to take the dare and he knows very well what her answer will, must be. In a short time she discovers that the funds will stretch for two tickets, if only one way. But these are the fast days with laws of their own and hippie ideals are the rule, so 'yes' is the answer and now is the time, for the island of Fernando Poo.

Tickets purchased they make for the docks and evening is falling as rounding a warehouse they catch a first sight of their ship. A graceful liner white from stem to stern with three funnels of daffodil yellow. Lined up and waiting to greet them aboard are the Captain and chief officers in starched white uniforms. They are *mucho smarto* and give grave little bows, but beneath this dignified mien Smith notices a flicker of puzzlement in their eye. They are used to a highly conventional clientele while Miriam and Smith have flung Roman disguises to the winds. Their hair blows loose and Smith has shed his cardboard suit and is Indian-shirted once more, but it is Miriam's chiffon harem trousers that catch their Latin eye.

There are few other passengers, mostly civil servants and minor diplomats with families returning from leave. These officials eat with the Captain, and Miriam and Smith dine alone in the large first-class restaurant. Under the big chandeliers a waiter serves course after course—three times a day.

The voyage lasts for twenty-two days and as the destination draws near the heat begins to rise, the air thickens and a brazen sun glares ruthlessly down sending those beneath to seek the cool sanctuary of shadow.

Cadiz

Squabble, squabble, squabble. Miriam and Smith are squabbling.

Still smarting about the upper legs from her experience at Her Majesty's pleasure she wants to replenish her stock of knickers. Smith however, is determined to explore the ancient streets and alleyways where pirate once mingled with privateer 'till who could tell the difference?

'We can have a look around after we've got my knickers,' says Miriam. 'There's plenty of time.'

Smith thinks that she should take care of her knicker problem herself, and tells her so.

They squabble.

The squabble becomes over-heated and rises in tones of ever greater exasperation until — enough is enough, for different objectives they part in a huff. She to shop, and he to search the alleyways for signs of the old swashbuckling days.

The ship has called for a few hours at the port of Cadiz before the last long leg of the voyage.

'Be back in two hours,' the Purser had warned them and Smith, eager to explore this home of sea-dogs and buccaneers leads the way ashore when this contentious situation had occurred and left him alone. Neither is successful in their forays, Smith had fruitlessly tramped the narrow cobbled streets for seamen's taverns all in vain and she, as she breathlessly pants when they meet at the docks:

'I've been chased by a gang of boys,' she complains, they followed me round the streets throwing stones, I don't know what they were shouting but I think it had something to do with my see-through chiffon trousers.

Smith looks down to where her "trousers" hang like a faint pink haze about her all but naked legs.

'I really had to run,' she says crossly.

'Your harem pants got up their Catholic noses,' observes Smith.

'What do you know of Catholicism?' she snaps, still angry over his knicker attitude; and they squabble.

Since there are no immediate decisions to be taken the squabble reverts to a vague background hum, until disturbed by a very disturbing sight. For as they pass the gates to the docks they see that the wharf lies empty.

Their ship has gone!

'We were late.' says Miriam, and Smith sees now that this must be so, blithely watchless, he had explored the streets of the town with not one thought for the time. They walk to the end of the pier and sit with swinging legs at its edge.

'We've blown it,' says Smith. An undeniable fact with which Miriam seems in accord, for in this instance at least, she offers no quibble.

They sit gazing morosely out to sea where the ship can still be distantly seen, a yellow funnelled white toy receding towards the horizon. This is a reality shift for Smith, another moment of truth, and he immediately begins rearranging his future.

'Back to London I suppose,' he thinks, and relishes the idea of sitting outside a Notting Hill café once more while watching the Portobello Road pass by. In fact he is now quite looking forward to the return, until Miriam gives him a nudge.

'It's stopped,' she says. 'Look!' and she points out to sea.

Smith steps back from his new future for a moment and sees that the white smudge is no longer receding and its frothy wake is broken. The ship lies still and Miriam and Smith fall silent. Then—emerging from behind the ship a black speck comes into view and speedily arrows its way to where they sit. The Captain through binoculars looking has seen them as he peers eagle-eyed from the bridge; he has sent the pilot boat back to collect them and is now in a terrible rage.

Taken out to the ship they leave the wildly tossing pilot boat and cling to the ladder which the crew have unrolled for them. Miriam is shrieking as she clings for her life and Smith, a few rungs below is still half-submerged each time the rollers smash against the towering side of the ship. At the top of the ladder the Captain is waiting to give them the vent of his wrath, waving and shouting. His arms are expressive and a seaman translates at his side.

'He is saying that you have disrupted his schedule and maybe caused the ship to miss the tide.'

With heads hanging low they go below and decide to keep out of sight for the rest of the trip.

The Island

The island first appears as a low grey-green line on the horizon, but as the ship draws nearer the line becomes a ragged scrawl transformed in turn into a dense mass of jungle vegetation which covers the rising slopes of the interior. From there it stretches down to the palm-fringed shore where tides come in among the mangrove trunks to wash the flotsam of branch leaf and coconut which litter the beaches. The boat steams round the island which as yet shows no sign of human life until, rounding a high headland a harbour comes into view, and clustered around it a small town.

From amongst lofty palms the cathedral of Santa Isabel sends its even loftier tower and around it lie the streets of the old Spanish colony. As the ship swings around to tie up at the wharf the waterfront hoves into sight, a long line of sleazy bars and warehouses and a teeming mass of black humanity to choke the main street and throng the dockside. The gangway is lowered and they swarm aboard making straight for the hold, from where a long ant-like conga of sack-bearing natives soon emerges to wend its way ashore.

They carry on a continuous high-pitch babbling conversation which passes up and down the line and is punctuated here and there with frequent laughter. Smith watches as, still speaking in tongues, the front of the line reaches up a slope to the street above and beyond, while from the hold the sack-on-back figures are still emerging. The Captain and the Purser once more make their stiff little bows as Miriam and Smith step tentatively ashore.

Their legs are a little wobbly as they pass along the crowded street where they are dismayed to find themselves the centre of attention. It is as if their like has never been seen before. Especially Miriam. A circle of curious spectators surround their every move and comments are exchanged without guile, while pointing fingers follow them as they make their way through the crowds. This is insufferable, and they search frantically around for sign of a hotel. To get off the street as soon as possible now seems desirable but hotels seem few, until in a side street a house on a corner and a notice board with the magic word: 'Rooms.'

The rent is affordable, but only for one night, since the money situation is not too good. Without thought to the future they have engaged in a major act of folly which only now is beginning to reveal itself. In fact they have put themselves into a very difficult situation indeed and that night they explore the waterfront bars looking for leads.

'I can get a job in a bar,' says Miriam confidently, and approaches the proprietor of several establishments. But she is trouble they know, for pale-skinned women are unknown on these streets and the Spaniards keep their ladies far from this bawdy seamen's world. There would be fights for her favours and amongst their rough clientele worse could happen. The barmen just don't want to know. Back in the room their desperation grows as they contemplate the full significance of where their nonchalant act has taken them.

'At the worst,' says Miriam, 'I can telegraph my family for some money for the fare home.'

Smith isn't too happy with this and has already decided to look for some work on the morrow. First thing next day they look for somewhere cheaper to stay and discover a line of concrete cubicles on the outskirts of town where the migrant dock labourers sleep. They can afford a couple of nights in one of these boxes, each of which contain two bare iron beds; a mattress apiece; a not very clean sheet, and a permanent swarm of heavy-duty mosquitoes.

Smith however has no luck finding work but has spoken with one or two American seamen in a bar near the docks. The men had encouraged him to go to a local agent and find a job on one of the rig-supply boats based in the port. From the bar Smith had seen their white dream ship still tied up at the dock, and he remembers the chandelier-hung restaurant where they had elegantly dined another lifetime ago it seems, so near and yet now so impossibly far away.

Meanwhile, Miriam contacts her people by phone and finds them unwilling to send more than her own fare home.

'You must take the opportunity,' says Smith. Already he knows that he will do much better here alone. An experience in a bar along the waterfront the evening before had speedily convinced him of this. The bar had been full of seamen; mostly American, Spanish and French. Black ladies of the night draped themselves provocatively along the bar and mingled at the tables, whilst in a far corner a little smoochy-smoochy dancing took place. Leaving Miriam at the bar he had gone to the toilet to be confronted inside by a stubble-jowled Spaniard with a dirty red bandanna tied around his head. The man had no front teeth and spoke in broken English, but Smith had been in no doubt of his intent. He had wanted to talk with Miriam alone. 'I've not seen white meat in three years.' he says.

This had seemed a little intrusive to Smith.

'She's not cattle,' he had replied, for the man had spoken with a suggestive leer.

'Then can you defend her?' the man said, patting a large knife on his belt.

Moments of truth have been coming thick and fast to Smith recently and now this is another. Ignoring the man he had returned to the bar, albeit with eyes a little more open to the difficulties he now faces. He has brought a honeypot into a nest of wasps.

And so... 'You must definitely go,' he tells Miriam. 'I can get a job and earn my fare here much easier alone.'

They do not quibble, the decision has obviously been taken from their hands and Miriam goes off to finalise her arrangements. With her moist-eyed damsel in distress technique she gets a lift to the mainland with a Captain she meets who owns a light plane, and from there can pick up a flight to anywhere she chooses.

Albion Unbound

Alone now, Smith spends a last night in the concrete box. Tomorrow he must get a job or sleep out, something he must avoid at all costs since he has by now become a little more aware of the island's fauna. On first arriving Miriam and he had discussed the possibility of taking off into the jungle and doing a Tarzan and Jane, it had seemed to them the obvious hippie thing to do. But they quickly came to learn that food is scarce out beyond the town and its local farms, and whilst Miriam might do a reasonable Jane; Smith had doubted his Tarzan abilities. What is worse, the spiders they hear are lethal. Smith awakes in the morning determined to test the advice given to him by some seamen he had met in a bar.

'Go and see our agent,' they had urged. 'Tell him that you've been discharged for political reasons from a ship over in Douala on the mainland. Nigeria is in a state of war and Europeans are not in favour at the moment.' They tell tales of violence along the coast, and claim that heads from the conflict drift over to the island and can often be seen floating like coconuts in the town harbour.

Smith leaves his box for what he hopes is the last time and makes his way back down to the harbour. Out here the shanty town is primitive and African housewives shout to him from the glassless windows of the palm-leaf huts which line the road into town. As he descends the hill he overtakes several small groups of local men. He has never seen degrees of relaxation in the human body such as they display. Loose jointed they amble along, their arms flopping around anyhow and definitely not marching. In fact, the rhythmic slop of their flip-flops, apparently the standard footwear here, give Smith the distinct impression that they are actually dancing. It is some kind of bodily anarchy, where limbs are so carelessly hung that they may at any moment take off by themselves, each with a life of its own. Smith is fascinated by the happy-go-lucky panache they express with every move.

The men for the most part are dressed in shirts and shorts or sarongs sewn from coarse flour sacks upon which the stencilled lettering can still be seen. This seems to be the staple cloth here, since Smith has already noticed that the fishing canoes around the harbour have sails made from the same material. The indigenous inhabitants are, therefore, a far cry from his usual acquaintances of African descent, the familiar Notting Hill version of his time: loose hung gabardine two-piece suit with peg-bottom trousers; dazzling white shirt and volcano tongue of a tie, this sartorial vision topped off with the sharpest of hats with the brim turned down just so.

He passes many of these groups until, arriving at the office he finds a young Scandinavian with a brisk manner who sits behind his desk and listens doubtfully to Smith's story.

'Vat ship?' he barks, and Smith is taken momentarily aback; he had not thought of this. He knows however, that there must be no hesitation here, and a name slips smoothly from his tongue; the first to come into his head. It is a name full of significance in his inner cosmology, which over the past year or so has accommodated several dramatic inclusions.

The notion of "Flower Power" and its associated messages arising in the streets around San Francisco's Height Ashbury and nourished by the balmy air of California, had travelled like wildfire across the Atlantic to evoke a similar response among London's young crop of bohemians, social radicals and other more quirky dissidents. The ancient shamanistic lore of the North American Indian mingling with the Maharishi glow of eastern metaphysics, while above all the Woody Guthriesque voice of Bob Dylan singing of meanings far beyond the grasp of poor old "Mr Jones", and setting the arms manufacturers quaking in their boots with his "Masters of War."

However, although generating a powerful influence, these American dreams arrived to encounter some equally powerful myths of the home-grown variety. Indelibly grounded in the bedrock of the sceptred isle, and triggered by this new infusion of freedom's ideals, these mythical figures rose to inspire a new and somewhat more Celtic philosophy.

Out of the hoary past and mists of fable a round table had emerged, and there sat King Arthur and his court of valiant knights. Great Merlin stood upon a hill with arms outstretched, bestowing the King's goodwill upon the green and pleasant land below. And later, Blake, to prophesy the New Jerusalem and send a clarion call for giant Albion to awaken from his centuries-long sleep; rise bodily up from that English landscape in which he has lain hidden for so long, and with one mighty arm drive the money-changers from the temple, and with the other smite those dark satanic mills to dust. The old straight tracks and ley-lines; stone circles primed with energy and star alignments, still generating their mystic fascination to those who measure with the ancient yard and pay a Druid's homage across the Salisbury Plain to Stonehenge. The Chartists too their mark have left upon the island's psyche, and Tom Paine's call for common sense still echoes through old England's bones.

From this maelstrom of native exotica Smith has cobbled together his own inner cosmology which he is always happy to invoke, and now at the agent's question he turns to this ghostly pantheon of hippie ideals; speaks the first name that comes to mind, and... '*The Albion*,' he says.

The man looks puzzled, but cannot check his tale since ships from the mainland seldom call in at the island. Were this a city office Smith's ploy would no doubt quickly unravel, but here, in this rusty corrugated shack on this out-of-it island, standards are fortunately lax. The man gives Smith the reluctant benefit of a yawning doubt and enters him into his book.

'Can you cooking do?' he asks as he writes.

With nothing to lose Smith says yes at once. He had put many a reasonable stew together back in the basement of the Free School with ingredients garnered from the Portobello Road when the market stalls had gone, and is pretty sure he can boil an egg. The agent scribbles on a scrap of paper and hands it over.

'See Captain Vilson,' he says.

Spam Again

To one side of the harbour a long jetty fingers out from the shore at which several company supply boats are berthed. Smith wanders along looking at their names which all seem prefixed with the word *Ocean*. The boats are squat, grey and powerful looking, with upperworks and high wheel-house rising like hunched shoulders near the bows, whilst the rear is flat and low with a heavy-duty gantry overhanging the stern. The boats look well kept to his eye as he passes them one by one, the paintwork is fresh and the decks neat. He looks at the scrap of paper which the agent had given him and there reads: "*Ocean Supply*."

Now that he is half way along the jetty he can see that at the far end lies a boat entirely unlike its fellows. Rust streaks its sides and upperworks and a filthy slime hangs below the galley porthole. A man sits on an upturned box on the cluttered deck, he wears a grubby red bandanna tied about his head and as Smith approaches he gives a toothless leer. It is the man who had threatened him while with Miriam in a bar only a few days ago. Smith gives no sign of recognition but sincerely hopes that this will not turn out to be his destination. It isn't, for, on looking up he sees *Ocean Supply* written large on the soaring prow of the cleanest, neatest, and proudest looking boat in this small but tough-looking fleet.

Coming aboard he is interviewed by Captain Wilson, a tall laid-back Texan with his jeans tucked into cowboy boots. Smith is shown his berth and the galley, a large room with big ovens and wall-to-wall stainless steel fridges. The crew are ashore at the moment and won't eat tonight, but tomorrow there will be an early breakfast before putting out for an oil-rig which they must reach in time feed the oilmen a meal.

'Make them sandwiches,' says the mate. 'They'll be coming aboard as soon as we tie up to the rig.'

Smith sleeps well that night, his bunk is cosy and the contrast with the concrete box is delightful. Not so delightful however, is the dark hour at which the mate wakes him. Smith is not used to having to get up. He has so far, apart from several insufferable years in the army, arranged his life so that such a thing is unthinkable. Each day he rises when the moment seems right, a willing gesture and full of curiosity as to what this new day might bring in the way of adventure, or that staple diet of existence—food. The mate's urgent shout, 'C'mon boy, time to get the range heated up,' sounds like a rancher hustling up the cowpokes from the bunkhouse. Reluctantly Smith has to exit his cosy berth, and dragging on his trousers in the pre-dawn light makes his way up to the galley. He turns on the top plate at the oven and gets out the eggs and oil. He had been told the night before that the crew are very fussy about their eggs and if they're not done right it can spoil their whole day. Smith nervously watches as the men come into the galley and crowd around the stove where each man stands behind him issuing precise instruction.

'Easy over, easy over,' they say, and, 'Now! NOW!'

Smith fumbles around but can't seem to please any of them.

'No! No! Sunny side up,' others complain.

Breakfast passes somehow and the crew go off to their work, their day thoroughly spoiled, and Smith begins to wonder if he has taken on more than he can handle, but he turns his attention now to lunch. Meanwhile, the boat has left the harbour for a two or three hour journey to a rig which stands on giant legs some few miles out to sea. The weather out here is rougher and the waves smash themselves like giant hammers against the boat's sides as its powerful twin diesels drive it remorselessly forward. Smith staggers around the kitchen as he cuts long French loaves in half and hacks great steaks from a massive block of industrial-strength spam he has taken from the fridge. He sets a large tray piled high with these "sandwiches" on the mess table at the far end of the galley, and when the oilmen come aboard they chomp their way lustily through the bread and spam and swill it down with coffee. They seem from their guttural jargon to be Danes or Swedes and are hung about with straps and snaplocks, their tools and spanners holstered like six-guns hanging from sturdy leather belts, their faces black as coal miners'. Their work clothes stink of oil and they have definitely not washed their hands before sitting down to eat. This meal becomes a routine over the next few weeks as the boat plunges from rig to rig, bringing succour by way of Smith's spam sandwiches.

Fortunately, they are so hungry that they seem not to notice the lack of variation, although the same cannot be said for the crew of *Ocean Supply*. Their pay is high and they eat ashore when not aboard, therefore Smith has only to cater for the on-duty crew which at first seems easy enough. He serves spam, egg and chips the first week, which they eat without comment, but by the second week he is beginning to collect surly looks from these rednecks from Oklahoma and “Good old boys” from Texas and Mississippi. The tension builds up while a low level muttering begins to make itself heard and Smith knows he must soon provide something more pleasing by way of diet and embarks upon a series of experiments.

He fills a large saucepan with chips of which there are great bags available in the fridge. Boiling the chips until soft he crushes them finely with a heavy ladle and... Hey Presto! Mashed potatoes. He serves the mash up that night with spam and some peas from a large tin he has found in the store room. The men stare at their plates as he dishes out the food, but he can see beneath their show of tolerance that they are not for a moment fooled. Smith avoids eye contact during this time but after a few more days of spam and mash the grumbling begins again. Desperately casting about he hits upon a brilliant idea: spam fried in egg batter, with — and this he feels is a stroke of genius — the choice of mash or chips. But time is running out for him and he knows it. He must make a radical change in the cuisine.

He is humping a sack of chips from the fridge one day when his eye alights on the top shelf and there, in frosty white rows, is a plentiful supply of frozen chickens. His spirit rises as he realises that here is the solution to all his problems and a sure way to win the approval of his disgruntled clientele. He removes six chickens and places them like small icy boulders on the oventop. He had heard somewhere that chickens must be roasted very slowly. ‘Maybe three or four hours,’ he thinks, and setting the range at medium heat he puts the chickens in the oven.

‘There’ll be chicken tonight,’ he announces as he struggles with the latecomers’ eggs. He still cannot get them just as they like but this proclamation galvanises them into great shows of camaraderie. He is their friend after all and they clap him on the back and a certain buoyancy is apparent in their manner. Every hour or so Smith looks in the oven and gives the chickens a bit of a prod, they are coming on nicely and assuming a rich dark brown colour and the smell permeates the galley with a tantalising aroma. When the men come for their evening meal they are all smiles, cracking jokes and rubbing their hands together in anticipation as they sit themselves at the table and look hopefully at Smith when, like a magician he opens his magic box.

Swinging wide the oven door he lifts out the chickens and places them on top of the range and the men can hardly contain their excitement as they gaze upon this succulent sight. Smith takes up a serving fork and knife and plunges them into the first chicken. It feels a bit odd and the meat strangely brittle. Pulling the chicken apart he finds the flesh is dry as a cinder all the way through and crackles into leathery pieces wherever he tries to cut; these chickens are dry as museum mummies and nowhere amongst them can he find a shred of edible meat. But the men are still waiting, and apart from making an abject confession, he has no choice but to play the game to the end and serve them up.

The crew stare at their plates with bulging eyes their red necks getting redder by the second and their eyes send waves of hatred towards Smith as he stands trying to look nonchalant at his stove. He thinks of a poem by Shelley which he recites silently to himself, and their murderous shafts fall away, fall away. Their murderous shafts fall away. — For today.

Next day comes a message from the Captain: he wants to see Smith in his cabin right away. He sits with his fancy boots propped up on his desk and delivers Smith an ultimatum.

'The men are plumb wore out with your spam, egg and chips,' he says. 'They ain't liking it at all. They want proper meals from now on and what's more they're demanding fresh coconut pie, and if they ain't getting it they threaten to feed your English meat to the sharks.'

Coconut pie? Smith has never heard of it and wouldn't know where to begin.

'And another thing,' says the Captain finally, 'You can go ashore and get your hair cut!'

'Cut my hair?' says Smith. He has heard this bourgeois mantra somewhere before but had not expected to hear it chanted in such an out-of-the-way place as this. The order gets up his nose and his radical instincts are aroused. 'Get my hair cut? Certainly not!' he announces, and the Captain has his response ready made.

'Then I guess you're fired boy,' he says in his lazy cowboy drawl.

Smith takes it on the chin; he has four weeks' pay unspent and is not too daunted by this outcome. Returning to his bunk he collects his gear and goes for the last time ashore. As he passes along the pier he notices that the disreputable looking boat has moved its berth nearer to shore, thus indicating that in spite of its unkempt appearance it has some sort of function amongst its well-maintained brethren. The man with the red bandanna is leaning against the rear gantry talking with another seaman who looks even more villainous than himself. He is cleaning his nails with a large wicked-looking knife and flashes his toothless leer at Smith as he passes. But, free now, he walks up the slope to the waterfront and decides to give the agent another try. There is little else he can do.

Hairy Stuff

'Vell?' snaps the agent, looking up from his desk as Smith enters the office.

'I was wondering if you have another job for me,' says Smith. 'I've been sacked from the boat you sent me to.'

'Zis I already know,' answers the man. 'Captain Vilson has asked me to send another cook.' He looks irritated as he shuffles through some papers and seems not well pleased with Smith's performance.

'I have notting else,' he says sharply, — 'unless' — he pauses and looks doubtfully at Smith. 'A deck-hand haff you been?'

This is an opportunity Smith cannot miss and the lies come swarming through his teeth. He begins recounting the names of fictitious cargo ships and ports he has visited around the world, but the man doesn't want to hear and waves his hands impatiently.

'Ja, ja, ja,' he says. 'But I haff only one job to giff now for you, and if you take it you had better vatch yourself out.'

Smith nods his assent and the man goes on:

'A deck-hand on der trouble-maker's boat is needed and if you vant it der job iss yers.'

'Trouble-maker's boat?' says Smith.

'Zey get drunk and fight or smash tings up and zen... zey get sent to der trouble-maker's boat.'

Smith looks a bit worried but the man is unsympathetic.

'Vell?' he barks. 'Do you vant it der job or not?'

Smith does want it; he has nowhere near enough money to get home yet and doesn't want to spend what he has wastefully. He signs the agent's form and again is handed a slip of paper.

'Report to der Captain tomorrow,' says the agent, and as Smith turns to leave the man gives him a further warning.

'You must vatch it out.' he says, 'Der crew on zis boat iss bad men, ze dregs of ze company fleet and zey do not giff a 'oot.'

Smith returns to the waterfront and books into a small room over one of the bars. Lying on his bed that night he watches the neon bar-signs flash their coloured reflections on his ceiling, while the sound of drunken shouts, oaths and multilingual curses rise from the street below.

'Hairy stuff,' he thinks, and now he remembers the agent's words, 'Trouble-maker's boat.' He begins to wonder about this until a nasty suspicion collects on the outskirts of his mind. He doesn't want to look at it, and manages to deny it entrance until he falls asleep. But the next morning the ominous thought is back again, pressing against his awareness with renewed force.

He rises, pays his bill and walks through the early morning market down to the harbour. Stalls are set up by the road and he glances at the wares as he passes. Flip-flops tied with coconut string are heaped in piles on the stalls; fruit and vegetables lie spread out on blankets, and just before the market gives out stands the rat stall. Stretched on strings between two poles the rats hang in long rows. Heads uppermost, their tails descend in snaky fringes that ripple languorously in the morning breeze. Two or three African ladies, shopping baskets at the ready are feeling the rats, squeezing and pinching their haunches to find the plumpest for supper tonight.

'Rats,' thinks Smith. 'Why didn't I think of it,' and he imagines serving up fresh rat pie to the crew of *Ocean Supply*. The idea amuses him, but also brings him back to the present, and he directs his steps away from the rat stall and along the wharf to where the Company boats, looking spick and span in the early sunlight lie in a neat row, and again the suspicious thought arises to assail him. Uneasily he takes the scrap of paper from his pocket and reads the name written there. "*Ocean Service*," it says.

At the far end of the pier he sees the rust-raddled hull of the scruffy boat nosing into its berth while a red bandanna wearing deck-hand flings a rope ashore. Reading the names as he goes Smith passes each boat without finding his own until, reaching the last; he sees that there is only one remaining. Walking towards it the nasty suspicious thought, bursting through his defences is given all the evidence it needs. Through flaking rust and the oily streaks that smear its filthy sides he makes out the faint words: *Ocean Service* and knows his fate.

The crew are scrambling ashore, a malignant-looking collection of ruffians who pass him with a piratical swagger as they make off into town. The man with the red bandanna is hitching a rope to a bollard and gives his gap-toothed leer as Smith ascends the rickety gangplank. There are boards missing from the floor and it wobbles violently as he comes aboard.

Go To!

The Captain of *Ocean Service* is a far cry from Smith's previous skipper. No poncey cowboy boots adorn his feet which are ensconced in rough seamen's boots. He is a giant Swede whose barrel chest is barely contained within a dark blue jersey with just enough wool remaining to hold its many holes together.

He wears a once white Captain's cap on the back of his head and turns his huge stubbled jaw towards Smith as he enters the cabin. He swivels around in his chair and away from the bottle of rum and a glass which alone occupy the top of his desk; he looks Smith up and down with a stony eye and it is plain to see that he is not impressed by what he sees. Reaching behind him for the glass he takes a generous swig, belches and says: 'You vill be called for yer vatch later.'

Smith thinks about this and imagines himself scanning the horizon for rocks or other ships, he has had plenty of practice: birds and delectable young ladies he has watched by the score and therefore doesn't think this will be too difficult. He stands silently waiting for more, but the Captain abruptly dismisses him by turning around and refilling his glass, the interview is over and Smith leaves the cabin. Outside the Mate is waiting for him. He is a gaunt Frenchman with a permanent black beetle-browed scowl and a tight little goatee beard to match. He speaks little or no English but his gestures are eloquent. Now he chooses one such from his repertoire and demonstrates it to Smith. Hunching his shoulders and raising one arm he points sternly below.

'Go to!' he roars.

Smith goes below to the crew's quarters and finds himself a bunk. The men are ashore until evening but meanwhile he has work to do. Once he has stowed his gear the Mate thrusts a hammer and chisel into his hand and pointing to the rusty scuppers orders Smith to get started. 'Go to!' he shouts aggressively and Smith gets to work. Later when the crew come aboard he tries to give a hand as they cast off; he helps pull up the gangplank and tries to look busy but hasn't a clue about his supposed role. That night he retires early to his bunk and, lulled by the distant smooth roar of the diesels is soon fast asleep.

'Englishman!'

The roaring voice is loud and much too close to Smith's ear. He opens a bleary eye and beholds the Mate standing over him. The Frenchman brings his shoulders to the level of his ears and points imperiously upwards.

'Englishman!' he shouts again. 'Go to!'

It is Smith's watch and he quickly jumps up and puts on his clothes. Meanwhile the Mate stands glowering at him until he is ready and then leads off. Out on deck the night is wild and the boat is pitching heavily. Smith follows the Mate along the bucking deck clinging to any handhold he can find while the Mate, with agile gorilla-like movements shambles effortlessly before him.

Reaching forward they arrive at the wheelhouse which sweeps in long spacious arcs against the night sky. The Mate seizes hold of a series of metal rungs which lead upwards into the darkness and rapidly hauls himself to the top. Smith has no head for heights, but under the circumstances has no choice but to follow and taking hold of the lower rung begins to climb. Once beyond the shelter of the lower structure the wind howls around him and he is buffeted by strong gusts which almost lift the shirt from his back, but he clings grimly on and forces himself to the top.

And A Star To Steer Her By

Inside the wheelhouse the Captain and Mate stand side by side behind the helmsman. It is so dark that Smith can only just make out their forms.

'694,' or, '820,' shouts the man at the wheel.

Smith has hardly heard and is wondering about this when... 'Repeat der bearings!' the Captain roars.

Now he understands, and not having taken them in, shouts out a few numbers at random. He allows his tongue to flop about in his mouth as he does this in order to make them near unintelligible, whilst taking many pains to get the authoritarian tone right. At this the helmsman relinquishes the wheel and Smith, still playing it by ear steps into his place. He had not expected this.

Between the spokes of the wheel the binnacle shows as a dim greenish-yellow light which illuminates the compass as it floats in a bath of oil. The boat is rising forward to mount the waves through which it ploughs and the compass rolls from side to side, but the needle barely registers any change of direction.

Smith stands with widespread legs, partly to maintain his balance and partly to impress the Captain and Mate with his seamanlike body language. All seems well. 'It's easy,' he thinks. 'Just like steering a car.' He is congratulating himself on his expertise when he notices that the compass bearing is slowly drifting to the left. He turns the wheel to the right to compensate, but still the needle swings left. He turns the wheel again but there is no response, so follows with yet more. Then, as he watches, the compass comes at last to a stop, hesitates for a while, and then begins swinging back to starboard. Satisfied, he watches as, gathering speed it approaches the bearing. But now he sees to his horror that it will widely overshoot the mark and frantically he tries to compensate. But too late, the compass spins around way past the bearing and seems will never stop.

Smith panics and turns the wheel to port and port and port again, and it is only after several full turns of the wheel that the compass slows, stops, and then begins its remorseless return. And now he sees what he has done; the bearing comes around to port, and rushing faster port and port and port she goes. With Smith at the helm the ship turns right around; and round and round and round she goes, somewhere off the coast of Africa.

Behind him Smith is aware of an ominously grim silence; he has been ignominiously rumbled, and it is glaringly obvious that he has never steered a ship before in his life. Now the Captain steps forward and takes the wheel roughly from his hands and with a few deft flicks this way and that brings the boat back on course. 'Do you see dat star?' he rasps, pointing forward through the wheelhouse window. 'Juss keep it in line with der bowsprit.'

Smith looks out and there, bobbing around above the bowsprit which points vertically upward from the plunging prow, he sees a bright star which far outshines all others. The Captain steps aside and Smith takes the wheel again.

'Don't try to steer by der compass.' The Captain barks, stepping back alongside the Mate, and Smith, released now from that treacherous instrument watches his star. It sways around in small arcs above the dark finger of the bowsprit, sometimes veering left and again to the right, but he finds a small touch of the wheel here or there is sufficient to recapture the errant spark. Within ten minutes he has the best of it and can relax a little, while the Captain to his cabin goes and leaves him with the Mate.

'829!' he bellows, when at the end of his watch the next man, a Spaniard, comes to relieve him.

'*Dos Cinco siete!*' shouts the man in reply as he takes the helm, and the Mate, speaking neither English nor Spanish cannot fault the logic, but seems satisfied by the shipshape spirit in which these formalities had been enacted. As he goes below Smith feels much empowered by his newly learned skill.

'I could steer an ocean liner now no problem,' he thinks.

Bad Language

The next few weeks are a crash course in seamanship and Smith watches the other deck hands closely as they work; copying their actions as best he can and picking up these skills as he goes along. Soon he can throw a weighted line with the best of them, gauging the force of wind instinctively when casting the lead, and when the boat noses into port he jumps ashore to throw a couple of expert half-hitches around the nearest bollard. Bronzed now by the merciless sun he invests in a new white T-shirt, and with locks shorn into a diplomatic crew cut he feels like a seaman at last. To his relief the man with the red bandanna makes no attempt to approach him, contenting himself with his toothless leer whenever they pass. It is a knowing leer, an eloquent reminder of his lascivious desire for Miriam, and he knows that Smith gets the point.

The rust that flakes the scuppers and upperworks of *Ocean Service* now becomes the main focus of Smith's attention, set to work by the Mate each day with chisel, hammer and paintbrush, he chips and scrapes and paints and paints. He is alone in this task, since the Mate knows that knives might be drawn should any other of the crew be ordered to the task. Smith however, carries no knife and so cannot resist orders.

One night in a bar along the waterfront an altercation occurs between a local pimp and the man with the red bandanna; knives had come out and the pimp had been taken to the dispensary in a very bad way, while red bandanna goes to the lock-up to await transport to Spain for trial. His replacement comes aboard with a jaunty air; another Spaniard, neat and efficient looking with slicked-back hair and the lithe step of a flamenco dancer. A friendly man he speaks some English and soon teaches Smith the subtler nuances of their trade. And one day he teaches much more...

Smith had been having coffee in the galley one day when the cook, also Spanish, had spilled some hot soup on his foot and '*Puta Madre,*' he had cursed.

'Puta Madre,' Smith had whispered to himself, and later up on deck 'Puta Madre,' complains when sent to chip and paint. However, the new deck-hand has much more than this up his sleeve, for there came a day when he too SWORE.

There came from him an oath as thunder splits the sky in two. It burst between his clenched white teeth and hung like lightning in the air. '*Cadmon Dios!*' Fierce it was and sharply on the air it rang and set Smith's ears a ringing. 'Cadmon Dios!' He whispers it in awe and taking it in careful hands retires within to contemplate and relish this new thing. He practises under his breath until he has them just right, and soon his speech becomes peppered with Spanish expletives: a plaintive 'Puta Madre,' here, or an outraged 'Cadmon Dios!' there gives him, he thinks, a little authenticity.

He is now beginning to feel at ease with the work and decides he can afford a little recreation, and one day when they have made the day trip across to the mainland at Douala to pick up the Company mail he stays aboard while the crew go ashore to top up on alcohol. When all is quiet he slips ashore and wanders along the jetty to where a few young Africans are sitting around on a pile of empty oil drums. He raises two fingers to his mouth in the universal gesture of smoking and one of the boys jumps to his feet. Grinning broadly he points to his wrist and raises an index finger high, while pointing at the ground with the other. One hour, here; the gestures are unmistakable. Smith nods and the boy runs off.

Well within the hour the boy comes running back followed at a small distance by an amazing sight. Like a great galleon with all sails billowing to the wind he comes. Swathed in red and orange robes topped with enormous flashing sunglasses, gold chains hung about his neck and with watches on both wrists, a giant African swaggers along the jetty towards them. His dazzling teeth bared in a grin he halts and holds forth his hand. Smith thinks he wants to shake, but he is mistaken, for the man's clenched fist opens and there is a great hairy ball of Congo green bush, as much as the large hand will hold. Smith takes it reverently and raises his eyebrows in question. The man understands his eyebrows immediately and holds up the fingers of both hands. Ten Pesetas, a paltry sum. Smith takes out a ten and hands it over and another five for the boy. Everyone seems happy and Smith returns to the boat while the man sails off into his own private sunset. Back aboard he takes out the hoard and carefully wraps it in a piece of newspaper. He has enough here to last him forever.

Artistic Pursuits

The rough surface is virgin white, unblemished as yet while it waits for the act of creation. Projecting diagonally from the lower left hand corner a fat pink object intrudes onto the unsullied white field. A close observation, however, reveals it to be Smith's thumb. It grips the watercolour paper firmly, as a brush laden with blue enters from above and sweeps the paint in one unbroken swathe across the top of the paper. Now washed, fresh dipped and replete with water it cuts a liquid path directly beneath the blue. Back and forth it washes till from above the blue begins to seep and spread its tentacles below. An instant sky which, rich in colour and deep in tone above, yet trails away downwards diluting as it goes, until only the barest hint of colour remain to reach an as yet undefined horizon.

He dabbles with this newborn sky and wonders if a touch of watery red might signify a sunset. It is an afternoon off and uninterested in going ashore he often comes to this shady angle beneath the wheelhouse, where he gets out his small box of watercolours and a pad. He keeps these things out of sight around the crew who are extremely macho and would consider him a ponce for even owning them. But here, hidden from all eyes he now indulges himself, and is just about to try for a sunset when a rough voice breaks his concentration.

'Englishman!' it roars. 'Go to!'

The Mate, prowling the deck and looking for trouble has stumbled upon Smith, and seeing him wielding his brush with such skill has conceived a brilliant idea. He will send him over the side with a pot of black paint to touch up the name of the boat. Two deck hands are already at work, tying ropes to either end of a plank of wood. When this is done they lower it over the side and secure the ropes to stanchions. The Mate stands in the bows glaring at Smith. Drawing in his neck like a tortoise he raises an arm and points to the hole through which the anchor stretches its chains to the seabed below. He thrusts his black beard aggressively forward and... 'Go to!' he shouts.

Smith pokes a cautious eye through the hole and looks down to where the slim plank hangs far below. He doesn't like heights, but before he can voice his doubts a deck hand steps forward and ties a rope firmly about his waist. Now he has no choice, he is supposed to be a deck hand after all, and to show fear now would mean the end of his fare home. Gritting his teeth he ducks backwards through the hole and dangling at the end of the rope is lowered until his feet touch the plank. Once he is safely seated the rope is withdrawn, a pot of paint and a brush is lowered on a line, and he is on his own.

Whatever happens he decides, he will use only one hand for the job; while the other will never leave its white-knuckled grip upon the plank's supporting rope. The huge letters of *Ocean Service* are now but a few inches from his face, their paint eaten away by the sea salt and rust obliterates most of the words, but he gets to work with the black brush and, having completed the letter "O" to his satisfaction, moves on to the "C". Already he feels more confident, adjusting his body weight to the swaying plank until his fear ebbs entirely away. It is a beautiful day and he begins to comprehend the idyllic nature of the task; made now perhaps even more idyllic when he remembers that in his back pocket is a ready rolled joint of Congo bush. He pulls it forth and lights up. Then, taking deep and satisfying drags he quickly smokes the lot. The grass works wonders on his perspective and he becomes totally absorbed; getting his black edges clear-cut while eradicating blips with a rag tied around the end of his brush. As he works he sees that the letters had originally been but crudely formed and decides to give them a little style with the addition of neat Roman serifs to the letters, and he takes great pains to get the points sharp.

He is putting the final touches to the last "E" when, forgetting to keep his left hand clamped on the rope, he reaches with it for a smaller brush and the plank wobbles. Just in time he grabs the rope, but the brush slips from his hand and falls below. His heart is beating in his mouth, he had almost fallen, and although he can swim it is not wise to do so in these waters. He looks down and what he sees makes all his former fears seem laughable, and causes the contents of his bowels to seek an emergency exit strategy. For there, swimming in lazy circles below him are several large sharks; occasionally they turn upon their sides and direct a cold and predatory eye upon him. The sharks are watching Smith and waiting for him to slip. He holds the rope tightly with both hands now and freezes with fear.

Stoned horrors with real sharks!

Now the flimsy plank, cracked and split along its length is about to fail him, while the rope to which he clings he sees now is old and frayed. He does not look down again, with eyes tightly shut he tries to shout, but his voice comes out as a croak. He tries again and again, his voice becoming stronger with desperation, but the crew are all below and will not hear him anyway. He is saved at last by a sound from above and looking up sees the silhouette of a head protruding like a black coconut against the darkening sky above the scuppers. It is the Mate. 'Englishman,' he shouts. 'Go to!'

Smith wishes he could but cannot move a muscle. Soon however, a rope comes snaking down and tying it securely about his waist he is soon hauled back through the anchor hole to the deck above. He feels like kissing it in gratitude for his deliverance but refrains from such a demonstration; it would not be understood. He gets to his feet and is confronted by the Mate who stands pointing sternly below. 'Go to!' he roars again. And now at last he can.

A Touch Of Zen

Smith has heard of a cinema somewhere in the town, and one evening when they have tied up after a day out amongst the rigs he washes, puts on a clean

T-shirt and makes for the gangplank with the rest of the crew. His path is barred however by the Mate who stands belligerently in his way.

'Englishman!' he shouts. 'Go to!'

Smith is getting tired of this; he has no idea what the man wants and decides to have it out with him there and then. Lying on the deck is a coil of rope. 'Go to this?' he asks, pointing at the rope and raising his eyebrows in a questioning manner. 'Or go to this?' pointing to a pot of paint lying nearby? The Mate continues to glare angrily at him as, with just a touch of Zen, Smith sits down on the deck and removing a shoe holds it up to the Mate and... 'Go to this?' he asks.

The Frenchman's face, already weather-beaten and scoured by sun and salt-laden wind to a ruddy hue, now attains a purple tinge as he regards Smith with a venomous eye while perversely ignoring Smith's eyebrows. But, as the crew stand around watching this inexplicable scene and the Mate mutters in frustrated rage, the natty Spanish deck-hand bends down to Smith's ear. *Cadmon Dios*! He grits. "E says you are to go ashore at once.'

Slowly Smith puts his shoe back on and stands up. He gives a lop-sided grin to the Mate who stares at him in baffled rage. He will never make Englishmen out.

Shoot-Out On Main Street

Once ashore, Smith hunts down the cinema. It is a church-like rusty corrugated-iron building covered at ground level with tatty posters of old cowboy films. He joins the Africans as they queue outside and notices that the American oilmen have arrived early to secure their favourite seats. Soon he finds himself at the box-office where he purchases a cheap ticket and a bag of nuts. Shown upstairs he is surprised to find himself high up among the best seats in the house. All around him the Africans chat excitedly and crack their nuts until the lights go down and a low anticipatory moan dwindles to silence.

The film starts. It is a black and white western with a plot that rapidly develops into a crisis situation. But the Africans seem not to be much interested in the early stages, or perhaps, not understanding the dialogue have no idea what is happening, for they continue to talk amongst themselves while their nuts crack like pistol shots, but nobody says: 'Shush!'

Now on the screen things is lookin' pretty mean, and the villains, riding through the town and firing into the air are hollerin' fit to bust, while the respectable inhabitants cower behind their locked doors. The Africans love it; jumping up and down they shout and throw their nuts at the actors on the screen, from where they bounce back to fall upon the American oilmen who sit downstairs; crouched in the first two rows their faces straining almost vertically upwards in order to see the screen; the worst seats in the house, for which they are willing to pay the premium price in order not to sit with the Africans. The owner of the cinema is an African himself and the humour is sublime.

At the end of the main street a lone horsemen has now appeared and at sight of him the gang stop their boisterous din and even the Africans cease their clamour as the lone figure halts and dismounting, ties his horse to the saloon bar rail. Now he turns and for the first time his face can be clearly seen. It is hawk-like, the slitted eyes cold as chips of ice and the mouth set in unsmiling stone. He walks slowly towards the gang who begin to mutter and throw uncertain glances at each other. Who can this be? Who dares alone to challenge them in this way?

One of the gang, encouraged by his fellows, dismounts, and walking a few paces forwards stands with hands hovering over his six-guns. The stranger comes on until only a few yards separate them. A heavy silence has fallen as the two men watch each other closely, but while the villain crouches with fingers a mere inch or two from his pistol butts the stranger seems entirely relaxed, even taking out his makings and rolling a one-handed cigarette while he waits. This show of disdain is more than the villain can bear, and with a muttered curse his hands fly to his guns and he draws. Although his hands move very fast they seem but slow-motion in comparison with the other. The stranger, still in the act of lighting his cigarette with one hand, moves with the other at lightning speed and draws so fast that it is impossible to follow the hand's blurred trajectory. Two shots ring out, so closely together as to seem one, and the villain's pistols fly from his hands and spinning through the air come to earth as useless clumps of twisted metal. Now the Africans are going crazy and a storm of nuts fly over the balcony. At this point the gang leader gets his first sight of the stranger's pistol. He sees that it has two barrels and can fire both simultaneously. There is only one man who totes a weapon like this and can use it with such consummate skill. 'Two-barrel Tomkins,' he mutters, and then: 'It's two-barrel Tomkins,' he warns. 'C'mon boys, let's get out of town.'

As the bandits wheel their horses in a cloud of dust and go galloping away, the Africans go berserk. They weep and laugh and throw their arms around each other with joyful exuberance and Smith, swept along by the excitement in which he is surrounded, jumps and shouts and hurls his nuts too. He has a wonderful time.

Blow The Man Down

Walking back to the boat through the mimosa-scented twilight a thirst comes upon him, and he decides to drop into one of the waterfront bars for a beer. He enters the first one he sees and sits drinking at the bar whilst casting a leisurely eye over the clientele. Slinky black girls, their bosoms and bottoms bursting like ripe fruit from their scanty dresses dance with the Scandinavian and Spanish seamen on a tiny dance floor, whilst doing their best to steer their drunken partners through the back door where, amongst the palm trees' shadows with trembling knees they offer maybe much more. Over in a corner the Americans sit by themselves. The U S of A men are from the deep South and draw the line at even dancing with them.

Smith is taking contented sips of his beer when he gives a violent start for there, sitting in another corner and unseen until now he spies the Mate. He sits alone at a table amongst a forest of empty bottles and has obviously taken more than a wee drop, since he sprawls loosely in his chair glowering around the bar and oozing aggression from every pore. Smith hopes that he will not be noticed, but hope, as he knows from long experience, is a fragile premise and can in very few circumstances be relied upon. Hopelessly then, he watches as the Mate's drunken eye comes inevitably to rest upon him, and he sees the naked hatred in his face. Slowly the Frenchman hauls himself to his feet and begins making his clumsy but determined way towards Smith. He is a fearsome sight and tough as the bar's customers are, they obligingly make way for him. Smith has seen enough, and not even waiting to finish his beer he is gone.

Coming aboard the boat he makes for his bunk, intent on a diplomatic early night. He falls asleep quite soon but is awakened a few hours later by a roaring voice and the sound of smashing glass. The Mate, fighting drunk has come aboard and is smashing up the galley. Pots and saucepans go flying out onto the deck as he throws them around and bottles are hurled to break in fragments against the scuppers and above all his voice rages in a soaring paean of warlike challenges. Two deck hands scurry past Smith where he lies abed; they lie full length upon the deck and squeeze themselves beneath a row of bunks and Smith wonders if he should join them. But now the Mate, having vented some of his fury upon the galley is taking the remainder elsewhere. Up to the bridge he staggers and there attempts to dismantle the Captain. It is a bad move, for the Captain, a mountainous Swede, with one swipe of his ham-sized fist blows the man down.

Next morning the Mate is still out of it and is carried ashore to the dispensary while the Captain sends up to the office for his replacement.

Pancho

Smith is reading in his bunk; it is evening and the crew are ashore. A loud creaking comes from the gangplank above and he feels a minor tremor as somebody steps heavily aboard. It is too early to be a returning crewman, and he wonders who it might be. Footsteps now traverse the deck and go aft to halt at the stern. Smith gets up to take a look, he is alone and, oh, the horror, it may be the French Mate returning for vengeance. He mounts the companion-way and comes stealthily up on deck. Evening has fallen and fortunately the jetty lights are few. Creeping aft he dodges from shadow to shadow until, concealed by the starboard funnel he gets a clear view across the deck. There stroking his big black Pancho Villa moustache, twirling the ends he stood: a barrel-chested Mexican; the new Mate.

He has a long cheroot clamped between his teeth and now leans on the stern rail gazing out across the moonlit harbour. The tinsel-lit town casts a dancing reflection across the still water but the raucous bars along the waterfront are too distant to break the silence. Smith comes out of hiding and strolls to the rail some yards from the Mexican where he too lights up. The man turns his head and removes his cheroot.

'*Buenos noches*,' he says in a friendly manner.

'Good evening,' says Smith in return.

'Ah!' says the Mexican with delight, 'eenglish!'

He does in fact speak quite good English and is pleased to have someone with whom to converse and improve his grasp of the language. He is an affable man and right away Smith christens him "Pancho." He likes it, and soon it catches on with the crew who, hearing Smith use the name soon begin calling him Pancho too, and he beams with pleasure when thus addressed. Over subsequent days Smith gets to know him quite well and they soon generate a good rapport. He hates the Americans and doesn't think much of the French and Spanish, but for some reason he has a profound respect for England, and one day he takes Smith aside and makes a request.

'When my tour here is feenish,' he says, 'I may go to London and I want you to teach me how to speak as they do, and then they weel think I am eenglish too.'

Smith wants to help out but doesn't think working-class London with a Mexican accent will get him very far or produce the required effect. 'Let me think about it,' he says, and a day or so later hits upon the best option for the exercise. Taking Pancho to the far end of the crew's quarters where they cannot be overheard, they begin lesson one.

'First,' says Smith. 'Whenever someone does you a good turn, you say: "Jolly good show, old bean."

'Cholly good shew, ol' been,' repeats Pancho, doing his best to imitate Smith's pompous tone.

That's right, old bean,' says Smith, giving him all the encouragement he can. 'Jolly good show.'

'Next,' goes on Smith, when he is sure that Pancho has got it just right. 'If someone is in trouble, perhaps their car has broken down or their mortgage company has foreclosed on the house, you say: "Bai Jove old chap, what a terrible ghastly bore."

Pancho practises hard and soon, with Smith's help becomes familiar with many other common English expressions, even using them on the deck-hands when he sets them to work.

Dash it all, old chap,' he says when catching one of them skiving below. 'That's not cricket, old boy.'

Sailing By

The harbour at Santa Isabel sweeps round in a long graceful curve and culminates in a slim-fingered peninsula; pointing seawards it dwindles into a final flat-topped headland upon which sits a modest lighthouse. A figure stands leaning upon a railing which runs the length of the esplanade and from there seems to be idly watching the sunset. Smith is just returning from a long walk out to the lighthouse and the sunset is outrageously over the top as usual; at any moment it looks as if a vast-bodied opera singer will burst forth from the multi-hued clouds to launch into a mighty earthshaking aria.

He looks downwards to where the seagoing fishing canoes lie gently pulling against their anchor ropes. Like Viking ships they are long-bodied and wide at the beam with a grass-roofed cabin woven into a hoop amidships. Forward is a slim mast which supports a triangular sail of patched flour sacks and at the stern a long steering oar is lashed in place. The boats are crewed by around eight men each and now they are having supper. Sitting at long tables beneath the central shelter they shout across the water to each other and their voices reach Smith but faintly. Now he looks at the boats with growing interest and the sunset loses its charm as an idea flits briefly through his mind, sudden as a swallow it is one moment there, and then gone. He snatches it back for a detailed examination and likes what he sees.

'It could be done,' he thinks. With one of these boats he could sail back home, the crew would work for next to nothing to get to England. He could sail right up the coast of Africa keeping in sight of land all the way; disembarking each evening to make camp, or sleeping aboard whilst anchored in peaceful lagoons along the way. He is warming to the idea and imagines the long voyage northwards to the Canaries, Gibraltar and Spain. Then with France lying starboard and home on the port, up the English Channel and into the mouth of the Thames. As dawn is breaking they reach Margate; the island of Canvey; past Dartford and Woolwich they sail, while the rising sun dispels the mist and tips the two rows of flashing paddles with red. A stiff morning breeze fills their sail and the river is choppy, but Smith, used now to the rocking of the boat stands in the stern with the steering oar beneath his arm as they pass beneath Tower Bridge. His heart beats faster now as Charing Cross hoves into view and... 'Ungowah!' he shouts to the crew. They turn and cast a puzzled eye upon him; he has no idea what the word means, but hearing it shouted frequently in the market place back at Santa Isabel he has taken it to heart, and being the only African word he knows he uses it freely on such occasions as this.

'Ungowah!' he shouts, and pointing a commanding finger towards the pier, 'UNGOWAH!' he shouts again.

The paddles used so heroically on their long journey dip in unison and guide the boat expertly in towards the steps of the pier. They are soon tied up fast and with the sail lowered and neatly stowed they jump ashore and climb the steps to the embankment, where the erstwhile crew now stand and stare with wonder at the pompous buildings and busy red early-morn buses.

Smith pays off the crew, five pounds apiece does the trick, plus the number of the Brixton bus where they're sure to make good friends to fill them in on England, perhaps even becoming minor celebrities of a sort. He shakes hands all round and turns towards Embankment Underground, while the Africans depart speaking amongst themselves in tongues, their flour sack skirts and plastic flip-flops looking strange beside Big Ben. Smith looks around to watch them cross the road. A tiny group and slightly overawed, they turn and with flashing spears wave a last farewell before disappearing towards Parliament Square.

Return Of The Seafarer

Meanwhile back at Santa Isabel Smith is leaning on the harbour rail dreaming of his journey home. The idea seems definitely feasible and he is possessed by the desire to test it out. He descends the steps to a narrow strip of beach and walks along to where two or three of the native vessels are tied up. Bringing out a fifty-peseta note he approaches a small group of fishermen sitting on a rickety bamboo wharf. He raps his knuckles on one of the craft, holds up the note and raises his eyebrows in question.

They shake their heads. The boat is not for sale. Nevertheless, one of the men stands up and gesturing Smith to follow him leads off up the beach to where another boat is pulled out of the water and beached. The man gives it a rap then holds up the fingers of both hands; clutching and opening them a number of times. Smith counts and makes a rough estimate; he is asking around thirty pounds for the boat. Smith nods and climbs aboard, it is old, but the timbers are sound. He walks up and down the low deck a few times to get the feel of it and stands in the stern to try out the steering oar. He can pay the asking price with ease and already has a sense of ownership.

Indicating that he will return the next day with the money he leaves the harbour to work out the final details. 'I will need a small compass,' he thinks and returning to his boat finds Pancho lying on his bunk below.

'I'm buying a boat.' says Smith, 'and wondered if you can tell me where I might find a small compass.'

'Where are you going old boy?' asks Pancho.

'England,' days Smith, and begins unfolding his plan.

A look of consternation crosses Pancho's face as he listens, and deepens as slowly he comprehends the scale of the enterprise. Finally he sits up and delivers his opinion.

'*Caramba!*' he explodes. '*loco hombré,* You weel not last one day, old boy, you are mad to even think such a thing.'

'Why is that?' asks Smith, dismayed by the discouraging response.

Pancho looks exasperated. 'The currents along the coast are treacherous' he explains. 'They weel push you onto the rocks, and contrary winds weel blow you far out to sea.'

Now Smith remembers the towering waves which slam themselves like sledgehammers against the sides of *Ocean Service* whenever they leave the protection of the harbour and he realises his naiveté. Pancho shakes his head seriously. 'You weel not last one day old bean.'

Smith's dream, fatally fractured by Pancho's words of wisdom collapses around him and he quietly says goodbye to Charing Cross pier.

'Well,' he says reluctantly. 'You're probably right.'

However, grateful to Pancho for saving him from his latest misbegotten folly, he adds: 'I say, old chap, jolly decent of you to tip me the wink.'

Mutiny

A new circumstance is looming just below Smith's event horizon of which he is blissfully unaware, yet it will transform his situation beyond his wildest dreams. It first shows itself when two deckhands fall sick and neither is capable of standing a watch, leaving the natty Spaniard and Smith to steer the boat. They share the task between them, standing four hours on and four off on a two-day trip to reel in some deep-sea buoys and strip them of barnacles. Now having completed the mission they are returning to port. Smith is at the helm and dawn is breaking as he peers through the wheelhouse window trying to keep a straight course through the marker buoys that warn of shoals lying off the harbour. Seriously tired, his eyes are heavy and he can barely keep them open, and were it not for the Captain's silent presence on the bridge he would be asleep on his feet.

Reaching port they tie up and Smith relinquishes the wheel gratefully. 'Now for some sleep,' he thinks, but first some breakfast. He makes his way to the galley dreaming of fried eggs and plenty of toast, but when he enters the cook points at the clock and shakes his head. Smith is too late it seems, breakfast time is long past and the cook will not put himself out. Smith is outraged by this sullen disregard for his plight. He has steered this ship of villains through the night and now definitely considers himself worthy of some breakfast. His indignation now takes the helm and... 'I want my breakfast!' he shouts, banging his fist down on the table.

The cook is a Spaniard and doesn't take kindly to this; he picks up a large carving knife from the range and storms across the galley with murder in his hot eyes. Smith is trapped in a corner and cannot escape, so rising to his feet he makes a sensible move. Raising both arms in surrender he capitulates.

'OK, no breakfast,' he says. The cook doesn't understand the words but the gesture is unmistakable, and accepting Smith's surrender he reluctantly retires to his range.

But Smith hasn't finished; he cannot let it go and decides to seek help from the Captain who he is sure must support his request. Climbing up to the bridge he knocks loudly on the cabin door. A disagreeable grunt comes from within and when he enters the Captain is filling his log. Bent over his desk, the bottle of rum within reach he doesn't even look round as Smith makes his case. 'It is too late fer breakfast,' he shouts when Smith has finished. 'If yer vant to eat yer must go ashore.'

'That's it,' thinks Smith. To be treated like this is too much and he loses his rag completely. Throwing caution to the winds he shouts back in anger: 'Then go steer you own bloody boat!'

The Captain stands up and turns around in a fury and Smith thinks that he too will be blown down. But luckily the big Swede controls himself, fists clenched at his sides his voice comes out in an unrestrained roar. 'Get out,' he bellows. 'GET OUT! YER FIRED!'

Deliverance

Collecting his gear from below and nothing loath, Smith goes ashore and directs his steps to the agent's office. He does not expect much help there having blown both of his jobs, but it might be worth a try. The agent looks up as he enters.

'Dere iss no more job fer you,' he snaps. 'So, vere do you vant to go?'

'Where can I go?' asks Smith, puzzled by the question and the man explains. It seems that he has served enough Company time to qualify for a short leave, and its planes leave from an inland air-strip taking its workers to destinations far and wide.

'So,' says the agent. 'Vere do you vant to go?'

Smith contemplates the many choices on offer, but what he really wants is a cup of good English tea and so: 'London,' he says hopefully.

The agent is unfazed by this. 'OK,' he says, opening a drawer and bringing out a book of passes. He fills one in, signs it and affixes the Company seal.

'Der plane leaves at eight o'clock tomorrow morning,' he says, handing Smith the pass. He looks Smith up and down with a cold calculating eye. 'And ven you come back I sink dere vill still be no job fer you,' he says meaningfully. But Smith has no intention of coming back. Fortune has smiled upon him and he is sure he will find many other less stressful situations to occupy him. Later that evening he relaxes with a beer on the balcony of a seamen's hostel where he has booked in for the night, and as darkness falls he watches the bats flicker in ragged black clouds about the scraggy palms which line the street below.

Morning comes early and he is soon up and on his long trek out to the airfield. It lies two or three miles inland but he has given himself plenty of time. The path runs through jungle and once out of town he gets a little nervous. Were he to meet with some large carnivore he would be helpless. However, he eventually arrives at the airstrip unmolested where the Company plane sits on the runway, engines warming up and the passenger door open. The plane is an old Dakota, oil-streaked and in need of a new paint job. He walks across the sandy strip, climbs the steps to the passenger cabin and there, just before he enters the plane he turns around and standing on the top steps breathes in one last pungent lungful of Africa.

Inside the plane Smith finds a window seat amongst the dozen or so oilmen who are already aboard and watches from his window as the pilot guns his engines. From the exhausts of the two prop engines great flames shoot back along the runway and for a moment Smith thinks the plane is on fire, but no one else in the cabin seems to be taking this pyrotechnic display amiss. Now the plane moves forward gathering speed until it lifts, soaring clumsily above the jungle below and Smith sees to his horror that in the wing below his window the rivets which punctuate its length are rattling around loosely in their sockets and a green mould inhabits every nook and cranny of the wing. Nevertheless, he closes his eyes and consigns himself once more into the hands of providence and is soon fast asleep.

He wakes. He sleeps. He wakes. He sleeps again. He wakes again and looks below. It is morning and a mist hangs in the air; then sprawling houses red and neat, the early post and milk. And now he sees it's winter here, the fields all cloaked in white as the plane swoops down to London town and 1967 in the snow.

Thereafter he carries in his head an indelible memory of that pungent jungle smell and the subtle scent of mimosa at dusk. Quiet back streets where wisteria loops its blossom through filigree wrought-iron and the long waterfront where babbling African voices clamour around the seething bars. It is no wonder then that the voices raised in party mood from Chief Mopo's garden have brought these memories to life once more and sent him into such a deep and complex reverie. He comes back to the balcony at the embassy with a start, awakened from his trance by a rustling in the leaves which shroud the end of the balcony beside him.

Double Trouble And Strife

Looking around he sees P. B. Rivers emerging from amongst the foliage. His eye is fixed intently on Smith who, having only just surfaced from his monumental reminiscence suspects that something is expected of him.

P. B. Rivers clears his throat. 'As I said,' he says dryly. 'You are mixing up the two examples.'

Smith hurriedly recapitulates the proposition, and in so doing is given a sudden insight into P. B. Rivers' approach and he realises that, having accepted the parameters of this existential point of view, he is now fully justified in establishing a few of his own.

'Yes, but supposing they are the same,' he persists. 'Then the father would also be honour-bound to reveal to the mother his relationship with his son-in-law's girlfriend, who we already know is having it off with someone else.' Smith has now absorbed enough of P. B. River's technique to challenge him with a few propositions of his own. 'Question:' he says. 'Would his wife's father be upset? Question: would her mother be able to take it? Question: Would it be better for him to pack a small case and do a runner?'

P. B. Rivers likes this, he laughs. 'I liken situations of that sort to barrels of gunpowder and when the sparks fly;' he knits his eyebrows and... 'Boom!' he shouts. 'Sensitives living as far away as Bushy Park or Ealing would feel the psychic tremors from such explosive revelations.' Smith stares at him, not quite sure how mad he is, but P. B. Rivers continues, looking down on the Africans with a benign and lofty smile. 'They're all the same,' he says. 'The whole thing is a can of worms.'

But Smith is pleased with his efforts to engage with P.B. Rivers' subtle insight into the human predicament.

'Maybe I'm not so stupid after all,' he thinks.

Old Man's Power

A month or so later the Guild is contacted by a Buddhist group who are bringing to England the Dalai Lama's boyhood teacher, now a venerable old man. Hearing of the success of Ubron's stay they wish to use the salon for a teaching with the frail old man, and send a dozen or so Tibetan monks to prepare for the visit. They scurry around in their maroon robes, cleaning and polishing the salon and front hall until they consider it worthy for their master. The great day arrives and by early evening the forecourt is becoming choked with cars, and there is some disturbance in the road outside as they turn in through the embassy gates.

'What time is the Dalai Lama arriving?' Johnny Banana Head asks, looking up from his *AtoZ*.

'It's not the Dalai Lama himself,' says Smith, watching through the kitchen window at the confusion outside. 'It's the old man who was his teacher.'

But Johnny isn't listening, his nose already back in his book.

'Why don't you go and sort out the cars in the forecourt?' Smith says. 'They'll take notice of you in that overcoat.'

'Right, I'll go and direct the traffic,' Johnny says, doing up his silver buttons and puffing out his chest. Someone finds him an old Gas Board peaked cap which had been languishing in a cupboard and now, his long hair pulled behind he almost looks the part. However, once outside, far from confining his activities to the forecourt he strides straight to the centre of the road outside and stops one line of traffic to allow cars to cross into the embassy gates, and before long has created a tailback stretching far down the road. The frustrated drivers honk their horns furiously as Johnny, his Gas Board cap pulled sternly over his eyes, struts imperiously about and with many compelling hand gestures holds them at bay.

Alerted by this blockage a police car comes hooting and flashing down the middle of the road, and with a dramatic screech of brakes pulls up onto the pavement outside the embassy. The doors fly open and two constables leap out. They approach Johnny at a half-run and one of them takes him roughly by the arm and swings him around.

'What do you think you're doing?' bellows the policeman.

'I'm directing the traffic,' says Johnny, his innocent moonface lacking all guile.

The policemen exchange looks and a nod passes between them. Johnny is obviously a nutter and the Gas Board hat doesn't help.

'Why are you directing the traffic?' asks the second policeman.

'Because the Dalai Lama is coming,' says Johnny, who still has it wrong.

'Oh yeah, yeah, the Dalai Lama,' says the first policeman with heavy sarcasm. 'Come on, get in the car,' and they begin to drag poor Banana Head towards their car.

'No wait,' shouts Johnny, struggling to get free. 'Look! Here he comes now.'

He points down the road and the policemen freeze as a large black limousine full of Tibetan monks sweeps up and pulls around through the embassy gates. The front door of the house opens and a hoard of shaven-headed monks come pouring out. They sink as one to their knees as the door of the car is opened, and, swathed in the robes of his order the old man descends, followed by various hierarchical officials similarly garbed.

The policemen are dumfounded. They stand gaping at the small ceremony of welcome now being performed in the embassy forecourt. The old man's power has emptied for one brief moment even the busy minds of the policemen. Eventually, one of them attempts to pull himself together and regain some semblance of authority. Unfortunately, in the face of these events he has difficulty in framing the appropriate attitude. Finally, scraping the bottom of the barrel he gives Johnny a dismissive push from behind, sending him stumbling away. The policeman's voice is furious.

'Well all right then,' he shouts.

'But don't do it again!

Parting Of The Ways

Brett has just returned from India with a magnificent Hiren Roy sitar, made this time for sure by the master himself, and such is the power of the instrument's resonance that he has difficulty putting it down.

'Everything about it is perfect,' he tells Smith, who has come up to Brett's room to view this new wonder. 'The sustain goes on for ever and the tone is the best I've ever heard.'

At last he is happy. He has found the instrument of his dreams and to cap it all, he has obtained a role as resident sitar player at an expensive Indian restaurant in Knightsbridge. He runs his fingers up and down the tones of a raga. 'All it needs,' he says, 'is a little adjustment to the bridge'.

Suddenly he puts down the sitar and jumps to his feet. 'I must ring and tell Polly about this,' he says, then leaves the room to head downstairs for the telephone.

Polly is Brett's girlfriend. She wields great influence over him and he treats her with much respect. 'She is a very serious Buddhist,' he says, 'and she meditates eight hours every day.' He looks sternly at Smith as he says this, and draws himself up importantly, as if having such a fanatical Buddhist for a girlfriend endows him with added social status. Polly is now in America where she has gone for a long austere retreat. But now, Brett's fantastic new sitar and a regular spot at a classy Indian restaurant have excited him beyond prudence.

'I must ring Polly and tell her,' he says.

Smith sits on the floor and awaits his return. The sitar lay before him gleaming in a rich dark chestnut lacquer, and the ivory inlays sketch a lacy path up the neck and around the ample gourd. He feasts his eyes upon it until he hears footsteps in the corridor outside. Brett stumps into the room looking as if his world has caved in, and a bitter dourness clouds his face.

'What's up?' asks Smith, sensing that Brett has received some mighty blow to his esteem.

'I told her,' he says. 'I told her about my sitar and all about the job in the restaurant.'

'What did she say then?' asks Smith.

'She was very sarcastic,' says Brett, and here he mimics her voice as if she were a squawking parrot. 'She said, '*Oh, that's very nice Brett. What a good little boy you are*.' And then she put the phone down on me.'

He walks over to the window and stands for a while looking out in silence, then...

'That's it,' he says bitterly. 'I've had it with Buddhism.'

No Laughing Matter

A large axe is buried deeply in the man's skull and the handle projects over his right shoulder. He is angry about something there is no doubt about that, for his voice quivers with suppressed frustration and he splutters as he speaks.

He has been brought to this condition by an unusual request from Sukie, who has been pestering Smith for some time in a similar manner. She is plying him with coffee and croissants one morning, when in a conspiratorial manner she first pops the question.

'I am interested to get some laughing-powder,' she says, and Smith suspects she is winding him up. But no, she gazes back at him seriously.

'There's no such thing,' he says.

'Oh yes,' says Sukie. 'You buy 'er in packet and blow it round the room and everybody laugh.'

Smith likes the sound of this but still has his doubts. He casts his mind back to his schooldays and the comic world of japes and wheezes. But nowhere among that subculture of stink-bombs and exploding cigars can he remember such a thing as laughing powder. Nevertheless, Sukie's utter conviction that it exists undermines his conviction that it does not, and he compromises.

'Well I've never heard of it,' he says.

Some days later she brings the subject up again.

'We can buy 'er in joke shop,' she says.

'Buy what?' asks Smith.

'Laughing-powder.' says Sukie. 'And you must come wiz me in case I am lost.'

This sounds like an interesting expedition, and Smith agrees to accompany her to a shop which they locate in the vicinity of the British Museum. The weather is fine as they strike out across Regents Park, and Smith wants to make a small detour past the wolf cages; he wishes to conduct an important experiment.

Sometime before their recent estrangement, Leon Bloch had given Smith a recording of Siberian wolves. A microphone had been hidden near a wolf den which had captured a whole night of the most sensational howling. From the opening deep baritone of a grizzled but still powerful elder, right through the spectrum of female contraltos and adolescent sopranos, to a final cascade of juvenile yaps from the nursery. It is a sublime chorus of voices and Smith finds it musically awesome.

'What if I play the tape to the wolves in the zoo?' he thinks. The wolves inhabit a large open-air enclosure that parallels the main boulevard through the park.

'If I play the tape to them it will re-connect them to their ancestral roots and maybe give them a bit of a lift.' The idea has been recurring of late and now seems a good opportunity to put it into practice. He packs the tape and a small player into his bag, 'I can kill two birds with one stone,' he thinks. 'First the invigoration of wolves, and then the hunt for laughing-powder.'

They cut across a canal bridge to the park beyond and head for the main boulevard, where the wolves can be seen lying amongst trees towards the back of their enclosure. One wolf however, stands alone by the fence. It gazes out across Camden Town with a far-away look, as if it sees a distant vista of craggy mountains capped with snow-clad firs.

Smith takes out his taperecorder, and standing closely against the outer barrier holds it as near to the wolf as he can. He presses the play button and the first of a series of wild howls emerge. Unfortunately, the speaker of his machine is so small, that out here in the immensity of the park its voice is frail and tinny. He feels a twinge of guilt. What is he doing barging into the presence of this nobley grey eminence with his trivial plastic toy? To make matters worse, the wolf now turns its head and looks — not at the tape-recorder, which is still emitting its tinny screeches — but directly at Smith himself. For one nanosecond, or possibly less, the wolf's glance flickers on him before, dismissing him as if he were an ant, it turns its head away and resumes once more its scrutiny of the distant mountains and snow-bound forests of Camden Town.

'It might work if I get a bigger speaker,' thinks Smith, as they leave the wolves and continue along the boulevard. He is about to return the recorder to his bag when he sees, coming slowly towards him an elderly Labrador. The dog's owner is walking some way behind and Smith sees another opportunity to test his theory.

'Dogs, unlike wolves, are domesticated,' he thinks, 'and therefore may respond more favourably to the sound of the wild. I think I'll give it a go.'

As the dog approaches with an aged but determined plod he holds out the tape recorder.

'Do you mind if I play this to your dog,' he shouts to the owner, who regards him suspiciously. Before the man has a chance to say no, Smith presses the play button and holds the recorder to the dog's ear. It takes no notice whatsoever, but continues its weary plod without missing a beat and Smith is confounded. Now the dog's owner passes in the wake of his geriatric pet.

'It's no good playing that to him,' he snaps as he goes by. 'He's as deaf as a post.'

Smith gives up, switches off the recorder and puts it back in his bag. Already the howls have been attracting the attention of passers-by and a few loiter expectantly in their vicinity. Hurriedly leaving the wide avenue, Sukie and Smith cut an oblique path towards Portland Place and on through Fitzrovia beyond. 'Well,' thinks Smith. 'Maybe we'll have better luck with the laughing powder.'

They are passing along a narrow street lined one side with quaint old shops, whilst on the other the British Museum looms like an ancient Greek cinema, when Sukie gives a delighted shriek. 'Look! Look! There,' and she claps her hands in excitement. She is pointing at a colourful selection of weird masks, skeletons, top hats, wands and other items from the world of carnival and illusion. The shop window is crammed with a fascinating display of tricks and disguises. Sukie pushes through the shop door and somewhere a small bell tinkles. A door opens at the rear of the shop and a man emerges.

He spreads his hands on the counter, and with a benevolent smile asks Sukie how he may help her. The man has a rubber axe fixed to his head with a concealed spring, and a deep recess in the blade allows it to fit snugly across the top, while giving the illusion of being sunk deeply into his skull.

'Please I would like to buy some laughing powder,' says Sukie. But the man has difficulty understanding her French accent, and he frowns, an expression which Smith considers more suitable considering the axe.

'I beg your pardon,' he says.

'She wants some laughing powder,' says Smith, who wonders how much longer he can keep a straight face.

'Yes and I would like to 'ave two packet please,' says Sukie firmly.

Now the man has understood. 'Laughing powder,' he says. 'There's no such thing.'

His face has gone from the initial benign expectation to puzzlement, and now suspicion lurks in every line, while the axe provides a surreal and hilarious context to all three expressions.

Sukie hasn't come this far to be brushed off so easily, she is sure that the elusive powder exists.

'Oh please,' she wails, raising her hands to the man as if in prayer. 'I just want a small packet; you must have some somewhere if you look.'

But the man is getting angry with her. 'There's no such thing!' he shouts, banging his fist down on the counter again. 'I've got sneezing powder, or itching powder, but there's no such thing as laughing powder.' He is getting very red of face and the axe wobbles when he bangs down his fist.

Sukie is now close to tears, she is convinced that the man has laughing powder concealed somewhere in the shop. She puts her hands to her face and weeps, 'Oh please, please,' she wails through her fingers. But the man is seriously put out; he thinks they have come here to pull his leg, a thing he must often endure, and the axe quivers wildly as he points to the door. 'Get out,' he says.

Sukie, sobbing bitterly, leaves the shop and Smith, who has managed not to laugh once, follows her.

'Well, there you are,' he says, when they are once more in the street. 'There's no such thing as laughing powder.' But Sukie is unmoved by the episode.

''E was maniac,' she says tearfully, 'and somewhere there is anozzer shop which 'ave it.'

'I know,' she says enigmatically. 'I know.'

Siren Song

Harry Flame's quest for poetic truth had of late been leading him into ever stranger modes of perception, where, beneath the surface of common-day experiences a murky world of subliminal intentions battle for supremacy. News has just arrived, however, of poor Harry's demise. Found half-naked in a wintry field and dead of exposure near the isolated Welsh cottage which he squats from time to time. What siren voice had sung to him on that fatal night had left no traces, but he had followed its song out into a bitterly cold landscape on his last walk and found at the end a final release from his suffering. He had turned up at the embassy only the summer before, looking gaunt and exuding a general air of resentment. A small room had been put at his disposal, but he had been unable to settle, spending most of his time hanging around in the kitchen casting malevolent glances at all who enter. Harry had once more fallen amongst the pygmies.

One bright spot had occurred during his brief stay, when the idea of giving a poetry reading at the embassy had taken hold and he had generated a little enthusiasm for the project. Smith had offered to help him with the posters, producing his collection of lettering transfers to accomplish this. But Harry, sorting through the different styles had rejected the lot and wanted to buy some of his own choosing. Together they had ventured forth to an art shop in Baker Street where he searched through drawer after drawer. The shop-assistant had tried to help, bringing forth many different designs, all of which Harry turns down. Smith had watched fascinated as the assistant exhibited first helpfulness, then irritation, and finally barely suppressed anger as Harry prevaricated among the now disordered drawers.

Eventually the man had stalked off in a huff, and Harry had been left kneeling on the floor amongst a litter of sheets sighing and muttering hopelessly to himself. Smith, who was beginning to think that Harry was being a little too fussy, suggested that although presentation is important the reading itself is the main issue and proposed that as a solution he should perhaps be satisfied with the least offensive of the type faces. Harry had let forth a groan.

'You just don't understand,' he sighed, and Smith, who had heard this weary retort many times before couldn't disagree since he knew it to be true. But as usual it is a truth that is of little help.

They had been in the shop for over two hours and the assistant had begun to close up. Returning, he then began to replace the scattered sheets in the drawers and Harry, no time left is forced to make a choice. They leave and returning to the embassy start putting the poster together. Smith has by now become quite proficient at poster-making but Harry, with his own private and incomprehensible criterion makes the task a nightmare.

'No, no,' he complains, his voice tired with the effort of explaining to this fugitive from the monkey house. 'The lines are too close together,' or: 'They're too far apart,' and Smith wonders why he had ever let himself in for this, while Harry paces the room muttering, 'Oh God! Oh God!'

Several rejected posters lie on the floor and the sheets of lettering have run out.

'You'll just have to choose one of these,' says Smith, and leaving Harry alone to decide, makes good his escape.

The next morning, resolving to get some action he finds Harry still unsure. 'I think this one may be all right,' he says. 'But on the other hand this one might be the best.' A pause and then... 'Or this.' He tentatively holds forth two posters and Smith, determined to stay clear of Harry's quagmire snatches the nearest. 'Right,' he says firmly, and before Harry can change his mind abruptly leaves the room and mounting his pushbike rides off to get it photocopied.

The great day draws near and Harry begins to get nervous, but the posters have been sent out and everyone wishes him well.

'We've sent them to all the people who might be able to help you,' says Tralee. 'If they turn up who knows what might come of it.'

But Harry, irrevocably addicted to his jaundiced view of the world scowls and looks with pity upon her naiveté. One day to go and the salon has been arranged for the event which will launch him on a new beginning, and in the afternoon he goes for a long walk to decide what poems he will read on the morrow. Returning, he enters the kitchen to find Smith having a bite to eat.

'It's off.' he announces in a doom-laden voice. 'I'm not doing the reading.'

'You can't pull out Harry,' says Smith, exasperated beyond belief. 'We've sent out the posters and it's too late to change it now.'

But Harry is adamant. 'You don't understand what levels I'm working on,' he says wearily. 'You see I was walking in Kensington Gardens this afternoon and came upon a set of ornamental gates celebrating the wedding of Princess Margaret, and the date of this occasion, inscribed above the gates falls exactly on the date of my reading. So I can't possibly do it.'

'But what does it matter when she was married? It's you that have the initiative now,' argues Smith, feeling betrayed by this last minute turnabout.

'You still don't understand.' Harry's voice has a tone of finality about it. 'I'm not a courtier. They can ring their own fucking bell!' His mind is made up and for Smith this convoluted reasoning is the last straw. 'OK Harry, it's your life.' he says, and spends the rest of the day making innumerable phone calls to the people on the mailing list and cancelling the event. By late evening he is pretty sure he has reached most of them, and a day or two later Harry, carrying his scruffy suitcase of poems leaves the house without another word. And now comes news of his death. Near naked in the arms of a wintry night.

Tralee has been inconsolable, weeping her way through several days as she mourns his passing. She had been very fond of him, going out of her way many times in the past to help and encourage him through the clouds of paranoia which had hung intermittently around his head. But poor Harry had been even then beyond all such help, since an earlier episode or two as a mental patient in the hands of psychotic psychiatrists, ever-ready with the electrodes had addled his brain and embittered him even further.

Smith casts his mind back to a long-ago event when Harry, lying solemn of visage in an open coffin had been carried upon the stalwart shoulders of six young fellows, their hair long and shaggy above the motley of hippie clothes, and lo! It is the mid-Sixties again and Harry is representing the death of the London hippie underground newspaper, *International Times*, otherwise known as *IT*.

The police have just raided and closed down the paper and a movement is quickly afoot to engage in a magical act. The symbolic enactment of the death and rebirth of *IT*. But who will provide the body in this worthy cause? A willing acolyte to be born aloft in a coffin down into the underworld and later to be resurrected as the hero of the hour? The hand of fate hovers as the issue is discussed, and its finger hesitates for a while before falling on the head of Harry Flame.

He takes the whole thing very seriously indeed. This is the kind of symbolic role he feels appropriate to his function as prophet, seer and poet. He relishes the attention which now comes his way and a faint sense of grandness is apparent in his manner. The coffin, painted black, is constructed of a rough timber frame covered with hardboard, and Harry, having with an air of great importance laid himself flat within, is hoisted aloft and carried amongst a sea of young hippie faces along the Portobello Road to Notting Hill Gate tube station, where it descends the entrance stairs and surrounded by a throng of gaily dressed revellers surges past the bewildered ticket collector, down the escalator and onto the platform.

This is the journey into the underworld and Harry, still in the coffin, is carried aboard a train and laid on the floor between the doors. A trip to Westminster and the Cenotaph for ceremonial purposes is then accomplished without mishap, and the coffin with attendant mourners again descends the escalator for one circuit of the Circle Line to represent the magical transformation. Then the triumphant coffin will emerge once more at Notting Hill station bearing the resurrected life and replenished energy of *IT*.

The other passengers seem to regard the coffin as some kind of student stunt and look on with tolerant amusement. But Harry, mission almost accomplished is becoming agitated and seems to be having second thoughts. Smith, who has accompanied him closely in this escapade leans down and asks him what is wrong.

'I don't think I'm up to it,' moans Harry weakly and begins to sit up.

'Don't get out of the coffin whatever you do,' says Smith. 'All you have to do is lie still.'

Harry however is afflicted by serious doubts about his involvement.

'You don't understand,' he groans. 'I'm not really pure enough for this role and I will be made to suffer if I go through with it.'

He begins struggling to get out and several pairs of hands are needed to restrain him, but he is becoming manic and eventually, breaking free he sits down on a passenger seat.

'There's only two more stops to go,' says Smith. 'Come on Harry, don't let us down now.'

But Harry's head is sunk in his hands impervious to all attempts to get him back in the coffin.

'Oh God,' he mutters. 'I can't do it, I can't possibly do it.'

Notting Hill is now reached and Harry, still prevaricating, forces the whole entourage to embark upon a second circuit of the line. It is now obvious that he will never get back into the coffin.

'Someone else will have to do it,' says Tim Jacobson, who has undertaken to act as High Priest in this enactment. 'We can't allow the ceremony to fail; it will be bad for future morale.'

Smith tries once more.

'Look Harry,' he pleads. 'You are now responsible for the success or failure of the whole thing. Everything depends on you.'

But his words have no effect.

'I'm not pure enough,' moans Harry, and Smith can see that his efforts are hopeless and gives up.

Notting Hill is coming round once more and they cannot waste any more time, a hasty discussion takes place and since no one else is willing Smith reluctantly lay down in the coffin. When their destination arrives the coffin with its new occupant is once more lifted high, and leaving Harry, (loyally accompanied by Tim Jacobson) to continue his fruitless journey, it is carried up the escalator and out into the Portobello Road. Its emergence is greeted by cheers, and amidst an excited throng is carried back in triumph until, arriving at a quiet back street it is dismantled and thrown into a skip. 'We were in the train for over four hours,' says Tim later. 'Harry couldn't face his failure to go through with it, and so we spent the whole afternoon going round and round on the Circle Line.'

Now that Harry is dead it seems appropriate that an evening should be dedicated to his poetry and extraordinary life where those who knew him well might gather to remember. But it is not until later in the year that the event takes place, a dark November evening which due to circumstances falls upon the fifth. Many poets arrive at the embassy to read and reminisce, while in the garden Roman Candles erupt, Silver Rain falls, and rockets take to the skies to burst among the stars.

'They're all for Harry,' says Tralee, looking up at the display. But Smith, knowing that Harry would violently reject any association with the government agent-provocateur Guy Fawkes, cannot deny that circumstances are sometimes mischievously apt.

Fancy Footwork

Tralee runs a small car and her driving can be at times a little erratic, resulting in the vehicle somewhat resembling a four-wheeled rock-cake. She and Smith are passing along Camden High Street in the battered car when a charity shop catches her eye and she pulls over to the curb and gets out. Smith follows her into the shop and makes for the men's corner where he may find something cheap. But nothing on the rail is interesting; a couple of old-fashioned double-breasted suits with bucket-size trouser bottoms are not to his taste.

Looking up to see how Tralee is getting on his glance passes through the front window where a parking warden is just about to write out a ticket for her car. The warden is a lady with cropped blond hair beneath a peaked-cap and her stance exudes officialdom. He calls to Tralee and points out of the window. She takes one look and is already half-way to the door, and Smith, recognising her Valkyrie stride knows there could well be trouble in the offing. He watches as Tralee, her ragged zigzag skirt whirling around the elegant but scruffy high-laced boots, storms out of the shop and descends on the unsuspecting warden.

Tralee is a lady who will not allow her natural sense of civil rights to be violated whatever the conditions or circumstances. She had for example in the Sixties, whilst peacefully attending an anti-Vietnam war demonstration outside the American Embassy in Berkeley Square, witnessed a policeman giving an elderly man a bit of truncheon. Leaping in passionate outrage upon the keeper of the peace she had dealt him several sharp blows about the ears with her tambourine, before being hauled off and inserted into a Black Maria by some of his colleagues. Smith knows all this. But the warden doesn't.

'I've only been in the shop one minute and I'm going now.' Tralee tells the warden who barely looks up from her busy pen.

'You're on a yellow line,' says the lady pompously, a hint of scorn riding her wilful lip. 'And I've already written out the ticket.'

'Well, you can tear it up,' says Tralee dismissively as she opens the car door with the obvious intention of driving off. Smith leaves the shop in a hurry and is making ready to leap aboard when he sees that the warden will have none of this. She moves in front of the car to block its escape and begins detaching the ticket. This move infuriates Tralee who now loses her rag completely.

'You stupid parasitic cow!' she shrieks, and flings herself towards the warden, who, seeing this whirlwind of fury coming in her direction takes a step back in alarm, but she is too late. Tralee's foot comes flashing out in a high kick, her boot catches the warden's clipboard from below and the next moment it is flying upward, shedding as it does so the tickets and stickers which come loose and taken by a wind flutter wildly around them.

This exhibition of fancy footwork however, is only the prelude to the main attack. For the next moment her arm swings round in a sideswipe which smites the warden's hat from her head and sends it flying through the air in a high arc. The trajectory of the hat takes it out across the road and when it falls has only time to bounce once before the wheel of a passing bus squashes it flat. There is some applause from the small crowd which has gathered, and a faint cheer or two shows Tralee that she has some allies amongst them.

The policeman who now appears however, is definitely on the side of the parking warden who is tearfully trying to gather up her tickets and retrieve her ruined hat from the road. The hat is a complete write-off and the warden holds it out to the policeman as evidence. Tralee is booked and appears before a magistrate, where she is fortunate enough to receive only a severe reprimand and the imposition of a stiff fine. But she leaves the court undaunted, her inner-volcano untamed.

Orpheus Unbound

Getting up early one morning Smith enters the kitchen to find Brett busy with a mop and bucket of water. He is washing the red tiles of the floor and has placed all the chairs onto the table while he mops beneath. Smith, being as yet unable to sit, stands near the stove where he makes a cup of tea, watching silently until Brett has finished and then taking a seat at the table. They do not speak since Brett rarely engages in conversation. He is a monosyllabic man whose mind is focused on his sitar to the exclusion of everything else.

Putting away the mop Brett leaves to return shortly afterwards with his sitar. He lays it upon the table and taking a chair sits gazing silently upon it. He has just returned from India where he had gone to acquire a new instrument, setting his mind on obtaining a Hiren Roy, the legendary maker of the finest sitars in India. So far he has said nothing of his journey; he is a loner and not much interested in chat unless it concerns sitars. Once this subject is breached however, he will describe in great detail the trouble he is having with the bridge of the instrument.

'I have to get the curve exactly right,' he will say, 'to produce the best tone.' He spends days at the kitchen table filing away at the bone top of the bridge, closer and closer to the optimum point.

'I think I can get it a little bit better,' he says, loosening the strings to release the bridge. Out comes the file and with a few light strokes he will shave a tiny fraction from the curve. Reassembling the instrument he plucks the strings a few times and his face drops.

'I've blown it,' he will say. 'I've taken too much off.'

The sitar is once more stripped down and he will spend the next few days fashioning a fresh piece of bone, rubbing away with the file until once more he is approaching the optimum point, and unable to resist, will fall to the temptation of giving it just one more scrape of the file in his attempts to reach the elusive perfection which he seeks.

'How was India?' Smith asks. Brett looks up with a startled expression.

'What?' he says.

'How did you get on in India?' Smith asks again.

'Oh yeah. Er OK,' says Brett, returning to his filing, and Smith knows he will have to push harder to get anything from him.

'Where did you go?' He asks after another long silence. 'Calcutta,' says Brett and making a great effort recounts the circumstances of his journey as he works.

Arriving in Calcutta he had made his way immediately to the master's workshop where he is told that it will take several weeks to build a sitar for him. He considers this. He only has a short visa and must leave India for a week or so before being eligible to renew it. Therefore, rather than returning all the way to London he will fly to Bangkok and spend the required time there. Now he enters into an agreement with the sitar maker and hands over the purchase price, then sits upon the floor in the playing position to be measured for the instrument. The old man walks around him muttering in Hindi, followed by his apprentice son who writes down his father's instructions: the slope of his shoulders, the tilt of his head and the curve of his knee, are combined into a formula which will produce an instrument perfectly balanced only in the hands of Brett.

Leaving the workshop he seeks a room in a cheap hotel and after locking up his bag and the sitar he has brought with him goes in search of a chai shop where he can sit and lay his plans. The streets of the city are seething in the hot sun, but he soon finds a shady looking place which is serving chai. He enters and sits on a bench against a wall sipping from his tea and considering his situation. He can stay in India for some weeks before leaving for Bangkok, after which his visa can be renewed and he will return to collect the new sitar. Now he can relax, enjoy India and practise on his old instrument in the hotel room. The prospect is a pleasant one and when he leaves the chai shop his spirits are buoyant.

'Please to be giving me some money.'

It is a feminine voice, the tone low and sweetly laced with musk. A woman stands in his path. She is around twenty-five or so and clinging to her sari is a little girl who looks up at him mischievously. The woman's eyes regard Brett serenely as if there is no question of a refusal and Brett, still euphoric at the prospect of the new sitar is in an expansive mood. Taking out his wallet he gives her a five-rupee note, which she accepts gracefully and expresses her gratitude by placing her palms together and bowing her head briefly. Now she looks up, smiles at him, and again he hears the bewitching music of her voice. 'Please,' she says, 'coming with me and I will make you a cup of good chai.'

Brett could listen to her voice all day long and wants to hear more, so nothing loath follows her through a labyrinth of back streets until she reaches a stretch of pavement where live the poorest of the city. Stopping half-way along she indicates an unoccupied space; this is where she lives. She unrolls a small carpet and invites him to sit while the little girl rummages amongst a stack of cooking pots for the tea-making equipment. Soon a small paraffin stove is roaring under a saucepan of water, and when the chai is made he receives the cup she offers and takes a sip. It is a quality brew, and leaning his back on an adjacent wall he stretches out his legs and looks around him.

The street is not busy and the traffic is light, mostly bicycles and motorised rickshaws. He casts his eye along the pavement and sees that the space in which he sits is but one in a long row which stretches along the street in both directions. Some of these spaces are occupied by individuals, and others by small families in which mothers tend their pots and oversee their small children. The lady, whose name is Vhariti, invites him to stay and eat with them that evening and he goes off to buy some sweets for dessert. Later, he sits by the light of a hurricane lamp and joins them in a meal. All along the pavement lanterns are flickering into life, each illuminating a small group of figures clustering around steaming pots.

When the meal is over his hostess introduces him to her neighbours who reside about two feet away on the next carpet. Mr and Mrs Mukarji make a great fuss and immediately chai must be brewed. He drinks cup after cup, as neighbours from further down the pavement come to pay their respects to the strange westerner who deigns to sit with them in the street. Brett now feels entirely at home, the little girl already seems to have attached herself to him and gazes up at him with undisguised curiosity, and when later he leaves they will not let him go without promising to visit on the morrow bringing, they demand, his sitar.

The next day he returns and after an evening meal plays an impromptu recital which attracts a sizeable audience from amongst the pavement dwellers. Such are their pleas for him to stay that he agrees to spend the night amongst them wrapped in a borrowed blanket. In the morning he is awakened by the clinking of cooking pots and the shouts of small children, while their mothers set to work searching for fleas in their hair and dousing them with buckets of water as they stand naked and shrieking with delight over a drain in the gutter.

He raises his head and sees Vhariti holding a cup of fresh chai and he sits up to take it from her. Their closest neighbours, some still wrapped in blankets, wave and wish him a good morning asking if he slept well, and he enjoys the deference which they show to him; they are treating him as if he is a prized possession. He spends the morning playing with the little girl, while Vhariti bustles around cleaning pots and disappearing on short expeditions to beg among the tourists for enough money for the evening meal.

Brett is now reluctant to leave, enamoured by Vhariti's sonorous voice and the charm of Rupa the little girl, who seeks constantly to capture his attention by bringing him an endless stream of offerings which she lays in front of him: small scraps of cloth, round pebbles and oddly shaped twigs, and when he looks at her she can hardly contain her delight. Later in the morning he plays his sitar for a while, and then, leaving it in care of Vhariti, he returns to the hotel, collects his bag and hands in the key. He is going to spend as much time as possible on the pavement.

The weeks fly by and he is beginning to feel like a family man, contributing towards the food and looking after little Rupa when Vhariti is away. By now he is a local figure amongst the pavement people who greet him by name as he strolls along the street. Eventually however he must leave for Bangkok, and the evening before his departure he provides food for a feast which they share with their neighbours. In the morning, he walks the length of the street bidding his friends farewell and promising Vhariti and Rupa that he will return in a couple of weeks.

A week later he is sitting in a bar in Bangkok when he is approached by a petite Thai girl who asks him to buy her a drink. She is stunningly beautiful with long glossy black hair and devastating brown eyes. They fall into conversation and she invites him back to her room when her shift at the bar is over, and so delightful are her charms that in the morning he cannot tear himself away and she seems pleased for him to stay. Her room is tiny, hardly big enough for the futon which lies in the middle of the floor. Otherwise it is empty, apart from a shrine made from a painted wooden box containing a small Buddha and a vase of flowers which she tends morning and evening with much chanting and burning of incense.

Brett is now enjoying himself immensely, taking long walks around the city and spending hours playing his sitar in the girl's room. Her name is Chan Pen which she tells him means "Full Moon". Soon however he must leave and return to India, and one day when Chan Pen is out he decides to check his sitar case, but where is it? His sitar lies covered with a silk cloth across the bottom of the futon but the case is nowhere in sight. His eye falls upon a large cupboard recessed into the wall where Chan Pen keeps her dresses. It is the only place where the case can be, but trying the handle he finds it locked.

Now he is a little worried. He had intended to go whilst she is out, leaving her a note and some money, but without the case he is trapped, since the sitar is a delicate instrument and will not survive rough treatment. He has also had a glimpse or two over the last few days of a different side to the delectable Chan Pen. She keeps, he has noticed, not without a twinge of apprehension, a wicked-looking dagger atop the shrine and has of late become a little bossy, speaking sharply to him when he fumbles with his chopsticks and spills rice on the floor. Also, when they take an evening stroll together, she holds his arm possessively as she parades him up and down the street past the strip clubs where the leering bouncers who stand outside wave a greeting to her as they pass. She seems to be friends with everyone on the street, and he feels too nervous to confront her when he leaves.

That evening when she returns from her work at the bar, she is sitting on the futon whilst brushing her long black hair which falls in a thick curtain around her forward tilted head.

'Where's my sitar case?' Brett asks, trying to sound as casual as possible.

The room is silent but for the measured strokes of the brush then, from beneath the glossy waterfall of hair the voice of Chan Pen slices sharp as a razor blade.

'What you wan case for? You don need no case.'

Now Brett knows for sure he is in trouble and deems it advisable to keep his mouth shut while he considers his position. Later, lying next to her on the futon he comes to the conclusion that he must act now. The room is dark as he stares at a ceiling, lit only intermittently by the flickering colours from the street outside where the strip clubs and bars blink their garish neons. He listens to the breathing of Chan Pen until he is certain she is asleep.

Beginning to move with exaggerated caution he slowly edges from the bed ready at any moment to feign sleep should she wake up. It takes an age before he can stand up and he doesn't dare put on his trousers; should she wake and catch him dressing she may, he suspects, go berserk. Silently he rolls up the trousers and bundles them around his shoes and wraps the silk cloth about his sitar. Then he begins making his way slowly towards the door, halting with bated breath whenever a floorboard creaks. But Chan Pen seems fast asleep, even snoring a little and Brett has now reached the door. Cautiously he turns the knob and slowly opens it onto the stairwell. If she wakes now he can have no excuse and is sure she will go straight for the knife.

The stairwell is lit on each landing by a single low-wattage bulb and he must be careful that he doesn't bang the sitar against the bare concrete walls. His feet pad silently on the stairs as moving a little faster he makes good his escape. Having reached the bottom of the first flight he has just put his foot upon the top step of the next, when from the room he has just left comes a terrifying scream of rage. It echoes down the stairwell and sends a cold shiver through him. Now he has the real horrors and begins stumbling down the stairs as fast as he can.

At the next landing the scream once more comes howling after him, though now it seems much closer. Looking up he sees Chan Pen leaning over the railings; her mouth is open in a wide and fearsome grimace while her wild and now demonic eyes stare down at him from amongst the disarranged hair. Again she screams as Brett fumbles and slips in his haste to get away. Now her anger is so great that she begins banging her head against the concrete wall, and hearing this dull repeated thud he cannot resist a look behind him. Blood runs in thick streams down her face and the scream emerges with animal ferocity. But by now Brett is halfway down the street, shoes and trousers in one hand, sitar in the other and shirt tails flying.

He tries not to run as the piercing screams echoing from the stairwell have alerted the bouncers and thugs who seem to make up her circle of friends, and they look towards the source of the sound. Fortunately an empty cab, prowling the streets for custom stops when he steps into the road, and he bundles the sitar into the back and jumps in. 'Airport,' he gasps urgently, and takes a look through the back window. One of the heavies has just emerged from the stairwell and shouts angrily down the street then breaks into a clumsy run towards the cab. The taxi driver, seeing that something is amiss and not wishing to lose his fare guns his motor and carries Brett swiftly to the airport where he is able, minus his sitar case, to get a seat on the next flight out.

The shrill sound of bicycle-bells and the horns of rickshaws mingle with the clatter of pots and shouts of children, while the pungent smoke of cooking fires swirl around Brett as once more he takes his ease on Vhariti's carpet. Still disturbed by the Bangkok episode, he begins to breathe a little easier. He has already paid one or two calls on the sitar maker to see how his instrument is progressing. The gourd for the soundbox has been cut to shape and the long neck fitted with glue and wooden pins. It will take a week or so more to finish, and while he waits he avails himself of Vhariti's hospitality.

Now he feels a desire to help her rise above her hand-to-mouth existence, and since he has some money from the sale of his old sitar he wonders how best to accomplish it. She has just handed him a fresh cup of chai and as he sips the brew he is struck by an idea: he will build her a tea-stall with which she can earn herself and Rupa a decent living. Proposing this idea to her he points out the advantages: it will allow her in a short time to rent a room and get her off the street. She looks dubious at this, the idea of leaving the street and living alone in a room she finds daunting, and she does not relish the idea of saying goodbye to Mr and Mrs Mukarji.

'Well,' he says. 'At least it will earn you a little more money and you will be able to give up begging.'

He has his eye on a small plot of pavement at the end of the road which is vacant; it would be an ideal place for a chai-stall since it is at the junction with a main road and will thus provide plenty of customers. He goes off and engages a couple of labourers to do the work and buys sufficient lumber to complete the job. Within a few days a simple stall has been erected and on a smooth piece of board he has painted in large letters: *Rupa London Snack Bar*. It looks splendid, and by the time his sitar is finished and he must leave, Vhariti is serving chai to a constant stream of customers.

Standing at the stall sipping from a cup he feels very proud of his efforts as he watches her standing behind a row of glasses while she tends the steaming urn. She makes the chai in the usual Indian fashion. A woollen sock is sewn around the top onto a hoop of stiff wire. The sock is then half-filled with tea-leaves and boiling water poured into the top, and, filtering through the sock the tea drips rich and strong into a glass held beneath. However, he is looking forward to his return to London and the embassy with his new sitar. The instrument looks wonderful, gleaming with fresh lacquer and resplendent with finely worked bone decoration. Lying in its velvet-lined case with the maker's name inscribed on a small plate attached to the end of the fingerboard, it is his dream come true. Once again there is a farewell feast and in the morning after many goodbyes he leaves for the airport.

Now in the kitchen of the embassy he takes up the sitar and begins to play a raga. It sounds magnificent to Smith's ears, the tone rich and sonorous, but Brett seems not entirely happy and after a while he puts it down.

'It's not quite right,' he says. 'The tone doesn't have enough edge to it. I think it is the bridge.' Smith has heard this many times before and is pretty sure what is coming. Brett dismantles the sitar and removes the bridge; out comes the file and he begins to alter the curve across the top. The process is so delicate that a few very light strokes are all he dares to make. Replacing the bridge and strings once more he plays a few notes. The tone is dull and has lost all resonance; replacing the sitar on the table he sits staring morosely at it then.

'I've blown it,' he says with a sigh. 'I took too much off.'

Some weeks later Smith finds Brett in the kitchen. Again he is sitting at the table with file and sitar. Noticing that he has of late been looking rather dejected he asks him if there is anything wrong. Brett as usual is reluctant to talk, but with a little more prompting he reveals that he now suspects that the sitar maker had taken advantage of him as a naive westerner and given the task of making the instrument to his son. Therefore, it does not have in his eyes the credibility of having been constructed by a master-maker. The notion is depressing him and his mood is not helped by recent news from India.

He has just received word from Vhariti. The British Prime Minister has paid a flying visit to Calcutta on his way to a summit meeting and the local authorities have had a big clean-up in the streets through which his entourage of limousines must pass. Armies of workmen with paint and brushes had swarmed along the streets painting everything in sight, and the *Rupa London Snack Bar* has been dismantled and removed lest the great man's eye be offended. Vhariti, however, says she doesn't care, since she prefers begging anyway.

Tweet Tweet

Tweet tweet
Quack quack
Too-whit Too-woo
Chirp chirp
The birdies sing
And pigeons koo.

Johnny Banana Head has just handed this poem to Smith. He has scrawled it on a piece of paper torn from a notebook and now watches closely for a response. Smith finds the poem quite a catchy little number, but has one small criticism.

'You've spelt "Coo" wrong,' he says.

'Who says so?' asks Johnny. 'The pigeons?'

'Oh, no,' thinks Smith, and sees at once that he has walked right into Banana Head's trap.

'Spelling "Coo" with a "C" is merely a convention,' says Johnny. 'It should always be spelt with a "K", since "C" is arbitrary and can be pronounced either as "S" or "K", which makes it difficult for foreigners who might suppose that pigeons say "Soo-soo soo Soo-soo".

Smith looks around for a handle on this but can't find one, and Banana Head, sensing his vulnerability, presses on.

"K" is one of the most powerful sounds in the alphabet,' he says. 'That's why the Germans like it so much, but "C" is weak unless it is pretending to be "K". Now he has a fanatical gleam in his eye. 'This is how the powers-that-be have pulled the teeth of all those words which once resonated with the subtler worlds.'

Smith isn't trying any more, he has never heard Johnny articulate so succinctly, and without a handle to his name, allows himself to be carried along by his irrefutable logic.

'Take Music,' says Johnny. 'Or Magic; both words which once had bite by reason of ending with "K". Now, tamed and emasculated to end ignominiously in "C", a letter entirely without resonance. However,' he goes on. 'The operation didn't entirely succeed, since although both Music and Magic now end with a "C" on paper, they are both pronounced as "K".

Smith can't actually disagree with any of this and therefore capitulates by making an offering himself. 'What about "Kok-a-doodle-doo?' he asks hopefully. But Johnny isn't listening. 'Whenever you come across one of those words with a "C" pretending to be a "K", think of it as a "K" when you say it, and feel the stirring of the old power which once enervated the language of Adam.'

Johnny is waving his arms about now and Smith backs off a little, his simple pigeon criticism has lifted Johnny's lid and he looks for a means of escape. He begins taking minuscule steps backwards, slowly increasing the distance between them until Johnny is talking to himself.

'Phew,' he thinks. 'I asked for that,' and he decides to lift no further lids on Johnny's poetry. Nevertheless, a wayward seed has been planted and back in his room it stirs into life.

'Maybe I'll make a cup of koffee,' he thinks.

He feels a little sorry for Johnny, 'How can he allow himself to get obsessed with stupid things like that?' he thinks. But the notion propagates like a virus amongst his synapses and despite himself he begins looking for all the words ending in "K". Running down the alphabet he discovers that "K" is indeed a most powerful letter, and certainly linked to the patanormal.

'The Duck for instance,' he thinks. 'A raucous bird, with an abrupt and definite "K" at the end of its "Quack." Or Luck, a mixture of good fortune and divine providence. And what about Muck, how filthy can you get? Then there is Puck, Shakespeare's spirit of wanton mischief. And lastly Suck, the first primal instinct of the new-born child.'

Although he knows there are likely to be more, he needs no further examples to see that the evidence is irrefutable, and what's more he has detected the process by which the "K" is being lost. In all these cases a "C" has crept up right behind the "K", from where it can easily take over.

'Banana Head is right after all,' he thinks. 'Only the pigeons know the right way to spell "koo".

Inner Light

Having now spent some years at the embassy, Ace has shed many of the inhibitions which his earlier sheltered upbringing had imposed on him. Living amongst the other embassy residents has widened his view of the world and he has attained a little street-cred from the association. For instance, he now uses only one knife to spread his bread with butter and honey, thus cross-contaminating both pat and pot with a nonchalant air that seems to say: 'It's my honey and butter mate, and I'll even use my fingers if I feel like it. A newborn bolshie attitude that he displays with panache.

However, he begins to feel the lack of challenge since nobody at the embassy tut-tuts him and couldn't care less how many knives he uses. Ace now wants to go back out into the world and test his new confidence. Whilst he chafes at the bit in this way a friend tells him of a farmer in Cornwall who has a caravan in a field which he is renting out, so Ace gets in touch with the man and secures a tenancy. Packing his bag and violin he takes his leave to embark on a completely new Odyssey, and though everyone wishes him well they will all sadly miss the sound of his cheapo-Chinese-factory-fiddle.

Ace keeps in touch frequently after this, ringing the embassy to recount the circumstances of his new life.

'It's fantastic down here,' he says, excitedly. 'I've met a lot of interesting people and quite a few musicians who like the sound of my fiddle, so I'm doing a lot of playing with them.' It seems Ace has landed on his feet and everything is going his way. However, a few weeks later he runs into a major problem and telephones Smith seeking his advice.

A guru has appeared in the nearby town to set up his base, and he is beginning to make quite a stir amongst Ace's friends. The guru is a shaman who had learned his skills amongst the Aborigines of the Australian interior. He is a powerful man with a formidable charisma, and one by one Ace's friends come under his spell and accept initiation as his disciples. Ace nevertheless has his reservations and holds out until he is the only one of his circle to remains outside.

'I find it too difficult to believe,' he says. 'The shaman says that they have all lost their souls, which have been scattered throughout the galaxy, and that each soul has come to rest on a different star. He, however, has the power of astral travel, and he can go out to each star and bring back their soul.' He pauses, then... 'And he only charges £350.'

Smith laughs at this but Ace is serious. 'The problem is,' he goes on. 'That my friends won't speak to me anymore. They say that I am a coward and a wimp and that I'm too afraid to step upon the spiritual path when the opportunity occurs.'

'Have you got £350?' asks Smith.

'No,' says Ace.

'Then just say you can't afford it,' suggests Smith.

'I already tried that,' says Ace. 'They immediately clubbed together and raised the money for me, and they mean so well that I find it difficult to refuse.'

'Just go along with it then,' advises Smith. 'If they want to buy your soul back from some star and are willing to finance the operation, why not indulge them? After all they are your friends.'

Ace is still somewhat uneasy. 'But I haven't told you everything,' he says. 'Before he astral travels the shaman must make a connection with the disciple, which he does by inserting this rod with coloured lights up their arse!' He sounds a trifle indignant.

In his initial days at the embassy the word 'arse' was not in his vocabulary, and were he to find the word unavoidable would whisper it with a hand held to his mouth. Now such restriction no longer inhibits him and he says the word with just a hint of relish. 'He tells them that it straightens out their auras,' he says.

'How many people have had the coloured lights up their arses?' asks Smith.

'About ten,' says Ace. 'In fact all my friends, and now he has forbidden any of them to speak with me. He has declared me a non-person and says that I am a negative influence on them.'

Just then Tralee passes the phone and Smith decides to get a second opinion. 'Listen to this,' he says to her, and lays out the circumstances of Ace's situation. Tralee is in a hurry and a little impatient, but she makes up her mind immediately. Snatching the receiver from Smith's hand she gives Ace her opinion.

'Ace,' she says. 'You should have the coloured lights up your arse.' She declares this very firmly, and handing the phone back to Smith walks off.

'Well, there you are,' says Smith. 'That was an impartial opinion, but I don't really know enough about shamanism myself to be of much help to you. However, if you do decide to accept the teaching, make sure you know first how big these coloured lights are.'

Over the next few weeks Ace feels more and more isolated, alone in his caravan and now without any friends at all, he misses their company, until a new and unforeseen situation arises. The local town hall hosts a concert for a visiting orchestra and the lead violinist knows one of Ace's erstwhile friends. He reveals that he knows of the shaman back in his home town, and he tells them that he is an ex-door-to-door salesman who has never been to Australia in his life. 'He's an utter fraud,' he says. 'A charlatan who has fooled many people and you shouldn't believe a word he says.'

The disciples are gutted. Their wonderful new spiritual reality crumples around them and they are desolate. A while after this shameful exposure Ace begins to notice one or two of them giving him a smile when passing, and later an occasional knock comes to his caravan door. Sheepishly an exdisciple will enter and even accept a cup of tea.

'They're all coming back,' says Ace. 'And now they think that I was very wise for not taking the initiation. They seem to be full of admiration for me and listen to everything I say as if *I* am a guru.'

'Well maybe you are,' says Smith.

'But it's very embarrassing for me,' says Ace, 'and I don't know what to do about it.'

'You should stick coloured lights up their arses,' says Smith. 'That'll teach them not to be so bloody silly.'

Traffic Master

The residential streets behind the embassy are quiet tree-lined backwaters and traffic is light. The odd rat-runner seeking a faster route or the occasional delivery van is all that disturbs their tranquillity. It is late spring, and the cherry and plum trees are shedding their blossom; the petals falling to lie in a thin patina across the old paving stones, or collect like pink snow in drifts along the gutters of the street in which Smith stands watching Moss cross the road.

As the boy steps out his head begins swivelling like an owl; side to side it turns, never ceasing this movement until he reaches the other side. There he turns and waits while two cars pass, and then embarks on the return, his head endlessly turning back and forth as he goes. He is learning his road drill, and Smith has devised a programme which he hopes will give Moss a good foundation for tackling this precarious art.

The Highway Code, once the benchmark for safety, with its 'Look right, look left, look right again,' is of course now hopelessly obsolete, not to say highly dangerous. In those days a car might enter a street and begin grinding its slow way through the gears while building up momentum, giving comfortable warning of its coming together with a wide margin of error. Now the cars like sleek spaceships slither almost silently around a corner and with barely a murmur can be upon the unwary pedestrian like a beast to its prey.

To counter this high-tech onslaught requires an extension of those hoary old instructions, which, were they acted upon now would likely lead to a sudden and messy end. Therefore, when crossing the road, Moss and Smith turn their heads from right to left continuously until reaching the far side. They have been practising these manoeuvres now for a week or so, and Moss seems to have the head-swivelling habit well established and can transverse these back streets alone, albeit under the watchful eye of Smith.

'And now,' he thinks, 'for the main road.'

This is an entirely different proposition, since the road which passes in front of the embassy carries heavier traffic and the gaps for crossing occur less frequently. Moss holds Smith's finger as they cross and re-cross, but he has the responsibility of choosing when it is safe to do so. Eventually Smith decides that he has the hang of it and that his judgement is reliable.

Now the time has come for Moss to make the crossing alone, and they stand for some time while cars, lorries and coaches swish by, and then... 'Now?' says Moss, as a long lull occurs, and, 'OK,' says Smith. Moss steps off the curb and head swivelling constantly walks confidently across the broad road. At the far side he stops, but by now the lull is menaced from both directions by oncoming traffic and it is some time before another gap appears and he can make the return.

Over several days this exercise is repeated endlessly until Smith is confident enough in Moss' judgement to make the final test. Smith will close his eyes at the curb while Moss decides when the time is right, and then lead Smith, still with his eyes shut, across the road. This is as much a test of Smith's confidence as of Moss' skill, but one afternoon finds them standing at the curb whilst the traffic hurtles by.

'Ready?' asks Smith. 'I'm closing my eyes now.'

Moss takes his finger and Smith listens to the traffic's roar, now that he can see nothing he begins to doubt the wisdom of this act. However, to throw in the towel now would undermine Moss's confidence, so he listens as a large vehicle swished by, then another, and a car, and another. Then, apart from a distant hum, silence. He feels Moss's grip on his finger tighten, and like a blind man he is pulled forward to step out from the curb and into the unknown.

He tries not to hurry and governs his step to match Moss's casual walk, but he desperately wants to open his eyes; even a small peep would ease this tension. He manages to resist the temptation however, until at last he feels the far curb at his feet and steps gratefully up onto the safety of the pavement. He opens his eyes and looks down to see an expression on Moss's face such as, for all the money in the world, cannot be purchased at the local toyshop.

Some few days later Moss shows off his newly awakened traffic awareness to Katarina, although his natural precociousness has already taken his expertise to what even Smith might consider an extreme. Katarina knows nothing of his new skills, and when they go out she keeps his hand tightly held in her own lest he, like a thoughtless child, make a sudden dash into the road, something which, as a fully-fledged traffic-master he is now quite incapable of. Moss knows better than to argue with Katarina and accepts this limitation philosophically. On the day in question they make a visit to the local doctor where Katarina will pick up some pills for a minor ailment. Seeing Moss playing happily with some children in the waiting room, she had decided that it was safe to leave him for a minute or two while she visits a nearby shop for some bread and milk.

'I won't be long,' she tells him, but he hardly looks up from his game.

Having made her purchases she makes her way back until reaching the major crossroads half-way up the hill to Hampstead. Coming to a halt she waits for the green man to show. The crossroads is a forest of traffic-lights, made more complex by left and right filtering lights, and even when the green man shows the pedestrians cross fearfully, as if venturing out into no-man's land where a sniper may pick them off.

As she waits for her light she looks diagonally across and there, standing at the far curb is Moss, and he is alone.

Deciding to come and meet his mother he had left the doctor's and had made his way down the hill to the crossing, and now Katarina's heart is in her mouth as, not daring to call out, she watches her son in horror.

Moss, meanwhile, seems entirely unconcerned and is watching the traffic-lights intently. Red, red, green, amber, the forest of lights flash in incomprehensible patterns and the pedestrians cluster while waiting for their signal. Then, to Katarina's further horror, Moss suddenly steps nonchalantly from the curb and begins walking in a casual manner diagonally over the middle of the crossroads. Katarina is holding in a scream as Moss, taking his time reaches the opposite pavement and comes to stand at her side.

'I came to meet you.' he says, but Katarina, her anger mixed with relief, gives him a good telling off.

'Don't you ever do that again,' she shouts angrily. 'You could have been killed.'

Moss is puzzled by this. 'But I was counting,' he says.

'What do you mean?' says Katarina, barely listening; she is still shaking from her fright.

Moss points to a set of lights. 'When those ones go red,' he explains. 'They all go red for seven seconds, and I can get across easy before I get to seven.'

Katarina isn't having any of this. 'Well I'm telling you never to do it again,' she says.

But Moss has misunderstood and thinks his mother doubts his mathematical abilities.

'Well, I can count up to seven,' he says truculently.

'That's not the point,' says Katarina crossly. 'It's dangerous.'

But Moss considers himself an expert on the subject. Still missing the point he puffs out his chest a little. 'And I can count up to even more than that,' he boasts.

What Now?

Caspar and Wirril have become engaged in a philosophical bout. They are wary of each other and yet within moments close in and lock antlers. Caspar is the essence of English good manners but he knows that Wirril, if provoked, may take refuge in some irrefutably absolute dimension which Caspar may be disinclined to enter. Also present is Smith who is observing the encounter with interest but so far has said nothing. He is wondering how soon Wirril will put in the metaphysical boot. Caspar had merely remarked that most, if not all of his life was in the past.

'What past?' says Wirril, putting in the metaphysical boot immediately.

'Oh no,' thinks Smith. 'Here we go.'

Caspar considers this kind of directness a mite impolite, he would prefer to approach these profound matters obliquely, and reach such conclusions in a rather more whimsical way. However, a little flustered, he rallies his manners and gives Wirril an answer:

'The past I remember,' he says, and back comes Wirril's boot:

'Memory is just a thought,' he says. 'And what's more, it's a thought you're having now.'

Caspar cannot refute this, but philosophical propriety demands he keep his end up, and with a degree from Cambridge in the subject he feels bound to honour the classical laws of dialectics.

'Not necessarily,' he says. 'It might be a thought I'm going to have in the future.' He knows that he has now put himself out on a limb, but he is saved from ignominy by Smith, who, unable any longer to hold his tongue utilises it to articulate an interjectory statement.

'The future is a word coming out of my mouth now,' he says.

'No it isn't,' says Wirril, rising impeccably to the challenge. 'Since it is me who is speaking now, and you can't even say that it was coming out of your mouth because there is no was.' Wirril is warming to his favourite subject: 'The thing is,' he says. 'You can't even say now, now, because you will quickly see that the moment you say it, it's already gone.'

'I wonder how fast it's going,' says Smith dreamily, and Caspar, the master of whimsy seizes the opportunity to regain his academic authority.

'Oh, around 186,000•281 miles per second I should think,' he says.

Conversation Piece

P. B. Rivers is up in town for a few days. He is staying at the embassy while he scours the local shops for existential bric-a-brac for his second-hand shop in Hastings. 'I have become a purveyor of attitudes,' he says, rummaging in a carrier bag and bringing out a piece of china. 'Look at this teapot for instance,' he goes on. 'What attitude do you suppose it has?' Smith looks at the pot but can see nothing particularly striking about it. 'It just looks like a teapot to me,' he says.

P. B. Rivers put the pot down on a table and stands back. 'Can't you see the way it sits? he says. 'Don't you see a kind of reluctance in its stance.' Smith looks again and now he begins to see what P. B. Rivers means, for there is a certain surliness in the way it squats; it looks as if it is not going to budge an inch for anyone. 'But,' P. B. Rivers goes on, 'there is a dichotomy in its attitude, for look how it seems to be leaning and thrusting forwards its spout, as if only too willing to start pouring, but this is only a front to cover its basic attitude of resentment. This teapot is seriously disturbed.'

Do you tell all this to your customers?' asks Smith.

'Of course,' says P. B. Rivers. 'The teapot itself is worthless, but for a twisted attitude like that my customers will pay well. There are many other curious pieces in my shop. For instance: I have an old wardrobe that has been in a state of acute and shameful embarrassment since the day it was made, and I have a malevolent hat rack that, were it endowed with the power of movement, would love to get its hands around the neck of the nearest person. On the other hand I have a deliriously happy chamber pot, and a rather saintly armchair which is not for sale. Every object has a stance,' he says, 'and I am an interpreter of their attitudes, which means that my shop is doing rather well at the moment.'

P. B. Rivers visit has coincided with the arrival of Johnny Banana Head whose intensity of manner catches his attention at once.

'What's he into?' he asks Smith, pointing across the garden where Johnny is snoozing away the afternoon on a garden bench.

'That's Johnny Banana Head.' says Smith. 'He's an intellectual and not easily understood.'

'Perhaps I'll go and have a talk with him.' says P. B Rivers, and Smith gives him all the encouragement he can.

'He has a brilliant mind,' he says. 'And his analytical conclusions have to be carefully studied to appreciate them to the full.'

P. B. Rivers is now very interested indeed, and leaving Smith he crosses the garden and stands looking down at Johnny.

'Ahem,' he coughs, and Banana Head opens his eyes. He sits up and makes room for P. B. Rivers who takes a seat.

'It's a nice day,' says P. B. Rivers by way of an opener.

'They're all nice,' says Johnny. 'I like them all very much.'

'Well I suppose the word "nice" could be improved on,' says P. B. Rivers making his first major stab. 'But as we know none of these words really make much sense.'

Johnny disagrees. 'They all make some sense,' he says.

P. B. Rivers however has already started, and unwilling to lose any momentum continues:

'Take for example the word "tree," he says. 'What does it mean?'

'The tree is a green one-legged thing.' says Johnny.

'That's eight words,' says P. B. Rivers. 'See what I mean?'

Johnny looks blankly at him, then tries to explain.

'First,' he says. 'There are many kinds of trees. And look here.' He pulls his *AtoZ* from his pocket and opens it at the back.

'I've made a list of all the streets with tree names.' He begins reading from the list: '*Acacia Avenue. Birch Grove. Willow Road...*' But P. B. Rivers lays a restraining hand over the book.

'No,' he says. 'That isn't what I meant. That isn't what I meant at all. I'm talking about the meaning of words.'

Johnny brushes this aside. 'Well,' he says. 'It was you who brought trees into it.'

'I only used the word "tree"', says P. B. Rivers. 'What kind of tree is entirely irrelevant to the argument.'

Banana Head looks at him in amazement. How could this imbecile have misunderstood him so completely?

'Look,' he says. 'If they suddenly changed the name of *Elm Terrace* to *Chestnut Grove* and then again to *Beech Close* the whole of our postal system would fall apart.'

Now P. B. Rivers begins to raise his voice. He thinks Johnny is maybe a little deaf.

'What I mean is,' he shouts. 'Every word needs several other words to give it its meaning. Without this support no single word has any meaning at all.'

Johnny however, is very patient. 'Come with me,' he says. 'I can show you a good example of what I mean. I can take you to *Acacia Avenue*, and it's only just around the corner.'

'Yes but take the word "corner"', says P. B. Rivers, ignoring Johnny's interruption. 'What does it mean? Can you convey its sense without resorting to other words? If you can't, then alone it is meaningless.'

'That's because you won't come with me,' says Banana Head, catching on at last. 'You're afraid to confront the evidence.'

'What evidence?' says P. B. Rivers, thrown a little off course by this challenge.

'Round the corner,' says Johnny. 'You can come and look, and meaningless or not you will see it: *Acacia Avenue*.'

P. B. Rivers gives up. Already he knows that he will never get through to Johnny who cannot see the wood for the trees. 'He must be a bit retarded,' he thinks, and Johnny, sensing that the opposition has given way, begins again to turn the pages of his *AtoZ*. His finger comes to rest on a dense maze of streets. 'And look at how all the streets beginning with " S" twist and turn like a snake.'

P. B. Rivers has drawn off a little, but Johnny cannot be stopped:

'The snake is highly symbolic,' he says. 'And it is the Old Testament which first established its importance.'

He looks up, but P. B. Rivers has gone.

'He can't concentrate on the real issue,' thinks Banana Head. 'Either that or he's some kind of retard.'

The Gate Of Dawn

For thousands of years,' says Ram O'Neil, 'the ancient religions of India have been worshipping false representations of the divine.'

Smith is making an overnight visit to Ram's land around Loch Ness and they are contemplating an impressive array of images of the *sri yantra*, a major symbol in the Indian pantheon which litters the table in the shed where Ram retires to do this kind of work. Books lie scattered on the table, their pages open to show coloured photographs of the ancient sign rendered in their primal colours, and postcards of temples from all over the hinterland of the subcontinent show these images in many variations and styles.

'Have you notice something?' asks Ram.

Smith looks at the diagrams, an arrangement of interlocked triangles, but sees nothing amiss and shakes his head.

'It's all to do with shape power,' says Ram. 'The *sri yantra* is an archetypal shape which, when perfectly constructed, creates a positive resonance. But if it is ill-proportioned it has no more value than so much graffiti. However,' he goes on, 'the proportions of these images here are all different one to another,' he says. 'As if they've forgotten how to construct the *yantra* geometrically and are just copying each other.' He picks up a book. 'Look at this one,' he says, his finger tapping the page. 'This is early 13th century and you can see that it's a fudge and no better than any of the later ones, which means they lost the secret a long time ago.'

As he talks he begins unrolling cartridge paper and gathering pencils, rulers and compasses to him. 'The whole point of sacred geometry,' he says, 'is that the proportions must be perfect, otherwise like all these examples they have copied each other's mistakes and passed on the errors.'

Smith says nothing but watches as Ram takes up his compasses.

'I think I know how it works,' he says. 'My bet is that it's based on intersecting circles and where they cross marks the points of the triangles of the yantra.'

They have spent the whole night in the shed and now dawn is not far off, and Smith decides to go for a walk and watch the arrival of morning across the loch before leaving to get a coach back to London. 'I'm just going for a walk before I go,' he says, and turns to leave.

'Oh, one thing,' says Ram, looking up from the circles he has begun to draw. 'Please stay away from the woods, my friend Tom Davidson is staying for a while and doesn't want to see any strangers. If anybody turns up he always goes up to the woods with a tent until they're gone. Ram looks serious as he goes on. 'The thing is he's a bit of a lunatic, and if anybody disturbs him up there he gets a bit out of hand and upsets the whole place for days.'

Smith leaves the shed; he has no interest in any woods and intends to climb a nearby hill overlooking the loch. It is still quite dark and he wants to watch dawn break across the water. Climbing higher into the heather he turns occasionally to look back and sees the lighted window of Ram's shed diminishing below him, while ahead the brow of the hill looms in a black hump against the stars.

From the top of the hill the deep waters of the loch are far below, where they brood in a still and awesome silence. The stars, seen through the clear lens of a northern clime, crowd the arching field of deep space above and jostle in multitudes to display their atomic finery. Smith's mind is struck dumb by the combination of this profound silence, and the awe-inspiring scale above, but he begins picking out the constellations until he notices that the sky is beginning to pale, as if somewhere a gate has opened to let in the light and a ruddy sheen touches the edges of the far side of the loch. He turns to go, and leaving hears a thrush break the silence with a long stream of complicated intervals. He has witnessed the last hour of darkness and watched Orion chase Cassiopeia across the night sky above Loch Ness.

Turning his back on the loch he takes a different route back to the shed. Striking around the hill and down the farther side he finds himself amongst thick bushes on the edge of a small wood. Picking his way through the outer fringe of trees he can still hear the now far-off song of the thrush, but here in the wood the deep hush of night still lingers. Then, faintly, on the periphery of his hearing, he detects another sound; a distinct piping tone comes echoing from deep within the wood and Smith, curious, makes his way quietly through the trees towards its source. The piping grows louder as he cautiously advances, rising strongly to a soulful long drawn-out wail, then fading through sinking tones until the merest whisper flutes the air.

Moving forward Smith now sees a small clearing just ahead, and there at its centre a man sits upon a fallen tree whilst playing on a bamboo flute. The man's back is turned to him and Smith wonders who it can be, but held back by a sense of unease he hesitates before stepping out to introduce himself. The piper, unaware of his presence, continues to embellish the breaking dawn while Smith stands hesitant. Then with a start he spies something which he had overlooked. A small tent is pitched at the edge of the clearing, and now he knows who the piper is.

'It's Ram's nutty friend,' he thinks, as he hurriedly withdraws back amongst the trees. But he is too late. The man stops playing and lowers his flute, his attitude stiffens and Smith can tell that he has been detected; the piper has somehow become aware of his presence. Even as he retreats he glimpses the man in the act of turning around and he dives back into the bushes as fast as possible.

Returning to the shed he finds Ram in an exultant state.

'I've cracked it,' he says, rummaging amongst a litter of discarded drawings. 'The triangles are set upon the points of these intersecting circles.'

Smith looks at the drawings and begins to see the principle, but so far these are only rough sketches and Ram is already stretching a fresh sheet of paper onto his table. 'This,' he says. 'Is going to be the first correct sri yantra drawn for thousands of years, and I have to will myself into the right mood to construct it. Once started I must not be interrupted or I will lose my concentration and have to begin all over again. This is a sacred task and the mind must be serene when it is undertaken.' He picks up a ruler and closes his eyes for a moment, then bends over the paper, reaches for his compasses and places the point for his first perfectly proportioned circle.

This is a good moment for Smith to leave. He has heard the postman's van in the lane outside and the driver is used to picking people up here and giving them a lift into town. He bids Ram good luck with the great work, but Ram is already focusing his mind for the long and meticulous task ahead. Down in the lane Smith arranges his lift, but before getting into the van he turns around to have a last look across the acres of heather that surround the croft.

What he sees fills him with horror, for somebody is storming along the path from the woods, and what is worse he is making straight for the shed. It is Ram's nutty friend and he looks furious. In a minute or two all hell will break loose amongst Ram's intersecting circles while the perfected sri yantra will have to wait for another day.

In later years Ram never mentions this episode, but Smith, although never forgetting the dreamlike quality of his encounter in the woods says nothing. He later puts the whole thing down to his quirky and perhaps even warped imagination which leaves him at times unsure of anything at all.

A Difficult Choice

Just within the forecourt of the embassy are the representations of order and chaos lying one each side of the entrance. To the right a neat sand-garden is carefully raked each morning; the parallel furrows spiralling outward from a central cluster of large stones until arriving at a peripheral circle of jagged marble rocks. To the left, a wilderness of coarse uncut grass and tall rank weeds, in the centre of which stands an old plum tree whose lower branches dip to meet the unkempt growth below. Between these two symbolic extremes the occasional resident passes and each time this occurs a sleek head cautiously lifts above the weeds and casts an eye upon them.

It is Genaro, a blue-brindled lurcher who lives on the far side of Primrose Hill. Genaro, in spite of his daily two tins of 'Bonzo' is always hungry, and this spot beneath the plum tree provides a convenient sanctuary which he frequently occupies before a nightly hunt among the rich pickings to be had from the upmarket dustbins of this affluent neighbourhood. He knows most of the residents by sight and his sharp ears have even picked up some of their names.

Just now the front door opens and Jack Rawlings steps out followed by Morgiana and Penny their toddling daughter. Genaro's ears flatten against his skull as he raises his head and his two keen eyes, lifted just above the tangled wilderness, watches them closely.

Unlike Caspar, who has dallied for so long orbiting Morgiana's flame from a safe distance, Rawlings had taken one look and plunged helplessly, wings aflame, straight into the heart of Morgiana's fire. Caspar is now right out of it. While Rawlings, not a man to hang about when such issues are at stake further seals the tryst and makes his mark with Penny, the fruit of this potent conjunction. Genaro watches them pass but bides his time till dusk, when he knows that Toledo and Tiberius will sally forth upon an evening's hunting.

Toledo and Tiberius collect vegetables and the odd choice morsel from the dustbins behind a select grocer shop in the local high street. In the kitchen they later construct opulent stews which they offer to residents or guests alike. One evening after an Indian concert a woman and her husband linger a while talking with the residents. She is curious about the house and asks Smith who owns it.

'Mr Richard Arnold is the owner,' says Smith. 'But I don't think he is around at the moment.'

'Well he must be a generous man to throw his house open in this way,' says the lady.

Generous is not a word Smith would use in reference to Mr Arnold, but he nods and smiles which seems to satisfy her. She wears an expensive fur coat and her manner is imperious. Her husband, an unreconstructed businessman says little, but he follows her into the kitchen where the residents are about to partake of a richly endowed stew courtesy of Toledo and Tiberius.

'Would you care for some goulash?' says Toledo, immaculate in a dark blue blazer and white shirt. Like a butler he bends formally at the waist and the lady is enchanted. She sits down in the chair which he pulls out for her and her husband sits beside her. Tiberius now appears at her side with a bowl of stew and she gets to work at once, making sounds of approval as she tastes the aromatic contents.

Tiberius is deadpan, but Toledo's conquistador beard is harbouring a wicked little grin. Smith however, sitting opposite her is in a philosophical mood. As he tucks into the stew his thoughts turn to the fundamental dynamics of this scenario. He analyses the situation carefully and comes to an intriguing insight.

'If she knew this is a squat,' he thinks. 'She would do a runner at once. And if she finds out where the ingredients for the stew came from she would probably throw up on the spot.' He ruminates further, as if exploring a curious mathematical problem. 'But what if she discovered these two things simultaneously? Would she throw up first and then do a runner? Or would she have sufficient bodily control to hold it in until she reaches the street?'

Looking closely at the woman he discerns, beneath the patronising poshness a degree of iron in her manner, which bespeaks of at least a modicum of self-discipline. This reassures him somewhat, for if somebody gives the game away and she throws up, then it is better that she does it in the street.

The Last Tail

Some time after this while nosing around the dustbins in the high street, the blue-brindled lurcher Genaro had seen Toledo and Tiberius making their way along the lamplit high street, and something in their manner had aroused his interest. He had seen at once that they were not quite what, on the surface, they seem to be. Tiberius shambles loose-limbed with arms flopping around anyhow, while his eyes, lacking all guile gaze innocently forth. But there are no flies on Tiberius and his logic is devastating. Toledo marches along, his good arm swinging and his pointed black conquistador beard thrust confidently forward, as if about to assault the fortress of Montezuma himself, and single-handed at that. Genaro however, is not so easily fooled, and, a connoisseur of body language, he detects a subtle furtiveness in their manner.

Alerted by this canine insight he watches as they turn down a dark alley which runs behind a row of shops. The alley is filled with shadow, dark, but for the occasional glint on a dank cobble from the full and lemon-yellow moon which hangs low over the far end. The two skulking figures creep in silhouette against its mellow disc. And they are doing the shrinking thing.

'They're doing the shrinking thing,' thinks Genaro, and loping across the street he enters the mouth of the alley.

The shrinking thing only brings a slight discomfort these days, although it is a subject about which Genaro is still a little touchy, but for years now it has not seriously bothered him. It is a disability which in the past had given him considerable grief, for try as he might, he had found himself utterly unable to produce the effect. Everyone else seemed to have no trouble with it and obviously knew some secret technique: people; dogs; birds, all growing smaller and shrinking as they move away. All, that is, but Genaro. He had spent long hours as a puppy sucking in his stomach and holding his breath behind the garden shed. Head sunk deeply into his shoulders and joints pulled tightly in he had willed himself to shrink; and all to no avail. Finally he had no choice but to accept the limitation, but he still feels a minor twinge of jealousy on occasions such as this.

Staying close to the wall he follows as the pair tiptoe along and stop at a gate. Tiberius reaches high to grip the top of a wooden fence; pulling himself over he disappears into the darkness below and Genaro knows now for sure that they are up to no good. Presently Tiberius opens a door in the fence and Toledo slips through and into the backyard of a grocer's shop. Genaro lies down at a little distance and waits. A rustling sound now comes from within the gate and soon Toledo and Tiberius reappear, each carrying a black bin-liner bulging with plunder. Genaro's ears prick up as they pass closely by and his nose twitches at the rich aroma issuing forth from the bags. He remains still until they have shrunk back down the alley leaving, he notices, the gate still somewhat ajar. He slinks across the alley, pushes open the gate, and enters.

The yard is quite small and he cannot miss the row of dustbins lined up against the far wall. They are filled almost to overflowing and a plethora of delectable smells so pungent he can almost taste them are wafted towards him. Taste them he does, beginning with a few choice slices of near-fresh salami. The rich and spicy meat quickens his hunger and thrusting his long nose further into a bin he pushes aside a layer of loose cabbage leaves. Again he strikes gold as he homes in on a slightly broken pork pie. These are top quality pickings, for most of the shopping around here is done by the chauffeur don't you know, and the slightest dent in tart or pie produces a tone of disdain delivered from beneath a lifted nose; they wouldn't touch it with a bargepole. The pie goes down well, but there is still room for some more, and now his eye alights upon a snake-like form hanging from amongst the shadows of a dustbin at the far end of the row. He moves stealthily closer and notices that the snake is segmented evenly along its length and glistens pinkly in the pale moonlight.

'Sausages!' The thought comes with an electrical thrill and an ancient impulse, buried long deep by his quasi-domestic life and the endless tins of 'Bonzo' takes possession of his limbs. Taking two swift paces forwards he seizes his prey by the tail and, with an involuntary flick of his jaws cracks the string of sausages like a whip and snatches them from the clutches of the dustbin. The lid of the bin flies into the air and crashes to the concrete with a horrendous clatter and Genaro is off. Through the gate he darts as if pursuing a devious hare; once outside he swings sharply sideways then with a last flick of the tail is gone.

The Iron Fist

An official looking envelope drops through the letter box. It is a summons demanding Smith's appearance in court once more for non-payment of rates and their solicitor applies immediately for Legal Aid. The summons is followed shortly by a letter from the Foreign Office which refers to his agreement with Colonel D— and encloses a document for his signature. He sees at once that the matter has now passed into hands more ruthless than those of the Colonel. For underneath the agreement to vacate the house when the Cambodians return is another item almost lost amongst the small print at the bottom: "*You will vacate the house for any other reason which the Foreign Office deems appropriate*".

Smith is disappointed. His gentlemanly agreement with the Colonel on which they had shaken hands, and more importantly the spirit in which it had taken place, is now sullied by this blatant chicanery. The Colonel's hand had been the velvet glove and this the iron fist which wore it. He wonders if perhaps they hoped, as an ignorant squatter, he might be unable to read, and therefore naively put his signature to anything, but he passes it on to Mr Priest to deal with.

'I've sent it back and asked by what authority it was issued,' says Mr Priest a few days later. 'But be on your guard for further developments there's more behind this than meets the eye.'

He is right, and not long afterwards a copy of the Diplomatic and Consular Premises Act which has recently been granted by Royal Assent arrives, together with a notice that the Secretary of State has through deed poll invested title to the house in himself and is demanding its vacation immediately, whereupon he has the duty to sell it on the open market at his soonest convenience.

'We must find someone else to represent the house over this,' says Mr Priest, 'in order to keep the rates case entirely separate, otherwise they will tend to reinforce each other, an effect which they will take advantage of if we give them the chance, so... who is it going to be?'

The question is deliberated over the next few days to discover who will stick his neck out and take on the Secretary of State; but it is a daunting proposition. Toledo, whose impeccable conquistadorial manner might well cause the great man's knees to shake is ruled out, since his citizenship might be placed in jeopardy. Caspar's Feng Shui nature puts him as far away from courtrooms as space allows, and Brett—? Smith imagines Brett in the witness box.

'Are you a resident at the aforementioned address?' The magistrate asks.

'What?' says Brett.

No, he has little idea of these developments and cannot commit himself to anything beyond his beloved sitar. Who then will take the dare and be their champion now that the gauntlet has been thrown down?

'I'll do it,' says Ace, stepping forward, the timidity of his early years at the embassy now stiffened by association with its reprobate members. And so Sir Ace accompanies Smith to the next conference and enters his name into the lists. Mr Brace will handle both cases to make sure that they remain distinct, and when the rates hearing takes place battles with his opponent as they hurl ancient statutes and obscure items of precedent at each other across the courtroom. The Council have an array of legal minds in their cause and a team of researchers combing the archives for ammunition, but Mr Brace, on a small fee from Legal Aid cannot afford such luxuries and must rely entirely on his wits. The gods however, continue to smile, and he emerges unscathed and even triumphant from the onslaught with the magistrate, unconvinced by Westminster's arguments, finding in favour of Smith, and warning the Council that any further proceedings against him could well be regarded as harassment.

But the Council cannot let it go, doubtless with good reason, worrying that should Smith create a precedent the entire population might then claim to be squatters and renege on their rates; and no sooner has the court found in his favour than they file notice of appeal.

Private Parts

Meanwhile, Sir Ace is girding his loins for his coming joust which will occur a few days hence. Smith remembers sitting with him in the kitchen years before when Ace had just moved in. He had been recounting the story of a recent altercation with a local shopkeeper who had tried to cheat him, and several of the 'Guild' are present.

'I nearly said "b—" says Ace, whispering the letter "b" whilst covering his mouth with his hand. They are on him like a shot.

'What do you mean, "b—"? says Smith, and Ace looks sheepish.

'Go on, say it.' Morgiana urges. At which Ace, covering his mouth again says something which no one can hear.

'Louder,' they shout.

'Take your hand away from your mouth.'

Ace drops his hand and it is obvious that he is making a supreme effort of will.

'Bollocks!' he says in a tiny voice.

'Louder! Louder!'

They press him from all sides and again the word emerges, a little stronger, but there is still room for improvement. They push him to his limits and suddenly.

'*BOLLOCKS!*' he roars at the top of his voice, and sits back somewhat shocked by this out-of-character behaviour.

He receives a storm of applause and a kiss from Morgiana, and for some days afterwards a slight swagger had been apparent in his gait.

'But God knows,' thinks Smith, 'what his mother would say.'

Compared to those early days Ace has acquired a little street cred.

'You know, when I first came here,' he says, years later, 'I thought you were a gang of villains and desperados.'

'And now?' Caspar asks.

Ace hesitates as the realisation dawns that he has not changed this opinion, and therefore must himself have become... he cannot face the completion of this logical outcome and Caspar, a desperado for sure but no hooligan, is in this instance too much of a gentleman to press him further.

Mr Brace assures Ace that he will not be called to the witness box since he will fight the case purely on technicalities.

'And these,' he says. 'Are very complicated indeed.'

Mr Brace intends to challenge the Secretary of State's right to invest the property in himself and begins his preparations for the final battle.

Hornet's Nest

The Bishops Avenue is situated in an opulent district on the exclusive heights of Hampstead. The recalcitrant sons and younger brothers of oil-rich sheikhs inhabit the vast mansions which lie along its expansive flanks, while deposed presidents bicker for the choicest locations. There is little traffic in this early spring afternoon. An occasional Rolls or Bentley whispers down a driveway in the dutiful hands of a chauffeur, while the odd Mercedes leaves the environs as a butler goes off to collect an extra case of caviar from Harrods. And rare the footstep falling on the broad and unworn pavement which lines the avenue's stately route.

Around a graceful curve in the wide road there now appears a clapped-out Volkswagen beetle. Dented and battered it rattles along in the bolshie hands of Morgiana. Beside her sits Smith, and in the back seat is Penny. Morgiana uses the car to collect and deliver the carpets which she repairs, and almost certain now that their days at the embassy are numbered they hunt for a new house.

Smith has spent the last few weeks on his pushbike scouring the streets of north London in the hope of finding a vacant property. But times have changed, and the days when derelict houses sat like ripe plums amongst their weeds seem to have passed. 'Let's use my car,' says Morgiana. 'We can cover more ground that way.'

She scans the street to the right while Smith, sunk almost to the floor in his broken seat cranes his head around to survey the left. So far they have seen nothing which might indicate abandonment. The lawns are shaved to perfection and the windows sparkle in the sun; but there in the driveway of an enormous mansion which has just come in to view a large pile of sand catches Smith's eye. The sand itself is only mildly interesting; maintenance in properties of this size require almost constant attention. This pile of sand has, however, further qualities which ignite his interest immediately.

Dandelions burst like golden stars against the tawny hue of the sand, and here and there a daisy sparkles amongst a thin screen of grass which sprouts in scattered clusters on the summit of the mound.

'Stop for a bit here,' says Smith. 'This looks interesting.'

The house is a dream, a spacious curving front faced by six tall fluted pillars which support a Grecian-style facade. But the sweeping gravel driveway has succumbed to virulent weeds and has not been disturbed for a considerable time.

'I'm going to have a look at this one,' he says, and leaving Morgiana in the car to watch for trouble gets out and cautiously enters the driveway, ready at a moment's notice to apply his usual techniques should an irate householder appear. He will say the first thing that comes into his head and if that doesn't work do a runner.

All seems quiet and no dogs bark as he approaches the house; from close up he can see that the windows are dull and curtainless. A path leads along the side and he follows this until an immense garden comes into view. Statues stand along pathways which lead among overgrown lawns to a central plaza where urns sit upon ornate pedestals around a central fountain.

'With the grass cut and a peacock or two we could do something with this,' he thinks.

The back of the house is as silent as the front, and he begins to look for a loose or broken pane of glass which might smooth his entry. Arriving at the backdoor he peers through the glass and sees at a glance that the house is indeed empty. Huge floor spaces devoid of all furniture stretch before his eye, the walls breached here and there with open archways giving access to even more. But how to get in? He looks down at the lock and notices something he had overlooked. A key projects conveniently beneath the doorknob and he gives it a turn.

The door swings open and he is in, his feet sinking into the rich pile of a shaggy white carpet which lines the floor as far as eye can see. Going to the front door he opens it and stands beneath the white pillars beckoning Morgiana to come in.

'Come and have a look.' He keeps his voice low and Morgiana, her engine still running should a quick getaway be necessary switches off and brings the now toddling Penny up the drive. They explore the house and wonder if again their luck is in. Will the "Guild" rise once more and fill this film star's palace with choice music and enlightening conversation? Morgiana chooses a suite of rooms for herself which overlook the elegant garden through a magnificent sweep of windows, while Smith discovers and claims a lofty room at the top of a tower with views all round: a vista taking in the Heath from Kenwood to Parliament Hill and the meadows of the lower reaches towards the west. St Paul's and King's Cross stand like old coral in the hazy distance, while around them a new growth of concrete and glass flaunt their modern facets to the sky. Leaving the house they lock the backdoor and pocketing the key return to the car. Morgiana, absorbed already in plans for her new room drives them back to the embassy.

Since Smith has the key to the house they can now move in anytime, but Toledo, when he hears the good news wants to see it at once. He runs an old Citroen and offers to drive them over.

'But it will be dark when we get there so we can't go in,' says Smith. To show a light prematurely may attract attention before they are ready to deal with it, and he has yet to change the lock on the front door. Toledo concedes this point; he will just have a look, and so they drive up the long hill to Hampstead and turn into the Bishops Avenue.

Discreet streetlamps are coming on in the late dusk as they approach the curve beyond which lies the house, and darkness gathers beneath the trees which line the road. But something strange is happening as they round the bend, for where there should be shadows in the falling night a glaring blaze of light spills into the road ahead. The dream house as it comes into view is floodlit, a dazzling white facade and beneath the pillars several dark-suited figures stand sentry with folded arms and face the street.

Toledo stops the car and Smith winds down the window for a better look. The crackling of walkie-talkies fill the night as from the bushes along the driveway more sober-suited men break cover and move purposefully towards the car. The nearest, a fellow with a crewcut wearing a headset and dark glasses keeps his hand hovering at the breast of his open jacket, and Smith suspects there is something nasty tucked beneath his arm as he speaks in guttural accents into the mouthpiece of the headset. Toledo has experience of these kind of people, and even as Smith says, 'Let's go!' the old car rumbles into life and makes off as fast as it is able.

'We stirred up a hornet's nest there alright,' remarks Smith as they drive back to the embassy. 'There must have been electronic surveillance operating, or perhaps a neighbour caught sight of us and made a report.'

Toledo is philosophic about the matter and considers it lucky they had not moved in and brought that lot down on them, and Smith cannot but agree; yet feels nevertheless a definite pang at the loss of his tower room idyll. This is, however, Smith's last attempt to find a new place, the dearth of empty properties and the reaction at The Bishops Avenue seem to him like omens. Now well past middle age he sees no future in continuing in this way.

'I don't want to be crawling in through windows when I'm sixty,' he thinks, and decides after much ruminating on the options, to retire into a less controversial lifestyle in the common-or-garden world, where shopping rules and Christmas comes but once a year.

'I can wear my suit and disappear into the crowd,' he thinks, and then: 'But I don't think I'll ever be any good at Bingo.'

St Crispin's Day

The bar is in an old-fashioned pub in a backstreet somewhere along the Strand. Against a background of polished mahogany and cut-glass mirrors well-dressed city gents of the legal profession and company directors discreetly relax in the respectable atmosphere; there is no television and football is definitely not on the agenda. Sitting around a small table in a far corner are Mr Brace, Ace and Smith. They are taking advantage of a short adjournment in the first part of Ace's hearing and are having a conference to assess the situation so far.

'I can give you little hope the way things are developing,' says Mr Brace. 'The Act on which they make their claim went through by Queen's Assent in 1988, so they have been preparing their ground for some time; all I have been able to do is question the meaning of the original legislation.' He takes a sip of his whisky. 'Personally I consider them to be misusing the Act, but that is merely my opinion, against which we have a government department with all its powers and frankly speaking I must tell you that we cannot win.'

Smith had suspected as much, and for some time now has considered these legal charades as nothing more than a device for putting off eviction for as long as possible.

'You see,' Mr Brace goes on, 'the Secretary of State has made his claim through Act of Parliament and will eventually just override my objections, and unfortunately I have nothing to counter with unless —', he pauses and takes another sip of his whisky.

'Unless you make a counter-claim.'

Smith is not sure what he means.

'How?' he asks.

'By claiming the house under the law of adverse possession; you've been in occupation well over the twelve years required and have every right to do so. Your claim would then antedate the Act and the government's case would collapse.'

Smith is not happy with this. The old dream of handing the house back to the Cambodians still lingers and more: should he become the owner he will become liable for the rates which he cannot possibly collect. Also, the house is rapidly deteriorating, the long winters without central heating have encouraged the rot which is spreading beneath the floor of the salon and annexe hall. The scale of work required is beyond their resources, and that is not to speak of the roof which is shedding tiles like leaves in autumn and only expensive scaffolding would give access. Smith explains all this to Mr Brace who looks at him as if he is mad.

'Well sell it then, because if you don't they will.'

Seeing Smith's hesitation he goes on.

'You can buy another house and begin again; it is the only card you have left to play. But I cannot advise you, I can only show you the alternatives.'

Smith is still doubtful. It could be a can of worms and he needs something more than a clever argument; he tries a piece of simple skulduggery.

'Suppose,' he asks, 'you were actually advising a client who was more or less in the same position as myself, what would you advise him to do?'

Mr Brace doesn't hesitate a second, banging down his whisky glass and half-rising to his feet he punches the air with his fist and shouts, '*GO FOR IT!*'

It is St Crispin's Day and he Henry V before Agincourt; this is what Smith had needed. 'Right,' he says, stirred by Mr Brace's stunning performance, 'we'll go for it.'

The discreet atmosphere of the bar however, in which a low murmur of modulated voices barely rise above the cigar-flavoured hush has been disturbed by Mr Brace's vibrant call to arms, and his dramatic gesture, in which he had seemed for a moment to be carrying high a great flaming sword, whilst his ruddy face shone with an ardent rebel fire has not passed unnoticed. Disdainful looks come their way from the pinstriped gentry, but Mr Brace seems unworried, flushed of face and pleased at last that he has something to fight with he lays out his plans.

'We'll get an affidavit sworn out tomorrow and once that is filed the case is dead.'

As they leave, hostile faces look at Mr Brace as if he is a yobbo and regard Ace and Smith in the same manner, but Mr Brace, the light of battle in his eye cleaves through this rabble of bores in great style, his two esquires following in his lordly wake.

Featherstick

The atmosphere in Regent's Park derives partly from the large scale and sense of distance in perspective. No small iron-railed sanctuary this; assailed and punctuated by the noisy din of traffic, where the internal combustion engine reigns in sonic supremacy; but wide plains of grass above which a vast blue sky hosts a succession of glorious cloud formations. No longer chopped into straight-edged segments by intruding architecture, or reduced to an occasionally glimpsed puff against grimy brickwork and the sad facades of talentless glass. Here they soar grandly and can be viewed in their several-mile-long entirety; a daily full-dress performance of which the sky rarely seems to tire.

Entering the park from the canal an edging treeline gives way to rolling English prairie, where the guttural roar of lion and the shrieking trump of elephant echo across the greensward from the Zoological Gardens. At the centre of this plain descends an almost unnatural silence and the far-off hum of the city drops below the buzz of a passing fly.

Running ahead, Moss is waving high the featherstick which he and Smith have just constructed. It has three components: a stick, a feather or two, and a piece of string, and these ingredients are the items for which they hunt when beginning their afternoon walks. Sometimes a stick will be found first, and then a feather or a piece of string, the combinations sufficient to supply a constant source of unique micro-events. Today has yielded first a strip of red plastic ribbon from a building site, then a fairly straight shaft of willow, and lastly two brown and white pigeon feathers and one of glossy black from an obliging crow. With his penknife Smith shaves the stick of minor twigs, and with the ribbon binds the feathers tightly onto one end of the shaft leaving two long ends to trail, and now Moss dances ahead with this shamanistic emblem held high in his hand.

'Featherstick!' he shouts.

Walking towards them across the grass there now come a man and another small boy of a similar age to Moss. As they approach the boy becomes first aware, and then fascinated by the featherstick which Moss is waving. He gazes at it in wonder and pulling at the man's hand says. 'Dad, what's that?' The Dad pays little attention and gives Moss but a cursory glance. The boy however is intrigued beyond measure, and even more so when Moss begins spinning around and twirling the featherstick high, then with a stamp of his foot abruptly halts to hurl it like a spear into the sky.

The stick rises smoothly, feathers fluttering wildly, the streaming ribbons red and swirling gracefully against the blue until, pausing at mid-trajectory the unadorned end of the shaft dips and the stick begins its earthward plunge. The little boy is frantic with excitement; tearing away from his father's hand he rushes across to where the stick has fallen and in one movement scoops it possessively from the ground. Raising it expectantly to his eyes a look of disgust comes into his face, and the wonder in his gaze dies in an instant as he casts it contemptuously back to the ground.

'It's only some old feathers tied on a stick,' he says dismissively, and stomps back to his Dad in a thoroughly disgruntled manner.

A Glorious Ride

The Royal Court of Justice in the Strand is an imposing place, its lofty pillars and vaulted arches of cathedral proportions, giving the barristers who stride around in wig and gown the look of a strange order of monks. The public gallery high above looks down into the well of the court where the action is taking place and a large contingent from the embassy line its benches in force. The case proceeds and in due course the Government's claim on the embassy is repeated and the arguments of the previous hearing regurgitated once more. This process takes the entire morning and the court then adjourns for lunch.

'We must allow them to commit themselves irrevocably to their line of attack,' says Mr Brace, 'since your claim will predate the Act and thus alter the entire situation.'

Mr Brace is enjoying himself, aware of the admiring looks he is collecting from Morgiana, Katarina, and Tralee and he blushes, but his eyes sparkle with pleasure. They are in a coffee bar not far from the court and the entire cast from the embassy fill a large table in the window of the café.

'Do they suspect what's coming?' asks Caspar, and Mr Brace looks for a moment slightly worried.

'Well yes,' he says, 'we are bound to reveal the grounds for our stance, but the claim for adverse possession is inviolable and there's nothing they can do about that, since your occupation was officially registered almost fifteen years ago when you paid the first electricity bill.' He sips his coffee and again a look of concern returns to his face.

'However,' he goes on, 'I would have expected them to restructure their position in relation to that information and they have not done so, which is puzzling. It means either they are fools (which I can assure you they are not), or there is some item in the Act which they think can subvert your claim; if so then neither I nor my office have been able to identify it.'

He stands up; there are a few details he must prepare for the afternoon's bout and they wish him luck. As he leaves he gives them a serious look.

'It's you who need the luck,' he says, 'I know where I'll be sleeping tonight, but don't worry,' and now he appears confident again, 'I will be confounded if they managed to wriggle out of this one.'

The afternoon's hearing begins with a final recitation of the Government's case and Mr Brace rises to his feet. He in turn repeats his brief and the tension in the public gallery increases as he approaches the moment when he will deliver his bombshell.

'However,' he says, 'the Court now has Mr Smith's affidavit invoking a claim for adversarial possession of the property under the Statute of Limitations period of twelve consecutive years' occupation, and the Consular and Diplomatic Premises Act therefore can have no jurisdiction.' He sits down and the Judge asks the Government team if they have anything further to add before he passes judgement.

The Government barrister rises to his feet and begins refuting Mr Brace's arguments one by one. He does this in a bored manner, as if he is tired of the whole thing, a mere ritual which, as far as he is concerned can only lead to Mr Brace's defeat. 'And finally,' he says, 'there is the matter of Mr Smith's affidavit and claim for possession. Were the house a private property, I should have to concede victory to my learned friend. However, the house in question is of a diplomatic nature and therefore falls under the jurisdiction of the Foreign and Commonwealth Office and thus into the domain of the Crown.' He allows a short silence to develop before dropping a bombshell of his own.

'Crown property has immunity from the twelve-year adversarial possession Act and is, rather, subject to a limitation period of thirty years.'

Mr Brace is confounded and the house is lost.

'I'm sorry,' he says, 'the bastards moved the goalposts, there's nothing more we can do.'

'Well', thinks Smith, 'I backed a losing horse, but what a glorious ride it's been.'

'You can appeal if you wish,' says Mr Brace, 'but I can tell you now that it will be to no avail and only serve to buy you some time.' Time as it happens is exactly what is needed at this point. Eight or so people must now re-enter the world and find private accommodation, since squatting seems no longer a viable option, and they lodge notice of appeal immediately. The result a few months later is a foregone conclusion and shortly thereafter they are given two weeks to vacate the house.

The Last Word

Having already moved their personal possessions out they spend the last night in a vigil at the house, partly from a feeling of loyalty and partly to fulfil their intention to see it through to the end. Leaving before it is absolutely necessary would be like deserting an old friend and they intend, as a formality, to let the eviction take place as the completion of a magical act, or at least a piece of theatre. A few old friends turn up, amongst whom is Tim Jacobson, High Priest of the Harry Flame coffin episode; he has been showing more than a passing interest in Tralee over the past few weeks and is now considered to be her official escort. Tim is a volcanic blues piano player and thus a good catch for Tralee, who's volatile upheavals he counters with impressive eruptions of his own.

In the morning Morgiana makes a large pot of coffee which they drink in the kitchen, aware of the ghosts of past times when it had been filled with the chatter of excited voices as they praised the master subtleties of some illustrious musician, or questioned the sanity of the evening's lecturer. The walls of the house are saturated with the echoes of their salad days, soon to be nothing but a memory.

'This is the moment,' says Toledo, 'when we must burst like a seedpod. It is the will of the gods.'

A stirring notion, and Toledo's dauntless manner, in which for a fleeting moment he assumes his conquistadorial stance, drives away the hungry ghosts and fills the air with the freshness of an unminted future. The long drawn-out appeal has allowed everyone to find alternative accommodation and no one will be on the street. These are the last moments of the "Guild" and their long association together, and as the fatal hour of nine approaches Smith looks from the window and sees a white car pull into the forecourt.

A blue light is affixed to the top and on the side is a crest surrounded by the words: "Westminster City", and beneath in larger letters, "SHERIFF'S OFFICE." The car is driven by a large black man who now lets down his window, lights up a cigarette and sits with his rolled-up shirt-sleeved elbow propped on the sill and Smith, unwilling to give an inch decides to act.

He goes out and strides purposefully across the forecourt; playing the part of householder to the end he bends down at the car window and says the first thing that comes into his head.

'Are you going to be here long?' he asks, aware as he speaks that these might be the last words spoken in their epidrama. They are. For the man looks up at Smith, and a wide good-humoured smile creases his face.

'Man,' he says in a lazy drawl.

'Ahm gonna be here for a l—o—o-ong time.'

'Enough,' thinks Smith, this contact with the forces of law and order, no matter how tenuous, or for that matter improbable, completes the magic, and he need remain no longer. Returning to the house he turns to the familiar faces collected together for perhaps the last time and announces stoically. 'Well, that's it,' and steps through the front door.

Down by the gate he sees a small group of photographers from the tabloids; the court case has been attracting some attention in the press and now they wait with equipment ready. But a look of disappointment is apparent as they lower their cameras. No armoured police with battering rams to drive the dirty squatters out, but what looks like a Sunday morning stroll before church and their frustration is obvious.

Behind Smith Katarina makes her elegant and unhurried way, her hair arrayed to her satisfaction and her nails honed to perfection. Moss rides his two-wheeled bicycle which he has just mastered and wobbles along behind her, while Penny is mounted upon her tricycle under Morgiana's eye; and as the others emerge they look perhaps like a large and respectable family as they walk for the last time across the forecourt.

The impression had only been broken somewhat when Smith, standing by now on the pavement outside, hears the voice of Tralee ring passionately down the street. Unable to contain herself at the sight of the photographers she delivers a broadside in passing.

'Philistines!' she screams, a word which they seem not to understand, for they exchange puzzled glances and Smith notes that he had not had the last word after all. On the pavement they stand together for a long poignant moment before wishing each other well and going their ways.

Smith pens a mental verse:

'Salad Days'

While the sun shone,
We danced.
As the bubble of delight
Rose to undreamed heights
We laughed and loved
Beneath the cherry blossom.
And when the bubble burst
We fell to common earth,
Like astronauts
Still dancing.

'Well, that's enough of that,' he thinks, and noticing a nearby sizeable gap in his thought processes, slips quickly through.

*

The end

Key to Pseudonyms

All names in these tales have been changed. However, the characters involved are closely modelled upon the actual residents of the embassy and the events described occurred as represented.

Ace..................Allan Samuel, classical violinist and sometime member of Third Ear Band
Albert Clere..........Robert Beer, artist, author of *The Encyclopedia of Tibetan Symbols and Motifs*
Andy...............Aidan Andrew Dunn, visionary bard of London, author of *Vale Royal*
Brett..Robert Elliot, sitarist
Bella de Lorne..Carol DeVaughn, poet and dancer
Bones....Tim Arnett, Professor of Experimental Biology at University College London
Caspar.......John Cox, co-developer of the astronomy catalogue imaging program Starry8
Count Marco de la Paloma..........Sir Mark Palmer, 5th Bart, leader of New Age wagon train
Dylan Jones..John Dyas
George O'Grass......................George Andrews, beat poet, author *The Book of Grass*
Harry Flame...Harry Fainlight, lyrical poet
Jake Naylor......................................John Taylor, musician and instrument maker
Jason...Jasper Newsome, ornithologist and saddhu
Jay Marcel...John Michell, author of *The View Over Atlantis*, *Eccentric Lives and Peculiar Notions* etc.
Johnny Banana Head...John Hay
Jack Rawlings...John Rowley, co-ordinator of special events for the Gandhi Foundation
Katarina..Natasha Jackson, screen print artist
Leon Bloch.............Noel Cobb, poet, psychologist, founder of the yearbook *Sphinx: A Journal of Archetypal Psychology and the Arts*
Lilith..Evelyn Honig, video artist
Morgiana........................Judith Rowley (née Morgan/Beck), oriental carpet restorer
Moss...Tom Jack Hennessey, embassy first-born
Mick daSilva..................Nicholas Carr Saunders, author of *Alternative London*, *E for Ecstasy* etc, founder of Neal's Yard
McCafferty...Mike McCafferty, street poet
Miriam.........................Hillary Lipsig (Rohde), author of *The Other Side: A Memoir*
Nick Warren...Mike Davis
Oberon...Norbu Rinpoche, Dzogchen Master
P. B. Rivers...Peter Hoffman, rabid existentialist

Paul Bloomfield..Peter Bloomberg, musician
Penny...Poppy Rowley, embassy second-born
Phineas..Frank (Ciaran) Clarke, musician and piano tuner
Ram O'Neil..Neil Oram, poet and author of *The Warp*
Jubal Smith..DaveTomlin, musician
Scipio Hawkins...........................John Hopkins (Hoppy), photographer and political activist, co-founder (with Barry Miles) of *International Times*
Seamus McFinn.......John Sharkie, poet, author of *Celtic Mysteries: The Ancient Religion*
Strimmer...Russell Denton, Phil Masters in *The Warp*
Sukie...Sophie Grandval, painter, botanical illustrator
Toledo..Bruno von Ehrenburgh, alchemist
The three Psykos...Metaphysical fascists
Tiberius...Tobias Braun, engraver
Tom Jacobson..Tony Jackson, painter
Tralee..Su Rose, astrologer and literary connoisseur
Wade Davenport...........................DaveWade, author of *Geometric Patterns & Borders*
Wirril...Maurill Wiritunga, Indian flautist
Woody..Keith Woolnough, Islamic scholar
Zen Glenn...Glen Sweeny, later leader of Third Ear Band